MODERN CORPORATE FINANCE

MODERN CORPORATE FINANCE

Theory and Practice

Fourth Edition

DONALD R. CHAMBERS
Lafayette College

NELSON J. LACEY
University of Massachusetts

To our families, with love.

Printed in the United States of America.

10 9 8 7 6 5 4 3 2 1

ISBN 0-7380-0770-6

Hayden McNeil Publishing, Inc.
47461 Clipper
Plymouth, Michigan 48170

Lacey, 0770-6, W03

CONTENTS

PREFACE

Dell Computer is a stunning success story. Dell Computer's founder and current chairman/CEO Michael S. Dell began his company as a 20-year-old student at the University of Texas in the early to mid 1980s. Dell detected a need for customized PCs and began a company that used direct sales, low prices, and quality service and that has soared in value. In 2001, Dell Computer's annualized revenues soared past $32 billion and the market value of its common stock was over $60 billion.

Managing the stunning growth of Dell Computer required both the vision of Michael Dell and the experience of seasoned executives. Like Dell Computer, the fourth edition of *Modern Corporate Finance: Theory and Practice* attempts to combine a forward-looking vision of corporate finance with the tried and true practices of the past. Like Dell, this text attempts to deliver a product that meets the needs of the consumer as clearly and efficiently as possible.

This text emphasizes the modernist movement in finance, which is based on systematic methodology with an emphasis on deductive reasoning and empirical validation. The modernist movement produces a market-value-based approach to finance, which emphasizes shareholder wealth maximization, options, and agency relationships. While this movement has, without question, expanded the frontiers of knowledge in finance, instructors have lacked a framework from which to teach these concepts at the introductory level. To date, undergraduate finance texts based on the modernist approach have been written from graduate texts. Thus, our text fills an important void in the market—a modernist book written for the introductory level of study.

The Text and Its Features

The text contains a number of distinctive features. First, it focuses on the most essential points of finance theory and reinforces these points with hands-on applications. Second, the text focuses on essential material. This contrasts with other corporate finance texts whose 25 to 30 chapters organized under eight to ten broad headings leave the instructor with the arduous task of sorting through what is relevant and what is extraneous to meeting course objectives. Third, each chapter contains two demonstration problems that take the student step-by-step to the solution, review questions, extensive problem sets, and discussion questions to be used both inside and outside the classroom.

Chapter Organization

The 20 chapters that make up the text introduce modern corporate finance, cover the firm's investment decision, the firm's financing decision, and then related topics. Chapter 1 provides a framework from which to view the corporation and its objectives. Chapter 1 also presents an innovative approach that derives, through economic principles, a set of decision rules for corporate managers making decisions for shareholders. Chapter 2 discusses contracts and markets, including the concept of efficient markets, and sets forth the view of ownership through the corporation with contracting and agency relationships.

The next five chapters focus on time value and capital budgeting. Chapter 3 covers the basics of the time value of money for both single cash flows and annuities. Chapter 4 examines the valuation of financial securities. Chapter 5 draws an important distinction between financial assets and real assets, discusses how value can be created, and introduces the various techniques of capital budgeting. The second edition brings two chapters on capital budgeting earlier in the book to be with Chapter 5: Chapter 6 details the estimation of project cash flows, while Chapter 7 covers advanced topics in capital budgeting.

Chapters 8 to 10 focus on risk. A common theme in Chapters 8 and 9 is the separation of total risk into systematic and unsystematic components, and the use of the capital asset pricing model to "price" systematic risk. Chapter 10 introduces call options and discusses how the firm's equity can be viewed as an option on the firm's assets. The material on options sets the stage for an understanding of bankruptcy and issues of firm financing.

Chapters 11 to 13 cover the firm's financing and dividend decisions. Chapter 11 discusses financing in perfect markets, while Chapter 12 discusses financing in imperfect markets. The dividend decision is the subject of Chapter 13. Taxes and bankruptcy are highlighted throughout these three chapters.

Chapter 14 through 20 offer a menu of special topics from which instructors can rank-order according to their own preferences. To the extent possible, these chapters have been designed so that they can be used at nearly any point in the course after the first chapters. Chapter 14 on corporate ethics remains as a stand alone chapter in the second edition and covers this increasingly timely topic in a unique way. Chapters 15 through 17 cover more traditional finance material: financial analysis, working capital management, and corporate financial planning. These three chapters represent an expansion of coverage of this material relative to the first edition. Chapters 18 to 20 cover three special topics: international finance, mergers, and financial engineering. Chapter 20 in financial engineering is an entirely new chapter in the second edition providing both an introduction to the topic and expanding the text's coverage of options to include put options and profit/loss diagrams.

Windows and Workshops

A special feature of the text is the boxed material in "Windows" and "Workshops." Windows provide extra detail related to the chapter material without interrupting the flow of the chapter. They are available to be "opened" and studied at the appropriate time. Workshops present step-by-step financial problem solving. Workshops are used to embed fundamental principles in finance, such as operating leverage and financial leverage, within chapters.

Supplements

Instructor's Manual

Created by Donald R. Chambers and Nelson J. Lacey, this teaching resource includes answers to all review and discussion questions; and detailed solutions to all problems, also designed for classroom distribution. For a copy, please email chambers@lafayette.edu.

Acknowledgments

We would like to thank the wonderful people at Hayden-McNeil who helped make this third edition possible including Pat Olson, Brett Sullivan and Colleen Bonadeo.

We would like to thank the following professors who assisted us in the development of this manuscript and provided valuable suggestions and comments:

Eric Amel, Arizona State University
Theodore A. Anderson, University of California at Los Angeles
W. Brian Barrett, University of Miami
Michael W. Becker, Valparaiso University
Richard H. Borgman, University of Maine
Ben Branch, University of Massachusetts at Amherst
K. C. Chan, Ohio State University
P. R. Chandy, University of North Texas
Jeffrey S. Christensen, Kent State University
David B. Cox, University of Denver
Ken B. Cyree, Bryant College
Vernon Dixon, Haverford College
Edward A. Dyl, University of Arizona

Robert M. Edmondson, Barton College
Henk, von Eije, University of Groningen
Mary E. Ellis, St. John's University
Thomas H. Eyssell, University of Missouri at St. Louis
Richard J. Fendler, Georgia State University
Manak C. Gupta, Temple University
Delvin D. Hawley, University of Mississippi
John A. Helmuth, Rochester Institute of Technology
Kendall P. Hill, University of Alabama at Birmingham
J. Ronald Hoffmeister, Arizona State University
Craig G. Johnson, California State University at Hayward
Steve A. Johnson, University of Texas at El Paso
Jarl G. Kallberg, New York University
Nikunj Kapadia, University of Massachusetts at Amherst
Dilip D. Kare, University of North Florida
Hossein B. Kazemi, University of Massachusetts at Amherst
William H. Lepley, University of Wisconsin at Green Bay
David Loy, Illinois State University
John A. MacDonald, SUNY Albany
Teye Marra, University of Groningen
Joe Messina, San Francisco State University
James A. Miles, Pennsylvania State University
David B. Milton, Bentley College
Lalatendu Misra, University of Texas at San Antonio
Sanjay Nawalkha, University of Massachusetts at Amherst
Timothy W. Nohr, Oklahoma State University
Larry G. Perry, University of Arkansas
Philip R. Perry, SUNY Buffalo
David C. Porter, University of Wisconsin at Whitewater
Ashok J. Robin, Rochester Institute of Technology
Arlyn R. Rubash, Bradley University
Thomas Schneeweis, University of Massachusetts at Amherst
John A. Settle, Portland State University
Jacobus T. Severiens, Kent State University
Mark J. Shrader, Gonzaga University
Robert A. Strong, University of Maine
David Y. Suk, Rider University
Sam Szewczyk, Drexel University
Gary Tallman, Northern Arizona University
Raj Varma, University of Delaware
James O. Washam, Arkansas State University
Allen L. Webster, Bradley University
Walter J. Woerheide, Rochester Institute of Technology
Thomas S. Zorn, University of Nebraska at Lincoln

Donald R. Chambers
Nelson J. Lacey

MODERN CORPORATE FINANCE

CHAPTER 1

INTRODUCTION TO MODERN CORPORATE FINANCE

The Walt Disney Company is one of the world's most recognized corporations. With annual sales of more than $25 billion, with more than 120,000 employees, and more than 2 billion shares outstanding, as well as worldwide distribution of merchandise, film, and video, the operation of the company presents a formidable task. What rules guide financial managers at companies like Disney?

This question provides an appropriate starting point with which to introduce *Modern Corporate Finance: Theory and Practice.* Our text builds a foundation of knowledge through principles that can be used to address corporate financial issues such as these:

- How can corporate managers attempt to satisfy the wishes of hundreds of thousands of the firm's investors dispersed throughout the United States, Europe, and beyond?
- To which new projects should the firm commit resources?
- Given that projects often take years to develop, how can the passage of time be incorporated into the decision to invest?
- Given that return on investment must be estimated, how can risk be incorporated into the decision to invest?
- Because cash inflows and cash outflows often occur in different cycles, how can the cash cycle be best managed?
- Can the particular mix of financial securities issued to finance projects affect the overall value of the firm?
- Does the set of rules change when projects are managed outside the United States?

Although these are complicated questions, the economic principles that underlie all of them are few in number and have common elements. Chapter 1 introduces these principles by defining modern corporate financial management and addressing the following questions:

What is finance?

Who uses finance?

What do financial managers do?

What is meant by *modern*?

What is the goal or purpose of the corporation?

Chapter 1 also discusses the economic foundations of finance and overviews the process of building models.

Modern Corporate Finance

Imagine that you are in the final interview for a job—your best job opportunity yet. This last appointment is with the company's president, who is a young entrepreneur who has driven the small company with record results. After reviewing your résumé, the president says: "I see you list finance as the focus of your studies over the past several years. I have two questions for you: First, how would you define *finance*? Second, because business administration is your major, what is the goal of a corporation and why?"

modern corporate finance
An approach to the study of finance that integrates financial decisions of business firms within a logical framework.

Defining finance and understanding the goal of the corporation provide an ideal backdrop for introducing **modern corporate finance.** Modern corporate finance is an approach that integrates financial decisions of business firms within a logical framework and teaches you to think clearly about the discipline of finance—to see the "big picture." This text accordingly builds a foundation for problem solving within the business enterprise.

There is a temptation to want to reduce the study of finance to a cookbook approach, developing a set of procedures and following them step by step to solve a particular problem. Our approach to modern corporate finance begins differently. It first teaches the student to understand the problem, and then to organize a solution to the problem through the use of models.

For example, consider the problem of investing corporate funds. The solution is to invest if the benefits of the investment exceed its costs. The model that will be introduced to measure costs and benefits is *net present value (NPV)*. When it is correctly applied, the net present value model will guide corporate managers to choose projects that add value to the firm.

Once a model has been introduced, this text will then emphasize the development of practical applications. After each concept has been presented, techniques will be introduced accordingly to use the model to solve real-world problems.

Example 1.1 ________ As an overview, let's take a brief look at the types of financial decisions that confront all organizations, large or small. For a multinational firm like Ford, this might be a decision to enter the downsized sport-utility vehicle market currently dominated by Japanese automobile manufacturers. Before devoting the resources needed to build factories, to hire labor to design and build the vehicles, and to embark on a campaign to market the vehicles, Ford must weigh the costs of this decision against the anticipated outcome carefully. The owner of a neighborhood furniture store might similarly consider the purchase of a larger delivery truck to provide better customer service.

How do firms make these decisions? The choices can affect their fortunes for better or worse. In Ford's case, success in sport-utility sales will enable the firm to garner a larger share of the market, thereby increasing overall profits. In the case of the furniture store, the failure to purchase the truck could mean being forced out of business by competitors who spend more on services for their customers. In both cases, financial decisions play a key role in building a competitive advantage in the marketplace. This book provides you with the means to analyze these decisions.

The Meaning of Modern Corporate Finance

Aristotle wrote: "Those who wish to succeed must ask the right preliminary questions." In our case, the preliminary questions relate to the meaning of the words in the title *Modern Corporate Finance.* As a vehicle for getting started in your study of finance, we will examine each of the words in the title to develop some working definitions and some themes that organize the rest of the book. Thus, the starting point in this introduction is the investigation of the word *finance.*

What Is Finance?

Finance is an extension of economics. This does not mean, however, that studying finance is identical to studying economics. Economics is the foundation of finance just as physics is the foundation of engineering or even of riding a bicycle. People do not need to have a thorough understanding of physics to learn to ride a bike—they just need to know a few principles. Finance similarly relies on a few economic principles to develop powerful decision-making tools for virtually every business decision.

Let us begin with a definition of economics: **Economics** studies the interaction of people with regard to scarce resources. Stated another way, economics is the study of the allocation of scarce resources, including how resources are produced and consumed by the participants in the economy.

economics
The study of the allocation of scarce resources or, more precisely, the study of how people, acting individually or through the businesses and governments they form, make decisions regarding the production and use of scarce resources.

finance
Applied economics or, more precisely, the economics of time and risk.

Finance takes underlying economic principles and projects them into more practical tools by incorporating the passage of time as well as uncertainty or risk. With this in mind, we can build a definition of finance from the definition of economics: **Finance** can be defined as applied economics or, more precisely, as the economics of time and risk.

The primary topic of corporate finance, accordingly, is how corporate financial managers make decisions today that affect outcomes that occur through time, including risk. For example, a decision to invest money today in a bagel-making machine in order to sell bagels in the future is a decision involving time. Further, there are no guarantees that bagel sales will meet projections inasmuch as competition, uncertain economic conditions, and changing tastes and preferences of consumers add risk to this investment decision.

valuation
The process of placing a value on, or determining the worth of, resources such as buildings, equipment, and ideas; the central process of finance.

An underlying theme of this text is that financial decisions are best made based on market values. **Valuation** is the process of placing a value on or determining the worth of resources, such as buildings, equipment, and ideas; *market values* are values determined in the marketplace. Decision making itself can be viewed as valuation. Someone who decides not to undertake a particular project has essentially placed a negative value on the idea. On the other hand, people accept ideas for which they perceive there is a positive overall value.

For example, the decision to purchase a bagel-making machine may be viewed as the comparison between the value of the machine to the baker and the value of the money needed to purchase the machine. Because all disciplines within business, such as marketing, accounting, management, and production, require valuation and decision making, finance is core to understanding business.

The insight provided by finance is that decision making and valuation in the presence of both time and risk can be handled through the use of a few basic principles of economics—principles used by people in everyday life. This book trains you to recognize economic principles within seemingly complex problems in corporate finance, and demonstrates that solutions to problems are straightforward extensions of these principles.

Who Uses Finance? Because everyone who makes economic decisions through time and with risk uses finance, the study of finance is often divided by the type of user. This book is about *corporate* finance; therefore, it emphasizes the financial decisions faced by corporations and their financial managers. Because corporations comprise such a large and important portion of the U.S. economy, corporate finance is the most common type of finance course. In contrast, other finance books and courses discuss the decision making faced by households (personal finance, consumer finance, or investments), governments (public finance), or specialty areas such as banking or international finance.

The study of corporate finance can be characterized by three types of decisions. As shown in Figure 1.1, financial management is viewed as integrating the major tasks of raising money, called the *financing decision;* investing money, *the investment decision;* and managing cash, the *working capital decision.*

Example 1.2 ________ In the instance of the bagel-making machine, first, the decision to purchase the machine is an example of the investment decision. This decision would be made on the basis of the cost and the projected benefits that the machine would bring. Second, how to pay for the machine is an example of the financing decision. The sources available for payment include the savings of the in-

FIGURE 1.1 The Role of Financial Management

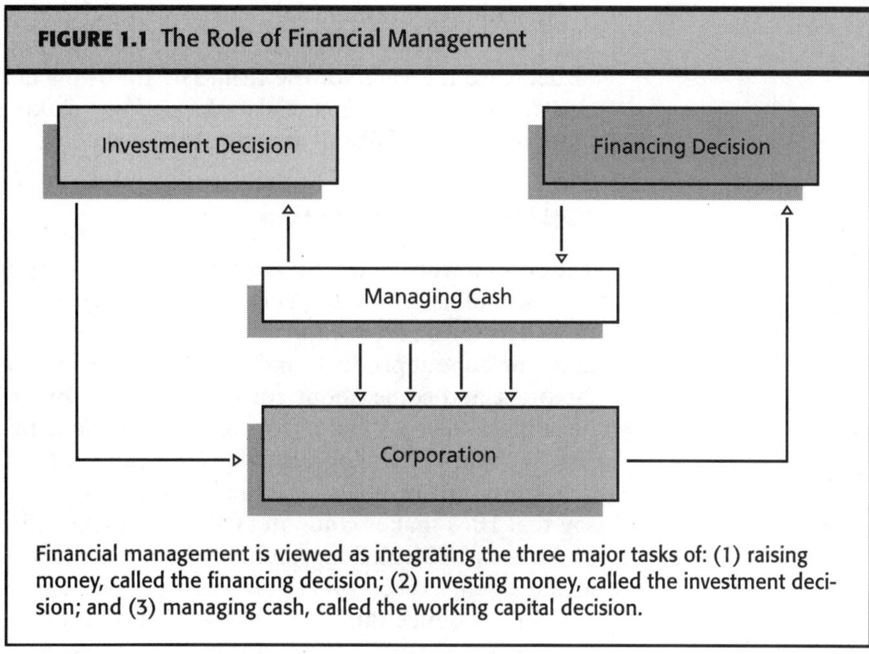

Financial management is viewed as integrating the three major tasks of: (1) raising money, called the financing decision; (2) investing money, called the investment decision; and (3) managing cash, called the working capital decision.

dividual who will own the machine, funds from individuals who become part owners of the machine, a loan from a bank, or loans from other investors. Third, how to keep the machine running throughout the year involves working capital decisions, which become important in situations where costs and benefits do not match up over time.

What Do Financial Managers Do? At a conceptual level, financial managers gather information, analyze the information, and then make decisions based on market values. On a practical level, the duties vary based upon the level of the manager and the area of decision making.

For example, the highest-level managers make the firm's major decisions regarding financing, investment, and working capital management. The financing and investment decisions would typically be the most important, such as where to obtain the funds and in which projects to invest.

Lower-level financial managers perform financial analyses that serve as the relevant input in making major decisions. For example, financial analysts study decisions such as which projects to recommend to top management, how best to pay the firm's bills, and where to put the firm's extra cash. Financial analysts monitor and regularly evaluate various aspects of the firm's operations, such as whether customers are creditworthy and should be allowed to purchase products on credit. Many financial managers perform these tasks for investment firms and banks, as well as for traditional manufacturing or service corporations.

Regardless of a financial manager's level and area, the objective of the analysis is the same—to determine whether the proposed action will increase or decrease the value of the firm. The following chapters provide a foundation for performing financial tasks and for making the financial decisions that underlie virtually all aspects of business.

Defining the Corporation

The second word in the book title, *corporate,* is significant because the focus of this book is on the financial decisions of businesses, specifically corporations. The term *corporation* means different things to different people. Some may think about products and services, some about employees, buildings, and factories, and some about corporate slogans or logos. Indeed, it is hard to hear the names of major corporations without thinking of their products: IBM, computers; Kellogg, breakfast cereal; Ford, cars and trucks.

A corporation, however, is actually none of these things. Whereas we can say that IBM makes computers, Kellogg makes cereal, and Ford makes cars and trucks, IBM, Kellogg, and Ford are really just names that define specific arrangements or contracts between people. Those within the corporation certainly produce things, but the corporation itself can serve only as a conduit between people. Viewed this way, the corporation is a legal entity—a collection or nexus of contracts—and as such is different from some other types of business organizations.

corporation
A distinct legal entity defined by the contracts between individuals such as owners, creditors, workers, suppliers, consumers, those in the surrounding communities, and those in all levels of government.

In summary, a **corporation** is a collection of contracts set up by one or more persons for the purpose of engaging in economic activity. These contracts might specify labor agreements, customer agreements, or agreements between business organizations and local governments and communities. The corporation itself, however, serves only as a link or connection between these various contracts.

Forms of Business Organization In addition to the corporation, the other two general types of business organizations are the *sole proprietorship* and the *partnership.* Corporations have certain qualities that make their financial decisions more complex than those of the other two. This section will compare the contracts that define each type of business organization.

sole proprietorship
A type of business organization in which an individual, acting alone, conducts business. Because the individual does not create a formal business organization agreement, the legal rights and responsibilities of the sole proprietorship are equivalent to the rights and responsibilities of the person who owns the business.

A **sole proprietorship** exists when an individual, acting alone, conducts business. Because the individual does not create a formal business organization agreement, the legal rights and responsibilities of the sole proprietorship are equivalent to the rights and responsibilities of the person who owns the business. For example, the income of the business is taxed directly as income of the owner when he or she files a personal tax return.

Other obligations of the sole proprietorship, including repaying borrowed money, fulfilling promises such as warranties, and paying costs of lawsuits, are the same as those of the person who owns the business. Thus, the sole proprietor is personally liable for all debts incurred by the business and puts all of his or her personal wealth at risk when operating a business—an aspect known as *unlimited liability.*

partnership
A type of business organization formed when two or more individuals join together to conduct business. Although no formal contractual agreement is required to form a partnership, the members will often voluntarily draw up a legal agreement specifying the rights and responsibilities of each partner.

A **partnership** is formed when two or more individuals join together to conduct business. Although no formal contractual agreement is required to form a partnership, the members will often voluntarily draw up a legal agreement specifying the rights and responsibilities of each partner. These rights and responsibilities include an understanding of how funds will be raised, how profits will be divided, and how the partnership will be dissolved. For tax purposes, the income or losses of the partnership must be reported on each partner's personal income tax returns.

As with a sole proprietorship, a partnership can expose its owners to unlimited liability—the responsibility to repay all obligations of the partnership such as borrowed money, unpaid expenses, and legal costs—even if the money required extends beyond the partners' investment in the business and into their personal wealth; however, a common type of partnership is a *limited partnership.* It releases or protects certain partners who may not participate in running the business, known as *limited partners,* from liability above and beyond their personal investment in the partnership. The partner who sets up the limited partnership and who is not protected from unlimited liability is the *general partner.*

In contrast to both the sole proprietorship and the partnership, the corporation is an organization that must be formed by legal agreement. The corporation is a distinct legal entity defined by the contracts between the individuals who make up the corporation. These individuals include owners, creditors, workers, suppliers, consumers, those in the surrounding communities, and those in all levels of government.

The relationship between owners and creditors is an example of one of the contracts that constitute a corporation. In the corporate organization, the owners are protected from losing more than their investment. In other words, the owners enjoy what is termed **limited liability.**

limited liability
Protection for the owners of a corporation against losing more than their original investment.

Another important feature of the corporation is that earnings from the business are taxed at corporate rates by both the state and federal governments. The earnings are then taxed again at the personal level if and when they flow through to the corporation's owners. In general, this *double taxation* of corporate earnings is viewed as a disadvantage of the corporate form.

A special type of corporation known as the *S corporation* allows relatively small corporations to avoid the double taxation of corporate earnings by flowing all of the corporation's earnings directly to the personal tax returns of the owners (without being subjected to corporate income taxes). Other distinctions between these three general forms of business organizations are summarized in Window 1.1.

While the technical definition of a corporation includes a collection of contracts, there are other ways to view the typical contractual relationships of a corporation. We call these the balance sheet view, the cash flow cycle view, the organizational view, and the modernist view. A discussion of each follows.

WINDOW 1.1

Types of Business Organization

This window compares and contrasts the three major types of business organizations: the sole proprietorship, the partnership, and the corporation.

Sole proprietorships are by far the most common type of business organization. Of the 23.6 million businesses in the United States in 1997, more than 17 million, or 73 percent, were organized as sole proprietorships.* Advantages of the sole proprietorship include legal simplicity, a lack of required paperwork and financial reporting, and an ability to charge any losses in the business against the proprietor's outside income to reduce taxable income.

There are, however, disadvantages to sole proprietorships: In addition to unlimited liability (i.e., the proprietor may be held personally liable for all debts incurred by the business), the reliance on a single individual limits both capital-raising ability and continuity. Sole proprietorships must usually rely on bank loans and personal savings for investment funds. This explains why sole proprietorships tend to be small businesses, which account for less than 5 percent of total business receipts of U.S. business activity in 1997. In addition, because it relies on a single individual, the sole proprietorship usually dissolves when its owner retires or dies.

Partnerships share many of the advantages and disadvantages of the sole proprietorship. They are simple to organize, require little paperwork, and enjoy tax benefits; however, they suffer from unlimited liability, limited sources for investment funds, and a lack of continuity. Unlike sole proprietorships, the partnership has the ability to draw from a slightly larger pool of talent and capital, but it suffers from potential conflicts between the partners. Partnerships accounted for less than 7.5 percent of the total number of U.S. businesses in 1997, and only 7.2 percent of total U.S. business receipts.

The corporate organization addresses many of the disadvantages of both the sole proprietorship and the partnership. Corporate owners (shareholders) enjoy limited liability because their losses are limited to their investment in the business. The corporation can more easily raise investment funds by issuing stock or by borrowing, in the form of debt. In addition, the life of the corporation is not limited to one person or a few key people, and, finally, the corporation can benefit from professional management.

There are, however, disadvantages: Corporations require significant amounts of paperwork and regulation, and they are often subject to financial reporting requirements such that all aspects of the business must be documented and available to the public. In addition, profits from the business are taxed at the corporate level by state and federal governments, and are taxed again at the personal level if and when they flow down to the corporation's owners.

In summary, there are advantages and disadvantages to each type of business organization. It is clear that the corporate form is conducive to large business operations. While comprising only 20 percent of total U.S. businesses in 1997, the corporation accounted for 88 percent of total U.S. business receipts and 72 percent of total U.S. profits.

*Statistical Abstract of the United States, 2000. U.S. Census Bureau

assets
Everything that can produce value for the firm, including buildings, equipment, land, patents, inventories, and cash.

debt
Obligations of the firm including accounts payable, bank loans, and bonds. Another name for these obligations is liabilities. Those who hold these claims are known as debtholders, creditors, or bondholders.

equity
The difference between the value of assets and value of debt. The equity of the firm is its common stock, and those who hold equity are often called stockholders, shareholders, or equityholders.

The Balance Sheet View of the Corporation The balance sheet view of the corporation has as its roots the financial statement with the same name. The corporation is viewed as a collection of **assets** (things owned), **debt** (things owed), and **equity** (the difference between what is owned and what is owed):

$$\text{Assets} = \text{Debt} + \text{Equity} \tag{1.1}$$

Assets include everything that can produce value for the firm, including buildings, equipment, land, patents, inventories, and cash. Debt represents the obligations of the firm, including accounts payable, bank loans, and bonds. Another name for these obligations is *liabilities,* which are held by individuals known as debtholders, creditors, or bondholders. The equity of the firm is its common stock, and the people who hold equity are often called stockholders, shareholders, or equityholders. The stockholders, as owners of the equity, are the owners of the firm. Equity is sometimes referred to as a *residual claim* because it represents something that is left over after the claims of all debtholders have been satisfied.

Formula 1.1 of the balance sheet reduces to its simplest terms the relationship between assets, debt (liabilities), and equity. In practice, however, a balance sheet can look complex because such a variety of categories and formats are used. Assets, liabilities, and equity are often broken into subcategories, and these subcategories can be broken down further.

Figure 1.2 shows the balance sheet of an actual corporation, the Walt Disney Company, and we have highlighted the three major categories. Disney reports fourteen categories of assets that totaled more than $43 billion in 2001, six categories of liabilities that totaled just under $21 billion, and five categories of equity that totaled more than $24 billion. The categories are highlighted to reflect the formula given by Assets = Liabilities + Equity. This allows you to see the balance sheet's big picture as portrayed by an actual company. In other words, Figure 1.2, like all other balance sheets, is simply a listing of assets, liabilities, and equity.

Figure 1.2 values each item using its accounting value. In other words, the value assigned to each entry, such as equipment, is based upon accounting rules. The accounting value is typically the initial cost of an item with possible regular adjustments using accounting rules such as depreciation.

Formula 1.1 can be rearranged to show the balance sheet view from the perspective of the equityholders:

market values
Values that the marketplace would place on items. Market values contrast with historical values, which are the values placed on items when they were originally purchased.

$$\begin{aligned}\text{Market Value of Equity} = {} & \text{Market Value of Assets} \\ & - \text{Market Value of Debt}\end{aligned} \tag{1.2}$$

Formula 1.2 places equity on the left-hand side and adds the word *market* to the formula. **Market values** are the values that the marketplace would place on items, and they contrast with accounting values, which were discussed earlier. To illustrate, the value of an individual's ownership in an auto

FIGURE 1.2 The Walt Disney Company's Balance Sheet

The Walt Disney Company's Consolidated Balance Sheets
(in millions)

September 30	2001	2000
Assets		
Current Assets		
Cash and Cash Equivalents	$ 618	$ 842
Receivables	3,343	3,599
Inventories	671	702
Television costs	1,175	1,162
Deferred income taxes	622	623
Other assets	600	635
Total current assets	7,029	7,563
Film and television costs	5,235	5,339
Investments	2,061	2,270
Parks, resorts and other property, at cost		
Attractions, buildings and equipment	19,089	16,610
Accumulated depreciation	(7,728)	(6,892)
	11,361	9,718
Projects in progress	911	1,995
Land	635	597
	12,907	12,310
Intangible assets, net	14,540	16,117
Other assets	1,927	1,428
	$ 43,699	$ 45,027
Liabilities and Stockholders' Equity		
Current Liabilities		
Accounts payable and other accrued liabilities	$ 4,603	$ 5,161
Current portion of borrowings	829	2,502
Unearned royalties and other advances	787	739
Total current liabilities	6,219	8,402
Borrowings	8,940	6,959
Deferred income taxes	2,730	2,833
Other long term liabilities, unearned royalties and other advances	2,756	2,377
Minority interests	382	356
Commitments and contingencies		
Stockholders' equity		
Preferred stock, $.01 par value		
Authorized – 100 million shares, Issued – none		
Common stock		
Common stock –Disney, $.01 par value		
Authorized – 3.6 billion shares, Issued – 2.1 billion shares	12,096	9,920
Common stock – Internet Group, $.01 par value		
Authorized – 1.0 billion shares,		
Issued – 45.3 million shares as of September 30, 2000	—	2,181
Retained earnings	12,171	12,767
Accumulated other comprehensive income	10	(28)
	24,277	24,840
Treasury stock, at cost, 81.4 million and 31 million Disney shares	(1,395)	(689)
Shares held by TWDC Stock Compensation Fund II, at cost		
Disney – 8.6 million and 1.1 million shares	(210)	(40)
Internet Group – 0.9 million shares as of September 30, 2000	—	(11)
	22,672	24,100
	$ 43,699	$ 45,027

Source: Company records. Data from www.disney.com.

mobile is equal to the market value of the auto minus the market value of the loan (the debt) against the auto:

$$\text{Auto Owner's Equity Value} = \text{The Market Value of the Auto} - \text{Market Value of the Auto Loan}$$

The auto owner has taken on debt (an auto loan) and has used the proceeds of the debt to buy the automobile. The person owns the auto subject to the terms of the debt, such that the person's equity or ownership in the auto must be reduced to reflect this debt obligation. If the owner does not make the loan payments, the debtholder will claim (repossess) the auto. In fact, if the auto is worth considerably less than the loan amount, the auto owner may find it in his or her interest to stop making payments, declare bankruptcy, and let the debtholder reclaim the auto.

The owners of a corporation's equity, like the owners of the auto, hold the claim to the corporation's assets, subject to the claims they have voluntarily surrendered to the debtholders in the process of borrowing money. If the value of the firm's assets is greater than the total payments promised to repay borrowed money, then the stockholders will continue to make payments to the debtholders. If the value of the firm's assets is less than the total payments promised on borrowed money, however, then the stockholders will stop making promised payments by declaring bankruptcy and will thus allow the debtholders to take ownership of some or all of the firm's assets.

cash flow
Cash moving into the firm (cash inflow) or cash leaving the firm (cash outflow). Net cash flow is defined as the difference between cash inflows and outflows.

The Cash Flow Cycle View of the Corporation We can also view the corporation through the cash flow cycle, where **cash flow** is defined as cash moving into the firm *(cash inflow)* or cash leaving the firm (cash outflow). Net cash flow is defined as the difference between cash inflows and outflows. In contrast to the balance sheet view, the cash flow cycle view takes the assets, liabilities, and equity of the firm and, in effect, sets them in motion.

The accounting statement known as the *income statement,* with its revenues, expenses, and profit, is somewhat similar to the cash flow cycle with its inflows, outflows, and net cash flows. In an income statement, the activity of a firm is seen as producing revenues, causing expenses, and generating profits, where profits are defined by:

$$\text{Profits} = \text{Revenues} - \text{Expenses} \tag{1.3}$$

There are significant differences between cash flows and accounting numbers, however, such as revenues and expenses. For example, in an income statement, an expense can be included when there is a promise to pay for something, even if the money has not yet been paid. Further, many cash flows, such as the purchase and sale of land and buildings, are shown on an income statement only to the extent that the transaction produces a profit or loss. Thus, the revenues and expenses found in the income statement can differ significantly from the cash inflows and outflows of the firm.

FIGURE 1.3 The Cash Flow Cycle View of the Firm

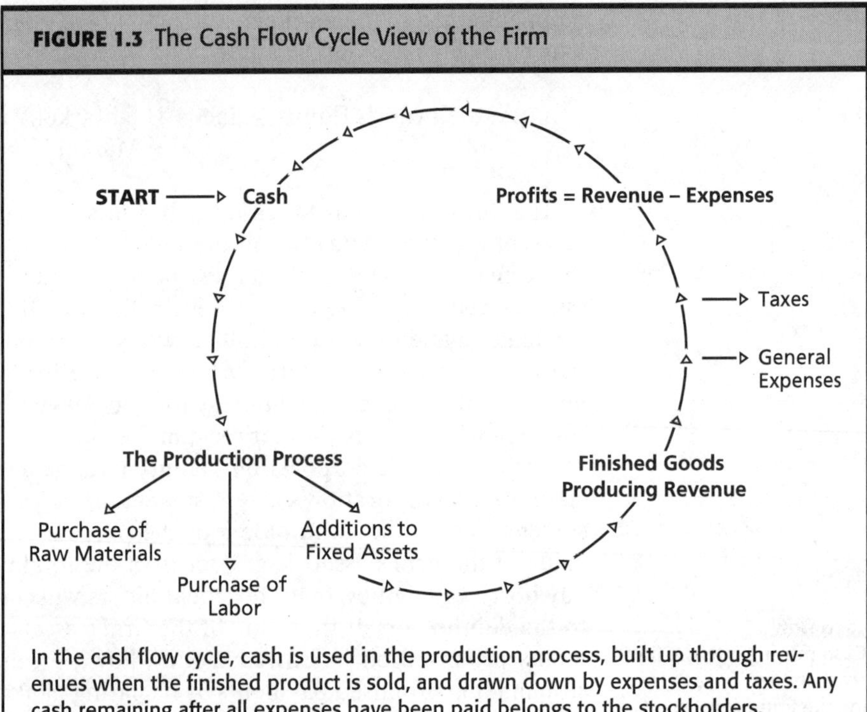

In the cash flow cycle, cash is used in the production process, built up through revenues when the finished product is sold, and drawn down by expenses and taxes. Any cash remaining after all expenses have been paid belongs to the stockholders.

We illustrate the cash flow cycle with a highly simplified example in Figure 1.3. The cycle starts in the upper left-hand corner with cash, either borrowed in the form of debt or supplied as equity by the stockholders. Cash is used in the production process to purchase raw materials, to replace equipment, and to purchase labor. By following the arrows in Figure 1.3, you will see that cash is built up through revenues when the finished product is sold, and is drawn down by expenses and taxes. Any cash revenue remaining after all cash expenses have been paid is a net cash flow that belongs to the stockholders.

Formula 1.3 represents a highly simplified cash flow statement. In practice, the firm's cash flow cycle is complex and can be erratic. A problem with cash flow analysis for a specific interval of time is that it can be severely affected by transactions that produce large cash inflows or outflows but have little effect on the firm's value—such as the sale of a building at its market value. Further, significant economic events with no immediate cash flow effects, such as losing a major lawsuit, would not be included in the firm's financial statement unless the cash were paid immediately.

The income statement attempts to correct the distortions caused by measuring cash flows over a specific interval of time. Accountants use complex rules and practices to attempt to measure and report the economically noteworthy changes in value. Accounting procedures are far from perfect, however, and some people argue that accounting numbers add more distortions than they correct.

FIGURE 1.4 The Walt Disney Company's Income Statement

The Walt Disney Company
Consolidated Statements of Income
(In millions, except per share data)

Year ended September 30	2001	2000	1999
Revenues	$ 25,269	$ 25,418	$ 23,455
Costs and Expenses	(21,670)	(21,660)	(20,030)
Amortization of intangible assets	(767)	(1,233)	(456)
Gain on sale of businesses	22	489	345
Net interest expense and other	(417)	(497)	(612)
Equity in the income of investees	300	208	(127)
Restructuring and impairment charges	(1,454)	(92)	(172)
Income before income taxes, minority interests and the cumulative effect of accounting changes	1,283	2,633	2,403
Income taxes	(1,059)	(1,606)	(1,014)
Minority interests	(104)	(107)	(89)
Income before the cumulative effect of accounting changes	120	920	1,300

Source: Company records. Data from www.disney.com.

The income statement reports the components of revenues and expenses, breaking them down into subcategories. For example, in the income statement of the Walt Disney Company shown in Figure 1.4, Disney reports of revenues for 2001 of approximately $25.3 billion, and expenses of approximately $21.7 billion. Profits, given in the income statement as net income, are approximately $0.12 billion. This allows you to see how an actual company presents an income statement.

Thus, both cash flow cycles and income statements attempt to measure a firm's economic changes as they occur over a specific interval of time. Both procedures have their benefits and flaws. However, in the long run it is cash flow analysis that portrays the most accurate picture, since it is cash flow, not accounting income, from which the shareholders ultimately benefit. In other words, when the analysis includes all time periods rather than a specific interval, it is cash flow analysis that correctly measures value.

Cash flow analysis portrays the most accurate picture since it is cash flow, not accounting income, from which shareholders ultimately benefit.

The Organizational View of the Corporation The corporation can also be viewed in terms of its organization. As shown in Figure 1.5, corporate owners and managers are usually different individuals, in contrast to sole

FIGURE 1.5 The Corporate Organizational Structure

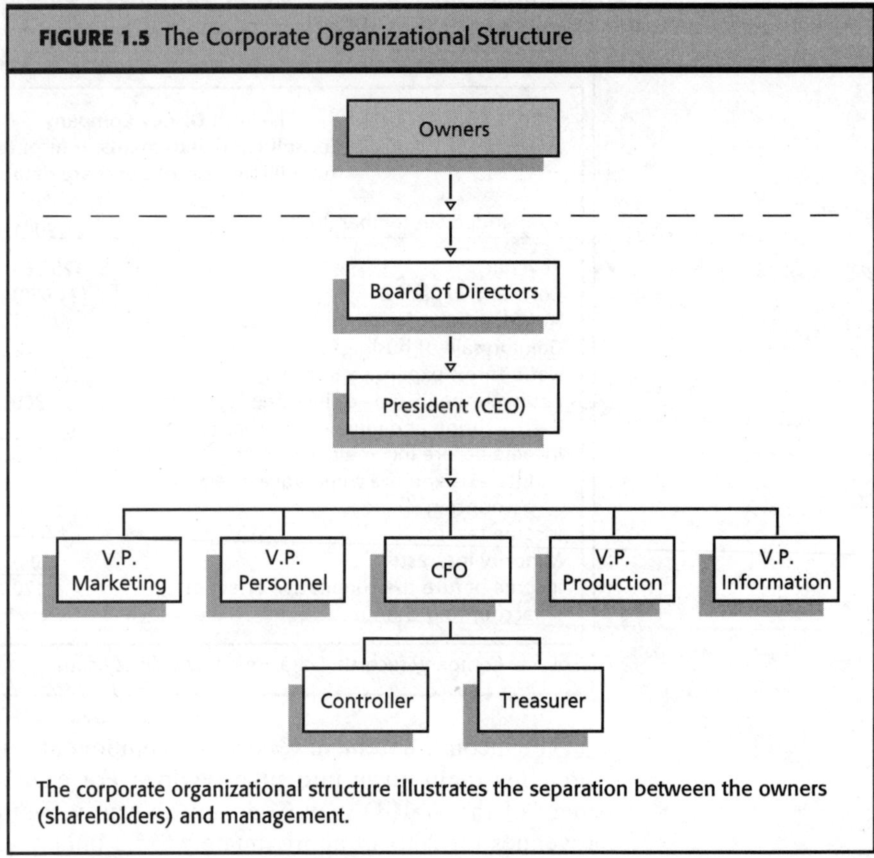

The corporate organizational structure illustrates the separation between the owners (shareholders) and management.

proprietorships and partnerships, whose owners and managers are usually the same individuals. The broken line in Figure 1.5 illustrates the separation between owners (stockholders) and top management in the corporate form of organization.

As owners of the firm, the stockholders have ultimate control over decisions regarding the firm's assets. This does not necessarily mean that the stockholders have the expertise or the desire to manage the firm on a day-to-day basis. Even if they had the desire and expertise, the number of stockholders is often so large that the very notion of stockholders making every decision is impractical and perhaps logistically impossible. This is illustrated in Table 1.1, which lists the ten largest U.S. corporations ranked by revenues generated (the Fortune 500) along with other pertinent financial information.

The largest U.S. corporation in terms of revenues is Wal-Mart. Wal-Mart had revenues in 2001 of almost $220 billion. The largest U.S. corporation in terms of the market equity value is General Electric (GE). In 2001, GE's market equity value was more than $400 billion. The tenth largest U.S. corporation ranked in terms of revenues is Philip Morris, with revenues just below $73 billion and a market equity value of just under $113 billion.

TABLE 1.1 Ten Largest U.S. Corporations Ranked by Revenues in 2001

Company	*Revenues (in millions)*	*Assets (in millions)*	*Market Value of Equity (in millions, as of 03/14/2002)*
Wal-Mart Stores	$219,812	$83,375	$ 277,543
Exxon	191,581	143,174	295,762
General Motors	177,260	323,969	47,463
Ford Motor	162,412	276,543	30,622
Enron	138,718	NA	186
General Electric	125,913	495,023	401,499
Citigroup	112,022	1,050,000	251,112
Chevron Texico	99,699	77,572	95,383
IBM	85,866	88,313	183,314
Philip Morris	72,944	84,968	112,495

Source: www.fortune.com

To overcome problems related to the diffused ownership of the typical corporation, the stockholders elect a board of directors to direct overall firm policy. The board selects a management team to participate in all major firm decisions, and the financial management positions shown in Figure 1.5 are part of that management team. Window 1.2 describes the typical functions of the top financial management team.

The Modernist View of the Corporation A theme throughout this book is the distinction between "traditionalists" and "modernists." Although the term *modern* or *modernist* will be more formally developed in the next section, we offer here a preview of finance from the modernist perspective. Modernists view the corporation as a set of contracts with three prominent characteristics:

1. Corporations can declare bankruptcy and therefore provide a protective shield in the form of limited liability to their owners.
2. Corporations are subject to corporate income taxes.
3. Corporations are often large enough that they require the owners (the shareholders) to hire managers to operate them. In this sense, the managers are known as *agents* of shareholders, and issues that relate to the relationship between managers and shareholders are known as *agency* issues.

Thus, when shareholders use the corporate form of business organization, their economic behavior may need to be adjusted to take into account the effects of these characteristics. In other words, bankruptcy, tax, and agency considerations may affect investment, financing, and working capital decisions. In the modernist view of the corporation, the essence of corporate finance is

WINDOW 1.2

The Top Financial Management Team

Almost every major decision within the firm involves the group of top managers known as the financial management team. The functions of the top management team are highlighted.

The Vice-President of Finance, or Chief Financial Officer (CFO)
In most larger firms, the VP of Finance is also known as the chief financial officer (CFO). The CFO formulates the major financial policies of the firm such as obtaining and investing funds. The CFO usually sits on committees of top management and is second only to the chief executive officer (CEO) in the corporate hierarchy in most corporations. The CFO is often heir apparent to the CEO or president.

The Corporate Treasurer
The treasurer manages cash within the firm. When the amount of cash held is greater than the amount currently needed, the treasurer will invest the excess cash in securities earning market rates of interest. When the amount of cash held by the firm is less than the amount of cash needed, the treasurer will borrow needed cash from sources such as banks. Thus, an important aspect of the treasurer's job is raising capital from outside sources.

The Corporate Controller
The controller prepares financial statements and manages the audits required to verify their accuracy.

how these three characteristics interact with the underlying economic principles of decision making in terms of time and risk.

Now that we have discussed in detail the terms *finance* and *corporation* and have considered the various ways of viewing the corporation, we will discuss what is meant by *modern* as we finish defining each term in *modern corporate finance.*

What Is Meant by *Modern*?

Finance has evolved over the past 40 years from a discipline close to accounting (the traditionalist approach) to one dominated by economic thought and reasoning (the modernist approach). In this development, finance has adopted the rules of science in suggesting plausible reasons for observed events, proposing theories to explain the events, and using data to test those theories.

One can trace parallels between the development of modern finance and modern medicine. In the Dark Ages, problem solving in medicine was unsystematic. If a person was sick, the physician might reason that because blood is an important carrier of materials throughout the body, it would be helpful to drain the bad blood and allow the body to produce new, good blood. This practice of bloodletting is now known to have been the cause of numerous deaths.

Let us take a closer look at how such medical practices as bloodletting could have become popular. A physician may have tried bloodletting on a patient who recovered (obviously not because of the bloodletting, but, rather, in spite of it) and inferred that the bloodletting was helpful. Based upon this single experience, or perhaps several such experiences, the physician taught other physicians to do the same.

Modern medicine has made great strides in the careful development of knowledge using rigorous experimentation. In other words, rather than relying on a few observations, the scientific researcher performs numerous tests to separate truth from coincidence. In addition, in a variety of other sciences, the great value of careful construction and testing of models has become clear. Once the foundation of understanding is in place, the simplified model can be used to solve real-world problems.

model
An abstraction from reality.

Because finance is not an experimental science, but one that relies on interpreting observations, it relies on **models**, as does economics. Models simplify problems and can be used to produce tremendous insights into the behavior of people within and through corporations. Thus, using underlying economic principles, finance develops models to explain how decisions are to be made.

Models should be evaluated by the extent to which they help us understand and solve complex situations. A particular model should never be criticized as being unrealistic. This point is so important and clear that Nobel

WINDOW 1.3

An Anecdote About Model Building

In order to understand that the *reality* of assumptions is not important, consider the following theory or model:

Assume that ice cubes can walk and open doors. Assume further that ice cubes are intelligent and that they prefer to be in a place that is as cold as possible. Under these assumptions, if you were to enter a house and wanted to find some ice cubes, where would you look for them?

Based upon the model's assumptions, we can deduce that the ice cubes would have moved to the freezer and that we could find the ice cubes if we looked there.

Nobel Laureate Milton Friedman points out that the model is useful because it explains or predicts something we need to know: where to find ice cubes. The model is very unrealistic, however, because we know that ice cubes cannot move or think.

The point of the anecdote is that the usefulness of a model should be based upon how well it helps us to understand a result, not on whether the assumptions are realistic. In fact, the definition of a *model*—an abstraction from reality—tells us that the model will have unrealistic assumptions. If a theory has no unrealistic assumptions, then it is reality rather than a model.

Prize Laureate Milton Friedman developed an example with which it could be illustrated. We offer Window 1.3 as an anecdote about model building.

Modern scientific knowledge is best constructed by carefully developing models and rigorously testing their ability to explain behavior. For example, using modern scientific principles, researchers have developed extremely successful models for explaining the prices of financial securities known as options (to be discussed in detail later in the book). In contrast, a careless researcher simply makes a few observations or perhaps even examines only a single case and attempts to infer knowledge.

The Goal or Purpose of the Corporation

We have already defined and described modern corporate financial management. We will now discuss corporate goals. Given the definition of the corporation as a collection of contracts, defining corporate goals really does not make much sense. People have goals, contracts do not. The issue can be stated better from the perspective of the goal of a particular person *with respect to* a corporation.

The various people who contract through the corporation have potentially very different goals. For example, an employee of the firm may desire a high salary, job security, and a good working environment. A supplier of raw materials may desire bulk purchases with a long-term commitment. A debtholder may desire that the firm live up to the agreement as specified by the debt contract. A member of the community where the corporation is located may desire that the corporation control noise during nighttime hours.

In attempting to define the goal of a corporation, it is probably most useful to identify the goal of the people who organized and own the corporation. From the perspective of finance these are the stockholders. This issue will surface throughout the text, so let us explore some of the concepts.

Corporate Ownership

In a pure legal sense a corporation is owned by its stockholders, but the claim that stockholders own the corporation goes beyond that of a legality. Because the stockholders are entitled to the wealth of the corporation once the contractual claims of others have been satisfied, they are the true owners of the firm.

What, then, is the goal of the shareholders of a corporation? Corporate finance teaches that the goal of the shareholders, and in fact the goal of the entire firm, is *maximization of shareholder wealth.* In other words, shareholders want the market value of their shares of stock to be as high as possible.

The principle of shareholder wealth maximization may appear to describe greedy, money-centered attitudes; however, shareholder wealth maximization in actuality means being efficient at doing whatever shareholders desire. In other words, if a manager operates a corporation in a manner that maximizes shareholder wealth, then the manager must be satisfying shareholder goals.

stakeholder view of the corporation
The view that the corporation can be influenced by—and therefore to some extent owned by—anyone who has a stake in the corporation's actions.

It must be said that alternative viewpoints exist. One such alternative viewpoint is that the corporation can be influenced by—and therefore to some extent owned by—anyone who has a stake in the corporation's actions. This view, often called the **stakeholder view of the corporation,** is expanded in Window 1.4 through a discussion of Ben and Jerry's Homemade,

WINDOW 1.4

The Stakeholder View As Seen Through Ben and Jerry's Homemade

The stakeholder view of the firm states that the corporation can be influenced by—and therefore to some extent owned by—anyone who has a stake in the corporation's actions. In other words, it is argued that the goal of the firm should be to benefit all stakeholders, not just the stockholders.

A firm that in some ways personifies this view is Ben and Jerry's Homemade Holdings, Inc., of South Burlington, Vermont. Although Ben and Jerry's makes ice cream, the unique aspect of the firm is their approach to business—an approach called "caring capitalism." In addition to Ben and Jerry's product mission (to make good-tasting ice cream) and their economic mission (to increase the value of their shareholders' wealth), the firm operates under a specific social mission:

To operate the company in a way that actively recognizes the central role that business plays in the structure of society by initiating innovative ways to improve the quality of life of our employees and a broad community: local, national, and international.

One of the ways the company works toward its social mission is through the Ben and Jerry's Foundation, created to distribute 7.5 percent of pretax profits to projects that are committed to social change (e.g., Center For Environmental Equity, Sweatshop Watch, and the Institute for Social Ecology).

The key to Ben and Jerry's Homemade is that the corporation's actions are still controlled by its owners. Many stakeholder advocates attempt to force corporations to adopt goals other than shareholder wealth maximization through government regulation.

The view of modern corporate finance is that there is nothing valuable about Ben and Jerry's social mission. This does not mean that these efforts are not worthy; rather, it says that individuals do not need to work through a corporation to attain these goals. In other words, caring capitalism can also be performed through philanthropic giving by the shareholders of firms that maximize shareholder wealth. The maximization of shareholder wealth is a goal that will allow the firm to concentrate its efforts on their product line, leaving the firm's shareholders to satisfy their own social agenda.

Inc., an ice cream manufacturer founded on a business principle called "caring capitalism."

The question of ownership is an issue of legal and philosophical concepts. The argument set forth by the modern finance viewpoint is clear and persuasive: Corporations belong to the shareholders and to the shareholders belongs the right to determine the goals of the corporation. This is referred to as **shareholder wealth maximization.**

shareholder wealth maximization
The financial objective of the corporation. This objective states that shareholders, as owners of the corporation, desire the market value of their equity to be as high as possible.

Does the goal of shareholder wealth maximization mean that managers should ignore employee and community concerns or even that all that shareholders can care about is money? The answers are, *no!* Maximizing shareholder wealth is in many cases comparable to producing products that people desire, at their lowest possible price, and at high quality, to be sold through convenient locations. Maximizing shareholder wealth is a goal that can result in job creation at competitive wages.

Owners Versus Managers

We have said that shareholders desire to have their wealth maximized by managers, but we must also realize that managers have their own goals. For example, managers may desire secure and lucrative jobs with attractive offices, travel, and freedom from pressures. However, some or all of these managerial goals may conflict with the shareholders' goal of having the highest possible market price for their shares.

The relationship between shareholders and managers is known as an **agency relationship.** An agency relationship exists when one or more persons (the *principal*) contract with one or more other persons (the *agent*) to perform a decision-making task for them. In the case of corporate finance, the shareholders are the principals and the managers are the agents. **Agency costs** are resources (including opportunity cost) utilized to align managerial goals with shareholder goals. In other words, the competing desires of shareholders and managers create conflicts and costs. One goal of the study of modern corporate finance is to understand these costs and to try to minimize them in an attempt to maximize shareholder wealth.

agency relationship
A relationship in which one or more persons (the principal) contract with one or more other persons (the agent) to perform a decision-making task for them. In the case of corporate finance, the shareholders are the principals and the managers are the agents.

agency costs
Resources utilized to align managerial goals with shareholder goals.

Now that we are equipped with this overview of modern finance, we will turn our attention to economic laws. Understanding economic laws and their implications is central to finance. Can you imagine trying to build an airplane without understanding the laws of gravity? It seems about as hopeless as trying to maximize shareholder wealth without understanding economic laws, markets, or valuation.

Economic Foundations of Finance

What skills are necessary to become a great pool player? Did you answer physics? Few people do, although great pool players understand physics (momentum, force, friction) better than most other people in the world. Most people do not analyze the ability of pool players in terms of physics. Rather, they assume that, through experimentation, thousands of mistakes are made until the essential principles become second nature.[1]

Just as pool players must understand the effects of physical laws, financial managers must understand the principles of economics when making investment, financing, and working capital decisions. Unlike pool players, most financial managers cannot afford the luxury of running a firm by trial and error, particularly when their decisions determine how millions of dollars will be invested. As many managers have discovered, financial skills are best attained through an understanding of the principles of economics within simplified models, then learning how to recognize and apply these principles to complex problems of the real world.

This section introduces the economic principles that form the foundation for financial decision making, most of which will seem familiar because they are part of the process you use in making everyday decisions. Financial managers use economic principles to make decisions. Investments made today often promise future cash inflows, and the period of time between the development of a project and its termination must be included in any project assessment. The financial manager must also include the effect of *uncertainty*—whether a project will perform as expected.

These economic principles also help us to understand financial markets. The financial manager relies on markets to raise funds to finance investments and uses the information in financial markets to assess the value of the firm. In the models that we will build to analyze investment, financing, and working capital management decisions, we need to know about the workings of markets. Financial theories have been developed in order to explain the way markets behave, and we will discuss them as part of this chapter.

Our goal is to describe, through principles, how shareholders behave in a simplified situation. It is extremely important that our knowledge be built carefully in order to avoid mistakes. As such, we first need to describe the conditions or assumptions that are essential in order for the economic principles of this chapter to hold. These conditions do not have to be true in *all* cases in order for the principles to be true or useful, but they allow the principles to be developed rigorously and provide a more complete understanding of the objective of shareholder wealth maximization.

Underlying Assumptions

Assumptions are the basis of models, and we start with the assumptions that underlie the economic principles of finance. First, we assume that people are

[1]Using the game of pool to illustrate the laws of physics and engineering first appeared in M. Friedman and L. J. Savage, "The Utility Analysis of Choices Involving Risk." *The Journal of Political Economy* 56, no. 4 (August 1948): 279–304.

rational. This means that individuals have preferences and that they act with available information and with some degree of intelligent logic to exercise their preferences. We know that this assumption does not hold for all people all the time, but it serves as a useful starting point.

Second, we assume that people have access to financial markets, and that these markets are well functioning. This means, essentially, that "the law of one price" holds—that the same asset can be purchased and sold by everyone at the same price. We further assume that markets contain some technical properties, such as the ability to trade at zero cost and the ability to divide products limitlessly, meaning that it is possible to purchase one half of a bond or one tenth of a share of stock.

With these assumptions, we are now ready to present our economic principles.

The First Principle: Positive Marginal Utility of Wealth

The first economic principle states that, given a choice, rational people prefer more wealth to less wealth, where *wealth* is defined as the sum of the values of all of the things owned. Because value can be measured through market prices, you can determine how wealthy you are by listing what you own, estimating what you could sell these things for today, and adding up the list.

positive marginal utility An economic principle stating that, given a choice, rational people prefer more wealth to less wealth, where wealth is defined as the sum of the values of all of the things owned.

Economists call our first principle **positive marginal utility** of wealth. *Utility* is the measurable happiness an individual derives from consumption. For instance, most people receive utility from eating ice cream. *Marginal utility* is the added utility from additional consumption of a product. Because positive means greater than zero, positive marginal utility of wealth means simply that people prefer more wealth to less wealth because more wealth will allow greater consumption in a well-functioning market.[2]

The first principle appears trivial until you realize that it holds not only for individual items but also for comparisons *between* items that trade in markets. For example, would a resident of Alaska prefer a $500 air conditioner to a $400 heater? The answer from our model is, *yes!* (Did this answer surprise you? If so, you were thinking more about the usefulness of the items to the Alaskan than about their *positive* marginal utility.) As long as the market for trading goods is well functioning, prices in the market are measures of the value of each item. Thus, the resident of Alaska could trade the $500 air conditioner for the $400 heater and pocket the $100 change. Choosing the $400 heater would be a violation of our first economic principle.

In fact, the ability to trade goods at market prices is key to our first principle. Well-functioning markets allow people to exchange whatever assets they own for assets that they prefer. They also allow workers to concentrate their productive efforts in areas where they have developed a comparative advan-

separation The ability to make certain decisions separately or independently from the preferences or tastes of the beneficiary.

[2]To some, positive marginal utility might be equated to greed. Most people, however, view greed as the excessive desire for wealth in relation to other desires. For example, greedy people might compromise their health or family for money. Positive marginal utility, therefore, is not quite the same as greed.

tage. This concept is known as **separation.** Separation refers to the ability to make certain decisions separate from or independent of the preferences or tastes of the beneficiary.

A farm provides a good example of separation. The farmer selects which crops to grow irrespective of what types of food the family wishes to eat. This is because the farmer knows that the family can go to the grocery store and best satisfy their individual tastes after maximizing the profit received from the harvest.

For the financial manager, the principles of positive marginal utility and separation have extremely powerful implications. Because all shareholders prefer more wealth to less wealth, and because wealth is measured through market prices, the financial manager can base *all decisions* on the *market value of the firm's stock price.* This is such an important statement that it merits emphasis. Managers may know little about the thousands of a firm's shareholders, but one thing they know for certain is that shareholders desire the firm's stock price to be as high as possible.

Given a choice between alternatives, shareholders desire the financial manager to make decisions that produce the highest market value for the firm's stock. A manager who causes the firm's share price to rise has made all of the firm's shareholders better off. On the other hand, a manager who causes the firm's share price to fall (e.g., by rejecting some project beneficial to the firm) has made all of the firm's shareholders worse off.

Given a choice between alternatives, shareholders desire the financial manager to make decisions that produce the highest market value for the firm's stock.

The Second Principle: Diminishing Marginal Utility of Wealth

diminishing marginal utility
An economic principle asserting that more and more units of consumption create less and less additional happiness when compared with previous units of consumption.

As we have stated, marginal utility is the added happiness derived from consuming a product. The second principle, **diminishing marginal utility,** implies that more and more units of consumption create less and less additional happiness when compared with previous units of consumption.

For example, virtually everyone would agree that it is worthwhile to purchase at least one pair of shoes because the advantages of wearing shoes are worth the price. Many people own several pairs of footwear because they find that the additional advantages to extra pairs of footwear exceed their costs.

Most people, however, discover an important principle when they consume—that the more individuals consume of a particular product, the less additional satisfaction they receive from each additional unit. The first pair of shoes provides a basic comfort need—an extremely high priority to most people. The second pair may also be important, but probably not as important as the first pair, and so forth.

At some point, the advantage offered by another pair of shoes no longer exceeds the disadvantages (primarily the cost) incurred when more shoes are purchased. Inasmuch as the person's preference for additional shoes approximately equals the market price of shoes, no additional shoes are purchased.

We can also express diminishing marginal utility in terms of wealth because wealth represents potential consumption. An added $1 of wealth becomes less and less important as a person becomes wealthier and wealthier.[3] Additional wealth would mean more to a person just before winning the lottery than it would mean just afterward. Notice that many multimillion-dollar lottery winners quit their jobs.

As with our first principle, diminishing marginal utility of wealth appears trivial until it is realized that the alternatives can include other products. An interesting result of well-functioning markets and diminishing marginal utility is that the relationship between market prices of various goods reflects the preferences of virtually all the people in the economy with regard to those goods.

For example, if the market price of beef is twice the market price of chicken, then generally we will find that people prefer beef two times as much as they prefer chicken. Thus, a piece of chicken would need to be double the size of a piece of beef to be equally attractive to consumers. If this were not true, then people would be bypassing opportunities to make themselves wealthier—which violates our first principle of preferring more wealth to less. For example, if John liked chicken more than beef, he would exchange beef for chicken, making the other person happier and pocketing the change. The process would continue until the law of diminishing marginal utility forced his desire for chicken to only half of his desire for beef (or until he ran out of beef).

Common sense tells us that this principle does not work perfectly in the real world, most likely because some of the assumptions are violated. The market for meat might not be well functioning; therefore, the person cannot return it for exchange. On the other hand, some people may not eat any meat at all. Most financial markets, however, have close to ideal conditions under which our principles hold fairly well.

This explains why the most desirable products seem to cost the most. It is not a cruel conspiracy of the ruling class perpetrated on consumers—it is a result of basic economic forces. Luxury items of the past, such as salt, spices, and silk, are abundant today and are not expensive. On the other hand, some items that have been abundant, such as clean water, are becoming more and more rare and more and more expensive today.

It is more important to note that diminishing marginal utility is the reason that people limit the amount of risk they bear. The explanation is that risks offer *opportunities* for higher wealth but *dangers* of lower wealth. Most

---

[3]Declining marginal utility may not hold for some people in selective circumstances. For example, a drug addict appears at times never satiated by the product—always wanting more. Without declining marginal utility, consumption of a particular product will "explode" to the exclusion of most other products. Contrary to the rule, another unit is consumed even though it appears to other people that the disadvantages outweigh the advantages.

people find that for a particular dollar investment, the unhappiness that would result from lost wealth is greater than the happiness that would result from added wealth. Diminishing marginal utility causes investors to take added risk only when it is compensated by higher expected return. A full explanation of this topic will be presented in the chapters on risk (Chaps. 8 and 9).

The Third Principle: Diminishing Marginal Return

diminishing marginal return
An economic principle whereby, at some point, the commitment of additional resources becomes detrimental to the firm with the result that the firm is forced to limit its investment to some optimal level.

In addition to deciding where to invest, financial managers must also decide when to stop investing—that is, the point at which the commitment of additional resources becomes detrimental to the firm. **Diminishing marginal return** forces a firm to limit its investment and output to some optimal level.

Just as added happiness diminishes with additional consumption, productive opportunities diminish with additional investment. *Marginal return* is the amount of additional value, expressed as a percentage, that a business can produce. *Diminishing marginal return* is the concept that, for a given business, there is a point at which higher production becomes more and more expensive without additional facilities, employees, land, markets, and so forth. A firm will invest up to the point at which the benefits earned on the next project are just equal to the additional cost of investment. Diminishing marginal return ensures that this will occur. Once this point is reached, the disadvantages associated with producing another unit can become greater than the advantages of production.

A firm will invest up to the point at which the benefits earned on the next project are just equal to the additional cost of investment. Diminishing marginal return ensures that this will occur.

Models have been developed to assist financial managers in making investment decisions and finding the optimal level of investment. These tools are known as *capital budgeting* models and are the topic of Chapters 5 through 7.

The Fourth Principle: Conservation of Value

conservation of value
An economic principle stating that the market value of a combination of commodities must be equal to the sum of the market values of all of the commodities in the combination.

Conservation of value states that the market value of a combination of commodities must be equal to the sum of the market values of all the commodities in the combination. (This principle is alternatively known as *value additivity* or *the law of one price*.) For example, suppose that the market price of apples is 25 cents and that the market price of oranges is 20 cents. At what price would two apples trade? At what price would an apple and an orange together trade? The principle of conservation of value would force the answers to be 50 cents and 45 cents, respectively.

If the combinations sold for more than the answers given, say 75 cents, anyone could make an instant profit by buying the fruit individually, and forming and selling the combination. The apple and orange could be bought separately for 45 cents. If they could be sold together for 75 cents, then there would be an instant profit of 30 cents.

Because people prefer more wealth to less wealth, why would they pay 75 cents for the combination when they could create it themselves for 45 cents? The answer is that they would not. In the market for apples and oranges described earlier, we would expect the law of the conservation of value to hold exactly. In large, well-functioning markets such as the financial markets in the United States, we would expect the law to hold very closely. Thus, breaking apart financial assets does not create value, destroy value, or transfer value. Window 1.5 illustrates the law of conservation of value in the market for stripped Treasury bonds. From the law of conservation of value, we know that the value of the total Treasury bond is equal to the "stripped out" parts.

A Summary of the Four Economic Principles

Economic principles provide a foundation for investment, financing, and working capital decisions. The first principle of *positive marginal utility* of wealth states that more wealth is preferred to less wealth, where wealth is measured by market prices. Given positive marginal utility of wealth, the financial manager will always choose the alternative that produces the highest market value for the firm's stock when making decisions for shareholders.

The second principle, *diminishing marginal utility* of wealth, states that the more a product is consumed, the less satisfaction it will bring. Diminishing marginal utility of wealth teaches us that market prices are accurate indicators of how people perceive value, and that risk bearing must be compensated with higher expected return.

These two principles are illustrated in Figure 1.6, which is called a *utility function* and demonstrates the relationship between utility and wealth. Utility is placed on the vertical axis and wealth is placed on the horizontal axis. In theory, each rational person in a well-functioning market has a utility function that links wealth and happiness, with everything else (e.g., health) held equal.

The first economic principle—positive marginal utility of wealth—is demonstrated in Figure 1.6 by a function that is always *upward sloping.* The second economic principle—diminishing marginal utility of wealth—is demonstrated by the way the curve decreases in its slope from left to right (i.e., is *downward curving*).

The third principle, *diminishing marginal return,* demonstrates that limits exist to the production of goods and services such that at some point the benefits of producing one additional unit are equal to the cost of production. This principle defines for the financial manager the level of production and the level of investment that maximize shareholder wealth.

WINDOW 1.5

Conservation of Value and the Stripping of Treasury Bonds

We observe the principle of conservation of value in the market for securities issued by the United States government. A type of U.S. government security called a *Treasury bond* offers investors two different kinds of payments: (1) relatively small interest payments received at specific points in time, and (2) a relatively large, one-time principal payment made at the time the security matures. For example, a 10-year Treasury bond might be purchased for $1,000 and offer to the investor interest payments of $100 per year for 10 years, and a principal payment of $1,000 when the bond matures in 10 years.

Although many investors are satisfied with receiving these payments, some may desire to receive only one payment. For example, parents of young children may wish to forego the series of interest payments in preference to a single payment in 10 years to cover college tuition and expenses.

In order to satisfy the needs of all potential investors, the U.S. Treasury provides a program in which it "strips" the interest and principal payments off some Treasury bonds and sells the payments separately to various investors who prefer to purchase only a single payment. The law of the conservation of value would suggest that the sum of the market prices of these separate securities, known as *Treasury strips,* should approximate the price of the total Treasury bond from which they were stripped. This is what we observe.

The stripped Treasury bond market provides us with an opportunity to illustrate an important implication of the principle of conservation of value. Think for a moment about the U.S. Treasury's strips program. By stripping the bond, the Treasury has not created anything of value; rather, it has simply cut up the cash flows offered by the Treasury bond. After all, is a pizza cut into twelve pieces more valuable than the same-size pizza cut into eight pieces?

Of course, investors who desire to invest in a part of the Treasury bond rather than the whole bond will compensate the Treasury for its work in stripping the bond (e.g., the paperwork, advertising, labor, and capital expenditures). The compensation, however, will not go beyond the costs of these efforts. In this case, the advantage gained from stripping the bond (the compensation) will exactly equal the disadvantage (the cost).

This must be the case in well-functioning financial markets. If for some reason the Treasury were compensated beyond its cost, then stripping would make it better off and would make investors who purchase the separate payments worse off because they would have paid too much. These actions would surely invite private corporations to come in and make their own shareholders better off by providing similar stripping services at lower cost. The increased competition would force down the compensation to the Treasury. In addition, if investors refused to pay to the Treasury an amount of compensation equal to the cost of stripping, neither the Treasury, nor anyone else, would supply these services.

FIGURE 1.6 A Utility Function

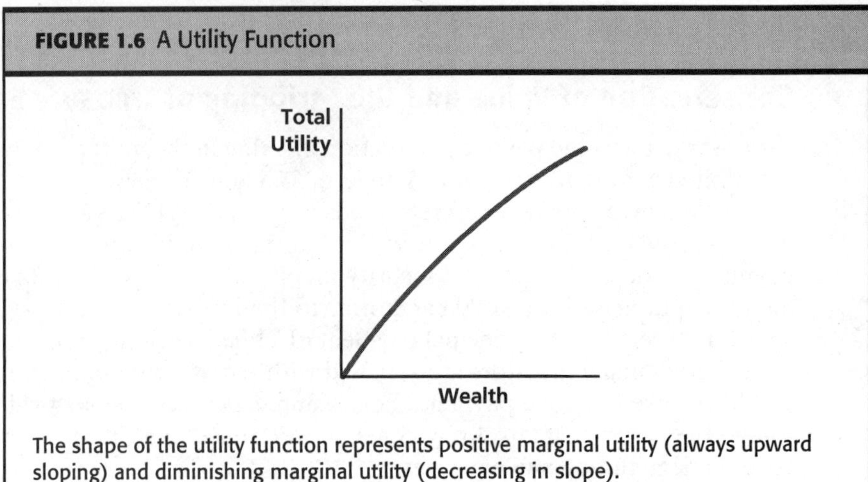

The shape of the utility function represents positive marginal utility (always upward sloping) and diminishing marginal utility (decreasing in slope).

Finally, the fourth principle, *conservation of value,* states that the value of two or more assets combined is equal to the sum of the values of the assets if they were separated. This principle implies that identical assets must sell for identical prices, and that in well-functioning markets, breaking apart financial assets does not create value, destroy value, or transfer value.

We will demonstrate next how economic decisions can be simplified by way of a model. Workshop 1.1 illustrates how the principles of positive marginal utility and diminishing marginal utility can be used to model how an individual decides which products to consume and how much to consume. Workshop 1.1 provides a foundation for analyzing corporate financial problems involving decision making, which will be developed further later in the book.

Time and Risk

The economic principles introduced earlier at first appear to apply only to cases of comparing two or more products at the same point in time, with no risk involved. In the real world, the financial manager must select investments that increase shareholder wealth. As we have said, benefits must be weighed against costs through time. Real-world investment decisions, however, can become complicated. Resources must be committed today to produce a product or service that will be brought to market in the future. In addition, because benefits and costs must be estimated, there is risk that benefits will be lower than anticipated or that costs will be higher than anticipated. The timing and risk of the cash flows expected from an investment will influence its value. Modern finance teaches that these simple economic

WORKSHOP 1.1

Economic Principles and Decision Making

Most people enjoy pizza, but nobody eats pizza continuously and limitlessly. How do people make the decision of whether and how much to consume? In this workshop we demonstrate the simple utility-based economic model that explains consumption decisions. If we analyze behavior using the principles of positive marginal utility and diminishing marginal utility, we can make some predictions about the amount of pizza people will buy and even the amount of other products they will consume.

Consider Bill, who enjoys pizza and root beer. Let us suppose that the utility function given in Figure 1.6 measures the pizza-eating happiness curve for Bill. Pizza costs $1 per slice. Data used to construct Bill's utility curve are given in Table 1.2. A "util" is a fictitious unit of happiness that allows us to describe a degree of happiness with a number.

TABLE 1.2 Bill's Pizza-Eating Utility

Slices of Pizza	*Increase in Happiness*	*Total Happiness*
1	10 utils	10 utils
2	8 utils	18 utils
3	7 utils	25 utils
4	6 utils	31 utils
5	3 utils	34 utils
6	2 utils	36 utils
7	1 utils	37 utils

Bill derives 10 utils of happiness from eating the first slice of pizza, but less and less happiness from each successive slice. His additional happiness starts to tail off after eating the first slice, and drops from 10 utils to 1 util by the seventh slice of pizza. Notice that Table 1.2 illustrates the principles of both positive marginal utility and diminishing marginal utility. Positive marginal utility is illustrated by the fact that added consumption always results in added happiness. Diminishing marginal utility is illustrated by the fact that the added happiness decreases at higher and higher levels of consumption.

At what point should Bill stop consuming pizza? This depends on his income level and other consumption choices. If Bill has limited income, then he should stop eating pizza when he can use the next $1 to derive more happiness from another product than that offered by the next pizza slice.

An alternative consumption choice for Bill is root beer, which costs $1 per glass. Table 1.3 presents Bill's root beer drinking utility.

WORKSHOP 1.1 (continued)

TABLE 1.3 Bill's Root Beer Drinking Utility

Glasses of Root Beer	*Increase in Happiness*	*Total Happiness*
1	9 utils	9 utils
2	4 utils	13 utils
3	3 utils	16 utils
4	2 utils	18 utils
5	1 util	19 utils

Given the opportunity to decide between pizza and root beer, what should he do? With limited income and an objective of being as happy as possible, his choice becomes clear. He should first eat one slice of pizza and then switch to root beer, as the second pizza slice offers him 8 utils of happiness, but the first glass of root beer offers him 9 utils of happiness.

When should Bill stop consuming root beer? As before, the answer depends on his income level and his consumption choices. If he has a choice of pizza and root beer, and if he has a third dollar to spend, then he should switch back to pizza, as the next slice offers more happiness as compared with the next glass of root beer.

Let us now allow for trading of commodities at market prices. Bill, who often clips coupons from the newspaper, brings a coupon to the local pizza parlor entitling him to a free beverage—no purchase necessary. The pizza parlor offers as beverages root beer at $1 a glass and orange juice at $2 a glass. We know from Table 1.3 that root beer delivers happiness to Bill. Orange juice, unfortunately, does not. What should Bill do?

The answer is clear if the pizza parlor allows Bill to trade commodities at market prices. He should use his coupon for orange juice, and trade back the orange juice for one slice of pizza and one glass of root beer. Of course, Bill must make consumption decisions involving many more than two products. The principles of positive marginal utility and diminishing marginal utility can be extended to incorporate any number of choices.

principles are equally appropriate for more complicated choices involving time and risk.

Time Value and the Concept of Different Commodities

Most people would not trade a double cheeseburger for three potato chips because they view the one double cheeseburger as being more valuable than the three potato chips. Should a corporate manager invest $100,000 today in return for $125,000 in 10 years? Logic might suggest yes—$125,000 *is* greater than $100,000. This logic is flawed, however, because it fails to recognize that, like the comparison of double cheeseburgers and potato chips, dollars received at different points through time are actually different commodities with different values. The correct answer is found by determining whether \$100,000 today has a higher value than \$125,000 due in ten years.

Because dollars through time are different commodities, they cannot be added to or subtracted from each other when making financial decisions. In order to analyze time value correctly, we need to change the future cash flow into an equivalent value in today's dollars and then make the comparison. Just as three potato chips are not worth three times as much as one double cheeseburger, \$125,000, to be received in 10 years is not 25 percent more valuable than \$100,000 to be received today.

Methods exist that allow precise market values to be placed on dollars that occur in different time periods. These methods help us to understand the *time value of money.* They also permit financial managers to use simple economic concepts to make decisions today regarding investments promising dollars to be received in the future. Once future cash flows have been transformed into present market values, separation can be applied to the decision-making process. In this context, *separation* refers to the idea that financial managers are satisfying all shareholders when they maximize the value of the shareholders' wealth.

Risk and the Concept of Different Commodities

Most financial decisions have some degree of risk. How can financial managers make decisions with such risks? Just as dollars through time are different commodities with different values, the promise of a risky cash flow is a different commodity compared with the promise of a safe cash flow. To put this another way, an investment that promises \$100 in 1 year with certainty might be viewed as more valuable than an investment that promises \$150 in 1 year with uncertainty.

For example, consider a cheese manufacturer whose limited manufacturing operations can produce either American cheese or Brie, but not both. Cost and sales estimates show that both are good investments, but that project Brie is expected to produce more future dollars as compared with project American cheese. Is Brie the product of choice?

The decision is not easy to make because Brie sales in the United States are uncertain, whereas sales of American cheese are virtually guaranteed. The difference in risk makes the investment in project Brie different from the investment in project American cheese. Because a safe dollar has a higher value than a risky dollar, project American cheese, although expected to produce fewer future dollars, might be the preferred choice.

Models exist to evaluate cash flows with different degrees of risk. These models, generally termed "valuation under uncertainty," comprise the material in the chapters on risk. These tools permit financial managers to merge uncertainty with rather simple economic principles. Once again, proper use of these tools permits the concept of separation. In this instance, separation refers to the ability of financial managers to make decisions that satisfy all shareholders by maximizing the shareholders' wealth. Thus, even decisions involving risky investments can be made on behalf of shareholders without having to worry about individual attitudes toward risk.

Summary

- Modern corporate finance is a two-step approach to problem solving within the business firm. The first step builds a foundation of understanding through the use of simplified models. The second step emphasizes practical applications of the model.
- Finance is defined as the economics of time and risk. The primary topics of corporate finance are how managers make financial decisions involving the passage of time and risk.
- The study of corporate finance can be characterized by three major types of decisions: the financing decision, the investment decision, and the working capital decision.
- The corporation is a collection of contracts organized by individuals for the purpose of engaging in economic activity. Those who normally contract through the corporation include owners (stockholders), creditors (debtholders), employees, suppliers, consumers, community residents, and the people who comprise all levels of government.
- Modernists view the corporation as a set of contracts with three distinguishing characteristics: (1) the corporation offers limited liability to its owners, (2) the corporation is subject to corporate income taxes, and (3) corporate owners (shareholders) hire professional managers to run the firm on a day-to-day basis. Managers are agents of the shareholders.
- Shareholders desire to have their wealth in the firm maximized. This goal requires managers to perform in a manner consistent with this goal.
- The economic principles that form the foundation of finance are positive marginal utility, diminishing marginal utility, diminishing marginal return, and the law of conservation of value.
- In well-functioning markets, market prices are not artificially determined but are the product of these basic economic principles.
- Managers need to know very little about the shareholders they represent in order to make optimal decisions for them as a group. Shareholders wish to have the market value of their claim maximized, which permits separation. Separation holds even when decisions involve different commodities, the passage of time, or uncertainty.
- Cash flows through time are best viewed as different commodities that cannot be directly added to or subtracted from one another. In a similar way, promised cash flows of different risk are different commodities that cannot be directly compared.

Demonstration Problems

Problem 1

The following chart describes the happiness or utility that Mary derives from fruit:

Quarts of Blueberries	*Total Utils from Blueberries*	*Quarts of Strawberries*	*Total Utils from Strawberries*
1	50	1	20
2	80	2	30
3	105	3	35
4	120	4	38
5	132	5	39

If quarts of blueberries and quarts of strawberries each sell for $2 and if Mary has $8 to spend, how will she spend the money if these are her only choices and if she decides to spend it all?

Solution to Problem 1

Step 1: The first step is to begin with no dollars spent and to determine whether the first two dollars should be used to buy blueberries or strawberries. It is implicitly assumed that Mary does not now have any quarts of fruit and therefore no utils from either type of fruit. The chart reveals that the first quart of blueberries would provide 50 utils of happiness and that the first quart of strawberries would provide only 20 utils of happiness. Thus, to maximize utility, Mary would first purchase a quart of blueberries.

Scorecard: 1 blueberries, 0 strawberries, $6 remain

Step 2: The second step is to compute the added happiness that another quart of blueberries would give Mary now that she already has one quart of blueberries. The chart reveals that two quarts of blueberries give her 80 utils, which is an increase of 30 utils from her current level of 50 utils. Thus, the incremental or marginal utility from another quart of blueberries is 30 utils. Because this is greater than the 20 utils a quart of strawberries would provide, Mary decides to purchase another quart of blueberries.

Scorecard: 2 blueberries, 0 strawberries, $4 remain

Step 3: The third step is identical to Step 2 except that we now begin with 2 quarts of blueberries. A third quart of blueberries would provide a total of 105 utils, or in other words a marginal increase of 25 utils. Because this is still greater than the marginal utils provided by the first quart of strawberries, Mary will maximize her utility by purchasing still another quart of blueberries.

Scorecard: 3 blueberries, 0 strawberries, $2 remain

Step 4: The final step is to determine what should be done with the last $2. A fourth quart of blueberries would provide a total of 120 utils, an increase of only 15 utils. Because this is less than the 20 utils provided by the first quart of strawberries, Mary decides to purchase a quart of strawberries with her last $2.

Scorecard: 3 blueberries, 1 strawberries, $0 remain

Final Solution: Mary should purchase 3 quarts of blueberries and 1 quart of strawberries for a total utility of 125 utils (105 utils from blueberries and 20 utils from strawberries).

Problem 2

Mary (the same person from Problem 1) has a garden with limited productive capabilities. The garden can be cultivated to raise either 1 quart of blueberries or 4 quarts of strawberries. Which alternative should Mary produce given that both alternatives require the same effort and costs? Assume that the market for fruit is well functioning and that the prices and preferences given in the first problem are applicable to this one.

Solution to Problem 2

Step 1: The first step is to recognize the importance of the assumption that the market for fruit is well functioning. This means that quarts of fruit can be purchased and sold at market prices with no taxes, fees, or any other sort of penalty. We can now view the productive capabilities of Mary's garden in terms of market prices. One quart of blueberries has a market value of $2. The 4 quarts of strawberries have a combined market value of $8. Thus, growing strawberries is the production alternative that produces the highest market value.

Step 2: The final step is to realize that $8 will provide Mary with more utility than $2. In Problem 1 we found that Mary can receive 125 utils from properly spending $8. Mary can only receive 50 utils from spending $2. It is not important that producing and consuming 1 quart of blueberries provides more utils (50 utils) than producing and consuming 4 quarts of strawberries (38 utils) because in a well-functioning market Mary can exchange the fruit that she is most capable of growing for the fruit that she most prefers to eat.

Final Solution: Mary should grow the 4 quarts of strawberries, sell them in the market for $8, and then spend the $8 in the manner that gives her the maximum utility.

Review Questions

1. How does finance differ from economics?
2. Explain the contractual differences between corporations, partnerships, and sole proprietorships.
3. What is the role of the stockholders in the organization of a corporation?
4. List and discuss three important characteristics of the corporation.
5. Who owns a corporation, and what is its goal?
6. What is an agency relationship?
7. Discuss the implication of positive marginal utility to the financial manager.
8. Discuss the implication of diminishing marginal utility to the financial manager.
9. Discuss the implication of diminishing marginal return to the financial manager.
10. Discuss the implication of the law of conservation of value to the financial manager.
11. Explain why, in well-functioning markets, a vegetarian might prefer $100 worth of beef to $90 worth of vegetables.
12. To what does the concept of separation refer?
13. Why is a "safe" dollar worth more than a "risky" dollar?

Problems

1. You are in a fabulous new discount store that accepts returned merchandise for exchange, with no questions asked and with a smile. In fact, if you desire they will even refund the retail price of an item. Through a local radio station you have won a free compact disc of your choice. Which of the following CDs will you select?
   a. Greatest Chants of the 11th Century $14.99
   b. Greatest Rock Hits of the 20th Century $12.99
   c. Saddest Country Hits of the 80s $11.99
   d. Most Exciting Vice-Presidential Memoirs $19.99
2. You are in a fabulous financial market where financial securities trade without transaction costs. You own one hundred shares of a firm called Machiavellian Motors, which sells for $20 per share. The chief executive officer (CEO) of Machiavellian Motors suddenly makes an announcement. Which of the following announcements and reactions would you prefer?
   a. The firm has been bought out. The CEO says that there is nothing that can be done to prevent it and predicts that the new owners will destroy the company. The price of the stock rises to $35 per share.
   b. The firm is altering its financial strategy in a move that the CEO predicts will generate huge gains in the future. The price of the stock remains at $20 per share.
   c. The firm is dramatically changing its product lines in a move that the CEO predicts will save the company. The stock price falls to $19 per share.
   d. The firm is fighting a takeover bid with every means at its disposal in order to protect itself from a corporate "raider." The price of the stock falls to $18 per share.
3. Maude loves to eat cookies and ice cream at the local soda shop. Maude's utility (happiness) from these two products can be expressed as follows:

Number of Cookies	*Total Utils from Cookies*	*Number of Scoops*	*Total Utils from Ice Cream*
1	10	1	16
2	18	2	22
3	25.5	3	24
4	31	4	25
5	36	5	25.5
6	40	6	25.7

(Beyond six cookies and six ice-cream scoops, Maude gets pretty sick.)

   a. If each cookie and each ice-cream scoop cost $1 each, what will Maude buy if she has $1? What if she has $2? How about $3 or $5 or $7?
   b. If the price of ice cream rises to $2 per scoop while the price of each cookie remains at $1, what will Maude buy if she has $2? What if she has $5?
   c. In general, what happens to the amount of ice cream that Maude eats as the price of ice cream rises relative to the price of cookies?
   d. Fill in the blank: If the price of ice cream rises to being X times more expensive than cookies, then Maude will switch to eating cookies until the marginal

utility from eating ice cream is ____ times the utility she gets from eating cookies.

e. In general, when the price of a particular item rises substantially, will people stop consuming it, consume less of it, consume the same amount, or consume more of it?

4. Farmer Ben knows that feeding a grain supplement to his cows will produce more milk according to the following schedule:

Total Pounds of Supplement Used	*Total Extra Pounds of Milk*
1	5
2	9
3	12
4	14
5	15
6	15.5

a. Ignoring all other issues, how many pounds of grain supplement should Farmer Ben feed the cows if the price of milk is $0.20 per pound and the price of the grain supplement is $0.50 per pound?

b. How many pounds of grain supplement should Farmer Ben feed the cows if the price of milk remains at $0.20 per pound but the price of grain supplement falls to $0.30 per pound? What if the price of grain supplement rises to $0.70 per pound?

c. Fill in the blank: In more general terms, suppose that the price of grain supplement is X times as expensive as milk. Farmer Ben should feed the grain supplement until each pound of grain supplement produces ____ more pounds of milk.

d. If a milk shortage develops, what would you expect to happen to the price of milk?

e. If the price of milk rises, what would you expect to happen to the amount of grain supplement manufactured and used? What will happen to the amount of milk produced?

f. If the price of grain supplement is exactly 3.25 times the price of milk, what do you know about every cow with regard to its ability to produce more milk using grain supplement?

Discussion Questions

1. Respond to the following statement:
The objective of the firm—to maximize shareholder wealth—is extremely narrow minded. This objective suggests that shareholders are more important than other groups of people who comprise the corporation. Corporate objectives should be directed to all groups, not just shareholders.

2. A U.S. senator said that a certain corporation was causing alarming levels of pollution, and that the corporation should be punished. Given our definition of the corporation, can the corporation pollute and can it be punished? If not, then who pollutes and who should be punished?

3. Recall Milton Friedman's ice cube example:
   Assume that ice cubes can move about (opening doors, etc.), assume that ice cubes desire to be as cold as possible, and assume that ice cubes are intelligent enough to know where it is cold. Using this theory, where would one look for ice cubes when entering a house?
   a. Which of the following conclusions can be rationally deduced from the foregoing assumptions? (more than one answer can be correct)
      (1) Ice cubes can be found in the freezer.
      (2) Some ice cubes will travel to the Arctic where it is cold.
      (3) Ice cubes can stay alive in boiling water.
      (4) Ice cubes can be purchased in bags from any convenience store.
   b. Which two of the conclusions in Part (a) could survive empirical scrutiny? In other words, which two conclusions accurately predict what we observe in the real world?
   c. Which one of the conclusions in Part (a) is both reasoned through deduction and can survive empirical scrutiny?
4. Adam loves people and his desire in life is to please them. Adam is always trying to do the things that others will appreciate the most and asking from others the things that cause the least burden. His brother Smithy loves money. Smithy is always trying to make as much money as possible and spend as little as possible. How will the decisions and actions of these two brothers differ when it comes to (a) selecting a career, (b) producing goods, and (c) consuming goods?
5. The law of conservation of value states that the market value of a combination must equal the sum of the market values of the items in the combination. This appears to suggest that mergers don't make sense because the market value of the firms combined is simply equal to the market values of the firms separately. How can this be true given the wave of mergers over the last 10 years?

CHAPTER 2

MARKETS AND CONTRACTS

Corporations do not exist in a vacuum; rather, they are part of a larger economic system. Financial managers making investment, financing, and working capital decisions within a corporation must have a basic knowledge of the components and interrelationships of that economic system.

For example, Disney's decision to expand into Europe and construct EuroDisney required the accumulation of vast amounts of land, buildings, and equipment. Who would hold legal title to the new assets? Where would various levels of the government fit in?

Financial newspapers, magazines, and television programs often discuss the economic system in a manner that makes it appear complex and confusing. Various organizations such as industrial corporations, financial firms, governments, and markets are often viewed as if they are living organisms with desires and emotions. Similar organizations are often grouped together and discussed as if the organizations themselves behave like people. For example, we might read that the banking sector has been hurt by a poor economy and is seeking help from the government.

This chapter lays a foundation to understanding the economic system in a logical manner. Our approach provides a highly simplified and somewhat unusual description of the economic system.

In Chapter 1 it was demonstrated that managers should attempt to maximize shareholder wealth by making the firm's share price as high as possible. In order for this decision rule to be meaningful, however, managers must understand how prices are determined in the market. Modern corporate finance assumes that prices observed in markets are rational measures of value, based upon all available information.

Financial markets and financial institutions link people who wish to invest money with people who need money, such as those starting a new corporation or expanding an existing corporation. For example, a bank receives money from various depositors, pools the money, and lends it to a variety of users of funds. In this example, a bank serves as a financial institution that links people who wish to invest money with people who wish to borrow money.

When a bank or other financial organization serves as a link between people, this is known as *intermediation,* which is a term derived from the word *intermediary,* a go-between. As this chapter discusses, there are many reasons for people to desire intermediation. For example, when a bank intermediates between its depositors and persons borrowing money on a credit card, the bank provides liquidity to the depositors and convenience to the borrowers.

In practice, the interrelationships can become quite complex because more than one financial institution, such as a bank, mutual fund, or pension fund, stands between the investor and the user of the funds. For example, workers who invest in a pension program may be providing funds for a project they have never heard of that may be located thousands of miles away. Perhaps the pension fund used the money to purchase a certificate of deposit at a bank which, in turn, loaned the money to the government of another country that, in turn, loaned the money to one of its industrial corporations.

Our discussion of the economic system will assist your understanding of the system by demonstrating that ultimately all relationships can be viewed as extensions of the simple ownership of assets by people. Our analysis expands from the simple case of a corporation directly controlled by shareholders to a more realistic portrayal of today's economic system. Modern finance views the entire economic system as various sets of contracts between people with regard to underlying assets. The purpose of these contracts is to establish who has the rights to enjoy the benefits produced by the total assets of the world.

This chapter has four main sections describing the economic system. In the first section we will discuss the concept of market efficiency and its implications to financial managers. In the second section we will discuss the direct and indirect ownership of assets. People want to own assets for the value or consumption that they provide. For example, owning a house provides the owner with the benefit of shelter and is an example of direct ownership of an asset. On the other hand, owning 100 shares of Disney's stock is an indirect form of asset ownership in which the investor hopes to benefit indirectly from the assets held inside the Disney corporation. The economic system is the vehicle through which people can acquire indirect ownership of assets. In learning about the financial markets and institutions that comprise the financial system, you will learn to view the entire economic system as linkages between people regarding assets such as land, buildings, equipment, ideas, and so forth.

In addition, the second section will describe governments as sets of contracts that link people together. The government is an organization that has tremendous influence on the way a firm can conduct its business because governments tax and regulate individuals and businesses. No financial decision should be made without analyzing the impact of taxes on the outcome. Thus, in a nutshell, the second section describes the economic system as sets of contracts.

The third section discusses the financial markets in which financial contracts are traded.

The fourth, and final, section provides a detailed look at the process of contracting by examining the contracts and conflicts between shareholders and managers. The conflicts that arise between these groups are known as *agency conflicts,* and the costs of these conflicts are known as *agency costs.*

Overall, our approach is to spend less time describing the details of tax laws and types of securities, which change through time, and more time describing the underlying principles, which do not change. At the same time, we will review enough of the major facts about U.S. tax laws and markets to provide a common base for discussion.

Market Efficiency

This section provides a detailed look at the behavior of markets, specifically at the process by which prices are determined within markets. As we said in the introduction, managers must understand how prices are determined in order to make decisions that increase the firm's stock price. Modern corporate finance assumes that prices observed in markets are rational measures of value, based upon all available information. We will now discuss situations in which this assumption can be expected to hold, such that financial managers have a meaningful understanding of how to implement the objective of share price maximization.

Many of us have encountered get-rich-quick schemes at one time or another. For instance, viewers of late-night television may be familiar with stories of how fortunes can be made trading certain commodities or real estate with relatively little effort and with a surprisingly small investment. When approached with such opportunities, most clear-thinking people understand that these advertisements are too good to be true.

Get-rich-quick schemes do not work because things of value cannot be purchased on the cheap; that is, the price of obtaining an asset must be (approximately) equal to the asset's value. Although an occasional exception may briefly exist in some markets, modern corporate financial management offers principles that will hold under normal circumstances.

efficient market
A market in which assets are traded at prices that equal their values, based upon all available information.

In the broadest sense, the concept that the price of an asset is equal to its value is known as *market efficiency.* An **efficient market** exists when the assets in the market are traded at prices that equal their values, based upon all available information.

There is growing support for the idea that most major U.S. financial markets—for example, stock markets and bond markets—are rather efficient. It is not possible to "beat the market" consistently in an efficient market because prices already reflect all available information. Countless tests have been performed and published generally demonstrating that various investment strategies are unable to earn consistently superior returns and, therefore, that major markets tend to be efficient.

Think for a moment about the thousands of finance professors, corporate investment analysts, and free-lance investors who are equipped with powerful computers, huge databases of price histories, and advanced statistical techniques. If markets were not reasonably efficient, would not many of these people be tremendously wealthy from their own investment success?

Competition is so fierce in these markets that most people have little or no chance of consistently outperforming others by buying assets trading at prices that are too low or by selling assets trading at prices that are too high. Both buyers and sellers use available information to make decisions, so it should be of no surprise that actual prices will reflect all the information that is available. Competition eliminates prices that are both too high and too low. Did you ever notice that when gas stations are located close to each other they tend to have more similar prices than when they are far apart?

It is important that market prices be based upon available information rather than upon emotions or trends. To maximize the value of shareholders' equity, financial managers must understand how the market prices the stock and respond accordingly. If market prices reflect all available information, then managers will find that the only way to maximize shareholder wealth is to make decisions in which the net result of all of the implications of the decision will be positive. In other words, managers must make decisions in which all benefits will exceed all costs because the market price will reflect all information. If markets were priced irrationally or emotionally (i.e., if some relevant information were ignored), then the financial manager either would not know what to do or could manipulate the market price by making otherwise detrimental decisions, taking advantage of the market's mistakes. For example, if a professor assigned grades at random, students would have no incentive to perform well on exams. Financial managers must similarly understand the process by which market prices are determined in order to make proper decisions regarding the management of the firm.

The theory of market efficiency is a solid starting point upon which to understand financial markets. For financial managers, the major implication of market efficiency is that the firm's stock price is an accurate reflection of value, and therefore that decisions should be made in such a way that all the advantages of the decision exceed all the disadvantages.

Market efficiency is discussed in Window 2.1—from the perspective of the individual investor, rather than from the perspective of the financial manager because it is easier to understand market efficiency from the perspective of the investor. The role of market efficiency in this text, however, is to provide a logical basis upon which to construct a meaningful model of how to manage a firm's finances. Regardless of the perspective, we will use the term *market efficiency* to describe the tendency of assets in a particular market to sell at their correct value based upon available information.

Table 2.1 in Window 2.1 summarizes a point that is central to discussions of market efficiency: whether or not a market is efficient relates to whether prices within the market reflect given information. In order to facilitate discussion of market efficiency, the three forms or levels of market efficiency

WINDOW 2.1

Market Efficiency and the Individual Investor

The idea that financial markets are efficient (i.e., it is impossible to identify consistently prices that are too low or too high) is actually a shock to many students. Many people believe that sharp investors have the knack of identifying good buys, perhaps due to years of exposure to advertisements and other claims that seem to be based on the idea of "outsmarting the market." The concept of market efficiency implies that "beating the market" on a consistent basis over a long period of time cannot be done.

Financial theorists debate among themselves about the efficiency of markets. To apply the definition of market efficiency to most markets, financial theorists have separated the concept of market efficiency into three forms, or levels, that differ by the kind of information available to market participants. These are the *weak form,* the *semi-strong form,* and the *strong form.*

Further, there are three major types of investment analysis—technical analysis, fundamental analysis, and modern portfolio theory—each of which can be related to the three levels of market efficiency and the information used. The three levels of market efficiency along with the three major types of investment analysis and the information used are presented in Table 2.1.

TABLE 2.1 Market Efficiency and Investment Analysis by Type

Type of Market Efficiency	*Type of Investment Analysis*	*Information Set*
(1) Weak	Technical analysis	All publicly available past prices and trading volume.
(2) Semi-strong	Fundamental analysis	All publicly available information including financial statements, analysts' recommendations, and past prices and trading volume.
(3) Strong	Modern portfolio theory	All publicly available information and inside information.

An appreciation of the levels of market efficiency requires some history in investment analysis. One of the first techniques of security selection, and a technique still utilized by some investors today, is *technical analysis.* In technical analysis, information concerning past prices and trading volume is used to try to predict future price movements. People who use charts to find good buys are often referred to as *chartists* because they make graphs or charts from past data. Chartists look for patterns in past price movements in order to decide which securities to buy and sell.

WINDOW 2.1 *(continued)*

For instance, a chartist might study patterns of stock price movements and conclude that stock prices tend to move in distinct *waves,* with the result that brief periods of price movements in one direction are often followed by reversals in the other direction. Technical analysts might chart the movements of stocks over some previous period of trading in order to identify those that are prime candidates for reversal. A key to many technical trading strategies (e.g., the reversal strategy) is that the only thing that matters in predicting future stock price is its past price pattern. To illustrate this, let us explore the use of technical analysis to determine whether to invest in Boeing or Sears. A chartist would begin by plotting past prices of both Boeing and Sears on a graph. The chartist would then try to predict future price movements from these patterns of prices. For example, Boeing's price chart might resemble a classic buy pattern, whereas Sears' price chart might provide no buy or sell signal. In this case, the chartist's decision would be to invest in Boeing and not Sears.

A more recent type of investment technique, called *fundamental analysis,* attempts to find the true value of a security using publicly available information such as financial statements. Fundamentalists look for securities whose market price differs from their true price.

For example, fundamentalists might examine a company's financial statements to identify information known as *financial ratios.* One popular ratio, for example, relates the current profitability of the firm to its current stock price. According to various ratios, the analyst might believe that the current stock price of Boeing is too high given the firm's fundamental financial situation, and from this analysis might decide not to include Boeing in the portfolio.

Finally, in the last 20 to 30 years, there has been a movement toward *modern portfolio theory.* This does not attempt to choose underpriced securities using publicly available information; rather, it attempts only to control risk. Modern portfolio theoreticians believe that the only way to beat the market is to have information not available to the general public. According to modern portfolio theory, investors who do not possess such information should not expect to outperform other investors consistently.

In our example of Boeing and Sears, the modern portfolio theoretician would not be concerned with charts or with the fundamental financial characteristics of either company. According to modern portfolio theory, the only concern would be to choose securities in a way that properly controls risk. Risk will be discussed in Chapters 8 and 9.

introduced in Window 2.1 are used. Each form or level relates to a different set of information and, in effect, a different type of investment analysis.

For example, if a person believes that it is possible to pick winning stocks or to predict major market movements using a strategy from technical analysis (such as the shape of a price chart), then that person rejects the weak form of market efficiency. On the other hand, a person who believes that technical analysis is worthless in a particular market believes in or accepts the weak form efficiency for that market.

When people like a product and invest in a firm because they believe that other people will also like the product and that the firm's profitability will grow and produce exceptional returns, they are implicitly rejecting the semi-strong form of market efficiency. On the other hand, a person who ignores financial statements under the belief that the market absorbs all information as soon as it is released (and so why not let others do the analysis?) is supporting the semi-strong form of market efficiency.

Finally, most people believe that a person with inside information about a firm, such as secret merger negotiations, can consistently outperform other investors. This viewpoint rejects strong form market efficiency. Of course, there are legal considerations in using inside information—such as the likelihood of prosecution and punishment, if caught.

Inefficient Markets

inefficient market
A market in which assets trade at prices that do not reflect all available information.

In a well-functioning market, rational investors will drive markets toward the concept of market efficiency through their attempts to outperform other investors. Markets that are not well functioning can be **inefficient markets,** in which assets can trade at prices that do not reflect all available information, such as the stocks and bonds of very small companies, real estate, equipment, cars, and other assets for which it is difficult to find numerous buyers who are already familiar with the asset.

One of the most important aspects of finance is learning how to make decisions regarding assets in inefficient markets. In fact, the objective of shareholder wealth maximization is accomplished almost entirely by applying tools that enable a financial manager to purchase and utilize assets at inefficient prices. For example, a typical manufacturer purchases land, buildings, equipment, and raw materials with the goal of selling the manufactured output at a price that exceeds the combined costs of the inputs.

In an efficient market, competition drives away superior returns found through combining assets that trade in the market. The value of a combination of assets in an efficient market is found simply as the sum of the values of the assets that form the combination. The primary business of most corporations, however, is selling their product for *more* than its cost (i.e., the combined costs of the inputs necessary to make the product).

Example 2.1

The primary way for a computer manufacturer to maximize shareholder wealth is to put together relatively inexpensive pieces of plastic and metal into a functioning computer that can be sold for more than it costs to make. The computer manufacturer will be successful only if other manufacturers cannot quickly undercut prices because they lack the expertise, patents, existing manufacturing ability, reputation, or the like.

Superior returns can be consistently earned only when there is a lack of competition such that others cannot duplicate the business at a lower price.

Financial managers must learn to recognize where lack of competition or poorly functioning markets create inefficiencies that will enable shareholder wealth to be increased. In addition, financial managers need to understand that in an efficient market, competition drives away the opportunities for superior returns.

There are many reasons why competition can be reduced to the point at which prices become inefficient: Perhaps there are limitations on the number of people who can produce a computer because of patent protection or a highly sophisticated, required technology. The assets being traded could also require information that is not widely known or is extremely difficult to interpret. The assets in these markets can often sell at prices that create the opportunity for superior returns because there are a limited number of participants who have the necessary information to compete. A possible example of such an opportunity is provided in Window 2.2, where a company's first equity issue made available to the public increased in price by 243 percent in 1 day. In 1997 and 1998, the market began to question whether Boston Chicken did in fact represent a valuable opportunity. The stock price plummeted and the firm's continued viability was questioned.

WINDOW 2.2

Market Inefficiency? The Initial Public Offering For Boston Chicken

From the Boston Globe, *November 10, 1993, City Edition, Economy, p. 95. Headline: Buyers Go Wild For Pieces of Boston Chicken, by Maria Shao (Globe Staff). Reprinted courtesy of the* Boston Globe.

Boston Chicken had a lot to crow about yesterday.

The rotisserie-chicken chain that started in Newton in 1985 made a high-flying debut on the stock market. Shares of Boston Chicken, Inc., surged to a high of $51 a share from an initial offering price of $20 before closing at $48.50 on the NASDAQ. More than 8.7 million shares traded, making Boston Chicken yesterday's most active NASDAQ issue.

Boston Chicken, which moved its headquarters to Naperville, Ill., in 1992, had been expected to be a hot offering when it went public with 9.5 percent of its stock this week. The stock exceeded expectations on its first day of trading by closing 243 percent above the offering price.

"The valuation is hard to justify. There's not a lot of logic to that," said Kathy Smith, an analyst at Renaissance Capital Corp., a Greenwich, Conn., research firm specializing in new stocks.

Still, analysts say investors simply are enamored of the Boston Chicken concept and management. "The formula is good. It's a healthy alternative to McDonald's at close to McDonald's prices," said Smith.

Inefficient markets consistently offer opportunities for superior returns and the danger of large losses. The subsections that follow explain some of the major concepts involved in dealing with assets when there is rather limited information available to the market participants. This problem is often discussed in the context of **liquidity,** which refers to the time and cost necessary to sell an asset at its true value.

liquidity
The time and cost necessary to sell an asset at its true value.

Liquid Assets

A highly *liquid* asset can be sold at its true value very quickly. An example of a highly liquid asset is a U.S. Treasury bill. Traders in the U.S. Treasury bill market have full and immediate information regarding market value. An asset with low or poor liquidity, such as a house, usually requires considerable time before it can be sold at its true value. The time and cost required to sell a house is the time and cost necessary to locate willing buyers and for them to acquire information about the property.

An asset is *illiquid* if it is costly for buyers to understand fully the information necessary to make a purchase decision. The seller may have to search for a specialized buyer, take time to arrange a sale, or accept a lower sales price. The discrepancies between the information known to the buyer and to the seller are known as **information asymmetries**—because the people involved have different knowledge.

information asymmetries
Discrepancies between the information held by the buyer and the seller of an asset.

To repeat, highly liquid assets, like stocks, may take only minutes to sell at true values, whereas low-liquidity assets like a house may require months to sell at true value.

Liquidity and Corporate Finance

Liquidity has a different meaning when applied to an overall corporation. A corporation is liquid if it has sufficient cash, assets that are considered to be near-cash, and sources of credit to pay its bills and to invest in beneficial projects. An illiquid corporation does not have full ability to pay its bills or to invest wisely in new projects.

Liquidity is familiar to all of us from our own experiences as consumers. Most individuals carry cash that can be used immediately and have a checking account that allows payment on demand. Prudent consumers manage their liquidity by having enough cash on hand to meet short-term expenses and leaving the rest of the money in the bank for safety and to earn interest.

The problem of liquidity as it relates to decisions of the financial manager is similar to that of the individual. Corporations try to keep enough cash on hand to meet current needs while trying not to hold excessive amounts of liquidity—a process called *working capital management.* The goal of working capital management is to maximize shareholder wealth by providing an optimal level of liquidity as cost-effectively as possible. There is a large cost to having too much cash available: Cash tends to offer little or no return. There is also a large cost to having too little cash available: The cost of frequently replenishing the cash account or having too little cash to avoid penalties for late payment. The optimum cash balance can be found by finding the strategy that minimizes total costs. This topic is more fully developed in Chapter 16.

Acquiring Assets in the Financial System

One of the most important examples of clear thinking that finance teaches is that corporations, governments, and other organizations do not consume or produce scarce resources . . . people do! These organizations are simply conduits (connections) through which people transact or contract.

Corporations and other organizations are not people—they are sets of contracts—and they cannot invest or consume in a literal sense. People within the corporation certainly consume, but the corporation itself can only act as a vehicle for the transactions.

Assets are produced by, owned by, consumed by, and, therefore, ultimately belong to people. Individuals desire to own assets because of the benefits the assets can produce. The *financial system* is the means through which individuals can acquire or contract for indirect ownership of assets.

For example, a 30-year-old worker may earn $35,000 per year and need only $30,000 per year to live. The worker wishes to invest the extra $5,000 for a time in the future when the money might be needed more—such as retirement. That worker could invest the remaining $5,000 directly in assets such as land, buildings, or equipment; however, there can be many problems with direct ownership of assets. For example, there could be a difficult time finding assets that have a cost exactly equal to the amount of money that can be spared. The worker also might not have the expertise or interest in learning how to acquire, manage, and resell the assets directly.

The financial system provides an excellent alternative to direct ownership of assets by providing investors with the opportunity to own assets indirectly, such as through a bank. There are many benefits to indirect ownership. For example, through a convenient investment program, the individual is able to earn desired cash flow at some time in the future, such as retirement, and with a controlled level of risk and liquidity.

Markets for goods and services allow enormous economic advantages that are relatively easy to appreciate. Imagine our lifestyles and poverty if everyone had to produce his or her own food, clothing, medicine, and shelter. Financial markets are similarly, but less obviously, central to our economic prosperity. Financial markets and institutions are among the major developments that have advanced our lifestyles beyond those of primitive civilizations, which offered only limited opportunities for direct ownership.

Real Versus Financial Assets

real assets
Assets that directly produce or help to produce scarce resources. Examples include tangible assets such as land, buildings, and equipment, or intangible assets such as trademarks, patents, and human productivity.

People want to own assets for the benefits they offer. There are two primary types of assets. The first, called **real assets,** directly produce or help to produce scarce resources. These may be tangible real assets such as the land, buildings, and equipment used in the manufacture of goods. On the other hand, they may be *intangible* real assets such as trademarks, patents, and human productivity.

Real assets can also be divided between natural resources and man-made resources. Whereas both natural and man-made resources are necessary components of real assets, wealth differentials are comprised almost entirely of differences in man-made resources. In other words, most wealth differentials between societies at a point in time or across societies at different points in time can be attributed to technology and motivation.

Did you ever stop to think about why the medical care, books, food, and clothing that we enjoy today are superior in quantity and quality to those of every human being that existed more than five hundred years ago? Whereas it is sometimes easy to think about land and other types of tangible resources when we think about real assets, clear reasoning reveals that technology and other intangible, man-made resources are the driving forces behind modern wealth.

financial assets
Assets that represent claims on the cash flows from real assets. Examples include stocks and bonds issued by corporations to raise capital and finance investments.

In contrast to real assets, **financial assets** are claims on the cash flows from real assets, and they include the stocks and bonds issued by corporations to raise capital and to finance investments. A *share of stock* represents a percentage claim on the residual value of the firm, whereas a *bond* is a fixed claim on the real assets of a corporation. The bondholder is promised a fixed cash flow as long as the firm stays healthy, whereas the stockholder is entitled to whatever cash flow remains. Window 2.3 provides a brief overview of the different types of financial assets.

Financial assets are a form of indirect real asset ownership. In other words, the benefits from a financial asset must flow from the real asset to the owner. For example, a resort hotel is a real asset because it directly provides scarce resources such as shelter and recreation. A person who owns a resort hotel would have his or her name listed on the property deed. Instead of investing directly in a resort hotel, however, individuals can buy shares of stock in a company that owns such hotels, and thereby benefit indirectly from those real assets through the stock. Among the many benefits of such indirect asset ownership is the ability to sell the financial claim to another investor without changing the legal title to the hotel. By selecting the proper financial securities, individuals can have greater liquidity and convenience than could be obtained through direct ownership of the underlying real assets.

The top portion of Figure 2.1 illustrates that people can own assets directly. When individuals own houses, cars, or books, they are taking direct control of a real asset. The control is sometimes formally established through

WINDOW 2.3

Types of Financial Assets

Financial securities are broadly classified as *equity* and *debt* securities. One type of equity security is *common stock.* When individuals purchase common stock, they are purchasing a claim on the cash flows of the corporation. In exchange for their money, they are given part ownership in the company and a right to all residual earnings, which are often distributed as dividends. Another type of equity security is *preferred stock,* which represents a residual claim with priority rights to dividends and other distributions relative to common stock. Although under no strict obligation to pay dividends to preferred stockholders, the firm cannot pay dividends to common stockholders without first paying dividends to preferred stockholders.

In contrast to equity securities, debt securities (or *bonds*) promise a fixed return on investment, paid at specific intervals, as well as repayment of the original amount, called the *principal,* at the end of the bond agreement. The returns promised to bondholders must be satisfied first, with any residual going to the equity holders. For example, if a firm has issued a bond for $1,000 that pays interest at the rate of 10 percent over 10 years, then the annual interest payments are $100 per year over the entire 10-year life of the bond. At the end of the bond agreement, the issuer repays the $1,000.

Some debt securities are backed by specific assets of the firm. For example, *mortgage bonds* have collateral secured by a lien on real property. In the event that the firm has not sufficient amounts of cash to make promised payments on its debt, holders of mortgage bonds can use the value of the property to satisfy their claims. Another type of debt securities, known as *debentures,* have no specific collateral behind the promises, but are backed simply by the earnings power of the firm.

an ownership contract such as a car title or a deed to a property. In our example, we begin with the idea of a corner grocery store directly owned by a couple affectionately known in the neighborhood as Mom and Pop.

Years ago, when small grocery stores and other small businesses satisfied the ordinary needs of consumers, it was common for the businesses to be directly owned by a single family. (It is, of course, still common for households to take direct ownership of houses, cars, and personal property.)

In contrast, such other assets as those real assets necessary to operate a large supermarket or industrial firm are usually too large to be owned by one person and can be more conveniently owned through indirect means. The lower portion of Figure 2.1 shows the financial system performing intermediation between real assets and the people who ultimately and indirectly own them. The idea is that many of today's large supermarkets are not directly owned by a single person; rather, they are indirectly owned by many people through the financial assets (e.g., stocks and bonds) that have claim to the underlying real assets (e.g., land, buildings, equipment, inventory, and reputation).

FIGURE 2.1 Ownership of Real Assets by People

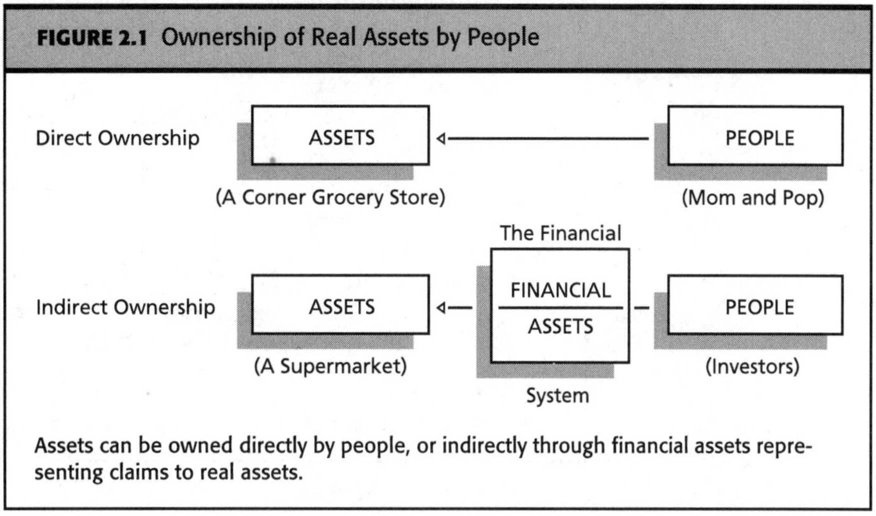

Assets can be owned directly by people, or indirectly through financial assets representing claims to real assets.

An essential point about Figure 2.1 is that the introduction of financial assets does not change the level of total wealth: Financial assets do not produce scarce resources. Financial assets, such as stocks and bonds, do not change the people or the real assets; they only serve as a convenient way to contract for ownership. The wealth of a society is comprised entirely of real assets. Financial assets are merely contracts that people create to facilitate the ownership of real assets.

We will now move to a basic legal form through which financial assets are created: the corporation. As illustrated in Figure 2.2, indirect ownership of real assets is usually accomplished by establishment of a corporation to serve as a conduit or buffer between real assets and the people who provide the funding for the assets, and therefore ultimately own the real assets. The corporation has legal claim to the real assets, and it flows the benefits of this ownership through to the holders of the firm's financial securities. The owners of these securities can then trade them without having to change the contracts regarding the ownership and management of the real assets. All wealth, however, ultimately flows from real assets to people. To repeat, the introduction of corporations and securities does not by itself alter the total level of wealth.

For example, as grocery stores grew into the huge supermarkets of recent decades, it became increasingly useful for them to incorporate. The ownership of the supermarket's real assets now flows through the corporation to the owners of its stock and bonds.

Figure 2.2 recasts the indirect ownership of real assets, as illustrated in Figure 2.1, into a situation that involves a single corporation that owns several supermarkets: Superstores Inc. You can see that the corporation is simply a conduit between real assets and people—a set of papers or contracts.

FIGURE 2.2 The Corporation as a Conduit between Real Assets and People

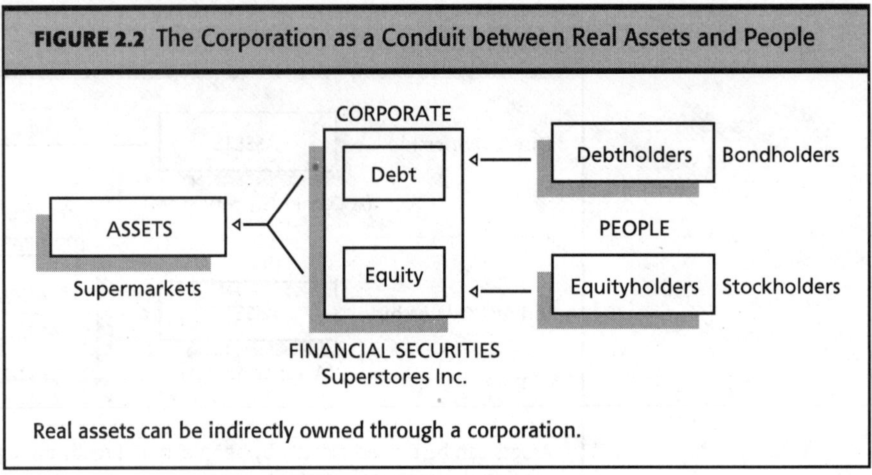

Real assets can be indirectly owned through a corporation.

We have already discussed some of the many reasons, such as convenience and liquidity, why people prefer indirect ownership of real assets. Why, then, do people use the corporation as the particular conduit or buffer to supply this indirect ownership? As illustrated in Figure 2.2 and discussed in Window 2.3, corporations usually offer financial securities represented by *debt claims,* which are fixed, and *equity claims,* which are residual. In general, the bondholders, who own the debt, bear much less risk than the stockholders, who own the equity. Corporations therefore offer investors the opportunity to invest with different levels of risk.

Asset Ownership Through Financial Intermediation

Investors can sometimes be burdened by direct ownership of corporate securities such as the stocks and bonds implied in Figure 2.2. These burdens can include an inability to sell the securities quickly at a fair price, the high costs of buying and selling securities, inappropriate risk taking, and, in some cases, high taxes. Investors can remove some or all of these burdens by investing in financial assets indirectly through financial intermediaries.

financial intermediaries Financial institutions, such as banks, savings and loans, and pension funds, that serve as a conduit between people and financial assets.

Financial intermediaries, such as banks, pension funds, and insurance companies, buy large amounts of securities issued by corporations and governments, and they flow the benefits of these financial assets through to the individuals who contribute capital to the financial intermediary. Adding financial intermediaries to our financial system as depicted in Figure 2.2 produces the more complex financial system depicted in Figure 2.3. The financial intermediary serves as a conduit between the people and the corporation's financial securities.

Because financial intermediaries pool the savings of a large number of small investors, they can provide a valuable service to investors by enhancing the liquidity of each investor, thereby reducing transactions costs, increasing

FIGURE 2.3 Financial Intermediaries between People and Assets

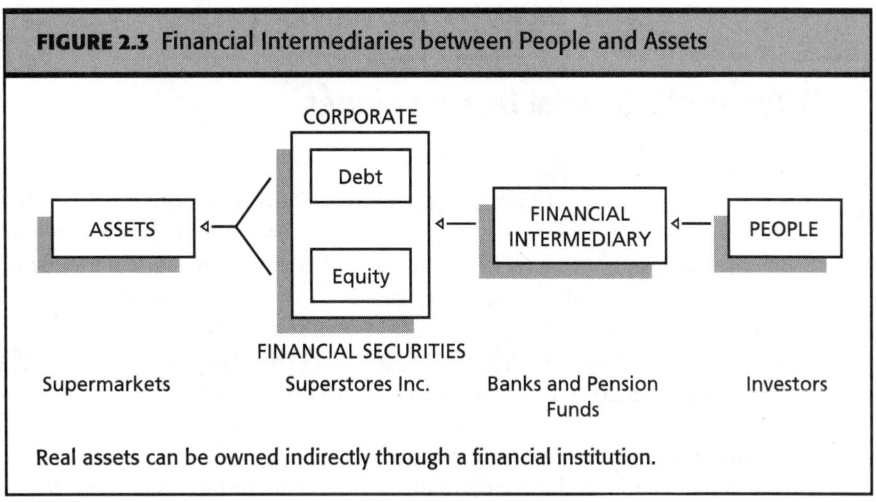

Real assets can be owned indirectly through a financial institution.

convenience, and assisting the investor to invest at a desired level of risk. For example, banks help provide investors with liquidity, convenience, and low-risk products. Pension funds provide investors with tax advantages. A corporation will often find it is cost effective and convenient to borrow directly from a financial intermediary with large issues of securities, such as commercial paper (see Window 16.1), that individual investors could not afford to purchase alone.

As Figure 2.3 depicts, corporations and financial intermediaries serve as buffers between individual investors and real assets (the supermarkets). The corporation (Superstores Inc.) is set up to manage the real assets and sell claims to the real assets in the form of financial securities. Financial intermediaries often serve as a secondary buffer by purchasing the corporation's securities and providing individuals with services such as liquidity, convenience, and professionally managed investments. Descriptions of types of financial intermediaries and the benefits that they provide are listed in Window 2.4.

The placement of financial intermediaries in the channel between people and real assets broadens our view of the contracts that comprise our financial system. The financial intermediary establishes new contracts with the individuals who invest through financial institutions—such as individuals who set up retirement funds—and with the corporations to whom it supplies funds. These new contracts can be financial securities such as shares in a mutual fund or certificates of deposit at a bank, or they can be financial contracts such as pension accounts and insurance policies.

Although financial intermediaries are organized as corporations, they differ from nonfinancial corporations in the types of assets they own. Financial intermediaries own *financial* assets, whereas nonfinancial institutions such as industrials, utilities, and transportation firms own *real* assets. In general,

WINDOW 2.4

Types of Financial Intermediaries

1. Commercial Banks

Commercial banks are corporations organized to accept deposits from individuals and make corporate and personal loans. Banks issue securities known as *demand deposits,* or checking accounts, to individuals and businesses, which facilitate transactions. Another popular security issued by banks is the *certificate of deposit* (CD). Commercial bank liabilities consist mostly of deposits made by individuals and businesses, such as those described earlier. Assets consist of a variety of loans to individuals, businesses, and state and local governments, as well as investments in U.S. government securities.

2. Savings and Loan Associations

Similar to commercial banks, savings and loans are businesses organized to accept deposits by individuals and businesses and to make loans. The major difference between the savings and loans and commercial banks is in the character of their loans. Unlike banks, savings and loans invest heavily in real estate and mortgages.

3. Pension Funds

Pension funds are financial intermediaries that obtain funds from employer and employee contributions and invest these funds in financial assets. Pension funds are a convenient means whereby employees may invest for their retirement. Pension funds invest most of their assets in common stock and long-term bonds.

4. Insurance Companies

Insurance companies are corporations that pool payments (*premiums*) from individuals into funds used to offset unpredictable losses. Life insurance companies protect individuals from the financial consequences of an unexpected death, and they generally invest premiums in common stocks and long-term bonds. Property and casualty insurance companies protect individuals and businesses against unpredictable risks related to fire, theft, and negligence, and they typically invest premiums in stocks and short-term bonds.

5. Investment Companies

Investment companies are businesses that manage pooled portfolios for investors. Types of investment companies, known generally as *mutual funds,* include those with a fixed number of shares to trade, called *closed-end funds,* and those with an open number of shares to trade, called *open-end funds.* Investment companies obtain funds through individual contributions, and invest them according to the stated objective of the fund. For example, one mutual fund may invest only in government bonds, whereas another may invest in the common stocks of more than 5,000 firms.

when we use the term *corporation* in this text we are referring only to nonfinancial corporations, even though, technically speaking, almost all financial intermediaries are incorporated.

Finally, it is common to have more than one financial intermediary and perhaps even more than one corporation serve as a buffer between an investor and the underlying real assets. This occurs when one corporation owns securities in another corporation or when one financial intermediary invests in the securities of another financial intermediary. In fact, it is typical for a corporation to invest money in a financial intermediary, such as putting excess cash in a bank account. Nevertheless, our view of the financial system remains conceptually the same. Corporations and financial intermediaries serve simply as sets of contracts joining real assets and the people who ultimately own them and therefore benefit from them.

Real Asset Ownership and Governments

Thus far we have tried to simplify the economic system by viewing corporations and financial intermediaries as sets of contracts or conduits through which people own real assets. We will show next that even governments can fit into this framework, beginning with the observation that governments, like corporations and financial intermediaries, are sets of contracts. As such, governments cannot ultimately own or consume real assets—only individuals can. We might sometimes think about a government as a collection of people or a major participant in the economy, but clear thinking reveals that governments are a system of contracts between people.

On the other hand, government programs and regulations influence people. Because this is a finance text we will concentrate on government's influence on the *economic* lives of its citizens. Governments, however, also influence citizens through noneconomic means such as civil regulations.

The economic role of government is best viewed through its influence on the ownership of real assets by people. Through taxation, federal, state, and local governments directly alter the asset ownership channels we observed in Figures 2.2 and 2.3. In addition, government regulations, such as environmental protection and food and drug laws, may indirectly alter the behavior of businesses and individuals and change both cash flows and the benefits that accrue from real assets. For example, pollution control devices may divert some of the cash flows derived from the real assets of the corporation to the purchase of equipment to reduce sulfur dioxide emissions, thereby lowering the residual value of the shareholders' claims.

In the case of the United States, the contractual relationships of government are rather clearly set forth in documents such as the Constitution, whereas in other societies the contract might be far less formal and not written down. For example, a military dictatorship might offer the following contract to its citizens: "Do as we say and we will be less likely to silence you."

Although governments differ, and some people might question whether a military dictatorship is legally a contract, virtually all governments have one

FIGURE 2.4 Governments as Conduits between Real Assets and People

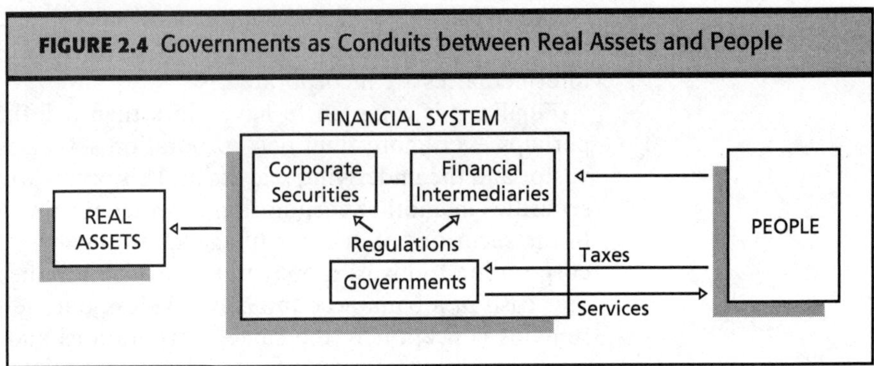

thing in common: their ability to tax. Taxes are a claim by one set of people—the recipients of governmental services—against another set of people—the taxpayers—on the basis of the contracts that comprise the government. Of course, we are all participants to various degrees as both recipients and taxpayers. Figure 2.4 illustrates the role of governments as indirect owners of real assets.

We can view the relationship of governments to other organizations in the financial system and to the individuals who own the assets as a set of contracts, extending our view of a collection of contracts still further. As in the case of corporations and financial intermediaries, governments do not produce or consume wealth, rather, they simply serve as sets of contracts between people with regard to the society's true wealth—its real assets.

An interesting aspect of Figure 2.4 is that taxes are the vehicle by which the ownership of cash flows from assets is transferred from direct ownership by people to ownership through the government. Because governments are only sets of contracts and cannot ultimately own assets, we can view taxes as transferring a portion of direct ownership by people to indirect ownership by society, through government as the intermediary. This view seems to run contrary to the traditional view of most governments in market economies. People certainly recognize that government ownership of assets occurs in communist countries, but they generally feel that in market economies the government does not own or control assets.

Example 2.2 Consider a profitable firm whose assets produce cash flow to its shareholders. A shareholder legally owns the firm and has a claim to the cash flow of the firm. The value of the firm economically is the cash flow generated from the firm's output. Thus, in an economic sense, ownership of an asset refers to who has the right to the benefits of ownership—in this case, who has the right to the money produced by the asset. In the United States, about 40 percent (depending on the state in which you live) of the cash flow from output is claimed in the form of taxes, including real estate, income, payroll, excise, and sales taxes. Taxation is a very important aspect of corporate financial management, and it is the subject of our next section.

Taxation

When a government imposes taxes on individuals and corporations, it causes the cash flows from the assets to be transferred from the taxpayer to the various recipients of government spending. The effect of taxes must be factored into all financial decisions, whether corporate or personal. For example, if you want to save money from a summer job to buy a car, you cannot simply add up your weekly salary and assume that you will have that amount to pay for the car. The federal government will require the deduction of income taxes and Social Security taxes, and your state and local governments may levy taxes on your income as well. Thus, you must deduct these taxes from your salary to determine how much you can spend for the car. You also should figure the sales and licensing taxes you will be charged by the state into your calculations to ensure that you will have enough left to pay them after you have purchased the car.

Let us also look at that summer job through the eyes of finance. A summer job may be viewed as a transaction in which a worker trades his or her time and energy, often called *human capital,* for money, which in turn will be traded for real assets. Taxation may be viewed as the process of claiming partial ownership of the worker's time and energy on behalf of the recipients of government spending. If aggregate tax rates are about 40 percent, then this can mean that government has a claim to approximately 40 percent of an employee's time, energy, and other assets. Note, however, that the worker also receives many benefits from government spending, such as highways, police protection, Social Security benefits, and military protection. Thus, governments are contracts through which people influence asset ownership.

Taxation exerts a powerful and often complex effect on most financial decisions, and the taxes that have the greatest such influence are the corporate and personal income taxes. Corporate and personal tax rates are legislated by Congress and change over time. In fact, the U.S. Congress changes the tax laws on average every 2 years. Representative tax rates at the time of this writing are shown in Workshop 2.1. Note that tax rates graduate such that the five income steps are taxed at progressively higher rates. This is the reason that the *average* individual or corporate tax rate, defined as total taxes paid divided by taxable income, is less than the *marginal* tax rate, which is defined as the tax rate applied on the last dollar of income.

Governments serve as conduits into which money flows in the form of taxation and out of which money flows in the form of spending. When taxation and spending levels temporarily do not match, the government can borrow to meet a deficit or invest to handle a surplus. In addition to these fiscal activities, the federal government can directly regulate economic activity.

Governments and Money

Money acts as another set of contracts between people regarding real assets. One individual will accept money in exchange for an asset, knowing that this money can be exchanged for another more desirable asset. As a medium or

WORKSHOP 2.1

Determining Personal and Corporate Income Taxes

This workshop will assist you in determining the amount of federal tax an individual must pay on earned income. Individuals earn income from salaries and wages, interest and dividends, rent, royalties, and gains on capital assets. The federal government does allow the individual to reduce taxable earned income through deductions, which currently include mortgage interest payments, state and local income taxes paid, and charitable contributions. Rather than itemizing these deductions, some taxpayers elect to take a *standard deduction,* which is a fixed sum to be deducted from total earned income in every year. Individuals will usually elect to itemize deductions if they pay interest on a mortgage, and they will usually elect to take the standard deduction if they have no mortgage.

Taxable income is defined as total earned income less deductions. The tax rate that applies to taxable income changes depending on the amount of taxable income. The tax system is *progressive,* taxing higher amounts of income at higher tax rates. For example, married individuals filing a *joint return* (husband and wife filing one return) would find five different tax rates for five brackets of taxable income. Although the exact ranges change each year based upon inflation, they look something like this:

Married Filing Joint Return, 2000

Taxable Income	*Tax Rate*
$ 0–$ 43,850	15%
$ 43,850–$105,950	28%
$105,950–$161,450	31%
$161,450–$288,350	36%
$288,350 and above	39.6%

A married individual with taxable income of $110,000 who filed a joint return would be taxed:

First $43,850 at 15%	$ 6,578
Next $62,100 at 28%	17,388
Next $ 4,050 at 31%	1,256
	$25,222

Just as individuals pay federal income tax based on income level, corporations, as legal entities, are also subject to federal income tax on their income. Like the individual tax system, the corporate tax system is progressive—tax rates rise with the level of taxable income, and the brackets change. The tax brackets are such that almost all profitable corporations pay tax at the highest marginal rate, say at or near 35 percent:

WORKSHOP 2.1 *(continued)*

Corporate Income Tax Rates, 2000

Taxable Income	*Tax Rate*
$ 0–$50,000	15%
$ 50,000–$75,000	25%
$ 75,000–$10,000,000	34%
$10,000,000 and above	35%

For example, a corporation with taxable income of $1,000,000 would be taxed $328,250, determined as follows:

First $50,000 at 15%	$ 7,500
Next $25,000 at 25%	6,250
Next $925,000 at 34%	314,500
	$328,250

Note that the highest corporate tax rate is about the same as the highest individual tax rate. Whether a person incorporates, incorporates as an S corporation, or remains as a sole proprietorship depends on individual circumstances and recent tax legislation.

tool of exchange, money greatly facilitates transactions in the economy, and is an accepted commodity by which people measure and exchange wealth.

Although coins containing precious metals such as gold and silver have value in and by themselves, the only value to most modern currencies such as the U.S. dollar is the value that people assign to it by their willingness to exchange it for valuable commodities. The value that people attach to money—like other goods—can fluctuate according to supply and demand. When the value of money drops, we observe that the price of virtually everything measured by money rises. We call this inflation.

inflation
An economic climate characterized by a decline in the value of money.

Inflation can be viewed as a decline in the value of money. For example, stating that inflation was 10 percent last year means that the value of money dropped by approximately 10 percent. On the other hand, *deflation* is the case (and a rarer one) when the value of money rises. We observe and measure the change in the value of money by observing the change in the *exchange rate* between money and other goods. In other words, we observe how prices change.

For example, one measure of the change in the value of money would be the exchange rate between money and automobiles. Another would be the exchange rate between money and haircuts. More useful measures, however, utilize a variety of goods that most people use. One such collective indicator, compiled by the Bureau of Labor Statistics, is known as the *consumer price index (CPI)*. It represents a fixed "market basket" of goods and services that an urban wage earner would buy, including food, housing, energy, clothing, transporation, medical care, and entertainment. The rate of change in the value of money as measured by the change in the CPI is given in Table 2.2.

The CPI measures changes in the value of money through time. A rise in the index means that inflation is occurring and the value of money is falling. The more rapid the increase in the CPI, the more rapid the decrease in the value of money. Comparing the CPI in 2000 with the CPI in 1980 tells us that money has lost approximately 56 percent of its value over these 20 years. Comparing the CPI in 2000 with the CPI in 1970 tells us that money has lost approximately 78 percent of its value over the 30-year period. The same amount of dollars that could purchase the basket of commodities in 1970 could buy only 22 percent of the basket in 2000.

The value of money changes in response to the same factors that cause other values to change: shifts in supply and demand. The supply of money is controlled by the federal government, and the government's printing of money and control over credit in the financial system are known as *monetary*

TABLE 2.2 Changes in the Consumer Price Index*

Year	*Value of the Index-January*
1970	37.9
1975	52.3
1980	78.0
1982–84	100.0
1985	105.7
1990	127.6
1995	150.6
1996	154.8
1997	159.5
1998	162.1
1999	164.8
2000	169.4
2001	175.7

For example, the price of the market basket of goods was 5.7 percent higher in 1985 than it was in 1982–1984, and 69.4 percent higher in 2000 than it was in 1982–1984.

*Bureau of Labor Statistics. All urban consumers. All items. U.S. City average. Seasonaly adjusted. The index represents a fixed market basket of goods and services available to the average urban wage earner. The market basket of goods is updated every few years. The major groups of commodities in the basket include food, shelter, energy, apparel, transportation, medical care, and entertainment.

activity. The demand for money is based upon factors such as the level of economic activity, new technologies, and people's attitudes toward the benefits of money. When the government causes the supply of money to grow at a pace that would otherwise outrun the demand, the price of money will fall and inflation will result.

Summary of Real Asset Ownership

All economic value must ultimately come from real assets and belong to individuals. As we have stated, the entire financial system of corporations, financial intermediaries, and governments can be viewed as sets of contracts through which the ownership of real assets flows.

Corporations are sets of contracts between people and are part of the financial system. Our main interest is with regard to nonfinancial corporations and their relationships to individual investors—the stockholders and bondholders.

As we focus on the decisions facing the financial manager, such as investment alternatives, financing for those investments, and working capital management, we will discuss some of the contracts between the corporation and the other individuals in the financial system in more detail.

Markets

A *market* is a conduit for exchange. When the market serves as a conduit for financial securities such as stocks and bonds it is known as a *financial market.* Such markets are our interest in this book because it is in financial markets that the financial manager issues securities to obtain financing and trades securities for working capital management. Further, the financial manager can use financial markets as a valuable tool in gathering information for the investment decision. We will describe the most important exchanges financial managers make in financial markets in this section.

primary securities
Financial securities issued by corporations and sold to investors for the first time. The market where primary securities are sold is called the *primary market.*

secondary securities
Financial securities already in existence and traded among investors. Trading in existing financial securities occurs in the secondary market.

Corporations can raise funds by issuing securities. Securities issued by corporations and sold to investors for the first time are called **primary securities,** and the market in which primary securities are sold is called the *primary market.* Investors who purchase securities often wish to exchange these securities for cash or other securities, and markets exist to make such trades. Existing financial securities that are traded or exchanged are **secondary securities,** and this activity occurs in the *secondary market.* Note that the quotes in the financial pages of the newspaper report secondary market trades.

One benefit of having a secondary market is that it increases the liquidity of financial securities. Investors know that they can trade these securities with other buyers and sellers. Secondary markets for financial securities are usually *dealer* markets or *auction* markets. Both dealer markets and auction markets are ideal for trading financial securities, as these markets work best when handling numerous small trades.

dealer market
A market where individuals, known as dealers, buy and sell using their own inventory. The dealer earns a commission equal to the difference between the price the buyer pays and the price the seller receives.

In a **dealer market,** dealers buy and sell certain types of securities using their own inventory. In other words, the dealer buys and holds securities when there is a seller but no buyer, and sells off the securities when there is a buyer but no seller. The dealer earns a commission equal to the difference between the price the buyer pays (the *offer price*) and the price the seller receives (the *bid price*). Dealer quotes from around the country are linked together through an automatic quotation system known as National Association of Securities Dealers Automatic Quotations (NASDAQ), which allows for an inexpensive and quick search for the best bid and asked prices.

Example 2.3 Consider a dealer who holds an inventory of shares in a stock known as Imex. The NASDAQ system lists Imex currently trading at bid $12.00, offer $12.50. This means that the dealer is willing to buy Imex at $12.00 per share, and sell Imex for $12.50 per share, thereby earning a commission of 50 cents for each share traded, the difference between the bid and offer price.

Nearly all bonds, in addition to some stocks, trade in dealer markets. Although many corporate bonds are listed on auction markets, only a small fraction of the volume is traded on these organized exchanges. Because most bond trading occurs among financial institutions like insurance companies, pension funds, and mutual funds, it is much easier to negotiate such transactions through the dealer market.

auction markets
Markets conducted at centralized locations. In auction markets, an auctioneer records bids and offer prices and notifies the two parties when trades match.

Dealers may be spread out across the country. In contrast, **auction markets** are conducted at centralized locations. In auction markets, an auctioneer records bid and offer prices and notifies the two parties when trades match. In other words, rather than buying securities from sellers, holding them, and waiting for a buyer, the auctioneer serves as a matchmaker for buyers and sellers willing to transact at the same price.

The firm operating the auction charges a fee on each transaction, known as a *transactions cost* or *commission,* as payment for providing the service. With the auction process, because all trades occur at the same place, buyers and sellers can be assured that they are receiving the best price available.

For trading of common stock, the central location is known as a *stock exchange.* Stock exchanges may be either national or regional. The New York Stock Exchange (NYSE) and the American Stock Exchange (AMEX) are national exchanges. There are five registered U.S. regional stock exchanges: the Boston, Philadelphia, Midwest, Pacific, and Cincinnati exchanges.

Most of the trading on these exchanges is done by *stockbrokers* who represent their clients, although there are some private traders, known as *floor traders* and *specialists,* who trade on their own accounts. The exchanges are equipped with elaborate telecommunications systems that allow quotations of all transactions to be transmitted almost instantaneously to the offices of member brokers.

The New York Stock Exchange is the largest organized auction exchange in the United States. It accounts for between 80 and 85 percent of the dollar volume of trading on organized exchanges in this country. More than 2,000 common and preferred stocks, representing more than 1,500 companies, are listed for trading. In addition, more than 2,000 bond issues are listed; however, trading in bonds in this as well as in other organized exchanges is light.

direct trading markets
Markets where sellers and buyers trade directly among themselves.

Although most financial securities trade in dealer or broker markets, other assets are traded in different types of secondary markets. **Direct trading markets** are markets where sellers and buyers trade directly among themselves. Sellers and buyers search for each other—perhaps by advertising, through the Internet or electronic mail, or simply by word of mouth. Financial securities are rarely traded in direct trading markets. However, the Internet may be changing the way that people will trade in the future by matching buyers and sellers in an extremely cost-effective manner.

brokered trading market
A market in which the buyer and seller employ an agent, called a *broker,* who matches them for a fee.

A final type of secondary market is a brokered trading market. In a **brokered trading market,** the buyer and seller employ an agent called a *broker* to facilitate the trade. The broker matches a buyer with a seller for a fee, offering this specialized service at a cost that is usually lower than the cost buyers and sellers would face in direct trading markets. In some markets, such as real estate, this arrangement works rather well. The broker acts to reduce the cost of trading and can pass some of those savings to both parties.

Contracting

As we have said, modern finance views the entire financial system as sets of contracts between people with ultimate regard to real assets. In fact, all economic activity can be viewed in the context of explicit or implicit contracts. This section will take a detailed look at the simplest case of how people contract with regard to economic activity.

Contracts between stockholders, bondholders, employees, governments, and other groups of people within the corporation are often spelled out in legal agreements. For example, a *bond* is a contract specifying the asset (if any) backing the bond, the principal and interest payment schedule for the bond, and the firm's obligations if promised payments cannot be met. In contrast, other contracts are more flexible, and often unstated. For example, stockholders who have received dividends in the past have no stated guarantee that these dividends will continue in the future.

The process of creating contracts can be analyzed utilizing agency theory. As discussed in Chapter 1, *agency theory* investigates how one person, called the *principal,* contracts with another person, called the *agent,* in a situation involving decision making. For example, in a corporation, shareholders—the principals—form contracts with managers—the agents—to make decisions on behalf of the shareholders regarding the management of the firm. In this section we demonstrate some of the costs of the principal–agent relationship and ways that principals can minimize these costs.

The Principal–Agent Relationship

This section examines the principal–agent relationship existing between shareholders and managers. As in all relationships, a potential conflict exists between what the principals desire and what the agents want to do. The goal of agency theory is to find the contract between a principal (shareholder) and an agent (managers) that maximizes shareholder wealth.

Principals want the agents to make decisions that most satisfy the principals; specifically, shareholders want the stock price maximized. Managers clearly have other goals, such as job security, high wages, and a pleasant life style. Conflicts can arise when managers make decisions that are not aligned with the objectives of the shareholders.

Agency Costs

Agency costs come in two types: (1) the costs of trying to get the agents to do what the principals want, and (2) the lost opportunities caused by conflicts too expensive to resolve.

To demonstrate these costs, assume that shareholders—the principals—in a particular firm believe that it is in their best interest if managers—the agents—do not take home office supplies for personal use. To prevent theft of office supplies, shareholders might incur costs such as inventory lists, identification tags, and security guards. These are examples of the first type of agency cost listed earlier—the cost of trying to get managers to do what the principals want.

It would typically not be worthwhile, however, to take inventories of small office supplies, such as pencils. Although the personal use of office supplies is considered by shareholders to be theft, these items will not be monitored and pencils will be wasted. The wastes involved with the disappearance of these small items are examples of the second type of agency cost—the cost of unresolved conflicts.

For simplicity, we will view agency theory as seeking to minimize the total costs attributable to the inherent conflicts of an agency relationship. An optimal contract between a principal and agent resolves only those conflicts that can be solved in a cost-effective manner.

Agency Relationships and Compensation Plans

compensation plan The contract between the principal and agent stating how the agent will be paid.

The primary tool that principals use to minimize agency costs is the compensation plan. The **compensation plan** is the contract between the principal and agent stating how the agent will be paid.

Agency theory teaches shareholders how to contract with agents using compensation plans that minimize agency costs. Typical compensation plans are salary and bonus agreements. One problem with traditional compensation plans is that they do not adequately interrelate the desires of the managers with the desires of the shareholders when bonuses are minor or when-

TABLE 2.3 The Top 10 Paid Chief Executive Officers in 2001. (All values in thousands.)

Executive and Company	*Base Salary*	*Bonus*	*Total Annual Comp*	*Total Long-term Incentives*	*Total Direct Comp*
1. Michael E. Lehman Sun Microsystems	$ 600	$ 0	$ 600	$ 36,601	$ 37,201
2. Mark H. Swartz Tyco International	$ 969	$ 2,500	$ 3,469	$ 28,900	$ 32,369
3. Larry R. Carter Cisco Systems	$ 424	$ 0	$ 424	$ 29,009	$ 29,433
4. Anthony S. Thornley Qualcomm	$ 529	$ 350	$ 879	$ 19,408	$ 20,287
5. James G. Stewart Cigna	$ 702	$ 600	$ 1,302	$ 14,133	$ 15,435
6. Dennis L. Winger Applera	$ 427	$ 202	$ 629	$ 11,985	$ 12,614
7. M. Scot Kaufman MBNA	$ 1,600	$ 3,601	$ 5,201	$ 5,541	$ 10,742
8. David L. Shedlarz Pfizer	$ 773	$ 737	$ 1,510	$ 7,908	$ 9,418
9. David A. Viniar Goldman Sachs	$ 600	$ 8,381	$ 8,981	$ 0	$ 8,981
10. John R. Joyce IBM	$ 0	$ 650	$ 1,169	$ 5,436	$ 6,086

Source: www.businessweekonline.com

*Defined as salary plus bonus plus other compensation not related to stock gains, in thousands.

they are based upon imperfect measures of performance, such as accounting profits. The result can be poor performance on behalf of the shareholders, rather than shareholder wealth maximization.

One way in which shareholders can maximize their wealth is to select managers carefully and to compensate them with a well-designed compensation plan, such as a salary combined with a significant bonus based upon stock performance. Example 2.4 clarifies these concepts. An example on a grand scale is provided in Table 2.3, which shows the top 10 paid chief executives in 2001. Executive compensation is broken into two categories: regular compensation (salary plus bonus) and compensation determined by changes in the stock price. As illustrated in Table 2.3, linking pay to the firm's stock price is an important part of CEO compensation.

Example 2.4 ________ George is an executive at MBI who works in a big office at the firm's headquarters. He is a valued employee at MBI, but like most employees he favors his own interests and goals over those of the corporation. George loves to golf, and he has two alternatives at the office: (1) work or (2) practice golf-putting. On balance, George would rather putt than work.

MBI shareholders want George to work, and they believe that the firm will benefit from having George work rather than putt, according to the following schedule:

Number of Hours Worked Per Day	*Total Daily Dollar Benefit to MBI*
0	$ 0
1	$ 70
2	$130
3	$180
4	$220
5	$250
6	$270
7	$280
8	$281

MBI shareholders are considering one of three alternative employment contracts to offer George for the upcoming year:

- *Alternative #1:* Pay George $25 per hour regardless of whether he works or not.
- *Alternative #2:* Pay George $25 to work and pay a guard $10 per hour to watch him work.
- *Alternative #3:* Pay George $10 per hour regardless of whether he works or not and an additional $15 for each hour worked if his output is determined by the shareholders to be satisfactory, which would preclude the need for the guard to watch him work.

George and the firm together must agree upon how many hours per day he will be employed (i.e., go to work), but George alone must decide actually whether to work or practice putting during this time.

Alternative #1 is unsatisfactory because the firm will pay George $200 per day and will receive no value whatsoever. George will choose to go to work 8 hours each day at a wage of $25 per hour. George, acting in a manner based upon his own perceived interests and goals, will not work but will become a great putter.

As shown in Table 2.3, Alternative #2 produces a benefit for the firm no matter how many hours George works.[1] For example, the gain is $80 per day if George and the guard are hired for 4 hours per day ($220 benefit to MBI's shareholders less $100 of wages to George less $40 of wages to the guard) and $1 per day if George and the guard are hired for 8 hours per day ($281 benefit to MBI's shareholders less $200 of wages to George less $80 of wages to the guard). According to the benefit schedule in Table 2.4, under Alternative #2 MBI would benefit most if George and the guard worked 4 hours per day.

[1]The example does not consider any resentment George might feel by having a guard watch over him. Resentment, in the form of a loss of commitment on the part of the employee or in employees leaving the firm, must be considered in an actual compensation plan.

TABLE 2.4 Compensation Plan #2: Hire the Guard

Total Hours Worked per Day	*Daily Benefit to MBI*	*Daily Wages to George*	*Daily Wages to the Guard*	*Net Benefit to MBI*
1	$ 70	$ 25	$10	$35
2	$130	$ 50	$20	$60
3	$180	$ 75	$30	$75
4	$220	$100	$40	$80
5	$250	$125	$50	$75
6	$270	$150	$60	$60
7	$280	$175	$70	$35
8	$281	$200	$80	$ 1

Alternative #3 builds in a bonus incentive similar to the long-term compensation shown in Table 2.3 on executive compensation. George knows he will make $10 per hour whether he works or not, but he will receive an additional $15 per hour for satisfactory performance. Let us now assume that George will spend all his hours working if he is given the bonus. For example, if George works 4 hours per day the gain to MBI is $120 ($220 benefit to MBI's shareholders less a total of $100 wages to George), and if George works 8 hours per day the gain to MBI is $81 ($281 benefit to MBI's shareholders less a total of $200 wages to George). The benefit schedule as it relates to Alternative #3 is provided in Table 2.5. According to this benefit schedule, under Alternative #3, MBI would benefit most if George worked 5 hours per day.

You can see that the bonus plan has replaced the need for a guard as a proper incentive for George to work and not putt. The firm would choose to allow George to work 5 hours per day, or 1 hour more than that chosen under Alternative #2. Compared with Alternative #2, the optimal number of hours worked provides an additional wage to George of $25 ($125 versus $100) and provides an additional $45 net benefit to MBI ($125 versus $80).

Of course, this simplistic example fails to incorporate many real-world complexities of bonus plans. For example, bonuses can be costly to implement, and George may learn how to cheat and receive bonuses even when the shareholders do not attain the goals they really desired. Judging from compensation plans that corporations choose to adopt, however, bonus plans appear to have advantages that outweigh the disadvantages.

The compensation plan of choice will be the plan that minimizes the total costs of conflicts, or that minimizes agency costs. In this example, the plan that minimizes agency costs is the plan that maximizes the benefit to the firm's shareholders.

TABLE 2.5 Compensation Plan #3: The Bonus Incentive

Total Hours Worked per Day	*Daily Benefit to MBI*	*Fixed Daily Wages*	*Bonus Wages*	*Net Benefit to MBI*
1	$ 70	$10	$ 15	$ 45
2	$130	$20	$ 30	$ 80
3	$180	$30	$ 45	$105
4	$220	$40	$ 60	$120
5	$250	$50	$ 75	$125
6	$270	$60	$ 90	$120
7	$280	$70	$105	$105
8	$281	$80	$120	$ 81

Summary

- Efficient markets are markets in which prices reflect available information.
- The liquidity of an asset is usually related to how difficult it is for buyers to understand information concerning the asset. Liquidity and the costs of information are important aspects of corporate financial management. Working capital management is the process of providing an optimal level of liquidity in as cost-effective a manner as possible.
- Corporate finance occurs within an economic system. The economic system comprises corporations, financial intermediaries, government, and markets that serve as conduits between people and real assets.
- Corporations are conduits between real assets and people via financial assets because they issue financial securities and purchase real assets.
- The existence of financial intermediaries and markets, also part of the financial system, makes it easier and more cost effective for people to own and trade their financial assets, which ultimately represent claims on real assets.
- Governments are also sets of contracts between people with regard to real asset ownership. Taxes are a claim by recipients of government services against taxpayers on the basis of contracts that comprise the government.
- The relationship between stockholders and managers is our example of the contracts formed in the financial system. This relationship is known as an agency relationship. The objective of shareholders is often to minimize the total costs—called agency costs—of the inherent conflicts. Compensation plans are a tool for minimizing agency costs.

Demonstration Problems

Problem 1

Fran wonders which income tax would be greater: the income tax paid by a married couple with $200,000 of taxable income or the income tax paid by a corporation with $200,000 of taxable income. Use the tax rates in Workshop 2.1 to find the solution.

Solution to Problem 1

Step 1: In order to compute the taxes for a married couple with $200,000 of taxable income, we must sum the amounts paid under the various rates shown in Workshop 2.1: taxes of 15 percent must be paid on the first $43,850 of income, 28 percent on the next $62,100 of income, 31 percent on the next $55,500 of income, and 36 percent on the final $38,550 of income. These amounts are summed as follows:

First $43,850 at 15% tax rate:	$ 6,578
Next $62,100 at 28% tax rate:	$17,388
Next $55,500 at 31% tax rate:	$17,205
Last $38,550 at 36% tax rate:	$13,878
For a total of:	$55,049

Step 2: In order to compute the taxes for a corporation with $200,000 of taxable income, we must follow a very similar procedure using the rates also found in Workshop 2.1.

First $50,000 at 15% tax rate:	$ 7,500
Next $25,000 at 25% tax rate:	$ 6,250
Last $125,000 at 34% tax rate:	$42,500
For a total of:	$56,250

Final Solution: The married couple would pay a lower tax ($55,049) than the corporation ($56,250).

Problem 2

Marjorie is a trusted employee whose productivity declines as she becomes tired each day. After careful observation of her work performance, her manager prepared the following chart:

Daily Number of Hours Worked by Marjorie	*Total Number of Work Units Completed*
1	100
2	190
3	270
4	340
5	400
6	450
7	480
8	500

Marjorie's total cost to the firm is $11 per hour. Each work unit completed is worth $0.21 to the firm. Ignoring all other possibilities and considerations, for how many hours should the firm hire Marjorie per day?

Solution to Problem 2

Step 1: Because Marjorie's productivity begins high and then tails off, begin by assuming that Marjorie is being hired for zero hours each day and then examine whether it is worthwhile to add hours. This is accomplished by first computing the total value of Marjorie's output at each work level as the product of the number of work units completed and the value to the firm of each work unit ($0.21):

Daily Number of Hours Worked by Marjorie	*Total Number of Work Units Completed*	*Total Value of Completed Work*
1	100	$ 21.00
2	190	$ 39.90
3	270	$ 56.70
4	340	$ 71.40
5	400	$ 84.00
6	450	$ 94.50
7	480	$100.80
8	500	$105.00

Step 2: Next, compute the *incremental,* additional, or *marginal* value of the completed work for each hour of labor. This is found by subtracting the value of the labor before the extra hour of work from the value of the labor after the next hour of work. For example, the first hour of work created a total value of $21.00. Because no hours of work produce no value, the additional value produced by the first hour is $21.00. Another hour of work for a total of two hours per day would create a daily benefit of $39.90. Subtracting the benefit of $21.00 from the first hour of work would produce an incremental benefit of $18.90. This value may also be found by multiplying the number of additional work units (90) times the value of each unit ($0.21). The process is summarized in the following chart:

Daily Number of Hours Worked by Marjorie	*Total Value of Completed Work*	*Incremental Value of One Hour of Work*
1	$ 21.00	$21.00
2	$ 39.90	$18.90
3	$ 56.70	$16.80
4	$ 71.40	$14.70
5	$ 84.00	$12.60
6	$ 94.50	$10.50
7	$100.80	$ 6.30
8	$105.00	$ 4.20

Step 3: The final step is to compare the incremental or marginal benefit from each hour of Marjorie's work with the incremental or marginal cost to each hour of work. The incremental cost is $11.00 per hour for each hour; therefore, the solution is found by finding when Marjorie's productivity falls below $11.00 per hour. Because the fifth hour of work produces $12.60 of value and the sixth hour produces only $10.50, the correct answer is five hours.

Notice that the firm would receive a profit (the value received would exceed Marjorie's pay) no matter how many hours Marjorie worked; however, the solution of five hours produces the maximum profit. This can be checked by subtracting the total wage cost from the total benefit at each level of work:

Daily Number of Hours Worked by Marjorie	*Total Value of Completed Work*	*Total Wage Cost*	*Total Profit*
1	$ 21.00	$11.00	$10.00
2	$ 39.90	$22.00	$17.90
3	$ 56.70	$33.00	$23.70
4	$ 71.40	$44.00	$27.40
5	$ 84.00	$55.00	$29.00
6	$ 94.50	$66.00	$28.50
7	$100.80	$77.00	$23.80
8	$105.00	$88.00	$17.00

Final Solution: Hire Marjorie for five hours per day.

Review Questions

1. What is the implication of market efficiency to the financial manager?
2. Distinguish between real assets and financial assets. Give examples of each to support your views.
3. How do equity securities differ from debt securities?
4. List the characteristics of dealer and auction markets.
5. In agency theory, explain why the shareholder is known as the principal and the manager is known as the agent.
6. Describe the two costs of a principal–agent relationship.
7. With respect to agency relationships, what is the objective of the particular compensation plan?

Problems

1. Rank the following assets from most liquid (1) to least liquid (3).
   a. An antique car
   b. IBM Corporation common stock
   c. Modern gold coins
2. Label the following items from SAC Corporation's perspective as being real assets (R) or financial assets (F):
   a. Accounts receivable: money owed to SAC Corporation by other corporations who have purchased products on credit.
   b. SAC Corporation's administration building, which houses the finance department.
   c. SAC Corporation's corporate checking accounts.
   d. Land purchased by SAC Corporation from a local finance company.
   e. SAC Corporation's inventories of raw materials.
3. Identify the groups of people who financially gain or suffer in the following financial transactions:
   a. Bigstuff Corporation uses a technical loophole to avoid paying $2,500,000 in real estate taxes to the county government.

b. Dangerous Products, Inc., unexpectedly loses a $20,000,000 lawsuit for punitive damages for selling faulty snow angels to the City of West Rochester. Assume that Dangerous Products, Inc., is uninsured and that the city retained the prestigious local law firm of Gopher, Thummuny, & Runn.
c. Through a technical error, Creditor Corporation permanently loses track of the fact that it is owed $1,000,000 by Debtor Corporation.
d. U.S. Senator Barrelpork slips in a provision to a bill that passes and grants $9,000,000 to the Town Government of Herbanna for a particular project.

4. J.P. Moneybags is a wealthy, married investor with annual taxable income of $125,000. (This is his income after all deductions and exemptions have been subtracted.)
   a. How much will J.P. pay in federal income taxes using the tax rates in Workshop 2.1?
   b. If J.P. has an extra $1,000 of income, how much of this will go toward federal income taxes?
   c. How would you answer questions (a) and (b) if J.P. falls on hard times and has only $10,000 per year of taxable income?
5. Cassidy Corporation is a pet products corporation with annual taxable income of $1,100,000.
   a. How much will Cassidy Corporation pay in federal income taxes using the tax rates in Workshop 2.1?
   b. If Cassidy Corporation has an extra $1,000 of income, how much of this will go toward federal income taxes?
   c. What would your answers be to questions (a) and (b) if Cassidy Corporation's business "goes to the dogs" and has only $60,000 per year of taxable income?
6. The current price of Nifty Nellie Corporation's (NNC) common stock is $20 per share. Churnem Brokerage Corporation charges a transactions cost of 2.5% of the total amount of a transaction. For example, on the purchase of 10 shares of stock for $200, the transaction cost would be $5.00.
   a. What would 200 shares of NNC's common stock cost?
   b. How much would an investor receive from selling 200 shares of NNC's common stock?
7. The bid price of Lucy Corporation common stock is $10.25 and the offer price is $10.75.
   a. How much will an investor have to pay to buy 100 shares of Lucy Corporation common stock directly from the dealer?
   b. How much would an investor receive from selling 100 shares of Lucy Corporation common stock directly to the dealer?
8. Nick has run the sports department of an old family-owned department store in Philadelphia for years. The firm's new, modern computer system allows top management to compute profits for each department quickly and accurately. Nick is very talented, but management has noticed that Nick has priorities in life other than producing profits for the firm. In fact, Nick spends several hours each day reading newspapers, drinking coffee, and talking on the phone with friends.

   The department currently earns $1,000 per day and Nick is paid $100 per day. Top management is confident that Nick could produce higher profits for the firm according to the schedule in columns 1 and 2:

(1) Additional Hours Worked Per Day	*(2) Additional Daily Profit to the Firm*	*(3) Extra Daily Salary Demanded by Nick*
1	$100	$10
2	180	25
3	230	45
4	250	70
5 or more	250	He quits

Top management thinks that Nick could be encouraged to work harder if he were given a financial incentive. Column 3 in the table shows the amount of dollars he would need to earn to work additional hours. They do not want to lose Nick because he is so talented.

a. How many additional hours a day should the firm try to get Nick to work?

b. What would be the method (i.e., compensation plan) of getting Nick to work the additional hours?

c. What do you think would happen if the firm simply demanded that Nick produce higher profits by threatening to fire him if he didn't?

d. Do you have any other ideas of how Nick could be motivated or encouraged to produce higher profits?

9. Rockhenge Corporation has a huge number of clerical workers. Rockhenge has been able to attract and retain clerical workers for years despite offering a slightly lower pay rate than their competitors. An external investigation conducted by a consulting team indicated that many workers are engaging in the following practices at Rockhenge:

- Taking home office supplies
- Making personal long-distance phone calls
- Mailing personal correspondence through the company mailroom
- Failing to purchase parking stickers (the company charges employees to park in the company parking lot)

The practices appear to be common to most of the employees and even appear to be sanctioned by the managers as part of a low-key management style.

The consulting team estimates that Rockhenge loses $250,000 per year due to these practices. The consultants recommend that for a one-time cost of $50,000 and an annual cost of $127,500, the firm could prevent all such abuses by employing auditors and other control measures. Ignoring ethical implications, should Rockhenge accept the recommendation?

Discussion Questions

1. If you believe in market efficiency, then you believe that investors have little or no chance of consistently outperforming other investors in well-functioning markets. Some stock investors, however, have done what market efficiency says cannot be done—they have regularly "beaten the market." Does this mean that well-functioning markets are inefficient?

2. Your instructor takes a $100 bill and burns it in front of the class. Describe: (1) the net effect of this action on human wealth, (2) any wealth transfers that took place, and (3) what this teaches us about inflation and monetary policy.
3. Can a corporation treat people unfairly?
4. Are silver and gold bars financial assets or real assets? Explain.
5. What is the difference between a communist society and a capitalist society with a 100 percent tax rate on income? If communism is wrong, how high do tax rates need to become before capitalism is wrong?
6. Select some valuable assets and discuss (a) whether the value of each asset is more from natural resources or from human effort, and (b) what humans contributed to the asset's value.
7. Without anybody else's help, how would you do the simple task such as transport some drinking water?

CHAPTER 3

THE TIME VALUE OF MONEY

Jack and Diane could hardly believe their eyes when they saw the Lotto jackpot numbers come up on the television screen. They had played the same six numbers for years and not once had they come close to winning. Tonight they held a winning ticket to a million-dollar lottery payout. Diane looked at Jack and said, "It's hard to imagine—us as millionaires!"

Although the couple has every reason to rejoice over their good fortune, the fact is that the lottery prize will not make them millionaires. You see, the couple will soon learn that the prize will be paid out at the rate of $50,000 a year for 20 straight years. Because the jackpot is not paid in a lump sum, but through time instead, the value today of their lottery prize is far less than its marquee value of $1 million.

Exactly how much is Jack and Diane's prize worth? We can answer this question once we have studied the techniques for calculating the **time value of money.** We will also see how the time value of money can be incorporated into financial decision making. These topics are the focus of this chapter.

time value of money
An economic principle stating that dollars to be received or paid out through time are different commodities that cannot simply be added together or subtracted from each other.

Time Value

The lessons from the first two chapters can be integrated into a single decision rule: Good investments are those whose benefits exceed costs, where costs and benefits are measured in market prices. This rule is consistent with the objective of shareholder wealth maximization as well as with the economic principles introduced in Chapter 1.

How, then, are benefits and costs valued in the market when they occur at different points in time? Said differently, if the value of a cash flow depends upon when it is received or paid, then how is that value determined? This will be the theme of the next few chapters.

Just about every financial decision, including investment, financing, and working capital management decisions, must take into account the passage of time. It is common for corporations to invest money today but not receive a return for years. Financial managers have long recognized the importance of time value when making investment decisions.

As Jack and Diane will learn, a dollar[1] to be received in the future is not as valuable as a dollar in your hand today. In fact, dollars received and dollars paid through time are different commodities that cannot be directly compared. For example, we offer the following proposition: Send $100 to the authors and we will return to you $1,000. Is this a good trade? By the way, as part of the deal, the authors get the $100 today, and you get $1 a year in each of the next 1,000 years.

Although we would be receiving dollars now and paying dollars over the 1,000-year term of our contract, these dollars are actually different commodities. Even if you were certain that the authors would deliver the dollar per year for the next 1,000 years to you and your heirs, most people would not make the trade because the commodity of $100 today is more valuable than the commodity of $1 per year for the next 1,000 years. In fact, under normal market conditions, the value of receiving $1 per year for 1,000 years is close to $10.[2]

Dollars Through Time as Different Commodities

Why is the value of a dollar in your hand today different from the value of a dollar due in your hands in 10 or 20 years? The answer is best found by viewing dollars at different points in time as different commodities or assets rather than as the same asset.

First, let us think about money. Money is simply a medium or tool of exchange. A dollar has no value other than what people will accept in exchange for it. This is very different from a doughnut, which has value to its owner even if it cannot be traded. For example, would you rather be stranded alone on an island with a $100 bill or a doughnut?

Like most assets, the value of money changes through time. The value of a dollar today is obviously $1. But what about the value today of a dollar that won't be received for 10 or 20 years—how much is it worth? As we will show, at ten percent interest rates, a dollar due in 10 years is worth only about 40 cents today, and the value of a dollar due in 20 years is worth only about 15 cents today!

The relative value of money received through time can be understood by thinking of the relative value of any commodity. Why is a big red apple worth more than a small green wormy apple? The answer is that people prefer to eat big red apples and that big red apples are harder to grow. Because they are harder to grow, farmers have to charge more for them, but people are willing to pay the extra cost because they like the taste. There is no logic in

---

[1]Throughout the text we will often refer to cash as "dollars," although the concepts presented in this book are applicable to the currency of any country.

[2]We used an interest rate of 10 percent to arrive at $10. Different interest rates will lead to different present values, as we will discuss further in the chapter.

claiming that all apples must have equal values, regardless of quality, because, technically speaking, they are all apples.

There is similarly no logic in claiming that dollars must have equal values regardless of when they are to be received because technically speaking they are all dollars. Dollars in hand today can be put to use immediately, whereas people must wait to utilize dollars to be received in the future. To put this another way, there is an **opportunity cost** associated with waiting to obtain dollars through time. It is interesting, though, that $1 million due in 145 years can be purchased for about $1 today! Does it not just make you want to put a few bucks in the bank and get your body frozen for a few centuries?

opportunity cost
An alternative forgone because a particular course of action is pursued.

Investing Dollars today can be traded for future dollars. This is called **investing.** Investment is deferred consumption because the investor decides not to consume or spend the money today; rather, the investor decides to trade the money today for a particular amount of money to be received in the future.

investing
The trading of dollars today for dollars in the future (deferring consumption).

Borrowing Market participants can also trade future dollars, for example, in the form of future paychecks, for dollars today. This is called **borrowing.** Borrowing is the opposite of investing. The borrower obtains money today in exchange for promises to return a particular sum of money in the future.

borrowing
The trading of dollars in the future for dollars today.

In the case of investing, the investor may enter the financial marketplace and purchase future dollars today at a cost per dollar of less than $1. The exact cost of each future dollar will depend upon both the length of time before the dollar is received as well as market conditions. For example, the investor may find that dollars next year can be purchased today for 90 cents, such that $900 can be invested today and $1,000 will be received in 1 year.

In this example, there is a temptation to say that because $900 was traded for $1,000, the investor will receive a profit of $100. In fact, this is precisely the way *accounting profits* are defined. Dollars to be received through time or paid out through time, however, are different commodities that cannot simply be added together or subtracted from each other. Claiming that a $100 profit has been earned does not make economic sense. For instance, if Jack trades the family cow for five beans, it makes no sense to claim that Jack produced a profit of four food units because he traded one food unit for five food units. It also does not make sense to claim that a person who trades one watermelon for five grapes has produced a profit of four pieces of fruit. The reason that such profits do not make sense is that we are comparing different commodities or assets.

> Dollars to be received through time or paid out through time are different commodities that cannot simply be added together or subtracted from each other. There is a relation, however, by which equivalent values can be found.

Discounting Cash Flows

If cash flows at different points in time are indeed different assets with different values, then how can we make meaningful comparisons between dollars that arrive at different points in time? This is the central issue within the study of the time value of money.

The answer is that all cash flows must be changed into dollars *at the same point in time.* The most common solution is to take all cash flows and to convert them into the value of the cash flows in today's dollars. This procedure is called **discounting** cash flows to the present.

discounting
The process of turning future cash flows into current cash flows.

Discounting can be accomplished by taking future dollars to a financial market and converting them into current dollars using the prices provided by the marketplace. The longer you must wait to receive future dollars, the less those future dollars are worth to you today. For instance, the marketplace might tell us that the value today of receiving $1.00 in exactly 1 year is $0.93. We now have a basis of comparing these two different commodities: $0.93 today is equivalent to $1.00 due in one year. The marketplace might also tell us that the value today of receiving $1.00 in exactly 2 years is $0.86, and that the value today of receiving $1.00 in 3 years is $0.79. In fact, we can envision a marketplace of cash set up to turn any future amount of money into a present value. Note that as we extend the time horizon into the more and more distant future, the value today of receiving those dollars in the more distant future becomes smaller. This is illustrated in Figure 3.1.

FIGURE 3.1 Discounting Cash Flows

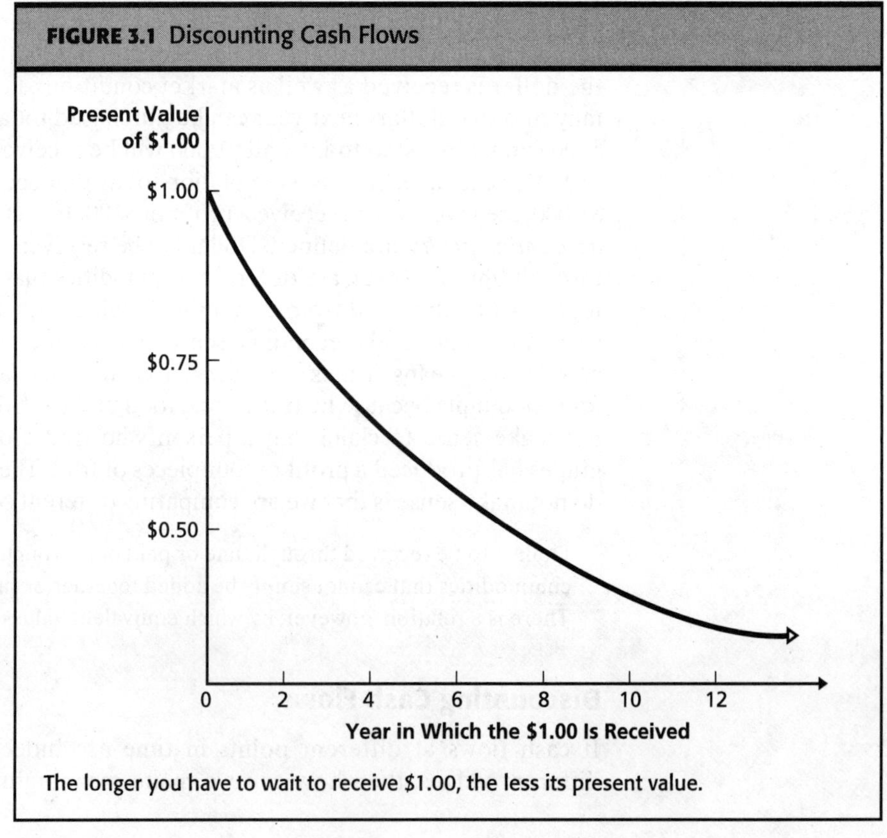

The longer you have to wait to receive $1.00, the less its present value.

The longer you must wait to receive future dollars, the less those future dollars are worth to you today.

Compounding Cash Flows

compounding
The process of turning current cash flows into future cash flows.

It can also be useful to turn current dollars into future dollars. This process is called **compounding** the cash flows. The main difference between discounting and compounding is the point of reference, which in discounting is today, but is at some future point in time in compounding.

We can continue with the example of a financial marketplace to illustrate compounding. For instance, the marketplace might tell us that the value in exactly 1 year of $1.00 invested today is $1.08, and that the value in 2 years of $1.00 invested today is $1.17. Under these conditions, the marketplace is telling us that $1.00 today is equivalent to $1.08 in 1 year, and that $1.00 today is equivalent to $1.17 in 2 years. We can utilize the financial marketplace to turn any present amount of dollars into future amounts of dollars. Note that as we extend the time horizon out into the more and more distant future, the future value of investing $1.00 today becomes larger. This is illustrated in Figure 3.2.

FIGURE 3.2 Compounding Cash Flows

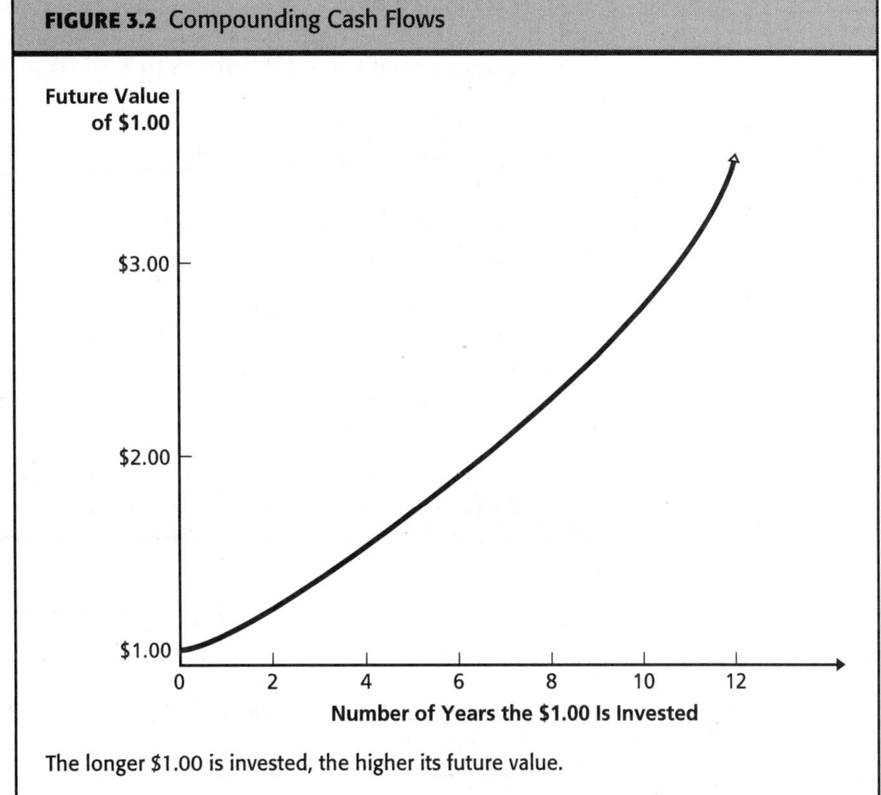

The longer $1.00 is invested, the higher its future value.

The line in Figure 3.2 could describe a student who borrows $25 for a date as a freshman in college by charging the evening to a credit card. Four years later that debt might grow to $50 if unpaid. Four additional years later, the student is finishing medical school. If unpaid, that $50 might now have grown to $100. If unpaid and allowed to continue to grow on the credit card, that debt could easily reach $20,000 by retirement. (Quite an expensive date!) In essence, the student, in following this scenario, is trading $20,000 of retirement consumption for $25 of current consumption.

Time Lines

time lines
A way to view the process of discounting and compounding dollars through time. Discounting is the process of pulling cash flows left along the line, whereas compounding is the process of pushing the cash flows right along the line.

Time lines provide an excellent view of the process of the time value of money. Time value of money problems may be viewed as pulling cash flows back in time (*known as discounting*) or pushing cash flows forward in time (*known as compounding*). Figure 3.3 illustrates the problem of determining the present value of $100 due in 5 years. Finding a *present value* may be viewed as pulling the $100 from the right toward the left of the time line. Whenever cash flows are pulled back to the left they diminish in magnitude. Figure 3.3 illustrates that the present value of the $100 to be received in 5 years is $62.09 under certain market conditions.

Next, Figure 3.4 uses the concept of a time line to turn a present value into a future value. Finding a *future value* may be viewed as pushing forward a cash flow from left to right, causing it to increase in magnitude. Here, under certain market conditions, $100 grows to $161.05 in 5 years.

All time value of money problems may be viewed as pulling (discounting) or pushing (compounding) cash flows along a time line.

Interest Rates and Present Value

Thus far, time value has been discussed using the price of future cash flows. In many cases time value is expressed with *interest rates,* not with prices. When dollars or cash flows are pushed and pulled along a time line, the rate at which the cash flows grow or diminish is determined by current interest rates prevailing in the market. An interest rate is the rate at which these

FIGURE 3.3 The Time Line View of Discounting

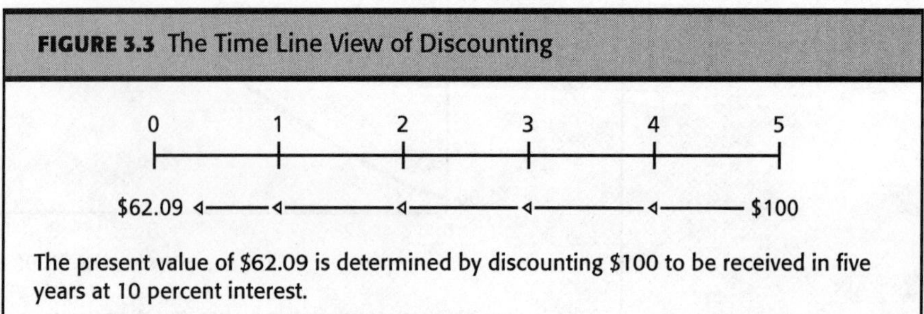

The present value of $62.09 is determined by discounting $100 to be received in five years at 10 percent interest.

FIGURE 3.4 The Time Line View of Compounding

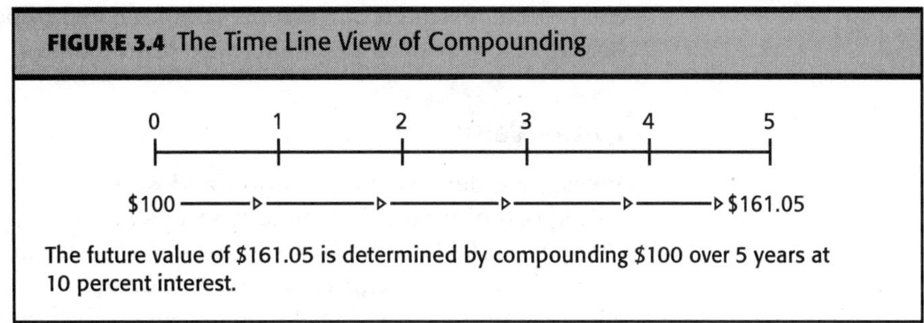

The future value of $161.05 is determined by compounding $100 over 5 years at 10 percent interest.

cash flows grow, in the case of future values, or diminish, in the case of present values.

Interest rates are used to express the time value of money in an easy-to-understand manner. For example, instead of a bank saying that $1.00 invested today will grow to $1.08 in 1 year, the bank may advertise an interest rate of 8 percent. This means that investors can expect to receive their original amount of money back plus an earned 8 percent in 1 year. Whether expressed as prices or interest rates, the concept of the time value of money is the same.

A Summary of Time Value

As we have said, dollars or cash flows to be received at different points in time are different commodities that should not be added to or subtracted from each other. Adjusting for time value may be viewed as pushing and pulling dollars or cash flows along a time line. Pushing values forward in time makes them larger; pulling values back in time makes them smaller. Moving cash flows to a single reference point in time allows for proper comparison of these different commodities, and provides for proper financial decision making.

Given an interest rate, the process of discounting and compounding can be determined with precision. The mechanics and mathematics of time value have been vastly simplified by financial calculators and computers. In fact, calculators and computers can do all the time value work for us!

Now that you understand the concept of time value, learning the mechanics is a straightforward process.

The Techniques of Discounting and Compounding

This section will discuss and illustrate two methods with which to compute present values and future values using interest rates: (1) formulas and (2) financial calculators or computers. The second method will be referred to as the *financial calculator method* for simplicity, although the same techniques can be demonstrated on personal computers with special software. We will illustrate each method, beginning with future values.

Future Values

Investing is delayed consumption, and waiting to consume can be considered an opportunity cost. Someone who invests gives up spending today by exchanging today's dollars for more dollars in the future. The interest rate is a convenient way of expressing the opportunity cost of waiting to consume and the rate of growth in the investment. Given any present dollar amount and any interest rate, the investor can determine the precise amount of future dollars to which the investment will grow in a given number of years.

Example 3.1 ________ Consider Ivan, who has $1,000 to invest and who takes his money to the local bank. Current market conditions allow the bank to offer Ivan an interest rate of 8 percent on his money. Ivan invests his $1,000 in the bank and informs the teller that he will return in 1 year to pick up his $1,080.

How did Ivan know that his $1,000 will grow to $1,080 in 1 year? Because the rate at which present dollars will grow in the future was given at 8 percent, and $1,080 is 8 percent more than $1,000. Although this calculation is easy to perform, others are not. For example, how much would Ivan have in 1 year if he deposits $1,150 in the bank account at 8 percent? Because this is harder to do, it is necessary to solve this and other future value problems with a formula.

Simple Interest: The Formula Method Let the notation PV stand for present value, FV_1 stand for the future value in year 1, and r stand for the interest rate. In the previous example PV is $1,000 and r is 8 percent. The following formula solves for the FV_1:

$$FV_1 = PV\,(1 + r) \tag{3.1}$$

The right-hand side of Formula (3.1) is actually two parts put together. For instance, we could write:

$$FV_1 = PV + (PV \times r)$$

The formula for future value combines the original amount, PV, with the amount of interest earned on the investment, $PV \times r$.

Using Formula (3.1), we see that Ivan's $1,000 investment will grow to:

$$FV_1 = \$1{,}000(1.08) = \$1{,}080$$

If Ivan deposited $1,150 in the bank account instead of $1,000, his investment would grow to:

$$FV_1 = \$1{,}150(1.08) = \$1{,}242$$

simple interest
The dollar amount of interest received on the original investment only.

Formula (3.1) is known as the **simple interest** formula because interest is received only on the original investment. If after 1 year Ivan decides to spend the \$80 of interest earned in the account and reinvest the \$1,000 for another year at 8 percent, then he will have \$1,080 at the end of that year as well. The amount of simple interest earned (\$80) did not change because Ivan invested \$1,000 the second year, the amount equal to his original investment. As long as interest rates stay at 8 percent, Ivan can continue to remove and spend the \$80 of interest earned each year and continue to turn \$1,000 of present dollars into \$1,080 of future dollars.

Compound Interest: The Formula Method Suppose that Ivan decides to delay consumption further by investing the \$1,000 in a bank account earning 8 percent for 2 years. The difference now is that Ivan decides not to remove the \$80 of interest earned in year 1 but, instead, to leave the interest in the account for the second year. What will his investment grow to in 2 years? At first glance the problem appears to be a trivial extension to the previous one above. If his investment earns \$80 in interest over 1 year, then one might guess that the investment would earn an additional \$80 in year 2 for a total of \$160 in interest over 2 years, and \$1,160 in total.

compound interest
The dollar amount of interest earned not only on the original principal but also on interest earned over previous periods.

The amount of \$1,160, however, will understate the future value of the investment because of compound interest. **Compound interest** includes interest earned on interest. In the second year Ivan will also earn interest on the \$80 earned in the first year, and his \$1,000 will grow to an amount greater than \$1,160. With compounding, the investment grows to a future value in the first period, and then the entire future value earns interest in the second period.

One way to solve future value problems with compounding is to use Formula (3.1) and to break the problem into two parts:

Part 1: Determine the future value at the end of the first year:

$$FV_1 = PV(1 + r) = \$1{,}000(1.08) = \$1{,}080$$

Part 2: Determine the future value at the end of the second year starting with the result of Part 1:

$$FV_2 = FV_1(1 + r) = \$1{,}080(1.08) = \$1{,}166.40$$

Notice that the preceding formulas use different subscripts for FV. The subscript refers to the future time period, such that FV_1 is the future value in year 1, and FV_2 is the future value in year 2. The subscripts are useful in keeping track of cash flows through time.

With compounding, the future value of \$1,166.40 in year 2 is \$6.40 greater than our first guess of \$1,160.

The two-step procedure for compounding interest can be reduced to one step by substituting the variable FV_1 in step two with $PV(1 + r)$:

$$FV_2 = PV(1 + r)(1 + r)$$

which is equivalent to:

$$FV_2 = PV(1 + r)^2$$

In determining the future value in year 3, we can extend our example by allowing a third year's interest earned on the original investment of $1,000:

$$FV_3 = FV_2\,(1 + r)$$

By substituting $PV(1 + r)^2$ for FV_2, we get:

$$FV_3 = PV(1 + r)(1 + r)(1 + r), \text{ or}$$
$$FV_3 = PV(1 + r)^3$$

Now that we see the pattern, we can move directly to the general formula for determining future values with compound interest:

$$FV_n = PV(1 + r)^n \tag{3.2}$$

where n is the number of periods interest is compounded. Formula (3.2) adds the general subscript n to the future value, and can be used to generate *any* future value given three pieces of information: (1) a present value, (2) an interest rate, and (3) a time period.

Returning to Example (3.1) and using Formula (3.2), we again determine that Ivan's future dollar amount after 2 years will be:

$$FV_2 = PV(1 + r)^2 = \$1{,}000(1.08)^2 = \$1{,}000(1.1664) = \$1{,}166.40$$

and his future amount after three years will be:

$$FV_3 = PV(1 + r)^3 = \$1{,}000(1.08)^3 = \$1{,}000(1.2597) = \$1{,}259.71$$

This solution is provided in detail in Table 3.1.

The general formula will work for any future time period. For example, if Ivan would like to invest his $1,000 toward his retirement in 30 years, and if interest rates stay constant at 8 percent, then he will turn his $1,000 of present dollars into $10,063:

$$\$1{,}000(1.08)^{30} = \$1{,}000(10.063) = \$10{,}063.$$

TABLE 3.1 Compounding Interest over 3 Years

Year	*Starting Amount*	*(1 + r)*	*Ending Amount*
1	\$1,000.00	(1.08)	\$1,080.00
2	\$1,080.00	(1.08)	\$1,166.40
3	\$1,166.40	(1.08)	\$1,259.71

Compound interest can make a significant difference in investment when the time period is long.

Financial Calculator Method The advantage of financial calculators is that they are quick and accurate, and most come with well-written instruction manuals that explain how to calculate future values. The most common mistake in using a financial calculator is failing to clear the memories as described in the calculator's instruction manual. We will briefly review the keystrokes applicable to most simple financial calculators.[3]

Formula (3.2) is composed of four variables: the present value (*PV*), the number of future time periods (n), the interest rate (r), and the future value itself (*FV*). Financial calculators require the input of any three of these variables to solve for the fourth.[4] For example, if you enter into a calculator \$1,000 for *PV,* 8 percent for r, and 30 for n, the calculator will compute the *FV* to be approximately \$10,063. The keystrokes will probably be something like this: (Clear calculator) \$1,000, *PV,* 8, %*I*, 30, *n*, *CPT, FV.*

Some financial calculators produce answers with negative values. Users of these calculators need to experiment to learn when to ignore the negative sign and when to input a negative sign.

Computers can also be used to calculate a future value. They can also be extremely useful in solving more complex financial problems. The computational tasks of this chapter, however, are relatively simple, and it is actually easier to solve them with a financial calculator. Window 3.1 discusses some of the aspects of using computers to solve financial problems, which we will do in subsequent chapters. For Chapter 3, it is easier to use a financial calculator.

---

[3]Some financial calculators ask for different keystrokes in different order. You must refer to your calculator's reference manual if the keystrokes presented here do not apply.

[4]Financial calculators have keystrokes with these variables typed on them (e.g., *PV* for present value and *FV* for future value). Your calculator's keystrokes for the interest rate (r) and time period (n), however, may not match our notation. Consult your instruction manual for the proper keystrokes for all necessary inputs. It is common for the calculator to use %*I* for r.

WINDOW 3.1

Using Computers to Solve Financial Problems

Some financial tasks are so complex that the power of a personal computer is highly advisable. We will provide here an overview of the spectrum of ways in which financial problems can be solved using a computer.

Regardless of the computer used, it is the software that differentiates the financial applications. Every software solution does essentially the same thing: It takes the known variables, such as the interest rate, cash flow, and number of years, and "crunches" the math, using the appropriate formula. What differs is the sophistication and method by which the software receives the known variables from the user.

1. **Programming Languages.** Some simpler financial tasks, such as the tasks in Chapter 3, can be solved using functions that are a normal part of programming languages. These functions can be assessed from commonly available libraries of functions or subroutines.
2. **Spreadsheets.** Spreadsheets are software packages that provide useful frameworks with which users can solve problems—especially financial problems. Microsoft's Excel and other brands of software offer a myriad of functions that solve virtually all of the time value of money tasks of this text. Additional functions can be added to solve virtually any financial problem. The spreadsheet software manufacturers and other software firms have developed powerful, low-cost, and user-friendly spreadsheet-based solutions to amazingly complex problems.
3. **Personal Finance and Investment Software.** Numerous software products have been developed specifically to provide easy to use interfaces to users with financial tasks. Some of the software products focus on personal finance. Other products attack the challenging tasks faced by investment professionals.

For the purposes of Chapter 3, virtually all computer approaches have the same general overview. For example, in the case of computing a future value, the user will need to input the cash flow, the length of time, and the interest rate. The computer does the math and returns a solution. The big difference between products is the method and ease of exchanging the information from user to computer, and back to the user.

Nevertheless, one example might help: In the case of computing a future value, most computer software will ask the user to input the appropriate values into the arguments of a function such as:

$$FV(PV, r, n)$$

The user inputs a cash amount or argument in the place of PV, an interest rate in the place of r, and a number of years in the place of n. The computer then returns the future value.

The most common mistake in using a financial calculator is failing to clear the memories, as described in the calculator's manual.

Nonfinancial calculators with the keystroke y^x can be used easily to solve the expression $(1 + r)^n$ in the future value formula (Formula 3.2) for any value of r and n. For instance, we can use the y^x key to solve $(1.08)^{30}$. The keystrokes typically used would be: *1.08*, y^x, *30*, = .

An advantage of using a financial calculator is that it can be used to solve for any one of the four variables given the other three. Thus, you are not confined to solving for the future value; rather, you can instead solve for the interest rate or length of time, given the other three variables. For example, if you wished to know how long it would take for $1,000 to grow to $10,000 if the interest rate were 8 percent, you would input these values and the calculator would solve for the answer of approximately 30 years. If you wished to know at what interest rate $1,000 would grow to $10,000 in 30 years, you would input the variables *PV*, *FV*, and *n*, and the calculator would solve for the interest rate of approximately 8 percent.

Some computer software, unfortunately, is a little more difficult to use when searching for different variables within the same equation or relationship. Thus, for example, if the user knows the future value and is searching for one of the other variables, such as the interest rate, then he or she will need to use a different function. The function specifically might look something like:

$$\text{rate}\ (PV, FV, r)$$

In this case, the user inserts the three known variables inside the function's parentheses and the calculator or computer computes the interest rate. As software writers provide easier interfaces, perhaps even the tasks of Chapter 3 will be more easily solved using a computer than by using a financial calculator.

More Frequent Compounding We have assumed to this point that interest was compounded on an *annual*, or once-a-year, basis. For instance, when Ivan left his $1,000 in the bank account in year 2, compounded interest was earned from year 1. In an environment where financial institutions compete for deposits, some banker is bound to suggest that it would be better for Ivan if the bank compounded his interest more frequently—say, every 6 months, or every month, or even as frequently as every day. In fact, why not compound the interest every second? This must be good for the investor because the more frequent the compounding, the greater the effect of compounding on future value.

Because financial institutions do compete for depositors' funds, it is common for banks and other savings institutions to compound interest more frequently than once per year. It is our job now to make the necessary adjustments to our future value formula to allow for more frequent compounding. Two adjustments need to be made to Formula (3.2). First, the interest rate, given by r, must be divided by the number of times interest is compounded within the year. For example, if interest is compounded quarterly (four times a year), then an 8 percent annual rate becomes a 2 percent quarterly rate. If interest is compounded daily, then an 8 percent annual rate becomes a .022 percent daily rate (8% ÷ 365) . If we let m be the number of times per year interest is compounded, then the expression $(1 + r)$ in Formula (3.2) becomes $(1 + r/m)$ in the adjusted future value formula.

Second, the expression $(1 + r/m)$, which was originally raised to the power n, must now be raised to the power n times m. Incorporating both of these changes, the adjusted future value formula becomes:

$$FV_n = PV\left[1 + \frac{r}{m}\right]^{mn} \qquad (3.3)$$

Let us return to Example 3.1 and Ivan's investment of $1,000 in a bank account earning 8 percent interest for 2 years. If Ivan's bank compounds interest once per year, m in Formula (3.3) is equal to 1, and Ivan's future value is:

$$FV_2 = \$1{,}000\left[1 + \frac{0.08}{1}\right]^{1\times 2} = \$1{,}166.40$$

the same future value as before. If Ivan's bank were to compound interest quarterly, however, then m is equal to 4 and his new (and improved) future value would be:

$$FV_2 = \$1{,}000\left[1 + \frac{0.08}{4}\right]^{4\times 2} = \$1{,}171.66$$

This future value is $5.26 greater than it was in the case of annual compounding. This is illustrated in Figure 3.5.

Why stop at quarterly compounding? Suppose instead that the bank compounds interest daily,[5] meaning that today's interest begins earning new interest tomorrow. For daily compounding, m is equal to 365 and Ivan's new (and even more improved) future value becomes:

$$FV_2 = \$1{,}000\left[1 + \frac{.08}{365}\right]^{365\times 2} = \$1{,}173.49.$$

Compounding more frequently than once per year can be accomplished using a financial calculator, by converting the annual interest rate and the number of years into a periodic interest rate and the number of time periods. For example, Ivan's investment of $1,000 for 2 years at 8 percent using quarterly compounding can be found using the keystrokes similar to this:

(Clear calculator) $1,000, *PV*, 2, *%I*, 8, *n*, *CPT*, *FV*.

[5]Most banks compound interest daily.

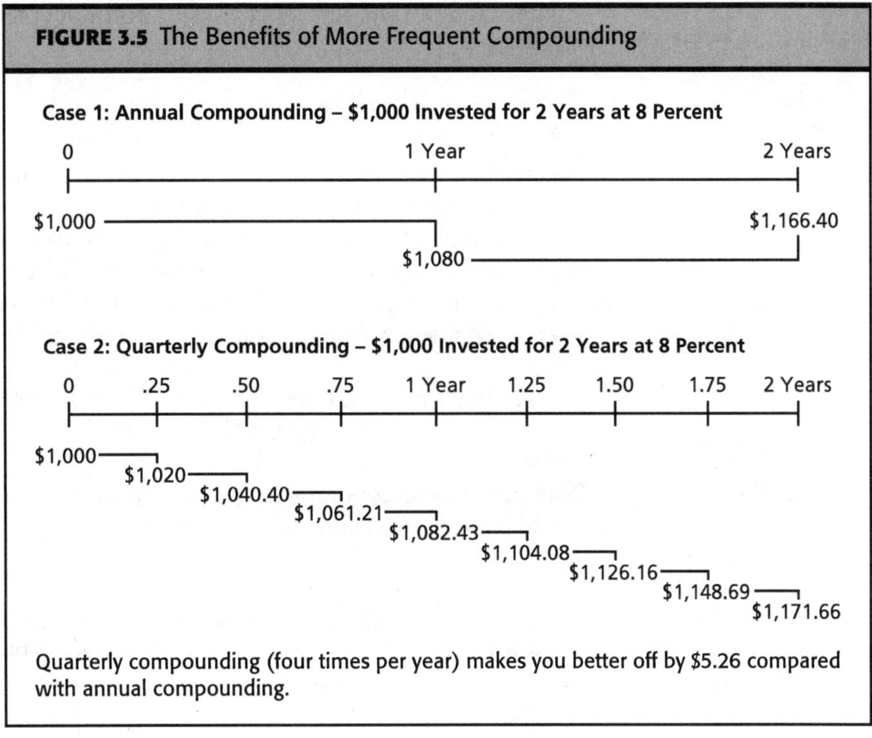

FIGURE 3.5 The Benefits of More Frequent Compounding

More sophisticated software will often do the conversion for the user if the user inputs the number of compounding periods per year (in this case, 4).

In our examples, more frequent compounding produces higher future values for Ivan. Note that daily compounding produces higher future values than quarterly compounding. Is there any way to make Ivan even happier? For instance, can we not break a year into even smaller pieces (i.e., 8,760 hours, 525,600 minutes, or 31,536,000 seconds)? At the extreme, we can define compounding on a *continuous* basis (e.g., over every fraction of a second)!

Future value Formula (3.3) can still be used for small periods of time, but it becomes quite cumbersome. For instance, if we choose to compound every hour, then an 8 percent annual rate becomes a 0.000009132 percent hourly rate, and the future value becomes (rounded):

$$FV_2 = \$1{,}000\ [1 + .000009132]^{8760 \times 2} = \$1{,}173.51.$$

This rate becomes even smaller if we go inside of a hour and compound over minutes, seconds, or even over fractions of a second. Eventually we would near a point where interest is earned continuously. For the case of continuous compounding, the value m in Formula 3.3 approaches infinity, and $[1 + r/m]^m$ approaches e^r, where e is the base for natural logarithms and is approximately equal to 2.71828.[6] Formula (3.4) allows for continuous compounding:

$$FV_n = PV[e^{rn}] \tag{3.4}$$

Financial calculators and computers do not generally contain built-in continuous compounding function keys. Most calculators however, have the keystroke e^x, which allows for easy computation of Formula (3.4). Calculators without the key e^x but with the key y^x can be used to solve Formula (3.4) using 2.71828 for y.

For example, if Ivan's investment earned 8 percent continuously for 2 years, then his new future value would (rounded) be:

$$FV_2 = \$1,000(2.71828^{.08 \times 2}) = \$1,000(2.71828)^{.16}$$
$$= \$1,000(1.1735) = \$1173.51.$$

With continuous compounding, Ivan's account grows by 2 cents more than it would have grown using daily compounding.

---

[6]For the technically minded reader, this footnote provides the derivation of the continuous compounding Formula (3.4). Formula (3.3), or the future value formula with nonannual compounding, is:

$$FV_n = PV\left[1 + \frac{r}{m}\right]^{mn} \tag{a}$$

This formula can be transformed into an alternative form by letting $w = m/r$:

$$FV_n = PV\left[\left\{1 + \frac{1}{w}\right\}^{w}\right]^{rn} \tag{b}$$

Formula (b) can be written more generally as:

$$FV_n = PV\,[f(w)]^{rn} \tag{c}$$

The function $f(w)$ can now be evaluated for different values of w. For example, when $w = 1$:

$$f(1) = [1 + (1/1)]^1 = 2.0000$$

when $w = 12$:

$$f(12) = [1 + (1/12)]^{12} = 2.6130$$

and when $w = 365$:

$$f(365) = [1 + (1/365)]^{365} = 2.71457$$

We can also evaluate w at the limit of infinity:

$$\text{Limit } f(w) \approx 2.71828$$

$$w \Rightarrow \infty$$

The value 2.71828 is the base number for natural logarithms and is given by the symbol e. Therefore, with continuous compounding, we obtain Formula (3.4):

$$FV_n = PV\,[e^{rn}]$$

Effective Annual Interest Rates It is sometimes difficult for investors to choose among different investments given different stated interest rates and compounding intervals. For example, would you rather invest $1,000 for 1 year to earn 7 percent compounded annually or 6.85 percent compounded daily? While you might be tempted to go with the higher stated interest rate of 7 percent, it turns out that you are slightly better off at 6.85 percent daily compounding.

To help investors make choices like the previous one, we can transform all quoted interest rates (i.e., 7 percent annually or 6.85 percent daily) to an **effective annual interest rate.** The effective annual interest rate is given by:

effective annual interest rate
An interest rate expressed as if it were earned once per year.

$$\text{Effective Annual Rate} = \left(1 + \frac{r}{m}\right)^m - 1 \tag{3.5}$$

Formula (3.5) builds compounding frequency into the quoted interest rate in order to compare quoted rates each with different levels of compounding. Thus, if you were faced with the choice of 7 percent compounded annually or 6.85 percent compounded daily, then you would calculate the effective annual rate on each and choose the investment with the higher effective annual rate.

$$\text{Choice \#1: 7\% Annually: } \left(1 + \frac{.07}{1}\right)^1 - 1$$
$$= 0.07 \text{ Effective Annual Rate.}$$

$$\text{Choice \# 2: 6.85\% Daily: } \left(1 + \frac{.0685}{365}\right)^{365} - 1$$
$$= 0.0709 \text{ Effective Annual Rate.}$$

Choice #2, with daily compounding, is preferred because it has the higher effective annual rate. Many financial calculators have keys that will perform this conversion automatically.

A Quick Summary of Future Values It may be useful at this point to stop for a brief overview. Compounding is designed to push the cash flows toward the future into larger dollar amounts. Future values may be calculated using simple interest (with no compounding of interest), annual compounding, or even more frequent compounding. The solutions may be found by using an ordinary calculator, a financial calculator, or a computer with financial software.

Present Values

How can Jack and Diane, who have just won the $1 million lottery prize, determine what their winnings are worth today? Recall that the prize is represented by a stream of cash flows to be received in the future. Because these cash flows are different commodities, we should not simply add them together to calculate total value. The technique introduced in this section, *discounting* cash flows, uses the present time as a reference point and determines the value of all cash flows with respect to this reference point.

Discounting: The Formula Method Many of the procedures used in discounting are similar to the procedures used in compounding. For example, the four variables that are needed for compounding—*PV, FV, r,* and *n*—are the same variables used to discount cash flows. In fact, the basic present value formula is the future value formula rearranged so that *PV,* instead of *FV,* appears on the left-hand side:

$$PV = \frac{FV_n}{(1+r)^n} \tag{3.6}$$

Formula (3.6) uses division rather than multiplication. Finding a present value is like compounding in reverse. We know the dollar amount to be received in the future, we know how long the wait will be to receive the money, and we know the interest rate that we could earn if we were to open a bank account. We do not, however, know the value of those future dollars today (i.e., what we would have to put into the bank account today in order to receive those future values).

To discount a cash flow, divide the known future value by the quantity $(1 + r)^n$. As long as the interest rate is positive, *PV* will be less than *FV.* This follows from the earlier example where the value today of receiving $1.00 in 1 year was $0.93, and the value today of receiving $1.00 in 2 years was $0.86. Given a market interest rate of 8 percent, we can use the present value formula to show how we arrived at these values:

$$PV = \frac{\$1.00}{(1.08)^1} = \text{(approximately) } \$0.93, \text{ and}$$

$$PV = \frac{\$1.00}{(1.08)^2} = \text{(approximately) } \$0.86.$$

In the case of compounding, the higher the interest rate, the higher the future value. In the case of discounting, however, the higher the interest rate, the lower the present value. If market interest rates in the preceding example are 12 percent instead of 8 percent, then the present value will be lower than before:

$$PV = \frac{\$1.00}{(1.12)^1} = \$0.89, \text{ and}$$

$$PV = \frac{\$1.00}{(1.12)^2} = \$0.80.$$

FIGURE 3.6 The Present Value of a Dollar at Different Discount Rates

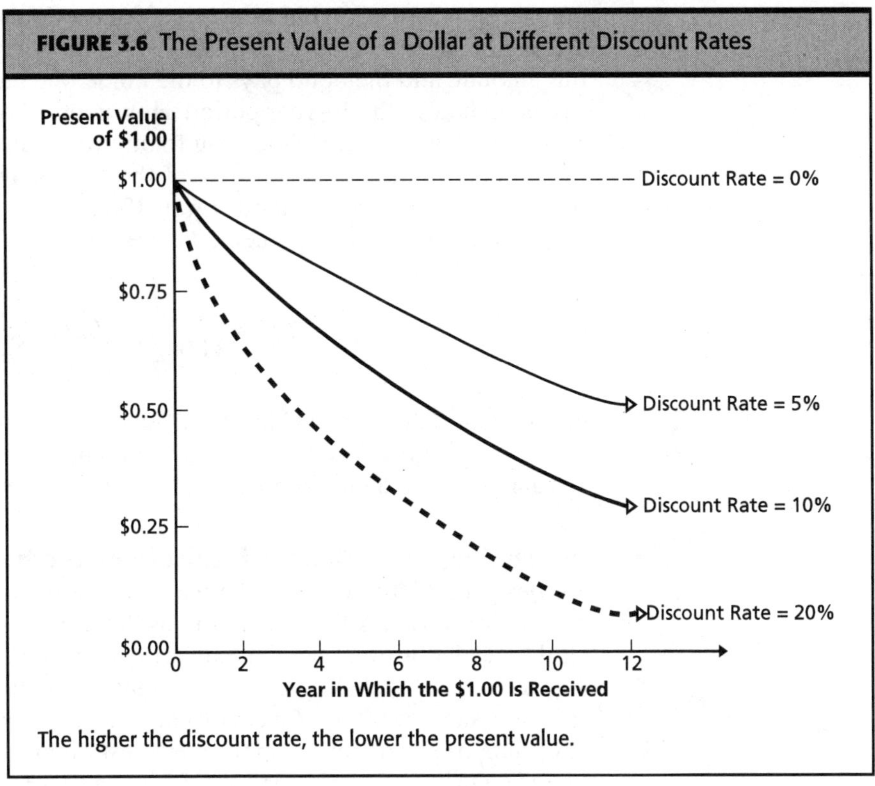

The higher the discount rate, the lower the present value.

Why are the present values lower for higher interest rate levels? Let us use our knowledge of compounding to answer this question. Given a choice, anyone would prefer a bank account that pays 12 percent interest over one that pays 8 percent because the future value will be higher if money is invested at 12 percent. Now let us shift the problem around and think about present values: If you have to wait a year to receive a dollar, your opportunity cost of waiting for the dollar depends on what you could have done with a dollar in your hand today. One alternative is to put the dollar in a bank account now. Because your opportunity cost of waiting for the dollar is greater the higher the interest rate, higher interest rates make the present value lower.

discount rate Another name for the interest rate. Because to discount is to deduct, the discount rate is used to reduce a future value to a present value.

This is the reason the interest rate in present value calculations is sometimes known as the **discount rate.** To *discount* is to deduct from the value. The higher the rate of discount, the larger the deduction from the future value amount, and the smaller the present value. The relationship between the discount rate and present values is shown in Figure 3.6.

Example 3.2 Friendly Freddy's car dealership, which is in need of new customers, announces the following bonus offer: a free $500 U.S. savings bond to anyone purchasing a new car within the next 30 days. Sound enticing? Although the savings bond is purportedly worth \$500, you must wait 10 years to receive this amount, and the bond pays to the holder an amount far less than \$500 if cashed in before the 10-year period. How good a bonus is this?

Before this offer persuades you to buy your car at Friendly Freddy's, you should determine the value today of the free savings bond. While it is true the bond will pay \$500, you must wait 10 years to receive full value. Given a market interest rate of 8 percent, the present value of the savings bond is:

$$PV = \frac{\$500}{(1.08)^{10}} = \$231.60,$$

or less than half of the value of the advertised bonus. Note that if Friendly Freddy gave you \$231.60 in cash, you could put it in the bank and get \$500 in 10 years. It is still a nice bonus, but not quite as nice as originally thought.

Discounting: The Financial Calculator Method Financial calculators are designed to perform all the work necessary for discounting. As in the case of future values, the calculator has the formulas built in and can perform all the needed arithmetic. For example, suppose that Friendly Freddy's Car Agency offered a slightly different bonus scheme: a \$500 savings bond that can be cashed in after 7.5 years to any customer who buys a car within 30 days. Suppose also that the market interest rate is 8.3 percent, not 8 percent. Inputting the values \$500 for *FV,* 7.5 for *n,* and 8.3 for *r* into the financial calculator will generate the *PV* of the new bonus as \$274.95.

Nonfinancial calculators can still be of great assistance in performing present value analysis. As long as your calculator has the y^x key, your nonfinancial calculator can solve for the denominator in Formula (3.6) for any set of values of *r* and *n.* If, as in the preceding case, *r* is 8.3 percent and *n* is 7.5 years, then the present value of \$500 is:

$$PV = \frac{500}{(1.083)^{7.5}} = \frac{500}{(1.8185)} = \$274.95.$$

The keystroke y^x will allow any value to be raised to any power. Most nonfinancial calculators have the keystroke $1/x$, which makes discounting even easier. To determine the present value, first raise one plus the interest rate to the power, and then hit the keystroke $1/x$. Multiplying by the *FV* provides the present value.

More Frequent Discounting Recall continuous compounding, where interest is earned every fraction of a second. We can also consider the case of continuous discounting. Formula (3.6) can be transformed to account for continuous discounting:

$$PV = \frac{FV_n}{e^{rn}} \tag{3.7}$$

where e is the base to the natural logarithm and is approximately equal to 2.71828. Most calculators have the keystroke e^x, which allows for easy calculation of Formula (3.7.) Calculators without the e^x key but with the y^x key can solve Formula (3.7) using 2.71828 for y.

For example, in Example (3.2), Friendly Freddy's Car Agency offered a $500 savings bond that will mature in 10 years. Suppose also that the market interest rate is 8 percent compounded continuously. Inputting the values $500 for FV, 10 for n, and 8 for r gives $224.66.

Just as the continuous discounting formula can be derived from the continuous compounding formula, we can transform formula (3.3) into a formula for discounting by rearranging the terms. Financial calculations can be used, as before, by dividing the annual interest rate by m and multiplying the number of years by m.

The Time Value for More Than One Cash Flow

We have thus performed time value of money problems for a single or lump-sum cash flow. A very common situation, however, is one in which a series of payments are either invested through time or are to be received through time—these are known as **multiple cash flow** problems.

multiple cash flow
More than one cash flow, as opposed to a lump-sum cash flow.

Compounding Multiple Cash Flows

Recall Example (3.1) and Ivan, the investor with $1,000 to invest in the bank today. The $1,000 came from savings Ivan accumulated while working a part-time job delivering pizza. Ivan is now completing his freshman year of college and plans to continue delivering pizzas through the end of his junior year. In addition to the $1,000 he has ready to invest in a bank today, Ivan will add to his investment at the end of each year over the next 2 years. He plans to close the bank account when he graduates in 3 years. Because the pizza business is growing, Ivan estimates that the deposit 1 year from today will be $1,250, and the deposit 2 years from today will be $1,500. How much will Ivan have when he graduates if interest rates stay at 8 percent?

As shown in Table 3.2, this multiple cash flow, future value problem is really three lump-sum future value problems in one. Case 1 considers the annual compounding of interest. We see that the first deposit of $1,000 grows to $1,259.71 in 3 years. The second deposit of $1,250 grows to $1,458.00 in 2 years. The third deposit of $1,500 grows to $1,620.00 in 1 year. The total future value can be found by summing the individual future values. The total future value of Ivan's investments is expected to be $4,337.71 at graduation.

Case 2 in Table 3.2 considers the continuous compounding of interest. The total future value of Ivan's investments with continuous compounding is

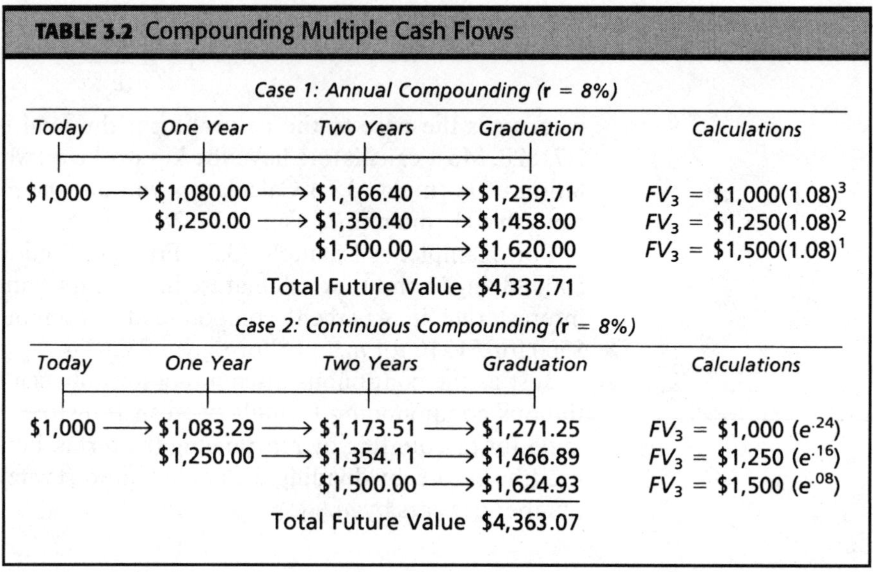

TABLE 3.2 Compounding Multiple Cash Flows

Case 1: Annual Compounding (r = 8%)

Today	*One Year*	*Two Years*	*Graduation*	*Calculations*
\$1,000 →	\$1,080.00 →	\$1,166.40 →	\$1,259.71	$FV_3 = \$1,000(1.08)^3$
	\$1,250.00 →	\$1,350.40 →	\$1,458.00	$FV_3 = \$1,250(1.08)^2$
		\$1,500.00 →	\$1,620.00	$FV_3 = \$1,500(1.08)^1$
		Total Future Value	\$4,337.71	

Case 2: Continuous Compounding (r = 8%)

Today	*One Year*	*Two Years*	*Graduation*	*Calculations*
\$1,000 →	\$1,083.29 →	\$1,173.51 →	\$1,271.25	$FV_3 = \$1,000\ (e^{.24})$
	\$1,250.00 →	\$1,354.11 →	\$1,466.89	$FV_3 = \$1,250\ (e^{.16})$
		\$1,500.00 →	\$1,624.93	$FV_3 = \$1,500\ (e^{.08})$
		Total Future Value	\$4,363.07	

$4,363.07, which demonstrates the desirability of continuous compounding over annual compounding.

Discounting Multiple Cash Flows

Recall Example (3.2) and the bonus offered by Friendly Freddy's Car Agency: a $500 10-year bond to any new-car customer within 30 days. Let us now consider a more elaborate bonus plan. In addition to the $500 10-year bond, Friendly Freddy's will offer an additional bond that pays $1,000 in 20 years, along with a third bond that pays $2,500 in 30 years. The total bonus money is $4,000, but how much is that worth presently if interest rates are 8 percent?

Table 3.3 provides the calculations to this multiple cash flow, present value problem. As the time line indicates, this is actually three present value problems in one. Receiving $500 in 10 years is worth $231.60 today, receiving $1,000 in 20 years is worth $214.55 today, and receiving $2,500 in 30 years is worth $248.43 today. The total present value of Friendly Freddy's bonus plan is $694.59.

We can use a similar procedure to calculate the present value of Jack and Diane's lottery prize. You will recall that Jack and Diane have won $50,000 per year for 20 straight years. To determine the present value of the prize, discount each of these payments to the present and add them up. These calculations are given in Table 3.4.

Given an interest rate of 8 percent, the present value of this Lotto prize is $490,907, which is about one-half of its stated prize value of $1 million. Notice that the present value of each of the $50,000 payments declines through time. The longer you have to wait, the less the payment is worth today.

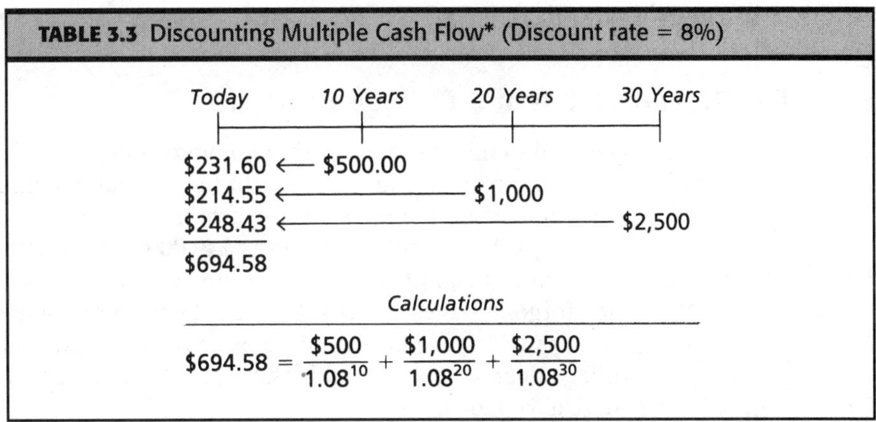
TABLE 3.3 Discounting Multiple Cash Flow* (Discount rate = 8%)

Calculations

$$\$694.58 = \frac{\$500}{1.08^{10}} + \frac{\$1,000}{1.08^{20}} + \frac{\$2,500}{1.08^{30}}$$

It turns out that a simpler method exists for discounting the multiple cash flow stream for Jack and Diane's lottery prize. A special feature of the lottery's cash payments is that they are all the same. Given *constant* cash payments through time, procedures exist to find the present value of the stream in one step. Constant cash flow streams through time, which are known as *annuities,* will be presented in the next section. First, however, an expanded example of discounting is presented in Workshop 3.1, where we consider the question of whether going to college makes financial sense.

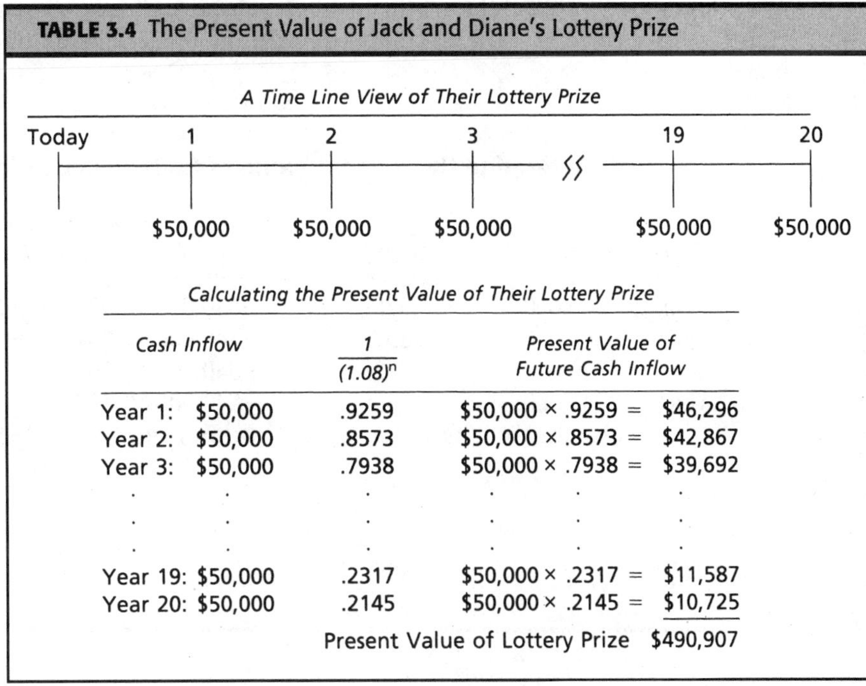
TABLE 3.4 The Present Value of Jack and Diane's Lottery Prize

A Time Line View of Their Lottery Prize

Today	1	2	3	…	19	20
	$50,000	$50,000	$50,000		$50,000	$50,000

Calculating the Present Value of Their Lottery Prize

Cash Inflow	$\frac{1}{(1.08)^n}$	*Present Value of Future Cash Inflow*
Year 1: $50,000	.9259	$50,000 × .9259 = $46,296
Year 2: $50,000	.8573	$50,000 × .8573 = $42,867
Year 3: $50,000	.7938	$50,000 × .7938 = $39,692
. . .	. . .	. . .
Year 19: $50,000	.2317	$50,000 × .2317 = $11,587
Year 20: $50,000	.2145	$50,000 × .2145 = $10,725
	Present Value of Lottery Prize	$490,907

WORKSHOP 3.1

The Present Value of a College Education

Have you ever stopped to think about whether going to college makes financial sense?* That is, are the costs of a college education worth the projected benefits? We will show how such a question can be answered in this workshop.

Let us assume that each year of college costs $40,000 in total expenses—$15,000 in added expenses (tuition, and all other college-related expenses) and $25,000 in forgone wages. (We include forgone wages as a cost because if you were not in college you would be working and receiving wages.) Given that these cost projections are reasonable, and given that the college degree you seek will take 4 years, the total cost of obtaining your degree is estimated at $160,000.

Although the costs appear large, we have yet to consider the benefits. It might be reasonable to expect that a college degree will increase your annual wage by $20,000 throughout your work life as compared with what you would be earning if you had not gone to college. That means that if you work for 40 years (say from the age of 23 to the age of 62) the "extra" income from your college degree will total $800,000 (40 years at $30,000 per year). Adding your wages together, however, and subtracting the sum of the costs is an accounting approach and is not equal to their true value.

The financial question we need to answer is whether $160,000 of college costs is worth the $800,000 of increased revenues. This multiple cash flow problem must transform all cash flows to a single reference point, in this case to present values. The following lists the multiple cash flows in the problem. Given an interest rate of 8 percent, we can convert future values into present values. College education costs are discounted first; then they will be compared with the present value of college education benefits.

Step 1: Determine the Present Value of College Education Costs

Cash Outflow	$\frac{1}{(1.08)^n}$	*Present Value of Future Cash Outflow*
Year 1: −$40,000	.9259	−$40,000 × .9259 = −$ 37,036.00
Year 2: −$40,000	.8573	−$40,000 × .8573 = −$ 34,292.00
Year 3: −$40,000	.7938	−$40,000 × .7938 = −$ 31,752.00
Year 4: −$40,000	.7350	−$40,000 × .7350 = −$ 29,400.00
Total Present Value of Future Cash Outflows		−$132,480.00

WORKSHOP 3.1 *(continued)*

Step 2: Determine the Present Value of College Education Benefits

Cash Inflow	$\frac{1}{(1.08)^n}$	*Present Value of Future Cash Inflow*
Year 5: +$20,000	.6806	+$20,000 × .6806 = +$ 13,612.00
Year 6: +$20,000	.6302	+$20,000 × .6302 = +$ 12,604.00
Year 7: +$20,000	.5835	+$20,000 × .5835 = +$ 11,670.00
Year 8: +$20,000	.5403	+$20,000 × .5403 = +$ 10,806.00
...	.	. . .
...	.	. . .
Year 44: +$20,000	.0338	+$20,000 × .0338 = +$ 677.00
Total Present Value of Future Cash Inflows		+$175,299.00

Step 3: Subtract Present Value of Outflows from Present Value of Inflows

Total Present Value of Future Cash Inflows	+$175,299.00
Total Present Value of Future Cash Outflows	−$132,480.00
	+$ 42,819.00

The table does not show the benefits between year 8 and year 44, simply to save space. (You could fill them in, if you are interested.) In terms of the benefits of a college education, the 40 years of increased wages have a combined present value of $175,299. In other words, if the prospective college student went to the financial marketplace he or she would be able to trade the 40 years of $20,000 benefits for $175,299 today. In terms of costs, the 4 years of $40,000 college payments have a present value of $132,480. The difference between the present value of benefits and costs will tell us whether or not the decision to earn a college degree makes financial sense.

The decision does make financial sense because the benefits exceed the cost by $42,819. The importance of the preceding procedure is that time value has been correctly used to make decisions involving cash flows at different points in time. This example showed that the financial benefits of college slightly exceeded the financial costs of college, when time value is considered for this particular high school senior. Ignoring time value, the decision appeared obvious because the unadjusted benefits were $800,000 and the unadjusted costs were only $160,000. Although the decision did not change after we worked the numbers, the magnitude of the difference between benefits and costs was greatly reduced by considering the time value of money.

---

*Of course, there may be issues other than money involved in deciding to attend college, such as the joy and noncareer usefulness of an education. Where else in life, other than as a college student, can you get 20 weeks of vacation per year, ignore reality, and sleep until 10 in the morning?

The Present Value of Annuities

Previous sections provided techniques for finding the present and future values of a single or multiple cash flow. Multiple cash flows were discounted separately and added together. We emphasized that computing present values was much like pulling, and diminishing, cash flows to the left along a time line, whereas computing future values was much like pushing, and increasing, cash flows to the right along a time line.

annuity
A series of equal cash flows to be received through time.

Annuities are a special type of cash flow stream. An **annuity** is a stream of equal payments through time. Examples of annuities include (1) monthly payments on certain types of consumer loans such as car loans, personal loans, and mortgages, (2) the stream of coupons offered in connection with financial securities known as bonds, and (3) dividend payments offered on certain types of stock. Most annuities have *finite* lives, which means that they stop at some predetermined point, although some annuities offer cash flows forever.

Example 3.3 ________

Suppose that your alumni office invites you to become a lifetime member of the alumni association soon after you graduate from college. The cost of lifetime membership is \$300 paid today, but the alumni association offers you the alternative of a payment plan. The payment plan requires payments of \$121 due at the end of each year for 3 years. The payment is a 3-year annuity, represented by the time line in Figure 3.7. Should you make the single payment of \$300 today or agree to the annuity payment plan? Assume market interest rates are 10 percent.

The present value of the single payment is of course \$300, as it is already in the present time period. If we knew the present value of the \$121 payment plan, we could compare the two payment options and choose the plan with the lower present value.

One way of determining the present value of the annuity plan is to discount each payment separately using the market interest rate of 10 percent and adding the three present values together:

$$PVA = \frac{\$121}{(1.1)^1} + \frac{\$121}{(1.1)^2} + \frac{\$121}{(1.1)^3} = \$300.91.$$

FIGURE 3.7 A Time Line View of an Annuity

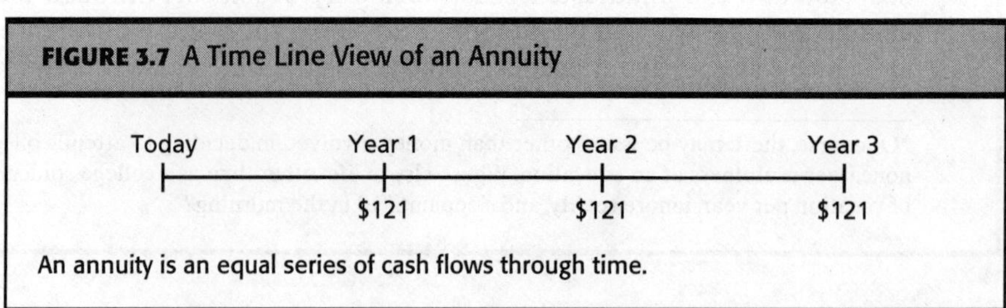

An annuity is an equal series of cash flows through time.

PVA stands for the present value of the annuity, which is three payments in this case. The payment plan has a present value approximately equal to the single payment.

The present values can also be solved using the financial calculator. Take a minute now to verify our answer of approximately $300 for the present value of the annuity using one or both of these methods.

Because the present value of the annuity is (approximately) equal to the alternative of paying $300 today, most people would be indifferent to the choice between writing a check today for $300 or paying through the annuity plan. Note that even though the annuity plan requires $363 total dollars to be paid (three payments of $121), the value to the alumni office of receiving $363 through time is equivalent to receiving $300.91 today, given the time value of money.

Developing a Shortcut Procedure for Annuities

This section develops a shortcut for finding the present value of annuities. The key to the shortcut is that the numerator in each of the three parts of the previous formula is the same. Because the numerator is a constant, we can factor out the common amount:

$$PVA = \$121\left[\frac{1}{(1.1)^1} + \frac{1}{(1.1)^2} + \frac{1}{(1.1)^3}\right] = \$300.91$$

The three fractions inside the brackets are equal to:

$$[0.9091 + 0.8264 + 0.7513] = [2.4869]$$

so that the solution to our present value problem becomes:

$$PVA = \$121[2.4869] = \$300.91$$

Thus, 2.4869 is the sum of three separate present values. If we can determine a way of calculating this sum directly, then we can solve the problem in one step. This is the annuity shortcut, and is shown next using the formula method and the financial calculator method.[7]

The Formula Method The general formula for the present value of an annuity is:

$$PVA = A\left[\frac{1}{(1 + r)^1} + \frac{1}{(1 + r)^2} + \frac{1}{(1 + r)^3} + \dots + \frac{1}{(1 + r)^n}\right]$$

[7]All annuities in this chapter are assumed to have cash flows that occur at the end of each period.

where A stands for the annuity amount, r is the market interest rate, and n is the period when the annuity stops. An algebraic solution[8] exists for the bracketed expression such that the PVA can be given by:

$$PVA = A\left[\frac{1}{r} - \frac{1}{r(1 + r)^n}\right] \tag{3.8}$$

Using Formula (3.8), we can solve for the present value of the alumni annuity in one step:

$$PVA = \$121\left[\frac{1}{.1} - \frac{1}{.1(1.1)^3}\right] = \$121(10 - 7.5131)$$

$$= \$121(2.4869) = \$300.91,$$

the same answer as before.

The annuity formula (Formula 3.8), which looks intimidating, is really quite manageable.[9] Most calculators are equipped with the keystroke y^x, which can solve for $(1 + r)^n$ given any combination of r and n. The rest is simple arithmetic.

---

[8]The annuity formula can be derived by using the concept of a geometric series. First let:

$$PVA = A/(1 + r)^1 + A/(1 + r)^2 + A/(1 + r)^3 + \ldots + At/(1 + r)^n$$

Now let $j = A/(1 + r)$ and $k = 1/(1 + r)$ so that the preceding equation becomes:

$$PVA = j(1 + k + k^2 + k^3 + \ldots + k^{n-1}) \tag{a}$$

Multiplying both sides of the above equation by k gives:

$$PVA \cdot k = j(k + k^2 + k^3 + \ldots + k^n). \tag{b}$$

Subtracting formula (b) from formula (a) gives:

$$PVA(1 - k) = j(1 - k^n) \tag{c}$$

Substituting back for both j and k gives:

$$PVA = \left[1 - \frac{1}{(1+r)}\right] = \frac{A}{1+r}\left[1 - \frac{1}{(1+r)^n}\right] \tag{d}$$

Multiplying both sides by $(1 + r)$ gives:

$$PVA \cdot r = A\left[1 - \frac{1}{(1+r)^n}\right] \tag{e}$$

Rearranging formula (e) gives the annuity Formula (3.8):

$$PVA = A\left[\frac{1}{r} - \frac{1}{r(1+r)^n}\right].$$

[9]A final note on the formula method. Formula (3.8) for the PVA can be written in several different ways; however, they all give the same result. Do not be surprised if a calculator handbook or another reference has an annuity formula that does not look exactly like ours.

The Financial Calculator Method The financial calculator method is simpler than the formula method. The present value of an annuity can be found by inputting the annuity amount A, r, and n into the financial calculator and computing PVA.[10]

The simplicity in using the financial calculator is well demonstrated in the case of annuities. For example, to determine the present value of the three-period alumni annuity, you would input the annuity amount (usually the keystroke PMT) as $A = \$121$, $r = .10$, and $n = 3$ years, and the calculator will determine the present value of the annuity to be \$300.91 (usually the keystroke *CPT* and *PV*). Of course, this is not magic. The calculator has the annuity formula (Formula 3.8) embedded in it, and simply replaces the variables A, r, and n with those of the specific situation. Remember to clear your calculator before starting a new problem. Many calculations express the answer as a negative number. It is important that you become familiar with your calculator's use of negative signs.

Beginning and Ending Payments

annuity due
An annuity with a first payment occurring at the beginning of period one.

Some financial calculators and other solution techniques raise the issue of whether cash flows (i.e., payments) occur at the beginning of each period or at the end of each period. The term **annuity due** is used to describe an annuity with a first payment occurring at the beginning of period one (i.e., today). In fact, using the beginning of a particular period is identical to using the end of the previous period. Thus, using an annuity due, or beginning-of-period cash flow assumption, is identical to shifting all cash flows back one period.

Throughout this text, we assume that cash flows occur at the *end* of the period. Thus, if your calculator has a beginning-of-period mode (e.g., BGN), then you should avoid it. If you do use beginning-of-period cash flows, be sure to add one to the number of periods to each cash flow.

The Future Value of an Annuity

This chapter developed present value techniques for multiperiod cash flows. Techniques have also been developed for future value as well as present value annuities.

To illustrate, suppose that you are bequeathed an inheritance of \$5,000 to be paid in installments of \$1,000 per year, with the first payment to come in 1 year. As part of the agreement, you cannot spend the money for 5 years. You can, however, let the local bank accumulate the funds for you, and the bank

---

[10]Most financial software for a financial computer would also ask these three inputs into a formula that solves for the present value of an annuity.

can guarantee a 6 percent interest rate to be earned on the funds over time. How many future dollars will you have to spend in 5 years?

This problem can be solved by taking the future value of each cash flow separately. For example, the first $1,000 payment will be received in 1 year and will be invested for 4 years:

$$FV_4 = \$1{,}000\,(1.06)^4 = \$1{,}262.48$$

Table 3.5 calculates the future value of each of the next four $1,000 payments, and sums them up to get the total future value of the five payments. Note that the last payment of $1,000 comes in year 5 and thus is already a future value.

Because the payments represent an annuity, a shortcut procedure exists to calculate the future value of the cash flow stream in one step. The formula for the future value of an annuity is:

$$FVA = A\left[\frac{(1+r)^n - 1}{r}\right] \tag{3.9}$$

where *FVA* is the future value of the annuity, *A* is the annuity amount, *r* is the interest rate, and *n* is the length of the annuity. Applying this formula for the inheritance gives:

$$FVA = \$1{,}000\left[\frac{(1.06)^5 - 1}{.06}\right] = \$1{,}000\left[5.6371\right] = \$5{,}637.10,$$

which is the same answer given in Table 3.5.

Remember that any calculator with the keystroke y^x can solve the bracketed expression with little effort, and thus can solve future value problems for any values of *r* and *n*. Most financial calculators can solve for the future

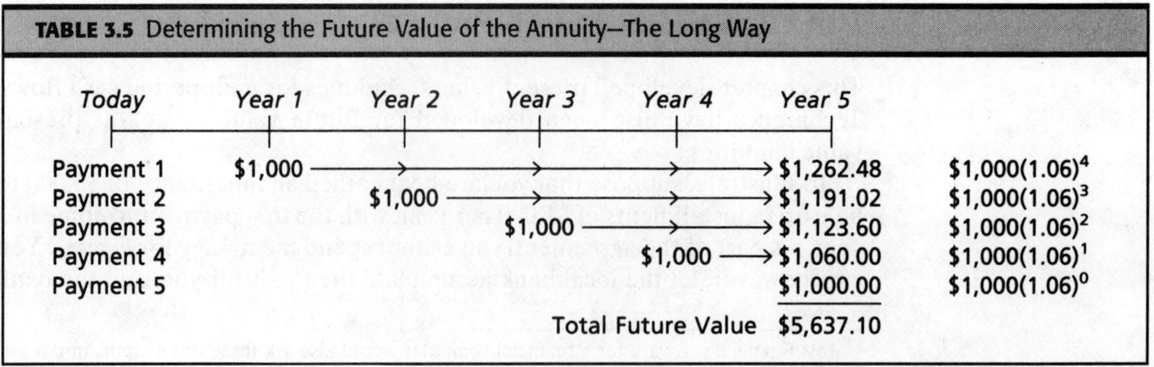

TABLE 3.5 Determining the Future Value of the Annuity—The Long Way

	Today	*Year 1*	*Year 2*	*Year 3*	*Year 4*	*Year 5*	
Payment 1		$1,000 →	→	→	→	$1,262.48	$1,000(1.06)⁴
Payment 2			$1,000 →	→	→	$1,191.02	$1,000(1.06)³
Payment 3				$1,000 →	→	$1,123.60	$1,000(1.06)²
Payment 4					$1,000 →	$1,060.00	$1,000(1.06)¹
Payment 5						$1,000.00	$1,000(1.06)⁰
					Total Future Value	$5,637.10	

value of the annuity by entering in the annuity amount, the interest rate, and the length of the annuity, and solving for *FVA:*

(Clear calculator) 1,000, *PMT,* 6, %*I,* 5, *n, CPT, FV.*

Solving for the Interest Rate

To this point we have emphasized problems that determine either future or present values. There are situations, however, in which you know present and future values and the length of time but do not know the interest rate. We show in this section how to solve for the interest rate.

The Echo Land Development Company is planning to buy a tract of land for \$118,000. Echo believes that it could sell the land 3 years from now for \$150,000. What rate of return would an investment that turns \$118,000 into \$150,000 earn?

We can use the future value formula (Formula 3.2) or present value formula (Formula 3.6) to solve for the interest rate. In either case, we rearrange the formula to get the interest rate on the left-hand side:

$$r = (FV_n/PV)^{1/n} - 1 \tag{3.10}$$

For the Echo Land Development, the interest rate on their investment is:

$$r = (150{,}000/118{,}000)^{1/3} - 1 = (1.2712)^{1/3} - 1 = .0832$$

so that r is 8.32 percent. This calculation can be challenging because it requires taking a value to the power 1/3; however, the keystroke y^x can be used to solve the problem. Taking a value to the 1/3 power is equivalent to raising to the power 0.333, so that 1.2712 raised to the 0.333 power is 1.0832.

Of course, the simpler method for solving for the interest rate utilizes the financial calculator. Remember that the financial calculator can solve for either *PV, FV, n,* or *r,* given any three variables. By inputting \$118,000 for *PV,* \$150,000 for *FV,* and 3 for *n,* the financial calculator will solve for *r* equal to 8.32 percent. Some calculations may require that one of the cash flows be entered as a negative number.

Solving for the Time Period

Finally, we will examine the case in which the present value, the future value, and the interest rate are known, but the time period is not known. For example, suppose your \$100 can be placed in a bank account to earn 10 percent interest compounded annually. Your goal is for the bank balance to accumulate to \$120. How long would the \$100 need to be left in the bank until it grows to \$120?

We can use the future value formula (Formula 3.2) or present value formula (Formula 3.6) to solve for the time period. In either case, we rearrange the formula to get the interest rate on the left-hand side:

$$(1 + r)^n = (FV_n/PV) \tag{3.11}$$

The unknown variable n appears as a power in Formula (3.10) and therefore requires that natural logarithms be used to determine a solution:

$$n \times ln(1 + r) = ln(FV_n/PV)$$

where *ln* stands for the natural logarithm. In the specific problem:

$$n \times ln(1.1) = ln(120/100)$$

$$n \times 0.0953 = 0.1823$$

$$n = 1.9131 \text{ years}$$

The simpler method for solving for the time period utilizes the financial calculator. Remember that the financial calculator can solve for either *PV, FV, n,* or *r* given any three variables. By inputting \$100 for *PV,* \$120 for *FV,* and 10 percent for *r,* the financial calculator will solve for *n* to be 1.9129 years.[11]

Summary

- The time value of money is a fundamental concept in finance. Dollars received in different time periods are different commodities and, as such, cannot be directly compared with each other for the purposes of making decisions. In order to compare dollars in different periods, we must transform their values to the same period, either to the present or to some point in the future.
- The formula for transforming present dollars to future dollars is:

$$FV_n = PV(1 + r)^n$$

- Compound interest is earned when interest is left to accumulate in an account through time. The amount of compound interest earned depends on the frequency in which interest is compounded, or by:

$$FV_n = PV\left[1 + \frac{r}{m}\right]^{mn}$$

[11]Some calculators will round this number up to the nearest integer. Others require that PV and FV be entered with opposite signs.

- The frequency of compounding spans the range of once per year (annual) to once every fraction of a second, or continuous compounding:

$$FV_n = PV(e^{rn})$$

- Discounting determines the value today of dollars to be received in the future. When discounting, the interest rate (r) is often referred to as the discount rate, or the rate at which future dollar amounts are discounted back to the present:

$$PV = \frac{FV_n}{(1+r)^n}$$

- Both discounting and compounding can be done with single payment amounts or with multiple cash flows. Multiple cash flow problems can be thought of as a series of single payment problems. Thus, it is possible to determine the value in the future of a series of cash flows, as well as to determine the value today of a series of cash flows to be received in the future.
- An annuity is a series of equal cash flows through time. The present value of annuities can be determined in one step using the annuity shortcut formula:

$$PVA = A\left[\frac{1}{r} - \frac{1}{r(1+r)^n}\right]$$

- Given the present value, the future value, and the time period (n), we can solve for the interest rate:

$$r = (FV_n/PV)^{1/n} - 1$$

- Given the present value, the future value, and the interest rate, we can solve for the number of time periods it takes for the present value to grow to a future value:

$$n \times ln(1 + r) = ln(FV_n/PV)$$

Demonstration Problems

Problem 1
Complete the following table:

	PV	*FV*	*r*	*n*	*m*
a	____	$100	6%	5	1
b	$100	____	5%	10	1
c	$50	$100	____	20	1
d	$50	$100	6%	____	1
e	____	$100	4%	10	4

Solution to Problem 1

The problems will be solved using both the formula method and the financial calculator method.

The formula method requires that the known values be plugged into the appropriate formula. With a little practice, using the financial calculator method is simpler. All five problems are solved by inputting the three known values and asking the calculator to solve for the fourth and missing value.

***Part (a):* (Finding a present value)**

Using the formula method, fill in the right-hand side of Formula 3.6:

$$PV = \$100/(1.06)^5 = \$74.726$$

Using the financial calculator method, insert the three known values and ask the financial calculator to solve for *PV*. Typical keystrokes would be:

(Clear calculator) 100, *FV*, 6, %*I*, 5, *n*, *CPT*, *PV*,

which produces the same answer of $74.726 (rounded).

***Part (b):* (Finding a future value)**

Using the formula method, fill in the right-hand side of Formula (3.2):

$$FV = \$100 \times (1.05)^{10} = \$162.89$$

Using the financial calculator method, insert the three known values and ask the financial calculator to solve for the *FV*. Typical keystrokes would be:

(Clear calculator) 100, *PV*, 5, %*I*, 10, *n*, *CPT*, *FV*,

which produces the same answer of $162.89 (rounded).

***Part (c):* (Finding an interest rate)**

Using the formula method, fill in the right-hand side of Formula (3.10):

$$r = (\$100/\$50)^{1/20} - 1 = 3.53\%$$

This is a little tricky, but it can be solved on most calculators using the following keystrokes: 100, /, 50, =, y^x, 0.05, =. Note that 0.05 is the decimal equivalent of 1/20.

Using the financial calculator method, insert the three known values and ask the financial calculator to solve for the %*I*. Typical keystrokes would be:

(Clear calculator) 50, *PV*, 100, *FV*, 20, *n*, *CPT*, %*I*,

which produces the same answer of 3.53% (rounded).

***Part (d):* (Finding the length of time)**

Using the formula method, follow the procedure at and after Formula (3.11) and solve for *n*:

$$n \times ln(1 + r) = ln(FV_n/PV)$$

This method requires the use of a natural logarithm key. If your calculator does not have one you will have to learn the trial and error method to be discussed in Chapter 4.

Using the financial calculator method, insert the three known values and ask the financial calculator to solve for the *n*. Typical keystrokes would be:

(Clear calculator) 50, *PV,* 100, *FV,* 6, %*I, CPT, n,*

which produces the same answer of 11.9 (rounded).

***Part (e):* (Finding a present value with quarterly compounding)**

When *m,* the number of compounding intervals per year, is greater than 1, two adjustments must be made. The value used for the interest rate must be divided by *m,* whereas the number of years must be multiplied by *m* in order to obtain the number of periods. Formula (3.3) shows this substitution.

Using the formula method, fill in Formula (3.3) and solve for *PV:*

$$FV_n = 100 = PV \times (1.01)^{4 \times 10}$$

$$PV = 100/1.48886$$

$$PV = \$67.165$$

The value 1.01 was found by dividing the interest rate (4%) by *m* (4) and adding 1. The exponent is solved using the y^x key as before.

Using the financial calculator method, the "trick" is to adjust the interest rate by dividing it by *m* and the number of periods by multiplying the number of years by *m.* Therefore %*I* is 1% (the quarterly rate), *n* is 40 (the number of quarters), and everything else is the same. Insert the three known values and ask the financial calculator to solve for the *PV.* Typical keystrokes would be:

(Clear calculator) 100, *FV,* 1, %*I,* 40, *n, CPT, PV,*

which produces the same answer of $67.165 (rounded).

Problem 2

Find the present value of an annuity of $100 per year to be received in years 1 though 20 using an interest rate of 4 percent. Find the future value of an annuity of $100 per year to be received in years 1 through 20 using an interest rate of 4 percent.

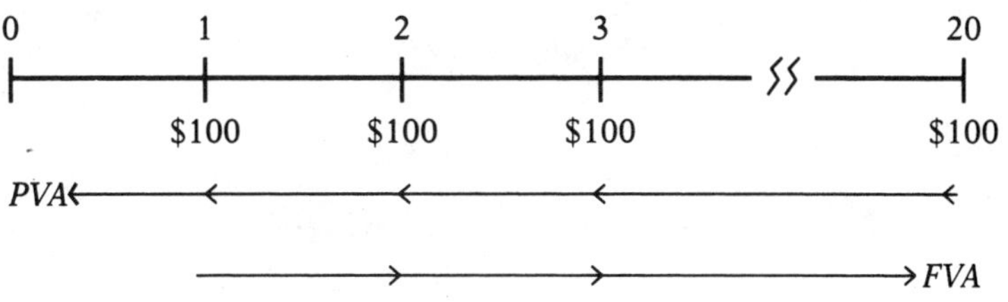

Solution to Problem 2

The present value of the annuity is solved by collapsing the 20 payments of $100 received at the end of each year into a single present value. This is accomplished by solving with Formula (3.8) where $r = 4\%, n = 20$, and $A = \$100$. Insertion of the variables using Formula (3.8) gives:

$$PVA = \$100 \left[\frac{1}{.04} - \frac{1}{.04(1.04)^{20}} \right] = \$100\,[13.5903] = \$1{,}359.03.$$

The same answer can be found by inserting the three known values into a financial calculator and solving for the *PVA*. Typical keystrokes will be:

(Clear calculator) 100, *A*, 4, %*I*, 20, *n*, *CPT*, *PV*.

The future value of the annuity is solved by collapsing the 20 payments of $100 invested at the end of each year into a single future value. This is accomplished by solving with Formula (3.9) where $r = 4\%, n = 20$, and $A = \$100$. Insertion of the variables using Formula (3.9) gives:

$$FVA = \$100 \left[\frac{(1.04)^{20} - 1}{.04} \right] = \$100\,[29.778] = \$2{,}977.80$$

The same answer can be found by inserting the three known values into a financial calculator and solving for the *FVA*. Typical keystrokes will be:

(Clear calculator) 100, *PMT*, 4, %*I*, 20, *n*, *CPT*, *FV*.

Review Questions

1. Why is there a time value of money?
2. Explain why investment can be called deferred consumption.
3. Why are cash flows to be received through time best considered different commodities?
4. What is compound interest? How does it work?
5. Explain why dollars to be received in the future have a lower value today.

Problems

Note: Unless otherwise indicated, use annual compounding in these problems.

Complete the table given the following information:

	PV	*FV*	*r*	*n*	*m*
1.	$100	—	.10	1	1
2.	$100	—	.10	2	1
3.	$125	—	.10	1	1
4.	$175	—	.15	20	1
5.	$175	—	.155	5	1

6. What is the future value of $1,000 in 2 years if it is invested at an interest rate of 8%?
7. If you borrowed $10,000 today for 5 years at 9% interest, how much would you have to pay back?
8. You deposit $500 in a 3-year savings certificate at 5% interest. At the end of the second year, the bank increases the interest rate on savings certificates to 6%. What will your initial deposit of $500 be worth in 3 years?

Complete the table given the following information:

	PV	*FV*	*r*	*n*	*m*
9.	$100	—	.10	1	2
10.	$125	—	.10	2	2
11.	$125	—	.12	1	4
12.	$125	—	.12	1	365
13.	$125	—	.155	1	12

14. Your boss, the treasurer for a small manufacturing company, wishes to deposit $50,000 for 2 years until the money is needed to replace some equipment. He would like you to analyze the investment opportunities offered by two savings certificates. One certificate offers 8% interest compounded annually while the other certificate earns 7.9% interest compounded quarterly. What is the future value of the $50,000 for each alternative?
15. What is the future value of $800 if it earns an interest rate of 6.5% compounded semiannually for 1 year? Repeat for 2 years, and again for 5 years.
16. What will $1,000 be worth in two years if it is compounded continuously at an interest rate of 8%?
17. You have seen an advertisement for an investment fund that offers 6% interest compounded continuously. At the moment, your savings account offers 6.5% compounded quarterly. What is the future value of $500 in 1 year for the fund and the savings account?

Complete the table given the following information:

	PV	*FV*	*r*	*n*
18.	—	$100	.10	1
19.	—	$150	.10	2
20.	—	$150	.12	1
21.	—	$150	.12	20
22.	—	$150	.155	5

23. What is the present value of $5,000 to be received in 2 years? The interest rate is 9%.
24. The parents of an 8-year-old child wish to deposit an amount today that will cover the child's first year in college. Tuition is estimated to be $15,000 when the child is a college freshman at age 18. If the interest rate is 10%, what amount needs to be deposited today?
25. You have just won a lottery prize and may choose between two alternatives:

    Choice A: Receive $2,000 1 year from today.
    Choice B: Receive $500 today and $1,500 1 year from today.

    What is the present value of each alternative, assuming an interest rate of 7%?

Complete the table given the following information:

	PV	*FV*	*r*	*n*
26.	$100	$110.00	—	1
27.	$150	$169.50	—	1
28.	$200	$213.00	—	1

29. A scholarship service wants to set aside an amount today to cover a particular student's college costs. The student will receive $15,000 per year for 4 years, beginning in 2 years. What is the present value of the entire scholarship amount, assuming an interest rate of 8%?

Complete the table given the following information using Formula (3.8):

	PVA	*A*	*n*	*r*
30.	—	$100	2	.10
31.	—	$100	5	.10
32.	—	$100	2	.17
33.	—	$150	20	.10
34.	—	$100	5	.105

35. What is the present value of 20 annual installments of $500 paid at the end of each year if the required rate of return is 9%?

36. Congratulations! You have just won a sweepstakes prize. The prize allows you to choose the method of payment.

Choice A: Receive $10,000 today.
Choice B: Receive $1,000 today and $1,000 at the end of each year for the next 12 years.

Which alternative has a higher present value? Use an interest rate of 7%.

37. If a deposit of $2,000 today will grow to $2,160 in 1 year, what is the interest rate that is being used?

38. How many years does it take for a deposit of $1,000 to grow to $2,000 if the money is in an account earning 8% interest compounded annually?

39. Your travel agent informs you that the agency can guarantee a trip to Australia for $2,500. You currently have $1,700 to devote to the trip. If bank accounts earn 6% interest compounded annually, how long will you have to wait to make the trip?

Complete the table given the following information and Formula (3.9):

	FVA	*A*	*n*	*r*
40.	—	$100	2	.10
41.	—	$100	5	.10
42.	—	$100	20	.10
43.	—	$100	2	.20
44.	—	$100	20	.20

45. A deposit of $100 is made at the end of each year for 9 straight years. The required rate of return is 9%. What will the total deposit be worth 9 years from today?

Discussion Questions

1. Respond to the following comment:
   The concept of the time value of money is a nice way to conceptualize economic decision making, but most real-world business decisions do not incorporate time value.
2. Respond to the following comment:
   Whenever you sell something for more than it costs, you have made a profit.
3. Respond to the following comment:
   I just learned that those big sweepstakes companies offer to grand prize winners the option of taking a smaller amount today instead of the larger amount that they really won. This just reaffirms my thinking that these companies will do anything to rip people off.
4. Provide a response to this statement:
   Annuities, shmuities! I think they are a big waste of time. I'm getting pretty good at single cash flow discounting, and the annuity formulas look too hard. I'll just stick to the single cash flow method.
5. The *Rule of 72* states that invested money will double in value whenever the number of years multiplied by the interest rate reaches 72.
   a. Is this approximately true?
   b. Can you prove this using the single cash flow future value formula for continuous compounding?

CHAPTER 4

THE VALUATION OF FINANCIAL SECURITIES

Megan Morrison, a financial analyst for Gecco Insurance Company, began the workweek with an interesting assignment: Gecco was considering purchasing a $47,134,572 bond issued by a relatively unknown cable TV company. The bond promises cash flows of $5 million per year for 30 years such that the total amount of future dollars offered by the security is $150 million (30 cash flows of $5 million each). Megan's job was to determine whether Gecco should invest in the security. Under current market conditions, interest rates are 10 percent.

Because the cash flows offered by the security are different commodities that cannot be added together, Megan is quite sure that she cannot make the decision by comparing the $150 million of total inflows with the $47,134,572 of outflow. Megan remembers from her finance course that future cash flows can be transformed into present values that can be added together. She knows specifically that the present value of any future amount can be determined by discounting these amounts at an appropriate discount rate. As Megan sits down to work the calculations, however, she is distressed by the thought of calculating present values for each of the security's 30 cash flows. Do easier procedures exist?

As demonstrated in Chapter 3, cash flow streams of equal amounts are known as annuities, and Megan is happy when she learns that the shortcut method for valuing annuities can be used for the Gecco bond. This shortcut will prove to be a big time-saver to Megan and anyone else calculating the price of bonds as well as other types of financial securities.

This chapter will expand the techniques for determining the present value of annuities. We will show that several types of *financial securities,* most generally bonds and sometimes stock, fit the definition of annuities. In addition, we will discuss how to calculate the required rate of return on a financial security.

Review of Discounting Annuities

Example 4.1 ________ Megan Morrison, the security analyst at the Gecco Insurance Company, was to determine if Gecco should purchase the bond that was being considered. Instead of working the problem as 30 separate lump-sum amounts, Megan recognized that the bond's cash flows comprise a 30-year annuity of $5 million payments. Given a market interest rate of 10 percent, she can determine the present value of this annuity in one step:

$$PVA = A\left[\frac{1}{r} - \frac{1}{r(1 + r)^n}\right] \tag{4.1}$$

where *PVA* is the present value of the annuity, *A* is the annuity amount, *r* is the interest rate, and *n* is the length of time of the annuity. For the Gecco bond:

$$\begin{aligned} PVA &= \$5\text{ M}\left[\frac{1}{.1} - \frac{1}{.1(1.1)^{30}}\right] \\ &= \$5{,}000{,}000[9.4269] \\ &= \$47{,}134{,}572. \end{aligned}$$

The present value of the bond's cash flows of $47,134,572 is exactly equal to the bond's price. The annuity formula allows Megan Morrison to complete her task quickly. Her report on the investment security ends: The market for these bonds is efficient in that the security's price is equal to the present value of the cash flows it offers—in other words you'll get what you pay for!

Special Annuities

In this section we will examine three special types of annuities, which will be shown to be useful in the valuation of certain financial securities.

perpetuity
An annuity with infinite life.

Perpetuities A **perpetuity** is an annuity with infinite life. This means that the cash flow stream of a perpetuity continues forever. The formula for the present value of a perpetuity can be derived from the annuity formula (Formula 4.1):

$$PVA = A\left[\frac{1}{r} - \frac{1}{r(1 + r)^n}\right]$$

Given that the perpetuity has infinite life, we can replace *n* in the annuity formula with infinity:

$$PVA = A\left[\frac{1}{r} - \frac{1}{r(1 + r)^\infty}\right]$$

The denominator in the second part of the bracketed expression explodes to infinity as long as the interest rate is greater than zero. Because any positive number divided by infinity is zero, the second part of the bracketed expression drops out, leaving the formula for the present value of the perpetuity (*PVP*):

$$PVA = A\left[\frac{1}{r}\right] = \frac{A}{r} \tag{4.2}$$

Thus, the present value of the perpetuity is simply the annuity amount divided by the interest rate.

Example 4.2 ________ Suppose that the bond held by Gecco, Inc., delivered to the firm \$5 million a year forever. The present value of this perpetual bond, given a market interest rate of 10 percent, can be determined through Formula (4.2):

$$PVP = \frac{A}{r},$$

whereby:

$$PVP = \frac{\$5\text{ million}}{.10} = \$50\text{ million.}$$

Compared with the 30-year annuity, the perpetual bond provides \$2,865,428 more in present value:

$$\$50{,}000{,}000 - \$47{,}134{,}572 = \$2{,}865{,}428$$

In other words, the present value of receiving an infinite stream of \$5 million payments starting in year 31 and continuing forever is only \$2,865,428 today. The reason the perpetuity's value is relatively close to the value of the 30-year annuity is that the additional payments of the perpetuity occur far into the future; thus, they have little value today. For example, the value of receiving \$5 million in 50 years with 10 percent interest rates is less than \$43,000 today; the value of receiving \$5 million dollars in 100 years is only about \$363 today!

constant growth perpetuity
A perpetuity that grows at a constant rate forever.

Constant Growth Perpetuities A **constant growth perpetuity** is a perpetuity that grows at a constant rate forever. For example, a perpetuity that starts at \$100 and grows at a constant rate of 5 percent forever would grow to \$105 next year:

$$CF_1 = CF_0(1 + g) = \$100(1.05) = \$105$$

where g is the growth rate of the perpetuity and CF_t is the cash flow in year t. This perpetuity would grow to $110.25 in the second year:

$$CF_2 = CF_1(1 + g) = \$105(1.05) = \$110.25$$

and would continue to grow by 5 percent each year thereafter.

It would appear to be a difficult task to value a constant growth perpetuity. Just think about sitting down to find a present value for an uneven stream of cash flows that continue forever. Because the growth rate is constant, however, we can determine its value in one step:

$$PVCGP = \frac{CF_1}{r - g} \tag{4.3}$$

where $PVCGP$ stands for the present value of a constant growth perpetuity, CF_1 is the perpetuity's cash flow in period one, r is the interest rate, and g is the constant growth rate of the cash flows. The formula does not work when the growth rate in the perpetuity is greater than or equal to the interest rate.

Example 4.3 Suppose you own land with a current annual rental income of $30,000 and with the expectation that the rental income would grow at the rate of 10 percent every year. The present value of this rental stream if interest rates are 15 percent would be:

$$PVCGP = \frac{\$33{,}000}{.15 - .10} = \frac{\$33{,}000}{.05} = \$660{,}000.$$

Note that we used $33,000 rather than $30,000 as CF_1 because the formula calls for the cash flow in period one. The current rental income is $30,000, but will grow by 10 percent to $33,000 next year. The present value of the land is $660,000.

Annuities Starting Beyond Period One Our treatment of annuities thus far has assumed that the first cash flow begins in the first period. For instance, consider again the alumni association offer (see Example 3.3). You were presented with alternatives of paying for a lifetime membership with $300 today or by making three annual payments of $121 starting in year 1. What if, however, the alumni association awards you a 1-year free membership, and offers a three-payment option of $121 starting in year 2 instead of year one?

The tools we will use to value this new type of annuity are similar to those used to value annuities starting in year 1. It is useful to think first about how we valued the original alumni annuity:

$$PVA = \$121\left[\frac{1}{(1.1)^1} + \frac{1}{(1.1)^2} + \frac{1}{(1.1)^3}\right] = \$300.91.$$

We discounted the first payment back one period, the second payment back two periods, and the third payment back three periods. Because the first payment was in year 1, the discounting process pulled all three cash flows back to period zero or to the present.

The new annuity is different because the first payment is made in period two, the second in period three, and the third in period four. Using the same tools as before will not pull all three cash flows back to time zero, rather it will instead pull the cash flows back to period one. In other words, the annuity formula values the annuity stream *one period before* the start of the annuity. If the annuity stream starts in period one, then this formula gives us the present value of the annuity. If the annuity stream starts in period two, then the formula gives us the value of the annuity at time one. If the annuity stream starts in period 20, then the formula will give the value of the annuity at time 19.

Annuities that begin beyond period one require a second step in order to compute a present value. In the first step, the annuity is valued using the same method as for an annuity that started at the end of year 1. For instance, in the alumni association example where the payments begin at the end of year 2, we would first compute the value of the annuity to be \$300.91. This is its value in year one, however, not year zero. The second step is to present-value the lump-sum amount obtained in step one back to period zero. This means converting \$300.91 to a present value:

$$PV = \frac{\$300.91}{(1.10)^1} = \$273.55.$$

The process of valuing the alumni association annuity is illustrated in Figure 4.1. Given the choice of the new annuity or paying \$300 today, you would prefer the new payment plan because waiting an extra year to make the first payment has value.

In the preceding discussion we analyzed how to find the present value of an annuity whose cash flows began in year 2. The mathematics of present value are so robust that we can extend this concept to finding the value of an annuity at any point in time.

FIGURE 4.1 Valuing an Annuity Starting in Year 2

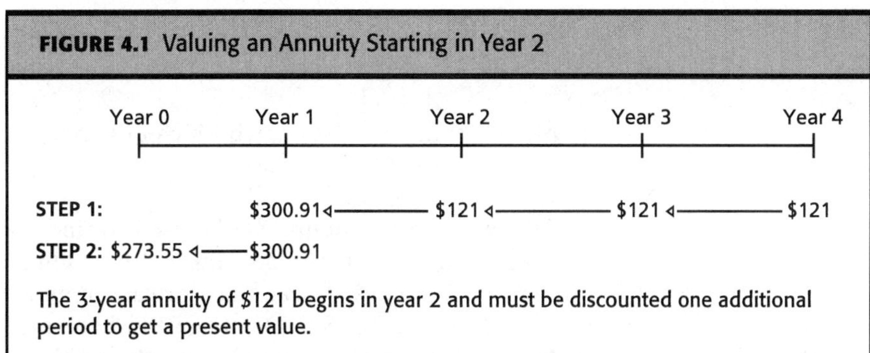

The 3-year annuity of \$121 begins in year 2 and must be discounted one additional period to get a present value.

The key is that these types of problems involve two steps. The first step is to collapse the annuity into a single value by applying the annuity formula. The second step is to move the value from step number one to any desired point on the time line by applying the single payment or lump-sum techniques of Chapter 3.

Example 4.4 Suppose that you are analyzing how much money must be set aside to pay \$10,000 per year toward each of the four years of a child's education. The money needed is shown using a time line, in which the years represent the age of the child:

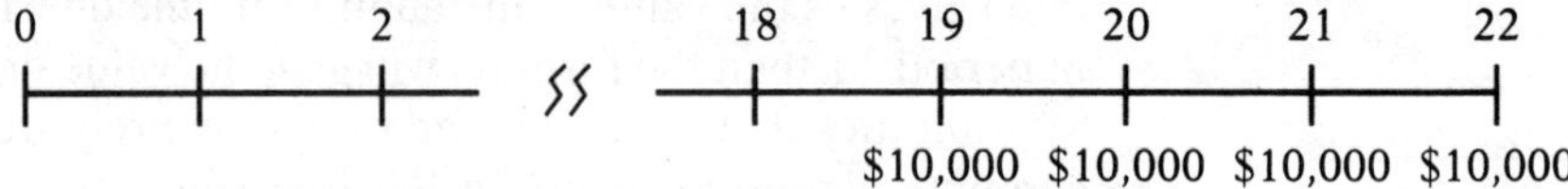

The first step is to apply the annuity formula to the four cash flows of \$10,000 each. Assuming an interest rate of 8 percent, the value of the annuity in year 18 is:

$$PVA = \$10{,}000\left[\frac{1}{.08} - \frac{1}{.08(1.08)^4}\right]$$

$$= \$10{,}000\,[3.3121]$$

$$= \$33{,}121.$$

At this point we may move \$33,121, the result of step number one, to any year that we desire. We already know that the four cash flows are equivalent to \$33,121 in the child's eighteenth year. This tells us how large a college fund the child will need at age 18 to exactly meet the 4-year cost of college. We can, however, state this value in terms of any year through present value or future value single payment or lump-sum techniques.

To find the value of the annuity at the child's birth, we pull the amount of \$33,121 back 18 years to time period zero:

$$PV = \$33{,}121/(1.08)^{18}$$

$$PV = \$33{,}121/3.996 = \$8{,}289$$

To provide today for your newborn child's college education, the amount of \$8,289 would need to be set aside.

This two-step procedure can be used to find the value of the annuity in any year desired. For instance, instead of pulling the annuity back to the present, we could push the annuity forward in time. Suppose that you need to borrow the amount of \$33,121 at age 18 when you enter college to cover the cost of your 4-year education. How much would you have to pay 4 years later when you graduate to satisfy the loan? Given an interest rate of 8 percent, this problem can he solved using future value techniques:

$$FV_{22} = \$33{,}121 \times (1.08)^4$$

$$FV_{22} = \$33{,}121 \times 1.3605 = \$45{,}061$$

The amount of $33,121 at age 18 is equivalent to $45,061 at age 22.

The key to solving annuities that start beyond period 1 is that the annuity is initially collapsed using as *n* the number of cash flows. Thus, in the previous example, *n* would be 4 reflecting the 4 payouts between age 19 and age 22. This collapsed value is the value in the year prior to the beginning of the annuity, or age 18.

Let's examine the previous example using a calculator and pricing the cost of a 4 year college education at a different year, say at age 12. First, compute the cost of a college education at age 18 with the following keystrokes: $10,000 for PMT, 4 for *n*, 8 for *r*, and solving for PV. The answer, $33,121, can now be discounted back 6 additional years to age 12 by inputting $33,121 for FV, 8 for *r*, and 6 for *n*. The answer is $20,872.

Another item of interest is the future value of an annuity that begins after year 1. The problem is solved much like the technique for present value except that in the first step the annuity is collapsed using the future value of the annuity. Importantly, future value is placed in the same year as the last cash flow. In our college education example, the future value of the 4 year annuity at age 22 would be $45,061.

Financial Securities

This section applies time value of money techniques to financial securities. To review, *securities* are financial assets rather than real assets because they are a claim on cash flows rather than a direct claim on real assets themselves. Financial securities are issued by corporations and governments in order to raise capital and are purchased by investors in order to convert current cash into future and larger cash flows.

Most fixed payment securities offer specific terms such as the amount of payment, the length of the payment stream, and the dates of payment. Investors in these securities know exactly the amount of each payment and when it is to be received. The law of one price from Chapter 1 tells us that the sum of the present values of these known cash flow payments must be the value of the security traded in the financial markets.

The interest rate used in the present value process will reflect the market's view of the value of the promised future cash flows relative to today's dollars. This process will clearly include an assessment of the risk inherent in the cash flows promised by the security, and the risk is incorporated into the interest rate or discount rate. Procedures for adjusting the discount rate for risk are addressed in Chapters 8 and 9.

U.S. Treasury Bills

U.S. Treasury bills Financial securities issued by the U.S. Treasury with maturities of 13 weeks, 26 weeks, or 52 weeks. They are offered with a minimum denomination of $10,000 and in multiples thereafter of $5,000 up to $1 million.

A **U.S. Treasury bill** (also known as a T-bill) is a promise from the United States Federal Government to pay a stated number of dollars at the end of a stated number of days. Window 4.1 provides detailed information on the institutional aspects of Treasury bill investments.

Treasury bills are purchased *at a discount,* which means that the investor pays a particular price today for the promise of receiving one cash flow when the security matures. The price or value of the T-bill is found by obtaining the present value of the single-payment cash flow over the stated length of time until maturity. Because Treasury bill maturities are quoted in days, the maturity must be converted to years by dividing the number of days to maturity by the number of days in a year. The present value of the T-bill can be determined using the formula or financial calculator methods from Chapter 3.

Example 4.5 ________ Consider a U.S. Treasury bill offering $10,000 at maturity in 91 days, or in 0.25 years (assuming 364 days in a year, to produce round numbers). Using an interest rate of 10 percent, the cash flows associated with the Treasury bill are illustrated by the time line in Figure 4.2.

The formula method requires substituting specific values for *FV, r,* and *n* into Formula (3.6) in Chapter 3:

$$PV = \frac{\$10,000}{(1.10)^{0.25}} = \frac{\$10,000}{(1.0241)} = \$9,764.54.$$

Calculating the Interest Rate of Treasury Bills

Sometimes the present value of the Treasury bill is known along with the future value and length of time. In this case it is possible to determine the interest rate. Returning to the T-bill examined earlier, suppose the Treasury bill's price of $9,764.54 was given, along with the future value of $10,000 to be received in 0.25 years. The Treasury bill's interest rate can be determined using Formula (3.10):

$$(1 + r) = [FV_n/PV]^{1/n}$$

$$(1 + r) = [\$10,000/\$9,764]^{1/0.25} = [1.02411]^4 = 1.10$$

The interest rate to be earned on the T-bill investment is 10 percent. A financial calculator provides the answer even more simply if you input *FV, PV,* and *n.*

Treasury bills are one of many financial securities that offer a single cash flow. Other examples include most U.S. savings bonds, most certificates of deposit issued by banks, zero coupon bonds, and stripped Treasuries, which are detailed in Window 1.5. The valuation of any single cash flow security will be similar to that of the Treasury bill.

WINDOW 4.1

The U.S. Treasury Bill Market

U.S. Treasury bills, or T-bills, are issued by and are obligations of the U.S. Treasury. Treasury bills fall in a class of securities known as *money market securities,* and they are issued with maturities of 13 weeks, 26 weeks, or 52 weeks. They are offered with a minimum denomination of \$10,000 and in multiples thereafter of \$5,000, up to \$1 million. The number or amount of T-bills issued at any one time is determined by the amount of maturing T-bills to be refunded, current monetary policy objectives (set by the Federal Reserve), and the Treasury's short-term financing needs.

Treasury bills are sold at a discount—determined by an auction—from face value. At maturity, the T-bill is redeemed by the holder for its full face value. This means that the rate of return is determined by the *difference* between the amount paid for the T-bill and its value at maturity.

One peculiar aspect of Treasury bills is how their prices are quoted for trading purposes and in the newspaper. Yields are quoted on what is known as a *bank discount yield* basis, dividing the amount of discount from par value (or face value) by the security's par value:

$$\text{Bank Discount Yield} = \frac{\text{Par Value} - \text{Purchase Price}}{\text{Par Value}} \times \frac{360}{\text{Days to Maturity}}$$

This calculation presents a problem for investors because the technique used to determine bank discount yields is different from the standard techniques discussed in Chapter 3. Because bank discount yields understate the rate of return on T-bills, investors must convert these yields to *actual or true yields* (for example, using simple interest):

$$\text{Actual Yield} = \frac{365 \times \text{Bank Discount Yield}}{360 - (\text{Bank Discount Yield} \times \text{Days to Maturity})}$$

Such conversion techniques are available to assist investors.

Although T-bill investors may wish to hold their securities until maturity, there is an active secondary market made by government securities dealers, who stand ready to buy and sell T-bills at their market price. Indeed, the liquidity of the T-bill market contributes to its popularity as an investment vehicle. Commercial banks, with their special liquidity needs, along with other financial institutions, state and local governments, the U.S. government, and individual investors, are major holders of Treasury bills.

Investment returns on Treasury bills are subject to federal income tax but are generally exempt from state and local taxes.

FIGURE 4.2 The Cash Flows of a Treasury Bill

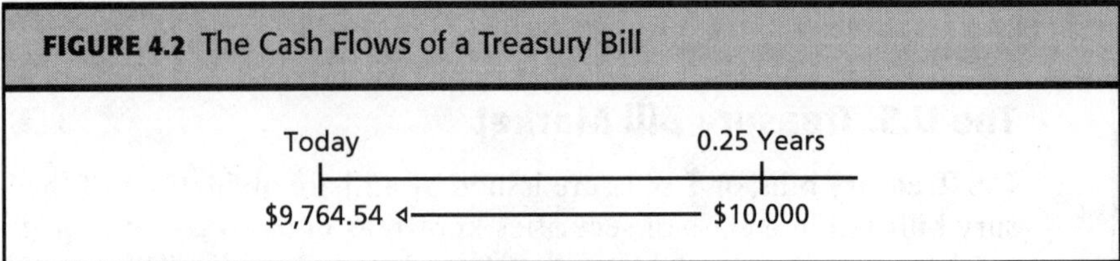

Coupon-Paying Bonds

bond
A long-term fixed payment instrument issued by a corporation or government.

coupon payments
The series of cash flows offered on bonds.

par value (face value)
The lump-sum amount paid to the holder of a bond at maturity.

A **bond** is a long-term fixed payment instrument issued by a corporation or government. Bonds are generally multiperiod cash flow securities that pay a series of **coupon payments** to the holder as well as a lump-sum amount at maturity. The lump-sum amount paid to the holder at maturity is the bond's **par value** or **face value** and is usually $1,000. Unlike Treasury bills, bonds, are long-term financial securities with maturities in the range of from 10 to 30 years. Window 4.2 describes some additional aspects of bonds.

The cash flow stream offered by most bonds can be broken into two portions: (1) an annuity portion made up of coupon payments, and (2) a lump-sum portion made up of the payment of the bond's par value at maturity. The price or present value of a bond is therefore the sum of the present value of its annuity stream plus the present value of the lump-sum par value payment at maturity.

Example 4.6 ________

Consider the Varma Corporation, which, in need of capital, issues a 15-year $1,000 par value bond with a coupon interest rate of 14 percent. A 14 percent coupon interest rate on a $1,000 par value bond translates into coupon payments of $140 paid to Varma bondholders each year for 15 years. Thus, the 15 coupon payments are a 15-period $140 annuity. The bond's payment of par value at maturity is a lump-sum cash flow of $1,000 in year 15. Combining the cash flows offered by the bond and taking their present value gives us the general bond valuation formula:

$$\text{Bond Value} = P_0 = \sum_{t=1}^{n} \frac{C}{(1+r)^t} + \frac{F_n}{(1+r)^n} \tag{4.4}$$

where P_0 is the present value of the bond, the *C*s are the stream of constant $140 coupon payments, F_n is the bond's $1,000 face value, *n* is the number of periods until the bond's maturity, and *r* is the market interest rate assumed to be constant over the bond's maturity. The summation sign indicates that the coupon payments are made over the time span 1 through *n*.

The present value of the Varma bond can be determined from Formula (4.4) given $C = \$140$, $F_n = \$1{,}000$, $n = 15$, and some value for *r*, the market interest rate. Because most bonds are issued with a coupon rate that matches the market interest rate, we will assume that *r* is 14 percent. The present value of the bond can now be determined using either the formula or financial calculator methods. We will illustrate both, starting with the formula method.

WINDOW 4.2

Some Background on Bond Investing

Bonds are securities that offer a stream of payments, known as *coupons,* and a return of the bond's face value at maturity. Bonds issued by the U.S. Treasury are known as *government* or *Treasury bonds*; those issued by state and local governments are known as *municipal bonds*; and those issued by corporations are known as *corporate bonds.* The par value of most bonds is $1,000. Maturities of bonds usually range from 10 to 30 years.

The bond's risk of *default*—nonpayment—is dependent on the economic viability of the issuer. At one end of the default spectrum are U.S. government bonds, which are considered to have zero default risk, due to the ability of the U.S. government to print money and to tax. At the other end of the risk spectrum are bonds issued by private corporations experiencing financial difficulty. High default-risk bonds are sometimes referred to as high-yield bonds or *junk bonds.* To help investors evaluate the default risk of non–U.S. Treasury bonds, services such as Standard and Poor's and Moody's provide a rating system ranging from AAA (very low risk of default) to D (in default). States and municipalities, with the power to tax, can be expected in most cases to sustain their economic viability and thus usually have low default risk when supported by general revenue. The default risk of corporate bonds will vary from very low to very high.

The tax treatment of the bond depends upon its issuer. The interest received from U.S. Treasury bonds is fully taxable at the federal level but is generally exempt from state and local taxes. Interest payments from municipal bonds are tax exempt at the federal level and may also be tax exempt at the state and local level if the investor resides in the state in which the bond has been issued. For corporate bonds, interest payments are taxable at the federal and state and local levels. Bonds purchased for a price less than the eventual sales price or redemption price are subject to a tax on the capital gain.

The general bond valuation model applied to the Varma bond is:

$$P_0 = \frac{\$140}{(1.14)^1} + \frac{\$140}{(1.14)^2} + \frac{\$140}{(1.14)^3} + \cdots + \frac{\$140}{(1.14)^{15}} + \frac{\$1{,}000}{(1.14)^{15}}.$$

Notice that bond valuation is really two problems in one. The present value of the coupon payments can be determined in the first step as a 15-year $140 annuity:

$$PVA = \$140\left[\frac{1}{.14} - \frac{1}{.14(1.14)^{15}}\right] = \$140[6.1422] = \$859.90.$$

In the second step, the present value of the return of par value at maturity can be determined as a $1,000 lump-sum payment in year 15:

$$PV = \$1{,}000\left[\frac{1}{(1.14)^{15}}\right] = \$1{,}000\,[0.1401] = \$140.10.$$

The present value of the bond is the sum of \$859.90 (the annuity portion) plus \$140.10 (the lump-sum portion), for a total of \$1,000. Investors purchasing the Varma bond have a security whose future cash flows are equivalent in total value to receiving \$1,000 today.

The financial calculator method may or may not require a two-part procedure, based upon the calculator's degree of sophistication. We will illustrate the two-part procedure that should work for most financial calculators. (You can check the handbook to see if your calculator has a one-step shortcut.) For the annuity portion, the values $A = \$140$, $n = 15$, and $r = 14$ percent are input into the calculator to compute the present value of \$859.90. This value is to be stored into the calculator's memory. The lump-sum present value is then determined by clearing the calculator's financial memories, inputting the values $FV = \$1{,}000$, $n = 15$, and $r = 14$ percent, and computing the present value to be \$140.10. Adding the two parts together gives \$1,000, the present value of the bond.

Bond Valuation with Semiannual Interest Payments The bond valuation model in Example 4.6 assumes that coupon payments are made annually. For example, if a bond was issued on July 1, 2002, with a maturity of 4 years, annual coupon payments would begin July 1, 2003, and would continue for an additional 3 years with the last payment occurring on July 1, 2006; however, this does not describe the coupon payment stream offered by most bonds.

Most bonds pay coupon interest twice per year, on a *semiannual* basis, such that investors receive coupon payments equal to one half the annual coupon payment every 6 months. A \$1,000 par value bond with a 10 percent coupon rate issued on July 1, 2002, would make its first semiannual coupon payment of \$50 on January 1, 2003, and continue to make semiannual payments of \$50 every 6 months for seven additional 6-month periods. The last semiannual coupon payment, to be made when the bond matures on July 1, 2006, is also the date that the bond delivers the lump-sum par value to the investor. This is illustrated in Figure 4.3.

The general bond valuation formula (Formula 4.4) can be used to value a bond that pays coupons annually *or* semiannually. Prices for bonds with semiannual payments are computed by defining a period as 6 months instead of 12 months. For example, let us return to the 15-year, 14 percent coupon bond from Varma Corporation discussed earlier. Because the variable n in the general bond formula is the number of periods until maturity, and because we are now defining a period to be six months, the new maturity is two times the number of years, or 30 periods.

The bond analyst must be careful to make all the proper adjustments when valuing a bond that pays coupons semiannually. The size of each annuity payment is one half the size of the annual coupon amount, and the interest rate must be adjusted so that the *semiannual* market interest rate, not the annual market interest rate, is used for r. Only the principal repayment of \$1,000 is left unadjusted.

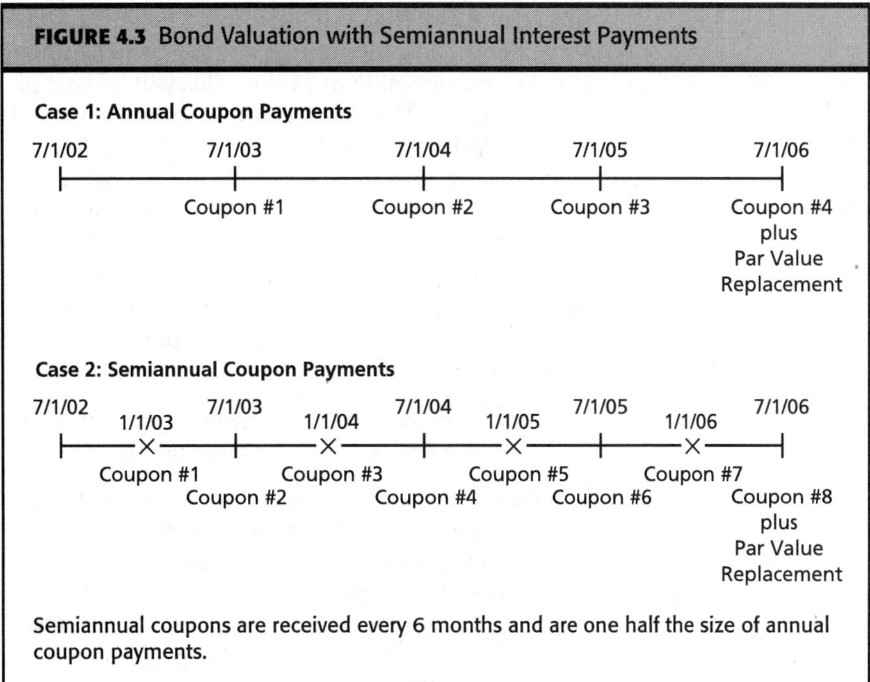

The cash flow stream for the Varma bond with semiannual coupons becomes:

$$P_0 = \frac{\$70}{(1.07)^1} + \frac{\$70}{(1.07)^2} + \frac{\$70}{(1.07)^3} + \cdots + \frac{\$70}{(1.07)^{30}} + \frac{\$1{,}000}{(1.07)^{30}}.$$

The semiannual annuity stream of \$70 is one-half the size of the annual annuity stream, the 30-period length of the annuity stream is twice that of the annual stream, and the semiannual market interest rate of 7 percent is half that of the annual market interest rate.[1] With these adjustments, the present value of the Varma bond can be determined in two steps:

$$P_0 = \underbrace{\$70\left[\frac{1}{.07} - \frac{1}{.07(1.07)^{30}}\right]}_{\text{Step 1: } PV = \$868.63} + \underbrace{\$1{,}000\left[\frac{1}{(1.07)^{30}}\right]}_{\text{Step 2: } = PV = \$131.37} = \$1{,}000.$$

[1]It is not technically correct to take an annually compounded interest rate, such as 14 percent, and divide it by 2 to produce a semiannual rate. The reason is that compounding causes 7 percent every 6 months to be more valuable than 14 percent every year. How much more valuable can be determined using Formula (3.5) for the effective annual interest rate in Chapter 3:

$$\text{Effective Annual Interest Rate} = \left[1 + \frac{r}{m}\right]^m - 1 = \left[1 + \frac{.14}{2}\right]^2 - 1 = .1449$$

Interest Rate Risk It was no coincidence that the present value of the Varma bond, whether it pays coupons on an annual or semiannual basis, was equal to its par value of $1,000. This will be true any time the bond's coupon rate is equal to the market rate of interest, which is usually the case when a firm like Varma issues *new* bonds to the market.

Bonds are known as *fixed payment securities* because their coupon payments are locked in at issue and do not change over the life of the bond. As time moves forward, the market interest rate may change but the bond's coupon rate does not—it is fixed throughout its life. For example, the market interest rate may change from 14 percent to any level above or below 14 percent, but the Varma bond will continue to pay coupon interest at the rate of 14 percent annually.

Bonds are known as fixed payment securities because their coupon payments are locked in at issue and do not change over the life of the bond.

Although the cash flows of the bond do not change, the discount rate that the market uses to price the bond can change. What happens to the value of a bond as market interest rates change? The answer to this question depends on the direction of the interest rate change. If market interest rates *increase,* then investors of Varma bonds will feel regret: Given the increase in the market rate, other firms similar to Varma will now issue their own bonds with coupon rates that match the new market rate, which is now higher than 14 percent. Because the 14 percent coupon rate attached to the Varma bonds stays fixed, Varma investors are stuck receiving a 14 percent coupon rate, whereas other investors enjoy higher coupons.

The amount of regret felt by the Varma bondholders will depend on the magnitude of the interest rate increase. Let us suppose that market interest rates climb to 16 percent the day after the Varma bonds are brought to the market.[2] One alternative that Varma investors have is to sell the Varma bond to another investor and to purchase newly issued 16 percent bonds. That is the good news! The bad news is that Varma investors will find that the value of their investment has fallen. The lower value reflects the fact that the Varma bond carries a lower coupon and therefore is not as valuable as new bonds being offered in the market.

To determine how much the price of the Varma bond will fall, we can use Formula (4.4) for bond valuation. Assuming semiannual coupon payments:

$$PV = \$70\left[\frac{1}{.08} - \frac{1}{.08(1.08)^{30}}\right] + \$1{,}000\left[\frac{1}{(1.08)^{30}}\right] = \$887.42.$$

Because of new market conditions, the old interest rate was replaced with the new market interest rate (16 percent annually, 8 percent semiannually).

[2]Such a sharp increase in the market rate overnight is a rare event. More realistic 1-day shifts in market rates are on the order of one tenth to one quarter of 1 percent (10 to 25 basis points). We use this large increase to better make the point of interest rate risk.

The price of the bond falls from $1,000 to $887.42. We say that the Varma bonds sell *at a discount,* which means that the price of the bond is below its par value. With the lower price, new bond investors are indifferent between paying $1,000 for a 16 percent coupon bond or paying $887.42 for the Varma 14 percent coupon bond. A comparison between the cash flows of the two bonds is illustrated in Figure 4.4.

You need not feel bad, however, for Varma investors. Because the relationship between bond prices and market interest rates is inverse, *falling* market interest rates cause the price of existing bonds to rise. Suppose that interest rates fall to the extent that the day after the Varma bond is offered new bonds come to the market offering a lower coupon rate, say 12 percent. The Varma bond continues to pay the original 14 percent coupon rate. Varma investors who wish to sell their bonds before maturity will find that the price of their bond has risen in value. We can use Formula (4.4) to determine how much the price of the Varma bond will rise (assuming no time has passed, so that the maturity is still 30 periods):

$$PV = \$70\left[\frac{1}{.06} - \frac{1}{.06(1.06)^{30}}\right] + \$1{,}000\left[\frac{1}{(1.06)^{30}}\right] = \$1{,}137.65.$$

The higher price reflects the fact that the Varma bond carries a 14 percent coupon and is therefore more valuable than other newly issued bonds trading in the market. We would now say that the Varma bonds sell *at a premium,* meaning that the price of the bond is above its par value. With the change in price, new bond investors are indifferent between paying $1,000 for a 12 percent coupon bond or paying $1,137.65 for the Varma 14 percent coupon bond.

The relationship between bond prices and market interest rates is inverse. Rising market interest rates cause the price of existing bonds to fall, and falling market interest rates cause the price of existing bonds to rise.

FIGURE 4.4 Rising Interest Rates and Falling Bond Prices

	Today	6 Months	1 Year	1.5 Years	//	14.5 Years	15 Years
Cash Flows – Varma	$887.42	$70	$70	$70		$70	$1,070
Cash Flows – New Bond	$1,000.00	$80	$80	$80		$80	$1,080

The new bond is issued with a higher coupon interest rate. The price of the Varma bond must fall.

Yield to Maturity

yield to maturity
A measure of the average rate of return that a bond will offer under current market conditions.

The previous section discussed how to determine a bond's price given the cash flow stream and a market interest rate. We will now show how to solve for the market interest rate given the bond's cash flow stream and price. The market interest rate, also known in this context as the bond's **yield to maturity,** is an accurate indication of the rate of return that the bond will offer until maturity under current market conditions.

Suppose you were given the opportunity to purchase the Varma bond for a price of \$887.42. Paying this price today entitles you to 30 payments of \$70, paid every 6 months, and a payment of \$1,000 in 15 years. If you purchased the bond, what rate of return would the investment earn, on average, over its life?

The answer is not 14 percent (the bond's coupon rate) because the bond is selling at a discount from its par value. Given that you can purchase the bond for an amount less than \$1,000 but receive \$1,000 at maturity, your rate of return will be higher than the 14 percent coupon rate if you hold the bond to maturity. The question is how much higher?

Let us use Formula (4.4) to see what we know about the investment in the Varma bond:

$$\$887.42 = \$70\left[\frac{1}{r} - \frac{1}{r(1+r)^{30}}\right] + \$1{,}000\left[\frac{1}{(1+r)^{30}}\right].$$

As you can see, our information on the Varma bond includes everything but the market interest rate or the bond's yield to maturity. This problem looks similar to solving for the interest rate in Chapter 3; unfortunately, things are not as simple as they were then because: (1) we have a multiple cash flow stream and (2) the cash flow amounts are not all the same due to the final principal repayment. No algebraic technique can be used to solve directly for r, leaving us with no choice but to use trial and error when using the formula method.

Trial and error means trying different market rates until we find the one that makes the present value of the Varma bond's cash flow stream equal to the \$887.42 price. For example, we can begin the search by substituting an annual rate of 20 percent (a semiannual rate of 10 percent) for r into Formula (4.4):

$$PV = \$70\left[\frac{1}{.10} - \frac{1}{.10(1.10)^{30}}\right] + \$1{,}000\left[\frac{1}{(1.10)^{30}}\right] = \$717.19.$$

With an interest rate of 20 percent, the bond's price of \$717.19 is below our search price of \$887.42. Because 20 percent is not the yield to maturity, the trial and error method asks for a new guess. The big question becomes: Should the next guess be higher or lower than 20 percent? The correct answer is lower than 20 percent because a lower interest rate will produce a higher price. Remember, our goal is to get the right-hand side equal to the original left-hand side value of \$887.42. Let us try 18 percent annually, or 9 percent semi-annually:

$$PV = \$70\left[\frac{1}{.09} - \frac{1}{.09(1.09)^{30}}\right] + \$1{,}000\left[\frac{1}{(1.09)^{30}}\right] = \$794.53.$$

An annual interest rate of 18 percent gets us closer to the search price, but it is still below \$887.42. The trial and error process requires still another guess, and will continue to require guesses until the interest rate is found that produces our search price of \$887.42. We know from a previous example that the search will end with a guess of 16 percent annually for *r:*

$$PV = \$70\left[\frac{1}{.08} - \frac{1}{.08(1.08)^{30}}\right] + \$1{,}000\left[\frac{1}{(1.08)^{30}}\right] = \$887.42.$$

We say that the bond's yield to maturity is 16 percent, meaning that if you purchase the Varma bond for \$887.42 and hold it to maturity, you will earn an interest rate (a *yield*) of 16 percent on average per year.

Students are often surprised to learn that in our sophisticated world we are forced to rely on the method of trial and error to solve the yield to maturity. One lesson this teaches is that sometimes even the most advanced algebraic techniques cannot produce a shortcut.

We can, however, sympathize with those who dislike the trial and error process and can offer a suggestion: Consider using a financial calculator with built-in programming capability. Many financial calculators can solve for the yield to maturity by performing the calculations of the trial and error process internally. Computer spreadsheet programs (e.g., Lotus 1-2-3 or Excel) offer similar capability. If you have a sophisticated financial calculator or access to a computer spreadsheet, solving for the yield to maturity becomes as simple as inputting the bond's cash flow stream and the price, and allowing the calculator or computer to do the rest. Some financial calculators require that the cash flow stream and the price be entered with opposite signs.

The Valuation of Common Stock

The second major category of financial securities is stock. Stockholders have claim to the cash flows of the firm only after all other claimants (e.g., employees, bondholders, suppliers, and governments) have had their claims satisfied. Stockholders are sometimes referred to as *residual claimants* because they have claim only to the residual cash flow.

dividends
The portion of the corporation's earnings paid out to the firm's stockholders, on a per share basis.

Stockholders derive their common stock investment return in the form of *dividends* and *capital gains.* Most firms pay **dividends**—per share distributions of the firm's earnings—on a regular schedule to their shareholders, but some

capital gains
The dollar gains that result when a capital asset is sold for more than it cost.

pay no dividends. **Capital gains** occur when shares are sold at a price above their original purchasing price. For example, the price of a firm's stock will rise when demand to invest in the firm increases due to the introduction of a new product. Thus, if you buy stock for $1 a share and sell the same stock in the future for $1.50 per share, you have realized a capital gain of $0.50 per share.

Unlike bonds, which offer fixed payments according to a specified schedule, neither dividends nor capital gains are fixed obligations of the firm. Thus, the process of valuing common stock is difficult because the key cash flows from stock—dividends and capital gains—must be estimated. In most models the price of the stock is the *present value of all estimated future cash flows.* Thus, because they calculate the present value of the cash flows, the model we will study here, and its variations, are termed a *discounted cash flow model.* The more sophisticated the model, the more realistic is the attempt to estimate the cash flows, but the more difficult the estimations become.

The Discounted Cash Flow Model

An explanation of the discounted cash flow model for stocks might begin with the assumption that the common stock is purchased today, and will be sold in 1 year. Consider Mirage, Inc., a firm that specializes in difficult-to-see processes. Claudia has come to know of this firm and believes it to be a good investment opportunity. She estimates that the stock price next year will be $20 per share, and she believes that the firm's dividend—now being paid at the rate of $2 per share—will stay at this level over the next few years. Given a discount rate of 15 percent, what price should Claudia be willing to pay for each share of Mirage's stock?

The *single-period* model is similar to the single cash flow present value model introduced in Chapter 3:

$$P_0 = \frac{DIV_1 + P_1}{(1+r)^1} \tag{4.5}$$

where P_0 is the current price or present value, DIV_1 is the dividend expected in year 1, P_1 is the stock price expected in year 1, and r is the discount rate applied to the investment. The value of Mirage stock given Claudia's estimates is:

$$P_0 = \frac{\$2 + \$20}{(1.15)^1} = \$19.13.$$

We would say that Mirage stock is estimated to be worth $19.13 per share. As long as other investors share these estimates, Mirage will trade in the market at approximately $19.13 per share.

Determining the Interest Rate As with bonds, if we know the market price along with other variables we can compute the model's interest rate.

Formula (4.5) can be solved for the interest rate investors are using to find the present value of Mirage stock:

$$r = \underbrace{\frac{DIV_1}{P_0}}_{\text{Dividend Yield}} + \underbrace{\frac{P_1 - P_0}{P_0}}_{\text{Capital Gain Yield}} \tag{4.6}$$

As with the case of bonds, the interest rate has special meaning when valuing common stock. The interest rate is an estimate of the rate of return investors expect when investing in a share of stock of a certain company, and it is composed of a *dividend yield* and *capital gain yield.* Given Claudia's estimates of a \$2 dividend and a \$20 stock price, and knowing that the current stock price of Mirage is \$19.13, we can determine the rate of return Claudia and other investors expect to receive:

$$r = \frac{\$2}{\$19.13} + \frac{\$20 - \$19.13}{\$19.13} = .105 + .045 = .15,$$

so that the rate of return investors expect on the investment in Mirage stock is 15 percent.

Extending the Holding Period One important feature of common stock is that it has no fixed maturity. We expect competitive firms to continue to operate far into the future. Claudia might therefore decide to invest in Mirage's stock today and continue to invest for more than 1 year. For instance, she might decide to invest for 2 years. How would she value the stock price given a 2-year investment horizon?

The 2-year common stock valuation model starts with the single-period formula and extends the formula to include a second year:

$$P_0 = \frac{DIV_1}{(1 + r)^1} + \frac{DIV_2 + P_2}{(1 + r)^2}$$

The value of the common stock today is derived from estimates of the firm's dividend payment for year 1 and 2, and an estimate of the firm's stock price in year 2. If Claudia estimates that dividends will stay constant at \$2 per share and that Mirage's stock price will rise to \$21 in year 2, then the value of Mirage stock today is:

$$P_0 = \frac{\$2}{(1.15)^1} + \frac{\$2 + \$21}{(1.15)^2} = \$19.13,$$

the same as before.

The discounted cash flow model can accommodate any holding period. For example, suppose Claudia wishes to hold Mirage stock for 3 years. In this case, the valuation model can be written:

$$P_0 = \frac{DIV_1}{(1+r)^1} + \frac{DIV_2}{(1+r)^2} + \frac{DIV_3 + P_3}{(1+r)^3}$$

The discounted cash flow model can be extended into an *n*-period model, where *n* is defined as some period in the future:

$$P_0 = \frac{DIV_1}{(1+r)^1} + \frac{DIV_2}{(1+r)^2} + \frac{DIV_3}{(1+r)^3} + \cdots + \frac{DIV_n}{(1+r)^n} + \frac{P_n}{(1+r)^n}$$

Because common stock has no maturity date, *n* is in theory infinity if, unlike Claudia, you have no intention of selling. Substituting *n* with infinity in the preceding model makes the model simpler. As *n* gets large, the present value of all cash flows to be received at or near this end point becomes small. When *n* becomes infinity, however, the present value of P_n in the model becomes zero and can be dropped from the model:

$$P_0 = \sum_{t=1}^{\infty} \frac{DIV_t}{(1+r)^t} \tag{4.7}$$

Formula (4.7) states that the present value of a share of stock is equal to the discounted value of the stock's expected stream of dividends. Formula (4.7) is written in a compact way, with the dividend stream beginning in period one and continuing to infinity.

Formula (4.7) is applicable for investors with short-term time horizons as well as for investors with long-term horizons. In other words, the investor's time horizon does not matter when determining security prices. To see this, recall the single-period model from Formula (4.5). From the perspective of a 1-year investor who might buy the stock next year, next year's stock price can be written:

$$P_1 = \frac{DIV_2 + P_2}{(1+r)^1}$$

meaning that any investor intending to purchase the stock in one year and sell the stock the year after will value the stock as shown earlier. Substituting P_1 from into the single-period formula (Formula 4.5) gives:

$$P_0 = \frac{DIV_1}{(1+r)^1} + \frac{DIV_2 + P_2}{(1+r)^2}$$

We can continue this line of reasoning by asking for a specification of P_2 in the preceding formula from the perspective of another 1-year investor. This would be:

$$P_2 = \frac{DIV_3 + P_3}{(1 + r)^1}$$

which when substituted for P_2 gives:

$$P_0 = \frac{DIV_1}{(1 + r)^1} + \frac{DIV_2}{(1 + r)^2} + \frac{DIV_3 + P_3}{(1 + r)^3}$$

The process of substitution can continue until we are left with the multiperiod Formula (4.7). Thus, our single-period model is actually a multiple-period model in disguise. Although it looks like the multiperiod model is applicable only to the long-term investor, it is actually applicable to investors with investment horizons of any length because the value of the stock is the value of its collective dividends even if they end up being received by different people over time.

Special Discounted Cash Flow Model—No Growth in Dividends The estimation of future dividends is a particular concern of stock valuation models. This concern can be simplified by assuming that future dividends will not deviate from the current dividend. Assuming constant dividends that continue forever greatly simplifies the multiperiod valuation model:

$$P_0 = \sum_{t=1}^{\infty} \frac{DIV_t}{(1+r)^t}$$

The only difference between the preceding formula and the discounted cash flow model, Formula (4.7), is the lack of subscript on the dividend variable. In other words, we assume here that $DIV = DIV_1 = DIV_2 = DIV_3 = \ldots = DIV_\infty$. This constant dividend stream is an example of a perpetuity inasmuch as the dividend continues forever. The present value of the stock according to the *constant dividend model* is simply the current dividend divided by the discount rate:

$$P_0 = \frac{DIV}{r}$$

To illustrate this special case, suppose that Mirage, Inc., which currently pays a dividend of \$2 per share, is expected to pay a \$2 dividend each year forever. If the rate of rate of return on Mirage stock is 15 percent, the present value of Mirage is:

$$P_0 = \frac{\$2}{.15} = \$13.33.$$

The preceding formula is an example of how standard formulas for discounting can be used to find the prices of financial securities. The common stock of firms that pay a constant dividend, as well as preferred stock, can be valued as a perpetuity; however, this model is usually too simplistic because most corporations change their dividend quite often. For example, growing firms can be expected to increase their dividend on a regular basis. The model, however, does accurately describe the cash flows from preferred stock, as preferred stock pays a constant dividend and is priced rather accurately using the perpetuity model.

The common stock of firms that pay a constant dividend, as well as preferred stock, can be valued as a perpetuity.

Special Discounted Cash Flow Model—Constant Growth in Dividends

It many cases it is more realistic to model a growth rate in dividends through time. The *constant growth in dividends* model assumes that dividends grow at the same rate in each period. Common stock offering a dividend stream that grows at a constant rate can be valued as a *constant growth perpetuity:*

$$P_0 = \frac{DIV_1}{r - g} \tag{4.8}$$

where DIV_1 is next year's dividend, r is the interest rate, and g is the constant rate of growth in the cash flow. The model can be used only in cases where r is greater than g. For example, if the \$2 dividend paid currently by Mirage is expected to grow by 4 percent forever, then the value of Mirage today would be:

$$P_0 = \frac{\$2.08}{.15 - .04} = \$18.91.$$

Note that the numerator in the formula is the expected level of next year's dividend, assumed to be equal to this year's dividend grossed up by the growth rate. Thus, \$2.08 is 4 percent higher than the current dividend of \$2.00 per share.

Common stock offering a dividend stream that grows at a constant rate can be valued as a constant growth perpetuity.

The constant growth perpetuity formula also provides insights into the interest rate used to discount common stock. We defined r earlier as the rate of return investors expect to earn on the common stock investment. A rearrangement of Formula (4.8) provides information on the components of that return:

$$r = \frac{DIV_1}{P_0} + g \tag{4.9}$$

The first component is the dividend return or dividend yield, which is defined as next period's dividend in relation to today's investment. This is easy to estimate for most stocks because information on the stock price and the dividends is readily available. The second component is the return derived from future growth and is much more difficult to estimate. Some analysts estimate future growth by:

$$g = \text{Plowback ratio} \times ROE \qquad (4.10)$$

plowback ratio
The percentage of the residual cash flow that is retained by the firm for growth purposes.

where the **plowback ratio** is the percentage of the shareholder's earnings or cash flow that is plowed back into or retained by the firm for growth purposes, and *ROE* is the accounting rate of return on the firm's equity. The intuition here is that the future growth rate in dividends will be based upon the amount of funds reinvested or retained for growth purposes times the rate of return the firm earns on equity. For example, the estimate of a 4 percent growth rate in dividends for Mirage stock could be derived from Formula (4.10) in the following way: First, the accounting rate of return on equity is estimated at, say, 16 percent, and the company has a policy of plowing back 25 percent of retained earnings to support growth:

$$g = .16 \times .25 = .04$$

Special Discounted Cash Flow Model—Nonconstant Growth in Dividends The final special model considers the more realistic case of *nonconstant growth* in dividends. Of course, changing growth rates in dividends bring us back to the general discounted cash flow in dividends model given by Formula (4.9). Suppose, however, that dividends can be assumed to grow by a certain rate for a set number of years, and then change to a different rate for each year thereafter.

Example 4.7 Suppose that the current \$2 dividend of Mirage, Inc., is expected to grow by 10 percent for 2 years, and then by 5 percent forever. The following process would be used to value Mirage stock per share:

1. Determine the present value of the dividends to be paid over the first 2 years:

$$P_0 = \frac{\$2(1.1)}{(1.15)^1} + \frac{\$2(1.1)^2}{(1.15)^2} = \$3.74$$

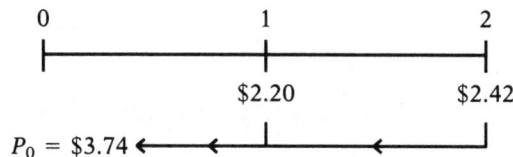

0	1	2
	\$2.20	\$2.42

$P_0 = \$3.74 \leftarrow$

2. Determine the stock price at the end of year 2 from the present value of the dividends expected from year 3 out to infinity:

$$P_2 = \frac{D_3}{r - g} = \frac{\$2(1.1)^2(1.05)}{.15 - .05} = \frac{\$2.54}{.10} = \$25.40$$

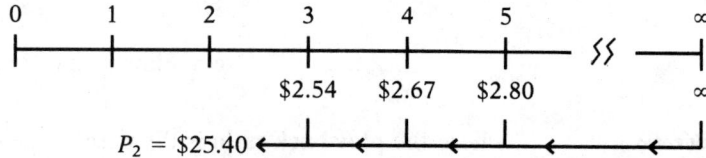

3. Determine the present value of the year 2 stock price:

$$P_0 = \frac{\$25.40}{(1.15)^2} = \$19.21$$

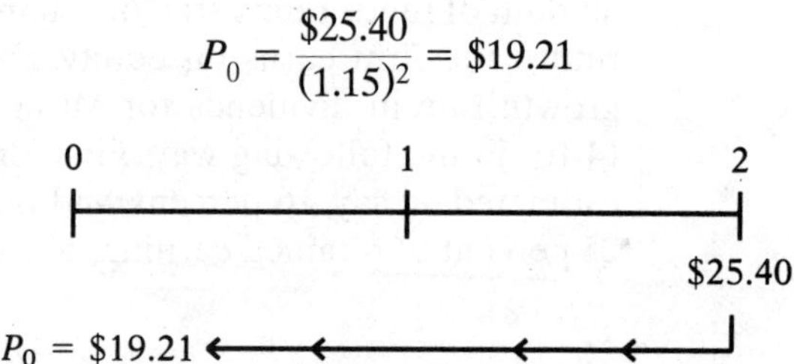

4. Add the present value of the year-two stock price to the present value of the first two years' dividends:

$$P_0 = \$3.74 + \$19.21 = \$22.95$$

As the example demonstrates, the process of determining the value of nonconstant growth in a dividend stock is greatly simplified by using a shortcut method, in this case by recognizing the constant growth rate in dividends from year 2 onward. Nonconstant growth is useful because it allows for more flexibility in dividend patterns while incorporating useful shortcuts.

Summary

- This chapter examines the valuation of financial securities. A number of cash flow models have been derived to assist in the valuation of these securities. These models include the *annuity*:

$$PVA = A\left[\frac{1}{r} - \frac{1}{r(1 + r)^n}\right]$$

the *perpetuity,* defined as an infinite set of equal cash flows through time:

$$PVP = \frac{A}{r}$$

and the *constant growth perpetuity,* defined as a perpetuity that grows at a constant rate through time:

$$PVCGP = \frac{CF_1}{r - g}$$

- Treasury bills promise one cash flow and can be valued using the *lump-sum technique* discussed in Chapter 3:

$$PV\text{ TreasuryBill} = \frac{F_n}{(1 + r)^n}$$

- Bonds offer a stream of cash flows. In order to value bonds, the stream of coupon payments paid by the bond is best valued as an annuity, whereas the payment of the bond's par value at maturity is best valued separately as a single cash flow or lump-sum cash flow:

$$\text{Bond Value} = P_0 = \underbrace{\sum_{t=1}^{n} \frac{C}{(1 + r)^t}}_{\text{Annuity}} + \underbrace{\frac{F_n}{(1 + r)^n}}_{\text{Lump Sum}}$$

- The value of bonds already outstanding is inversely related to any changes in market interest rates. When market interest rates rise, the value of outstanding bonds falls. When market interest rates fall, the value of outstanding bonds rises. This relationship derives from the fact that bonds are fixed-payment securities, and the promised cash flows from the bond do not change as market conditions change.
- The interest rate in the bond pricing formula is known as the yield to maturity. Yield to maturity is an estimate of the average rate of return the bond will offer given current market conditions.
- Common stock valuation is difficult because the stock's cash flow stream, given by dividends and capital gains, is not fixed. The general formula for valuing common stock is the discounted value of all future dividends:

$$P_0 = \sum_{t=1}^{\infty} \frac{DIV_t}{\left(1 + r\right)^t}$$

- Two special stock valuation models are the zero growth in dividend model and the constant growth model. The present value for *zero dividend growth* relies on the perpetuity model and is especially useful for pricing preferred stock:

$$P_0 = \frac{DIV}{r}$$

whereas the *constant growth* perpetuity model is useful for pricing common stock:

$$P_0 = \frac{DIV_1}{r - g}$$

- From the constant growth in dividends model comes an expression for the interest rate in common stock valuation models:

$$r = \frac{DIV_1}{P_0} + g$$

The interest rate, or the rate of return common stock investors expect to earn, can be broken into two parts: an expected rate of return on dividends and a return expected on the future growth of the firm.

Demonstration Problems

Problem 1

Compute the price of a 12 percent coupon bond with a maturity of 10 years if current interest rates are 8 percent. Assume that the bond's face value is $1,000 and use annual payments and compounding.

Solution to Problem 1

This typical bond problem is solved using both the formula methods and financial calculator methods. The problem involves three steps on many calculators. First, find the present value of the annuity stream formed by the coupon interest payments. Second, find the present value of the lump-sum principal payment. Third, add the two numbers together. Some financial calculators can do this in a single step.

Step 1: The bond offers 10 annual coupon payments of $120. The $120 figure was found by multiplying the bond's face (par) value, $1,000, by the coupon rate, 12%. The present value of this 10-year annuity can be found using the annuity method.

The formula method involves substituting $r = 8\%$, $n = 10$, and $A = \$120$ into Formula (4.1) and solving for *PVA*. Note that the interest rate used is a market interest rate, not the bond's coupon rate.

The financial calculator method involves substituting the three known values ($r = 8\%$, $n = 10$, and $A = \$120$) and asking the calculator to compute the *PV.* Typical keystrokes are:

(Clear calculator) 120, *PMT,* 8, %*I,* 10, *n, CPT, PV*

Either method produces a present value of $805.21. This interim result should be stored in the calculator's regular memory or written down. It is the present value of the coupon payments only.

Step 2: The bond's remaining cash flow, the $1,000 principal payment at year 10, can be discounted using the lump-sum techniques of Chapter 3. Formula (3.6) provides the formula with $r = 8\%$, $n = 10$, and $FV = 1{,}000$. The keystrokes for a typical financial calculator are:

(Clear calculator's financial memory only) 1000, *FV,* 8, %*I,* 10, *n, CPT, PV*

Either method produces a result of \$463.19, which is the present value of the principal payment only.
Step 3: Sum the answers to Steps 1 and 2. This can usually be accomplished by simply hitting a memory plus key after Step 2. If necessary, the sum may be found from writing down the answers to each step and then reentering them into the calculator to sum them.

Some more advanced financial calculators will allow this problem to be solved in one step by inserting the four known variables (r = 8%, n = 10, A = 120, and FV = 1,000) and computing the fifth variable, PV. Typical keystrokes would be:

(Clear calculator) 120, *PMT,* 8, %*I,* 10, *n,* 1000, *FV, CPT, PV*

Final Solution: Either way, the final answer is \$1,268.40.

Problem 2

A common stock has a current dividend of \$2.00, an annual growth rate of 5 percent, and a required rate of return of 15 percent. Using the growth perpetuity model, find its price.

Solution to Problem 2

The growth perpetuity model has four variables: the price (P_0), the next year's dividend (DIV_1), the required rate of return (r), and the annual growth rate (g). Most problems involving the model simply require the solution of one of the variables, usually the price, given the other three known variables. A common complication is that the current dividend, DIV_0, is supplied to the user rather than next year's dividend. The first step, therefore, is to transform the current dividend into the next year's dividend.
Step 1: The next year's dividend can be found from the current dividend because dividends are assumed to grow at the rate g:

$$DIV_1 = DIV_0 \times (1 + g)$$

Because we know that DIV_0 = \$2.00 and that g = 5%, DIV_1 is:

$$DIV_1 = \$2.00 \times (1.05)$$
$$DIV_1 = \$2.10$$

Step 2: The stock price can be found by inserting the known values into Formula (4.8) and solving for P_0:

$$P_0 = DIV_1/(r - g)$$
$$P_0 = \$2.10/(0.15 - .05)$$
$$P_0 = \$21.00$$

Final Solution: The stock price is \$21.00.

Review Questions

1. Explain how an annuity differs from a perpetuity.
2. Why are Treasury bills called pure discount securities?

3. Explain the relationship between bond prices and changing market interest rates.
4. How does the payment of coupons on a semiannual basis change the bond valuation model?
5. What is a bond's yield to maturity? How is it estimated?
6. Why is it generally true that bond valuation is easier than common stock valuation?
7. When is the perpetuity formula useful in common stock valuation?
8. What does *r* mean in the common stock valuation model?
9. What is the biggest shortcoming of the equity value model?

Problems

Note: Unless otherwise stated, assume annual compounding.

1. What is the price today of a 20-year zero coupon bond if the required rate of return is 12%? The bond's face value is $1,000.
2. What is the price of a 2-year bond that pays no coupon? The required rate of return is 12%, and the security has a par value of $1,000. Comment on why the price of the 2-year bond exceeds the price of the 20-year bond in the previous problem.
3. Calculate the value of each of the following three zero coupon bonds:

   Bond A: $1,000 par value, 5-year zero coupon bond. Required return = 7%.
   Bond B: $2,000 par value, 10-year zero coupon bond. Required return = 8%.
   Bond C: $5,000 par value, 20-year zero coupon bond. Required return = 11%.

4. What is the price today of a 2-year 9% coupon bond that has a par value of $1,000 and a required rate of return of 9%?
5. A $1,000 par value bond was issued one year ago with a coupon of 8%. The bond has five more years until maturity. What is the bond's price today if the required rate of return is currently 9%?
6. You are trying to price two bonds that have the same maturity and par value but different coupon rates and different required rates of return. Both bonds mature in 3 years and have par values of $1,000. One bond has a coupon of 5% and a required rate of return of 7%. The other bond has a coupon of 7% and a required rate of return of 9%. What should the difference in price between these two bonds be?
7. You are concerned about the value of a bond that you own. The bond was issued 5 years ago with a 7% coupon and was priced at its par value of $1,000. The bond matures 3 years from today.
   a. What is the bond's price today, assuming a current required rate of return of 10%?
   b. Why is the current market price below the par value?
8. You have invested in a bond that pays semiannual coupon payments of $40 and has a par value of $1,000. The bond matures in 1 year, and its required rate of return is 10% compounded semiannually. Determine the bond's present value.
9. A bond paying a coupon payment of $100 is currently worth 95% of the value it had when it was issued 1 year ago at a par value of $1,000. The bond has 3 years remaining until maturity. What is the yield to maturity?

10. What is the yield to maturity for a 5-year, 7.5% coupon, $1,000 par value bond priced currently at $940.65?

11. A bond with 2 years to maturity is priced today at $900. The bond's coupon rate is 8%, and its par value is $1,000. What is the bond's yield to maturity?

12. A bond with 10 years to maturity is priced today at 105.04% for every $100 of par value. The bond's coupon rate is 9%. Determine the bond's yield to maturity.

13. A $1,000 par value bond with an 8.5% coupon and 2 years until maturity is priced at $1,008.91. What is the bond's yield to maturity using annual coupons and annual compounding?

Fill in the missing information using Formula (4.8):

	P_0	DIV_1	r	g
14.	— —	$1.00	.10	.05
15.	— —	$1.00	.12	.11
16.	— —	$1.50	.09	.01
17.	— —	$1.50	.09	.08
18.	— —	$1.00	.19	.02

19. In 1 year, a stock is expected to pay a $2.11 dividend and be priced at $50 per share. What is the stock's price today if the required rate of return on the stock is 8%?

20. You expect a stock to pay a dividend of $1.59 and be priced at $38 in 1 year.
a. What is the stock's price today, assuming a required rate of return of 7%?
b. If the required rate of return is 6%, how would that change the stock's price today?

21. A certain stock has historically paid a dividend of $1.50 per year. If this pattern holds and the stock's price is expected to be priced at $100 in 2 years, what is its price today? The required rate of return is 7%.

22. After careful research, you estimate that each of two stocks will be worth $100 in 3 years. Stock A pays a dividend of $4 per year and is expected to stay at this level for the next 3 years. Stock B pays an annual dividend of $4 currently but it is expected to increase at a rate of 10% per year for 3 years. What is the price today of both Stock A and Stock B, assuming a 6.5% required rate of return?

23. You are considering buying one of two stocks, both of which are expected to be worth $100 in 2 years; however, you expect that Stock C will pay a dividend of $2 per year for 2 years, whereas Stock D will pay a dividend of $1 this year and $3 next year. Assuming a required rate of return of 8%, what is the difference in the price today of the two stocks?

24. What is the price today of a stock whose dividend is $3 per year forever? The stock's required rate of return is 7.5%

25. What would you be willing to pay for a stock that promises to pay a $20 annual dividend forever? The required rate of return is 8%.

26. Your uncle is interested in buying a certain stock, which he says is undervalued and should be worth $35 per share. He has asked for your help. The stock's dividend, currently at $1.10, is expected to increase at a rate of 5% per year forever. What should the stock be worth today, assuming a required rate of return of 8.5%?

27. A certain stock is priced at $30 per share today and is expected to pay a dividend of $1.50 in 1 year. The dividends are then expected to grow at a rate of 5% forever. What is the required rate of return on the stock?

28. You have been following two firms in the health care industry. You expect the dividend payment of both firms to grow at an annual rate of 5%. Dividend payments are currently \$1.00. Stock E is priced at \$10 today, and Stock F is priced at \$11.20 today. What required returns were used to price these stocks?
29. A firm provides an annual dividend that is consistently 2% of the value of its stock. The current dividend is \$0.25 per share and is expected to grow at a rate of 5% forever. What required rate of return is being used?

Discussion Questions

1. Provide a response to this statement:

   Chapter 4 stated that the present value of a perpetuity is a finite amount. That does not seem logical. The value of receiving some amount of money forever, even \$1, should be worth an infinite amount of money.

2. Provide an intuitive explanation to someone who has not taken a finance or economics course as to why the value of bonds already outstanding is inversely related to changes in market interest rates.
3. Provide a response to this statement:

   The common stock valuation model cannot be correct. I personally know of a stock that has never in its 20-year history paid a dividend, and yet its price is consistently above \$20 per share.

4. Suppose Microsoft's stock is selling for \$100 a share, and that approximately half of the firm's earnings are paid out as dividends. You own a share of Microsoft stock, and design a unique deal to a potential buyer of that share. The deal is this:

   The person buying the share of Microsoft gets to hold the stock; however, every future dividend that Microsoft pays goes to you (or your family, should you die). Anyone purchasing the stock must agree to this arrangement. Thus, all dividends (or any other distributions) for all future generations from that share of stock belong to you or your heirs.

   a. If the person who buys the stock from you cannot sell the stock to anyone else, how much would the share of Microsoft sell for under this unique arrangement?
   b. If the person who buys the stock from you can resell the stock to one person, how much would the share of Microsoft sell for under this unique arrangement?
   c. How much would the share of Microsoft sell for under this unique arrangement if there were no restrictions on reselling the stock?

CHAPTER 5

THE TECHNIQUES OF CAPITAL BUDGETING

Phelps Products is one of the world's leading producers of fiberglass.[1] Founded by William J. Phelps II in 1918, the company has grown from a family-operated concern to a multinational corporation with more than 10,000 employees and sales eclipsing the $1 billion mark; however, all is not well at Phelps. The company has been in serious decline for five straight years, and there is now talk of major cutbacks and even the possibility of bankruptcy.

The story of the rise and fall of Phelps is an interesting one. William J. Phelps II was a chemist and inventor who, when he was only 20 years old, developed a glass now known as fiberglass. Phelps obtained a patent for his process, and found that his product quickly became popular in all types of manufacturing operations. William Phelps played a major role in building the company, and was active in all facets of its operations until his death in 1985.

In 1985 the control of the company was in the hands of his two sons. Whereas they understood the business, they did not seem to have the skills to lead the company. For instance, they made a decision to open a new division of specialty products in 1986 without a careful analysis of the financial details. Although they could recall their father basing new product decisions on such things as "value present," "rate internal," and "back pay," they seemed to be more interested in making decisions based upon what felt right. They believed that investment decisions should be based upon the firm's strategic plan as they tried to position their firm for the global competition of the twenty-first century.

The new division was a disaster. The sons significantly underestimated the costs of production to the point that they were actually losing money on each unit sold. They did not take into account the fact that production delays increase costs today and at the same time postpone revenues for years into the

[1]The story of Phelps Products is a composite of real and fictitious events. All names and circumstances have been changed.

future. By 1995, it was clear that the investment in the new division was bringing the company down.

What the Phelps brothers spent billions of dollars to learn will be presented in this chapter. Investment decisions should be based upon careful analysis of all advantages and disadvantages—adjusted for time and risk.

The story of Phelps Products illustrates the investment decision of the firm, and the investment decision represents the single most important method of achieving the firm's objective—maximizing shareholder wealth. In this chapter we discuss how this objective can be achieved, and how the decision to invest can often change the wealth of the firm's shareholders.

Creating Value

Table 5.1 lists 10 firms whose successful investments have resulted in powerful brand recognition in the marketplace. Everyone has heard of these brands; indeed, many of us use these products and services every day. How did these firms judge the potential value of these brands? Why were these

TABLE 5.1 The 10 Most Powerful Brands in the World

Rank	*Brand*
1	Coca-Cola
2	Microsoft
3	IBM
4	GE
5	Nokia
6	Intel
7	Disney
8	Ford
9	McDonald's
10	ATT

Source: Interbrand, 2001, http://home.t_online.de/home/mario.wolff/brandvalue.pdf.

products and services brought to the marketplace whereas competing projects within the firm were never launched? These issues are the focus of Chapter 5.

Should a firm's shareholders approve of an investment opportunity within a corporation that promises to turn $100 today into $110 in 1 year? While it may be tempting to say *yes,* shareholders would be wise to consider this investment against other investment opportunities first. For example, shareholders might be able to deposit money in a bank and receive a return greater than the 10 percent offered by this investment. The bottom line is that we cannot say if a particular return on investment would (or should) meet with shareholder approval without additional information regarding alternatives.

Let us look at a more detailed example and one with which you are already familiar. Recall Megan Morrison from Chapter 4, the financial analyst for the Gecco Insurance Company, who determined that the bond being considered for purchase by the firm had a price equal to the present value of its future cash flow. In other words, the costs of the bond and the benefits of the bond were equal in present value terms. Most financial assets trade at prices so near the present value of their future cash flows that a corporation's managers have little if any ability to enhance shareholder wealth by trading them. We could say that the investment offers the exact return to the shareholders that they would expect to earn on other investments with similar risk—nothing more and nothing less. The bond investment accordingly does not create or destroy value for the shareholders, but keeps value unchanged.

Gecco's bond is reflective of most financial assets that trade in efficient markets: The price of the asset is equal to its present value. There is nothing special about the Gecco bond. Bonds trading in efficient markets offer returns that investors expect to earn on similar risk investments. This is the reason that modern corporate finance does not view the trading of financial assets to be as important as the management of real assets for the purpose of increasing firm value and therefore shareholder wealth.

Most financial assets trade at prices so near the present value of their future cash flows that a corporation's managers have little if any ability to enhance shareholder wealth by trading them.

A different type of investment is one in real assets (e.g., an investment in plant and equipment). Real asset investments are generally referred to as **projects,** and the analysis of projects is known as **capital budgeting analysis.** An important difference between real asset investment and financial asset investments is the competitive forces of the respective markets where the assets trade. Lack of competition creates the potential for a project to increase shareholder wealth. Whereas millions of individuals and corporations have excellent access to the financial markets where financial assets trade, only a relatively few have access to many of the real goods markets where real assets trade.

projects
Investments in real assets.

capital budgeting analysis
The analysis of projects within the firm, such as the purchase of new plant and equipment.

Lack of competition creates the potential for a project to increase shareholder wealth.

Example 5.1 You recognized the Eastman Kodak Company, a maker of cameras and camera equipment, as one of the firms with a powerful brand recognition listed in Table 5.1. Kodak's decision to manufacture and market a camera on a global basis is, realistically speaking, available to only a limited number of firms. Although, of course, there are thousands of firms for which a camera project might be possible, such a project would typically be considered only by a firm with a market reputation or expertise in a related technology. Moreover, when a project is available to only a small number of firms, there is a possibility that a lack of competition will create a superior investment opportunity, thereby increasing shareholder wealth.

Very few firms have the capital and market position to introduce successfully a new product such as an instant camera with its own film. Because so few firms have this alternative, the lack of competition creates the potential for large benefits—or large losses.

Patents represent another avenue by which firms establish a competitive advantage in the real goods market. Due to patent protection, there may be some projects that only a single firm can consider. For example, the NutraSweet™ subsidiary of the Monsanto Company held 75 percent of the artificial sweetener market worldwide in the 1980s, deriving its market power from a patent issued in 1969 on aspartame.[2] This example illustrates how patents can remove competition (in the short run) and create the potential for very large benefits, which may encourage a firm to undertake research/development and to compensate it, in part, for any large development costs.

Another source of superior investment opportunity could be the ability to compete in a market using superior management. For example, competitors within a particular industry or geographical region may have inefficient management, such that an efficiently managed firm might be able to increase shareholder wealth by expanding to compete against them. Thus, opportunities exist to invest in the real asset market and create wealth. How, then, can financial managers recognize wealth-creating projects? The rest of this chapter is devoted to answering that question.

Keeping Score

This section discusses alternative ways to measure value creation. The models developed assume that all of the costs and benefits of a project can be expressed as dollar values at various points in time. This concept is illustrated in the following time line. The project is represented by costs of $10,000 today and produces numerous future cash inflows:

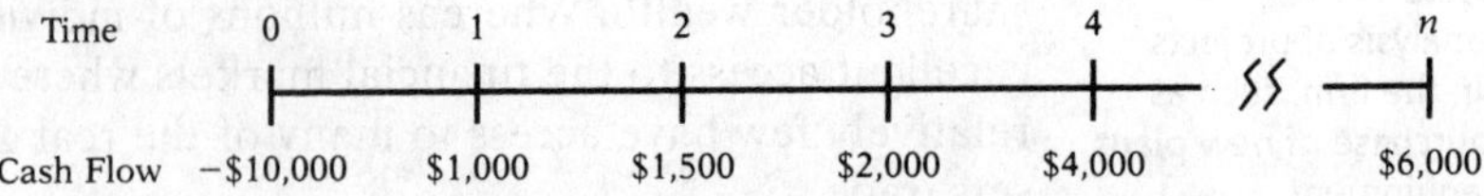

[2]The patent on NutraSweet expired on December 14, 1992. Competing firms can now market their own version of the product.

We will discuss later why it is reasonable to believe that any cost or benefit can be expressed in terms of dollars. The key for now is to understand that this chapter addresses a straightforward question: Given the cash flows of a project (as illustrated before), would acceptance of the project increase, decrease, or leave unchanged shareholder wealth?

The Required Rate of Return in Project Analysis

required rate of return
The minimum rate of return that an investor would accept in order to invest in a project of a particular risk.

Most capital budgeting models require the discount rate to be estimated. The discount rate is the interest rate used to discount future cash flows. Throughout this chapter we will refer to the discount rate as the required rate of return on a project. The **required rate of return** is the minimum rate of return that an investor would accept in order to invest in a project of particular risk. For example, bond investors require a higher rate of return on corporate bonds than on Treasury bonds. The reason for the differential is risk—the risk that a corporation will fail to meet promises is greater than the risk that the government will fail to repay an investor. In general, the higher the risk, the higher would be the required rate of return. Although we defer the full discussion of concepts of risk to later chapters, it is important to see that risk enters the capital budgeting analysis through the discount rate and estimations of the cash flows.

A Summary of Value Creation

To summarize, investments in real assets offer the potential for unique advantages and can allow firms to exploit projects whose benefits truly exceed costs. In cases such as these, we say that the project has increased shareholder wealth. On the other hand, firms also wish to avoid projects that decrease shareholder wealth.

We will discuss alternative capital budgeting models next. In general, capital budgeting models are designed to help identify and compare project costs with project benefits. The goal of capital budgeting is to identify those projects whose benefits exceed their costs.

Net Present Value

net present value
A capital budgeting model that compares the present value of the project's benefits with the present value of the project's costs. The difference between benefits and costs is the net present value of the project.

The premier capital budgeting model is called the **net present value** (*NPV*) model. One advantage of *NPV* is the way it incorporates the time value of money, measuring benefits and costs in terms of present values. *NPV* transforms all of the project's cash flows through time to the same commodity so that costs can be subtracted from benefits.

Our initial examples of *NPV* will assume that the costs of the investments are paid today at time zero. The initial investment might be the purchase of a machine or of raw materials necessary for production. The project's benefits will be represented by future cash flows received when the product or service is sold and payment is received. The future benefits are pulled back by discounting future cash flows using the required rate of return appropriate for the project. Costs are then compared with benefits:

$$NPV = PV \text{ of Benefits} - PV \text{ of Costs} \tag{5.1}$$

A positive *NPV* means that the project's benefits exceed costs, and the decision to undertake the project increases the value of the firm and shareholder wealth. A negative *NPV* means that the project's costs exceed benefits, and the decision to undertake the project would decrease the value of the firm and shareholder wealth. A *NPV* of zero means that the project's benefits are equal to costs, and the decision to undertake a project does not increase or decrease the value of the firm or the wealth of the shareholders. From the perspective of shareholder wealth maximization, positive *NPV* projects should be accepted, negative *NPV* projects should be rejected, and firms should be indifferent toward accepting or rejecting zero *NPV* projects.

The *NPV* rule follows from the fourth economic principle, the law of conservation of value. If a project whose benefits exceed its costs is added to the existing assets of a firm, then the value of the firm's assets with the project must equal the original value of the firm's assets plus the value of the project. In the case of a positive *NPV*, the firm's new asset value will be greater than its original asset value by the amount of the *NPV*.

The *NPV* Rule in Capital Budgeting

incremental cash flows Benefits that would not have been received, or those costs that would not have been incurred, if a project had not been undertaken.

It is best to view a project or any other type of financial decision as a set of cash inflows and outflows at various points in time. The cash flows are the incremental cash flows that result from undertaking the project, where **incremental cash flows** are those benefits that would not have been received, or those costs that would not have been incurred, if a project had not been undertaken. The next chapter will detail the issues involved in determining the precise cash flows of a project. For now, view the capital budgeting decision as whether or not it is beneficial to accept a given stream of inflows and outflows.

The net present value rule in cash flow form is:

$$NPV = C_0 + \frac{CF_1}{(1+r)^1} + \frac{CF_2}{(1+r)^2} + \frac{CF_3}{(1+r)^3} + \cdots + \frac{CF_n}{(1+r)^n} \tag{5.2}$$

where C_0 represents the initial (period zero) cash flow and is usually negative, CF_1 through CF_n represent the incremental future cash flows that result from undertaking the project and are usually positive, and r is the project's required rate of return.

Example 5.2

Consider a new comedy film being considered by Univers Studios. Univers estimates the cost of producing the film to be $25 million, all payable in the current period. Ticket sales are estimated to be $15 million in year 1 and $10 million in year 2, at which point the film will be taken out of circulation and its rights sold to cable companies for $8 million in year 3. No other revenues are expected after year 3. The project's required rate of return is 12 percent.

The cash flows for the film project and the project's *NPV* are shown in Table 5.2. The movie project's single cash outflow in the current period is $25 million, and the present value of the three future cash inflows, discounted at 12 percent, is $27.059 million. The *NPV* of the movie project is $2.059 million ($27.059 million minus $25 million) and should be accepted as it increases the wealth of Univers Studios' shareholders.

Workshop 5.1 illustrates how *NPV* calculations can be simplified when discounting special cash flow streams such as annuities. The workshop also presents a quick method for discounting an uneven cash flow stream. Many sophisticated financial calculators will solve for NPV directly. The user inputs all of the cash flows, inputs a discount rate, and then computes the NPV by hitting a single key, which is usually labeled NPV. Spreadsheets and other financial software will also compute NPV automatically. For the types of problems encountered in Chapter 5, financial spreadsheets and other sophisticated computer software offer tremendous speed and accuracy. They are well worth using once the concepts are fully understood.

TABLE 5.2 The NPV of Univers's New Movie Project (all values in millions)

A Time Line View of the Project's Cash Flows

Today	Year 1	Year 2	Year 3
−$25 M	+$15 M	+$10 M	+$8 M

Worksheet for Calculating the NPV

Year	*Cash Flow*	$\frac{1}{(1.12)^n}$	*Present Value*
0	−$25	1.0000	−$25.000
1	+$15	0.8929	+$13.393
2	+$10	0.7972	+$ 7.972
3	+$ 8	0.7118	+$ 5.694

Present Value of the Initial Investment	−$25.000
Present Value of the Inflows	+$27.059
Net Present Value	+$ 2.059

WORKSHOP 5.1

NPV with Even and Uneven Cash Flow Streams

Chapter 4 discussed and illustrated shortcuts when discounting particular cash flow streams. A good example of such a shortcut was the case of an equal cash flows stream through time—or the case of an annuity—where the entire stream was discounted in one step. If the cash flows in the *NPV* analysis represent an annuity, then shortcut methods can be used.

For example, consider a project whose initial investment is $25 million and which promises three annual cash inflows starting in year 1 of $12 million each. If the project's required rate of return is 12 percent, then the *NPV* can be determined as follows (all values in millions):

$$NPV = -\$25\text{M} + 12\text{M}\left[\frac{1}{r} - \frac{1}{r(1+r)^n}\right]$$

where the bracketed expression is the formula for the present value of an annuity. Substituting 12 percent for *r* and 3 for *n* provides the *NPV* of the project:

$$NPV = -\$25\text{ M} + \$12\text{ M}\left[\frac{1}{.12} - \frac{1}{.12(1.12)^3}\right] = -\$25\text{M} + \$12\text{M}\left[2.4018\right] = \$3.822\text{ M.}$$

Thus, given an annuity stream of cash inflows, *NPV* can be calculated in one step. In addition, when a project offers a level payment stream terminated by a lump sum, the computations can be done using the same mathematics as used in Chapter 4 for bond problems.

Although annuities make *NPV* analysis easier, we cannot always expect cash flow streams to be equal. In fact, a general rule is that the more complex the *NPV* analysis, the more likely it is for an uneven cash flow stream to result. Uneven streams of cash flows must be discounted one at a time. For those looking for a shortcut, we offer the following process for discounting an uneven stream on an ordinary calculator.

The idea behind the shortcut we are about to present is best seen with an analogy. Suppose a person was asked to take a truck and go pick up a number of packages down a particular road. Suppose that some of the packages were at a location 1 mile down the road, some were 2 miles down the same road, and so forth up to perhaps 5 miles down the road. What would be the most efficient method of hauling the packages (assuming that they could all be fitted on the same truck)?

Rather than make separate trips, it should be obvious that the best method would be to make a single trip for all the packages (unless the person was paid by the hour!). For example, the person could:

1. Drive to the furthest location and load the packages.
2. Drive back to the second furthest location and load the packages.
3. Drive back to the third furthest location, and so forth.

WORKSHOP 5.1 *(continued)*

When we discount future cash flows we are in effect moving the cash flows back to the present time. Rather than making a separate trip or present value for each cash flow, it is better to bring back all of the cash flows using a single trip.

Thus, a present value problem for a stream of uneven cash flows can be solved as follows:

1. Enter the final cash flow into the calculator.
2. Move the cash flow "back" 1 year by dividing it by $1 + r$.
3. Add on the second-to-last cash flow to the previous result.
4. Move the new result "back" 1 year by dividing it by $1 + r$.
5. Continue the process until the initial outlay is subtracted out.

For example, consider the following project and cash flows:

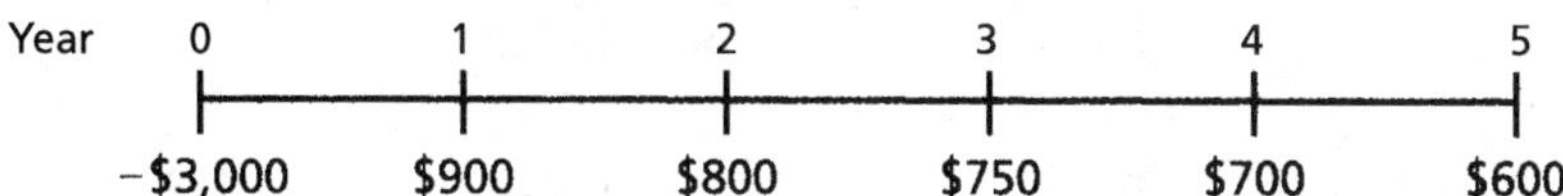

Using a discount rate of 12 percent, the keystrokes would be:

$$600 \div 1.12 = +700 = \div 1.12 = +750 = \div 1.12 = +800 = \div 1.12$$
$$= +900 = \div 1.12 = -3000 = \text{(the answer: } -\$239.52)$$

Quite a savings of time and a definite hit at a good party! In fact, the keystrokes can be further simplified on most calculators by noting that (1) many of the equal signs are unnecessary, and (2) it is easier to place $(1 + r)$ into the memory and then simply hit the recall memory key after each "÷." Because calculators vary, this shortcut may need some experimentation.

Competitors of *NPV*

NPV is the premier capital budgeting rule because it relates directly to the objective of maximizing shareholder wealth. For a variety of reasons, however, alternative models of capital budgeting are utilized by corporations. Some of these models are preferred because of their simplicity, others because of corporate tradition. This section discusses the competitors of *NPV*.

The Profitability Index

The profitability index (*PI*) is *NPV* in ratio form. Instead of subtracting the present value of costs from the present value of benefits, the present value of the benefits is divided by the present value of the costs (ignoring the negative sign):

$$PI = \frac{\sum_{t=1}^{n} C_t / (1+r)^t}{|C_0|} \tag{5.3}$$

profitability index
A capital budgeting model: A ratio constructed by dividing the present value of the project's benefits by the present value of the project's cost.

where C_t represents cash inflows through time, C_0 represents current cash flows and is usually negative, r is the discount rate, and t represents a period in time. The **profitability index** is a ratio of benefits to costs: a *PI* value greater than 1 defines a project whose benefits exceed costs, and a *PI* value less than 1 defines a project whose costs exceed benefits. A *PI* equal to 1 implies that costs are equal to benefits.

Example 5.3

The *PI* for Univers Studios' movie project is:

$$PI = \frac{\$27.059 \text{ million}}{\$25 \text{ million}} = 1.0824$$

The profitability index for the Univers movie project is greater than 1, which means that benefits exceed costs and the project is acceptable. Given that the PI is a ratio, it provides in percentage form the extent to which benefits exceed costs. As shown earlier, benefits are 8.24 percent greater than costs.

The final decision on the movie project is the same for both *NPV* and the *PI.* This is no coincidence! Any project with a positive *NPV* will also have a *PI* greater than 1, and any project with a negative *NPV* will also have a *PI* less than 1. Thus, in the analysis of a particular project, both the *NPV* and *PI* rules will lead to the same decision.

A potential shortcoming of the *PI* is revealed, however, when, instead of evaluating a single project, the firm evaluates groups of projects and must choose from a subset of the group. As a percentage, the *PI* may overstate the attractiveness of certain projects while understating the attractiveness of others. This shortcoming will be described in detail later in this chapter.

The Internal Rate of Return

internal rate of return
A capital budgeting model represented by the discount rate that equates the present value of the costs with the present value of the benefits from the project.

The most popular competitor to *NPV* is the **internal rate of return** (*IRR*) method. Computing the *IRR* is tantamount to answering the following question: If we viewed the project like a bank account, what interest rate would the bank have to offer in order to produce the same benefits and costs as the project? The *IRR* can also be described as the discount rate that makes *NPV* equal to zero, or alternatively the discount rate that equates the present value of the costs with the present value of the benefits from the project.

There are two steps to evaluating projects based on the *IRR:* (1) calculating the *IRR,* and (2) comparing the *IRR* to the required rate of return. Acceptable projects are those whose *IRR* is greater than the required return. Projects should be rejected if the *IRR* is less than the required rate of return.

Shareholders are indifferent when the *IRR* is equal to the required rate of return.

The first step is to determine the *IRR,* which is illustrated in Formula (5.4). Let C_0 be the project's initial investment, and CF_1 through CF_n be the project's future cash inflows. The internal rate of return is the interest rate that equates the right-hand side and left-hand side of the equation:

$$C_0 + \frac{CF_1}{(1+IRR)^1} + \frac{CF_2}{(1+IRR)^2} + \frac{CF_3}{(1+IRR)^3} + \cdots + \frac{CF_n}{(1+IRR)^n} = 0 \qquad (5.4)$$

There are generally two approaches to solving for the *IRR.* The first relies on a trial and error search process similar to that demonstrated for a bond's yield to maturity. The second allows the trial and error process to be performed by an advanced financial calculator or computer software programmed to execute the search for you.

Notice the relationship between Formula (5.4) and the *NPV* formula. Solving for the *IRR* may be defined as finding the discount rate that, when plugged into the *NPV* formula, gives an *NPV* of zero. It is important, however, to distinguish between the *IRR* and the discount rate used in the *NPV* method. The *IRR* gets its name because the rate is internal to the project. In the *NPV* model, however, the discount rate is a measure of the project's required rate of return (and comes from the market). Because the discount rate used in the NPV calculation comes from the market, it is external to the project (i.e., an external discount rate or an external required rate of return). In contrast, when using Formula 5.4 to find the *IRR,* the user searches internally or within the project for the unique discount rate (IRR) that makes costs equal to benefits. Once estimated, the *IRR* is compared with the external required rate of return from the market in order to make an accept–reject decision on the project.

Example 5.4

The amount of work required in determining the *IRR* depends on the project's cash flow stream and on the availability of a sophisticated financial calculator or computer. We will assume that a sophisticated financial calculator or computer is not available and demonstrate the *IRR* procedure using the trial and error process.

To determine the *IRR* of the Univers movie project, we insert the cash flows of the project into Formula (5.4):

$$-\$25M + \frac{\$15\ M}{(1 + IRR)^1} + \frac{\$10\ M}{(1 + IRR)^2} + \frac{\$8\ M}{(1 + IRR)^3} = 0$$

The *IRR* is the precise interest rate that satisfies the preceding equation. The trial and error process, illustrated in Table 5.3, selects an initial guess followed by subsequent guesses until the *IRR* is found.

With an initial guess of 10 percent the present value of the inflows of $27.911 million is greater than the $25 million outflow. Remember, our goal

TABLE 5.3 Determining the IRR by Trial and Error

Interest Rate	*PV of Outflow*[a]	*PV of Inflows*[b]	*NPV*
10%	\$25.000	\$27.911	\$2.911
11%	\$25.000	\$27.479	\$2.479
12%	\$25.000	\$27.059	\$2.059
13%	\$25.000	\$26.650	\$1.650
14%	\$25.000	\$26.252	\$1.252
15%	\$25.000	\$25.865	\$0.865
16%	\$25.000	\$25.488	\$0.488
17%	\$25.000	\$25.121	\$0.121
18%	\$25.000	\$24.763	−\$0.237

[a]The interest rate does not change the present value of the outflow because the outflow occurs at time zero.

[b]The inflows must be discounted individually. The shortcut method demonstrated in Workshop 5.1 will speed up the process.

is to make the numbers equal. Our next guess for the *IRR* should be higher than 10 percent because we need to lower the present value of the inflows. At 11 percent, the present value of the inflows is \$27.479 million, which is closer to \$25 million, but is still too high. The trial and error process continues until we hit a guess of 18 percent. At 18 percent, the present value of the inflows is \$24.763 million, lower than the \$25 million present value of the outflow. Thus, the *IRR* is between 17 percent and 18 percent. The exact *IRR* is 17.334 percent.[3]

The *IRR* of 17.334 percent is greater than the 12 percent return investors would require to earn on such a project. Because the *IRR* exceeds the required rate of return, the project will increase the value of the firm and should be accepted.

If an advanced financial calculator is available, the *IRR* can be found by inputting into the calculator the cash outflow and the series of cash inflows. The calculator will then grind through the trial and error process illustrated in Table 5.3 to solve for the *IRR* of 17.334 percent. Spreadsheets and other computer software will likewise perform the search given the cash flows and, in most cases, an initial guess at the solution.

Note that there are two specialized cases where computing the *IRR* does not require a trial and error method: The first is the case of a single cash outflow and a single cash inflow; the second is the case of an annuity of inflows.

[3]Interpolation can be used to find a better estimate of the *IRR*. In most cases, however, investment decisions using *IRR* will not require a precise solution; therefore the *IRR* can be approximated to the closest integer value.

In both cases, the *IRR* may be found by using the mathematical calculations given in Chapters 3 and 4.

net present value profile
A graph that demonstrates the net present value of a project at different discount rates.

The Net Present Value Profile The **net present value profile** graphs the trial and error process for finding the *IRR*. Learning the process of creating a net present value profile is essential for issues that arise later in the chapter—even if you have a calculator that solves for NPV automatically. The net present value profile for the movie project is presented in Figure 5.1.

The *NPV* profile locates the *IRR* graphically. Because the *IRR* is the discount rate that makes *NPV* zero, the *IRR* is represented by the point where the profile crosses through the horizontal axis measuring the discount rates. This occurs between 17 and 18 percent on the figure, which corresponds to our previous solution of 17.334 percent. Note also that at zero percent, the *NPV* is equal to the sum of the cash flows.

Payback

The capital budgeting methods discussed thus far are called discounted cash flow (DCF) methods. Net present value, the profitability index, and internal

FIGURE 5.1 The NPV Profile for the Univers Studios Movie Project

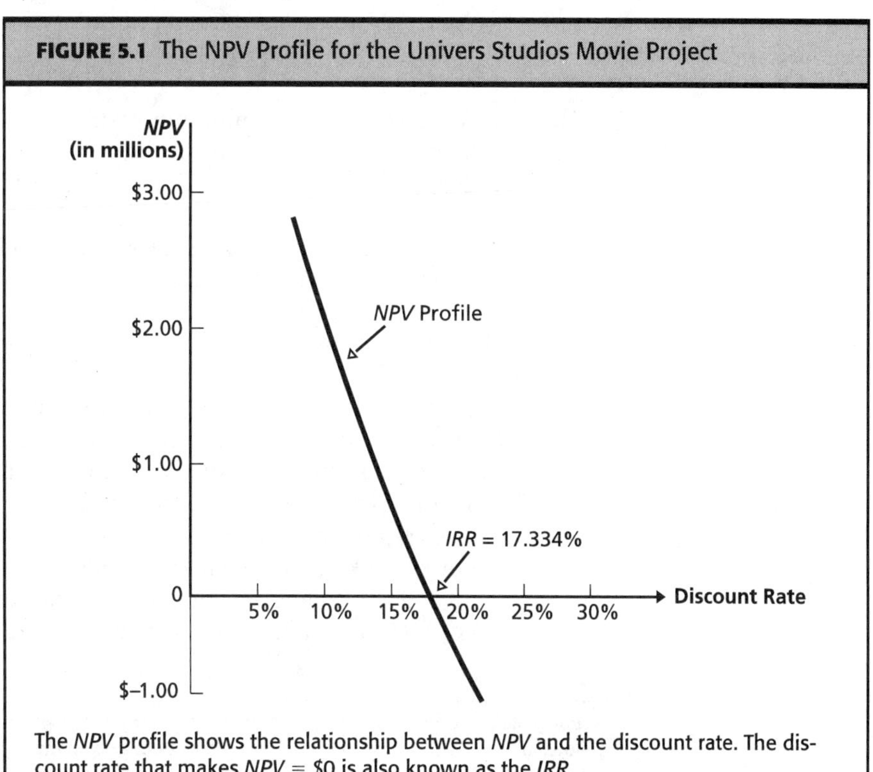

The *NPV* profile shows the relationship between *NPV* and the discount rate. The discount rate that makes *NPV* = $0 is also known as the *IRR*.

rate of return all discount future cash flows back to the present so that these cash flows can be properly compared. The payback model, discussed here, does not discount cash flows and thus fails to treat dollars through time as different commodities. As you might expect, we view this as a serious shortcoming. Nevertheless, surveys have found that corporations use the payback rule, especially in combination with other capital budgeting rules, when making investment decisions.

payback
A capital budgeting model that answers the question: How long will it take to recoup the initial investment?

Payback answers the question: How long will it take in order to recoup our initial investment? The shorter the period of time needed to get your money back, the shorter the payback. The simplicity of the payback model has a certain appeal. Indeed, it would not be surprising to find even the most ardent critics applying its logic when making certain types of financial decisions.[4] Further, compared with *NPV* and *IRR,* the concept of payback is easier to grasp and is therefore easier to apply. We warn against adopting the payback model, however, because of its simplicity. As we will soon see, simplest is not always best!

Example 5.5 ________ Recall the cash flows associated with the Univers movie project (values in millions):

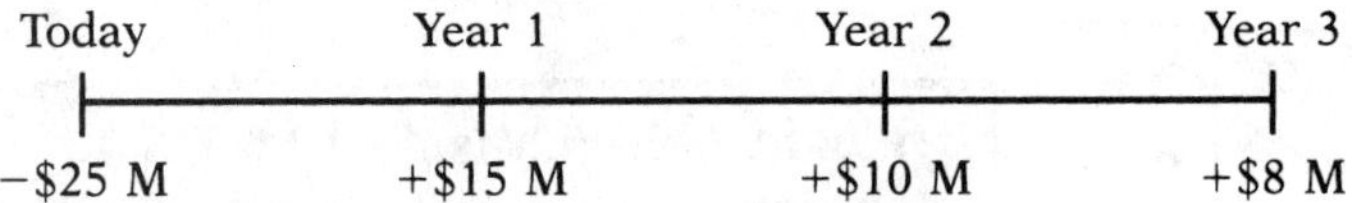

The project recovers the $25 million investment in 2 years, defining a 2-year payback. Univers must now use the information contained in payback to make an accept–reject decision on the movie project.

Is a particular payback, say 2 years, good or bad? To put it another way, would it be wise for Univers to accept projects with a 2-year payback, or should it only accept projects with a payback less than 2 years? If projects with a 2-year payback are acceptable, would a 3-year payback also be acceptable? What about a 10-year payback?

These questions reveal one of payback's shortcomings. Firms using the payback model to make accept–reject decisions on projects must decide on a payback cutoff criterion. For instance, setting the cutoff criterion at 3 years would lead Univers to accept the movie project; but this criterion is arbitrary. A payback acceptable to one firm could be unacceptable to others. Further, there is no direct linkage between a project's payback and its value. Projects accepted through the payback model could increase firm value, decrease firm value, or leave the value of the firm unchanged.

---

[4]For instance, homeowners will often put replacement decisions or energy conservation decisions in the context of payback. In fact, we wonder how many finance professors have justified a major household purchase, say the conversion of oil heat to natural gas, by applying the payback method.

A second shortcoming of the payback model is that it ignores all cash flows that occur after the payback period. This shortcoming is illustrated by examining the cash flows of two different projects, A and B:

	Today	Year 1	Year 2	Year 3	Year 4	Payback
Project A:	−$100	+$60	+$40	+$40	+$40	2 Years
Project B:	−$100	+$40	+$40	+$40	+$400	3 Years

Project A's payback is shorter and thus is superior to Project B's payback.[5] In fact, if the firm's payback criterion is to accept any project with a payback of 2 years or less, Project A would be accepted and Project B would be rejected. This decision, however, fails to consider Project B's huge cash inflow in year 4! Indeed, when considering all the cash flows, Project B is clearly superior to Project A. As we said, the payback model unfortunately fails to consider cash flows beyond the payback period.

We can expose this shortcoming of payback by comparing the *NPV* of the two projects. Using a discount rate of 10 percent:

$$NPV\text{ A} = -\$100 + \frac{\$60}{(1.1)^1} + \frac{\$40}{(1.1)^2} + \frac{\$40}{(1.1)^3} + \frac{\$40}{(1.1)^4} = \$44.98.$$

$$NPV\text{ B} = -\$100 + \frac{\$40}{(1.1)^1} + \frac{\$40}{(1.1)^2} + \frac{\$40}{(1.1)^3} + \frac{\$400}{(1.1)^4} = \$272.70.$$

From the standpoint of shareholder wealth maximization, Project B, with the higher *NPV*, is the clear winner.

The third and final shortcoming of payback is that it ignores the time value of money. This shortcoming is illustrated by examining the cash flows of two different projects, C and D:

	Today	Year 1	Year 2	Year 3	Year 4	Payback
Project C:	−$100	+$90	-0-	-0-	+$30	4 Years
Project D:	−$100	+$30	+$30	+$30	+$30	4 Years

Both projects offer a payback of 4 years, so that the firm using the payback method would view them as roughly equivalent. The payback model, however, adds and subtracts dollars through time as if they were the same commodity, thus violating the principle of the time value of money. From the standpoint of present values, Project C's cash flow stream is preferred because most of its inflows occur in year 1.

[5] Defining a 3-year payback for Project B assumes that all cash flows come at the end of the year. With more detailed information, we might be able to define payback more precisely. For example, if Project B's cash flows arrive continuously over the years, its payback would be 2.5 years.

We can again expose this shortcoming of payback by comparing the *NPV* of the two projects. Using a discount rate of 10 percent:

$$NPV\,\text{C} = -\$100 + \frac{\$90}{(1.1)^1} + -0- + -0- + \frac{\$30}{(1.1)^4} = \$2.31.$$

$$NPV\,\text{D} = -\$100 + \frac{\$30}{(1.1)^1} + \frac{\$30}{(1.1)^2} + \frac{\$30}{(1.1)^3} + \frac{\$30}{(1.1)^4} = -\$4.90.$$

From the standpoint of shareholder wealth maximization, Project C's *NPV* is greater than Project D's, and Project D decreases shareholder wealth.

The Accounting Rate of Return

Analysts who tend to focus on accounting numbers often evaluate projects according to the accounting rate of return model. The logic underlying the accounting rate of return is that an objective of the firm is to produce high profits on investments, so it is wise to invest in assets that produce high average profits.

accounting rate of return
A capital budgeting model defined by a ratio of average accounting profits over the project's life divided by some estimate of the average annual investment.

depreciation
The reduction in the book value of an asset using accounting rules.

The **accounting** (or average) **rate of return** is a ratio of some measure of average accounting profits over the project's life divided by some estimate of the average annual investment. Accounting profits are defined as revenues less expenses, taxes, and depreciation, where **depreciation** is a reduction in the book value of an asset using accounting rules. The average annual investment takes into account the decline in the investment through time due to depreciation. Once computed, the accounting rate of return is compared with some benchmark in order to decide if the project should be accepted or rejected.

Example 5.6 ________

Table 5.4 shows how the accounting rate of return is computed. Methods of computing the accounting rate of return differ. In Table 5.4, depreciation is calculated by the straight line method, whereby the initial investment of $90 million depreciates by $30 million per year. The annual investment starts in year 0 at $90 million and depreciates by $30 million per year to a value of zero at the project's end. Thus, the investment lasts for 4 years. The average annual investment is $45 million. The accounting rate of return is $13.33 million divided by $45 million, which equals 29.6 percent. The firm would then compare the accounting rate of return of 29.6 percent to some benchmark in order to decide if the project is acceptable or not.

The accounting rate of return method suffers from many serious shortcomings. First, like payback, it requires the use of an arbitrary decision rule. In our example, the firm must decide whether 29.6 percent is acceptable or not. There is no decision rule that can be applied equally across all firms, nor is there a way to link the accounting rate of return with firm value. Second, because accounting rate of return does not discount future cash flows, it violates the time value of money principle. The $20 million of profit in year 1 is added to the $10 million of profit in years 2 and 3 to get the total profit of $40

TABLE 5.4 Computing the Accounting Rate of Return (all values in millions)

Part 1: Determining Average Annual Accounting Profits

	Year 1	*Year 2*	*Year 3*
Revenues	\$100	\$70	\$70
Expenses Plus Taxes	\$ 50	\$30	\$30
Cash Flow	\$ 50	\$40	\$40
Less Depreciation	\$ 30	\$30	\$30
Accounting Profit	\$ 20	\$10	\$10

$$\text{Average Accounting Profit} = \frac{\$20 + \$10 + \$10}{3} = \$13.33$$

Part 2: Determining the Average Annual Investment (\$90 M outlay)

	Year 0	*Year 1*	*Year 2*	*Year 3*
Investment: Start of Period	\$90	\$90	\$60	\$30
Depreciation	\$00	\$30	\$30	\$30
Investment: End of Period	\$90	\$60	\$30	\$00

$$\text{Average Annual Investment} = \frac{\$90 + \$60 + \$30 + \$00}{4} = \$45.00$$

Part 3: Determining the Average Accounting Rate of Return

$$\text{Average Accounting Rate of Return} = \frac{\$13.33}{\$45.00} = 29.6\%$$

million. Reversing the timing of the cash flow stream would give us the same total profit, even though the time value is clearly different.

Third, the rate of return measure depends on the accounting rules used to depreciate the investment through time. The preceding project used the straight line depreciation method. The firm, however, could also choose to use some other depreciation method, and that choice would have a significant impact on the measure of return. Modernists strongly believe that cash flows measure value far better than accounting numbers.

NPV Versus *IRR*—Which Method Is Better?

The previous sections highlighted two models of capital budgeting, the *NPV* model and the *IRR* model. Whereas *NPV* is theoretically superior, the *IRR* enjoys widespread use. Both models are designed to determine whether the proposed project adds to or subtracts from the value of the firm. Unlike the

NPV model, however, which measures the change in firm value in dollars, the *IRR* measures the prospective return of the project to the firm.

In many circumstances, the two models lead us to the same conclusion—either to accept or reject the project—so it would not matter which model is used. An argument for using the *IRR* is that most financial managers prefer to speak of projects in terms of rate of return, not in terms of dollar values. A counterargument would recommend *NPV* because it measures the change in wealth as a result of undertaking the project.

The important distinctions between the two models arise when they lead to different decisions. In some circumstances, shortcomings inherent in the *IRR* model will direct the financial manager to accept a project that should be rejected, or to incorrectly rank one project as better than another. Thus, extra care must be taken when using the *IRR* in capital budgeting.

Accept-or-Reject Projects Versus Ranking Projects

accept-or-reject projects (independent projects) Projects whose accept-or-reject decision can be made without affecting other projects.

ranking projects (mutually exclusive projects) Projects whose accept-or-reject decision affects other decisions.

In order to clarify the reasons for preferring *NPV,* we begin by drawing a distinction between two types of decisions that might be made. **Accept-or-reject projects** represent decisions that can be made without affecting other projects. These are also known as **independent projects. Ranking projects** or **mutually exclusive projects** represent decisions that cannot be made in isolation because they affect other decisions. Projects are mutually exclusive if acceptance of one would preclude acceptance of the other. Whereas both the *NPV* model and the *IRR* model have no problems with accept–reject decisions, only *NPV* ranks mutually exclusive projects correctly.

Example 5.7 For marketing reasons Univers Studios might reason that producing the comedy film under consideration excludes the production of all other comedy projects for at least 6 months. They might only have enough directors, writers, actors, or facilities for one comedy project. Univers, therefore, cannot simply accept or reject each comedy movie; rather, they would have to decide on which comedy movie is best to produce. This will necessitate a ranking of movie projects because their mutually exclusive nature precludes the acceptance of more than one project.

Let us suppose Univers narrows its choice to two comedy movie projects, referred to as Movie Project One and Movie Project Two. Both are 3-year projects, and both require a rate of return of 12 percent. The two projects, however, have different cash flows streams. Movie Project One has an initial investment of $25 million and cash flows that decrease through time. Movie Project Two has an initial investment of $5 million and level cash flows. The cash flows of the respective projects are given in Table 5.5, along with their *NPV*s, *IRR*s, and *PI*s.

Movie Project One has a higher *NPV*; thus, the acceptance of One over Two results in a greater increase in firm value. Movie Project Two, however, has a higher *IRR*; thus, the acceptance of Two over One results in a greater percentage rate of return on the money invested. Of the two, shareholders should prefer Movie Project One because it results in a higher level of shareholder wealth. Movie Project Two might allow for higher bragging rights ("My rate of return beat yours"), but Project One puts more wealth in the shareholders' pockets.

The conflict results from the fact that *NPV* measures dollar gains, whereas *IRR* measures percentage returns. As a percentage, the *IRR* rule can produce more dramatic numbers for projects of smaller investments ($5 million vs. $25 million) and for projects with short time lengths. The *NPV* rule, which is a measure of the change in shareholder wealth as a result of accepting a project, does not suffer from these shortcomings; thus, it can correctly rank mutually exclusive projects.

The preceding conflict is known as the *scale problem.* The *IRR* model ignores the scale of the project. In other words, it correctly measures a rate of return, but is biased toward short-term, small-investment projects.

Scale can be exemplified as follows. Which is better, an investment that costs $1.00 today and pays back $1.25 in 6 months, or an investment that costs $100 today and pays $120 in a year? The *IRR* of the first project is 56.25 percent, whereas the *IRR* of the second project is 20 percent. The *IRR* method ranks the first project ahead of the second.

IRR, however, ignores scale differentials. Using a discount rate of 10.25 percent, the *NPV* of the first investment is $0.19, and the *NPV* of the second investment is $8.84. The *NPV* method recognizes that the first project's return is for a shorter time period and is based on such a small investment that there is little net benefit. Whereas these examples give the appearance that scale differences are easy to spot, in practice it can be difficult because scale is determined by both the magnitude and timing of the cash flows.

The profitability index also suffers from scale problems. Table 5.5 computes the profitability index of Movie Projects One and Two. Because the *PI* is also a ratio or percentage, *PI* can rank mutually exclusive projects incorrectly. Under the *PI* rule, Movie Project Two, with a *PI* of 1.201, is preferred over Movie Project One, with a *PI* of 1.082. Project Two has a higher net benefit expressed as a percentage of cost, but a lower *NPV.* The correct decision is to choose Movie Project One, which has the higher *NPV* project.

TABLE 5.5 Two Mutually Exclusive Movie Projects (all values in millions)

	Today	*Year 1*	*Year 2*	*Year 3*
Movie Project One	−$25	+$15.0	+$10.0	+$ 8.0
Movie Project Two	−$ 5	+$ 2.5	+$ 2.5	+$ 2.5

Capital Budgeting Models

Project	*NPV*	*IRR*	*PI*
One	$2.059	17.33%	1.082
Two	$1.005	23.33%	1.201

Methods exist to help the *IRR* and the *PI* rank mutually exclusive projects correctly. For example, a procedure known as computing the *IRR* of the incremental investment—a method of focusing on the marginal effects between two projects instead of analyzing the projects separately—will correct this shortcoming. The technique of incremental investment will be demonstrated in detail in Chapter 7.

In summary, situations exist when projects, judged individually to be acceptable, must be rank-ordered and must compete against each other. These are called *mutually exclusive projects.* In these cases, *NPV* will more accurately rank the projects and is preferred to the *IRR* and to the *PI.*

Capital Rationing

There is another reason that projects might need to be ranked. It is sometimes claimed that a firm cannot or should not accept all projects with positive *NPV*s. The explanation is that the firm has a shortage of capital to fund projects, caused either by an unwillingness of investors or lenders to provide additional capital or by an internal decision that the firm must limit growth. This is known as **capital rationing.**

capital rationing
A shortage of investment capital caused either by an unwillingness of external entities to provide additional capital or by an internal decision that the firm must limit growth.

Neither argument is persuasive when one considers the definition of *NPV.* The *NPV* of a decision should include all benefits and costs. If someone attempts to argue that a positive *NPV* project should be rejected, then what is really being said is that some costs were not included in the computation of the *NPV,* such as the costs associated with rapid growth. Remember, however, that an *NPV* analysis should include all costs and benefits.

For example, a firm might decide to spend only $25 million on new projects even if it means that positive *NPV* projects will be rejected. This usually means that management believes that investment beyond $25 million would strain the firm's ability to manage the investments correctly. Thus, there is a hidden cost in too much investment inasmuch as management's time will become stretched out over so many projects that all will not perform as well as planned. When the cost of too rapid growth is included in the analysis, management believes that projects bringing total investments to more than $25 million will have greater costs than benefits.

Modernists believe that even these costs should be estimated and inserted into the *NPV* analysis. Management can only be assured that they are maximizing shareholder wealth when all benefits and costs are included.

Nevertheless, practically speaking, projects are sometimes ranked and selected from best to next best, and so forth, until the capital runs out. In this case, ranking becomes especially important. We can expect conflicts in ranks between the *NPV* and the *IRR* rule if the time patterns of cash flows from the projects differ greatly or if the amounts or size of the capital investments are significantly different, or both. Once again, the source of the conflict rests with the *IRR* rule's inability to handle scale differences. *NPV*, accordingly, is the method of choice.

NPV Versus *IRR* for Nonstandard Projects

standard project
A project whose cash flow stream begins with one or more cash outflows and is followed only by cash inflows.

A final instance in which *NPV* demonstrates its superiority to *IRR* is the case of nonstandard projects. In this text we define a **standard project** as one that begins with one or more cash outflows and is followed only by cash inflows. For example, many projects involve the immediate purchase of assets followed by years of net benefits. Nonstandard projects are defined as all other projects.

borrowing project
A project whose cash flow stream begins with a cash inflow and is then followed by cash outflows.

multiple sign-change project
A project whose cash flow stream switches through time from inflows to outflows or outflows to inflows more than once.

There are two kinds of nonstandard projects: borrowing projects and multiple sign change projects. A **borrowing project** is a nonstandard project because it begins with a cash inflow and is followed by cash outflows. A **multiple sign-change project** is a project that switches through time from inflows to outflows or outflows to inflows more than once. The differences between standard and nonstandard projects are illustrated in Figure 5.2.

Distinguishing between standard and nonstandard projects facilitates a highly simplified comparison of *NPV* and *IRR*. While both methods work fine for standard projects, only NPV gives consistently correct answers for nonstandard projects. In fact, it is in the case of nonstandard projects that *NPV* demonstrates its clearest superiority over *IRR*.

Borrowing Projects As we said, borrowing projects are represented by a cash inflow followed by cash outflows. We call these projects *borrowing projects* because they are the opposite of investment. For example, a firm may decide to sell a portion of its manufacturing process and switch to buying the output from external sources. Proceeds of the sale will bring cash into the firm immediately, but the greater cost of purchasing rather than making will result in subsequent cash outflows.

NPV may be used and interpreted as before; however, *IRR* must be interpreted differently. In borrowing projects, a high *IRR* is bad rather than good because the *IRR* is revealing the cost of borrowing rather than the return on investment. In fact, for borrowing projects, the *IRR* decision rule is reversed: Acceptable projects are those whose *IRR* is less than the required

FIGURE 5.2 Standard Versus Nonstandard

	Time Period					
Type of Project	0	1	2	3	4	5
Standard	−	+	+	+	+	+
Nonstandard						
Borrowing	+	−	−	−	−	−
Multiple sign change	−	+	+	−	−	+

The + sign indicates a cash inflow, and the − sign indicates a cash outflow.

rate of return. *IRR* users must search for low *IRR*s when evaluating borrowing projects.

Example 5.8 Consider The Veggie Market Cafe (VMC), whose specialty is carrot cake. VMC has decided to sell its carrot shredder and to purchase its carrots preshredded. Because carrot shredders are in demand, the VMC can sell the machine for \$15,000. The firm, however, estimates that it must now pay an extra \$5,000 per year for preshredded carrots. If the VMC's carrot shredder was expected to last for 5 years, should they sell the shredder? Assume that there are no other relevant costs or benefits (the machine has no remaining value if they keep it for 5 years because it will be worn out), and that the required rate of return for the VMC is 10 percent.

The *NPV* and *IRR* of the decision to sell the shredder are provided in Table 5.6. The *NPV* is negative, directing the VMC to reject the project and to continue to shred its carrots. However, because the *IRR* is greater than the required rate of return, VMC might be tempted to accept the project. This is the wrong decision! For borrowing projects, the *IRR* decision rule is the reverse of the normal *IRR* rule—accept projects whose *IRR* is less than the required rate of return. Applying the corrected *IRR* rule for borrowing projects would lead to rejection of the project, the same decision reached by *NPV.*

Multiple Sign-Change Projects The second problem—multiple sign changes—is more troublesome. Whenever there is more than one sign change in the cash flow stream, more than one *IRR* may exist. In other words, there are probably two or more answers that can be found using the *IRR* formula. In fact, the number of possible *IRR*s will be equal to the number of sign changes. This result accords with Descartes "rule of signs" (e.g., there can be as many different solutions to a polynomial expression as there are changes in signs).

There is no problem with using *NPV* for multiple sign-change cash flow streams, but the *IRR* method becomes difficult to apply. When more than one *IRR* is calculated, which *IRR* should be used? There is no way for the *IRR* model to overcome this particular shortcoming.

TABLE 5.6 NPV *and* IRR *for Borrowing Projects*

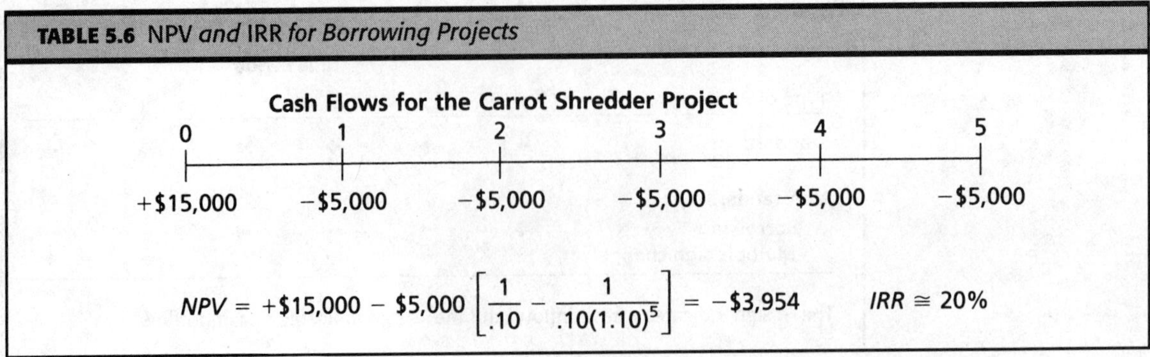

Cash Flows for the Carrot Shredder Project

0	1	2	3	4	5
+\$15,000	−\$5,000	−\$5,000	−\$5,000	−\$5,000	−\$5,000

$$NPV = +\$15{,}000 - \$5{,}000\left[\frac{1}{.10} - \frac{1}{.10(1.10)^5}\right] = -\$3{,}954 \qquad IRR \cong 20\%$$

Example 5.9 ________ Belchertown Waste Company is developing a temporary site for trash disposal. The landfill, which requires a \$5,000 investment to open, is expected to operate for 2 years and generate cash inflows of \$11,500 per year. In the second year the firm must spend \$18,050 to cap the landfill. The project's specific cash flows are given below:

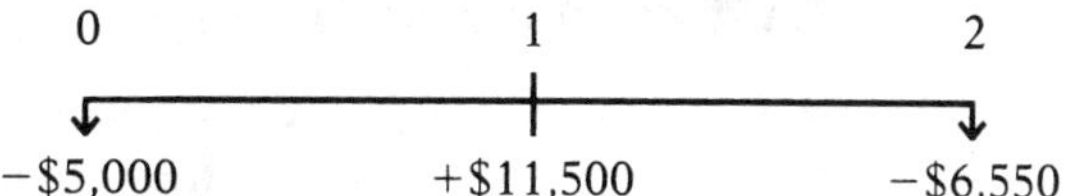

This project changes signs twice, once from negative to positive, and another from positive to negative. The two *IRR*s are 3.82 percent and 26.2 percent.

Both 3.82 percent and 26.2 percent satisfy our definition of the *IRR* because they produce an *NPV* of zero. Should Belchertown accept this project on the basis of the high *IRR* or reject it on the basis of the low *IRR?* In this case the *IRR* decision rule would not allow the financial manager to make an accept–reject decision.

The *NPV* profile for the Belchertown Waste Company is provided in Figure 5.3. This *NPV* profile looks very different from the one shown earlier. Note that the line crosses the horizontal axis twice, defining two different *IRR*s. The *NPV* method produces no such dilemma. Using 15 percent as a required rate of return, the *NPV* of the landfill project is +\$47.26 and the project is accepted.

FIGURE 5.3 NPV Profile for Belchertown Waste

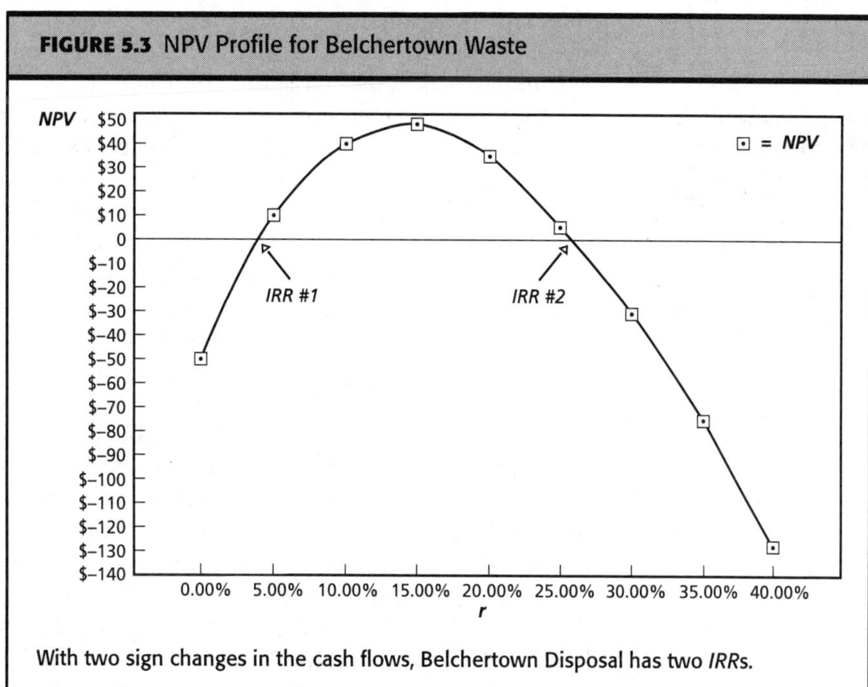

With two sign changes in the cash flows, Belchertown Disposal has two *IRR*s.

In summary, nonstandard projects provide rather strong reasons to prefer *NPV* over *IRR*. Although it is sometimes possible to correct for *IRR*'s shortcomings, the *NPV* method is preferred.

Estimating the Required Rate of Return— An Advantage to the *IRR?*

Although we have argued for *NPV* over *IRR,* little has been said concerning the difficulty of estimating the required rate of return, a key variable in *NPV* analysis. Because the *IRR* model needs only the cash flows and produces a discount rate, does this give an advantage to the *IRR?*

At first glance the answer appears to be *yes.* In reality, however, both models have the same demands because a decision for the *IRR* necessitates the required rate of return for comparison. This comparison rate—often referred to as the benchmark or **hurdle rate**—is the same rate used by *NPV* to discount cash flows. Because both methods need the required rate of return, the fact that this variable is difficult to estimate does not give one model an advantage over the other, but instead presents a challenge to both models.

hurdle rate
The required rate of return, or the interest rate used in the net present value model to discount future cash flows. It can also be used to determine that good projects are those whose internal rate of return is greater than, or hurdles over, the required rate of return.

Project Selection and the Required Rate of Return

A true conflict exists within the finance discipline in the debate over how the required rate of return should be measured. The answer of modern finance is that the required rate of return should be derived from the market and should reflect the rate of return investors in the market would require to invest in the project or an asset of equivalent risk.

weighted average cost of capital (WACC)
An attempt to measure the rate of return required by the firm to satisfy its sources of capital.

Traditional finance proposes an alternative: the **weighted average cost of capital (WACC).** In a nutshell, the *WACC* is an attempt to measure the rate of return that is required by the firm to satisfy its sources of capital. The *WACC* is discussed in detail and computed in Window 5.1. The logic is that any project that is accepted must be expected to be able to pay for the firm's cost of capital. If a project's *IRR* exceeds the *WACC,* then traditionalists reason that it must be good for the firm because it will be more than able to meet the capital expenses the firm now faces.

Although the weighted average cost of capital is intuitively appealing, closer inspection reveals its weakness. The equity and debt costs represent the rates required to be earned by the firm's shareholders and bondholders (i.e., by the firm's capital suppliers) on the firm's currently owned assets. In reality, most firms consist of a large mix of projects (e.g., can you think of a one-asset firm?). The *WACC* is therefore appropriate only for firms whose proposed projects are identical in risk to the existing firm's assets such that the required rate of return is the same for each. If the proposed project(s) do(es) not have identical risk with existing assets, then shareholders and bondholders will naturally revise their required rates of return, and the weighted average cost of capital will no longer be appropriate.

WINDOW 5.1

The Weighted Average Cost of Capital

The purpose of this window is to discuss the issues involved in using the weighted average cost of capital as the required rate of return in capital budgeting analysis. The view of modern finance is that the discount rate should be derived directly from the market. The view of traditional finance is that the cost of capital concept should be used.

The weighted average cost of capital is the cost of the firm's overall financing. In the case of an all-equity firm this would be the return that the firm's shareholders expect to earn on the common stock investment. (This number is often generated using one of the common stock models of Chapter 4.) If the firm has other securities, such as debt, then the cost of capital would be a weighted average of the costs of all the firm's securities. This is known as the *weighted average cost of capital.*

The weighted average cost of capital is a broad concept that covers a variety of ways to compute the costs of each type of security (their expected return) as well as a variety of ways of computing the weights. For instance, although costs were defined earlier as market-expected returns, some prefer using accounting numbers that measure the original return the market expected back when the securities were issued. There is also a debate as to the percentages that should be used to weight each security in the weighted average cost of capital. Some people advocate using accounting "book" values, some advocate target values that the firm strives toward, some advocate weights that seem to correspond to the project being analyzed, but most advocate the use of weights based upon current market values. In other words, the weight of each security type is found by dividing the total market value of that security by the total market value of the firm.

The most popular weighted average cost of capital approach taught in traditional corporate finance accordingly is the use of market returns on each type of security weighted by market proportions. For example, consider a firm whose assets are financed by both debt and equity in the ratio of 75 percent equity and 25 percent debt. The firm's cost of equity—the rate required to be earned by the firm's shareholders—is 20 percent. The firm's cost of debt—the rate of return required to be earned by the firm's bondholders—is 15 percent. The firm's overall cost of capital, or the *WACC,* would be*:

$$\begin{aligned} WACC &= [\%\text{ in Equity} \times \text{Cost of Equity}] + [\%\text{ in Debt} \times \text{Cost of Debt}] \quad (5.5) \\ &= [.75 \times .20] + [.25 \times .15] = .1875, \text{ or } 18.75\% \end{aligned}$$

Regardless of which costs and weights are used, the objective is the same. The user is attempting to calculate an overall cost of the capital to a firm and then to apply this cost to new projects.

The logic of computing and using the weighted average cost of capital (*WACC*) is that it measures how much the firm is paying for its capital. It would therefore appear

*The cost of debt may be stated in an after tax basis by multiplying the second bracketed expression in Equation (5.5) by (1 − Tax Rate). This modification recognizes that interest expense is tax deductible at the firm level; thus, the cost to the firm gets reduced to reflect the tax savings. A full discussion on tax savings from debt financing is in Chapter 12.

WINDOW 5.1 *(continued)*

that a firm that accepts a project whose return is greater than its *WACC* is making a correct investment decision because the new project is estimated to pay a higher return than is currently being earned by the firm. It would also appear that a firm that rejects a project whose return is smaller than its *WACC* is making a correct investment decision.

Appearances can be deceiving, however, especially when risk enters the picture. Differences in risks between projects can make it beneficial for a firm to accept a project whose return is less than its *WACC* and reject a project whose return is greater than its *WACC*. For now, we ask you to think of the required rate of return as a market rate, observed and/or measured in a financial market.

The problem of the *WACC* can be better seen in a standard example. It is possible to view a new car as costing, say, \$8 per pound. In other words, we can compute an average cost by taking the total cost of a particular car and dividing it by its weight in pounds. The *WACC* for a firm likewise measures an average cost of capital for the whole firm.

Serious mistakes can be made, however, when an average cost is applied to each component. For example, a car's stereo might be worth far more than \$8 per pound, whereas the oil and gas in it are worth far less than \$8 per pound. In fact, it does not make sense to use \$8 per pound to measure the value of any component in the car.

A firm with a *WACC* of 15 percent likewise should not automatically assume that all of its existing assets or any proposed investments have a required rate of return of 15 percent. It is logical to assume that some of the riskiest assets would have a higher rate of return and some of the safest assets would have a lower rate of return.

Summary

- The capital budgeting decision—the decision to invest in real assets or projects—represents the single most important decision in meeting the firm's objective of shareholder wealth maximization.
- In highly competitive markets, the price of an asset should equal its present value such that the benefits of investment equal its cost. This is the natural result of competition in which any potential for abnormal profits is competed away.
- Some real asset markets are not highly competitive because many projects are available to only a limited number of firms. It is this potential lack of competition for certain projects in terms of real assets that creates the possibility that a project can significantly increase (or decrease) shareholder wealth.
- Net present value, or *NPV*, is the present value of future cash benefits minus the initial investment or cost:

$$NPV = PV \text{ of Benefits} - PV \text{ of Costs}$$

NPV measures the change in the firm's total asset value as a result of undertaking a project. A positive *NPV* adds value to the firm and thus represents an acceptable project. A negative *NPV* subtracts value from the firm and thus represents an unacceptable project. An *NPV* of zero leaves value unchanged; therefore, it does not matter whether it is accepted or not.

- The internal rate of return (*IRR*) is the discount rate that equates the present value of the costs to the present value of the benefits, in other words the discount rate that sets *NPV* to zero:

$$C_0 + \frac{CF_1}{(1 + IRR)^1} + \frac{CF_2}{(1 + IRR)^2} + \frac{CF_3}{(1 + IRR)^3} + \cdots + \frac{CF_n}{(1 + IRR)^n} = 0$$

Projects with *IRR*s that exceed the required rate of return will add value to the firm and thus are acceptable. Projects with *IRR*s below the required rate of return will subtract value from the firm and thus are unacceptable. If the *IRR* equals the required rate of return, then its acceptance or rejection is irrelevant.

- Both *NPV* and *IRR* work fine for projects with an immediate cash outflow followed only by cash inflows (standard projects) that are also independent projects whose accept–reject decision will not affect other projects. For nonstandard projects or projects requiring ranking, however, the two methods can produce different decisions. Because the *IRR* method has inherent shortcomings that must be overcome to make correct decisions, it is suggested that the *NPV* method, which has no inherent shortcomings, be used in these cases.
- Other capital budgeting models do not apply a discounted cash flow approach. These include payback and the accounting rate of return. These models have serious weaknesses and should be used with extreme care.
- The required rate of return must be used either as an input in computing the *NPV* or as a benchmark with which to evaluate the *IRR*. The required rate of return should be estimated or observed in the financial marketplace on securities with risk similar to that of the project under consideration. An alternative to a market-determined required rate of return is the weighted average cost of capital (*WACC*), a measure of the average cost of capital to the firm. The *WACC* is inappropriate, however, when the project under consideration has a different level of risk than the average level of risk in the firm's existing assets.

Demonstration Problems

Problem 1

Mom and Pop Grocery Stores is considering the purchase of a frozen yogurt machine expected to produce the following cash flows:

C_0	C_1	C_2	C_3	C_4
−$5,000	+2,200	+2,800	+3,400	+1,000

In other words, the machine costs $5,000 today but is projected to produce cash inflows for the next 4 years as given. Using a required rate of return of 15 percent, compute the net present value, profitability index, and internal rate of return.

Solution to Problem 1

Net Present Value:

The *NPV* is found by substituting into Formula (5.2) with r = 15%. One method of solving the problem is to discount each of the four cash flows using the single cash flow present value techniques of Chapter 3, sum them, and then net out the project cost of $5,000.

Step 1:
Present Value of Year 1 Cash Flow of $2,200 = $1,913.04
Present Value of Year 2 Cash Flow of $2,800 = $2,117.20
Present Value of Year 3 Cash Flow of $3,400 = $2,235.56
Present Value of Year 4 Cash Flow of $1,000 = $ 571.75

Step 2:
Sum the preceding single cash flow present values: $6,837.55.

Step 3:
Net out the initial cost of $5,000 to compute the *NPV*:

NPV = +$6,837.55 – $5,000 = $1,837.55

Workshop 5.1 demonstrates a shortcut that significantly speeds up the process into a single step. The keystrokes are:

1000 / 1.15 = + 3400 = / 1.15 = + 2800 = / 1.15 = + 2200 = / 1.15 = – 5000 =,

which produces the same answer (rounded) of $1,837.55.

Profitability Index:

The *PI* is found as the absolute value (i.e., ignoring the negative sign) of the ratio between the answer to Step 2 and the project's initial cost of $5,000:

Profitability Index = $6,837.55 / $5,000.00 = 1.3675

Internal Rate of Return:

The *IRR* is found using trial and error search. The objective is to find the discount rate that produces an *NPV* of $0.
Step 1: Compute the *NPV* of the project at some initial value of the discount rate. Because we have already computed the *NPV* using a discount of 15% as $1,837.55, we will use this as the initial "guess."
Step 2: Use the result of Step 3 from the net present value to formulate an educated guess as to the next value to use in the trial and error process. Because the *NPV* at 15% was positive, we should try a higher discount rate, say 20%. Computing the *NPV* formula as earlier (except using a discount rate of 20%) produces an *NPV* of $1,227.62. The process is repeated until a discount rate is found that produces an *NPV* of near zero.

For example, because raising the discount rate from 15 to 20% only lowered the *NPV* from $1,837.55 to $1,227.62, our next guess should raise the discount rate about twice more than the initial raise from 15 to 20%. Trying a discount rate of 30% produces an *NPV* of $246.81.

Because the *NPV* is still positive, the next trial should use an even higher discount rate. Because the last trial (using a discount rate 10% higher) lowered the *NPV* by about $1,000, a reasonable estimate would be 33%. A discount rate of 33% produces an *NPV* of only $1.82. Thus, the *IRR* is approximately 33%.

Final Solution: All three techniques indicate that the frozen yogurt machine should be purchased.

Problem 2

Compute the weighted average cost of capital of Superstores Inc. The firm is worth $100 million with $60 million of equity and the remainder as debt. The common stock has a dividend yield of 5% (based upon next year's dividend) and a growth rate of 10%. The cost (yield) of the firm's debt is 12%. Find the weighted average cost of capital.

Solution to Problem 2

The weighted average cost of capital, *WACC*, is found using the formula from Window 5.1:

$$WACC = [\text{\% in Equity} \times \text{Cost of Equity}] + [\text{\% in Debt} \times \text{Cost of Debt}]$$

Step 1: The first step is to compute the percentages of equity and debt in the firm, often referred to as the weights. These are sometimes given directly. In our example, the weights are found by dividing the amount of the equity by the total value of the firm:

$$\text{\%in Equity} = \text{Equity Value / Total Firm Value}$$

$$\text{\%in Equity} = \$60\text{ M} / \$100\text{ M} = 60\%$$

The percentage in debt forms the remainder of 40% because they must sum to 100%.

Step 2: The second step is to compute the costs of the equity and debt. The equity cost is found in this problem using the tools presented in Chapter 4 and the constant growth perpetuity model. To be specific, the rate of return on common stock formula in Formula (4.9) shows that the required rate of return on (cost of) equity is the sum of the dividend yield (using next year's dividend) and the annual growth rate.

$$\text{Cost of Equity} = \text{Next Year's Dividend Yield} + \text{Annual Growth Rate}$$

$$\text{Cost of Equity} = 5\% + 10\%$$

$$\text{Cost of Equity} = 15\%$$

Although this problem gave the cost of debt, another problem could ask the student to compute the bond's yield to maturity using the tools presented in Chapter 4.

Step 3: The final step multiplies each weight from Step 1 times each cost from Step 2 and then sums them:

$$WACC = [60\% \times 15\%] + [40\% \times 12\%]$$

$$WACC = 9.0\% + 4.8\% = 13.8\%$$

Final Solution: The *WACC* is 13.8%.

Review Questions

1. Why are investments whose potential worth is higher than their cost more likely to be found in the market for real assets than in the market for financial assets?
2. Explain the evaluation of an investment decision using the concepts of costs and benefits.
3. Explain the net present value (*NPV*) method of evaluating projects. What is its acceptance criterion?
4. Explain the profitability index (*PI*) method of evaluating projects. What is its acceptance criterion?
5. Explain the internal rate of return (*IRR*) method of evaluating projects. What is its acceptance criterion?
6. What is a *NPV* profile? What information does it portray?
7. Explain the difference between standard and nonstandard projects. Why is the *IRR* method troublesome for nonstandard projects?
8. Explain the difference between an accept-or-reject project and a ranking project. What would be the cause of conflicting rankings between the *NPV* method and the *IRR* method?
9. What is capital rationing? How does capital rationing affect a firm's choice of acceptable projects?
10. What are the principal disadvantages of the payback method? What (if any) are the principal advantages?
11. What are the principal disadvantages of the accounting rate of return method? What (if any) are the principal advantages?
12. What is the weighted average cost of capital? How does it compare with the project's discount rate?

Problems

1. Given the following cash flows, determine the net present value (*NPV*), profitability index (*PI*), internal rate of return (*IRR*), and payback for each of the following five projects (assume a discount rate of 10%):

Project	C_0	C_1	C_2	C_3
A	−\$100	\$ 0	\$ 0	\$145
B	−\$100	\$115	\$ 0	\$ 0
C	−\$100	\$230	−\$120	\$ 0
D	−\$ 45	\$ 20	\$ 20	\$ 20
E	−\$100	\$ 30	\$ 30	\$ 90

2. A ski manufacturer is planning to purchase \$500,000 of materials to produce a new line of skis. The skis will be ready for sale in 1 year. If the company can sell 10,000 sets for a net cash flow of \$57.50 a set, should the line be produced? Compute the *NPV* of the project using a required rate of return of 10%, and assume that the skis are produced for one period only.
3. A consultant claims that she can increase employee productivity when automated billing procedures are introduced at law firms. For a \$50,000 fee, the consultant states that firm cash flow, now at \$1.5 million per year, can be improved to

$1.53 million per year for 5 years. Determine the *NPV* of the decision to hire the consultant. Use a required rate of return of 9%.

4. A cookie company wants to expand its retail operations. Based on a preliminary study, 10 cookie stores are feasible in various parts of the country. Cash flows at each store are expected to be $150,000 in the first year and grow at 10% per year for the next 4 years. Each store requires an immediate investment of $500,000 to set up operations. Assuming a required rate of return of 8%, what is the *NPV* of each store?
5. A magazine publisher wants to launch a new magazine geared to college students. The start-up costs are $700,000, and expected cash flows are $200,000 for years 1–4, at which time the magazine project will end. The required rate of return is 7.5%. What is the profitability index for this project?
6. A real estate developer plans to construct and then rent a 15-unit office building. The construction costs are $600,000, and cash flows on all units will be $100,000 annually for 5 years, at which time the project will end, and the developer will be able to sell the building for $450,000. Calculate the profitability index for the office building using a required rate of return of 12%.
7. The research division of a large consumer electronics company has developed a prototype of a radio that management has decided to produce if the *IRR* exceeds 11%. Production costs in the current period will be $1,399,100. The radios will produce a cash flow of $500,000 a year for 4 years. Use the *IRR* rule to determine if the project is acceptable.
8. A manufacturer of backpacks plans to introduce a new line. Equipment and production costs total $7,272,727. The company expects a cash flow of $20 per backpack. Sales are estimated at 100,000 in the first year, and are then expected to grow by 10% in each of the following 3 years. Should the company produce the backpacks if the required rate of return is 12%?
9. An aquarium wants to construct an addition for large tropical fish that will cost $714,568 today and will be completed in three years. Beginning in the fourth year, cash flows will be $400,000 per year for three straight years. What is the internal rate of return on the addition? Should the addition be built if the required rate of return is 11%?
10. A clothing manufacturer anticipates that the market for a certain popular T-shirt will continue to be strong for a few more years. The manufacturer, accordingly, is considering the purchase of equipment that would generate $100,000 in cash flow starting in 1 year and continuing through year 3. The machine itself costs $250,000. Initial expenses also include a one-time fee of $710 for a machine maintenance contract and $7,000 for setup and labor. What is the project's *IRR?* Should the equipment be purchased if the required rate of return is 10%?
11. A real estate developer has just bought an undeveloped parcel of land for $200,000. Although the real estate market is currently slow, he expects that the property will be sold in 2 years. If improvements costing $15,330 are made now and the land is sold in 2 years for $275,000, what is its internal rate of return?
12. A small accounting firm is considering the purchase of a computer software package that would reduce the amount of time needed to prepare tax forms. The software costs $1,500. The firm estimates that it will save $750 per year if the software is used.
    - **a.** What is the payback on the computer package?
    - **b.** The firm may instead buy a more sophisticated computer package for $3,000. Assuming the same $750 annual savings is relevant, what is the payback on this package?

13. A citrus farmer intends to plant additional lemon or orange trees. The trees would require a $500,000 investment and the farmer can expect to get $250,000 per year in cash flow from the orange trees that would start in year 3. On the other hand, the farmer could invest the same amount on lemon trees, which would provide $125,000 per year in cash flow starting in year 2. What is the payback for purchase of the lemon trees and the orange trees?

14. An investment at a new trucking firm costs $1,600,000 and is expected to last 5 years. The investment represents assets that will be depreciated $400,000 per year during years 1–4. Revenues are expected to be $600,000 for the first year and $800,000 for each of the next 4 years. Cash expenses will be $150,000 for the first year and then rise to $300,000 per year for the next 4 years. What is the accounting rate of return?

15. A snack food manufacturer is planning to introduce three new products simultaneously. Investments and per-year cash flows are given for each:

	Initial Investment	*Cash Flow per Year*
A. Potato chips	$ 5 million	$1.60 million
B. Popcorn	$ 2 million	$0.75 million
C. Granola bars	$11 million	$3.25 million

Assuming that the cash flows will be received for 5 years, compute the *NPV* and the *IRR* (to the nearest integer value) for each project. Use a required rate of return of 10%. Rank-order each project from best to worst.

16. An arts foundation is considering two proposals that have been submitted by its members:

Proposal 1: Buy a library of animated film classics for $15 million. The collection has to be restored, at no additional cost, which will take 3 years. In 4 years, film cash flows are expected to be $6 million a year for five straight years.
Proposal 2: Buy modern oil paintings for $1 million and then lease them to museums for $100,000 per year starting in year 1 and continuing for 4 years. In year 5, the paintings would be sold for $2 million.
Compute the *NPV* and the *IRR* (to the nearest integer value) for each project. Use a required rate of return of 9 percent. Which proposal is better?

17. A restaurant makes its own pizza crust. With the rising cost of labor, however, the restaurant is investigating the possibility of buying the pizza crust instead of making it internally. The equipment (with a remaining life of 5 years) and remaining ingredients can be sold immediately for $20,000. The restaurant would spend $5,000 per year for the crusts for 5 straight years. Assuming that the payment is due at the end of the year and that the required rate of return is 15 percent, compute the *NPV* for the decision to buy the crust. Now compute the *IRR* for the same decision. What is your recommendation?

18. The manager of a ski resort is planning to open a second site. Demographic and general economic predictions are encouraging for the next 3 years, but look bleak thereafter. Initial costs are $500,000, and cash flows are expected to be $200,000 per year for the 3 years. For the fourth year, however, a net loss of $100,000 is projected. What is the *NPV* and *IRR* for the new ski resort? Use a required rate of return of 10%.

19. A computer manufacturer must calculate its cost of capital before deciding on the appropriate method for raising new funds. The company has 58% equity financing at a required rate of return on equity of 13.5%. The remaining 42% is in debt financing at a required rate of return of 8%. What is the firm's weighted average cost of capital?

20. As chief financial officer you must approve or reject projects based upon the company's traditional capital budgeting method: the IRR. Your financial analysts recently calculated the cash flows that would be produced by two projects suggested by the marketing department. Half of the marketing team favored one project and half favored the other project. The cash flow analysis indicated the following cash flows for each project, one called Peanut Butter and the other Chocolate:

	Cash Flows in:			
	Year 0	*Year 1*	*Year 2*	*Year 3*
Peanut Butter	−$3,000	$ 0	$1,000	$ 0
Chocolate	$ 0	+$9,053	$ 0	−$9,053

Both projects look pathetic. The Peanut Butter project actually has more dollar outflows than inflows. The Chocolate project does not begin for another year and has future inflows equal to outflows. Nevertheless, in order to evaluate the projects in terms of company policy, you compute the internal rate of return of each project. Sure enough, the internal rate of return of Peanut Butter is −42.265%. The internal rate of return of Chocolate is 0%. Because your company requires a rate of return of 15%, you send out the bad news that both projects are rejected.

Several days later the whole marketing department runs into your office with some startling news: In a seminar on working together, they learned the value of teamwork, and they suggest that the two projects be put together to form one great project. None of the revenues or expenses will change, so the combined project looks like this:

	Cash Flows in:			
	Year 0	*Year 1*	*Year 2*	*Year 3*
Combined project	−$3,000	+$9,053	+$1,000	−$9,053

When plugged into the computer, the project produces an internal rate of return of 20%. Because this internal rate of return exceeds the company-required rate of return, it looks like both projects can go ahead.

a. Verify that the internal rates of return have been computed correctly.

b. Find the net present value of each project and the combination using a discount rate of 15%.

c. Discuss what you would do, and why internal rate of return did or did not work.

Discussion Questions

1. Think of two successful firms, and ask yourself what gives these firms a competitive advantage. Do you think they will continue to be in business in 10 years? Why or why not?

2. Respond to the following statement:
   NPV sounds great, but our firm finds it difficult to implement, mostly because we have little idea what required rate of return to apply. For this reason, we prefer to use IRR.
3. Respond to the following statement:
   It is clear that modern finance thinks little of the payback method; but I can tell you this. Our firm has done quite well for 50 years relying on that rule, and we intend to continue using it for the next 50 years.
4. The first step in capital budgeting is to convert all advantages and disadvantages into cash flows. Consider the following project where:

   - acceptance of the project will increase the probability of a serious injury or death to an employee,
   - acceptance of the project will increase the probability of a serious injury or death to a customer, and
   - acceptance of the project will cause pollution.

   NPV has been criticized by some as omitting important factors in the analysis. Can NPV be used for the foregoing project? Why or why not?
5. Comment on the following statement: *NPV* is a terrible and shortsighted financial tool because it ignores the long-term impacts of the decision.
6. How much would you pay for an idea that was guaranteed to pay a risk-free internal rate of return of 100% per year?

CHAPTER 6

ESTIMATING PROJECT CASH FLOWS

Rush Ryan, a senior vice-president of the Orange Electronic Company, was about to make the biggest decision of his career. Rush has the authority to move ahead with a project that could earn the firm large gains in market share. Orange's project, called "Project Prose," is a VCR that understands spoken commands.

Project Prose is similar in design to other VCRs, with one exception—a voicebox. Users speak into the voicebox and the VCR responds. For instance, once the voice mechanism is activated, the VCR would ask specific questions about taping an upcoming program, such as the time to start recording, the time to end recording, and the channel to record. Users could verbally tell the VCR to tape multiple programs over multiple days, and the VCR would play back those instructions for verification.

Marketing research performed by Rush Ryan and his staff found that a surprisingly high percentage of VCR owners do not prerecord programs, due mostly to an inability to follow the taping directions. It was thought that Project Prose's main appeal would be its simplified programming procedures.

The idea of developing a talking VCR originated at the Orange Electronic Company years ago. The firm has been secretly exploring the technology and has put $8 million into research and development. If Rush decides to attempt to develop Project Prose, an additional investment of approximately $53 million will be required. This would represent the largest single investment project in Orange Electronics' 20-year history. The firm estimates that once development is complete, even if successful, the first generation of Project Prose VCRs will not be ready for 12 to 18 months.

The question before the new-product division is whether or not to accept the project. Given its significance, each of the managers in Rush Ryan's division wants to be sure that the capital budgeting analysis is done carefully and correctly. The firm will base its decision on the project's estimated net present value *(NPV)*. *NPV* is a capital budgeting model that compares the present value of the project's benefits to the present value of the project's costs:

$$NPV = C_0 + \frac{CV_1}{(1+r)^1} + \frac{CF_2}{(1+r)^2} + \frac{CF_3}{(1+r)^3} + \cdots + \frac{CF_n}{(1+r)^n}$$

where C_0 is the cash flow in the current time period and usually represents the initial investment, CF_1 through CF_n are the cash flows from periods one through *n,* and *r* is the shareholder's required rate of return on projects of similar risk. Positive-*NPV* projects increase shareholder wealth and should be accepted. Negative-*NPV* projects decrease shareholder wealth and should be rejected. Zero-*NPV* projects neither increase nor decrease shareholder wealth.

As Rush and his staff work through the final analysis for Project Prose, they know that the decision to estimate the amount and timing of the project's cash flows will help determine the future of the Orange Electronic Company.

This chapter discusses the process of estimating project cash flows. Recall the simplicity of using the *NPV* model in capital budgeting from Chapter 5. The initial investment was given by a single cash outflow (C_0), and all subsequent cash flows were labeled project inflows (CF_1 through CF_n). Applying *NPV* was reduced to simple arithmetic.

Chapter 5 did not discuss, however, the process of estimating the cash flows that serve as the inputs to the *NPV* model. For instance, think for a moment about the VCR project called Project Prose. Estimating its *NPV* will require the firm to: (1) estimate the probability that the technology can be successfully developed, (2) approximate the demand for this new and unique product over its life, (3) turn all relevant costs and benefits into cash flow estimates, (4) determine when the project should be terminated, and (5) estimate the project's terminal cash flow. We could, of course, continue to enumerate complicating factors, but this short list serves to illustrate the complexity of cash-flow estimation.

This chapter illustrates the estimation of cash flows and is organized into four sections. The first section discusses what constitutes cash flow and presents a model and an example of cash-flow estimation. The second estimates cash flow and *NPV* analysis for Project Prose. The third section discusses the effect of errors in cash flow estimation. The final section presents "what-if" or sensitivity analysis as a way of dealing with cash flow uncertainty.

Estimating Project Cash Flows

Project cash flow lies at the heart of sound *NPV* analysis. Whether *NPV* is positive, negative, or zero matters little if the model's inputs are not reliable estimates of costs and benefits. The old cliché "garbage in–garbage out" has direct application here.

The first task in estimating cash flow is to identify those costs and benefits that are relevant to the particular project. As a rule, only incremental cash flows should be counted.

Only incremental cash flows should be counted—that is, the cash flows that will occur only if the project is accepted.

The rule of counting only incremental cash flows seems trivial. Even seasoned project managers, however, include costs and benefits that are not relevant and/or omit costs and benefits that are relevant. The highlighted rule will force managers to make a judgment on each potential cost and benefit. The rest of this section will discuss how those judgments should be made.

Incremental Cash Flow Versus Accounting Profit

incremental cash flows Dollar expenditures or dollar receipts that are the direct result of a particular decision.

Incremental cash flows are dollar expenditures or dollar receipts that are the direct result of a particular decision. When determining whether or not an expenditure or receipt is incremental, ask the question: Would the expenditure have been made or the receipt have been realized if the project had not been undertaken? If the answer is no, then the expenditure or receipt is incremental and relevant and should be included as part of the analysis. We can also define incremental cash flow for multiple project firms as cash flow to the firm with the project minus cash flow to the firm without the project.

Cash flow is sometimes confused with accounting profit, even though they can be very different. In fact, it is possible for a project to offer accounting profits while at the same time decreasing shareholder wealth (i.e., having a negative *NPV*). On the other hand, projects can have low accounting profits while increasing shareholder wealth (i.e., having a positive *NPV*). The reason for these apparent inconsistencies is that **accounting profit** is a measure of performance based upon accounting rules, whereas shareholder wealth and *NPV* are measures of performance that are based upon cash flow.

accounting profit Financial performance based upon accounting rules.

Project cash flows in a particular year are measured by adding up the dollars brought into the firm as a result of the project, and subtracting out the dollars that leave the firm as a result of the project:

$$CF_t = (PI_t - PO_t), \tag{6.1}$$

where CF_t is the cash flow in time period t, PI_t is the sum of the project inflows in time period t, and PO_t is the sum of the project outflows in time period t.

Example 6.1 ________

Superstores, Inc., is considering adding video rental departments in their stores. Video rentals have been introduced successfully by other supermarket chains, and the management at Superstores believes videos would complement their product line. The cost of adding a video department, mostly in equipment and video purchases, is estimated at $250,000 per store, which will be incurred immediately. Because of required renovations in the stores, rentals are not expected to begin until 1 year later. The rental facilities are expected to become obsolete in 5 years and to have no market value at that time. Based on market research, per-store revenues are expected to be \$146,000 a year, and per-store expenses are expected to be \$46,000 a year. Applying Formula (6.1), project cash flow per store is represented as:

$$\text{Annual Project Cash Flow} = (\$146{,}000 - \$46{,}000) = \$100{,}000$$

and the stream of cash flows for the video rental project is:

Superstores' Video Rental Project: Projected Annual Cash

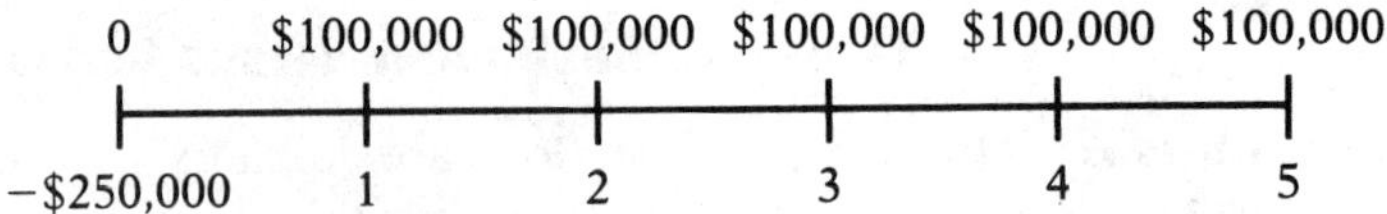

Cash Flow and Taxes

Formula (6.1) does not yet explicitly consider taxes. As discussed in Workshop 2.1, most major corporations, as legal entities, are subject to federal income taxes. Because most profitable corporations have taxable income that places them in the highest tax bracket, we assume that a tax rate such as 34 percent can be applied for all firms.

Let us begin by incorporating taxes into cash flow but by ignoring depreciation. The formula for cash flow after tax is:

$$CF_t = (PI_t - PO_t) - T_c(PI_t - PO_t),$$

where T_c stands for the corporate tax rate. Note that the amount of taxes paid (the second part of the formula) depends on the difference between project inflows and project outflows.[1] After-tax cash flow can be written more compactly by factoring out the common term $(PI_t - PO_t)$:

$$CF_t = (PI_t - PO_t)(1 - T_c) \tag{6.2}$$

Formula (6.2) shows that only a portion of project cash flow stays with the firm because the portion T_C leaves the firm in the form of taxes. The closer the tax rate, T_C, gets to 1.0 (100 percent), the smaller is the amount of project cash flow that stays with the firm.

[1]Formula (6.2) allows taxes to be positive or negative, depending on the difference between project inflows and project outflows. In our examples we will assume inflows greater than outflows such that taxes are always greater than zero. The U.S. corporate tax system has a negative tax feature, called *tax loss carryforwards,* that allows corporations to deduct from current year those income losses sustained in previous years.

Example 6.2

Return to Superstores' video rental project. The cash flows provided earlier were before tax. Given a tax rate of 34 percent, the annual after-tax cash flows from Formula (6.2) are:

$$CF_t = (\$146,000 - \$46,000)(1 - .34) = \$66,000$$

and the stream of cash flows is given on the following time line:

Superstores' Video Rental Project:
Projected Cash Flows After Tax

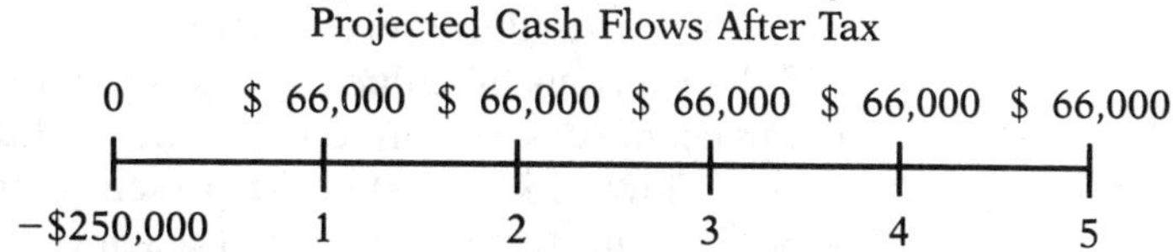

Depreciation (and Other Noncash Expenses) and Cash Flow

Earlier in the chapter we discussed the difference between accounting profit and cash flow. Accounting profits are sometimes difficult to measure and, compared with cash flow, appear to be more complicated. First, accountants usually treat sales as inflows whether or not the firm has received payment (i.e., whether or not the dollars have arrived at the firm), and they count certain expenses as outflows even if the firm has not yet paid for the expenditure (i.e., whether or not the dollars have left the firm). Second, accountants separate expenditures into two categories—expenses that can be expensed or deducted from revenues immediately, versus those that can be capitalized and deducted from revenues in increments through time. The term used to describe the accounting treatment of capital expenditures is **depreciation,** and different rules exist to determine how capital expenditures are to be depreciated.

depreciation
Reduction in the value of an asset.

Depreciation is an accounting number—the accountant's method of deducting an asset's book value through time. For example, Superstores, Inc., may determine that the $250,000 investment in the video rental project will be used up over 5 years, so we can generally think of the investment losing one fifth of its value cach year. A simple technique for depreciating the machine would be to subtract as depreciation one fifth of its original value of $250,000, or $50,000, per year. According to this simple technique, the accounting value of the machine would be $200,000 after 1 year, $150,000 after 2 years, and so on until the machine's value after 5 years would be zero. Other depreciation techniques will be considered later in the chapter.

Depreciation introduces a key difference between accounting profits and cash flow. In defining accounting profits, depreciation is treated as an expense throughout the life of the project. Using the simple depreciation method, annual revenues are reduced by the depreciation expense, $50,000, and per-year after-tax, profits are:

$$\text{Profit}_t = (\$146,000 - \$46,000 - \$50,000)(1 - .34) = \$33,000$$

The 5-year stream of after-tax profits is given on the following time line:

Superstores' Video Rental Project: Projected Accounting Profits After Tax

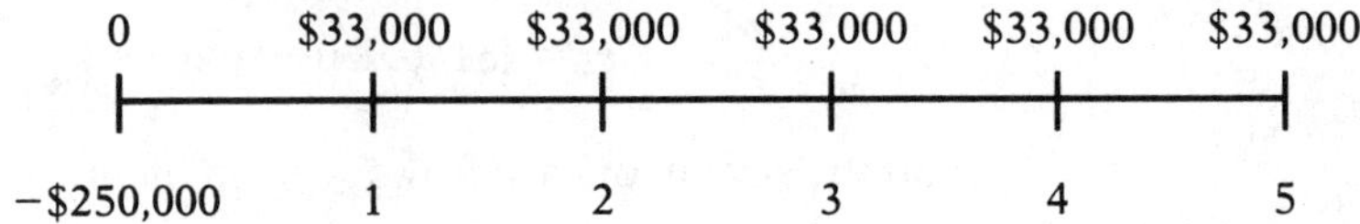

There are two differences between this time line of accounting profits and the previous time line of projected after-tax cash flows. First, the cost of the machinery is expensed over time, not deducted as an immediate lump sum outflow of $250,000 in the present time (time 0). Second, depreciation expense is subtracted from profits each year.

In contrast, cash flow analysis recognizes that depreciation is not an annual out-of-pocket expense because no money leaves the firm. Treating depreciation as a true expense would neglect the timing of the investment represented by the outflow in time zero. The issue is therefore one of timing and not of magnitude; cash flow recognizes the outflow when it occurs, whereas depreciation recognizes the outflow in increments through time.

There is one hitch. While not a true expense, depreciation is a determinant of cash flow. As an allowable business expense, depreciation reduces the firm's taxable income, and lower taxable income results in lower taxes paid. Depreciation therefore works to reduce taxes, which is a relevant cash outflow. The cash flow formula must be altered by incorporating depreciation's role in reducing taxes:

$$CF_t = (PI_t - PO_t) - T_c(PI_t - PO_t - D_t)$$

In the above formula, D_t is the amount of incremental depreciation expense caused by the project under consideration in period *t*. The formula demonstrates that depreciation reduces taxes and increases cash flow. We can also write this formula another way by factoring out common terms:

$$CF_t = (PI_t - PO_t - D_t)(1 - T_c) + D_t \tag{6.3}$$

Formula (6.3) can be factored to illustrate that depreciation is important only in that it reduces taxes.[2] Depreciation expense is removed from cash

[2]Another way to write the after-tax cash flow formula with depreciation is:

$$CF_t = (PI_t - PO_t)(1 - T_c) + T_c \times D_t \tag{6.3'}$$

This is sometimes called the "depreciation tax-shield" version of the cash flow formula because it treats depreciation solely as a shield against taxes. The depreciation tax shield is higher the higher the depreciation expense and the higher the tax rate. Formula (6.3') is algebraically equivalent to Formula (6.3).

flow in order to determine taxes owed, and is then added back to avoid double-counting the expenditure.

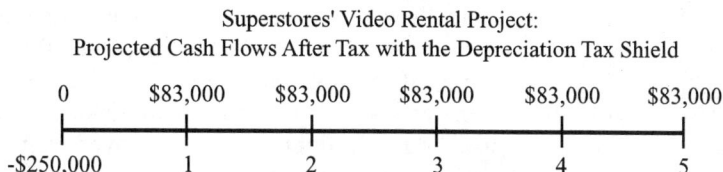

Example 6.3 For Superstores' video rental project, per-year after-tax cash flow including the depreciation tax shield is:

$$CF_t = (\$146{,}000 - \$46{,}000 - \$50{,}000)(1 - .34) + \$50{,}000 = \$83{,}000$$

and the stream of cash flows are given on the time following time line:

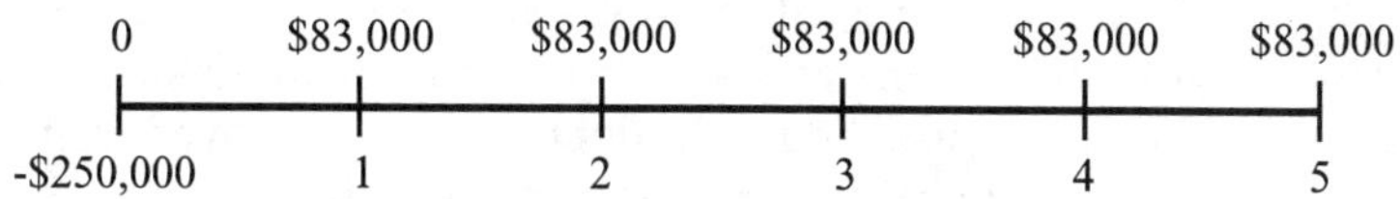

amortization
The reduction in the value of certain intangible assets.

depletion
The reduction in the value of certain assets, such as natural resources, as they are used.

Depreciation is not the only type of noncash expense. Other types include the **amortization** of the value of certain intangible assets (e.g., patents and licenses) over time, and the **depletion** of certain assets such as natural resources as they are used. Both amortization and depletion are similar determinants of cash flow because they act to reduce taxable income and subsequently increase cash flow. Accounting rules also provide for the advance recognition of certain revenues and expenses that have been agreed to but have not been completed. These accrued figures represent another difference between accounting numbers and cash flow. These issues, fortunately, can be addressed in a way similar to depreciation, but are beyond the scope of this chapter.

Sunk Costs and Cash Flow

sunk costs
Costs that have already been incurred and, as such, should not influence future behavior.

Did you ever hear the story of the gambler who spent his entire life trying to recover the $10 he lost on his first bet? The gambler was applying the empty logic that somehow the lost $10 should matter, whereas the correct way to view the lost $10 is as a sunk cost. **Sunk costs** are costs that have already been incurred and should not influence future behavior; accordingly, they should not be included as incremental cash flow.

For example, Superstores, Inc., may have spent $50,000 on market research to determine the feasibility of video rental facilities in their stores. Once those research and development costs have been incurred, they are irrelevant to future decisions and become sunk costs. Treating the $50,000 in research and development as relevant to the decision on whether to accept or reject the new project would be analogous to the gambler treating the $10 he lost in his first bet as relevant to subsequent bets.[3]

[3]For simplicity we are ignoring the tax consequences of decisions that expense previously capitalized sunk costs.

Project Side Effects and Cash Flow

project side effects Hidden but relevant costs or benefits that should be factored into cash flow.

Project side effects are hidden but relevant costs or benefits that should be factored into cash flow. Project side effects can be easily overlooked. An example of a relevant side effect was introduced in Chapter 5 under the heading capital rationing, where we discussed an often-overlooked cost related to excessive growth and the costs related to spreading management too thin. Firms that reject positive-*NPV* projects on the premise that capital needs to be rationed are implicitly incorporating these costs into the analysis.

Overlapping revenues are another example of a project side effect. This is especially important for firms with homogeneous product lines. For example, when introducing Lite Beer, the Miller Brewing Company reasoned that a portion of the revenue stream from the new "Lite" product would come at the expense of the revenues from its other beers. The amount of shared revenue should be identified and removed from the revenues of Lite Beer to determine incremental cash flow.

net working capital The difference between current assets and current liabilities.

Another relevant side effect is the additional investment in **net working capital,** or the difference between current assets and current liabilities. Examples of side effects related to working capital include additional investments in inventory, accounts receivable, and cash needed to support the project. These costs are typically incurred early in the project's life, with the full investment or some portion of this additional investment recovered when the project is terminated.

Summary of Cash Flow Estimation

Incremental cash flows are those costs that would not have been incurred, or those receipts that would not have been received, if the project had not been undertaken. Only incremental cash flows should be included in *NPV*. Applying this rule of thumb when estimating project cash flow will both assure that all relevant costs and benefits are included, and that costs and benefits not relevant to the project will be omitted. Once incremental costs and benefits have been identified, Formula (6.3) can be used to determine after-tax cash flow.

Estimating Cash Flow and *NPV* for Project Prose

initial investment phase The first phase of a capital budgeting analysis, which details the project's capital investment.

long-term cash flow phase The second phase of a capital budgeting analysis, which details the project's inflows and outflows throughout its life.

The chapter's opening section described the current situation at Orange Electronics: The firm is faced with an accept-or-reject decision on Project Prose, a VCR that understands spoken commands. Rush Ryan, a senior vice-president at Orange—along with his staff in the new project division—is now evaluating the project based on estimated cash flow and its projected *NPV*.

The analysis will be separated into three phases. The first phase, entitled the **initial investment phase,** takes into account the project's capital investment. An example of the format for cash flows that comprise the initial investment phase is shown in Panel A in Table 6.1. The second phase, called the **long-term cash flow phase,** considers the project's inflows and outflows

termination phase
The third phase of a capital budgeting analysis, which details the cash flows associated with the project's end.

salvage value
The value of a capital investment when the project is terminated.

throughout its life. An example of the format for cash flows that comprise the long-term cash flow stage is shown in Panel B in Table 6.1. Finally, the third phase, called the **termination phase,** takes into account cash flows associated with the project's end. One common type of terminal cash flow is the value of the capital investment when the project is terminated, known as **salvage value.** A format showing the types of cash flows that comprise the termination phase is shown in Panel C in Table 6.1.

The Initial Investment Phase

The decision to move forward with Project Prose will necessitate a significant investment over the next 12 months. These investments are listed in

TABLE 6.1 The Format for Cash Flow Analysis

Panel A: The Initial Investment Stage

	Year 0
1. Building renovations	______
2. Production equipment	______
3. Total plant costs (1 + 2)	______
4. Start-up costs	______
5. Working capital investment	______
6. Total initial investment (3 + 4 + 5)	______

Panel B: The Long-Term Cash Flow Stage

	Year 1	*Year 2*	. . . . .	*Year N*
7. Units sold	______	______		______
8. Price per unit	______	______		______
9. Project inflow (7 × 8)	______	______		______
10. Project outflow	______	______		______
11. Depreciation	______	______		______
12. Income before tax (9 − 10 − 11)	______	______		______
13. Taxes	______	______		______
14. Income after tax (12−13)	______	______		______
15. Depreciation	______	______		______
16. Net cash flow (14 + 15)	______	______		______

Panel C: The Terminal Cash Flow Stage

	Year N
17. Salvage value	______
18. Tax on sale	______
19. Net salvage value (17 − 18)	______
20. Recovery of working capital	______
21. Depreciation tax shield	______
22. Net terminal cash (19 + 20 + 21)	______

TABLE 6.2 The Initial Investment for Project Prose

	Year 0
1. Building renovations	$ 2,000,000
2. Product equipment	50,000,000
3. Total plant costs (1 + 2)	$52,000,000
4. Start-up costs	1,130,000
5. Working capital investment	7,500,000
6. Total initial investment (3 + 4 + 5)	$60,630,000

Table 6.2. It is anticipated that Project Prose will be housed in an idle building owned by Orange Electronics. Required renovations to the building include the installation of a new climate-control system and a newly designed layout of the production floor. It is estimated that these renovations will cost $2 million and will take approximately 6 months to 1 year to complete.

Once renovated, the building will be ready for production. The required investment will consist mostly of high-technology machinery, which is estimated to cost $50 million and will represent a significant portion of the project's required initial investment. Orange estimates that the first generation of Project Prose VCRs will be on store shelves within 12 months of the start of the project.

Finally, the initial investment includes *start-up costs,* which are defined as all other costs related to the project, and an investment in working capital. Start-up costs for Project Prose include employee and sales force training totaling an estimated $1.13 million.

The total initial investment for Project Prose, including building renovations, production equipment, training, and increases in working capital, totals $60.63 million.

The Long-Term Cash Flow Phase

The long-term cash flow phase illustrated in Table 6.1 is an expansion of Formula (6.3). The first generation of Project Prose VCRs is expected to be ready for sale within 12 months of the start of the project. It is expected that Project Prose will last 5 years, at which time the project will be terminated. These cash flows require substantial analysis. We start with depreciation.

Depreciating the Production Equipment The $50-million investment in equipment will be depreciated through time. As discussed earlier in the chapter, depreciation is a relevant noncash expense in that it provides a valuable tax shield to the firm.

depreciable base
The dollar amount of an asset that is depreciated through time.

In calculating depreciation, three decisions must be made: First, the firm must determine the investment's depreciable base. The **depreciable base** is the dollar amount of production equipment that is depreciated through time, and is usually the cost of the capital expenditure.[4] If the full amount of equipment is depreciated, the firm is estimating that the value of the equipment at the end of the project is zero. In other words, the depreciable base is the cost of the asset less its estimated salvage value. Second, the firm must determine the number of years it will take to depreciate the capital expenditure. This decision has been greatly simplified by a system known as the modified accelerated cost recovery system (MACRS). Detail on the MACRS will be given later. Third and finally, the firm must determine the timing of the depreciation. For instance, the firm can depreciate an equal amount each year, or an unequal amount, such that more depreciation is taken in the early years, and less depreciation is taken in the later years.

With these three decisions in mind, Orange Electronics has a number of alternatives in depreciating the VCR equipment. Given a depreciable base of $50 million, the firm can depreciate according to a *straight line depreciation schedule,* which depreciates in equal dollar amounts per year, or according to an *accelerated depreciation schedule,* which depreciates more of the investment in the early years and less of the investment in the later years.

The straight line method is the easiest to calculate:

$$\text{Straight Line Deprecation: } D_t = \frac{1}{n} \times \text{Depreciable Base} \tag{6.4}$$

where D_t is the depreciation in year *t,* and *n* is the life of the investment. Assuming an estimated useful life of 5 years for the video project, and a value of the investment in 5 years of zero, the straight line method produces depreciation per year of:

$$\text{Straight Line Depreciation: } D_t = \frac{1}{5} \times \text{ \$50 million} = \text{\$10 million}$$

Depreciating the equipment by $10 million per year for 5 years depreciates to a value of zero. To put this another way, the equipment is assumed to have no value at the end of the project.

A more attractive alternative to the firm would be to depreciate according to the **modified accelerated cost recovery system (MACRS),** developed to simplify the depreciation process for tax purposes. MACRS is adapted from the double-declining balance method of depreciation, which allows more rapid depreciation in the early years and less rapid depreciation in the later years. Because depreciation shields the firm's income from taxes, and because the shield is more valuable in early years due to the time value of money, MACRS provides a more favorable method of depreciation. Window 6.1 provides additional

modified accelerated cost recovery system (MACRS)
Accounting rules developed to simplify the depreciation process for tax purposes. MACRS is adapted from the double-declining balance method of depreciation, which allows more rapid depreciation in the early years and less rapid depreciation in later years.

[4]The depreciable base includes only the cost of equipment, and should not include expenses such as delivery and installation expenses. The depreciable base should also not include any tax credits such as the investment tax credit.

WINDOW 6.1

The MACRS Description Method

The Economic Recovery Act of 1981 defined methods of depreciation for federal income tax purposes. Because the system uses an accelerated method of depreciation, it was referred to as the *accelerated cost recovery system (ACRS)*. The Tax Reform Act of 1986 modified the ACRS and designed a new system called the *modified accelerated cost recovery system (MACRS)*.

Two objectives were accomplished by the depreciation methods given by ACRS and MACRS. First, they provided a standard by defining certain cost recovery periods rather than basing the depreciation schedule strictly on the asset's useful life. Second, the system allowed for more depreciation in the early years and less in the later years (i.e., allows for more rapid depreciation), a more valuable schedule given the time value of money. This was accomplished by allowing most machinery to be depreciated over 3–5 years. Five of the six recovery periods under MACRS are shown:

	Recovery Period				
Year	*3-Year*	*5-Year*	*7-Year*	*10-Year*	*15-Year*
1	33.33%	20.00%	14.29%	10.00%	5.00%
2	44.45%	32.00%	24.49%	18.00%	9.50%
3	14.81%	19.20%	17.49%	14.40%	8.55%
4	7.41%	11.52%	12.49%	11.52%	7.70%
5		11.52%	8.93%	9.22%	6.93%
6		5.76%	8.93%	7.37%	6.23%
7			8.93%	6.55%	5.90%
8			4.45%	6.55%	5.90%
9				6.55%	5.90%
10				6.55%	5.90%
11				3.29%	5.90%
12					5.90%
13					5.90%
14					5.90%
15					5.90%
16					2.99%

The particular recovery period is determined through the asset's useful life:

Useful Life of	*MACRS Recovery Period*
Less than 4 years	3 years
Between 4 and 10 years	5 years
Between 10 and 15 years	7 years
Between 16 and 20 years	10 years
Between 20 and 25 years	15 years
Greater than 25 years	20 years

WINDOW 6.1 *(continued)*

Note that, for example, the 5-year recovery period class gets depreciated over 6 years. This is due to the fact that one-half year's depreciation is recognized on all assets purchased during the year. Thus, for tax purposes, it is assumed that the asset is purchased halfway through the first year, such that a 5-year recovery system begins halfway into year 1 and lasts into year 6.

details on the MACRS. Project Prose, with an estimated life of 5 years, falls into the 5-year recovery period class. Table 6.3 shows the depreciation schedule that will be used for Project Prose.

Annual Cash Flow Estimates Table 6.4 derives cash flow estimates for Project Prose over its 5-year life. The numbers in the left margin pick up where Table 6.2 ends and follow the outline in Table 6.1. Net cash flow is computed using Formula (6.3):

$$CF_t = (PI_t - PO_t - D_t)(1 - T_c) + D_t$$

Project inflows are estimated by multiplying the number of units sold by the price per unit. For instance, it is estimated that Orange will sell 100,000 units in year 1 at a price of $500 per unit, defining cash inflows in year one of $50 million. Units sold are expected to change year to year because of market conditions. Orange estimates that sales will increase 20 percent in year 2 to 120,000 units, but due to competition (competitors are expected to respond with similar products in 2 years) will never go higher. Sales in year 3 are expected to remain at 120,000, but are then forecast to fall by 25 percent in year 4, and by an additional 33 percent in year 5.

It is expected that the price per unit will rise by 5 percent in year 2, but must then hold at that level in year 3. As demand weakens, Orange will have to cut the price per unit by 10 percent in year 4. Price per unit in year 5 is forecast to remain at its previous year's level. Project outflows include both

TABLE 6.3 Depreciating the $50-Million Investment in Project Prose

Year	*MACRS Factor*	*Depreciation (in millions)*
1	.2000	$50 × .2000 = $10.00
2	.3200	$50 × .3200 = $16.00
3	.1920	$50 × .1920 = $ 9.60
4	.1152	$50 × .1152 = $ 5.76
5	.1152	$50 × .1152 = $ 5.76
6	.0576	$50 × .0576 = $ 2.88

TABLE 6.4 Long-Term Cash Flows for Project Prose

	Year 1	*Year 2*	*Year 3*	*Year 4*	*Year 5*
7. Units sold	100,000	120,000	120,000	90,000	60,000
8. Price per unit	\$500	\$525	\$525	\$472.50	\$472.50
9. Project inflow (7 × 8)	50,000,000	63,000,000	63,000,000	42,525,000	28,351,418
10. Project outflow	30,000,000	35,200,000	35,200,000	27,010,000	21,340,567
11. Depreciation	10,000,000	16,000,000	9,600,000	5,760,000	5,760,000
12. Cash flow before tax (9 − 10 − 11)	10,000,000	11,800,000	18,200,000	9,755,000	1,251,851
13. Taxes (34 %)	3,400,000	4,012,000	6,188,000	3,316,700	425,289
14. Cash flow after tax (12 − 13)	6,600,000	7,788,000	12,012,000	6,438,300	825,562
15. Depreciation	10,000,000	16,000,000	9,600,000	5,760,000	5,760,000
16. Net cash flow (14+15)	16,600,000	23,788,000	21,612,000	12,198,300	6,585,562

fixed outlays, estimated at \$10 million per year, and variable costs, estimated to be 40 percent of total cash inflows. For example, estimated project outflows in year 1 are:

$$PO_1 = \$10{,}000{,}000 + .4(\$50{,}000{,}000) = \$30{,}000{,}000$$

Project outflows in years 2 through 5 are calculated in a similar way. Outflows fall as sales drop off, reflecting the variable costs of production. Taxes are levied at the rate of 34 percent.

The Terminal Cash Flow Phase

The final phase in estimating cash flow for Project Prose occurs in years 5 and 6. The terminal cash flows for Project Prose are given in Table 6.5. The numbers in the left margin pick up where Table 6.4 ends and follow the outline in Table 6.1.

Orange estimates that the machinery used for production can be sold on the market for 11 percent of its original value, or for \$5.5 million in year 6. The firm depreciated the equipment to a zero value. Thus, the book value of the machine at the end of year 5 is zero, while the market value of the machine is \$5.5 million. In cases such as these, the amount by which the selling price exceeds the terminal book value (\$0) represents a taxable gain to the firm. The \$5.5-million salvage value will net the firm \$3.63 million after tax.

The firm expects to recover a portion of its investment in working capital. It is estimated that the last of its inventory units can be sold to mail-order firms at a discount of 50 percent, or for \$3.75 million.

TABLE 6.5 Termination Cash Flows for Project Prose

	Year 5	*Year 6*
17. Salvage value		5,500,000
18. Tax on sale (34%)		1,870,000
19. Net salvage value (17–18)		3,630,000
20. Recovery of working capital	3,750,000	
21. Depreciation tax shield*		979,200
22. Net terminal cash flow (19 + 20 + 21)	3,750,000	4,609,200

*Depreciation tax shield = $ Depreciation × Tax Rate
= $2,880,000 × 0.34
= $ 979,200

Finally, Orange will depreciate the remaining 5.76 percent (see Table 6.3) of its equipment investment in year 6. Depreciation in year 6 will be used to offset a portion of the firm's income in that year.[5] Given a tax rate of 34 percent, the tax shield from depreciation in year 6 is:

$$\text{Depreciation Tax Shield in Year Six} = \$2{,}880{,}000 \times .34 = \$979{,}200$$

The terminal cash flows in years 5 and 6 are represented by the after-tax salvage value, the recovery of working capital, and the year-6 depreciation tax shield.

Total Project Cash Flows and *NPV*

Figure 6.1 summarizes the three cash flow phases by placing the project's net cash flows beneath a time line. These net cash flows will be used to estimate project *NPV.* Recall from Chapter 3, The Time Value of Money, that cash flows that occur through time cannot be added to or subtracted from each other. Our analysis of Project Prose has provided a cash outflow followed by six cash inflows. Because the cash flows occur in different time periods, they are different commodities that cannot be directly compared. To provide a meaningful comparison, the cash flows must be converted to some common time period, so we use the convention of transforming all cash flows to the present time. The initial investment will occur in year zero, and each of the six cash inflows must be pulled back or discounted to year zero.

Orange will use 10 percent as the project's discount rate or required rate of return. Table 6.6 computes the *NPV* for Project Prose.

[5]We are assuming that the equipment was depreciated during the first half of the year, and sold during the second half of the year.

FIGURE 6.1 A Cash Flow Time Line for Project Prose (cash flows in millions of dollars)

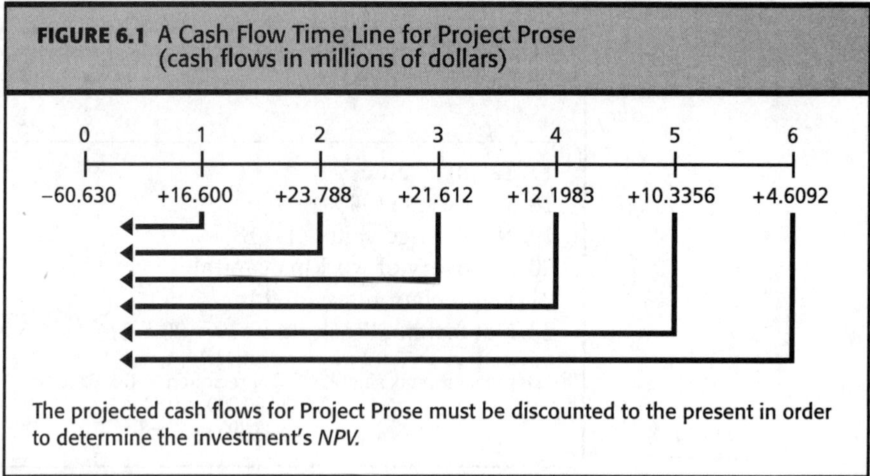

The projected cash flows for Project Prose must be discounted to the present in order to determine the investment's *NPV.*

The project's investment at time zero is $60,630,000, and the present value of the future cash flows, spanning years 1–6, is $68,337,000. Subtracting the present value of the estimated outflows from the present value of the estimated inflows defines *NPV:*

$$\text{Project Prose } NPV = -\$60{,}630{,}000 + \$68{,}337{,}000 = +\$7{,}707{,}000$$

Because the present value of benefits exceeds the present value of costs, the project has a positive *NPV* and is acceptable.

Has Everything Been Included?

Let us take a quick check of the cash flow analysis to make sure everything relevant has been included. We defined an incremental cash flow as any revenue source that would not have been received, or any cost that would not have been incurred, if the project were not undertaken. Our analysis was careful to include the obvious (investment in plant and equipment, fixed and variable expenses tied directly to the project, the revenue stream from sales, and salvage value) as well as the less obvious (start-up costs, tax benefits from depreciation, and additional investment in net working capital).

TABLE 6.6 *NPV* for Project Prose (*r* = 10%; cash flows in millions)

$$NPV = -\$60.630 + \frac{\$16.600}{(1.1)^1} + \frac{\$23.788}{(1.1)^2} + \frac{\$21.612}{(1.1)^3} + \frac{\$12.1983}{(1.1)^4} + \frac{\$10.3356}{(1.1)^5} + \frac{\$4.6092}{(1.1)^6}$$

$$NPV = -\$60.630 + \$15.091 + \$19.660 + \$16.234 + \$8.332 + \$6.4176 + \$2.6018$$

$$NPV = -\$60.630 + \$68.337$$

$$NPV = +\$7.707 \text{ million}$$

Rush Ryan calls his staff together to announce the good news of the positive *NPV.* At that time, however, a number of questions surface, the first concerning the facility to be used to house the production process. Whereas it is true that the building is owned by Orange and is currently vacant, someone recalls an offer made by the company across the street to rent out the space for storage. In fact, the company was to pay Orange $250,000 per year in rent for the use of the space. Would the lost rent not relate directly to the decision to accept Project Prose, and, if so, should the lost rent not be included as part of the cash flows of the project?

After some discussion, the consensus is that the forgone rent should be included into *NPV* as an opportunity cost. Because the rent payments are taxable to the firm, taxes at the rate of 34 percent must be subtracted. The after-tax amount of the lost rent payments is $165,000 ($250,000(1 − .34)). The present value of the five after-tax rent payments of $165,000 with an interest rate of 10 percent[6] can be determined through the annuity formula:

$$PVA = \$165{,}000\left[\frac{1}{.10} - \frac{1}{.10(1.1)^5}\right] = \$165{,}000\left[3.7908\right] = \$625{,}482.$$

The value today of the opportunity cost of lost rent payments is $625,482. This amount can be easily incorporated into project *NPV* because the annuity stream is in the form of a present value. The *NPV* adjusted for the inclusion of the opportunity cost of forgone rent is:

$$\text{Adjusted } NPV = \$7{,}707{,}000 - \$625{,}482 = \$7{,}081{,}518$$

Including this hidden cost does not change the decision, as *NPV* is still positive.

The second question raised by the staff concerns the customers of Project Prose. Will most customers be first-time VCR users who were waiting for the advent of a talking VCR, or will they be VCR users who would have purchased a new VCR even in the absence of Project Prose? If the former case is true, then the analysis does not change. If the latter case is true, then a relevant side effect has been introduced in the form of overlapping revenues, which will occur across the company's product line of VCRs.

A persuasive argument is made that Project Prose is so different from other VCRs on the market that most customers will purchase the product because of its uniqueness. This line of reasoning suggests that this potential side effect can be dismissed. The managers in the new-product division, however, understand that this issue is likely to become relevant in the future should Project Prose spawn new generations of talking VCRs.

---

[6]Using an interest rate of 10 percent to present-value the forgone rental payments assumes that the risk of renting out the space to another firm is the same as the risk of Project Prose. It is not a requirement that the two discount rates be the same. If the "rental" project is considered to be less risky than Project Prose, then a discount rate less than 10 percent is appropriate. If the rental project is considered more risky then a discount rate higher than 10 percent is appropriate. Remember, the discount rate reflects the return required on investments of similar risk.

Finally, someone on the staff mentions that the analysis has failed to consider the cost of researching and developing Project Prose. In fact, given that R & D expenditures totaled $8 million, the inclusion of these costs would reverse the accept-or-reject decision:

NPV Including R & D Expenditures: $7,081,518 − $8,000,000 = −$918,482

The $8 million in research and development is quickly dismissed as a sunk cost that should not be included in *NPV.* The R & D expenditures, which would have already been incurred regardless of the accept–reject decision of Project Prose, is not an incremental cost and therefore should not be part of cash flow.

At this point, Rush Ryan and his staff at Orange Electronics are satisfied that their cash flow analysis includes all relevant costs and benefits. It is the unanimous decision of the staff to recommend acceptance of the project to the board of directors at the next meeting. Rush is confident that the board will provide the final stamp of approval and that Project Prose will shortly become a reality.

Errors in Project Cash Flow Estimation

The first part of the chapter discussed what constitutes cash flow and presented a model of cash flow estimation. In this section, we will focus attention on the accuracy of cash flow estimates. Estimating incremental cash flows with values that are too high or too low will result in an inaccurate *NPV.*

The second part of the chapter provided estimates of project cash flows and *NPV* for Project Prose. As you recall, *NPV* is the change in shareholder wealth from undertaking a project. How confident, then, can the shareholders in the Orange Electronic Company be that the decision to produce a talking VCR will increase the value of their shares by $7,081,518?

The cash flows are estimates and are subject to error of a certain degree. Further, because Project Prose is a new product in the industry, the potential for error is greater.

When discussing the potential for errors in cash flow estimation, it is useful to differentiate between errors of two types: (1) managerial bias, and (2) misestimation, both of which will be discussed shortly.

Managerial Bias

managerial bias
The potential for managers to base their analysis on rosy or optimistic forecasts. Examples of managerial bias include high sales projections and/or low cost projections.

Managerial bias occurs when managers base their analysis on rosy or optimistic forecasts. Examples of managerial bias include high sales projections and/or low cost projections. Managerial bias will result in an *NPV* that is higher than would be expected under more realistic or unbiased cash flow estimates.

It is easy to see how managerial bias can come about. The time and effort spent by managers in developing a new project can create a situation in which managers wish to see their projects accepted. For instance, Rush Ryan of Orange Electronics has a personal stake in Project Prose. Because this project was developed by his staff, the project's success will in some part be his success as well. As this example illustrates, most projects suffer from some degree of managerial bias, the extent depending on the firm and the project being evaluated.

One way of eliminating or reducing managerial bias is to set up a system of checks and balances. For example, each new project may be subjected to questioning from outside or impartial managers. This would be similar to the questions concerning side effects raised by the staff in the new project division. One drawback with this approach is that impartial managers may lack the knowledge to ask the right questions.

Another way to remove or lessen managerial bias is to make arbitrary adjustments in order to project cash flows. For example, the firm may require that cash inflows be adjusted downward and cash outflows be adjusted upward. Acceptable projects would be those whose adjusted *NPV* is still greater than zero after the adjustments.

To incorporate managerial bias, Orange Electronics Company might arbitrarily adjust the initial cash outflow upward by 5 percent and adjust the present value of the cash inflows downward by 5 percent. Using the estimates from Table 6.6, the *NPV* adjusted for managerial bias becomes:

NPV[7] Adjusted for Managerial Bias: = −\$63,661,500 + \$64,920,015 = \$1,258,515

The adjustment has lowered significantly the *NPV* for Project Prose; however, including this adjustment does not change the decision to accept.

Misestimation

Misestimation is fundamentally different from managerial bias. In managerial bias, revenues are consistently biased upward and costs consistently biased downward. In misestimation, errors in the projection of revenues and costs can be in either direction.

misestimation
Errors in revenues and costs, either too high or too low. Misestimation reflects the fact that future events are uncertain and that actual outcomes may differ from expected outcomes.

Misestimation reflects the fact that future events are uncertain and that actual outcomes may differ from expected outcomes. For example, Figure 6.2 provides sales estimates of Project Prose against the probability of obtaining a particular sales level. This graph is of a particular type of probability distribution known as a normal distribution. The expected outcome is in the center of the distribution. The distribution is symmetrical so that the probability of an estimate above the expected outcome is equal to the probability of an estimate below the expected outcome.

The expected sales level is 120,000 units. As the distribution moves away from the expected outcome, the probability of obtaining sales at these levels diminishes. In fact, the probability of sales being greater than 200,000 or less than 40,000 in year 2 is almost zero; however, the probability that sales will fall within 10,000 units of the expected level of 120,000 is high.

Statistical techniques (e.g., confidence interval estimation) can be used to incorporate misestimation into *NPV*. For instance, managers can determine

---

[7]Included in net revenues is the opportunity cost of lost rent payments.

FIGURE 6.2 A Normal Probability Distribution for Project Prose

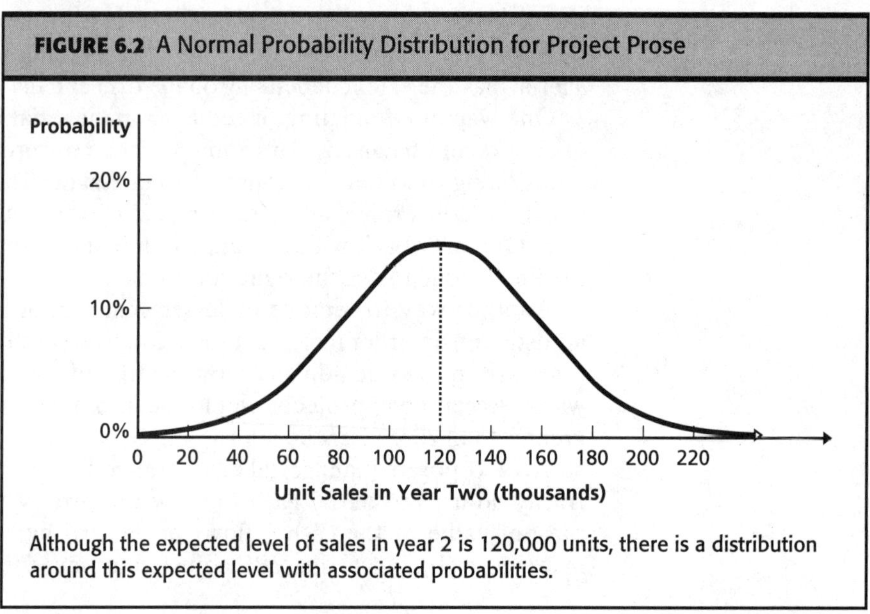

Although the expected level of sales in year 2 is 120,000 units, there is a distribution around this expected level with associated probabilities.

that they are 90 percent confident that *NPV* will be within a certain range. The statistical techniques that allow for such analysis, however, are beyond the scope of this text.

Sensitivity Analysis

Cash flow estimation is not an exact science, especially for estimates projecting a number of years in the future. In some cases management would like to know which variables merit a more detailed analysis. For example, if net present value is extremely sensitive to a particular factor, management should study this factor in more detail to develop a more precise estimate.

sensitivity analysis
A technique of isolating factors to which *NPV* is most sensitive.

"What-if," or **sensitivity analysis,** is a way of isolating such factors. Sensitivity analysis asks how sensitive *NPV* is to a change in a particular variable holding all other variables constant. For example, suppose that of all the cash flow estimates of Project Prose, the one that concerns Rush Ryan the most is the projected rate of growth in sales in year 2. Year 2 is a key year as it will gauge the market's response to a talking VCR and will determine the likely sales path through year 5. Rush Ryan wonders what the project's *NPV* would be if sales fell short of projection.

This question can be answered by performing a sensitivity analysis on year-two sales growth. Figure 6.3 shows the sensitivity of *NPV* to changes in the growth in sales over year two. Shown in the graph are sales growth rates between −30 percent (a decline in sales of 30 percent from the previous year given by 0.70) and +30 (a rise in sales of 30 percent from the previous year given by 1.30). The 12 points plotted on the graph are 12 *NPV*s, one for each growth rate in 5 percent increments in year-2 sales.

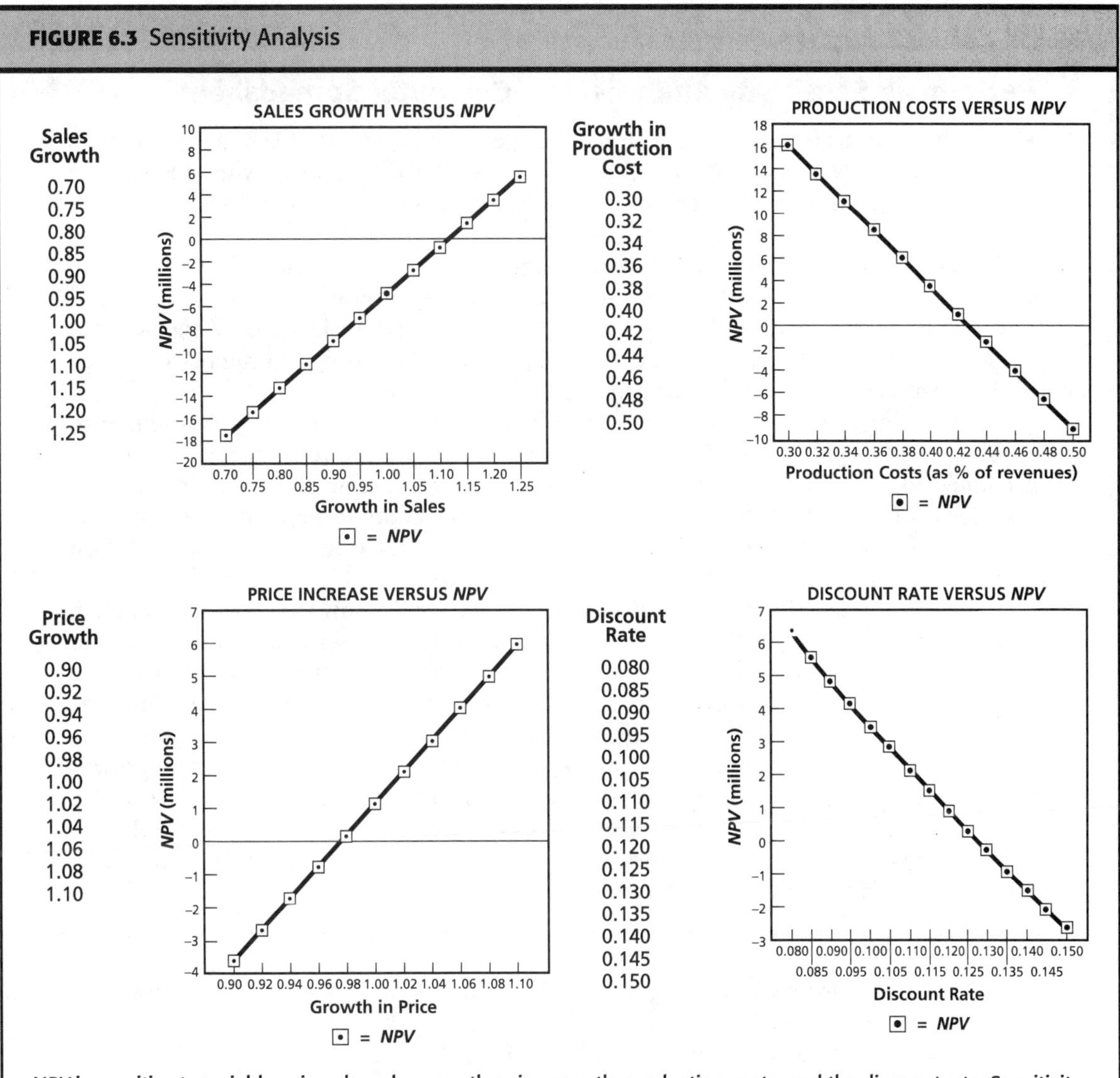

FIGURE 6.3 Sensitivity Analysis

NPV is sensitive to variables given by sales growth, price growth, production costs, and the discount rate. Sensitivity analysis provides answers to "what-if" questions such as: "What if price per unit must be set at a level *X*% below that forecast?"

We learn that *NPV* will reach as high as \$7.7 million if sales growth is 30 percent from this sensitivity analysis, but it will reach a low of −\$17.5 million if sales growth is −30 percent. The *NPV* "crossover" point or the point at which *NPV* turns from positive to negative is also of interest. This occurs at a growth rate in sales of approximately 12 percent.

Sensitivity analysis can be performed isolating any one input variable. Figure 6.3 also shows the sensitivity of *NPV* to projected price increases, to

WINDOW 6.2

Performing Sensitivity Analysis on a Computer Spreadsheet

Sensitivity analysis is tedious work. Each change in an input variable changes the cash flow stream and *NPV*. For instance, the sensitivity of *NPV* to sales growth in Figure 6.3 was examined against 13 different sales growth assumptions, leading to 13 different cash flow streams and 13 different *NPV*s.

Financial tools, which are called *computerized spreadsheets,* fortunately can perform sensitivity analysis with little input effort. Spreadsheet programs such as Lotus 1–2-3, Excel, and Quatro Pro are designed to perform repetitive tasks quickly and without mathematical error. When it is properly set up, a spreadsheet program can perform each of the sensitivity analyses illustrated in Figure 6.3 in seconds.

Constructing a computerized spreadsheet to perform sensitivity analysis is similar to constructing a large display of dominoes to be knocked down one by one. Each domino is connected to the next, so that knocking over the first domino starts a chain reaction that does not end until the last domino has fallen. The computer spreadsheet connects each cash flow value to the next such that changing one variable starts a chain reaction that does not end until every *NPV* has been recalculated.

The chain reaction in the spreadsheet requires each cash flow to be connected. Cash flows are connected from top to bottom (from cash inflows to net cash flow) through the after-tax cash flow Formula (6.3), and are connected from left to right (from year to year) through growth rate assumptions. For example, in the sensitivity analysis for sales growth, second-year sales are estimated as first-year sales augmented by some growth rate, third-year sales are estimated as second-year sales augmented by a new growth rate, and so on for each year of the project's life. In this way, changing the growth in sales over year 2 will change the sales estimates through year 5. With each new sales estimate comes a new set of cash flows and a new *NPV*. Recalculating *NPV* becomes as simple as pushing a few keys on the computer keyboard.

production costs, and to the discount rate.[8] Each of these graphs demonstrates *NPV* sensitivity to a change in a key input variable, holding all other input variables constant.

To summarize, sensitivity analysis allows managers to isolate *NPV* sensitivity to a change in a certain variable. A strength of sensitivity analysis is that it addresses, albeit in a crude way, uncertainty. A weakness is that it assumes that all other variables are held constant—it is static as opposed to dynamic. In a real-world scenario, we should expect many variables to change simultaneously. Finally, it should be noted that sensitivity analysis is tedious work, and, because of this, is usually performed using a computer and a spreadsheet. Window 6.2 discusses how the computer spreadsheet is used in performing sensitivity analysis.

[8]Readers will recognize the similarity between the sensitivity analysis on the discount rate and the *NPV* profile from Chapter 5. Another way to think of the *NPV* profile is that it measures the sensitivity of *NPV* to changes in the discount rate. The point at which *NPV* moves from positive to negative defines the project's *IRR,* or the discount rate that makes *NPV* zero.

Summary

- Incremental cash flows are dollar receipts or dollar expenditures that relate directly to a particular project.
- Much of the complexity in project analysis derives from determining which cash flows belong and which do not belong. This is especially true given the fact that certain cash flows, such as additional investment in working capital, managerial time, and overlapping revenues, are less obvious but relevant to the decision.
- Depreciation and other noncash expenses are important only to the extent that they reduce taxable income and therefore reduce the firm's tax liability.
- The formula for after-tax cash flow is given by:

$$CF_t = (PI_t - PO_t - D_t)(1 - T_c) + D_t,$$

  where PI_t and PO_t are the project inflows and outflows in time t, T_c is the tax rate, and D_t is the amount of depreciation expense taken in time t. Depreciation is first subtracted out for tax purposes, but is then added back in to produce after-tax cash flow.
- Errors in cash flow estimates can be traced to overly optimistic estimates on the part of managers (managerial bias) or to the fact that actual outcomes differ from estimated outcomes. Overoptimism on the part of managers will bias *NPV* upward and can be corrected by installing a system of proper checks and balances, or, arbitrarily, by adjusting *NPV* downward. Misestimation can be measured through a probability distribution that allows for statistical techniques, such as confidence interval estimation, to be defined.
- Sensitivity analysis allows managers to see the sensitivity of *NPV* to a change in one of the key input variables. It is useful in illustrating best- and worst-case scenarios, as well as for identifying the *NPV* crossover point, which is the point *NPV* shifts from positive to negative. The shortcoming of sensitivity analysis is that it is static, changing one variable and assuming that all other variables stay constant.

Demonstration Problems

Problem 1

A new automotive tuning machine would cost a repair shop $21,000 and would be expected to produce higher revenues of $11,000 per year and higher expenses of $4,000, based upon the additional work brought in. The machine is expected to last for 4 years, at which time it would be sold as scrap for $1,000. Compute the annual after-tax cash flows and the net present value by assuming a discount rate of 10%, a tax rate of 40%, and that the machine can be depreciated at $7,000 per year for each of the first 3 years.

Solution to Problem 1

After-tax net cash flows must be determined for the initial investment stage (Step 1), the long-term cash flow stage (Step 2), and the terminal cash flow stage (Step 3). Then they are combined in the final solution. The solution to this problem may be approached by plugging the missing values into Table 6.1, and readers may find Table 6.1 helpful. For this simple example, however, we will demonstrate the solution directly with the equations.

Step 1: The initial investment stage computes the after-tax net value of all immediate cash inflows and cash outflows. In this simplified example, the only immediate cash flow is the $21,000 outflow to cover the cost of the machine. Notice that this outflow is not tax deductible because it is a capital expenditure. The expensing of this outflow for tax purposes must take place each year using depreciation.
Step 2: The cash flows from the long-term cash flow stage are usually the most difficult and may be found using Formula (6.3) directly or one of its equivalent forms:

$$CF_t = (PI_t - PO_t - D_t)(1 - T_c) + D_t \tag{6.3}$$

PI_t for each year is the increased cash inflow of $11,000 per year. PO_t is the increased cash expense of $4,000 per year. D_t is the increased depreciation. For years 1–3, $D_t =$ $7,000. For year 4 D_t is $0 because we have assumed that the machine can be fully depreciated in the first 3 years. Let us start with years 1–3 by inserting the known values into Formula (6.3):

$$CF_1 = CF_2 = CF_3 = (11{,}000 - 4{,}000 - 7{,}000)(1 - 0.40) + 7{,}000$$

$$CF_1 = CF_2 = CF_3 = \$7{,}000$$

Finally, let us solve for year 4 (CF_4) by again inserting the known values into Formula (6.3) and remembering that $D_4 = \$0$:

$$CF_4 = (11{,}000 - 4{,}000)(1 - 0.40) + 0 = 4{,}200$$

Thus, the after-tax cash flow in years 1–3 is $7,000, while the depreciation is eliminating taxes, but falls to $4,200 in year 4 as the machine has been fully depreciated.
Step 3: Compute the cash flow for the terminal cash flow stage. This cash flow is the net after cash flows from ending the project. In this simple example, the only cash flows are the $1,000 that the machine can be scrapped for and the taxes due on this sale. Because the machine has been fully depreciated to a book value of zero (3 years of depreciation at $7,000 per year equals the total purchase price), the entire $1,000 of proceeds is taxable. At a tax rate of 40% the tax expense is $400 and the after-tax net cash flow is $600.
Final Solution: Insert the cash flows from each stage into the net present value formula using a discount rate of 10%:

$$NPV = -\$21{,}000 + \$7{,}000/1.10^1 + \$7{,}000/1.10^2 + \$7{,}000/1.10^3 + \$4{,}800/1.10^4$$

$$NPV = -\$21{,}000 + \$6{,}363.64 + \$5{,}785.12 + \$5{,}259.20 + \$3{,}278.46$$

$$NPV = -\$313.57$$

Notice that the CF_4 of $4,200 was added to the terminal stage cash flow of $600 to produce a single cash flow in year 4 of $4,800.

Problem 2

Repeat the previous problem, however, assume that the machine can be depreciated in 2 years at $10,500 per year. Assume that the firm can take advantage of any tax losses on this project in a particular year by offsetting the tax losses against taxable profits on other operations.

Solution

The important difference is that the timing of the depreciation will change from Problem 1, so the present value will change. We will repeat the entire problem with less detail and with the new depreciation numbers.

Step 1: The initial investment stage computes the after-tax net value of all immediate cash inflows and cash outflows. The new depreciation schedule has no effect on this stage, so the only immediate cash flow is still the $21,000 outflow to cover the cost of the machine.

Step 2: The cash flows from the long-term cash flow stage are found by substituting the new depreciation numbers. Recall that D_t is the depreciation. For years 1–2, $D_t =$ $10,500. For years 3 and 4 D_t is $0. Let us start with years 1–2 by inserting the known values into Formula (6.3):

$$CF_1 = CF_2 = (11{,}000 - 4{,}000 - 10{,}500)(1 - 0.40) + 10{,}500$$

$$CF_1 = CF_2 = \$8{,}400$$

Finally, let us solve for years 3 and 4 (CF_3 and CF_4) by again inserting the known values into Formula (6.3) and remembering that $D_3 = D_4 = \$0$:

$$CF_3 = CF_4 = (11{,}000 - 4{,}000)(1 - 0.40) + 0 = 4{,}200$$

Thus, the after-tax cash flow in years 1 and 2 is $8,400, but falls to $4,200 in years 3 and 4 as the machine has been fully depreciated.

Note that we are assuming that the firm is able to benefit in a tax sense from the full $10,500 of depreciation in each of the first 2 years even though the machine only produces a gross profit of $7,000 per year. This is because we are assuming that the "additional" $3,500 of depreciation can be used to reduce the overall taxes of the firm.

Step 3: Compute the cash flow for the terminal cash flow stage. This cash flow is the same as earlier, $600.

Final Solution: Insert the cash flows from each stage into the net present value formula using a discount rate of 10%:

$$NPV = -\$21{,}000 + \$8{,}400/1.10^1 + \$8{,}400/1.10^2 + \$4{,}200/1.10^3 + \$4{,}800/1.10^4$$

$$NPV = -\$21{,}000 + \$7{,}636.36 + \$6{,}942.15 + \$3{,}155.52 + \$3{,}278.46$$

$$NPV = +\$12.49$$

Notice that the *NPV* is now positive. This reflects the tax advantage of being able to depreciate more quickly and therefore to benefit from the time value of money.

Review Questions

1. Provide a definition of cash flow. Name two reasons that cash flow can differ from accounting profit.
2. Why is depreciation, defined as a noncash expense, included in the formula for estimating cash flow?
3. Describe briefly how a progressive tax system works.

4. What are sunk costs, and why are they not relevant in cash flow estimation?
5. List three common side effects when estimating cash flow.
6. What are the three phases of cash flow estimation? At which phase(s) would the depreciation tax shield enter in?
7. Why would a firm, for tax purposes, choose an accelerated depreciation method over a straight line depreciation method?
8. List the two types of errors in cash flow estimation and discuss briefly how they are different.
9. What is sensitivity analysis, and how is it useful in making accept-or-reject decisions on projects?

Problems

1. A marketing research firm with current sales of $400,000 does not expect any growth in sales for the next 2 years. The company, however, anticipates that expenses, currently at $200,000, will increase to $210,000 next year and to $220,500 the year after. Assuming a tax rate of 34%, determine the firm's current after-tax cash flow as well as projected after-tax cash flow over the next 2 years. Assume there is no depreciation.
2. A distributor of computer software instruction manuals plans to expand distribution. Annual sales are currently $2 million and are expected to be $2.1 million next year and $3.08 million the year after. Assuming that expenses are 80% of sales each year, what are the distributor's current after-tax cash flows and projected after-tax cash flows next year and the year after if the tax rate is 34%? Assume there is no depreciation.
3. MBI Corp. is considering purchasing one of two types of machinery. The first type, costing $800,000, is expected to last for 10 years. The second type, costing $1.2 million, is expected to last for 15 years. Assuming that straight line depreciation is used, and that the salvage values are zero, what is the annual depreciation schedule for each type of machinery?
4. For the MBI Corp. in Problem 3, recalculate the annual depreciation schedule for each type of machinery using the MACRS schedules in Window 6.1 assuming the recovery period = useful life.
5. A travel agent intends to update its computerized reservation system. State-of-the-art computer equipment costs $200,000 and is expected to be used for 4 years. There is no salvage value. What is the equipment's depreciation schedule for each of the 4 years, assuming that the MACRS is used and a 3-year recovery period?
6. The owner of two pizza restaurants needs to buy a new pizza oven for each restaurant. Each oven costs $300,000 and is expected to last 15 years.
   - **a.** Using the MACRS schedules in Window 6.1, determine the annual depreciation schedule for each oven over the first 5 years assuming a 15-year recovery period.
   - **b.** Determine the annual after-tax cash flow for the pizza restaurants over the first 5 years, assuming total cash inflows are a constant $1 million, total cash outflows are a constant $500,000, and the tax rate is 34%.
7. A manufacturer of recyclable paper and paper board is considering the replacement and upgrading of machinery that would improve efficiency. The new ma-

chinery costs $2.5 million and is expected to last for 5 years with no salvage value. Straight line depreciation will be used. Cash inflows, currently at $5 million per year, are expected to increase to $5,750,000 annually if the machinery is purchased. Assuming that the machinery can begin to increase cash inflows in 1 year, and company expenses are consistently 60% of cash inflows, what is the after-tax cash flow in each of the next 5 years? The tax rate is 34%.

8. A poster manufacturer wants to introduce a small-size line of movie, concert, and theater posters. To do so, however, requires new equipment, additional personnel, and increased advertising expenses. The equipment costs $2 million and will be depreciated on a straight line basis for 4 years. Annual cash inflows are expected to increase by $5 million in year 1, by $5.5 million in year 2, and rise 15% per year over each of the next 2 years. Costs for manufacturing, sales personnel, and advertising will increase by $3,800,000 in year 1, increasing by 5% annually in each of the next 3 years. What are the after-tax cash flows for the project? The tax rate is 34%.

9. A bus tour company wants to provide excursions to several national and international sports events that will be taking place throughout the country during the next few years. To make the buses more comfortable and the trips more popular, each of eight new buses will be equipped with a kitchen and a large video screen for movies and sports telecasts.

Each bus costs $200,000 and requires customized equipment that costs an additional $100,000 per bus. All the buses and the equipment have a recovery period of 5 years. An advertising campaign, which will start immediately, costs $750,000 and will be paid for immediately. Other start-up costs total $30,000.

The sports trips are scheduled for 3–10 days and will generate revenues of $100 per day per seat. For the eight video buses, total revenues are expected to be $3,168,000 for the first year and $3,484,800 for the second year (a 10% increase). Operating costs are 30% of total revenues. Personnel expenses, including driver salaries, are $650,000 in year 1 and will increase by 5% in year 2.

The company expects to discontinue operation of its video bus tours after the second year. Each bus will be sold to a university for $35,000–$30,000 for the bus itself and $5,000 for the equipment.

a. What are the cash flows for the initial investment period?
b. What is the MACRS depreciation schedule for the first two years for all of the buses and the equipment? Depreciate both down to zero, using the 5-year recovery period.
c. What are the after-tax cash flows for the 2 years that the bus tours will be in operation? The tax rate is 34%.
d. What are the termination cash flows in year 2?
e. If *NPV* analysis is used, should the buses be purchased? The required rate of return is 12%.

10. A car manufacturer is considering production of a convertible version of the former Volkswagen "beetle." The marketing VP, an enthusiastic former owner of a "beetle" himself, has been conducting market research on the project. Once the car is available, the marketing VP expects that 50,000 cars at $18,000 per car will be sold in the first year. Sales would then be anticipated to increase 8% per year over the previous year's level.

The cars will be produced and warehoused at only one of the company's several locations. Machinery will cost $100 million, has a useful life of 10 years, and will be depreciated on a straight line basis. Start-up costs, including mechanic's training, are another $13 million. Advertising expenses will amount to $5 million initially and remain at this level annually for the first 2 years. Manufacturing and employee costs will be 60% of revenues.

a. What is the after-tax cash flow in year 1 if 50,000 cars are sold? The tax rate is 34%.

b. What is the after-tax cash flow in year 2 if 50,000 cars are sold in year 1? The tax rate is 34%.

c. If sales in year 1 turn out to be 50% lower than expected, what is the after-tax cash flow for the first year?

d. The marketing VP wishes to project sales and expenses in a general economic scenario in which both unemployment and inflation are high. Sales would consequently be lower and costs would be higher. What is the net after-tax cash flow for the first year if sales are 50% lower and manufacturing costs are 80%, instead of 60%, of sales?

11. A small regional airline is performing sensitivity analysis to determine the effect of changes in the price of oil on its cash flow. Because of competitive market conditions, the airline cannot raise air fares if the price of oil increases but could lower fares if oil decreases. An increase in the per-barrel price of oil will consequently be absorbed by the firm, but a sizable decrease in the price of oil is anticipated to increase revenues. On particular routes, the firm estimates that 5 million passenger miles are recorded for 1 year. Each passenger mile generates $0.50 in revenue and $0.10 in after-tax cash flow, assuming that oil costs $19.00 per barrel. For each $1.00 increase in the per-barrel price of oil, after-tax cash flow drops by $0.02. For each $1.00 decrease in the per-barrel price of oil, one million passenger miles will be added.

a. At $19.00 per barrel, what is the total revenue and after-tax cash flow?

b. At $21.00 per barrel, what is the after-tax cash flow?

c. At $17.00 per barrel, what is the after-tax cash flow?

Discussion Questions

1. The *Wall Street Journal* makes two announcements on the Walker Corporation: First, Walker reported record-high profits for the last fiscal year. Second, Walker arranged a $50 million credit line over the same fiscal year from Citibank to get the firm through cash flow problems. How is it possible that these two events can occur simultaneously?

2. The Eastham Company uses straight-line depreciation. The firm reasons that it does not matter which depreciation method is used because the total amount of depreciation is the same under each method. Do you agree or disagree with Eastham?

3. Scnibble and Fizz, a firm with an entire line of dishwashing detergents, is advertising its newest dishwashing detergent project as *new and improved.* When analyzing project cash flows, you notice that the estimates on the new project make no adjustments for "side effects." From the limited information provided, what mistakes do you think the firm made in its analysis?

4. It was argued that managers have an incentive to see their own projects get funded (the managerial bias). Design an incentive scheme for project managers that will have the effect of reducing or even eliminating managerial bias.

5. The UpSmith Pharmaceutical Corporation announced the successful development of a vaccine that can prevent certain forms of cancer. The cost of each dose of the vaccine is inexpensive—as low as $1 by some estimates. The retail price of the vaccine per dose, however, is $100. UpSmith defends this high price as a way to recover research and development efforts connected with the cancer vaccine that spanned over 20 years. Is the firm correct in incorporating these R & D expenditures into the vaccine's sales price?

CHAPTER 7

ADVANCED TOPICS IN CAPITAL BUDGETING

Emily, the president of Visualized Construction, Inc., was responsible for analyzing the firm's new construction projects. In fact, Emily made all of the firm's business decisions. Her partner was in charge of on-site project management. Emily enjoyed her job and took pride in the fact that the firm was growing and successful.

Emily studied corporate finance while at college. The most important thing she learned was the net present value (*NPV*) rule—the premier method by which to make new project decisions. Emily had recently encountered a situation, however, in which her instincts led her to believe that *NPV* was providing the wrong answer.

She had been asked to consider the possible construction of two types of building projects. The first, Project Big, involved a very large building. Project Big appeared extremely lucrative and would be finished in about 2 years. The second, Project Small, involved 12 small office buildings. The second project would be finished in about 6 years.

Emily decided to base the decision on *NPV*. Project Big offered an *NPV* of $1 million, and Project Small offered an *NPV* of $1.5 million. Because her firm had only one qualified construction manager (her partner), she realized that these were mutually exclusive projects and that she had to decide which of the two (if either) to accept. Emily remembered that *NPV* was supposed to solve all ranking problems caused by scale differentials such as size and length of time. Nevertheless, her instincts told her that the 2-year project was better even though it had a smaller *NPV*.

Emily's instincts perhaps had more to do with her ambition to build a grandiose building than with corporate finance, or perhaps her instincts were wrong. Worse yet, perhaps the unthinkable was true—that the *NPV* rule as applied was not correct in its choice of projects!

Overview—Complexities in Capital Budgeting Analysis

Chapter 5 presented a highly simplified decision rule for financial managers: Accept all projects with positive *NPV*s and reject all projects with negative *NPV*s. In theory, *NPV* can be used to make all optimal investment decisions because the *NPV* rule measures the change in the wealth of the firm's shareholders by subtracting costs from benefits.

In practice, however, there are complexities that make it virtually impossible to reduce all decisions to a simple *NPV* analysis. This chapter will detail some common complexities that arise when making investment decisions using *NPV*. We will first consider the problem of using *NPV* to select between projects with unequal lives, such as the Visualized Construction example of deciding between a 6-year project and a 2-year project; this situation was not discussed in Chapter 5. Users should be aware that *NPV* must be calculated with care when deciding between unequally lived projects.

This chapter will also detail three other special situations that occur within capital budgeting analysis. They are least-cost decisions, inflation, and capital rationing. There are, of course, an unlimited number of complexities that can arise in investment decisions, and no textbook can fully prepare a student for all of them. Nevertheless, this chapter provides a good starting point for tackling some of the more common issues.

Projects with Unequal Lives

For the construction company forced to decide between a 6-year project and a 2-year project, the projects were mutually exclusive such that the firm could choose one, but not both. Mutually exclusive projects were introduced in Chapter 5 as a ranking problem, and a problem that could be solved by selecting the project with the higher *NPV*. In fact, you will remember that Chapter 5 indicated that when ranking projects, *NPV* was clearly superior to other criteria—especially the internal rate of return rule (*IRR*).

These results, however, only apply to a special situation in which a particular advantage to short-lived projects was assumed not to exist. Specifically, the analysis in Chapter 5 ignored the fact that a short-lived project might offer a firm the advantage of being able to begin a new project sooner than if a longer-term project were accepted. This section will attempt to incorporate this aspect into the analysis.

NPV Versus *IRR:* The Controversy Revisited

Chapter 5 discussed the problem of choosing between two mutually exclusive projects, necessitated perhaps because of the firm's limited space, limited management, or the fact that the projects fill the same market niche. It was demonstrated that the *IRR* can rank projects incorrectly if the projects have unequal scales, which were defined as having either unequal sizes in terms of dollar magnitudes or unequal lives in terms of length of time the projects will run.

Chapter 5 correctly demonstrated that earning, say, 26 percent on a large, long-term project might be preferred to earning 30 percent on a small, short-lived project. After all, would you rather have a summer job that lasted 8 weeks and paid $26 per hour or a summer job that lasted only 1 week and paid $30 per hour? We are sure you agree that the 8-week job is the one to choose. Chapter 5 showed that *NPV* would incorporate the scale differentials and would generate the correct ranking.

The Hidden Reinvestment or Replication Assumption

Our analysis has yet to consider the possibility that projects can be repeated. Returning to the summer job analogy, is there any situation in which you would prefer a 1-week summer job that offers $30 per hour to an 8-week summer job that offers $26 per hour? The answer is, *yes!* Suppose you know that, at the end of the first week, you can get another job paying $26 per hour for the remaining 7 weeks. Would it not be better to work 1 week for $30 per hour and then switch to another job for $26 per hour for the remaining 7 weeks?

Using this same line of reasoning, consider Emily and the choice she faces as president of Visualized Construction. What if Visualized Construction, at the end of Project Big, could begin a new project with a potentially positive *NPV?* In this case, the firm might be better off with Project Big in combination with this new project.

In capital budgeting, a simple *NPV* analysis can incorrectly rank unequally lived projects. This can occur if the firm ignores the fact that at the end of the shorter-term project the firm might be able to find new positive *NPV* projects. In finance, this is often called project reinvestment, although it might be better referred to as **project replication.**

project replication
An assumption that projects, at completion, can begin again offering the same *NPV.*

***NPV* and Replication** In a nutshell, simple *NPV* analysis assumes that investing in the short-term project will not allow the firm to be able to reinvest or get started on any other project with a positive *NPV.* Simple *NPV* analysis implicitly assumes that the selection of the short-term or long-term project will not change the firm's future investment opportunities. This seems rather unrealistic in the case of Visualized Construction during strong economic times because the two-year project would presumably allow the firm to begin another profitable construction project sooner than if management selected the 6-year project.

***IRR* and Replication** On the other hand, simple *IRR* analysis implicitly assumes that the firm will be able to reinvest all cash flows at the project's *IRR*. This is also unrealistic because it would be unusual for a firm always to have sufficient new projects into which it could reinvest each cash flow and which will earn the *IRR* of today's best project. For example, if Project Short is earning a high *IRR,* such as 30 percent, a simple *IRR* analysis implicitly assumes that all cash flows from future projects can be continually reinvested at the rate of 30 percent.

This chapter will discuss a more complex *NPV* analysis that permits the financial manager to utilize a replication assumption between the two extremes mentioned earlier and, therefore, is more realistic. This more complex *NPV* analysis is to be used in cases in which a financial manager believes that once the shorter-term project is finished, the firm will be able to begin a new project offering a similar *NPV*. Simply put, we will assume that the short-lived project can be replicated as soon as it is finished.

Solving the Problem of Unequal Lives

equivalent annuity approach
A method of comparing unequally lived projects by converting project *NPV* into an annuity stream. Under this approach, a particular level of wealth today (an *NPV*) is shown to be equivalent to receiving some constant level of wealth each year in the future. The preferred project is the one with the highest present value of the annuity string.

The purpose of this section is to detail an advanced capital budgeting approach called the **equivalent annuity approach,** which converts an *NPV* into an annuity stream. In other words, a particular level of wealth today (an *NPV*) can be shown to be equivalent to receiving some constant level of wealth each year in the future. This equivalent annuity allows projects with unequal lives to be directly compared with each other under the assumption that the projects can be replicated when they are completed.

To illustrate, Skyhigh Airlines is considering one of two projects, which both have an initial investment of $500,000. Project Short will last 3 years and has expected cash flows represented by a 3-year $258,136 annuity. Project Long will last 7 years and has expected cash flows represented by a 7-year $153,382 annuity. Cash flow streams and project *NPV*s using a 12 percent required rate of return are:

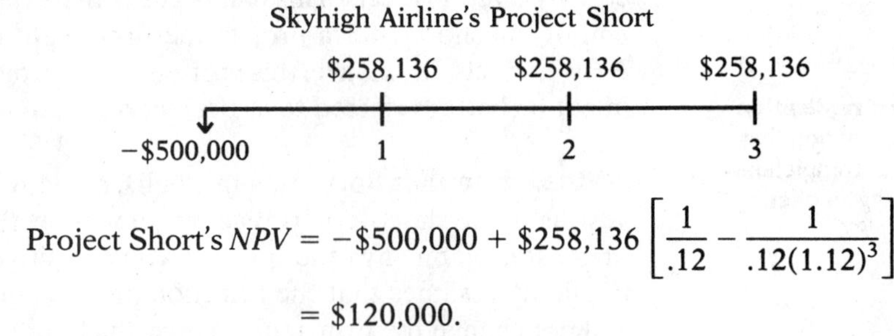

$$\text{Project Short's } NPV = -\$500{,}000 + \$258{,}136\left[\frac{1}{.12} - \frac{1}{.12(1.12)^3}\right]$$

$$= \$120{,}000.$$

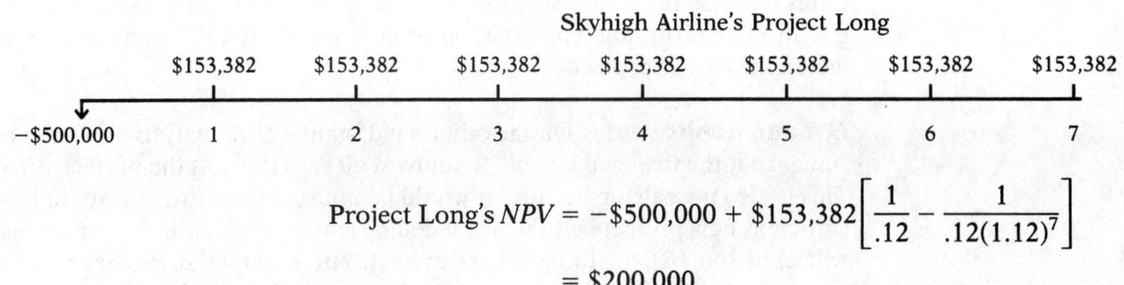

$$\text{Project Long's } NPV = -\$500{,}000 + \$153{,}382\left[\frac{1}{.12} - \frac{1}{.12(1.12)^7}\right]$$

$$= \$200{,}000.$$

Because these projects use the same facilities, the same personnel, and produce products that fill the same niche in the firm's product mix, only one project can be accepted. The financial managers at Skyhigh, however, believe that if the firm selects Project Short, then it can either repeat that project in 3 years or begin a new project in 3 years that would add similar value to the firm.

Remember that accepting a project with an *NPV* of $120,000 has the same effect on the value of the firm's assets as if the firm received an immediate gift of $120,000. Accepting Project Short, therefore, is just like receiving $120,000 in immediate cash, whereas accepting Project Long is just like receiving $200,000 in immediate cash. If the unequal lives of the projects did not matter, the simple *NPV* rule would show that it is better to take the $200,000 project; however, what if projects can be repeated? Should the Skyhigh managers accept a project that produces an *NPV* of $120,000 every 3 years or should they, instead, accept a project that produces an *NPV* of $200,000 every 7 years?

One Approach: The Common Ending Point One way to factor replication into the analysis is to repeat each project over and over again—stringing out each project on a time line. In this case, Project Short will repeat every 3 years, and Project Long will repeat every 7 years. The projects should repeat on the time line until they have a common ending point. The common ending point occurs in 21 years such that Project Short is repeated for a total of seven times and Project Long three times.

The next step is to discount the string of *NPV*s to the year the project starts. For example, Project Long is repeated for a total of three times over the span of 21 years, earning an *NPV* of $200,000 in year zero (today) along with two additional *NPV*s of $200,000 in year seven and $200,000 in year 14. The present value of the string of *NPV*s for Project Long is given by:

$$\text{Project Long's } NPV \text{ String} = 200{,}000 + \frac{200{,}000}{(1+r)^7} + \frac{200{,}000}{(1+r)^{14}}$$

Project Short can be replicated for a total of seven times over 21 years, and the present value of the string of *NPV*s is given by:

$$\text{Project Short's } NPV \text{ String} = 120{,}000 + \frac{120{,}000}{(1+r)^3} + \frac{120{,}000}{(1+r)^6} + \frac{120{,}000}{(1+r)^9} + \frac{120{,}000}{(1+r)^{12}} + \frac{120{,}000}{(1+r)^{15}} + \frac{120{,}000}{(1+r)^{18}}$$

FIGURE 7.1 NPV Using the Common Ending Point Approach (numbers in thousands)

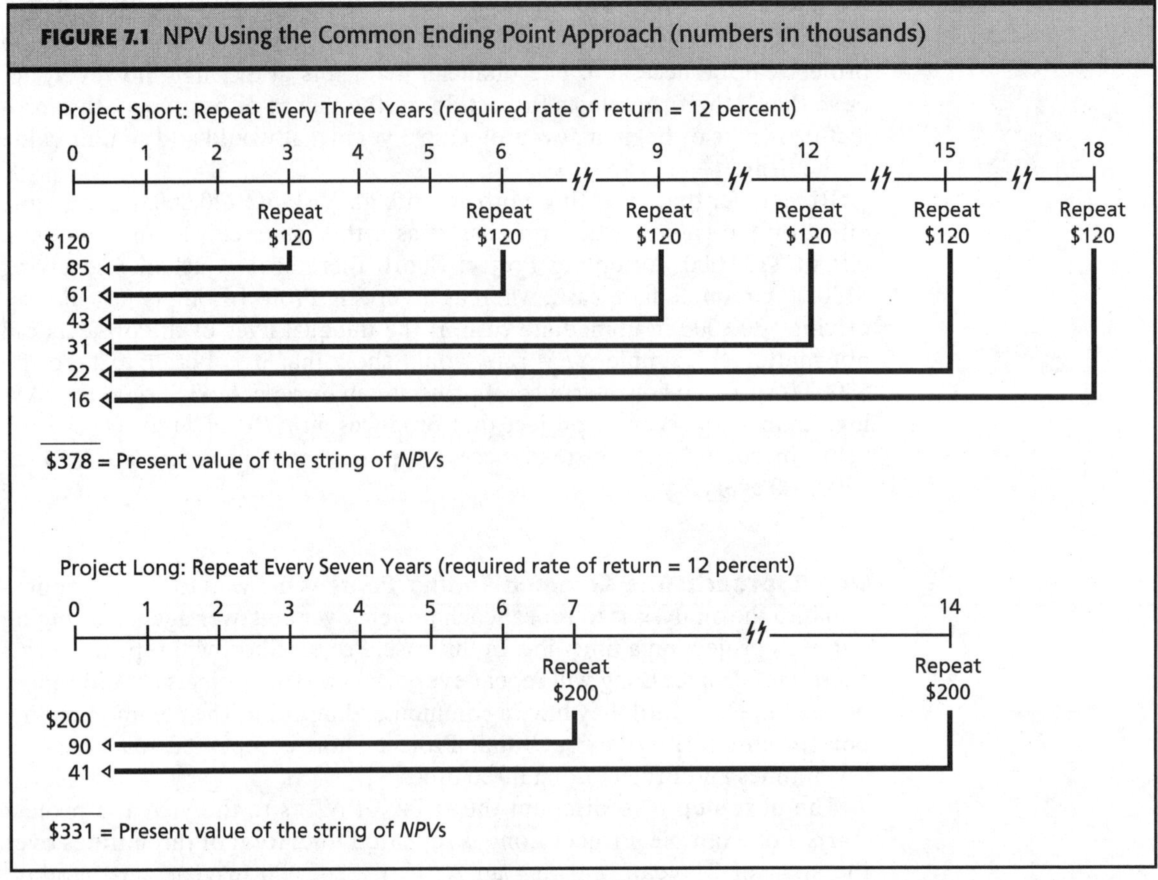

Comparing Project Long's *NPV* string against Project Short's *NPV* string will allow for *NPV* to incorporate correctly the replication assumption.[1] This **common ending point approach** is shown in Figure 7.1.

common ending point approach
A method of comparing unequally lived projects by replicating the projects until they have a common ending point. The preferred project is the one with the highest *NPV* string.

Given a required rate of return of 12 percent, the present value of the string of *NPV*s for Project Short is greater than the present value of the string of *NPV*s for Project Long. Thus, incorporating replication leads to a decision to select Project Short over Project Long.

A Better Approach: The Equivalent Annual Annuity Although it produces correct results, the common ending point approach can be quite tedious.[2] An easier way to compare these repetitive projects is to convert the

[1]Stopping at year 21 is sufficient even though these projects are assumed to continue indefinitely. Extending the analysis beyond year 21, say to year 42 or beyond, will change the magnitude of the respective *NPV*s, but not the ranking.

[2]For example, if one project ends in 7 years, but the other ends in 13 years, then the time line will be extended to 91 years, which is the year of the first common ending point.

FIGURE 7.2 Project Short's Equivalent Annuity

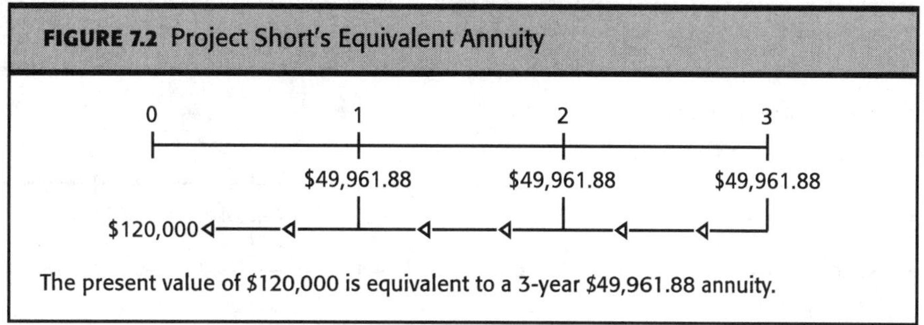

The present value of $120,000 is equivalent to a 3-year $49,961.88 annuity.

*NPV*s of each project into equivalent annuities, then to compare these annuities. For example, with an interest rate of 12 percent, we may use the annuity concept to convert Project Short's *NPV* of $120,000 today into a 3-year annuity of $49,961.88. This is shown in the form of a time line in Figure 7.2.

Receiving $120,000 today is equivalent to receiving $49,961.88 each year for 3 years. If we imagine Project Short being repeated every 3 years forever, then we can extend the time line out 6 years and beyond. This is illustrated in Figure 7.3.

Project Long can also be converted into an annuity of approximately $43,823.55. Note that in computing Project Long's equivalent annuity we used its 7-year life. Project Long's equivalent annuity and equivalent perpetuity are illustrated in Figure 7.4.

The usefulness of converting each *NPV* into an annuity of equivalent value is that it permits us to compare the projects directly. Accepting Project Short and repeating it every 3 years is equivalent to receiving $49,961.88 every year. Accepting Project Long and repeating it every 7 years is equivalent to receiving $43,823.55 every year. Now the comparison is easy. We accept Project Short because this is tantamount to receiving a higher cash flow in every year.

In summary, when a firm must decide between projects having unequal lives, it is often appropriate to assume that the projects can be replicated once finished and to use the equivalent annuity method, which converts each *NPV* into an annuity whose length is equal to the length of the project. The annuities are then compared and the project with the higher annuity is ac-

FIGURE 7.3 Project Short's Equivalent Perpetuity

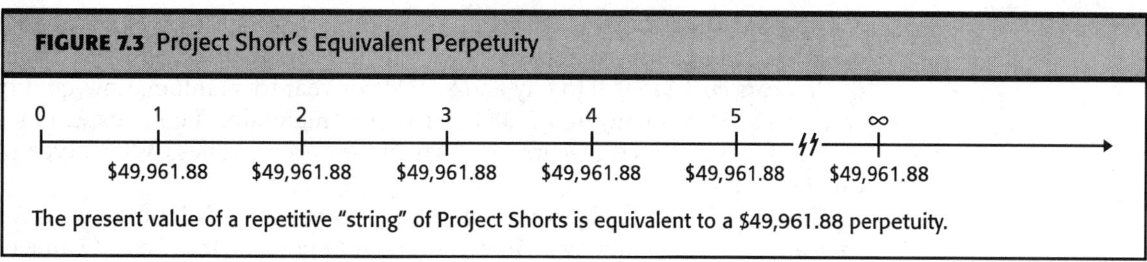

The present value of a repetitive "string" of Project Shorts is equivalent to a $49,961.88 perpetuity.

FIGURE 7.4 Project Long's Equivalent Annuity and Perpetuity

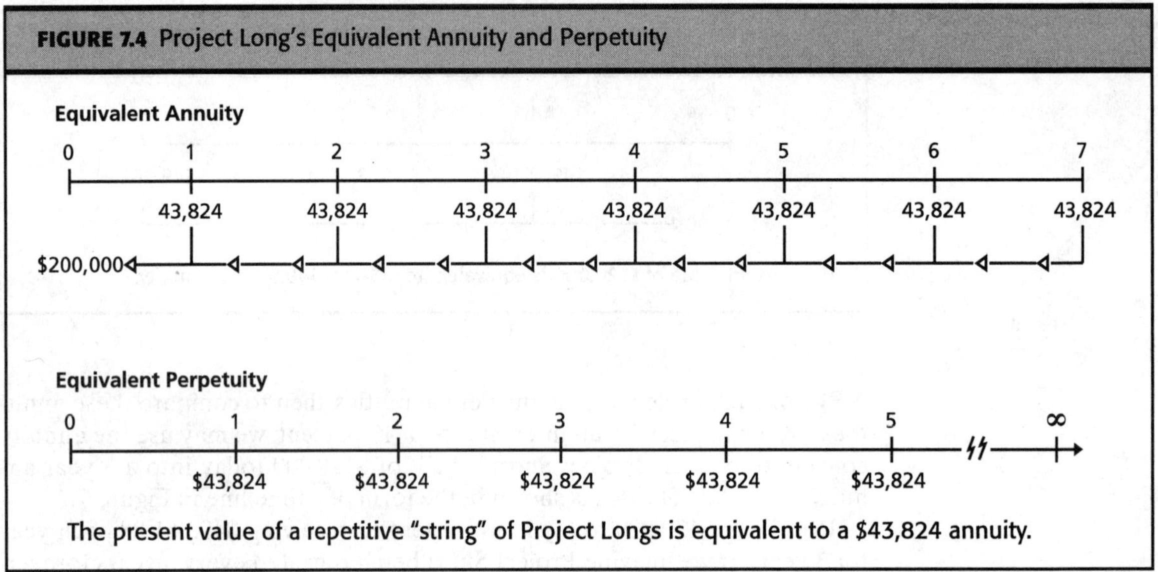

The present value of a repetitive "string" of Project Longs is equivalent to a $43,824 annuity.

cepted. This method should be used whenever the firm believes that the shorter project's quicker termination will permit the firm to commence projects of similar added value.

Least-Cost Decisions

Another common investment decision involves the comparison of projects producing the same cash inflows but at different costs. For example, a firm may be deciding between two production processes performing the same job and therefore producing the same benefits. The firm has already decided that it needs a production process; all that is being decided is which production process is best for the firm. In this case, the best process would be defined as the one that offers the lowest total cost when time value is included.

least-cost decision
A capital budgeting decision in which the best process is the one that offers the lowest total cost when time value is included.

The problem is solved utilizing a **least-cost decision.** Rather than computing the *NPV* of the alternative production processes, the firm computes the total present value of the costs and compares them.

Example 7.1 ________ Vertigo Cabs, Inc., of New York City, is debating whether to buy high-quality cars that will need fewer repairs or low-quality cars that will cost less. High-quality cars cost $15,000 to buy and $2,000 per year to maintain. Low-quality cars cost $10,000 to buy and $5,000 per year to maintain. The life expectancy of both types of cars is 3 years, after which they are worthless. Which type of car should they buy?

The answer is found by computing the present value of all of the costs for each alternative. Assuming an interest rate of 11 percent, the present value of the costs of the high-quality cars is found by adding the $15,000 cost of the car today with the present value of three $2,000 payments. The annuity formula can be used to determine these present values. The present value of the cost of high-quality and low-quality cars is:

PV Costs for High-Quality Cars

$$= \$15{,}000 + \$2{,}000\left[\frac{1}{.11} - \frac{1}{.11(1.11)^3}\right]$$

$$= \$15{,}000 + \$2{,}000\left[2.444\right]$$

$$= \$19{,}888.$$

PV Costs for Low-Quality Cars

$$= \$10{,}000 + \$5{,}000\left[\frac{1}{.11} - \frac{1}{.11(1.11)^3}\right]$$

$$= \$10{,}000 + \$5{,}000\left[2.444\right]$$

$$= \$22{,}220.$$

The least-cost alternative is the high-quality cars, whose higher purchase price is more than offset by their lower annual maintenance costs.

The values in the previous example should technically be listed as negative numbers because they are costs. By convention, however, they are listed as positive numbers and the decision is to choose the project with the smallest present value.

Least Cost and Unequal Lives

It is also common for least-cost comparisons to involve different lives. One alternative is usually more expensive but lasts longer than its cheaper and shorter-lived counterpart. Thus, the problem involves both the concepts of a least-cost analysis and an unequal-lives analysis.

Example 7.2 Consider Nittany Manufacturing Inc., which is deciding between two alternative manufacturing processes. Alternative A uses high-quality, all stainless steel equipment that costs $1.35 million, and has an expected life of 10 years and an annual operating expense of $250,000. Alternative B is a cheaper set of equipment that uses a variety of materials, costs only $750,000, and has a useful life of 5 years and annual operating expenses of $350,000. Which alternative is cheaper given that both alternatives produce equal-quality output?

The answer is found by combining the approaches of unequally lived project selection and least-cost decision making. The user computes the total present value of the costs and converts the costs into equivalent annuities. Using an interest rate of 8 percent, the answer is found by selecting the alternative with the lower annuity cost.

Let us apply this solution to Nittany Manufacturing's problem. First, the present values of the costs are:

Alternative A

$$= \$1{,}350{,}000 + \$250{,}000\left[\frac{1}{.08} - \frac{1}{.08(1.08)^{10}}\right]$$

$$= \$1{,}350{,}000 + \$1{,}677{,}520 = \$3{,}027{,}520.$$

Alternative B

$$= \$750{,}000 + \$350{,}000\left[\frac{1}{.08} - \frac{1}{.08(1.08)^{5}}\right]$$

$$= \$750{,}000 + \$1{,}397{,}449 = \$2{,}147{,}449.$$

Alternative A has higher total costs, but we must now adjust these costs for the fact that they cover 10 years of production rather than 5 years. We adjust for the unequal lives by converting each total cost into an equivalent annuity. Following the equivalent annual annuity approach outlined earlier in the chapter, the *PV* of the costs of Alternative A can be converted into a \$451,190 annuity:

$$\$3{,}027{,}520 = \text{Annuity}\left[\frac{1}{.08} - \frac{1}{.08(1.08)^{10}}\right]$$

$$\text{Annuity} = \$451{,}190,$$

whereas the *PV* of the costs of Alternative B can be converted into a \$537,842 annuity:

$$\$2{,}147{,}449 = \text{Annuity}\left[\frac{1}{.08} - \frac{1}{.08(1.08)^{5}}\right]$$

$$\text{Annuity} = \$537{,}842.$$

If these manufacturing processes can be repeated after completion, then we can think of these annuities as representing a perpetual string of costs. Alternative A is the best alternative in that it produces smaller annual costs. This example illustrates a common problem in corporate finance because the more expensive alternative often lasts longer. If this were not true, then the choice of technologies would be easy—always take the less expensive, longer-lasting technology.

Inflation and Investment Decisions

A topic of prime importance is the treatment of inflation in investment decisions. As Chapter 2 detailed, inflation occurs when the value of money falls, causing the prices of everything else to rise. In terms of project cash flows, inflation will affect estimated revenues as well as estimated costs throughout the project's life. Whereas Chapter 6 discussed the difficulty of estimating cash flows, inflation can make the task seem especially difficult.

Example 7.3 Let us first consider inflation in the context of personal finance—the retirement decision faced by independent business owners Matthew and Jennifer Fairmont. The Fairmonts have worked all their adult lives owning and operating a clothing store and building its reputation and clientele. The couple's only other asset is their house. They have reinvested everything that they have earned in the store or have spent it raising their children. As they both approach age 62, they began to question whether they could sell the business and retire.

The Fairmonts are sure of two things: First, they know they can sell the store for $650,000. Second, as they think about their retirement life-style, they know that they must supplement their social security benefits by about $30,000 per year, or $2,500 per month, based upon today's prices.

The Fairmonts have learned that they can use the $650,000 proceeds from the sale of the business to purchase a retirement annuity that will pay them $66,092 per year as long as either of them lives. The annuity is based upon a life expectancy of 30 years and an interest rate of 9.5 percent. The calculations of the annuity are shown in Table 7.1.

As shown, the retirement question can be solved by applying the present value of the annuity formula first presented in Chapter 3. The couple knows the present value of their funds ($650,000), has estimated the amount of time they wish to draw on these funds (30 years), and the rate of interest these

TABLE 7.1 The Fairmonts' Retirement Annuity

The Facts

Retirement nest egg = $650,000
Length of time of the investment = 30 years
Interest rate to be earned = 9.5%

The Problem

How much can they spend, per year, from their retirement nest egg?

The Procedure

Apply the present value of the annuity formula:

$$PVA = \text{Annuity}\left[\frac{1}{r} - \frac{1}{r(1+r)^n}\right]$$

$$\$650{,}000 = \text{Annuity}\left[\frac{1}{.095} - \frac{1}{.095(1.095)^{30}}\right]$$

$$\$650{,}000 = \text{Annuity}\ [9.8347]$$

$$\text{Annuity} = \$650{,}000/9.8347$$

$$\text{Annuity} = \$66{,}092$$

funds can earn in the bank throughout their retirement (9.5%). The annuity formula is used to solve for the annuity amount, or $66,092.

The Fairmonts' financial problem appears to have been solved because the annuity amount of $66,092 per year greatly exceeds their annual cash needs of $30,000, but the analysis has yet to consider inflation. What if high inflation occurs such that the fixed annuity of $66,092 per year purchases less and less each year? Could inflation make $66,092 a poverty level of income?

The Mathematics of Inflation

The tools of Chapter 3 allow for an analysis of the effects of inflation. As discussed in Chapter 2, price indexes are regularly computed using current prices to reflect the changing costs of overall purchases. Inflation is expressed using rates of growth. Mathematically speaking, the growth rate of inflation acts like the interest rate in present and future value analysis. For example, if on January 1 the price index stood at 100.0 and on December 31 the price index stood at 106.2, inflation, expressed as π, is 6.2 percent:

$$106.2 = 100(1 + \pi) \rightarrow (1 + \pi) = 106.2/100 \rightarrow \pi = .062$$

We can calculate the rate of inflation over various intervals by inserting the starting value price index as *PV*, the ending value price index as *FV*, the number of years as *N*, and solving for the interest rate. For example, returning to the Fairmonts, we can re-address their retirement income in the context of inflation. What rate of inflation, say over 10 years, would turn their $66,092 annuity into the same purchasing power as the $30,000 of income they desire in today's dollars? This can be found by solving the present value formula for the rate of return:

$$\$66{,}092 = \$30{,}000(1 + \pi)^{10}$$

$$(1 + \pi)^{10} = \$66{,}092/\$30{,}000$$

$$\pi = 2.2031^{1/10} - 1 = 0.0822$$

This means that if 8.22 percent inflation occurred each year for 10 years,[3] the purchasing power of the Fairmonts' income would decline to the same level of purchasing power as $30,000 today. In other words, $66,092 of income 10 years from now would be approximately equivalent to $30,000 of income today if inflation were 8.22 percent per year. A higher rate of inflation would push the purchasing power of the Fairmonts' income below $30,000, so that their retirement goal would not be achieved.

[3]We can analyze inflation's effect on purchasing power over periods other than 10 years. For instance, for time periods of 20 years and 25 years, the inflation rate that would reduce the purchasing power of $66,092 to $30,000 would have to be 4.03 percent and 3.21 percent, respectively.

Do the Fairmonts need to be concerned with the level of inflation that will occur over their retirement? As we will see, they can protect their retirement income from inflation rather well if they rely on the tendency of interest rates to adjust to the level of inflation.

Interest Rates and the Fisher Effect

In the late 1970s, inflation was causing prices to rise at more than 10 percent per year. The dollar you held in your hand on January 1 would buy 10 percent less of most goods and services by December 31 of the same year. Lenders who had lent money to borrowers at interest rates of less than 10 percent found that their money was not growing fast enough to keep up with inflation; it was actually declining in real value or purchasing power.

A property of interest rates called *the Fisher effect* became abundantly clear as people adjusted to the unprecedented levels of inflation in the United States. The **Fisher effect** states that the market interest rate can be separated into a real rate of interest and an expected inflation rate. Fisher called the market interest rate the nominal interest rate. It is the nominal rate that we usually use for computing present values.

Fisher effect
A theory of interest rates stating that the nominal interest rate is composed of the real interest rate plus the expected inflation rate.

real rate of interest
The interest rate earned after removing the effects of inflation.

The **real rate of interest** is the rate earned after the effects of inflation, and it reflects purchasing power rather than dollars. When economists use the term *real* they are referring to a number that indicates the physical quantity of goods and services purchased rather than the number of dollars used in that purchase. Given the concept of the real rate of interest, the Fisher effect is expressed as:[4]

$$\text{Nominal Rate} = \text{Real Rate} + \text{Expected Inflation Rate} \qquad (7.1)$$

Although it may take a little time for interest rates to adjust, generally speaking, the nominal interest rate adjusts to include inflationary expectations.

Estimating the Real Rate of Interest

From the Fisher effect, the real rate of interest is the nominal rate minus the expected rate of inflation. The real rate of interest is the price of borrowing and lending (with inflation removed). Although prices change in response to supply and demand, some argue that the real rate of interest is relatively stable and that it tends to range around 2–3 percent.

---

[4]Formula (7.1) is really just an approximation (when compounding is not continuous) and comes from the more precise formula:

$$(1 + \text{Nominal Rate}) = (1 + \text{Real Rate}) \times (1 + \text{Expected Inflation Rate}).$$

This formula differs from Formula (7.1) by including a cross-product term between the real rate and inflation rate. The cross product term is usually ignored, which makes the simple addition of the "real" rate with the expected inflation rate to get the nominal rate an approximation.

In other words, when there is a very low rate of inflation, such as 1 or 2 percent per year, we would expect nominal interest rates to be 4 or 5 percent. This is confirmed by applying the Fisher effect shown in Formula (7.1)—adding together the real interest rate and the expected inflation rate. During periods of high inflation, such as 10 percent, we would expect that interest rates would rise to 12 or 13 percent.

Using the Fisher Effect in Investment Decisions

Remember that the typical investment decision is made by discounting estimated future cash flows by market interest rates:

$$NPV = C_0 + \frac{CF_1}{(1+r)^1} + \frac{CF_2}{(1+r)^2} + \cdots + \frac{CF_n}{(1+r)^n}$$

Inflation can be viewed as having two effects on the preceding equation. First, inflation will cause the estimated cash flows to increase through time as the prices underlying the cash flows rise. Second, inflation is viewed as being a component of the interest rate, or r in the NPV formula.

For simplicity, let us look at cash flows of an investment that are expected to rise only by the inflation rate. We express this by inserting the inflation rate, given by π, into the numerator of the preceding NPV formula. Second, we replace the nominal interest rate in the NPV formula with its components, according to the precise form of the Fisher effect:

$$NPV = C_0 + \frac{CF(1+\pi)}{(1+\text{real})(1+\pi)} + \frac{CF(1+\pi)^2}{(1+\text{real})^2(1+\pi)^2} + \cdots + \frac{CF(1+\pi)^n}{(1+\text{real})^n(1+\pi)^n} \tag{7.2}$$

where CF stands for real cash flows, and real is the real rate of interest.

Notice that the expected inflation rate appears in both the numerator and the denominator of Formula (7.2). Thus, the terms containing the expected inflation rate cancel out and the formula can be rewritten as:

$$NPV = C_0 + \frac{CF}{(1+\text{real})^1} + \frac{CF}{(1+\text{real})^2} + \cdots + \frac{CF}{(1+\text{real})^n}$$

Rather than performing the analysis in actual or nominal dollars and with nominal interest rates, the analysis can be performed as if inflation did not exist. This is accomplished by using real dollars in the numerator, which is equivalent to estimating future cash flows as if inflation did not exist. The second step is to use the real rate of interest in the denominator—around 2 or 3 percent.

Example 7.4 Let us return to the Fairmonts' retirement decision and attempt to simplify the analysis, using real numbers. As discussed earlier, the Fairmonts, like everyone else, are very uncertain as to what the inflation rate will be over the next 30 years. They do expect, however, that they will need $30,000 per year measured in today's dollars (i.e., in terms of today's prices). The Fairmonts can obtain an estimate of the dollar amount needed today to meet their retirement needs by working with "real" cash flows and a "real" interest rate of, say, 2.5 percent. The amount needed to be invested today in order to be able to spend $30,000 in today's purchasing power for 30 years can be determined, through the annuity formula, by supplying the annuity amount ($30,000), the interest rate (2.5%), and the time period (30 years), and then solving for the present value of the annuity:

$$\text{Fairmonts' Need in } PV = \$30{,}000 \times \left[\frac{1}{.025} - \frac{1}{.025(1.025)^{30}}\right]$$

$$= \$627{,}909.$$

Since the Fairmonts anticipate having $650,000 of cash when they sell their business, it looks as if they'll be able to fund their retirement needs regardless of the actual subsequent inflation rate. They simply need to keep their money in short-term, very low-risk investments that will offer a return of around 2–3 percent above the current inflation rate. If the inflation rate rises dramatically, then the cash needs of the Fairmonts will also rise. By investing their money short term, however, the Fairmonts will be able to reinvest at the new, higher interest rates caused by inflation and will, therefore, be able to meet both the expenses caused by higher prices and the need to reinvest money to keep up with inflation.

Adjusting for Inflation in a Corporate Context

Corporate investment decisions need to incorporate inflation appropriately. As demonstrated in the retirement example, there are two ways to treat inflation: (1) use nominal dollar values along with nominal interest rates, or (2) use real dollars along with real interest rates.

Nominal decisions, which are the more common approach, use estimates of cash flows and interest rates that have the effects of inflation added into them. The key to implementing this approach is to make sure that the cash flows are estimated using the same inflation rate that is implied by the discount rate.

Real decisions estimate cash flows using today's dollars and apply a much lower interest rate, the real interest rate, as the discount rate. Economists estimate the real interest rate to be approximately 2–3 percent before risk adjustment. Thus, the effects of inflation are subtracted out of both the numerator and the denominator. Long-term decisions such as those concerning retirement can sometimes be more accurately estimated using the latter technique.

Capital Rationing

Our final advanced topic in capital budgeting is capital rationing. As discussed in Chapter 5, capital rationing is the concept that a firm limits the amount of money it will invest in new projects. Modernists look skeptically at capital rationing, believing that firms reject positive-*NPV* projects because of hidden costs, such as the inability of management to oversee excessive growth efficiently, rather than because of a lack of funding. What appears to be a worthwhile project would therefore in actuality put a strain on the firm's resources such that firm value would decline. Capital rationing is nevertheless often argued to limit investment, and it is discussed in detail in this section.

Capital Rationing and the Profitability Index

One approach to solving this problem is to rely on the profitability index. As discussed in Chapter 5, the profitability index expresses the *NPV* of the project as a proportion by dividing the *PV* of the cash inflows by the immediate cash outflows. Because *NPV* is measured as a proportion of its cost, the profitability index is reasoned to be the ideal way to rank projects when there is a need to ration capital.

Example 7.5 ______ Consider United Piano, which is a firm built on a successful history in the musical instrument industry but which expanded into other fields such as financial services in later years. The firm has $100 million of investment capital available for projects that it considers to be worthwhile. The financial managers of the firm's various divisions have compiled the list of prospective projects shown in Table 7.2.

TABLE 7.2 A List of Prospective Projects for United Piano

Project	*Investment (in millions)*	*NPV (in millions)*
A	$ 50	$20
B	$ 20	$ 5
C	$ 20	$ 4
D	$ 50	$12
E	$ 70	$ 6
F	$ 10	$ 2
G	$ 25	$ 1
Total	$245	$50

If each project were funded, the cost of investment would be $245 million. However, the firm will invest only up to $100 million. How does the firm decide which projects to accept?

Using the profitability index, United Piano's projects would be ranked as shown in Table 7.3. According to the profitability index, the financial manager should begin with the highest ranked project and accept lower and lower ranked projects until the capital has been fully allocated. In the preceding example, the firm would accept Projects A and B (because they are ranked first and second) but would then find that there would be insufficient funds to accept Project D (which is ranked third). The firm might add Projects C and F so that all $100 million is used.

This list of acceptable projects would unfortunately not maximize *NPV*. In this case, the total of the *NPV*s of Projects A, B, C, and F is $31 million. The firm would be better off skipping Project B and investing in only Projects A and D for a total *NPV* of $32 million.

In summary, the profitability index is a simple but imperfect attempt to solve the capital rationing problem. The problem is that projects typically must be either fully accepted or fully rejected—they cannot be partially accepted. A better approach is a procedure known as *integer linear programming*. The integer linear programming model as it applies to United Piano is presented in the chapter appendix. Integer linear programming is a rather sophisticated solution to the problem of capital rationing. As with all the techniques discussed in Chapter 7, however, there are times when simple *NPV* analysis is insufficient.

TABLE 7.3 A Ranking of United Piano's Projects Using the Profitability Index

Project	*Profitability Index*	*Rank*	*Cost (in millions)*	*NPV (in millions)*
A	1.40	1	$50	$20
B	1.25	2	$20	$ 5
C	1.20	4–5	$20	$ 4
D	1.24	3	$50	$12
E	1.09	6	$70	$ 6
F	1.20	4–5	$10	$ 2
G	1.04	7	$25	$ 1

Amount of capital to invest = $100 million

Decision: Invest in project A ($50 million invested, $50 million left)
Invest in project B ($20 million invested, $30 million left)
Bypass project D as not enough capital is available
Invest in project C ($20 million invested, $10 million left)
Invest in project F ($10 million invested, $0 million left)

Summary

- In the simplest model of the firm, the financial manager makes investment decisions by selecting those projects with a positive *NPV*. In theory, *NPV* can be used to solve any problem because it includes all costs and benefits.
- In practice, several more advanced tools of *NPV* analysis have been developed to solve common complexities. The problem of unequal lives for projects that can be replicated or projects whose completion would enable acceptance of other equally attractive alternatives can be solved using the equivalent annuity method. The financial manager simply converts the *NPV* of each alternative into an annuity based upon each project's life span. The annuities are then compared directly.
- Some problems that produce highly similar benefits can be compared on a least-cost basis. The alternative with the lower total present value of costs is usually the best. In cases of unequal lives, it is usually necessary to convert the costs into equivalent annuities.
- Inflation affects the future cash flows of a project and is difficult to estimate. If nominal values are used, then the financial manager should be careful that both the cash flows and discount rates reflect a similar inflation expectation. In some long-term decisions it may be useful to estimate cash flows and discount rates as real numbers. Real numbers subtract out the effects of inflation as if the inflation rate were zero.
- Capital rationing can be solved nicely by using a technique known as integer linear programming. Through this technique, which is illustrated in the chapter appendix, virtually all common aspects of capital rationing problems can be easily modeled and solved.

Demonstration Problems

Problem 1

Lafayette Corporation is considering two mutually exclusive projects with unequal lives. Lafayette anticipates being able to repeat each project each time it is completed. The cash flows are given as:

		Cash Inflows for Each Year				
Name	*Cost*	*Year 1*	*Year 2*	*Year 3*	*Year 4*	*Year 5*
Danny	−$10,000	+$9,000	+$7,000	+$ 0	+$ 0	+$ 0
Arnold	−$ 8,000	+$8,000	+$2,000	+$2,000	+$2,000	+$2,000

First, compute the simple net present values and the internal rates of return, then use the equivalent annuity approach in order to select the best project. Assume that the required rate of return for each project is 12%.

Solution to Problem 1

There are three separate analyses to be performed: simple *NPV*, *IRR*, and the equivalent annuity approach. These will be demonstrated in steps 1–3, respectively.

Step 1: Compute the simple *NPV*s by discounting all the cash flows at 12% and summing them. Project Danny has *NPV* = $3,616.07 and Project Arnold has *NPV* =

$4,566.70. These answers were found using the simple time value of money techniques of Chapter 3. Note that according to simple *NPV* analysis Project Arnold seems better because it has a higher *NPV.*

Step 2: Compute the internal rates of return using the techniques of Chapter 5. In other words, use a trial and error search for each project to find the discount rate that sets $NPV = \$0$. Project Danny has $IRR = 40\%$ and Project Arnold has $IRR = 43.76\%$. According to simple *IRR* analysis, Project Arnold appears better.

Step 3: Now compute the equivalent annuities taking into account that Project Danny is a 2-year project but Project Arnold is a 5-year project. Equivalent annuities are formed by transforming the given *NPVs* into annuity streams that have the same present value.

This is especially easy using financial calculators. For each project, we input the length in years, the interest rate of 12%, the *NPV* as the present value, and compute the annuity amount:

$$\text{Project Danny } PV := \$3{,}616.07, N = 2, \%I = 12, CPT\ PMT$$

The answer is $2,139.62.

$$\text{Project Arnold } PV := \$4{,}566.70, N = 5, \%I = 12, CPT\ PMT$$

The answer is $1,266.85.

Final Solution: The equivalent annuity method demonstrates that Project Danny is superior because its annuity amount is $2,139.62 per year, whereas Project Arnold's is only $1,266.85 per year.

Problem 2

Lafayette Corporation also struggles with a question of whether to use high-quality vehicles for their fleet that cost more to purchase, but less to operate. The cash costs of each type of vehicle are:

			Cash Outflows for Each Year		
Name	*Initial Cost*	*Year 1*	*Year 2*	*Year 3*	*Year 4*
High quality	−$16,000	−$1,000	−$2,000	−$3,000	−$4,000
Low quality	−$12,000	−$2,000	−$3,000	−$4,000	−$6,000

Compute the least-cost vehicle using a discount rate of 15%.

Solution to Problem 2

Step 1: Because both projects involve equal-length lives, this is a simple analysis of which of the two projects has the lower total present value of costs. Notice that all of the cash flows are costs. Thus, they should all be added together rather than netted from each other.

Step 2: Present-value all the costs from the high-quality alternative and sum them:

$$PV = -\$16{,}000 - \$1{,}000/1.15^1 - \$2{,}000/1.15^2 - \$3{,}000/1.15^3 - \$4{,}000/1.15^4$$

$$PV = -\$22{,}641.41$$

Step 3: Present-value all the costs from the low-quality alternative and sum them:

$$PV = -\$12{,}000 - \$2{,}000/1.15^1 - \$3{,}000/1.15^2 - \$4{,}000/1.15^3 - \$6{,}000/1.15^4$$

$$PV = -\$22{,}068.15$$

Step 4: Because our objective is to minimize costs, the project with the smallest present value should be selected.
Final Solution: Select the low-quality alternative as it has the smallest total present value of costs = −22,068.15.

Review Questions

1. Why are some sets of projects mutually exclusive while others are not?
2. How does the *NPV* rule dictate a choice among mutually exclusive projects when projects cannot be repeated?
3. Why might it be true that a project with a lower *NPV* is preferred to a project with a higher *NPV?*
4. How does the equivalent annual annuity approach help solve the unequal lives problem?
5. *True or false:* Accepting a project with an *NPV* of $1 million has the same effect as the firm receiving a $1 million gift today.
6. How does the equivalent annuity approach differ from the common ending period approach?
7. What is the Fisher effect?
8. Distinguish between the real rate of interest and the nominal rate of interest.
9. Provide an estimate of the real rate of interest.
10. Should firms use nominal or real dollars in capital budgeting?
11. What is capital rationing?
12. Explain how the profitability index is used to solve the ranking problem.
13. [Based on the chapter Appendix] What is integer linear programming?
14. [Based on the chapter Appendix] What is the purpose of the objective function and the constraints in the integer linear programming model?

Problems

1. Project Jethro has an *NPV* of $100,000 and is expected to last 4 years. Using a discount rate of 10%, convert this *NPV* into an equivalent annuity.
2. Using a discount rate of 12%, convert the following *NPV*s to equivalent annuities based upon the project lives.
   a. Project Carter with an *NPV* of $10,000 lasting 1 year.
   b. Project Reagan with an *NPV* of $25,000 lasting 2 years.
   c. Project Roosevelt with an *NPV* of $30,000 lasting 4 years.
   d. If the White House Corporation can select only one of the projects and if the corporation believes that there will be opportunities to begin new projects with similar *NPV*s once a project terminates, which of the projects should be accepted? Why?

3. Project Enquirer has an *NPV* of $875,000 and is expected to last 5 years. Project Star has an *NPV* of $1.225 million and is expected to last 7 years. Both projects have a discount rate of 15%. Use the equivalent annuity approach to determine which project should be accepted.
4. Bundy Corporation has two projects under consideration that would use the same facilities and management team: Project Al and Project Peg. The cash flows of the projects are given as follows:

Project Name	*Initial Cost*	*Cash Inflows* Year 1	Year 2	Year 3	Year 4
Al	10,000	7,000	6,000		
Peg	20,000	8,000	9,000	10,000	12,000

Bundy Corporation realizes that the shorter life of Project Al would be an advantage because it would enable the firm to begin another profitable project quicker than if Project Peg were accepted because Project Peg takes longer to finish. Both projects have a discount rate of 10%. Use the equivalent annuity approach to determine which project should be accepted.
5. Island Corporation has two projects under consideration, both of which fill the same niche in its product line: Project Thomas and Project Croix. The cash flows of the projects are:

Project Name	*Initial Cost*	*Cash Inflows* Year 1	Year 2	Year 3
Thomas	200,000	90,000	160,000	
Croix	200,000	80,000	90,000	190,000

Island Corporation asks you to select the better project using the equivalent annuity approach. Both projects have a discount rate of 8%. Determine which project should be accepted.
6. Paterno Corporation specializes in building production facilities in cold and remote locations. The production facilities manufacture equipment used to reel in fishing lines and nets (known as "linebackers" in the industry). The firm is considering two projects for which it has been asked to work. The first project, labeled "Ground," would involve shipping materials by ground and would take 4 years to complete. The other project, labeled "Air," would be much quicker, but more expensive. The cash flows are given as:

Project Name	*Initial Cost*	*Cash Inflows* Year 1	Year 2	Year 3	Year 4
Ground	800,000	300,000	300,000	400,000	500,000
Air	2,000,000	2,000,000	900,000		

Select the better project using the equivalent annuity approach. Both projects have a discount rate of 12%.
7. Three alternatives produce identical benefits to the firm but have the following costs:

Project Name	Initial Cost	Year 1	Annual Cost Year 2	Year 3	Year 4
A	100,000	10,000	10,000	10,000	10,000
B	120,000	8,000	6,000	4,000	2,000
C	40,000	40,000	40,000	40,000	40,000

Using a discount rate of 14%, compute the total present value of each alternative. Which is cheapest?

8. Jordan Airlines is considering two alternatives for maintaining its fleet of small private jets. The first alternative is to contract with a major airline to perform the necessary maintenance for an annual cost of $1.2 million. The second alternative is for Jordan to construct its own facilities and establish its own maintenance program. The second, "do-it-yourself" alternative will cost less each year (only $500,000), but has large costs to get started—management estimates that it will involve an initial investment of $9 million. The time horizon of the problem is 20 years because a new fleet of jets will be purchased and the facilities and program will have to be completely revised by that time. Which alternative has the lowest present value of costs, given a 13% discount rate?

9. Rose Resorts is debating which type of slot machine to buy for its new casino in Atlantic City. There are two types: a high-quality model that costs $12,000 and is expected to require $1,500 per year of maintenance, and a low-quality model that costs $8,000 and is expected to require $2,000 per year in maintenance. Both machines are expected to last 10 years. Using a discount rate of 15%, compute the total present value of the costs of the two alternatives.

10. Three alternatives produce identical benefits to the firm but have unequal lives and different costs:

Project Name	Initial Cost	Year 1	Annual Cost Year 2	Year 3	Year 4
Short	100,000	10,000	10,000		
Medium	160,000	10,000	8,000	6,000	
Long	200,000	40,000	40,000	40,000	40,000

Using a discount rate of 10%, compute the total present value of each alternative and then convert them into equivalent annuity costs. Which is cheapest?

11. Returning to Problem 9, if Rose Resorts determines that the high-quality machine would last 15 years and that the low-quality machine would last only 10 years (with initial costs and annual maintenance costs unchanged), which machine would have the lower equivalent annuity cost?

12. Shark Entertainment Corporation has two alternatives under consideration that would provide major entertainment and considerable benefit to the firm. The benefits of the alternatives are equal, but their lives and costs are different. One alternative, code-named "Transfer," will last 2 years. The second alternative, code-named "Senior," will last 4 years. The costs of each of the projects are:

Project Name	Initial Cost	Year 1	Annual Cost Year 2	Year 3	Year 4
Transfer	100,000	90,000	160,000		
Senior	50,000	80,000	120,000	180,000	240,000

Shark Entertainment Corporation asks you to select the better project using the equivalent annuity approach. Both projects have a discount rate of 15%. Determine which should be accepted.

13. Inflation rates can be computed for overall indexes or for individual items. Compute the inflation rate implied by each of the following pairs of prices.

Item	*Year*	*Price*	*Year*	*Price*
Consumer price index	1940	42.0	1950	72.1
Consumer price index	1950	72.1	1960	88.7
Consumer price index	1960	88.7	1970	116.3
Consumer price index	1970	116.3	1980	246.8
Consumer price index	1980	246.8	1990	385.0
Milk	1965	$1.00	2000	$2.25
Gasoline	1965	$0.35	2000	$1.25
Beer	1975	$1.25	2000	$3.00
House	1950	$5,000	2000	$125,000
Computer	1985	$5,000	2000	$ 1,500
Tuition (public)	1975	$2,000	2000	$ 5,000

14. Use the approximate formula for the Fisher effect given in Formula (7.1) to determine the missing values:

Nominal Rate	*Real Rate*	*Expected Inflation Rate*
a. ____	3%	5%
b. ____	2%	15%
c. 10%	4%	____
d. 8%	____	6%

15. Use the precise formula for the Fisher effect in order to revise your answers:

$$(1 + \text{Nominal}) = (1 + \text{Real}) \times (1 + \text{Expected Inflation})$$

Nominal Rate	*Real Rate*	*Expected Inflation Rate*
a. ____	3%	5%
b. ____	2%	15%
c. 10%	4%	____
d. 8%	____	6%

16. Keuka Corporation is considering a project that costs $1 million and will produce benefits for 5 years. The first year cash inflow can be rather accurately estimated at $240,000, measured in today's dollars. If the actual first- through fifth-year cash flows are assumed to be the same size ($240,000), what would the *NPV* of the investment be if the appropriate discount rate is 15%?

17. Return to Keuka Corporation in Problem 16. Now assume that the cash inflow will rise each year with inflation. Assume that the inflation rate is 10%. Thus the first-year cash inflow will be found by multiplying the $240,000 by (1 + 10%) to obtain $264,000. After the first-year cash inflow of $264,000, each cash inflow is expected to rise by another 10%. Compute:

a. The second-year cash inflow = _____

b. The third-year cash inflow = _____

c. The fourth-year cash inflow = _____

d. The fifth-year cash inflow = _____

(*Hint*: Each cash inflow must be determined by applying the inflation rate to the previous year's cash inflow.)

e. Now compute the *NPV* using the cash inflows above, the original project cost of $1,000,000, and the discount rate of 15%.

f. Why did the *NPV* change relative to problem 16?

g. Which computation of *NPV* is more reliable?

18. Returning once again to Keuka Corporation (problem 16), let us compute the *NPV* using real cash flows and real interest rates. We thus use the original cash flow estimate of $240,000 for each of the 5 years. To start, we approximate the real rate of interest by subtracting the inflation rate (10%) from the nominal interest rate (15%) and obtaining 5%.

a. Compute the *NPV* using these real cash flows and the real discount rate (5%).

b. Compute the *NPV* using the real cash flows and a discount rate of 4.55%.

c. Can you verify that the discount rate used in Problem 18(b) is found by computing the real rate of interest using the precise form of the Fisher effect?

d. Ignoring rounding errors, compare your answers to Problems 16, 17(e), 18(a), and 18(b). Which is (are) correct?

19. Brooksmel Corporation is considering offering a pension alternative to its employees that is indexed to inflation. In other words, each employee would receive a pension that is increased each year in order to keep up with the inflation rate as measured by the consumer price index. Of course, employees who opt for this plan would have to be willing to accept a lower starting pension. Brooksmel's CFO is attempting to compute the cost of this pension to the firm. Consider Gene, who has worked for Brooksmel for years and is considering retirement soon. For math simplification, consider that Gene's life expectancy is only 8 years.

a. Compute the present value of Gene's pension if he opts for a fixed pension of $8,000 per year and the interest rate is 10%.

b. If Gene opts for a pension indexed to inflation, his "base pension" would be $5,000. All of his actual receipts would be higher than this figure and would depend upon the inflation rate. For example, if the inflation rate is 5%, then his first-year pension would be $5,250, which is found by multiplying $5,000 by (1 + 5%). If the inflation rate continues at 5%, his second-year pension would be $5,512.50, and so forth. Project his eight annual pension receipts, assuming that the inflation rate starts and stays at 6%.

c. Let us now solve the problem in real terms. Compute the present value of Gene's pension using a fixed annual cash flow of $5,000 and a discount rate of 4%. This approximate real rate of interest was found by subtracting the 6% inflation rate from the nominal interest rate of 10%.

d. In order to obtain an exact solution, find the real rate of interest using the precise form of the Fisher effect and solve Problem 19(c) again with the new rate.

20. Plastex Corporation is considering expanding but wishes to control growth by imposing a limit on capital expenditures of $500,000. The capital investment opportunities are:

Investment Opportunities of Plastex Corporation
(all dollar values are in thousands)

Project	*Cost*	*NPV*	*Profitability Index*	*PI Rank*	*First-Year Cash Flow*
1	$200	$50	1.25	1	$ 0
2	$200	$40	1.20	5	$ 5
3	$400	$99	1.2475	2	$10
4	$100	$17	1.17	7	$ 2
5	$100	$19	1.19	6	$ 3
6	$ 50	$12	1.24	3	$20
7	$ 50	$11	1.22	4	$15

a. Use the profitability index to select projects subject to the constraint that the firm can only invest $500,000. In other words, use the *PI* ranking to accept the best project, the next-best project, and so forth until the money is completely used. If a project's cost brings the total cost over the $500,000 limit while money remains, then skip the project and attempt to add a cheaper one.
b. Compute the total of the *NPV*s of the projects selected earlier.
c. Use your common sense to figure out a better solution—one that produces a higher total *NPV* but still uses only $500,000. Compute the sum of the *NPV*s of this better solution.
d. Why do the answers to Problem 20 (a) and (c) differ and why is the profitability index method flawed?

21. [Based on the chapter Appendix] Using the following notation:

NPV_i = the net present value of Project i

X_i = the decision variable produced by the software, which has a value of 1 if the project should be accepted and 0 if it should be rejected

C_{0i} = initial cost of Project i

C_{ti} = cash inflow (+) or outflow (−) in period T for Project i

a. Express the objective function of Problem 20.
b. Express the constraint that all the initial costs of the accepted projects must be less than or equal to $500,000.
c. Express the constraint that all the first-year cash flows of the accepted projects must add together to be at least $25,000.
d. Express the constraint that Projects 3 and 4 use the same facilities, so only one of them can be accepted.
e. Express the constraint that the company is required by previous contracts to produce a certain good, which means that the company must accept either Project 4 or 5 (or both).
f. Express the constraint that no more than three projects can be accepted from the group of projects which require supervisors (Projects 3–7).

22. Based on the chapter Appendix, use integer linear programming software to solve for the optimal solution to Problem 20 without incorporating any of the additional constraints in problem 21.

Discussion Questions

1. If *NPV* has as many difficulties as discussed in this chapter, then why should we not learn a different capital budgeting method?
2. Why is it said that using the equivalent annuity method implicitly assumes project replication?
3. In least-cost problems, the present values are always negative. Why would any firm accept a decision when the cash flows are all negative?
4. Based on the chapter Appendix, when would normal linear programming be a better solution than integer linear programming for the capital rationing problem?
5. What is the exact formula for the error introduced by using the approximation for the real interest rate in the Fisher effect equation?
6. It is said that, when using continuously compounded interest rates, the Fisher effect is given exactly by the equation:

   $$\text{Nominal Interest Rate} = \text{Inflation Rate} + \text{Real Interest Rate}$$

   Why would this be true?

APPENDIX

INTEGER LINEAR PROGRAMMING

A mathematical technique known as *integer linear programming* is ideally suited for solving the capital rationing problem. Once the problem is set up, the power of a computer can be used to search for those projects that should be accepted or rejected. Projects that are acceptable are assigned a value of 1, whereas projects that are rejected are assigned a value of zero. The word *integer* refers to the technique's ability to accept a project in total or to reject the project. In other words, the technique will not allow some fraction of the project to be accepted while some fraction is rejected. This is ideal for our problem.

We illustrate the technique of integer linear programming using the variables X_1 through X_n, where X_1 signals whether Project One should be accepted, X_2 signals whether Project Two should be accepted, and so forth. When X_1 is assigned the value of 1, Project One is accepted. When X_1 is assigned the value of zero, Project One is rejected, and so forth.

The Model's Objective Function

We first state the objective of the problem. For United Piano (Example 7.5), the objective is to select the combination of projects that produces the highest total *NPV.* The total of the *NPV*s is determined by multiplying each project's *NPV* by its decision variable ($X_i = 1$ to accept, $X_i = 0$ to reject) and summing them:

$$\text{Maximize} \sum_i NPV_i \times X_i$$

The purpose of the technique is to compute which projects should be accepted and which projects should be rejected by setting their decision variable, X_i, to either one or zero. Notice that the preceding equation adds the *NPV*s of all the accepted projects together because acceptable projects have a value of X_i equal to 1, whereas unacceptable projects have a value of X_i equal to zero.

The preceding equation is known as an *objective function* because it expresses what the user of the model wants to optimize—in this case the sum of the *NPV*s of the accepted projects.

The Model's Constraints

The integer linear programming model also needs constraints to be placed on the decision variables. Constraints are equations that place limits on the values of the decision variables. Without constraints, the model would accept all projects with positive *NPV*s. First, linear programming automatically restricts each decision variable to be greater than or equal to zero:

$$\text{Constraint One: } X_i \geq 0, \text{for all projects}$$

Next, we would usually restrict each of the *X*s to be less than or equal to 1 because it would be rare that we would have a project that we would be able to accept more than one time.

$$\text{Constraint Two: } X_i \leq 1, \text{for all projects}$$

Because integer linear programming restricts the *X* variables to integer values, the two sets of constraints listed earlier force the *X*s to have a value of either 1 (acceptance) or zero (rejection).

We can now address the issue of capital rationing directly. United Piano's problem is that they have only \$100 million to invest. We can express this constraint by requiring that the solution have initial cash flows that spend no more than the budgeted amount:

$$\text{Constraint Three: } \sum_i X_i \times C_{0i} \geq -\$100{,}000{,}000$$

where C_{0i} is the initial cash flow (C_0) of Project *i*. Thus, the total initial costs of all accepted projects, given by summing $\{X_i \times C_{0i}\}$, must not exceed in absolute value the amount specified by the user. Because the cash flows are negative, we constrain the sum to be greater than a negative number. In other words, the sum must be less negative than the budgeted number.

The objective functions and constraints mentioned earlier would guide the computer program into providing the optimal solution to the simplified typical capital rationing problem.

Other Constraints

One important advantage of using integer linear programming to solve capital rationing problems is that many other potential restrictions can be easily incorporated.

For large projects it would be common for cash flows to be negative for several years. Thus, the financial manager might want to restrict the sum of the cash flows across projects to be no less than a certain amount in each of the first few years. For example, to constrain the projects to cost no more than $10 million in the first year, to break even by the second year, and to produce a cash inflow of $20 million by the third year, the financial manager would include the following constraints:

$$\text{Constraint Four: } \sum_i X_i \times C_{1i} \geq -\$10{,}000{,}000$$

$$\text{Constraint Five: } \sum_i X_i \times C_{2i} \geq \$0$$

$$\text{Constraint Six: } \sum_i X_i \times C_{3i} \geq \$20{,}000{,}000$$

Other potential constraints could be that certain combinations of projects could not be accepted together. Projects sharing the same building, personnel, or product niche might have to be limited so that only one of them would be accepted. For example, if Projects 1 and 2 were mutually exclusive because they required the same building, we would impose the following constraint:

$$\text{Constraint Seven: } X_1 + X_2 \leq 1$$

If only two of the projects, 3, 4, and 5, could be accepted because they used the same personnel, then we would impose the following constraint:

$$\text{Constraint Eight: } X_3 + X_4 + X_5 \leq 2$$

Finally, perhaps market research or agreements with customers would require that the firm continue to supply at least one of the products produced by certain projects such that at least one of projects 2 and 3 has to be accepted:

$$\text{Constraint Nine: } X_2 + X_3 \geq 1$$

Other constraints could be included to consider project interaction.

A Summary of Integer Linear Programming

Integer linear programming is a powerful answer to the problems of capital rationing and project interactions. With the widespread availability of personal computers and the increasing ability and willingness of financial managers to use them, it is clear that integer linear programming is destined to become the standard technique.

This appendix demonstrated how the integer linear programming model can be used in a business situation. The complete integer linear programming model is shown in Table 7.4. Given the model's objective function and its series of constraints, the computer will find the ideal set of projects that maximizes *NPV*.

TABLE 7.4 The Integer Linear Programming Model

The Problem

United Piano must decide which of the seven projects in Table 7.2 in which to invest.
United Piano cannot invest more than \$100 million.

The Basic Model

Objective function: $\sum_i NPV_i \times X_i$, subject to the following constraints:

$X_i \geq 0$, for all projects

$X_i \leq 1$, for all projects

$$\sum_i X_i \times C_{0i} \geq -\$100{,}000{,}000$$

The More Advanced Model

Objective function: Maximize $\sum_i NPV_i \times X_i$, subject to the following constraints:

$X_i \geq 0$, for all projects

$X_i \leq 1$, for all projects

$$\sum_i X_i \times C_{0i} \geq -\$100{,}000{,}000$$

$$\sum_i X_i \times C_{1i} \geq -\$10{,}000{,}000$$

$$\sum_i X_i \times C_{2i} \geq 0$$

$$\sum_i X_i \times C_{3i} \geq \$20{,}000{,}000$$

$$X_1 + X_2 \leq 1$$

$$X_3 + X_4 + X_5 \leq 2$$

$$X_2 + X_3 \geq 1$$

CHAPTER 8

RISK AND DIVERSIFICATION

Traveler's checks are used as an inexpensive and convenient way of protecting against theft. To the traveler, the time between the purchase of the checks and the use of the money seems short. For the firms that issue traveler's checks, however (e.g., American Express), their revenue comes from the interest income earned between the time they receive payment for the checks and the time the checks are used. This period is called float, and the longer the *float,* the more interest earned.

In gleaming office towers in major financial centers sit managers whose job is to invest these funds. Their job sounds simple—shopping for the places to store the money at the highest interest rate. These managers, however, must contend with their number-one enemy every day—risk. High returns must be produced in order to be competitive, but with the promise of high returns comes risk. For example, the money invested may never be returned because the borrower might go bankrupt, or the money received may be less than expected because interest rates have changed. The bottom line is that understanding risk and determining an appropriate rate of return for bearing the risk are central to today's financial decision making.

The definition of *finance* as the economics of time and risk indicates that risk plays a major role in investment, financing, and working capital management decisions. This chapter will introduce models that allow assets to be classified according to their risk level. Once risk has been identified, other models, such as net present value, can be used to incorporate both time and risk when making corporate financial decisions.

A Conceptual Analysis of Risk

Let us begin by recalling the corporate objective of shareholder wealth maximization and by noting some of the key results from the earlier chapters in the book. Financial managers, acting as agents of shareholders, should invest when the cash flows representing benefits exceed the cash flows representing costs. Comparison of dollars through time can be made only by discounting future dollars into present values. Promises of risky dollars are similarly not the same commodity as promises of safe dollars, and a transformation must be made to adjust for risk. Once we learn to transform risky dollars into safe dollars, basic economic principles can be used to make decisions consistent with the goal of the firm—shareholder wealth maximization.

Risk was introduced in Chapter 1 through the economic principle of diminishing marginal utility. Diminishing marginal utility implies that investors arc risk-averse and establishes a foundation for studying risk-taking behavior. Risk-averse investors bear risk only if rewarded. If investors are risk-averse, then the required return on a risky project will be greater than the required return on a relatively safe project.

One of the main objectives of this chapter is to show how risk can be incorporated into the *NPV* model. This chapter and Chapter 9 combine statistical measures of risk with modern portfolio theory. Modern portfolio theory demonstrates that the risk of an asset held alone is different from the risk of an asset held as part of a diversified group of assets. A new model, called the *capital asset pricing model,* will use modern portfolio theory to estimate an appropriate discount rate for risky cash flows.

Here is a sneak preview of two important results that will be developed in these next two chapters on risk:

portfolio
A combined holding of at least two assets.

1. The risk of an asset held alone is measured differently from the risk of an asset held as part of a group of assets. A group of assets is known as a **portfolio.** The risk of an asset held as part of a portfolio can be fully measured using a risk measure entitled *beta,* which will be defined in Chapter 9.
2. Risk enters the net present value model through the discount rate or interest rate. The discount rate appropriate for a specific asset depends upon the asset's beta and is found using the capital asset pricing model. This model will be fully developed in Chapter 9.

The key to understanding risk, therefore is to understand this new risk measure, entitled *beta,* and to understand the capital asset pricing model, known by the acronym CAPM (often pronounced: cap em). Although the end result will be straightforward, it is useful for students to understand the reasoning behind the tools used to obtain this end result. We begin with the concept of uncertainty.

What Is Uncertainty?

uncertainty
The inability to forecast which outcomes or states of nature will occur in the future.

Uncertainty is the inability to forecast future outcomes or future states of nature. For example, consider Risk, Inc., a new company whose only project is an attempt to develop a powerful new technology to remove ice cream stains. If the company is successful, then we know that the stock will rise to \$10 per share—the favorable outcome (or state of nature). If the technology fails, the stock will drop to \$0 per share—obviously the unfavorable outcome (or state of nature). Risk, Inc. is currently being offered to the public at \$5 per share. The uncertainty in this example is that we do not know which of the two outcomes, $10 per share or $0 per share, will occur.

What Is Risk?

risk
The variation in value among uncertain outcomes.

Let us now assume that Mr. Smart has refused to place his money in Risk, Inc.'s, stock despite the advice of a stockbroker. We would say that Mr. Smart has decided not to expose his money to this substantial risk. **Risk** is variation in value among uncertain outcomes—in this case the difference between $10 and $0 per share.

Not all securities contain risk. For example, a U.S. Treasury bill promises a guaranteed dollar amount regardless of what happens to Risk, Inc.'s new technology or to anything else. We call the Treasury bill investment riskless, as it promises cash flows with certainty.[1] How does Mr. Smart decide in which asset—Risk, Inc. or Treasury bills—to invest? To answer this question, we must consider how investors view risk.

Risk-Averse Behavior

risk-averse
Unwilling to accept risk without the expectation of reward.

Most investors share similar behavior when it comes to risk—they do not enjoy bearing it. This does not mean that people will not take risk; rather, it means that they demand extra return for bearing risk. When individuals will accept risk if and only if the expected return is increased, then we say they are **risk-averse.** The vast majority of money in the United States is invested with the attitude that the riskier the investment, the greater must be its expected return or reward.

This is not to say that all investors are risk averse all the time. For example, a **risk-neutral** investor will be indifferent between two investments that have the same expected return even if the risk levels of the investments are different. **Risk-seeking** investors will actuallly prefer higher risk given choices with the same expected payoff. Further, we may observe that an investor who is risk-averse by day enjoys taking different types of risk by night, such as buying a lottery ticket or playing casino blackjack. This behavior is due perhaps to the entertainment value that the ticket or game offers. Nevertheless, throughout this text, we will assume that investors behave in a risk-averse manner.

Where Risk Aversion Comes From For centuries there was no solid explanation for why people are risk-averse. Then, in the 1730s, Swiss mathematician Daniel Bernouilli provided an explanation using our second economic principle, diminishing marginal utility.[2] As we have said, diminishing

---

[1]Finance ignores things like thermonuclear war and revolution.

[2]Those readers interested in the development of our understanding of risk through the ages will enjoy reading the book *Against the Gods, the Remarkable Story of Risk,* by Peter L. Bernstein (New York: John Wiley, Inc.).

marginal utility means that as people become wealthier and wealthier, a particular amount of money tends to be less and less important to them. For example, to a person who can barely meet the basic economic needs of life, $10 may seem like a great deal of money; however, if that same person were to become wealthy, $10 will be much less important.

Given diminishing marginal utility, in Bernouilli's explanation, the happiness gained from increases in wealth is less in magnitude than the happiness lost from decreases in wealth. Put simply, people view an unrewarded risk as undesirable because the potential winnings have less value than the potential losses.

Measuring Risk Aversion Using Utility Analysis Let us return to Mr. Smart. When contemplating the shares of Risk, Inc., Mr. Smart thought about how nice it would be to receive $10 per share and how unpleasant it would be to lose his money. Mr. Smart was applying the economic law of diminishing marginal utility to the investment decision.

Figure 8.1 contains the utility diagram from Chapter 1. It represents the assumed relationship between happiness and money. The two key aspects

FIGURE 8.1 Mr. Smart's Utility Curve

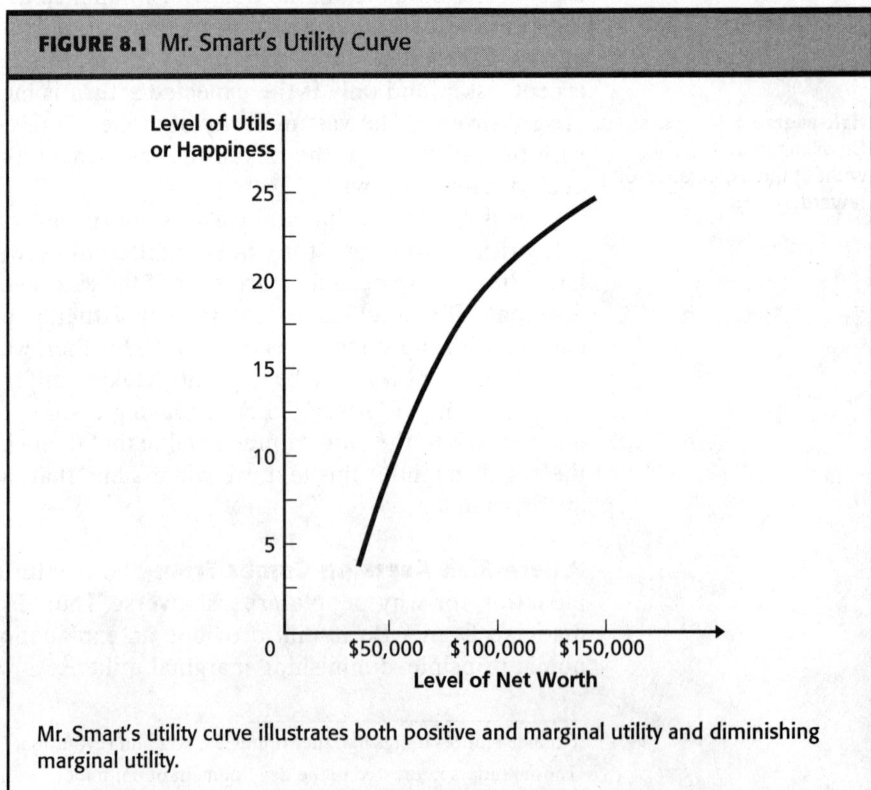

Mr. Smart's utility curve illustrates both positive and marginal utility and diminishing marginal utility.

to utility theory are positive marginal utility—more money means more happiness—and diminishing marginal utility—a given amount of money means less and less additional happiness as people become wealthier and wealthier.

Figure 8.1 includes utility values for Mr. Smart. Suppose that Mr. Smart's total wealth is $100,000, without an investment in Risk, Inc. If he purchases 10,000 shares of Risk, Inc. for $5 per share, his wealth would either rise to $150,000 if the stock rose to $10 or fall to $50,000 if the stock fell to zero. In terms of dollars, the risk offers equal potential gains and losses of $50,000.

Utility diagrams translate dollar amounts into units (or an imaginary measure called *utils*) of happiness. In our example we have attached symbolic levels of happiness to each level of wealth. At $100,000 Mr. Smart enjoys 20 utils of happiness. If Mr. Smart's wealth rises to $150,000, then his happiness will rise to 25 utils. If, on the other hand, Mr. Smart's wealth were to fall to $50,000, then his happiness would fall to 10 utils.

When viewed in terms of happiness rather than dollars, we see that the potential gain from the investment, measured by five additional utils of happiness, is less than the potential loss from the investment of ten utils of happiness. Even though the dollar gains and dollar losses are equal, Mr. Smart's utility function reveals the problem with risk—the happiness that could be lost exceeds the happiness that could be gained. Given the characteristic of diminishing marginal utility, Mr. Smart is unwilling to take a risk that in dollar terms appears to offer equal potential for gains and losses.

Why Risk-Averse People Invest in Risky Assets Risk is a necessary part of life in general and economic activity in particular. Because most financial decisions involve some degree of risk, we find that risk-averse people will bear risk as long as they are rewarded for doing so.

One way that Mr. Smart could be rewarded for bearing the risk of Risk, Inc. would be if the probability of the stock's rising were greater than the probability of its falling. Another way would be if the stock sold for only $1 per share (instead of $5 per share) such that the potential gain of $9 in the favorable state of nature far exceeded the potential loss of $1 in the unfavorable state. It turns out that Mr. Smart's decision not to invest in Risk, Inc., was based on his assessment that the probability of the stock's price rising to $10 per share was small.

Risky investments will not always produce higher profits when compared with safe investments. If they did, no one would buy the safe investments. Rather, risky investments offer higher expected or higher average profits that are greater than those of safe investments. These higher expected profits could be a result of high probabilities of moderate success or moderate probabilities of enormously successful outcomes.

Thus, the theory of risk-taking is built upon a tradeoff between risk and expected reward. These tradeoffs between risk and reward are all around us and are made every day. For example, some people accept the risk of driving 80 miles per hour on an interstate highway because the rewards of driving at such a speed are greater than the risks. If the risks increased, say to double the fine for speeding, some people might reassess the risk and reward relationship and decide not to take the risk.

In the 1950s, Harry Markowitz, an economist, demonstrated the insights into the risk and reward tradeoff for financial securities using the tools of math and statistics. In 1990 he earned a Nobel prize for his work. The remainder of this chapter will use these tools.

Return and Risk on Individual Assets

An asset's return is often used as an indication of its performance. Positive returns indicate good performance, and negative returns indicate bad performance. Returns can be thought of as the change in value through time, expressed as a percentage.

Asset returns are defined as the change in value through time expressed as a proportion or as a percentage.

For example, consider Woolridge, Inc., a research firm whose stock price is \$20 per share today. The annual return on Woolridge, Inc., denoted $R_{w,}$ is expressed as a ratio of the change in price during the year to the old price at the start of the year:

$$R_w = \frac{[\text{End Value - Start Value}]}{\text{Start Value}} \tag{8.1}$$

If Woolridge's stock price rises to \$22 next year, the return would be:

$$R_W = \frac{[\$22 - \$20]}{\$20} = 0.10, \text{ or } 10\%$$

To convert a decimal, say 0.10, to a percentage, multiply the decimal amount by 100. For example, if the price of the stock fell from \$20 to \$19, then the return would be −0.05 or −5 percent.

If the investment includes more than one payment, such as a stock whose end value may include both a price plus a dividend payment, both payments should be added together to get the end-of-period value. These concepts are more thoroughly discussed in Window 8.1.

Distributions of Returns

We may now view the risk of an asset as uncertainty regarding the asset's return. Because the return on the asset is unknown, it is referred to as a

WINDOW 8.1

Measuring Security Returns

This window details the calculation of security returns. Many of these calculations were introduced in Chapter 3 as time value of money problems. The returns examined in this window relate directly to financial securities known as common stock and bonds, and will build from Formula (8.1).

Returns from common stock can come from dividend payments and changes in the stock's market value. The common stock return formula can be given as:

$$\text{Common Stock Return} = \frac{[\text{Dividend Received} + \text{Ending Price}] - \text{Starting Price}}{\text{Starting Price}}$$

For example, suppose you purchase a share of stock for \$20 and sell the stock next year for \$21. Over the interim, the stock pays a dividend of \$2. The percentage return on the stock investment is:

$$\text{Common Stock Return} = \frac{[\$2 + \$21] - \$20}{\$20} = 0.15, \text{ or } 15\%$$

We could get more precise and break the return into its two components: a dividend return (sometimes referred to as a dividend yield) and a capital gain. In the preceding example, the dividend return is 10 percent and the capital gain return is 5 percent.

The selling price could of course be less than the buying price. In this case, the second component of return would be negative and we would say that the investment produced a capital loss.

Returns from bonds can come from coupon payments and changes in the bond's price when it is sold. The bond return formula can be given as:

$$\text{Bond Return} = \frac{[\text{Coupon Payment} + \text{Ending Price}] - \text{Starting Price}}{\text{Starting Price}}$$

For example, suppose you purchase a 10-year maturity bond at par for \$1,000 that pays a \$120 coupon annual payment. Suppose also that at the end of the year the bond's price has fallen to \$996 (*Quick Quiz:* In what direction did market interest rates move?) and you decide to sell the bond at this time. The return on the bond investment is:

$$\text{Bond Return} = \frac{[\$120 + \$996] - \$1{,}000}{\$1{,}000} = 0.116, \text{ or } 11.6\%$$

We could get more precise and break the return into its two components: a coupon return and a capital loss, as we sold the bond for a price less than we paid for it. In the preceding example, the coupon return is 12 percent and the capital loss is 0.4 percent.

WINDOW 8.1 *(continued)*

In both examples, the time period of investment was 1 year, and the rate of return was an annual return. (*Note:* It is common to quote returns on an annual basis.) There is nothing common or conventional, however, about measuring returns over 1-year intervals. Some investors buy stock and sell the stock in less than 1 year; some even buy stock and sell it the next day! The same is true for bonds.

Although the return formulas can be altered to calculate the return over any number of days, it is conventional to report returns as if they were earned over the entire year. For example, an investor who earns a return of 3% over 3 months might wish to know what the return would have been if the investment were held for the period of 1 year. Returns over any time period, fortunately, can be transformed into annualized returns in one of two ways:

$$\text{Simple Annualized Return} = R_t \times 365/t$$

or

$$\text{Compound Annualized Return} = (1 + R_t)^{365/t} - 1$$

where R_t is the return over the holding period, and t is the number of days in which the investment was held. For example, t is 1 day in the case where stock is sold the day after it is purchased. The difference between the two annualized return formulas is that the second formula assumes that interest is compounded during the year, but the first formula does not.

Returning to the preceding stock example, suppose that you purchase a share of stock for \$20 and sell the stock in 6 months (182 days) for \$21. Over the interim, the stock paid a dividend of \$2. Although your holding period is 6 months, what is the annualized return on the stock investment?

It is best to break the problem into two steps. First, apply Formula (8.1) to obtain the holding period return. Next, apply either the simple annualized return or the compound annualized return formula to annualize the holding period return:

Step 1:

$$\text{Holding Period Return: } R_t = \frac{(\$2 + \$21) - \$20}{\$20} = 15\%$$

Step 2:

$$\text{Simple Annualized Holding Period Return} = 0.15 \times 365/182 = 30\%$$

or

$$\text{Compounded Annualized Holding Period Return} = (1.15)^{365/182} - 1 = 32.35\%$$

WINDOW 8.1 *(continued)*

The effect of compounding interest can be seen from the difference in annualized holding period returns. Under simple interest, the 15 percent return earned over the half-year period is doubled to get the annualized holding period return. With compounding, the annualized return is more than double the half-year return because the interest earned over the first half-year is assumed to be reinvested along with the original investment over the second half of the year.

This procedure works for any time period, be it one day or 1,000 days; however, investors should be aware of the potential for enormous returns when annualizing returns earned over short periods. For example, suppose you buy a share of stock today for \$5.00 and sell it next week or in 7 days for \$5.125 (no dividends are earned). The annualized holding period return would be:

$$\text{Annualized Holding Period Return} = \left[\frac{\$5.125}{\$5.00}\right]^{365/7} - 1 = 2.6239 \text{ or } 262.39\%.$$

This return is realistic only if the investor believes that it is possible on a continuing basis to purchase the stock and sell the stock in 1 week for a higher price.

random variable
In finance, a variable whose value in the future is unknown.

normal distribution
A probability distribution with a symmetrical or bell-like curve.

random variable. The relationship between the possible returns of a random variable and the probability of obtaining these possible returns is known as a *probability distribution.* Figure 8.2 illustrates a random variable's return using a special type of distribution called the **normal distribution.**

The normal distribution illustrated in Figure 8.2 and another similar distribution known as the log-normal distribution are the primary distributions used for return analysis. These distributions are used in developing a framework for describing how an investor would make decisions regarding the tradeoff between risk and the reward for bearing risk.

Statistics contains many useful tools for analyzing the tradeoff between risk and reward. The two primary tools we will use are: (1) the mean or expectation to describe the level of return offered, and (2) the standard deviation or variance to describe the dispersion or degree of uncertainty of the return.

Mean Returns

mean or expected value
The average of all possible values weighted by their probabilities of occurrence.

We are all familiar with the concept of an average such as a grade point average. *Mean* is another term for *average,* and *expected value* is another. The three terms can be used interchangeably.

The **mean** return or **expected value** is the middle of the outcomes on a probability-weighted basis. The formula for the mean return or expected

FIGURE 8.2 The Normal Distribution of Returns

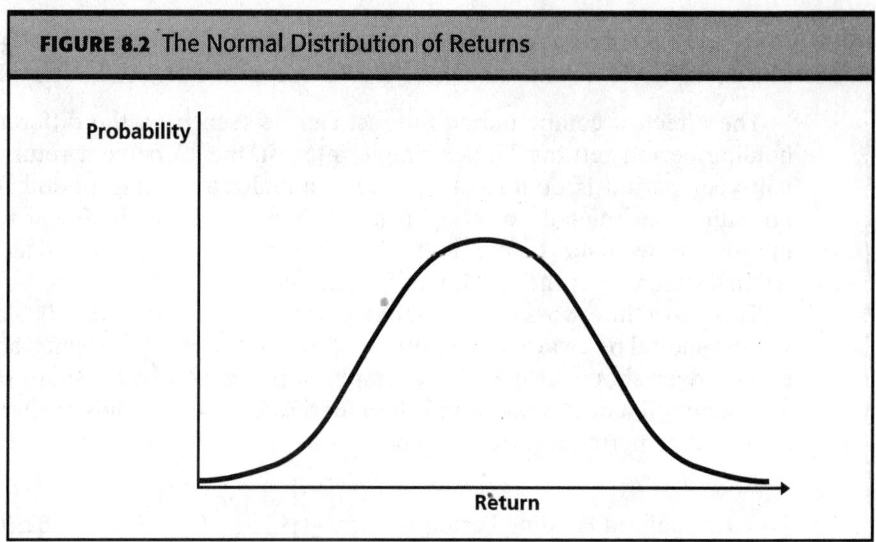

value is the sum of the expected returns in each state of nature multiplied by their associated probabilities:

$$E(R) = \sum_{i=1}^{n} R_i \times Prob_i \tag{8.2}$$

where $E(R)$ is the expected or mean return, i stands for a particular state of nature, n is the total number of states of nature, R_i is the asset's return in state i, and $Prob_i$ is the probability that state i will occur.

Example 8.1 We can calculate the expected or mean return of Risk, Inc., using Formula (8.2). The stock price of Risk, Inc., is currently $5 per share. The uncertainty associated with an investment in Risk, Inc., is captured by the two states of nature. In state success the stock price will rise to $10, and in state failure the stock price will fall to $0, defining the return in each state:

$$\text{Return in State Success: } R_S = \frac{\$10 - \$5}{\$5} = 100\%$$

$$\text{Return in State Failure: } R_F = \frac{\$0 - \$5}{\$5} = -100\%$$

In order to compute Risk, Inc.'s, mean return it is necessary to know the probability of either state occurring. If the two states are equally likely such that the probability of each state is 0.5, then the expected or mean return would be 0%:

$$E(R) = (-100\% \times 0.5) + (100\% \times 0.5) = 0\%$$

If the probability of the \$10 outcome were 60% and the \$0 outcome were 40%, then the expected or mean return would be:

$$E(R) = (-100\% \times 0.4) + (100\% \times 0.6) = 0.20, \text{ or } 20\%$$

In real situations, the number of possible outcomes is far greater than two and the probabilities associated with these possible outcomes are difficult to estimate. The concept, however, remains unchanged.

Example 8.2 ________ Consider Project A and Project B. Project A is an investment in machinery to manufacture a product with a relatively stable market. Project B is an investment in machinery to manufacture a luxury product that is more sensitive to economic conditions. The returns from each have been estimated for four possible states in the economy: recession, slow growth, moderate growth, and prosperity. The estimates are shown in column 1 of Table 8.1.

Both projects are expected to produce returns of 0 percent in a recession; however, in prosperity the return on Project A would be 10 percent, whereas the return on Project B would be 15 percent. These estimates may derive from a sophisticated computer analysis or they may be completely subjective.

The next step is to estimate the probability of each state and is usually relatively subjective. Once estimated, these probabilities are multiplied by their respective returns to obtain weighted values. As shown in Table 8.1, the sum of these weighted values is the mean or the expected value. The mean of Project A is 6 percent, and the mean of Project B is 7 percent.

The Standard Deviation of Returns

The mean is a measure of an average, not a measure of risk. Two investments can have very different risk levels. We need a measure of the amount of

TABLE 8.1 State-Dependent Returns from Projects A and B

	(1) *Annual Return*		*(2)* *Probability of State Occurring*	*(3)* *Probability-Weighted Return (2) × (3)*	
State of Nature	**Project**			**Project**	
	A	**B**		**A**	**B**
Recession	0.00	0.00	0.20	0.000	0.000
Slow Growth	0.06	0.05	0.30	0.018	0.015
Moderate Growth	0.08	0.10	0.40	0.032	0.040
Prosperity	0.10	0.15	0.10	0.010	0.015
Expected Value				*0.060*	*0.070*

standard deviation and variance
Statistical measures of dispersion and variability.

dispersion of the returns around the mean return to measure risk. Such risk measures are known as the **standard deviation** and **variance.**

The variance and standard deviation can be computed using the following formula or by using a calculator or computer that has the formula programmed into it:

$$Variance = \sigma^2 = \sum_{i=1}^{n}\left[(R_i - E(R))^2 \times Prob_i\right] \tag{8.3}$$

$$Standard\ Deviation = \sigma = \sqrt{\sum_{i=1}^{n}\left[(R_i - E(R))^2 \times Prob_i\right]} \tag{8.4}$$

where the Greek letters σ^2 (sigma squared) and σ (sigma) stand for the variance and standard deviation, respectively, R_i is the asset's return in state i, $E(R)$ is the expected or mean return, i stands for a particular state of nature, n is the total number of states, and $Prob_i$ is the probability that state i will occur.

Example 8.3 ________ Look again at Projects A and B. Project A has a mean return of 6 percent, whereas Project B has a mean return of 7 percent. Notice that the returns expected in the respective states are different. In the case of Project A, the difference in return between the best and worse states of nature is 10 percent. The difference is 15 percent for Project B. Figure 8.3 illustrates the dispersion of the returns of Projects A and B. The distribution for Project A appears tighter, whereas the distribution for Project B appears wider.

The calculation of the variance and standard deviation of Project A and Project B is shown in Table 8.2. Columns 1 through 3 of Table 8.2 come directly from Table 8.1. They indicate (1) the estimated return from the projects under each state (R_i), (2) the probability of each state occurring ($Prob_i$), and (3) the estimated return under each state multiplied by the probability of that state occurring ($R_i \times Prob_i$) for each project, respectively. The sum of

FIGURE 8.3 The Distribution of Returns of Projects A and B

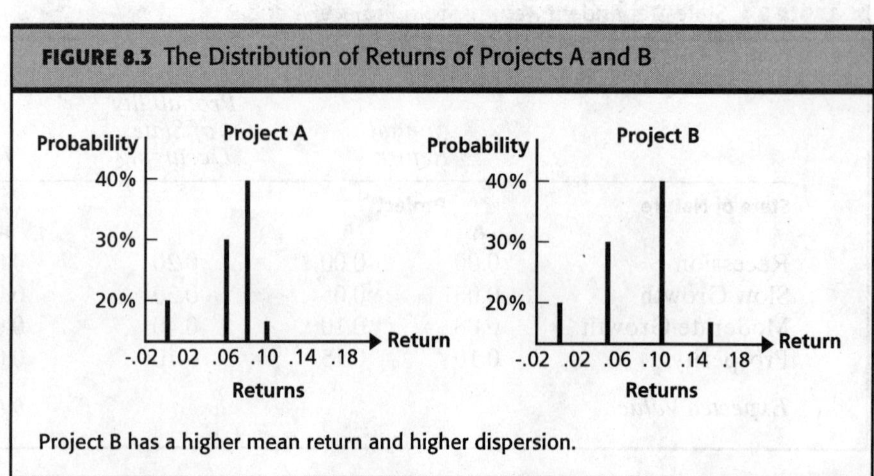

Project B has a higher mean return and higher dispersion.

TABLE 8.2 The Standard Deviation of Returns for Projects A and B

State of Nature	(1) *Estimated Return*	(2) *Probability of State*	(3) *Weighted Return*	(4) *Return Deviation*	(5) *Squared Return Deviation*	(6) *Weighted Squared Deviation*
Project A						
Recession	0.00	0.20	0.000	−0.06	0.0036	0.00072
Slow Growth	0.06	0.30	0.018	0.00	0.0000	0.00000
Moderate Growth	0.08	0.40	0.032	+0.02	0.0004	0.00016
Prosperity	0.10	0.10	0.010	+0.04	0.0016	0.00016
		Expected Value = 0.060			Variance = 0.00104	

Standard Deviation = $\sqrt{0.00104}$ = .03225

State of Nature	(1) *Estimated Return*	(2) *Probability of State*	(3) *Weighted Return*	(4) *Return Deviation*	(5) *Squared Return Deviation*	(6) *Weighted Squared Deviation*
Project B						
Recession	0.00	0.20	0.000	−0.07	0.0049	0.00098
Slow Growth	0.05	0.30	0.015	−0.02	0.0004	0.00012
Moderate Growth	0.10	0.40	0.040	+0.03	0.0009	0.00036
Prosperity	0.15	0.10	0.015	+0.08	0.0064	0.00064
		Expected Value = 0.070			Variance = 0.00210	

Standard Deviation = $\sqrt{0.0021}$ = .04583

these weighted values is the expected return of Project A and Project B as previously demonstrated in Table 8.1.

Column 4 calculates the return deviation, $R_i - E(R)$, of each estimated return from its expected return. Column 5 squares each deviation. In column 6, each of the squared deviations is multiplied by the probability of its occurrence ($Prob_i$). The sum of these weighted squared deviations is the variance of the distribution. The standard deviation is calculated as the square root of the variance.

The larger the standard deviation, the wider the probability distribution and the greater the risk. We see from Table 8.2 that the standard deviation of returns of Project A is 0.03225 and of Project B is 0.04583.

There are two primary methods of computing the variance and standard deviation. The first is to use a calculator or computer, which will do the work, and the second is to build a table similar to that shown in Table 8.2. We would encourage you first to learn the concepts by building tables similar to Table

8.2, and then to seek shortcuts such as those provided by computers or advanced calculators.

The Normal Distribution

There were only four possible states of nature for Project A and Project B, whereas there are an infinite number of states in the normal distribution. The meaning of standard deviation is well known in the case of the normal distribution. For a normally distributed variable, 68 percent of the outcomes fall within one standard deviation of the mean. For example, if the mean is 12 percent and the standard deviation is 20 percent, then we would say that, although we expect the return to be 12 percent, an actual return of 12 percent is unlikely. The best we can say is that the actual return will be somewhere between −8 percent and +32 percent 68 percent of the time. Further, for the normal distribution, 95 percent of the actual outcomes will fall within two standard deviations of the mean, and more than 99 percent will fall within three standard deviations of the mean. This is illustrated in Figure 8.4.

Risk and Reward

The mean and standard deviation are important in describing the returns offered by a risky asset. The mean appears to be a good measure of the reward that an investor anticipates. At first glance it also appears as though standard deviation is a good measure of risk.

Recall that the objective of this chapter is to develop a framework for analyzing the way investors make decisions between risk and reward. The concept that investors demand more reward for bearing more risk is illustrated in Figure 8.5. The remainder of this chapter as well as Chapter 9 will deter-

FIGURE 8.4 Interpreting the Standard Deviation Under the Normal Distribution

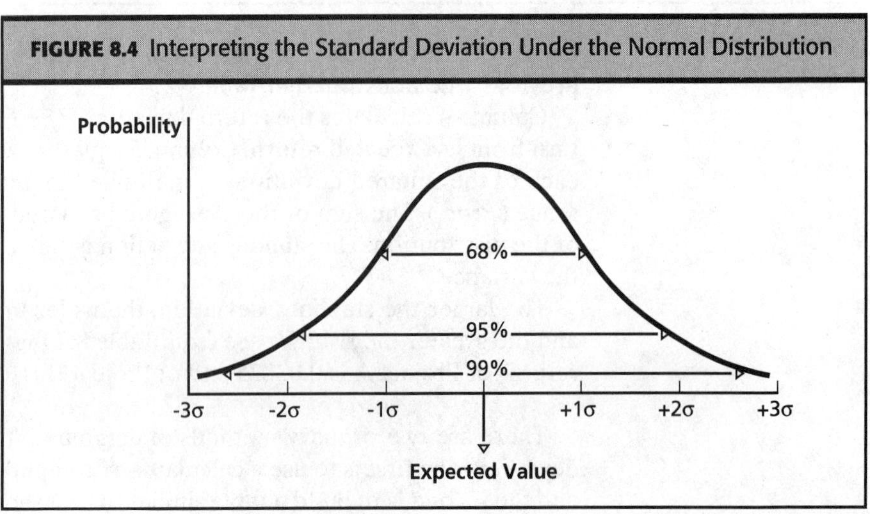

FIGURE 8.5 The Risk-Reward Relationship

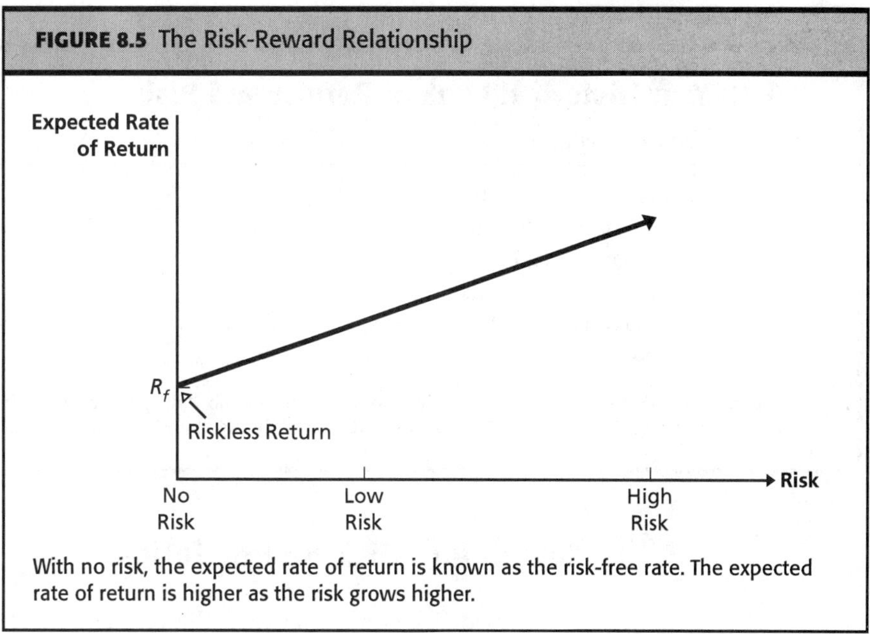

With no risk, the expected rate of return is known as the risk-free rate. The expected rate of return is higher as the risk grows higher.

mine the proper labels to each axis in Figure 8.5 and what the specific relationship should look like.

Let us return briefly to the discussion of how the investing public views risk. Earlier in this chapter we stated that the vast majority of money in the United States is invested with the attitude that the riskier the investment, the greater is its expected return or reward. Now that we have defined measures of return and risk, we can look to the historical evidence to see if this is true. This is shown in Window 8.2.

The summary provided in Window 8.2 confirms our earlier description of the risk–reward relationship. The higher the risk of the investment as measured by its standard deviation, the higher its return. Although Window 8.2 does not show year-by-year returns, the greatest dispersion of annual returns is found in small common stocks, where returns ranged from +143 percent in 1933 to −58 percent in 1937.

The Problem with Standard Deviation as a Risk Measure

Although the standard deviation at first appears to be a good measure of risk, it has a serious flaw. This flaw, to be demonstrated in the next few subsections, will be revealed when risky assets are combined. When two or more risky assets are combined, the standard deviation of the combination will, in most cases, be less than the average standard deviations of the individual assets. To develop this point further it is necessary to learn some of the results of portfolio theory—an important subset of modern finance.

WINDOW 8.2

A 70-Year Historical Look at Return and Risk

Security Type	*Mean Return*	*Standard Deviation*
1. Small Common Stocks	17.7%	33.9%
2. Large Common Stocks	13.0%	20.3%
3. Corporate Bonds	6.1%	8.7%
4. Government Bonds	5.4%	5.7%
5. U.S. Treasury Bills	3.8%	3.2%
6. Inflation	3.2%	4.5%

Source: Used with permission. [Certain portions of this work were derived from copyrighted works of Roger G. Ibbotson and Rex Sinquefield.]

Return and Risk on Portfolios

The previous sections analyzed the calculation of the expected return and the standard deviation of returns for individual assets. It is common, however, for investors to hold groups of assets called *portfolios.* This section performs similar analysis for portfolios.

Portfolio Returns

The return of a portfolio can be computed by combining the returns of the assets in the portfolio. We refer to the assets in a portfolio as its constituent assets, much as an elected state or national representative refers to the people in his or her district as constituents. If the assets are held in equal proportions, then the portfolio return is the simple average of the individual returns. If the assets in the portfolio are not held in equal proportions, however, then each asset must be weighted by its percentage representation of the total portfolio value.

Actual Returns Consider a portfolio with only two stocks: Disney and ATT. Inasmuch as it is necessary to know the percentages of the portfolio's market value represented by each of the stocks, let us assume that 60 percent of the portfolio's market value is in Disney stock, and the remaining 40 percent is in ATT stock.

The return of the portfolio in a given time period can be found by adding 60 percent of Disney's return and 40 percent of ATT's return. For example, if Disney's return is 20 percent and ATT's return is 10 percent, then the portfolio's return is 16 percent.

In order to prepare for some more complex concepts to follow, it is useful to introduce some notation. We will denote the percentage of a portfolio's value in a particular asset (such as asset *i*) as w_i. The letter *w* stands for weight and the subscript *i* refers to a particular asset. The formula for w_i is given by:

$$w_i = \frac{\text{Market value of the investment in asset } i}{\text{Market value of the entire portfolio}} \tag{8.5}$$

The formula for the return of a portfolio (denoted R_p) may therefore be expressed as the weighted average of the returns of the portfolio's constituent assets:

$$R_p = \sum_{i=1}^{n} w_i \times R_i \tag{8.6}$$

where R_p stands for the return of a portfolio, R_i is the return on constituent asset *i,* and *n* stands for the number of assets in the portfolio. The summation sign indicates that the weighted returns are summed across the number of constituent assets in the portfolio.

Another way of calculating the return of a portfolio would be to calculate its total market value at the beginning of the period and again at the end of the period, and then applying Formula (8.1). This method, however, does not illustrate the points of this chapter well and turns out to be slower than the procedures shown in Formula (8.6).

Expected Returns As in the case of actual returns, the mean or expected return of a portfolio depends upon the mean or expected returns of the portfolio's constituent assets. In fact, the procedures are identical. The mean or expected return of the portfolio, $E(R_p)$, is a weighted average of the mean returns of the constituent assets as shown:

$$E(R_p) = \sum_{i=1}^{n} w_i \times E(R_i) \tag{8.7}$$

Expected returns operate just as we would hope. The portfolio's expected return is a blend or weighted average of the expected returns of the constituent assets. Thus, if an asset is added to the portfolio that has a higher expected return than the portfolio's other assets, then the portfolio's expected return would rise. On the other hand, adding a lower expected return asset would cause the portfolio's expected return to fall.

A First Look at Portfolio Risk

The simplicity of moving from returns on individual assets to the returns on portfolios unfortunately does not extend to the portfolio's variance and standard deviation. If it did, then this chapter would end at this point and

Chapter 9 would not even exist. This subsection is necessary because it explains diversification, which is a key concept in risk management. **Diversification** is the reduction in a portfolio's risk that occurs when assets are combined into a portfolio and some of the risks of the portfolio's constituent assets cancel each other out.

diversification
The reduction in a portfolio's risk that occurs when assets are combined into a portfolio and portions of the risks of the portfolio's constituent assets cancel each other out.

Diversification Consider a sunglasses corporation and an umbrella corporation. Each investment by itself would be risky because the sunglasses firm's success depends upon sunny days and the umbrella firm's success depends upon rainy days. An investor holding both stocks, however, would find little risk because one of the assets in the portfolio will perform well and will cancel out the bad performance of the other asset whether it rains or shines. Thus, a portfolio of the two assets would have much less risk than either asset held alone. In contrast, having a sunglasses corporation and a suntan lotion corporation in the same portfolio would provide less diversification because their risks would not cancel each other out. The amount of diversification in a portfolio will depend upon which assets are in the portfolio and how those assets behave relative to each other.

The Covariance

Given the preceding discussion, portfolio risk must incorporate a statistical measure of diversification known as **covariance**. The formula for covariance is similar to the formula for variance:

covariance
A statistical measure of the extent to which two variables move together.

$$\sigma_{xy} = \sum_{i=1}^{n} \left\{ \left[R_{xi} - E(R_x) \right] \left[R_{yi} - E(R_y) \right] \times Prob_i \right\} \tag{8.8}$$

The main difference between covariance and variance is that covariance includes two assets, given in the formula by subscripts x and y. Thus, σ_{xy} stands for the covariance between asset x and asset y. The variables R_{xi} and R_{yi} are the returns of assets x and y in state i, $E(R_x)$ and $E(R_y)$ are the expected or mean returns of assets x and y, and $Prob_i$ is the probability that state i will occur.

The covariance of two assets measures the degree or tendency of two variables to move in relationship with each other. If two assets tend to move in the same direction, then they are said to be positively correlated and they will have a positive covariance. If the two assets tend to move in opposite directions, then they are said to be negatively correlated and they will have a negative covariance. Finally, if they tend to move independently of each other, then their covariance will be zero.

Many students find the concept of covariance confusing at first. Thinking about the importance of diversification in reducing risk, however, makes the concept of covariance clearer. Covariance is a quantitative tool that helps us understand how much diversification will occur.

Example 8.4 The calculation of the covariance of returns for Project A and Project B, introduced earlier, is shown in Table 8.3. Columns 1 through 5 of Table 8.3 repeat the analysis shown in a previous table on computing variance. The main difference between the covariance in Table 8.3 and the variance in Table 8.2 is shown in column 6. In Table 8.3, column 6 computes the product of the deviations of each state-dependent return from its respective expected return. In other words, column 6 multiplies Project A's deviation from its expected return by Project B's deviation from its expected return. Each of the products of the deviations is then multiplied by the probability of each state occurring and is shown in column 7. The sum of the products is the covariance between Project A and B.

Covariance measures the degree of the relationship between two variables. Because covariance is based on products of individual deviations and not squared deviations, its value can be positive, negative, or zero. We see from Table 8.3 that the covariance between Projects A and B is 0.0014, indicating that the returns of Project A and Project B tend to move in the same direction.

There are two primary methods of computing covariance. The first is to enter the data into a calculator or computer, which will compute the statistic for you. The second is to build a table similar to Table 8.3. As with the calculation of variance, we would encourage you to learn how to compute the statistics using the second method. Once you understand how covariance is computed, you will probably want to use the calculator method, as it is much quicker and more reliable.

correlation coefficient
A statistical measure of the extent to which two variables move together. The correlation coefficient ranges from +1, or perfect positive correlation, to −1, or perfect negative correlation.

The Correlation Coefficient

A statistic related to the covariance is called the **correlation coefficient.** Like the covariance, the correlation coefficient measures the degree of associa-

TABLE 8.3 The Covariance of Returns Between Projects A and B

	(1)	*(2)*	*(3)*	*(4)*	*(5)*	*(6)*	*(7)*
State of Nature	*Probability*	*Return A*	*Deviation from Mean*	*Return B*	*Deviation from Mean*	*Product of Deviation (3) × (5)*	*Probability-Weighted Product (3) × (5) × (1)*
Recession	0.20	0.00	−0.06	0.00	−0.07	0.0042	0.00084
Slow	0.30	0.06	0.00	0.05	−0.02	0.0000	0.00000
Moderate	0.40	0.08	+0.02	0.10	+0.03	0.0006	0.00024
Prosperity	0.10	0.10	+0.04	0.15	+0.08	0.0032	0.00032
						Covariance =	*0.00140*

tion between two assets. The sunglasses corporation would be expected to have negative correlation with the umbrella corporation, whereas the sunglasses corporation would be expected to have positive correlation with the suntan lotion corporation.

The correlation coefficient takes the covariance and forces its value to be between −1 and +1. Negative one is the lowest correlation and indicates that the two assets are exact opposites, whereas +1 is the highest correlation coefficient and indicates that the assets are clones of each other. Values between these two extremes indicate different degrees of association. The fact that the correlation coefficient is bounded is an advantage because the value of the correlation coefficient itself describes the extent of the relationship or correlation between two variables.

The correlation coefficient is given by:

$$\rho_{xy} = \sigma_{xy}/\sigma_x\sigma_y \tag{8.9}$$

where the Greek letter ρ (rho) is the notation for the correlation coefficient between asset *x* and asset *y*, σ_{xy} is the covariance between asset *x* and asset *y*, and σ_x and σ_y are the standard deviations of assets *x* and *y*, respectively.

Example 8.5 ________ The correlation coefficient between Project A and Project B can be determined from the data in Tables 8.2 and 8.3.

$$\rho_{\mathrm{AB}} = \frac{\sigma_{\mathrm{AB}}}{\sigma_{\mathrm{A}}\sigma_{\mathrm{B}}} = \frac{.0014}{(.03225)(.04583)} = 0.9472.$$

Because the correlation coefficient is close to +1, its highest possible value, we say that returns expected on Project A and Project B are highly correlated with each other.

Calculating Portfolio Variance and Standard Deviation

Knowledge of covariance will come in handy when computing the variance of a portfolio. Although portfolios can be of any size, our examples will illustrate portfolio variance and standard deviation in the case of two assets. The formula for the variance of a two-asset portfolio (using returns and weights as defined in preceding subsections) is:

$$\text{Portfolio Variance} = \sigma_p^2 = w_x^2\sigma_x^2 + w_y^2\sigma_y^2 + 2w_xw_y\sigma_{xy} \tag{8.10}$$

where σ^2_p is the notation for portfolio variance, σ^2_x and σ^2_y are the variances of assets *x* and *y* respectively, σ_{xy} is the covariance between assets *x* and *y*, and w_x and w_y are the weights of asset *x* and asset *y* in the portfolio.

The standard deviation of the portfolio, given by σ_p, may be found by taking the square root of both sides of Formula (8.10). The formula demonstrates that the variance and standard deviation of a portfolio's return depends upon the variances of the constituent assets and their weights, as well as upon their covariance.

Example 8.6 Return to Project A and Project B, whose respective variances and covariances are provided in Tables 8.2 and 8.3. If an investor places an equal amount of money in each of the projects such that the portfolio weights are both 0.5, the portfolio variance from Formula (8.10) would be:

$$\sigma_p^2 = (0.5)^2(0.00104) + (0.5)^2(0.00210) + 2(0.5)(0.5)(0.0014) = 0.001485$$

and the portfolio standard deviation would be:

$$\sigma_p = \sqrt{0.001485} = 0.0385$$

Note that the combined portfolio standard deviation is less than the weighted average of the standard deviations of the two stocks, illustrating the risk-reducing effects of putting assets together in portfolios.

The Relationship Between Covariance and Portfolio Standard Deviation

Of the three terms on the right-hand side of Formula (8.10), the first and second terms represent the effect of the variances of the individual assets on the variance of the portfolio. Notice that all the components of these first two terms are squared so that they must be nonnegative. Portfolios that include stocks with high variances will therefore tend to have high portfolio variances.

It is the third term on the right-hand side of the formula (i.e., the part of the formula containing the covariance) that represents the key to how diversification works to reduce risk. As we have said, the covariance term may be positive, negative, or zero depending upon the correlation between the assets. To show the effect of covariance on portfolio risk, it is helpful to analyze three situations: (1) the highest possible covariance, (2) the lowest possible covariance, and (3) any covariance between the highest and lowest.

Figure 8.6 plots the standard deviations and mean returns of two assets given by asset X and asset Y. Asset Y has a higher expected return and higher standard deviation compared with asset X. The lines connecting points X and Y represent possible portfolios that can be formed using assets X and Y in various proportions or weights. For example, points closest to X represent portfolios comprised almost entirely of asset X, while points closest to Y represent portfolios comprised almost entirely of asset Y.

Perfect Positive Correlation Given the relationship between the covariance and the correlation coefficient, the highest possible covariance occurs when the assets' correlation coefficient rests at the upper limit, that of +1. This is called *perfect positive correlation.*

The dotted line between points X and Y on Figure 8.6 plots the possible standard deviations and mean returns achievable by combining asset X and

FIGURE 8.6 Diversification Between Two Assets

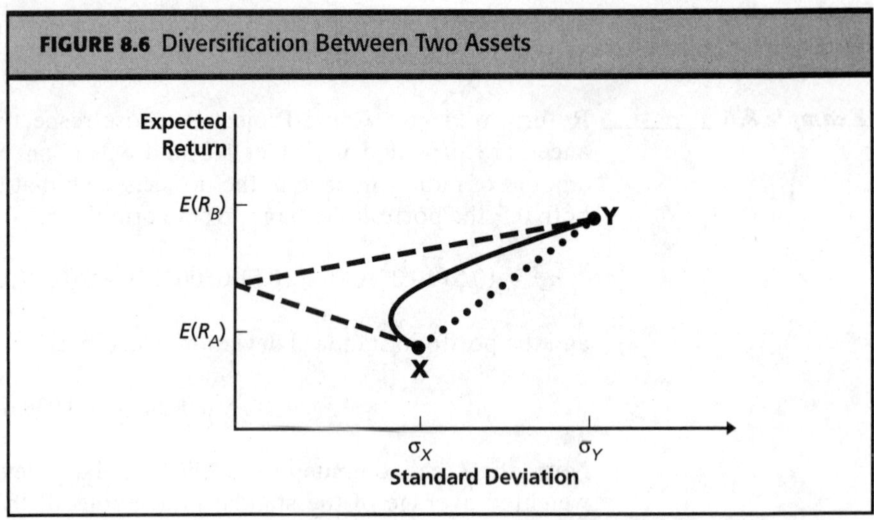

asset *Y* under perfect positive correlation. Notice that the dotted line is simply a straight line between the two assets. A straight line means that portfolio risk is a weighted average of the individual risks. This illustrates that there are no benefits to diversification when perfectly correlated assets are combined. The intuition is that diversification occurs when the risks of unusual returns of assets tend to cancel each other out. This never happens in the case of perfect positive correlation because the assets always move in the same direction.

Perfect Negative Correlation Given the relationship between the covariance and the correlation coefficient, the lowest possible covariance occurs when the assets' correlation coefficient rests at the lower limit, that of negative one. This is called *perfect negative correlation.*

The dashed line connecting points *X* and *Y* on Figure 8.6 plot the possible standard deviations and mean returns that would be achieved by combining asset *X* and asset *Y* under perfect negative correlation. Notice that the line between *X* and *Y* moves directly to the vertical axis, or the point at which the standard deviation is zero. This illustrates "ultimate" diversification—where two assets always move in opposite directions; therefore, combining them into a portfolio results in rapid risk reduction, or even total risk reduction![3]

Correlation Between the Extremes The final possibility is represented by the solid line in Figure 8.6. This is the more realistic situation in which the assets are neither perfectly positively nor perfectly negatively correlated; rather, they have some degree of independent movement. The solid line in Figure 8.6 best depicts the situations in this text that involve portfolios of stocks or real assets. The solid line is curved in nature, illustrating that combining risky assets

[3]Holding assets in inverse proportions to their standard deviations will result in total risk elimination.

into a portfolio produces some degree of diversification as long as these assets are not perfectly positively correlated. The line, however, will not touch the vertical axis and, therefore, will not completely eliminate risk.

Measuring Portfolio Risk with Diversification

diversifiable risk
The risk that can be removed through diversification.

nondiversifiable risk
The risk remaining even after assets are combined in a well-diversified portfolio. Also known as systematic risk or market risk.

The key point to diversification and risk is that when risky assets are combined into a portfolio, a portion of the portfolio's risk is diversified away. The risk that can be removed through diversification is called **diversifiable risk.** Diversifiable risk should be viewed as harmless in the sense that it can be removed by combining assets together.

Not all risk, however, can be diversified away. The risk that remains even after assets are combined in a well-diversified portfolio is called **nondiversifiable risk.** We will see in the next chapter that nondiversifiable risk is also known as *systematic risk* or *market risk.*

In Chapter 9, a new risk measure entitled *beta* is demonstrated. Unlike the standard deviation, beta measures only the nondiversifiable portion of the risk. Thus, beta focuses on only the risk that needs to be rewarded when assets are held as part of a portfolio.

Summary

- Risk is variation in value in financial outcomes. People do not want financial risk because their declining marginal utility causes the potential unhappiness from losses to outweigh the potential happiness from gains. Because of this risk aversion, people require a higher expected return on assets with greater risk.
- Statistics provides several useful tools for analyzing risk, including the mean, standard deviation, variance, and covariance. The expected return of a portfolio is a weighted average of the expected returns of the assets in a portfolio.
- The standard deviation of a portfolio is found using the variances, covariances, and weights of the assets in the portfolio. The standard deviation of a portfolio depends upon the covariances between the assets in the portfolio—in other words, the tendency of the assets to move in the same or opposite directions.
- When assets that are to some degree uncorrelated are put together in a portfolio, there will be a reduction in the portfolio risk. This reduction is due to diversification. Thus, in situations where different assets are less than perfectly correlated, diversification will reduce some risk and some risk will remain. The risk that is diversified away is entitled diversifiable risk, and the risk remaining is entitled nondiversifiable risk, systematic risk, or market risk.
- Beta is a measure of nondiversifiable risk, also known as market risk or systematic risk.

References

Bernouilli, D. *Econometrica* 22 (January 1954): 23–36.

Markowitz, H. M. *Portfolio Selection, Efficient Diversification, and Investments.* New York: John Wiley, 1959.

Demonstration Problems

Problem 1

The Mom and Pop Grocery Store is incorporated and has shares of stock that are now worth \$10 per share. A financial analysis of the store indicates four equally likely states or outcomes:

State	*Probability*	*Share Price*	*Dividend*
Struggling	0.25	\$ 5	\$0
Status Quo	0.25	\$10	\$0
Slow Growth	0.25	\$12	\$0
Good Times	0.25	\$14	\$1

Compute the mean, standard deviation, and variance of the returns of the common stock of Mom and Pop Grocery Store Corporation.

Solution to Problem 1

The solution is found by first computing the returns for the stock under each outcome or state and then plugging the returns (and their probabilities) into the tables or formulas given in the chapter. We will illustrate the table method because it is clearer.

Step 1: Convert the performance of the stock in each state to a return using the formula for common stock return given in Window 8.1. The four returns are computed as:

$$\text{Struggling Return} = [\$0 + \$\,5 - \$10]\,/\,\$10 = -0.50 \text{ or } -50\%$$

$$\text{Status Quo Return} = [\$0 + \$10 - \$10]\,/\,\$10 = 0.00 \text{ or } 0\%$$

$$\text{Slow Growth Return} = [\$0 + \$12 - \$10]\,/\,\$10 = 0.20 \text{ or } 20\%$$

$$\text{Good Times Return} = [\$1 + \$14 - \$10]\,/\,\$10 = 0.50 \text{ or } 50\%$$

Step 2: Plug the returns and probabilities into the table given in the chapter as a guide for computing statistics (Table 8.2 will do well):

State	*(1) Return*	*(2) Probability*	*(3) Weighted Return*	*(4) Return Deviation*	*(5) Squared Return Deviation*	*(6) Weighted Squared Deviation*
Struggling	−0.50	0.25				
Status Quo	0.00	0.25				
Slow Growth	0.20	0.25				
Good Times	0.50	0.25				

Step 3: Compute the mean return, which is found by multiplying each entry in column 1 by the corresponding entry in column 2, and fill in column 3. The mean is entered at the bottom of column 3 as the sum of all the entries in column 3:

State	(1) Return	(2) Probability	(3) Weighted Return	(4) Return Deviation	(5) Squared Return Deviation	(6) Weighted Squared Deviation
Struggling	−0.50	0.25	−0.125			
Status Quo	0.00	0.25	0.000			
Slow Growth	0.20	0.25	0.050			
Good Times	0.50	0.25	0.125			
			Mean = 0.050 or 5%			

Step 4: Fill in the remaining columns of the table. Column 4 is found by subtracting the mean (0.05) from column 1. Column 5 is found by squaring column 4. Column 6 is found by multiplying column 5 by column 2.

State	(1) Return	(2) Probability	(3) Weighted Return	(4) Return Deviation	(5) Squared Return Deviation	(6) Weighted Squared Deviation
Struggling	−0.50	0.25	−0.125	−0.55	.3025	.075625
Status Quo	0.00	0.25	0.000	−0.05	.0025	.000625
Slow Growth	0.20	0.25	0.050	0.15	.0225	.005625
Good Times	0.50	0.25	0.125	0.45	.2025	.050625
			Mean = 0.050 or 5%			

Step 5: Compute the variance by summing all of the numbers in column 6. The sum is 0.1325.
Step 6: Compute the standard deviation by taking the square root of the variance found in step 5, which is 0.364.
Final Solution: The mean is 0.05 or 5%, the variance is 0.1325, and the standard deviation is 0.364. The table method is simply a way of "walking through" the formulas. The answers may also be found using a statistical calculator.

Problem 2

SuperStore, Inc., is considering the purchase of two supermarkets at opposite ends of the town of Lehigh, Pennsylvania. The south store has an expected return of 0.12 and a variance of 0.0900, the north store has an expected return of 0.14 and a variance of 0.0625, and together they have a covariance of −0.0500. Compute the expected return (mean) and variance of the portfolio of returns found with $6 million invested in the south store and $4 million invested in the north store.

Solution to Problem 2

The mean or expected return can be found using Formula (8.7), and the variance can be found using Formula (8.10). Both equations require us to begin by computing the portfolio weights.
Step 1: Compute the portfolio weights by finding the percentage of the portfolio invested in each investment. Formula (8.5) provides the method:

Weight in South Store = $6,000,000 / [$6,000,000 + $4,000,000] = 0.60

Weight in North Store = $4,000,000 / [$6,000,000 + $4,000,000] = 0.40

Step 2: Compute the portfolio mean or expected return by plugging the weights and the expected returns into Formula (8.7):

$$E(R_p) = (0.60 \times 0.12) + (0.40 \times 0.14) = 0.072 + 0.056 = 0.128, \text{ or } 12.8\%$$

Step 3: Compute the variance by plugging the weights, variances, and covariances into Formula (8.10):

$$\text{Portfolio Variance} = (0.6^2 \times 0.09) + (0.4^2 \times 0.0625) + (2 \times 0.6 \times 0.4 \times -0.05)$$

$$\text{Portfolio Variance} = 0.0324 + 0.0100 + -0.024$$

$$\text{Portfolio Variance} = 0.0184$$

Final Solution: The expected return of 12.8% lies in between the expected returns of the individual stores. The variance of the combination (0.0184), however, is much less than the variance of either of the individual stores because of the very negative covariance between the individual stores and the resulting diversification.

Review Questions

1. Provide a definition of uncertainty using as an example the investment in a stock.
2. Provide an example of a security that contains risk as well as one that does not.
3. How do risk-averse investors behave when making investment decisions?
4. Describe declining marginal utility in the context of risk-averse behavior.
5. What does the standard deviation measure?
6. Why might the standard deviation be a flawed measure of risk?
7. The expected return of a portfolio is a weighted average of the portfolio's constituent securities. Is the same true for the standard deviation of the portfolio? Why or why not?
8. Explain why diversification reduces risk in a portfolio. Use as an example a portfolio made up of a sunglasses company and an umbrella company.
9. What does it mean when assets are perfectly positively correlated? How well does diversification work in this case?

Problems

1. Consider the following alternatives, all of which offer some chance of receiving one dollar at some time in the future:
   A. A safe dollar soon
   B. A risky dollar soon
   C. A safe dollar far into the future
   D. A risky dollar far into the future
   a. Which alternative is generally most valuable?
   b. Which alternative is generally least valuable?
2. Suppose that Olive Oil Corporation offered jobs working on an oil platform out in the ocean for $100,000 per year (with no vacations). The jobs are safe but very boring.

a. How many years do you think that a typical person would work on the oil platform? Why would they stop?
b. How many years do you think that a person would work on the oil platform after they won a million-dollar lottery? Why?

3. Melissa has been asked to report the amount of enjoyment that she receives from various levels of wealth. She reports her happiness in utils.

Wealth Level	*Happiness in Utils*
$100,000	10 utils
$200,000	40 utils
$300,000	50 utils
$400,000	56 utils
$500,000	61 utils

When Melissa's wealth is at risk, her happiness is equal to the expected number of utils. Thus, if she has a 50 percent chance of having $100,000 and a 50 percent chance of $200,000, her happiness is measured by multiplying the corresponding number of utils by each probability and summing them: $[(50\% \times 10) + (50\% \times 40)] = 25$ utils.

Suppose Melissa is offered an investment that has a 60% chance of giving her a profit of $100,000 and a 40% chance of causing a $100,000 loss.

a. If Melissa currently has $200,000, will she accept the risk?
(*Hint:* Compare her current utils with the expected utils of taking the risk.)
b. If Melissa currently has $300,000, will she take the risk?
c. If Melissa currently has $400,000, will she take the risk?
d. What is the logical reason that Melissa would refuse the risk at some levels of wealth and accept it at others?

4. Abbott Corporation stock sells for $20 per share and Costello Corporation stock sells for $10 per share. Compute the separate returns for the two stocks in each year:

a. Each stock rises by $4 in year 1.
b. Each stock falls by $2 in year 2. (*Hint:* The starting value for year 2 is the ending value from year 1.)
c. Each stock rises $1 in price and pays a dividend (cash payment) of $1 in year 3.

5. The returns on shares of Lewis Corporation and Martin Corporation are predicted under the following various economic conditions:

State of Economy	*Return on Lewis*	*Return on Martin*
Recession	−10%	−15%
Normal	+5%	+10%
Boom	+35%	+41%

a. If each economic state has the same probability of occurring, what are the expected returns of each stock?
b. If the economic outlook improves and the probability of a recession drops to 10%, the probability of normal growth drops to 30%, and the probability of a boom rises to 60%, what are the expected returns of each stock?

6. The returns on shares of Laverne Corporation and Shirley Corporation are predicted under the following various economic conditions:

State of Economy	*Return on Laverne*	*Return on Shirley*
Recession	−20%	−30%
Stagnant	0%	−5%
Moderate Growth	+10%	+10%
Boom	+30%	+65%

Each economic state has a 25% probability of occurring.

a. What are the expected returns of each stock?
b. What are the variances of each stock?
c. What are the standard deviations of each stock?

7. The returns on shares of Ernie Corporation and Bert Corporation are predicted under the following various economic conditions:

State of Economy	*Return on Ernie*	*Return on Bert*
Recession	−5%	−10%
Normal	+0%	+20%
Boom	+25%	+50%

There is a 50% chance of a moderate state and a 25% chance each for a recession and a boom.

a. What are the expected returns of each stock?
b. What are the variances of each stock?
c. What are the standard deviations of each stock?

8. The prices and dividends on shares of Rowan Corporation and Martin Corporation are predicted under the following various economic conditions:

State of Economy	*Probability of State*	*Price*	*Rowan Corp. Dividend*	*Martin Corp. Price*	*Dividend*
Recession	20%	$ 8	$0	$38	$0
Stagnant	30%	$10	$0	$48	$2
Moderate	40%	$12	$0	$63	$2
Boom	10%	$15	$1	$82	$3

The current price of Rowan Corp. is $10.
The current price of Martin Corp. is $50.

a. Compute the returns for each stock in each state.
b. What are the expected returns of each stock?
c. What are the variances of each stock?
d. What are the standard deviations of each stock?

9. The returns on shares of George Corporation and Gracie Corporation are predicted under the following various economic conditions:

State of Economy	*Return on George*	*Return on Gracie*
Recession	−10%	−30%
Moderate Growth	+10%	+10%
Boom	+30%	+65%

Each economic state has an equal probability of occurring.

a. What are the expected returns of each stock?

b. What is the covariance between the stocks?

10. The returns on shares of Jimmy Corporation and Walter Corporation are predicted under the following various economic conditions:

State of Economy	*Return on Jimmy*	*Return on Walter*
Recession	−20%	+40%
Boom	+30%	−20%

There is a 60% chance of a boom and a 40% chance of a recession.

a. What are the expected returns of each stock?

b. What is the covariance between the stocks?

11. Various attributes of three stocks are listed:

	Larry Corp.	*Curley Corp.*	*Moe Corp.*
Price	$20	$20	$40
Expected Return	18%	15%	12%
Variances	10%	5%	4%

The covariance between Larry Corp. and Curley Corp. is 0.03, between Larry Corp. and Moe Corp. is −0.01, and between Curley Corp. and Moe Corp. is −0.01.

a. What would be the weights of a portfolio that consists of 100 shares of each stock?

b. What would be the expected return and variance of a portfolio consisting of 50% Larry Corp. and 50% Curley Corp.?

c. What would be the expected return and variance of a portfolio consisting of 25% Curley Corp. and 75% Moe Corp.?

d. What would be the expected return and variance of a portfolio consisting of 50% Curley Corp. and 50% Moe Corp.?

12. Identify the true statements and the false statements.

a. The popularity of lotteries, casino gambling, and sports betting proves that risky securities are preferred by most investors even when they do not offer a higher return than safe securities.

b. The underlying cause of risk aversion is declining marginal utility.

c. Declining marginal utility proves that money is less important to rich people than to poor people.

d. Risky assets must offer lower expected returns than safe assets in a competitive market.

e. The expected return of a portfolio is the weighted average of the expected returns of the assets in the portfolio.

f. The variance of a portfolio is the weighted average of the variances of the assets in the portfolio.

g. The risk reduction attained through the diversification of a portfolio depends upon the covariances between the assets within the portfolio.

h. If enough securities are added to a portfolio, then all risk can be diversified away.

13. Suppose a portfolio has two assets. Asset 1 has a standard deviation of 0.0 and an expected return of 8%. Asset 2 has a standard deviation of 0.22 and an expected return of 18%. The covariance between them is 0.0 because asset 1 has a standard deviation of 0.0. Compute the expected return and standard deviation of a portfolio consisting of:

a. 25% asset 1 and 75% asset 2.
b. 50% asset 1 and 50% asset 2.
c. 75% asset 1 and 25% asset 2.
d. 100% asset 1 and 0% asset 2.

Discussion Questions

1. Casino games are designed such that the "house" has an advantage over the player. Another way of saying this is that from the player's perspective, the expected return on casino gambling is negative. Casinos are jam-packed every day with willing investors. This is proof that the assumption that individuals are risk-averse is false. Discuss.
2. Because casino gambling can be very risky for gamblers, is it not also very risky for the casino? Explain.
3. Because diversification works best for assets that are negatively correlated, we should see most investors holding negatively correlated assets in their portfolios. Do you agree?
4. How does the saying, "Don't put all your eggs in one basket," relate to this chapter?
5. Consider the St. Petersburg paradox posed by Bernouilli:

   There is a game in which one player flips a fair coin. If the coin reveals heads, the "house" (i.e., the person who sets up the gamble) will pay the player $2, and the game is over. If the coin reveals tails, it is tossed again. If the second toss reveals heads, then the house pays ($2)^2 to the player and the game is over. If the second toss reveals tails, the coin is flipped again. The game then continues until the first heads appears, and at that time the house pays the player the amount ($2)^n, where n *is the number of tosses required to reveal tails.*

   a. What is the expected payoff of this game? (*Hint:* Find the probability of each outcome and multiply this probability by the payoff. The sum of the probabilities times the payoffs is the expected payoff of the game.)
   b. As a player, how much would you pay to play this game?
   c. How can the difference in the answers to (a) and (b) be explained?

CHAPTER 9

MODERN PORTFOLIO THEORY AND THE CAPITAL ASSET PRICING MODEL

The news was quickly spreading around the annual shareholder meeting. It seems that the company's chief financial officer was found to have authorized large investments over the past 15 years that had never paid back a nickel. Further, it was determined that these investments had a 1-in-1000 chance of returning millions of dollars, and a 999-in-1000 chance of returning nothing. One shareholder summed up the mood when he said, "How could this possibly have been a good use of our funds?"

Most concluded that the CFO was speculating with shareholder money. Many likened the characteristics of this investment to that of buying lottery tickets—an investment with an extremely large payoff in one particular state of nature, but one with a very low probability of receiving such a payoff. The conclusion that the CFO was speculating, however, could not have been further from the truth. The "investment" turned out to be a fire insurance policy on the firm's headquarters. The insurance offered a large cash payment in the unlikely event of a fire, but because the policy offered a large cash inflow at precisely the time of a large cash outflow to the firm, the fire insurance investment had the effect of decreasing aggregate firm risk.

This example illustrates that the net result of an investment or expenditure on the total risk of the firm cannot be ascertained by looking only at the investment in isolation. The investment in the fire insurance policy seemed to have high risk, yet the investment reduced the total risk of the firm. Proper risk analysis requires a more sophisticated look at risk than simply measuring the variance of the cash flows of an individual investment.

This chapter continues our introduction to risk and builds on the main result of Chapter 8—that total risk can be separated into a diversifiable part and a nondiversifiable part. *Diversifiable risk* is the portion of risk that disappears as assets are combined in a portfolio. *Nondiversifiable risk* is the risk of a portfolio remaining after all possible diversifiable risk is removed.

Chapter 9 will discuss and illustrate a measure of nondiversifiable risk called *beta.* Finally, beta will be used to accomplish the major objective of risk analysis—determining how risk can be properly incorporated into investment, financing, and working capital management decisions.

Portfolio Management Theory

Portfolio management theory describes, among other things, how and why portfolio managers reduce risk. Financial managers use portfolio management theory to make decisions in a risky environment. To understand how risk enters these decisions, however, we need to know how investors in general—and the stockholders of the firm in particular—view risk.

The Markowitz Model: Risky Assets Only

The pioneering work of Markowitz (1952) determined that investors hold a variety of assets in a portfolio with the objective of diversifying away as much risk as possible. Markowitz extended the statistics of Chapter 8 to develop a portfolio management model. He also demonstrated that investors choose assets in such a way that the risk of those assets matches the investor's level of risk aversion.

In the Markowitz framework, highly risk-averse people, sometimes referred to as widows and orphans, would generally invest all of their money in relatively low-risk, high-quality assets. At the other end of the investment risk spectrum, less risk-averse people would generally accept high levels of risk by investing in lower-quality assets.

A Graphical Illustration The Markowitz model is illustrated in Figure 9.1. The shaded area represents all possible portfolios among all possible assets that investors can form. This is in contrast to Figure 8.6 in the previous chapter, which looked at combinations of two assets only. In other words, all possible or feasible portfolios are shown somewhere within the shaded region. The question is, however, which portfolio will they hold?

The answer to this question depends, in part, upon the preferences of investors. There are some portfolios within this shaded region, however, that no rational investor would hold. For example, consider the choice between portfolio A and portfolio Z in Figure 9.1. Investors will always prefer portfolio A to portfolio Z because portfolio A promises a higher expected return and has the same amount of risk. Now consider the choice between portfolio A and portfolio Y. Investors will always prefer portfolio A to Y because A carries less risk than Y but promises the same amount of expected return.

Extending these examples of choosing between two portfolios based upon return and risk leaves only those portfolios on the dotted line in Figure 9.1, which represent those diversified portfolios offering the highest return for a given level of risk or the lowest risk for a given level of return. Given the mil-

FIGURE 9.1 The Frontier of Risky Portfolios

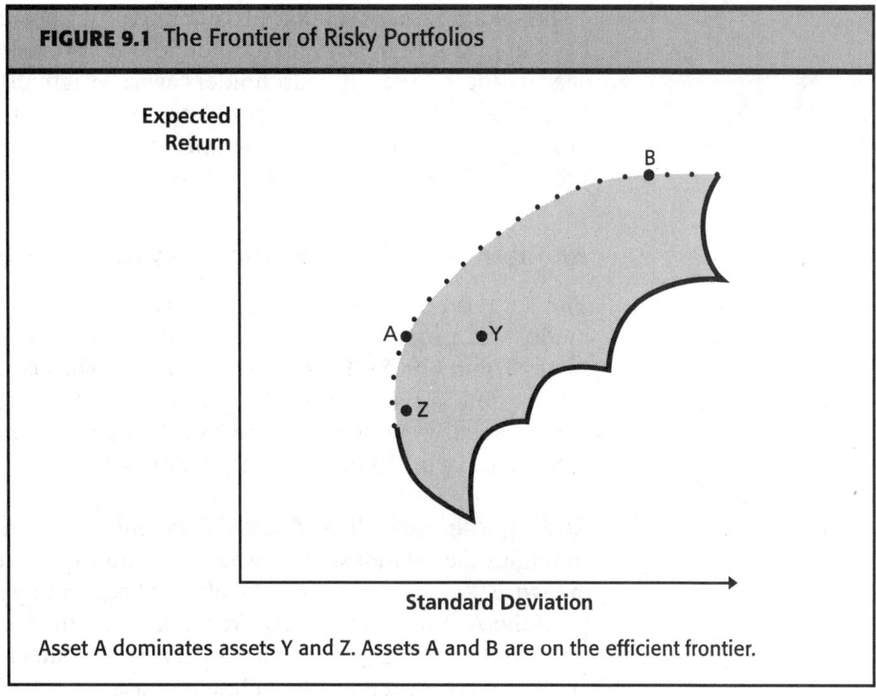

Asset A dominates assets Y and Z. Assets A and B are on the efficient frontier.

frontier of risky portfolios Portfolios of risky assets offering the highest return for a given level of risk, or the lowest risk for a given level of return.

lions of choices represented in Figure 9.1, only those portfolios that lie on the dotted line will be desired by investors. The dotted line is known as the **frontier of risky portfolios.**

Risk Preferences In the Markowitz framework, investors with different levels of risk aversion hold different portfolios along the frontier. For example, in Figure 9.1, highly risk-averse investors might end up holding portfolio A, but investors more tolerant of risk might end up with portfolio B. The risk-versus-return tradeoff is different at each point along the dotted line in Figure 9.1. Each investor therefore perceives a potentially different expected change in return for a given change in risk because the slope of the dotted line changes.

Corporate Financial Decisions The main result in the Markowitz framework is that the particular portfolio of risky assets held by the investor depends upon the investor's risk preference. This framework, however, presents a problem for corporate managers who must make decisions for shareholders with differing levels of risk aversion. Whose risk tastes should the manager satisfy when choosing among different investments? There is unfortunately no definitive answer to this question in the Markowitz framework.

For example, a particular project might be considered a great opportunity by the firm's high-risk shareholders, but too risky by the firm's low-risk shareholders. Even if shareholders were originally attracted to firms with particular risk strategies, a problem would occur if the firm uncovered a great opportunity that only the particular firm could exploit, but which had the wrong level of risk for most of its shareholders.

An Alternative Framework: Risky and Risk-Free Assets

The solution to the financial manager's dilemma in using the Markowitz model was provided through a slightly different framework introduced by James Tobin (1965). Tobin noted that portfolios could comprise risk-free assets as well as risky assets. We define a risk-free asset as a short-term, fixed income security with little or no risk of default. The ideal example would be a U.S. Treasury bill as detailed in Window 4.1.

Adding the Risk-Free Asset Combining risk-free and risky investments simplifies the relationship between risk and expected return. This is illustrated in Figure 9.2, where we show the effect of combining a risk-free asset with risky portfolio A. Note that the risk-free asset is on the vertical axis because its risk, measured by its standard deviation, is zero. The line between the risk-free asset and any risky asset is a straight line because no diversification takes place.

capital asset pricing model (CAPM)
A model that specifies the relationship between risk and expected return. In the *CAPM* model, the only risk that matters is nondiversifiable risk, also known as systematic risk or market risk, which is the variation in the asset's return that is correlated with the market.

This new relationship between risk and return is known as the **capital asset pricing model (CAPM).** According to the *CAPM* relationship, investors no longer choose only between the risky portfolios along the dotted line; rather, they choose how much money to put into risk-free assets and how much to put into risky assets. Points on the solid line near risky portfolio A represent portfolios with most of the money placed in portfolio A. Points in the middle tend to represent a balance between the risk-free asset and the risky portfolio A.

Adjusting for Risk in a CAPM Framework How do investors adjust for risk in a *CAPM* framework of risky and risk-free portfolios? The answer is different from that utilizing the Markowitz model, where investors searched for the particular portfolio of risky assets that matched their risk preferences. In the *CAPM* framework, investors adjust the risk in their portfolio by adjusting the percentages of their portfolio held in risky assets versus the risk-free asset.

asset allocation decision
The decision as to how much money to put in risky assets and how much to put in risk-free assets. According to the *CAPM* model, the asset allocation decision is the most important decision investors make in terms of risk.

According to the *CAPM,* the decision of how much money to put in risky assets and how much to put in the risk-free asset is the most important decision investors make regarding risk. This decision is usually called the **asset allocation decision.** For example, low-risk investors typically reduce their risk exposure by placing a limited portion of their money in risky assets and most of their money in the risk-free asset. Although some investors may try to adjust the level of risk by investing primarily in certain types of risky

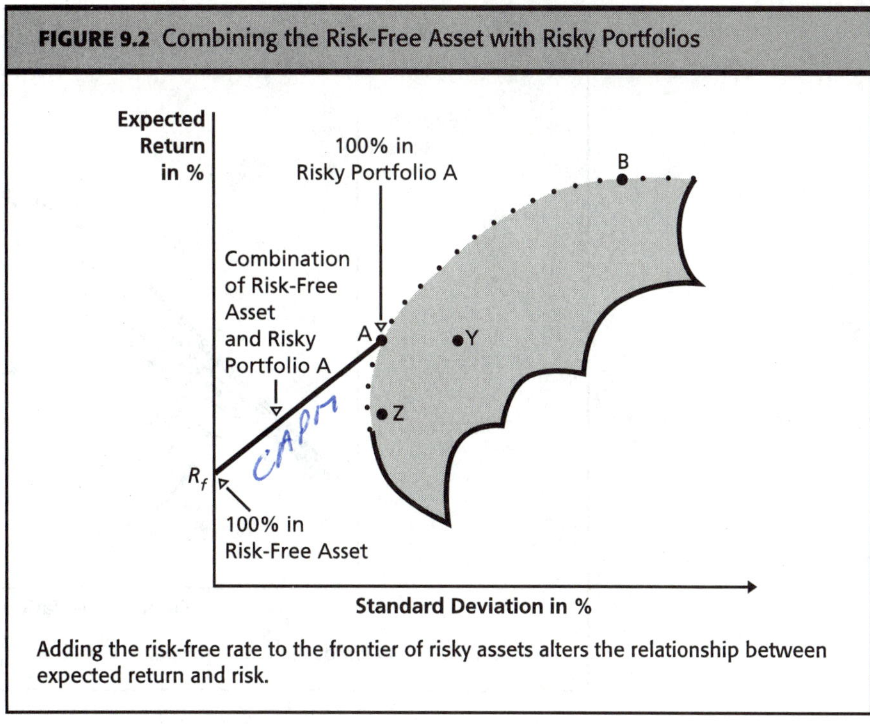

FIGURE 9.2 Combining the Risk-Free Asset with Risky Portfolios

Adding the risk-free rate to the frontier of risky assets alters the relationship between expected return and risk.

assets, the vast majority of money invested in U.S. capital markets is invested while making use of the risky-versus-riskless-asset decision as the primary risk-management tool.

The Market Portfolio

In the *CAPM* relationship, investors adjust risk by choosing among risky assets and the risk-free asset. The question becomes, which risky assets? From the millions of risky assets in Figure 9.1, our objective is to see why one portfolio exists that will satisfy the tastes of all investors. This unique portfolio is called the **market portfolio.**

market portfolio
The unique portfolio of risky assets along the efficient frontier that satisfies the tastes of all investors.

We already know that most of these risky portfolios can be eliminated from contention because they are clearly inferior to other risky portfolios. This led us to consider only those risky portfolios along the frontier represented by the dotted line in Figure 9.1. Given the availability of the risk-free asset, however, we know from Figure 9.2 that risk-versus-return opportunities are given by a straight line. Hundreds of straight lines could be drawn, each combining the risk-free asset with one of the risky portfolios along the dotted line. The key is to find which risky portfolio (and therefore which straight line) is best for investors. This is illustrated in Figure 9.3.

FIGURE 9.3 Choosing Among Risky Portfolios When the Risk-Free Asset Exists

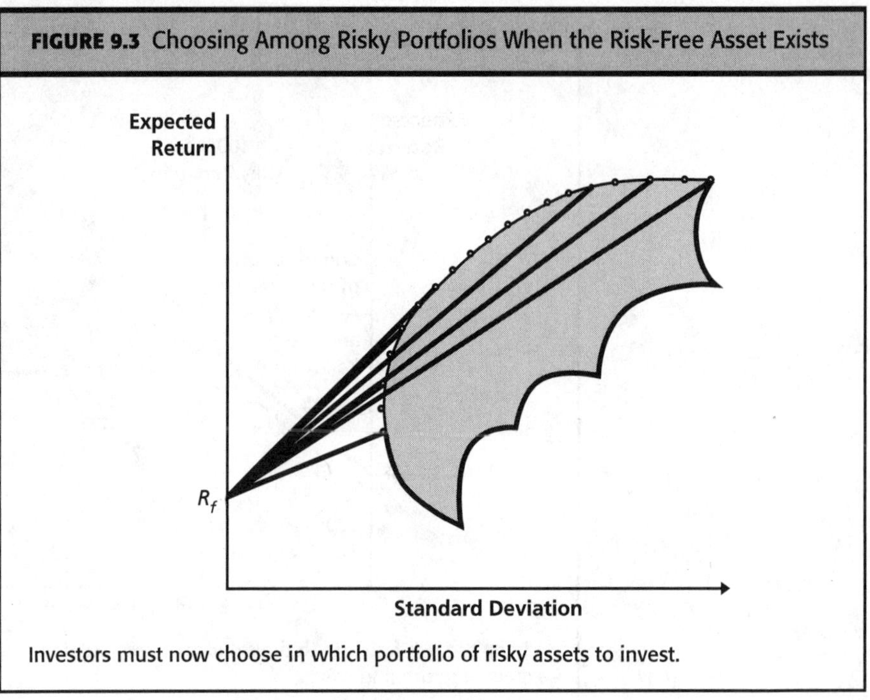

Investors must now choose in which portfolio of risky assets to invest.

capital market line
The particular combination of the risk-free asset and the diversified portfolio of risky assets offering the highest slope.

Using Figure 9.3, the choice of a particular risky portfolio is a matter of which straight line is best. To put it another way, the investor must decide which line offers the best combination of risk and return. We see that one line is best in the sense that it offers the highest expected return for a given level of risk. This unique line is known as the **capital market line** and is shown again in Figure 9.4. The particular risky portfolio along the capital market line is given the name portfolio M, which stands for the market portfolio. As we have said, the market portfolio is defined as the portfolio that includes all risky assets.

How did we know that this portfolio must be the market portfolio? Because every investor is striving for the same goal—the highest return for bearing risk—and because every investor is competing to purchase the same assets, we can deduce that portfolio M must be comprised of all risky assets, or the market portfolio.

Each asset in the market portfolio is held in proportion of its total value relative to the total of the values of all tradable risky assets combined. For example, if the stock of General Motors Corporation is 1 percent of all risky assets, then the market portfolio will be made up of 1 percent General Motors stock. The market portfolio is therefore made up of all risky assets held by all investors. More on the market portfolio is provided in Window 9.1.

FIGURE 9.4 The Market Portfolio

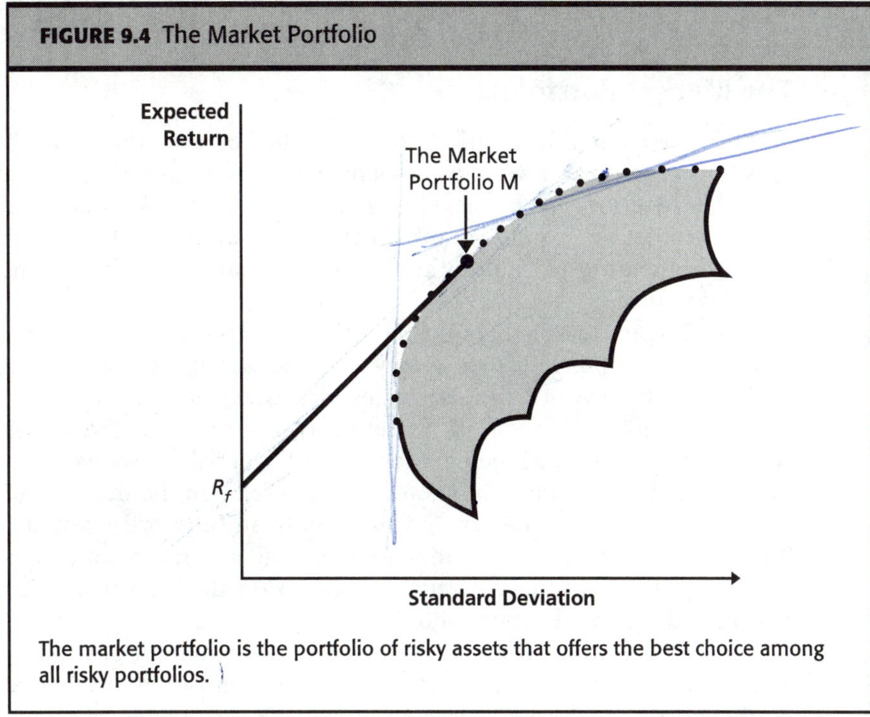

The market portfolio is the portfolio of risky assets that offers the best choice among all risky portfolios.

Summary and Illustration of Risk

The key result of the *CAPM* framework is that there are two potential types of risk within the total risk of an asset: (1) diversifiable risk, which is the variation in an asset's return that has no correlation with the overall market, and (2) nondiversifiable risk, also known as systematic risk or market risk, which is the variation in the asset's return that is correlated with the market. We will end this section with an illustration of this important concept.

Example 9.1 Suppose that an investor is considering the purchase of a very small grocery or convenience store. What are the risks this investor faces? What are the most serious risks and the less serious ones? Take a moment before proceeding and try to come up with a brief ranking of these risks.

Of course to some extent these answers are subjective and would depend upon specific circumstances, but here is our list:

1. The risk that another food store will open nearby.
2. The risk of poor management, fire, theft (customer or employee), storm, or other disaster.
3. The risk of a serious loss of traffic due to a new highway, a detour, a bridge in repair, and so forth.

WINDOW 9.1

The Market Portfolio

Our development of the market portfolio relied on both theory, or the way in which diversification reduces risk, and reasoning, or the way in which investors will search for the highest return given a level of risk. Does the market portfolio exist in the real world? Whereas we would not expect every investor to hold the market portfolio, there are several reasons to believe that the overall market portfolio is the key portfolio for most investors.

First, it seems reasonable to believe that if all investors are striving to diversify away as much risk as possible, then they will use all available assets. Second, because all investors will be driven by the same instincts, such as their desire for high returns and their aversion to risk, each risky asset must adjust in price through supply and demand forces such that it is included in the portfolio. If a risky asset were priced too high, then no one would demand it and its price would fall. On the other hand, if it were underpriced the demand would exceed the supply and the price would be driven upward. Third, even if some investors do not understand or choose not to apply modern portfolio theory, as long as the majority of investors do, the market will behave as if every investor holds the market portfolio.

Suppose, then, that you wanted to invest in the market portfolio. Can this be done? The answer is that you can get close enough in most circumstances. If you define the market portfolio in its strictest sense to include all tradable assets, such as all stocks, all bonds, all precious metals, all real estate, all art, and all other valued assets, then the answer is probably, *no.* A portfolio that includes everything does not exist.

If, however, you define the market portfolio to include a representative sampling of common stocks, then the answer is, *yes.* Large diversified common stock portfolios do exist. Three popular hypothetical portfolios that attempt to replicate the stock market are:

The S&P 500 Index: An index including 500 widely held common stocks. Stocks held in the S&P 500 are value weighted, such that the larger the firm, the larger its representation in the index.

The Nasdaq Composite Index: An index of stocks that trade over-the-counter (OTC). These stocks tend to be smaller than those included in the S&P 500 index. This index is also value weighted.

The Wilshire 5,000 Index: The broadest of stock indexes, the Wilshire index is made up of over 5,000 different securities, including all New York Stock Exchange and American Stock Exchange stocks, and most OTC stocks.

Other popular indexes include international stock portfolios. One important fact concerning all of these indexes is that they correlate highly with one another, providing some proof that they are all attaining the same goal—a portfolio that behaves as if it contained all assets. Investment companies set up mutual funds that replicate these in-

WINDOW 9.1 *(continued)*

dexes so that even small investors can invest in a representative portion of the market portfolio at low cost.

Finally, you may be surprised that the foregoing discussion did not include the most popular of all indexes, the Dow Jones Industrial Average. The reason it was not included is that it is an index of only 30 industrial firms. Even with its limited sample, however, studies have shown that the Dow index correlates highly with the larger indexes, suggesting that most of the benefits of diversification can be achieved through a small number of holdings.

4. The risk that the local neighborhood will decline in population, income, or tendency to use "convenience" stores.
5. The risk that the overall economy will slide into a serious recession.

Your list could contain other risks or have them in different order. We hope, however, that you agree with this important point: Most of the major risks that a convenience store faces are not related to the overall economy of the nation, or the world. In fact, if we were to guess, then we would estimate that only a few percentage points of the store's overall risk could be attributed to the systematic movements of national or world economies. This means that most of the major risks are diversifiable.

Let us now consider an investor who is considering purchasing stock in a corporation owning thousands of convenience stores throughout the world. What would the risks be that this investor would face?

It seems clear that the number-one risk would probably be the risk of a nationwide recession. Other risks could include concerns about potentially poor management, or competition from another convenience store chain, or a major change in consumer attitudes regarding convenience stores. What happened, however, to the risks of lost traffic or disasters? The answer is that they were diversified away. A chain of thousands of convenience stores will surely have a portion of their stores afflicted by such store-specific risks. On the other hand, a portion of their other stores will actually benefit by certain traffic pattern changes or as a result of disasters afflicting their nearest competitor.

A chain of thousands of stores will diversify most of the risks away, leaving primarily systematic risk. This illustrates *diversification*—the grouping of assets to reduce risk. In the case of large corporations, the corporations have hundreds or thousands of projects, whose diversifiable risks tend to vanish as the corporation is viewed as a whole. Further, the shareholders of the corporation can have tens or hundreds of different stocks in their portfolio—creating even more diversification.

The vast majority of the shares of common stock in the United States is held in large and highly diversified portfolios, such as pension funds, mutual funds, insurance companies, and endowments. Within these funds, the diversifiable risks of the individual stocks are completely removed. The systematic risk remains and is what concerns the investor. The owners of these stocks are most concerned with overall movements in the market. The required return of a common stock should not depend upon diversifiable risks, but upon the only type of risk that will ultimately affect the returns of the diversified investor—systematic risk. The consequence of this reasoning is that diversifiable risk can be ignored.

> The required return of a common stock or on a project within a large publicly traded corporation should not depend upon diversifiable risks but upon the only type of risk that will ultimately affect the returns of the diversified investor—systematic risk.

The next section details how systematic risk can be measured.

Beta

beta
A measure of systematic risk, or risk that cannot be diversified away by forming portfolios. To be specific, beta is a measure of correlation with the overall market.

We have detailed the importance of systematic risk and the unimportance of diversifiable risk; fortunately, a rather remarkable measure of systematic risk exists—a measure called **beta.** A beta of zero means no systematic risk, whereas a beta of 1 denotes the same level of systematic risk as the overall market. Given the beta of an asset, we may calculate the expected return of the asset by plugging the beta into the *CAPM* model:

$$CAPM\text{: } E(R_i) = R_f + \beta_i[E(R_m) - R_f] \tag{9.1}$$

where $E(R_i)$ is the expected return of asset *i*, R_f stands for the risk-free rate of return, β_i is the notation for the beta of asset *i*, and $E(R_m)$ is the expected return on the market portfolio. A proof of the *CAPM* is provided in the appendix to this chapter.

arbitrage pricing theory
A model of risk and expected return that includes multiple measures of systematic risk.

Scholars may debate whether the nondiversifiable risk can be captured using the single-risk measure of the *CAPM,* but the concept of pricing only nondiversifiable risk is well illustrated using the *CAPM.* More advanced models, such as the **arbitrage pricing theory,** discuss concepts that attempt to provide multiple risk measures for nondiversifiable risk.

Although the theory and development of the *CAPM* are rather complex, Formula (9.1) presents a simple relationship between risk and expected return.

Systematic Risk and Beta

Recall the statistical concept known as *covariance* from Chapter 8, which was defined as a measure of correlation between two variables. The beta of a stock or of any other investment is defined by the covariance between the stock's returns and those of the market, divided by the variance of the market's return:

$$\beta_i = Cov(R_m, R_i)/Var(R_m) \tag{9.2}$$

where *Cov* stands for covariance, *Var* stands for variance, *i* stands for an individual asset, and *m* stands for the market portfolio of all assets. From our notation used in Chapter 8, we can write the formula for beta as:

$$\beta_i = \sigma_{mi}/\sigma_m^2$$

The numerator of Formula (9.2) measures the amount of risk that an individual stock brings into an already diversified portfolio. The denominator represents the total risk of the market portfolio. Beta therefore measures systematic risk relative to the risk of the overall market. (The mathematics of computing both the covariance and variance have been fully covered in Chapter 8.) Window 9.2 provides an example of using these statistical measures to compute the beta for McDonald's Corporation.

There are several important features of beta. First, it can be easily interpreted. The beta of an asset may be viewed as the percentage return response that an asset will have on average to a percentage movement in the overall market. For example, if the market were to rise by 1 percent in response to certain news, a stock with a beta of 0.95 would be expected on average to rise 0.95 percent, and a stock with a beta of 2.00 would be expected to rise 2.00 percent. The risk-free asset has a beta of zero and its return would therefore not be expected to change with movements in the overall market. The return on a portfolio with a beta of 1 would be expected to change in the same amount as the change in the overall market.[1]

Example 9.2 ________ Table 9.1 lists the estimated betas of some well-known corporations. The highest betas are of Microsoft, General Electric, and IBM. Companies with high betas have stock returns that are highly sensitive to marketwide factors such as general economic activity and interest rates. The lowest betas are of Procter and Gamble and Anheuser Busch. Companies with low betas have stock returns that are less sensitive to marketwide factors.

The second feature of beta is that it is the slope coefficient of a linear regression of the returns of the asset as the *y* or dependent variable against the returns of the overall market as the *x* or independent variable. For those familiar with the concept of linear regression, you now have another way to compute beta.

[1]The same concept, of course, can be extended for movements in the market of more than or less than 1 percent. For instance, if the market falls 2 percent, then a stock with a beta of 1.5 would have an expected decline of 3 percent.

WINDOW 9.2

Calculating Beta

This window details the calculation of beta, given in formula form as:

$$\beta_i = Cov(R_i, R_m)/Var(R_m)$$

We know that our calculation will require a covariance and a variance term. The most common procedure in estimating beta is to use what is known as the ex-post method of calculation. In the ex-post method, historical data are used to estimate various statistics. This contrasts with the method discussed in Chapter 8, which used states of nature and their associated probabilities to estimate the statistics. The ex-post method is commonly used when the number of potential states of nature is enormous, and the ability to attach probabilities to those states is difficult.

In our example, we will show how to estimate the beta for the McDonald's Corporation, or Stock MD for short. Our first step is to collect past data for Stock MD and for the market portfolio, or Stock m. We will use a portfolio of large company stocks as a proxy for the market portfolio. Our example will use 9 years of past data, mostly for illustrative convenience. A better approach, however, would be to use more data points measured over shorter intervals of time, such as 60 monthly observations instead of nine annual observations.

The following worksheet provides the necessary calculations. These data are in decimal form, such that, for example, 10 percent is stated as 0.10.

(1) Year	(2) Return on McDonald's R_{MD}	(3) Return on Market R_m	(4) McDonald's Deviation $R_{MD} - \bar{R}_{MD}$	(5) Market Deviation $R_m - \bar{R}_m$	(6) Market Deviation Squared $(R_m - \bar{R}_m)^2$	(7) Cross Product $(R_{MD} - \bar{R}_{MD})(R_m - \bar{R}_m)$
1992	0.1207	0.0659	−0.0298	−0.0608	0.0037	0.0018
1993	0.1723	0.0631	0.0218	−0.0636	0.0040	−0.0014
1994	−0.0370	−0.0464	−0.1875	−0.1731	0.0300	0.0325
1995	0.3832	0.3093	0.2327	0.1826	0.0333	0.0425
1996	−0.0970	0.1646	−0.2475	0.0379	0.0014	−0.0094
1997	0.0495	0.2344	−0.1010	0.1077	0.0116	−0.0109
1998	0.6300	0.2540	0.4795	0.1273	0.0162	0.0610
1999	0.0231	0.1482	−0.1274	0.0215	0.0001	−0.0027
2000	−0.0843	−0.0532	−0.2348	−0.1799	0.0324	0.0422
Total					0.1327	0.1483
Average	0.1505	0.1267				

Columns 2 and 3 provide the annual returns over the 9-year period for McDonald's (stock MD) and for the market (stock m). In columns 4 and 5, each of the average or

WINDOW 9.2 *(continued)*

mean returns is subtracted from annual returns. For example, the value of −0.2475 in column 4 for 1996 is stock MD's return of −0.0970 less stock MD's average return of 0.1505. Column 6 squares each of the annual deviations of the market from its average return. Column 7 multiplies stock MD's annual deviation from its average with the market's annual deviation from its average (column 4 multiplied by column 5).

The covariance between McDonald's and the market is found by averaging column 7:

$$Cov(R_{MD}, R_m) = 0.1483 / 9 = 0.0165$$

The variance of the market is found by averaging column 6:

$$Var(R_m) = 0.1327 / 9 = 0.0147$$

The beta of McDonald's, from Formula 9.2, is:

$$Cov(R_{MD}, R_m) / Var(R_m) = 0.0165 / 0.0147 = 1.1224$$

Now that we have taken you through this rather lengthy procedure, we should mention that an easier method exists. Students with some background in statistics might recall that the formula for beta is the same as the formula for the slope coefficient of a linear regression of the returns of the asset (as the *y* or dependent variable) against the returns of the overall market (as the *x* or independent variable). Programs exist that will easily perform such a regression and produce an estimate of beta.

TABLE 9.1 Estimated Betas of Well-Known Corporations

Corporation	*Beta*
Microsoft	1.71
IBM	1.35
American Express	1.19
Ford Motor Company	1.15
General Electric	1.09
McDonald's	0.83
Anheuser Busch	0.14

Source: Company Profiles, data from www.biz.yahoo.com/ Yahoo Finance, www.yahoo.com

Third, the beta of a portfolio is a weighted average of the betas of the constituent assets. This is true even though the total risk of a portfolio is not the weighted average of the total risk of the constituent assets. Because beta measures only the systematic risk of an asset, and because the systematic risk does not diversify away as assets are combined into a portfolio, we can compute the portfolio beta as a weighted average:

$$\beta_p = \sum_{i=1}^{n} w_i \beta_i \tag{9.3}$$

where β_p stands for the beta of the portfolio, w_i is the percentage of the portfolio invested in asset *i*, β_i is the beta of asset *i*, and *n* is the number of constituent assets in the portfolio. We will provide a proof of Formula (9.3) in the chapter appendix.

In summary, beta measures systematic risk. It is used in the *CAPM* to compute an estimate of the expected return for a risky asset. Beta is easy to compute, interpret, and use in portfolio management.

Using Beta to Calculate Expected Rates of Return

This section will demonstrate how the corporate manager can use Formula (9.1), called the *CAPM,* to make financial decisions:

$$E(R_i) = R_f + \beta_i\,[E(R_m) - R_f]$$

The *CAPM* relationship provides an estimate of the return that investors expect to earn on a stock or project with a particular beta.

Previous sections have detailed the importance of systematic risk and how it can be measured using beta. Later in this chapter we will detail how to calculate the beta of a project. For now, let us assume that we know the beta. Once you've measured an investment's beta, how much return should you demand for holding the asset?

The *CAPM* relationship is represented by the straight line in Figure 9.5. The name of this relationship is the security market line *(SML)* or simply the capital asset pricing model itself. Remember, Figure 9.5 is simply a graphical representation of Formula 9.1. From Figure 9.5 we see that R_f, or the risk-free rate, is the line's intercept, and the bracketed expression $[E(R_m) - R_f]$ is the line's slope. The beta for asset *i* determines where on the line the asset is located.

There are three key points to know about the security market line. First, the expected return of an asset with a beta of zero is equal to the risk-free rate. The reason is that the risk-free asset also has a beta of zero and, from the law of conservation of value, competition will force assets of equal risk to offer the same expected return. Second, the expected return of an asset with a beta of 1 is equal to the expected return of the market as a whole. The reason is that, by definition, the beta of the market is 1, and owing to competition all other assets with a beta of one must offer the same expected return.

FIGURE 9.5 The Security Market Line

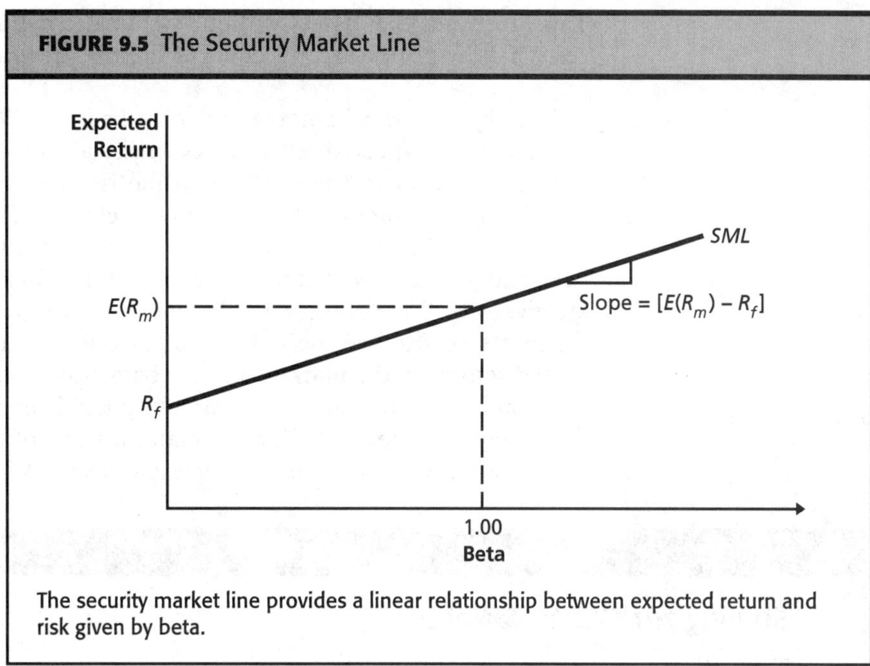

The security market line provides a linear relationship between expected return and risk given by beta.

Third, all other combinations of betas and expected returns lie along a straight line between and beyond these two points. This is explained in the chapter appendix.

Example 9.3 We can estimate the expected return of any risky asset by plugging its beta into Formula (9.1) along with an estimate of the risk-free rate and the expected return of the market. Let us illustrate the mechanics of using the *CAPM.* Consider two assets, A and B. Asset A has a beta of 0.7, and asset B has a beta of 1.0. The risk-free rate is 7 percent, and the return expected to be earned on the market portfolio is 15 percent. The *CAPM* provides an estimate of the expected return of the two assets:

$$E(R_A) = 7\% + 0.7[15\% - 7\%] = 12.6\%$$

$$E(R_B) = 7\% + 1.0[15\% - 7\%] = 15.0\%$$

It is no coincidence that asset B has a higher beta and a higher expected return. According to thc *CAPM,* assets with higher betas offer higher expected returns when compared with assets with lower betas. This must be true because beta is our measure of risk and we know that higher risk must be rewarded with higher expected return in a world of risk-averse investors.

Let us now consider asset C, whose beta is 0.0. From Formula (9.1):

$$E(R_c) = 7\% + 0.0[15\% - 7\%] = 7.0\%$$

This illustrates that assets without systematic risk (i.e., assets with betas of zero) have expected returns equal to the risk-free rate.

The objective of Chapters 8 and 9 has been met. We now have a way of determining the expected return of any risky asset using its beta, the expected return on the market portfolio, and the risk-free rate. Formula (9.1) is the foundation for your understanding of this chapter. The equation has four variables: (1) the expected return of a risky asset, (2) the risk-free rate, (3) the beta, and (4) the expected return on the market. In most *CAPM* problems, we are given any three of the variables and asked to solve for the fourth. Window 9.3 shows how to use the *CAPM* to solve for the risk-free rate, for the expected return on the market, and for beta. Students whose algebra is a little rusty should practice solving for all four possible missing values.

We have finished detailing the major aspects of the *CAPM,* and will now discuss some of its additional aspects and results. We conclude the chapter by

WINDOW 9.3

Solving for *CAPM* Variables

The *CAPM* presents a simple relationship between risk and return:

$$E(R_i) = R_f + \beta_i\,[E(R_m) - R_f]$$

The text illustrates that the *CAPM* can be used to estimate the return on an asset given three variables: (1) the risk-free rate of interest (R_f), (2) the expected return on the market portfolio $E(R_m)$, and (3) the asset's beta. For example, if the risk-free rate is 7 percent, the return on the market is 15 percent, and the asset's beta is 0.80, then the asset's return according to the *CAPM* is:

$$E(R_i) = 0.07 + 0.8\,[0.15 - 0.07] = 0.134$$

This window demonstrates that through algebraic manipulation, the *CAPM* can be used to solve for the risk-free rate, the return on the market, and for beta, given the other three variables

$$R_f = \frac{E(R_i) - \beta_i \times E(R_m)}{1 - \beta_i} \text{ so that } R_f = \frac{0.134 - (0.8 \times 0.15)}{1 - 0.8} = 0.07.$$

$$\beta_i = \frac{E(R_i) - R_f}{E(R_m) - R_f} \text{ so that } \beta_i = \frac{0.134 - 0.07}{0.150 - 0.07} = 0.8.$$

$$E(R_m) = \frac{E(R_i) + R_f(\beta_i - 1)}{\beta_i} \text{ so that } E(R_m) = \frac{0.134 + 0.07(0.8 - 1)}{0.8} = 0.15.$$

showing specifically how the *CAPM* can be implemented for projects in the firm's capital budgeting decision.

The *CAPM* and Corporate Risk Management

You may recall that, in the Markowitz model, different investors had different risk-return preferences. Whose preferences should a corporate manager utilize when a firm has many heterogeneous shareholders?

According to the *CAPM,* because the security market line is a straight line, all investors will have the same risk-versus-return tradeoff. This is true because the slope between risk and expected return is equal regardless of where on the line the investor decides to be. Thus, the corporate financial manager now has no problem in understanding the risk aversion of the shareholders—they are all equally risk-averse. This leads us to an important concept called **separation,** which means that corporate decisions such as risk analysis can be separated from stock ownership. The following information will explain why the model looks the way it does.

separation
The notion that corporate decisions can be separated from the preferences of the individual stockholder.

Why All Securities Lie on the Security Market Line

All securities lie on the security market line for two reasons. First, because of competition, investors are always looking for extra return without bearing added risk. The second reason is that because beta operates in a linear fashion, expected returns must be linear in beta.

What, then, about the role of competition? Suppose that you have some cash and are planning to add a stock to your portfolio. You are torn between three stocks, A, B, and C, but have enough money to invest in only one. Suppose, also, that when you compute the beta and expected return on each, and plot them on a risk—return graph, the risk—return tradeoff between the two stocks is as shown in Figure 9.6.

In deciding between Stock A, B, and C, the first decision to make is the level of systemic risk (or beta) you're willing to tolerate. Let's suppose that you're willing to consider any of the three stocks for investment. The next question is: Is there an obvious choice among the three stocks? You should see that Stock C is the obvious choice. Stock C will earn a return higher than what would be expected given its beta. The same cannot be said for Stock A or Stock B, as their return is lower than expected given their beta. You love a good deal, so you call your broker with an immediate request to purchase Stock C.

Such dreams, unfortunately, are unlikely to come true in competitive financial markets. The person intending to sell an asset would never sell Stock C at a price that would mean giving up superior return. There would therefore be pressure to buy Stock C rather than Stocks A and B, and a redusal to sell Stock C in favor of selling Stocks A and B. These pressures would combine to force the price of Stock C up (and therefore its expected return down) and to force the prices of Stocks A and B down (and therefore their expected returns up). These pressures would force the prices of Stocks A, B, and C to adjust until their expected returns were on the SML.

FIGURE 9.6 An Example of the Effects of Competition?

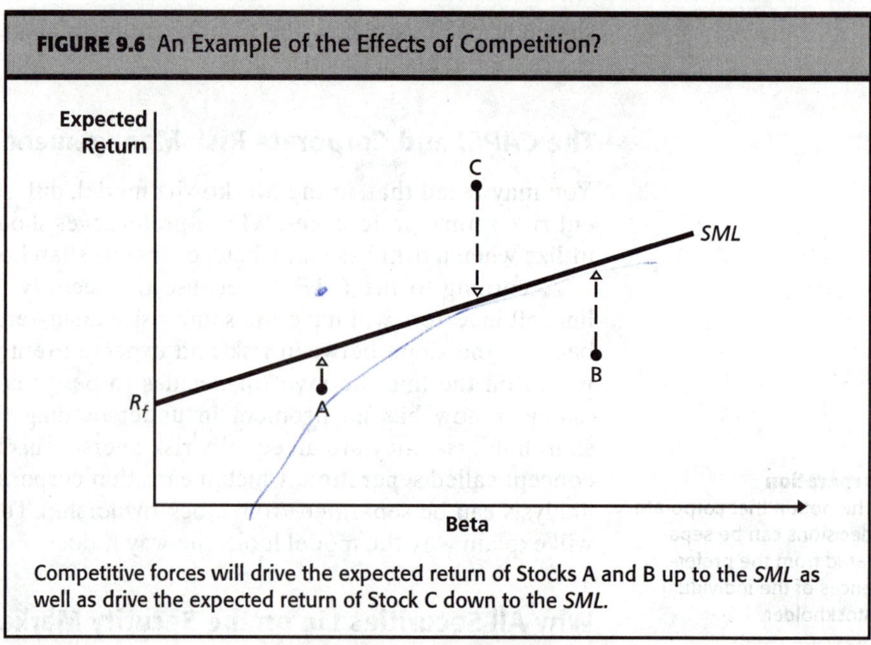

Competitive forces will drive the expected return of Stocks A and B up to the *SML* as well as drive the expected return of Stock C down to the *SML*.

The lesson to be learned is that U.S. capital markets comprise millions of investors, all operating with similar information and all looking for good deals. In such markets, stocks with identical betas will offer identical expected returns. This will be true for any level of beta, so that the relationship between beta and expected return for all stocks will be a continuous relationship like that given by Figure 9.5. The result that the line is straight is proven in the appendix.

Our analysis, like the *CAPM,* assumes that there is ultimately one type of risk—systematic or market risk. The *CAPM* is also based on the assumption that all investors operate with similar information. We know that this is not true for all stocks in all cases, but we believe it is true for most cases and offer the following evidence: Because we know of no portfolio managers who can endlessly increase their expected returns without bearing additional risks, we conclude that assets with equal risks must offer equal returns.

The *CAPM* and Capital Budgeting

We are now ready to tackle the final objective of the chapter—using the *CAPM* to make optimal capital budgeting decisions. As discussed in Chapter 5, capital budgeting decisions are best made using the net present value *(NPV)* model; therefore, our discussion focuses on applying the *CAPM* to *NPV* analysis.

The previous sections have established the point that if the beta of a project is known, its expected return can be estimated using the *CAPM.* In this section we will concentrate on how to estimate the project's beta. Once the beta of the project is estimated, we can use Formula (9.1), or the *CAPM,* to generate the project's expected rate of return. We can then use the estimate of the project's expected rate of return as the denominator in the *NPV* formula.

At this point, everything should be clear except how to estimate the beta of the project. It was shown in Window 9.2 that the beta of a stock can be calculated using a linear regression of the stock's returns on the market's returns. This would be impossible for almost any project, however, because projects are not publicly traded with a track record of historical returns.

The standard method of finding the beta of a project is to find a publicly traded corporation whose overall assets have a level of risk similar to the project under consideration. For example, if the project involved a certain industry, then the objective would be to find a corporation with as much of its assets as possible in the same industry as the project under consideration.

The project's risk will be equal to the risk of the similar firm's assets (the risk of the firm's assets is found by combining the risks of all of its securities). This is detailed in Window 9.4.

WINDOW 9.4

Determining Project Betas

In order to estimate the beta of a project when past project values cannot be observed, it is usually necessary to observe the publicly traded securities of a corporation with assets similar to the project.

Suppose, for example, that we are considering opening a brewery. We first find the market prices of securities of a publicly traded corporation whose primary asset is a brewery. Suppose we observe a brewery whose stock has a beta of 0.8 and debt with a beta of 0.1, where the beta of the debt is estimated in a fashion similar to the beta of a stock, as shown in Window 9.2.

We know that the value of the firm's assets must always equal the value of the firm's liabilities plus the value of the firm's equity. This is a result of our fourth economic law—the law of conservation of value. The beta of the assets must therefore equal the combination of the betas of the stocks and bonds as shown in Formula (9.3):

$$\text{Beta of Assets} = [(\%\ \text{Bonds}) \times \beta_b] + [(\%\ \text{Stock}) \times \beta_s]$$

where β_b is the beta of the brewery's bonds, β_s is the beta of the brewery's stock, and % stands for the percentage of the firm's assets financed by bonds or stock. For example, if the brewery has one third of its assets financed by bonds and two thirds financed by stock, from the information given earlier:

$$\text{Beta of Assets} = [(1/3) \times 0.1] + [(2/3) \times 0.8] = 0.567$$

Thus, the beta of the project would be 0.567, estimated by observing the betas of securities of corporations with similar projects already in place.

Thus, the *CAPM* provides an equation that allows the capital budgeting decision to be made in a way whereby shareholder wealth can be maximized. Let us review the steps in this process. First, estimate the beta of the project using a methodology such as that found in Window 9.4. Next, use the estimated beta, estimates of the risk-free rate, the expected return of the market, and the *CAPM* to estimate the required rate of return for the project. Finally, use the required rate of return as the discount rate in the computation of the project's *NPV*.

Summary

- Risk comes in two varieties: diversifiable risk, which will vanish and therefore can be ignored in terms of required rates of returns, and systematic risk, which does not vanish.
- Beta is a measure of an asset's systematic risk and is calculated by:

$$\beta_i = Cov(R_m, R_i)/Var(R_m)$$

  The numerator of beta's formula measures the amount of risk that an individual stock brings into an already diversified portfolio. The denominator represents the total risk of the market portfolio. Thus, beta measures the systematic risk of an asset in relation to the systematic risk of the market.
- Because the beta of the overall market is equal to 1, assets with betas greater than 1 signify a level of systematic risk greater than the overall market, and assets with betas less than 1 signify a level of systematic risk less than the overall market.
- Given an asset's beta, we can use the *CAPM* to determine the asset's required rate of return:

$$E(R_i) = R_f + \beta_i\,[E(R_m) - R_f]$$

  The *CAPM* should not be viewed as an extremely accurate and unquestioned method of finding this rate—rather, it should be viewed as a good tool for separating risks into those that do and do not require rewards and for estimating the amount of return that the market requires for bearing a particular level of systematic risk.

References

Lintner, J. "The Valuation of Risk Assets and the Selection of Risky Investments in Stock Portfolios and Capital Budgets." *Review of Economics and Statistics* 47 (February 1965): 13–37.

Markowitz, H. M. "Portfolio Selection." *Journal of Finance* 7 (March 1952): 77–91.

Sharpe, W. F. "Capital Asset Prices: A Theory of Market Equilibrium Under Conditions of Risk." *Journal of Finance* 19 (September 1964): 425–442.

Tobin, J. "Liquidity Preference as Behavior Toward Risk." *Review of Economic Studies* 25 (February 1965): 65–86.

Demonstration Problems

Problem 1

The common stock of SuperStore, Inc., has generated substantially different returns in the last 5 years. These returns are shown in the chart, along with the corresponding returns for the stock market as a whole.

Year	*SuperStore, Inc., Return*	*Market Return*
1	0.12	0.30
2	0.40	0.15
3	−0.10	−0.15
4	−0.20	0.00
5	0.38	0.45

Compute the beta of the common stock of SuperStore, Inc., based upon these 5 years of returns.

Solution to Problem 1

The beta of an investment is equal to the covariance of the investment with the market divided by the variance of the market. These statistics are now computed using the table method demonstrated in Window 9.2.

Step 1: Form a table similar to that in Window 9.2 and fill in the returns that are given:

(1) Year	*(2)* Return on SuperStore	*(3)* Return on Market	*(4)* SuperStore Deviation	*(5)* Market Deviation	*(6)* Squared Market Deviation	*(7)* Cross Product
1	0.12	0.30				
2	0.40	0.15				
3	−0.10	−0.15				
4	−0.20	0.00				
5	0.38	0.45				

Step 2: Compute the average return for both column 2 and column 3 (separately) by summing the returns in each column and dividing by the number of years (5). Thus, the average return for column 2 (SuperStore) is found by dividing the sum of the returns (0.60) by 5, equaling 0.12. The average return of column 3, the market, is found by dividing the sum of the returns (0.75) by 5, equaling 0.15.

Step 3: Subtract each average return from each column to form columns 4 and 5. If you have done the math correctly (and if the problem does not involve unequal probabilities), the sum of the deviation columns should be zero. This is a convenient method for checking your math.

(1) Year	(2) Return on SuperStore	(3) Return on Market	(4) SuperStore Deviation	(5) Market Deviation	(6) Squared Market Deviation	(7) Cross Product
1	0.12	0.30	0.00	0.15		
2	0.40	0.15	0.28	0.00		
3	−0.10	−0.15	−0.22	−0.30		
4	−0.20	0.00	−0.32	−0.15		
5	0.38	0.45	0.26	0.30		
Average	0.12	0.15				

Step 4: Complete the entries for columns 6 and 7. Column 6 is found by squaring each entry in column 5. Column 7 is found by multiplying column 4 by column 5. All of the entries in column 6 must be greater than or equal to zero. Be careful, however, to make sure that the entries in column 7 have the correct sign. Finally, average columns 6 and 7 separately to form the variance of the market in column 6 and the covariance between the assets in column 7. These columns are averaged by summing them and then dividing by the number of entries (e.g., 0.2250 / 5 = 0.0450 for column 6).

(1) Year	(2) Return on SuperStore	(3) Return on Market	(4) SuperStore Deviation	(5) Market Deviation	(6) Squared Market Deviation	(7) Cross Product
1	0.12	0.30	0.00	0.15	0.0225	0.0000
2	0.40	0.15	0.28	0.00	0.0000	0.0000
3	−0.10	−0.15	−0.22	−0.30	0.0900	0.0660
4	−0.20	0.00	−0.32	−0.15	0.0225	0.0480
5	0.38	0.45	0.26	0.30	0.0900	0.0780
Average	0.12	0.15			0.0450	0.0384

Final Solution: The beta is found by dividing the covariance (0.0384) by the variance of the market (0.0450), which equals 0.8533. Notice that the returns of SuperStore tend to move in the same direction as the market (the beta is positive) but not quite as much as the market (the beta is less than 1).

Problem 2

SuperStore, Inc., has four divisions based upon geography. Their financial analysts have computed the betas of the divisions as follows:

Region	*Beta*
Northeast	1.0
Southeast	1.2
Midwest	0.8
West	1.5

The risk-free rate is 5% and the expected return on the market is 14%. Compute the required rates of return for each division.

Solution to Problem 2

When an asset trades in a competitive market, its expected return must equal the required rate of return of the investors. In this question, we are looking for the required rates of return for divisions within a corporation. These required rates of return should be equal to the expected rates of return that an investor would earn in the marketplace on assets with similar betas. Thus, each required rate of return can be found using the *CAPM* as shown in Formula (9.1). The *CAPM* has four variables. This problem, like many others, provides three of the variables and requires that the fourth variable be computed.

Step 1: Copy Formula (9.1) from the text (or, better, from memory):

$$E(R_i) = R_f + \beta_i[E(R_m) - R_f]$$

Step 2: Fill in the two rates of return that are provided, the risk-free interest rate (R_f) and the expected return of the market [$E(R_m)$].

$$E(R_i) = 0.05 + \beta_i\,(0.14 - 0.05)$$

Step 3: Solve for the required rates of return by inserting the given betas:

Northeast Division: $E(R_i) = 0.05 + (1.0 \times 0.09) = 0.14$, or 14%

Southeast Division: $E(R_i) = 0.05 + (1.2 \times 0.09) = 0.158$, or 15.8%

Midwest Division: $E(R_i) = 0.05 + (0.8 \times 0.09) = 0.122$, or 12.2%

West Division: $E(R_i) = 0.05 + (1.5 \times 0.09) = 0.185$, or 18.5%

Final Solution: Each division has a required rate of return that depends entirely upon its beta. An investment with a beta of 1.0 requires 9% more return than a risk-free investment. For each 0.1 increase or decrease in beta, therefore, we should expect a 0.9% increase or decrease in the required rate of return.

Review Questions

1. Explain the difference between diversifiable and nondiversifiable risk.
2. Why do we say that some risky portfolios will always be preferred to others?
3. In the Markowitz framework, how do investors decide in which risky portfolio of securities to invest?
4. How do people adjust the risk of their total security holdings in the *CAPM* framework?
5. What is the name given to the unique risky portfolio that all investors are drawn to? Why is it given such a name?
6. Provide both a statistical and a nonstatistical definition for beta.
7. If the market were to fall unexpectedly by 1%, a stock with a beta of 0.75 would be expected to fall on average by 1%. True or false? Explain.
8. Draw the relationship given by the security market line. Label both axes.
9. Explain the procedure of using the *CAPM* in capital budgeting.
10. How is a project beta estimated?

Problems

1. What is the beta of the risk-free asset and what is the beta of the overall market?
2. The covariance between Eb Corporation's common stock returns and the return on the market portfolio is 0.06. The standard deviation of the market is 0.2. What is the beta of Eb Corporation's common stock?
3. Financial analysts have estimated the returns on shares of Drucker Corporation and the overall market portfolio under various economic conditions as follows:

State of Economy	*Return on Drucker*	*Return on Market*
Recession	−15%	−10%
Moderate Growth	+10%	+5%
Boom	+35%	+20%

The analysts consider each state to be equally likely.

a. Compute the expected return for each column.
b. Compute the variance of the market.
c. Compute the covariance between Drucker and the market.
d. Compute the beta of Drucker Corporation's stock.

4. Using Formula (9.1), called the capital asset pricing model or the security market line, if the expected return of the market is 16%, the risk-free rate is 6%, and the beta of an asset is 0.5, what is the expected return of the asset?
5. What would be the beta of the following portfolios?

a. 100% risk-free asset and 0% market
b. 75% risk-free asset and 25% market
c. 50% risk-free asset and 50% market
d. 25% risk-free asset and 75% market
e. 0% risk-free asset and 100% market

6. Use Formula (9.1) to supply the missing values:

	$E(R_i)$	R_f	β_i	$E(R_m)$
a.	___	8%	1.0	18%
b.	___	8%	0.5	18%
c.	___	8%	1.5	18%
d.	___	6%	0.8	20%
e.	___	7%	−0.9	15%
f.	14%	9%	___	19%
g.	12%	8%	___	24%
h.	22%	10%	___	18%
i.	−2%	8%	___	18%
j.	15%	5%	1.0	___
k.	10%	5%	0.5	___
l.	18%	9%	0.9	___
m.	22%	7%	1.2	___
n.	−2%	6%	−1.1	___
o.	6%	___	0.0	14%
p.	14%	___	0.5	18%
q.	25%	___	2.0	15%
r.	−5%	___	−1.5	14%

7. Various attributes of three stocks are listed:

	Arnold Corp.	*Ziffel Corp.*	*Douglas Corp.*
Price	\$25	\$40	\$35
Expected Return	10%	12%	14%
Covariances with the Market	0.03	0.04	0.05

The variance of the market portfolio is 0.04.

a. What would be the portfolio weights of a portfolio consisting of 100 shares of each stock?
b. What would be the expected return of a portfolio of 100 shares of each stock?
c. What is the beta of each stock?
d. What would the beta of a portfolio of 100 shares of each stock be?
e. What would the beta of a portfolio of these three stocks be if the expected return of the portfolio were 11%?

8. It is possible to compute means, variances, betas, and so forth using historical data as shown in Window 9.2. For our purposes the procedure is identical to the case of various economic states where each economic state is equally likely. Consider the following history of returns:

Year	*Homer Company*	*Large Company Stocks*
1	34.09%	14.63%
2	1.00%	2.03%
3	17.05%	12.41%
4	73.15%	27.26%
5	20.40%	−6.56%
6	51.84%	26.31%
7	30.50%	4.46%
8	2.22%	7.06%
9	11.43%	−1.54%
10	40.16%	34.11%

a. Compute the mean of each return series (*Hint*: Treat each outcome as having the same probability of recurring—in this case 10%).
b. Compute the beta of Homer Company (*Hint*: First compute the covariance between them and the variance of the market).

9. What combination of the risk-free asset and the market portfolio would have the same beta as the following stocks?
a. A stock with a beta of 0.5
b. A stock with a beta of 0.9

10. If the risk-free asset offers an expected return of 6% and the overall market offers an expected return of 18%:
a. What would be the required returns of the two stocks in Problem 9?
b. What would the required returns be of the two portfolios determined as answers to Problem 9?

11. If a stock had an expected return greater than it should according to the *CAPM,* would it be overpriced or underpriced? What should we expect to happen to its price in an efficient market?

12. Both Oliver Corporation and Lisa Corporation have debt with a beta of 0 and equity with a beta of 1.2.

a. What is the beta of Oliver Corporation's assets if the corporation's debt is 30% of its securities and the equity is 70% of its securities?
b. What is the beta of Lisa Corporation's assets if the corporation's debt is 50% of its securities and the equity is 50% of its securities?

13. The Haney Corporation is considering a major capital expenditure on a project. The current risk-free interest rate is 8% and the expected return on the overall market is 18%. What required rate of return should the corporation use as a discount to its *NPV* analysis if:
a. The risk of the project is identical to the risk of the assets of the Oliver Corporation in Problem 12?
b. The risk of the project is identical to the risk of the assets of the Lisa Corporation in Problem 12?

Discussion Questions

1. When is the expected rate of return equal to the required rate of return? When are they different?

2. *CAPM* theory leads to the conclusion that all investors hold the same portfolio of risky assets—the market portfolio. Today, billions of investment dollars are "indexed" or placed into portfolios that seek to replicate the market as a whole; however, some people do not diversify at all. What does this evidence say about *CAPM* theory? Explain.

3. Ricky "All Eggs in One Basket" Jordon has his cash invested in one stock. The beta of his stock is 0.5. Ricky concludes that his investment is half as risky as the market as a whole. Is he correct? Explain.

4. Respond to the following comment:

Our company's products are unique; therefore, the CAPM *is of little use to us in our capital budgeting analysis.*

5. Select a product, make an ordered list of the largest risks its producers face, and then estimate the extent to which these risks are diversifiable or systematic.

6. If an asset has a negative beta, will it offer a higher or lower expected return relative to the risk-free rate? Would anyone ever invest in an asset whose expected return is less than the risk-free rate?

7. Respond to the following comment:

The CAPM *is ridiculous; actual returns do not lie in a straight line against beta.*

APPENDIX

WHY EXPECTED RETURNS LIE IN A STRAIGHT LINE AGAINST BETA

The purpose of this appendix is to derive the *CAPM* with a minimum of math because some mathematical proofs of the *CAPM* are very difficult to follow. We will demonstrate that the linearity of beta and the formulas that use beta are sufficient to derive the *CAPM* under the potentially tricky assumption that assets with identical betas must have identical returns.

We will begin by proving that beta operates in a linear fashion, which is to say that the beta of a portfolio is a linear combination of the betas of the constituent assets. Recall Formula (9.2):

$$\beta_i = Cov(R_i, R_m)/Var(R_m)$$

This is the definition of beta and says that the beta of an asset depends upon its covariance with the market divided by the market's variance. Let us now look at the formula for the return of a portfolio of two assets using weights as in Chapter 8:

$$R_P = (w_1 \times R_1) + (w_2 \times R_2) \qquad \text{(A9.1)}$$

where R_p is the return on a portfolio, w_1 and w_2 are the percentages invested in assets 1 and 2, and R_1 and R_2 are the returns of assets 1 and 2.

The beta of the portfolio in terms of the portfolio's constituent assets can be found by inserting R_p from Formula (A9.1) in place of R_i from Formula (9.2):

$$\beta_p = Cov\{[w_1R_1 + w_2R_2], R_m\}/Var(R_m) \qquad \text{(A9.2)}$$

Formula (A9.2) becomes:

$$\beta_p = w_1\,[Cov(R_1,R_m)/(VarR_m)] + w_2\,[Cov(R_2,R_m)/\,Var(R_m)] \qquad \text{(A9.3)}$$

Recognizing the formula for beta, Formula A9.3 reduces to:

$$\beta_p = (w_1\beta_1) + (w_2\beta_2) \tag{A9.4}$$

As promised, we have proved that the beta of a portfolio is equal to the weighted average of the betas of the constituent assets. Note that Formula (A9.4) is simply the two-asset case of Formula (9.3). The math could be performed for any size portfolio.

Let us now assume that asset 1 is the risk-free asset with a beta of zero and that asset 2 is the overall market and therefore has a beta of 1. As shown in Formula (A9.5) the beta of this special portfolio reduces:

$$\beta_p = w_2 \tag{A9.5}$$

where β_p is the beta of a portfolio with w_1 percent in the risk-free asset and w_2 in the overall market.

Thus, the beta of the portfolio is equal to the percentage of the portfolio invested in the market. If the portfolio is 0% invested in the market, then the beta is 0, if it is 25% invested in the market then the beta is 0.25, and if it is 100 percent invested in the market the beta is 1.00.

The expected return of this portfolio can be found using the formula from Chapter 8 for the expected return on a portfolio:

$$E(R_p) = (w_1 \times R_f) + (w_2 \times E(R_m))$$

Inserting $(1 - w_2)$ for w_1, B_p for w_2, and rearranging produces the familiar *CAPM:*

$$E(R_p) = R_f + \beta_p\,[E(R_m) - R_f]$$

This equation demonstrates that the expected return of our portfolio, which has w_1 percent in the risk-free asset and w_2 percent in the market, *adheres* to the *CAPM*. The beta of the portfolio is β_p. If we assume that the expected return of all assets with equal betas must be equal, then the expected returns of all assets must lie on the straight line depicted in the *CAPM* equation. For beta values of less than zero or greater than 1, some concepts beyond the scope of this text would be required.

The critical assumption was that assets with equal betas must offer equal expected returns. This concept is detailed in the main text of Chapter 9. The implications of this concept are complex and beyond the scope of this text.

It is worth noting, however, that there may be systematic types of risk other than market risk. The arbitrage pricing model has been developed to demonstrate the effects of multiple sources of systematic risk. It is a useful concept for advanced courses, but for the purposes of this text one systematic risk factor (the market) is enough!

CHAPTER 10

INTRODUCTION TO OPTIONS

Thomas Donaldson, a senior finance major, has been managing his family's investment portfolio for 3 years with good success. His overall philosophy is to take well-calculated risks, and his latest strategy is to invest in stock options. To be specific, he is proposing a position in a combination of options known as a straddle. Here is how the straddle works: The investor purchases two types of stock options—a call option and a put option. The call option becomes profitable if the stock market goes up, and the put option becomes profitable if the stock market goes down. The straddle loses money if the stock market does not change substantially from its current position.

The reaction of the Donaldson family to this new investment strategy was summed up by his mother, who said, "Thomas, this sounds crazy. On the one side, we win if the market goes up, but on the other side, we win if the market goes down. It's like placing two wagers on the upcoming football game—one on the home team and one on the away team. How can we possibly come out ahead?"

Thomas explained that the genius of this strategy is timing: "The presidential elections are coming up, and most everyone expects a close race this year. While I can't predict who will win, I can say that the stock market will react strongly to the election results. The way I see it, the market goes way up if the Republican wins, in which case we make more money on the call option than we lose on the put option. On the other side, the market goes way down if the Democrat wins, making us more money on the put option than we lose on the call option. In other words, I know the market will move, and the straddle allows us to profit no matter what happens."

Understanding the straddle requires option pricing theory—the subject of this chapter. Chapter 10 introduces options on common stock, and links the concept of an option to the value of the equity of a firm. Much of the material in this chapter, from option terminology to the basics of option contracts, has not been introduced previously. Whereas the material may require more than one reading, options are such an important part of the study of finance that the time spent will be well worth the effort.

The Importance of Option Theory

There are three reasons why the study of options is important. First, options are a common component in many corporate finance decisions. For example, when a corporation purchases land, leases space, or makes major purchases such as airplanes, it is common for the corporation to obtain options for more land, more space, or additional airplanes that allow the corporation to lock in future purchase prices in the event of expansion. Further, corporations often attach options to their securities that enable the holder to buy more securities or to trade their securities for other securities.

The corporation may also issue securities and require that the purchaser allow the corporation the option to buy them back. Many of the corporation's contracts—including employment contracts, supply contracts, distribution contracts, insurance contracts, and so forth—contain provisions that allow one or more of the parties in the agreement to make a decision about whether or not to terminate, extend, or modify the agreement. These are all options.

Second, the financial markets allow widespread trading of options. Organized option trading, which began in 1973, now consists of hundreds of millions of contracts per year on more than a dozen U.S. options exchanges. For example, investors can use options to buy or sell financial securities including common stock, government bonds, and commodities. As mentioned earlier, the trading of options has exploded in popularity, and is an important building block in the risk management of corporations and investment portfolios.

Third, the corporate form of the business organization itself creates an option. The equity of the corporation is an option in the sense that shareholders can either continue to own a firm or can walk away from the corporation by declaring bankruptcy. Thinking about the equity of a firm as a call option allows for new insights concerning the value of the firm.

Our main objective in this chapter is to provide you with the tools necessary to understand how options are valued. We will begin with a discussion on the mechanics of options. The Black-Scholes Option Pricing Model—a dramatic breakthrough in finance—will eventually be presented. Finally, options will be applied to some of the most common situations in corporate finance.

The Mechanics of Options

The key to understanding the option contract is that, whereas many contracts require you to act, an option gives its holder the opportunity to act without an obligation. A financial option is a contract that offers the holder the choice either to accept a transaction or to decline the transaction. The terms of the option usually include a specific transaction price and a time limit or date of expiration.

This chapter emphasizes **call options.** A call option gives its holder the opportunity either to buy something, such as 100 shares of common stock at a certain price, or to do nothing and therefore not transact. The call option will include a time period, at the end of which the option expires or ends. Another common type of option, known as a **put option,** gives its holder the choice of either selling something or not transacting.

call option
A security that gives its holder the opportunity either to buy something, such as 100 shares of common stock at a certain price, or to do nothing and therefore not transact. The call option will include a time period at the end of which the option expires or ends.

put option
A security that gives its holder the opportunity either to sell something, such as 100 shares of common stock at a certain price, or to do nothing and therefore not transact. The put option will include a time period at the end of which the option expires or ends.

> A financial option is a contract that offers the holder the choice to either accept a transaction or to decline the transaction. The terms of the option usually include a specific transaction price and a time limit or date of expiration.

Options exist in many forms, and many have entered into option contracts without thinking much about them. For example, at one time you may have placed a fee, say $25, with a landlord to guarantee an apartment up to a certain date at a specified monthly rent. The fee (or deposit) essentially holds the apartment until you move into the apartment and pay another sum of money. This deposit is very much like a call option, as it gives you the right to the apartment at a specified price. If you act in time, you pay the next sum of money and the apartment is yours. If you choose not to act, you walk away from the rental deal, losing only the deposit.

There is a new vocabulary to learn when dealing with options for the first time. Window 10.1 explains much of the terminology in detail and highlights the most important terms that you will need to know to understand this chapter. You should review the option terminology in Window 10.1 before proceeding.

A Graphical Look at Options

Chapters 8 and 9 discussed the pioneering work in portfolio theory. The development of the theory assumed that prices of financial assets follow the familiar normal or bell-shaped distribution. The tails of the normal distribution run from negative infinity to positive infinity. In more modern and technical work, stock returns are usually assumed to form a related distribution entitled the **lognormal distribution.**

lognormal distribution
A statistical distribution in which the variables can take on only positive numbers.

The lognormal distribution, which is illustrated in Figure 10.1, looks similar to the normal distribution, but it is flattened or skewed to the right. In Figure 10.1, the potential range of stock prices on the horizontal axis from zero to positive infinity rather than from negative to positive infinity. Given limited liability, stock prices cannot go lower than zero.

Example 10.1 _______ Suppose that a call option on the stock in Figure 10.1 exists such that the option allows the holder to purchase shares of stock for $20. Using option terminology, we say that the option's exercise price is $20. Because the call option gives the holder the right to buy stock at $20, the value of the option will depend on the value of the underlying stock. The option is more valuable when the price of the stock is near or above $20 and has little or no value if the stock falls far below $20. For example, if the price of the stock should move to

WINDOW 10.1

Option Terminology

Call options give the buyer the right to buy an asset at a specific price on or before a certain date. For standard options on common stock, each option permits the holder to purchase 100 shares of stock. The purpose of this window is to review the terminology of options and option trading. Some of these definitions will be illustrated using actual call option prices taken from the *Wall Street Journal* for the IBM Corporation:

IBM Call Option Prices—May 11, 2001

NY Close	*Strike Price*	*May*	*June*
111 81	110	3 60	6 80
111 81	115	1 40	4 20
111 81	120	0 30	2 30

1. Strike Price or Exercise Price The price at which the stock underlying the call option can be purchased. The terms strike price and exercise price can be used interchangeably.

For the IBM option, three different strike or exercise prices are illustrated: \$110, \$115, and \$120. If you purchased the IBM \$110 strike option, you could, until expiration, purchase IBM stock for \$110 no matter the current price of IBM. It is typically the case that many different strike prices are available for each tradable option.

2. Option Premium The amount the buyer of an option has to pay for the right to purchase or sell the stock at the specified price by a specified date. The option premium is also referred to as the option price.

Six different premiums are listed for IBM. For the strike price of \$110, the call premiums are \$3.60 for May and \$6.80 for June. For the strike price of \$115, the call premiums are \$1.40 for May and \$4.20 for June. For the strike price of \$120, the premiums are \$0.30 for May and \$2.30 for June.

3. Expiration Date The last day an option can be exercised. The option becomes worthless after this date is reached. Option exchanges have exact times and dates that define expiration.

For IBM, two different expiration dates, May and June, are listed. IBM options trade on the American Stock Exchange, and these options expire at 4:00 P.M. on the third Friday of the month. The premium for the June option is always higher than the premium of the May option because the June option has a longer life.

4. In-the-Money Call Options Call options whose underlying stock price is currently above the exercise price.

For IBM, the market price on May 11, 2001 is \$111.81. Two of the six options listed are in the money. The \$110 exercise price is below the current stock price.

WINDOW 10.1 (continued)

5. Out-of-the-Money Call Options Call options whose underlying stock price is currently below the exercise price. These options will have some value as long as investors believe that there is a chance that the option will be in the money by expiration.

For IBM, the $115 and $120 exercise price options are out of the money. The value of IBM would have to rise above the exercise price in order for the option to have value at expiration. These out-of-the-money May and June IBM options have some value because investors believe that IBM's stock price might rise above $115 and $120 per share before expiration.

6. At-the-Money-Call Options Options whose underlying stock price is currently equal to the exercise price.

7. Call Option Writer The individual who created and sold the call option and agrees to deliver the option's underlying asset to the buyer at the strike price if demanded. For this guarantee, the call option writer receives the premium from the option buyer.

8. Covered Call Option Call option for which the writer owns the underlying stock.

9. Naked Call Option Call options for which the option writer has no holdings of the underlying stock.

10. Option Clearinghouse The corporation that handles all option transactions on the exchange. The clearinghouse guarantees that all prior commitments, especially those of the option writer, are fulfilled. If the writer fails to deliver the underlying stock to the buyer at the exercise price, the clearinghouse steps in and absorbs the loss. The clearinghouse therefore becomes the seller to every buyer. To safeguard the clearinghouse from losses, option writers are required to keep good-faith deposits, called *margin,* with the exchange.

11. Index Options Call options whose underlying security is an index of stocks instead of a single stock. The value of the call option rises and falls with an index of stocks, such as the S&P 500 index, instead of with a single stock like IBM.

12. Option Combinations One of the interesting features of options is their ability to be combined with stocks or with other options to create portfolios with different payout streams. Popular option combinations include:

Straddle: A call option and a put option on the same stock with the same exercise price and the same expiration date.

Strip: Two put options and a call option, all on the same underlying security, all with the same exercise price and expiration date.

Strap: Two call options and a put option, all on the same underlying security, all with the same exercise price and expiration date.

Spread: The purchase of one option and the simultaneous sale of another option on the same underlying security at a different exercise price or different expiration date.

FIGURE 10.1 The Lognormal Distribution

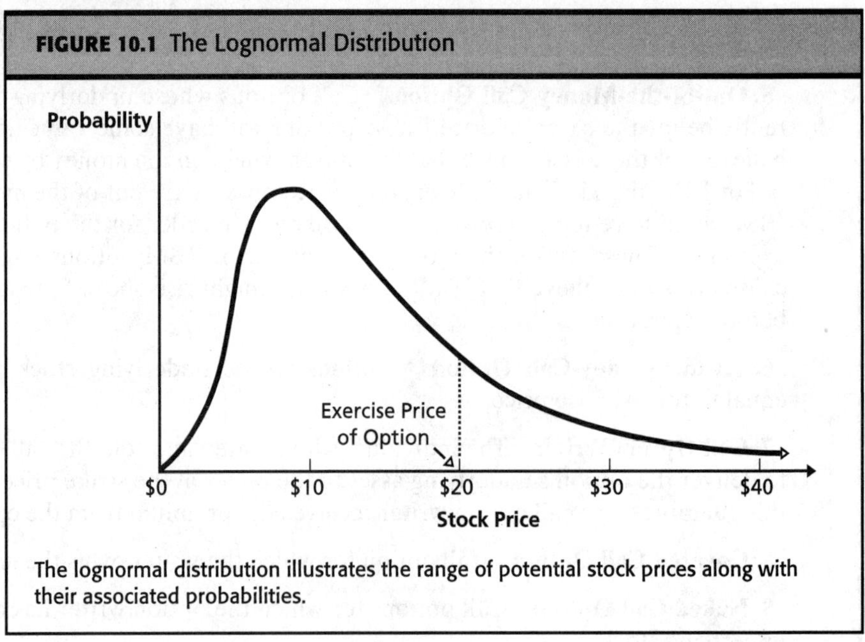

The lognormal distribution illustrates the range of potential stock prices along with their associated probabilities.

$25, the holder of the call option can exercise the option, purchase stock for $20, and sell the stock in the open market at $25, making $5 in the process.

Figure 10.2 illustrates the option payout distribution, or the value of the call option against the price of the underlying common stock. Notice that there is a significant chance that the option will be worth zero because the stock will be worth $20 or less. This is shown in the unshaded portion of the bottom diagram in Figure 10.2, and it illustrates the concept that at expiration an option whose exercise price is above the stock price is worthless. The logic is that because the option entitles its holder to buy the stock at $20, and because the stock can be bought in the market for $20 or less, there is no value to using or having the option. After all, would you be willing to leave a deposit with a landlord for the right to rent an apartment for $500 if the apartment can be rented without such a deposit for $450?

Note, however, that if the final stock price is above $20 the option has value. In fact, the greater the stock price, the more valuable the option. This is illustrated in Figure 10.3, where the value of the call option is shown with the price of the stock. Notice that the value of the option at expiration is $1 for each $1 by which the stock price exceeds the $20 exercise price. For example, if at the expiration date of the option the price of the stock is $8 over the exercise price, the option will be worth $8.

Figure 10.3 illustrates an important feature about call options. The worst that can happen when you purchase an option is that it expires worthless, resulting in a loss equal to the price or premium of the option. Said another

FIGURE 10.2 The Option Payout Distribution at Expiration

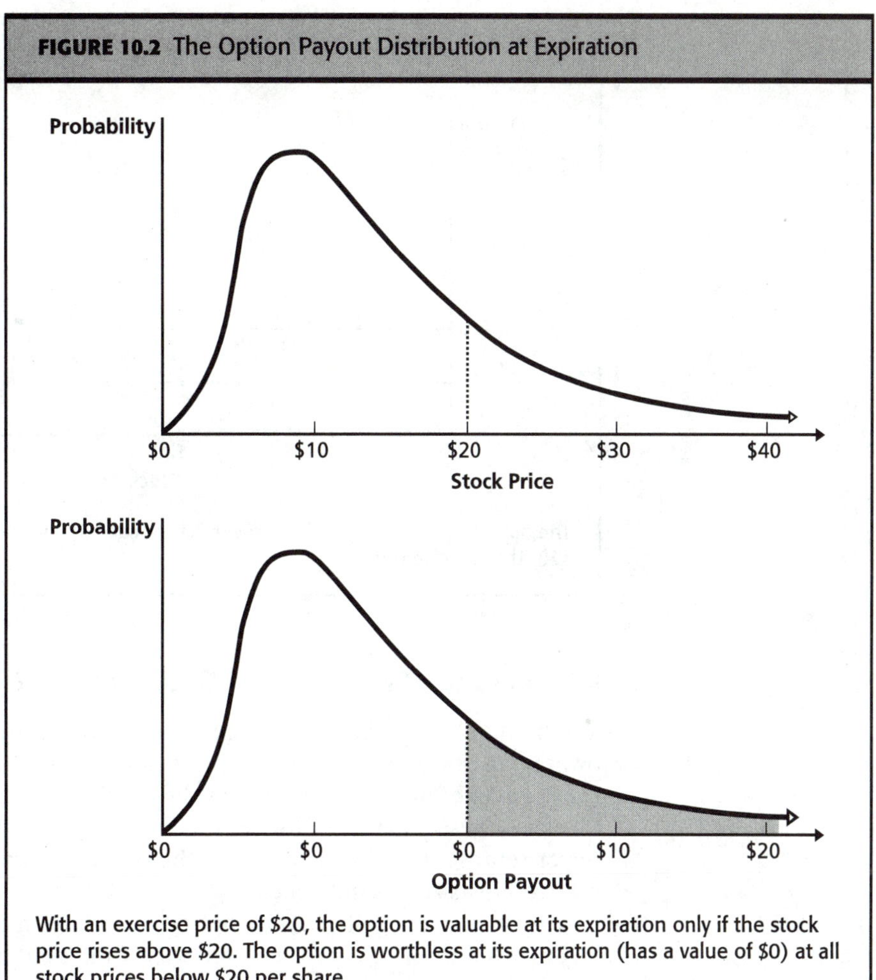

With an exercise price of $20, the option is valuable at its expiration only if the stock price rises above $20. The option is worthless at its expiration (has a value of $0) at all stock prices below $20 per share.

way, the most you can lose when you purchase the call option is the call premium, the price you paid for the option. Even if the stock price went to zero, you would lose no more than your original investment. An option can never have a negative value to its owner. Owning an option gives you the right to purchase stock at a specific price and carries no obligation.

> The worst that can happen when you purchase an option is that it expires worthless, resulting in a loss equal to the price or premium of the option.

At the other extreme, you will notice from Figure 10.3 that there is no limit to the potential value of the option. As the stock climbs in value, so does the call option. The stock price is not expected to grow from $20 to, say, $2000, but there is no theoretical upper boundary.

FIGURE 10.3 The Value of a Call Option at Expiration

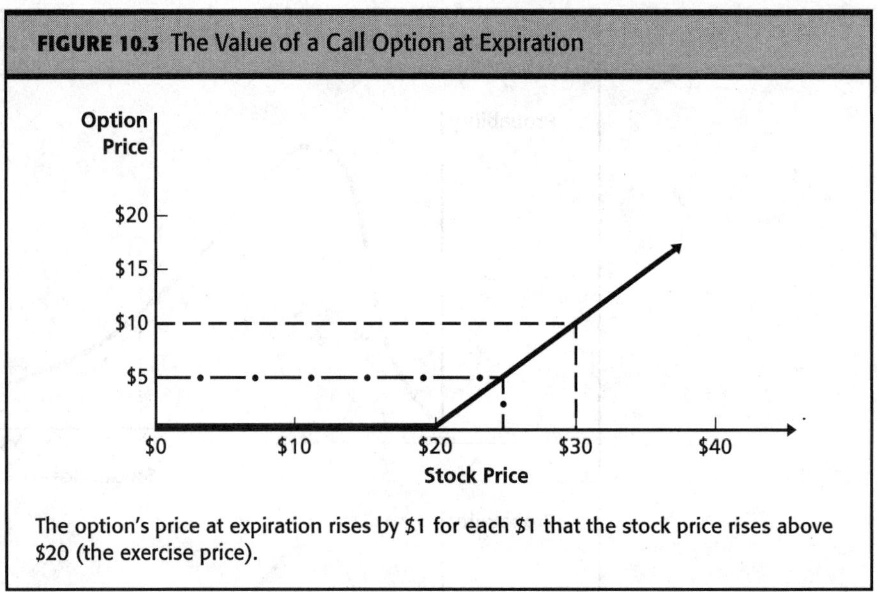

The option's price at expiration rises by $1 for each $1 that the stock price rises above $20 (the exercise price).

Who Pays the Profits to Call Option Buyers?

The limited loss potential and theoretically unlimited profit potential make owning an option an attractive opportunity to some investors. However, for every buyer of an option there must be a seller of the option who is obligated to make these payments to the buyer. Every dollar of gain to the option buyer represents a dollar of loss to the option seller. This is why options are referred to as zero-sum games.

Why would the seller of the option, who has an obligation to the option buyer, ever offer the buyer a security with limited losses and unlimited gains? (Remember that unlimited gains to the buyer means unlimited losses to the seller.) The seller or writer of an option in effect pays all the cash flows the option buyer receives. Thus, the worst thing that can happen when you write an option is that you will be responsible for paying out the buyer's (perhaps considerable) profits. The answer is that the seller is paid a fee, known as the *option premium,* for taking this risk, and the seller hopes that the stock price will not rise beyond the exercise price.

The seller or writer of an option in effect pays all the cash flows the option buyer receives. Thus, the worst thing that can happen when you write an option is that you will be responsible for paying out the buyer's (perhaps considerable) profits.

In summary, there are two participants in every option contract: the buyer and the seller. The positions of the two parties are mirror images in that any profit on one side must be offset by a loss on the other. Option buyers have limited loss potential and unlimited profit potential. Option writers have limited profit potential and huge or unlimited loss potential.

Call Option Pricing Prior to Expiration

At this point we have considered only the case of the option on its expiration date. Of course, options trade prior to expiration, as illustrated in Example 10.2.

Example 10.2 _______ Consider a coupon or certificate that allows you to purchase an airline ticket for $200 on or before a certain date. In the parlance of finance, this certificate is a call option that allows the holder of the option to purchase an airline ticket for the exercise price of $200. The certificate allows for travel during a certain vacation period, and ticket prices during that vacation period vary from year to year, based upon competition, the economy, and fuel costs. Past prices have varied from $100 to $300 per ticket; future ticket prices are unknown.

How much would such a certificate be worth prior to its expiration? It is clear that the certificate is worth something. In the event that ticket prices at travel time are greater than $200, the certificate will have value. There is a limit to the value of the certificate, however, because it is almost impossible for the airline ticket to rise above $300 by the next vacation period.

If you were buying the airline certificate (or call option), how much would you pay? If you owned several of the certificates, what events would cause you to make or lose money? Before introducing a model to help answer these questions, let us apply some common sense. The value of the certificates will rise if airline ticket prices rise or even if ticket prices become much more uncertain because of some international crisis. On the other hand, if ticket prices drop significantly, then the coupon will also fall in value and may eventually be worthless. A "ball park" value to the certificates could be $20 to $30 each. This type of rough analysis would be adequate for occasional transactions. Many economic exchanges, however, involve options too important to estimate. The next section will introduce a model that provides the sophisticated analysis required by modern corporate financial management.

The Black-Scholes Option Pricing Model

In the early 1970s Fisher Black and Myron Scholes derived an option pricing model, based upon a tremendous insight, that revolutionized both the study of option pricing and even the option industry itself. Today, with the help of the **Black-Scholes option pricing model,** option trading is a massive, highly sophisticated component of finance.

Black-Scholes option pricing model
A model for valuing options based upon five variables: the value of the underlying asset, the time to expiration of the option, the option's exercise price, the volatility of the underlying asset, and the risk-free rate of interest.

Newer models have been developed to fine-tune pricing in certain specific situations, but the Black-Scholes model is the industry standard. The next part of this section will explain the underpinnings of the Black-Scholes model.

Systematic Risk and Option Pricing

Like any asset, the value of an option is the present value of the future cash flows adjusted for time and risk. The key is to estimate the future cash flows and to find a proper interest rate for discounting. The Black-Scholes model proved that the price of the option did not depend upon whether the risk is systematic or unsystematic or upon people's attitude toward risk. Black and Scholes proved that options are priced as if no one cared about risk, or, in other words, as if everyone were risk-neutral rather than risk-averse.

The lack of distinction between systematic and unsystematic risk in the Black-Scholes option pricing model seems very strange given our treatment of risk. At first glance it would seem that the formula for the price of a call option would include beta or some other measure of systematic risk. It does not. And it is not that people do not care about risk: There is a good effect and a bad effect of systematic risk within an option, and these two effects cancel each other out.

The price of a call option on common stock may be viewed as the present value of the option's cash payouts at its expiration. These cash payments depend on the price of the common stock, which is also known as the price of the underlying asset. The good effect of systematic risk in the underlying asset is that high systematic risk, or high beta, translates into a higher expected rate of return for the underlying asset and therefore higher expected future cash flows from the option. The bad effect of systematic risk in the underlying asset is that high systematic risk in the underlying asset means that the future cash flows of the option will also have high systematic risk and therefore must be discounted at a higher rate.

The Black-Scholes magic is that these two systematic risk effects cancel each other out, leaving a model that generates an option price that seems to ignore systematic risk but actually works whether or not systematic risk exists.

Foundations of the Black-Scholes Option Pricing Model

Because many of the details of the Black-Scholes model are well beyond the scope of this book, we will summarize what is important. First, the Black-Scholes option pricing model is an accurate way of computing the price of an option that fully accounts for both the time value of money and risk. Second, there are five variables that determine an option price: (1) the price of the underlying asset, (2) the exercise price of the option, (3) the time to expiration, (4) the standard deviation of the returns of the underlying asset, and (5) the risk-free interest rate. Third, given these five variables, the model uses a complicated formula to provide an option price.

Because of its complexity, the model itself has been placed in the appendix to this chapter; however, it can be easily programmed into a computer or even an advanced calculator and therefore can be convenient to use. The user inputs the five variables and asks for the option price to be calculated. (Some readers may wish to study the appendix before continuing.)

The Five Variables in the Black-Scholes Option Pricing Model

This subsection examines in more detail the five variables that determine the value of a call option in the Black-Scholes model.

The Price of the Underlying Asset One of the most important relationships in option pricing theory is between a call option price and the price of the underlying asset because they tend to move in the same direction. In the Black-Scholes model, the price of a call option rises at an increasing rate as the price of the underlying asset rises. With everything else held constant, a call option premium will, in theory, rise more than 0 cents and less than $1 for each $1 rise in the underlying asset (prior to its expiration).

Figure 10.4 illustrates the relationship between a call option price and the price of the underlying asset, with everything else held constant. The difference between Figure 10.3 and Figure 10.4 is that the value of a call option is shown before expiration in Figure 10.4, whereas Figure 10.3 illustrates the value of the call option at its expiration date.

Notice that the slope of the call option is always positive, so that increases in the stock price always lead to increases in the call option price. When the stock price is very low, the slope of the line is nearly flat, which illustrates that the price of the call is less responsive to changes in the stock price at this range. In other words, for a near-zero stock price, the exercise price of the option is well above the current stock price, such that the option is way out-of-the-money and will not change much as the underlying stock price changes.

When the stock price is very high, the slope of the line is very steep, illustrating that the call price moves in a nearly one-to-one relationship with the stock price at this range. In other words, when the exercise price of the option is well below the current stock price and the option is way in-the-money, owning an option is not very different from owning the underlying security.

The Option's Exercise Price The exercise price of the option does not change throughout the life of the option; however, it is important to know

FIGURE 10.4 Call Option Sensitivity to the Price of the Underlying Asset

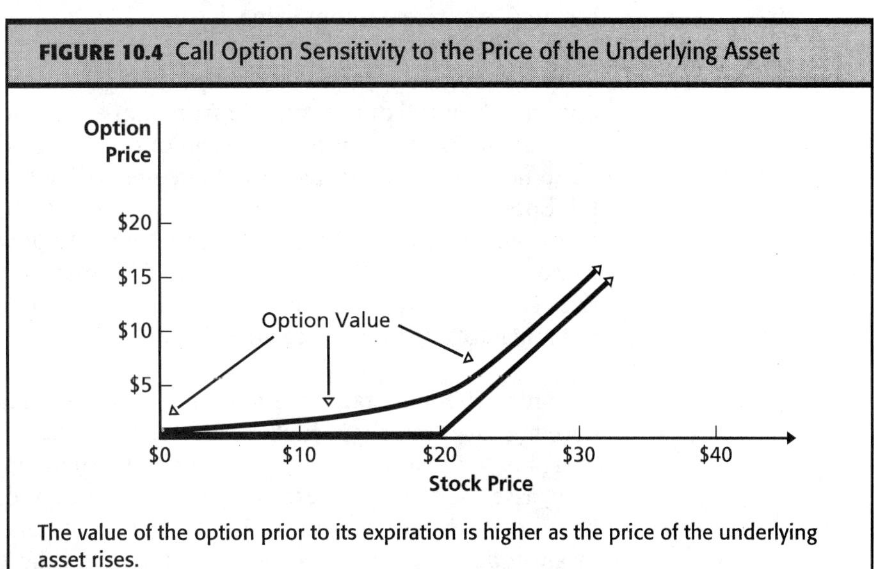

The value of the option prior to its expiration is higher as the price of the underlying asset rises.

the effect of alternative exercise prices in comparing different options. In the Black-Scholes model, the price of the call option is inversely related to the option's exercise price because the call option becomes more valuable as the stock price exceeds the exercise price. In other words, at expiration, the call option will only have value to the extent that the stock price exceeds the exercise price.

The Standard Deviation of the Underlying Asset The total risk or volatility of the underlying asset can be measured by the standard deviation of the returns of the underlying asset. The Black-Scholes model illustrates that call option prices rise as the standard deviation or total risk of the underlying asset rises. It may seem that this concept runs counter to the concepts of risk aversion detailed in Chapters 8 and 9 because the option price rises in response to increased risk, but it actually reflects the real essence of an option.

As we have said, an option is a claim on an asset that permits the holder to have large or unlimited profit potential with limited loss potential. The worst thing that can happen to an option holder is that the option expires without value and the option holder loses the entire investment in the option. The profit potential is limitless, however, because the holder benefits from price increases in the underlying asset.

Figures 10.2 and 10.3 illustrated the idea that a call option has the potential for limited loss and virtually unlimited profit. Thus, if the underlying asset becomes much more volatile, the option's upside potential will be increased, but the option's downside potential is limited; therefore, an increase in the underlying asset's standard deviation, which can be represented by a widening of the distribution in Figure 10.2, acts to benefit the call option holder, who gains higher profit potentials. The worst the option can do again remains to expire without value.

Example 10.3 Suppose that for your graduation present your rich uncle has given you the option to buy 100 ounces of gold from him at $400 an ounce. Note that if the price of gold stays at or near $400 an ounce, the graduation gift will have little to no value. If the price of gold begins to fluctuate wildly, however, then the option could become extremely valuable. As the holder of the option, you would rather see the price of gold fluctuate upward than stay stable because your option will have little value if it remains stable. If the price of gold rises substantially, then you have the chance at a great graduation gift, but not much to lose if the price goes down.

Figure 10.5 illustrates the idea that higher standard deviation in the underlying asset produces higher call option prices. The curve labeled "M" is designed to illustrate the relationship between an option price and its underlying asset price when there is a moderate amount of volatility in the underlying asset. The curve labeled "L" illustrates the same relationship in the case of an underlying asset with low volatility, and the curve labeled "H" illustrates the case of high volatility.

FIGURE 10.5 Call Option Sensitivity to Underlying Volatility

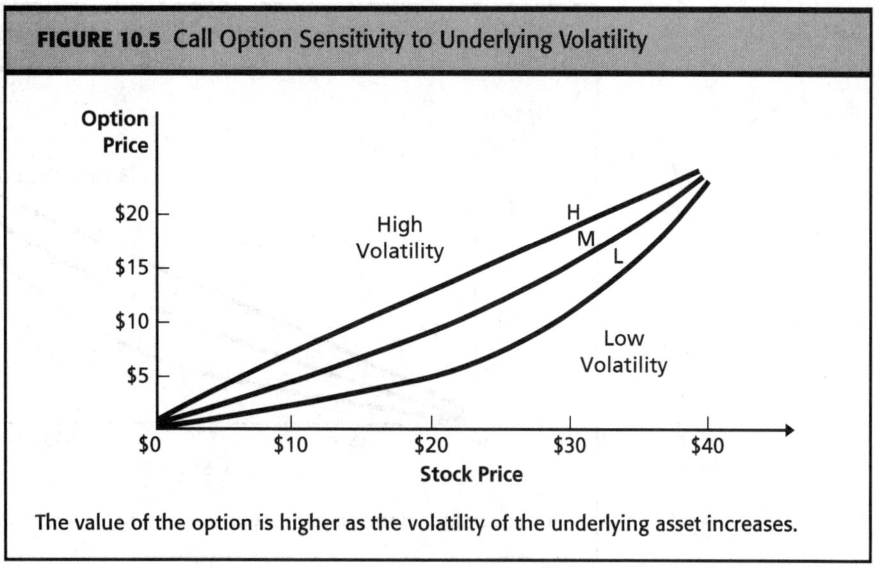

The value of the option is higher as the volatility of the underlying asset increases.

Figure 10.5 illustrates that regardless of the underlying asset's price relative to the strike price, the higher the volatility of the underlying asset, the higher is the price of the option, which is a point that will be utilized in future chapters.

The Time to Expiration The effect of time to expiration on the value of a call option is straightforward. Because most options allow the holder to exercise the option at any time during its lifetime, a long-term option is worth more than a short-term option. The importance of having more time to expiration is that it provides a longer period for the underlying asset to achieve substantial price movements. Remember: The key to an option is that it permits the holder to benefit virtually limitlessly from price movements in one direction, but it limits the losses from price movements in the opposite direction. Thus, a longer time to expiration gives the option holder a wider opportunity for the underlying asset to move. The effect of longer time to expiration is very similar to the effect of more volatility, as shown graphically in Figure 10.6.

The Risk-Free Interest Rate According to the Black-Scholes model the risk-free interest rate is also a determining factor in the price of options. To understand why the interest rate affects option prices, think again about what call options represent. Suppose that you believe a certain stock will increase in value in the future, and you have decided today to invest money in the stock. Your choice of investment is to buy the stock, or buy a call option on the stock.

If you buy the stock, then your investment today for each share of stock will be the current stock price. If you buy call options, however, then your investment today is the call premium, and your future investment if you exercise the option is the exercise price of the option. This comparison illustrates

FIGURE 10.6 Call Option Sensitivity to Time to Expiration

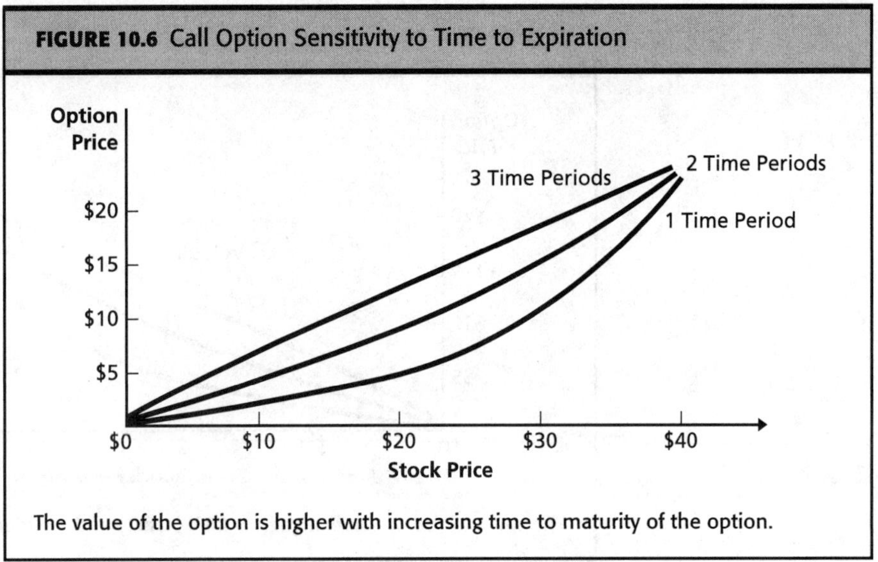

The value of the option is higher with increasing time to maturity of the option.

that buying options is like buying the stock on borrowed money—you have effectively bought now but do not have to pay the exercise price until later.

The higher the risk-free interest rate, the more advantage there is to owning a call option because the present value of the exercise price is less if the risk-free interest rate is higher. Thus, call option prices will rise slightly when the risk-free interest rate rises, and vice versa.

Summary of the Black-Scholes Option Pricing Model

We discussed each of the five variables that determine call option prices. Four of the variables—the price of the underlying asset, the standard deviation of the underlying asset, the time to expiration, and the riskless interest rate—were shown to be positively related to call option prices. Only the exercise price is inversely related to the price of a call option. The next section provides a simplified financial example of binomial—two-state—option pricing.

Option Pricing—A Two-State Example

Recall that Risk, Inc. from Chapter 8 had a chance of being worth either $10 per share or $0 per share, depending upon whether or not it was successful in developing a new technology. Let us assume the stock is now selling for $4 per share. The purpose of this section is to discuss how much a call option on the stock would be worth.

Let us consider two call options on Risk, Inc. In one case there is a call option on Risk, Inc. with an exercise price of $10, and in the other there is a call option on Risk, Inc. with an exercise price of $0. How much would these call options be worth?

The call option with a $10 exercise price would be worth $0, as there is no value to an option to buy something for $10 that has no chance of rising above $10 before the option expires. This is true, given that Risk, Inc. will be worth either $10 or $0. The call option with a $0 exercise price is worth the same as the value of the stock, or $4. The reason is that there is no chance that the stock will drop below the exercise price of $0. In this case, the call option is, in effect, identical to owning the stock.

A more interesting case is a call option on Risk, Inc. with a strike price between $0 and $10. For example, a call option with a strike price of $5 will pay either $5 if the stock price goes to $10, or $0 if the stock price falls to $0. In this simplified example the value of the call option on Risk, Inc. can be determined exactly. In this case, the call option pays off exactly half as much as the stock. If the price of Risk, Inc. stock rises to $10, then the call option is worth half its value or $5. If the price of the stock falls to $0, then the option is worth half its value, or $0. The call option, therefore, is worth exactly half as much as the stock, or $2. Two call options with a strike price of $5 would cost a total of $4, and offer the exact payoff as a share of the stock—also $4.

This example from a highly simplified two-state model demonstrates several points regarding option theory:

1. The price of an option does not depend upon whether the risk is systematic or diversifiable, and it does not depend upon the degree of risk aversion of market participants.
2. The upper bound to the price of a call option is equal to the price of the underlying asset. This was demonstrated in the case of a $0 exercise price, where the potential payout of the call option was identical to the potential payout of owning the stock. From the law of conservation of value, we know that identical cash flow streams must have identical values. In other words, in this case, the value of the call option must be equal to the value of the underlying asset.
3. The lower bound to the price of a call is zero. This was demonstrated in the case of a $10 exercise price. Because there was no chance of the option being in-the-money, the option would never have any value. The call option, however, can never have a negative value because the option buyer is not obligated to do anything.

An Application of Option Theory to the Equity of a Firm

We now examine how options can be used to better understand the value of the common stock of a firm. As discussed in Chapter 1, the balance sheet view of a firm using market values is:

$$\text{Equity} = \text{Assets} - \text{Liabilities}$$

The shareholders are best viewed as owning the firm's assets subject to the claims of debt holders. An alternative and extremely useful view of the position of equity holders is that they have a call option on the assets of the firm. If the firm's assets turn out to be worth more than the face value of the debt holder's claim, then the equity holders will exercise their option by paying off the debt holders and taking over ownership of the assets. On the other hand, if the firm's assets turn out to be worth less than the debt holder's claim, then the equity holders will walk away from the firm—or declare bankruptcy—allowing their option to the ownership of the firm's assets to expire worthless.

Thus, the ability of a corporation's equity holders to declare bankruptcy makes their position tantamount to owning a call option. Just as in the case of a traditional call option, if the assets do extremely well, then the equity holders can benefit greatly. If the assets do extremely poorly, then the losses of the equity holders are limited to the dollar amount they invested in the equity. The length of the equity holder's option is the time to maturity of the debt.

Figure 10.7 shows the relationship between equity values and asset values when the debt is maturing. Note the similarity between the payout to equity holders in Figure 10.7 and the payout to traditional call option holders in Figure 10.3.

Example 10.4 From Figure 10.7, suppose that the face value of the firm's debt is \$10 million. If the assets of the firm are worth less than \$10 million when the debt matures, then the equityholders will declare bankruptcy and the value of the equity will tend toward zero. On the other hand, if the assets are worth more than \$10 million, then the equityholders will pay to the debtholders their promised payment and the value of the equity will be the excess of the assets' original value over the \$10 million.

Table 10.1 illustrates the equity of the firm as a call option. The first column lists the five variables that determine an option price according to the

FIGURE 10.7 The Equity of the Firm as a Call Option

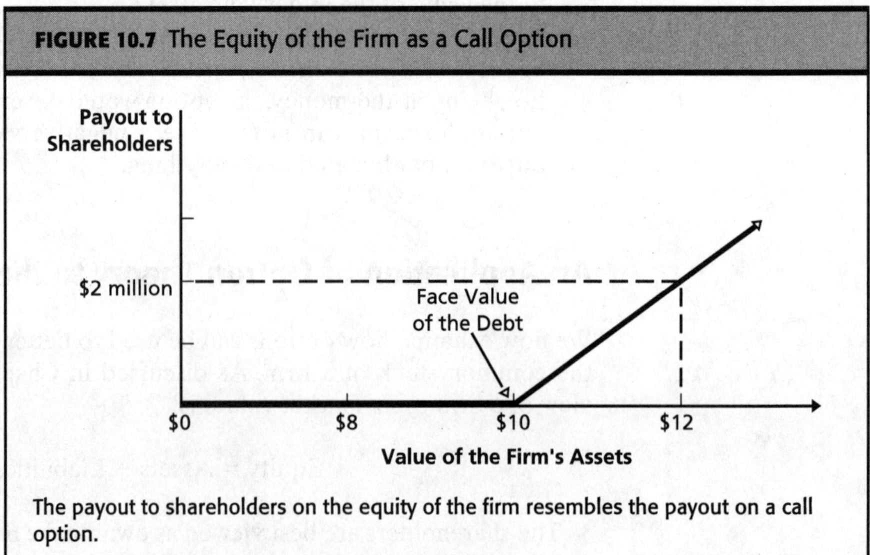

The payout to shareholders on the equity of the firm resembles the payout on a call option.

TABLE 10.1 Option Variables as Related to the Value of the Firm

Generic	*Call Option on Stock*	*Equity as a Call Option*
(1) The option's exercise price	Price at which stock can be purchased	Face value of debt
(2) The price of the underlying asset	Price of stock	Value of firm's assets
(3) The standard deviation of the underlying asset	Volatility of stock	Volatility of firm's assets
(4) The time to expiration	Time to option's expiration	Time to maturity of firm's debt
(5) The risk-free interest rate	Risk-free interest rate	Risk-free interest rate

Black-Scholes option pricing model. The second column lists the meaning of these five variables in the traditional case of a call option on a share of stock. The third column lists the meaning of the five variables when the equity in a firm is being viewed as a call option.

The idea that the equity of a firm should be viewed as a call option on the firm's assets is most useful when the firm has a substantial amount of debt and therefore a relatively high probability of bankruptcy. The concept is weakened by the tendency of most firms to have a variety of debt issues with different maturities and interest payment dates so that there is no single point in the future at which expiration will occur. Nevertheless, in Chapters 12 and 13, the application of option pricing theory to the equity of a firm will prove to be a useful method of understanding the effects of bankruptcy potential.

Summary

- This chapter has presented a brief introduction to option pricing. The essence of owning an option is that it provides the potential to benefit a great deal from a particular movement in the value of an underlying asset while limiting the potential loss to the option investment itself.
- To own an option the investor must pay a price, known as the option premium, for this ability to have potentially huge profits and limited losses.
- There is a powerful model for pricing options developed by Black and Scholes. The Black-Scholes model estimates an option price using five variables as inputs: (1) the option's exercise price, (2) the price of the underlying asset, (3) the standard deviation of the underlying asset, (4) the time to the option's expiration, and (5) the risk-free interest rate.
- Call options rise in value between \$0.00 and \$1.00 for each \$1 rise in the value of the underlying asset (everything else held equal) and fall in value between \$0.00 and \$1.00 for each \$1 fall in the value of the underlying asset.
- Call options rise in value when the standard deviation of the underlying asset increases and fall in value when the standard deviation of the underlying asset falls.
- The equity of a firm can be viewed as a call option on the firm's assets. If the value of the firm's assets is greater than the value of the firm's debt, then the equity-

holders will exercise their option, make promised payments to bondholders, and continue to hold the equity. If the value of the firm's assets is less than the value of the firm's debt, then the equityholders will choose not to exercise their option, walking away from the firm by declaring bankruptcy.

Reference

Black, F., and M. Scholes. "The Pricing of Options and Corporate Liabilities." *Journal of Political Economy* 81 (May–June 1973), 637–654.

Demonstration Problems

Problem 1

a. SuperStore, Inc. common stock is trading for $50 per share. Call options are being traded on the stock with a strike price or exercise price of $50. Find the value (payoff) to the call option at expiration for the following potential prices for SuperStore, Inc. stock: $0, $10, $20, . . . , $100.

b. Mom and Pop Grocery Store has $50,000 of assets and $50,000 face value of debt. Including the debt, therefore, the value of the store's equity appears to be zero; however, Mom is experimenting with some radically new marketing concepts that will significantly change the value of the store. Find the value to the store's equity (its assets minus its $50,000 debts) for the following potential values to the firm's assets: $0, $10,000, $20,000, . . . , $100,000.

Solution to Problem 1

These questions address the same issues that are addressed in Figure 10.3. In other words, given the value of the underlying asset, find the value of the call option (at expiration).

Step 1: From the text, the value of a call option at expiration is equal to zero if the underlying asset is worth less than the strike price, and it is worth the difference between the price of the underlying asset and the strike price if the underlying asset is worth more than the strike price; therefore, subtract the strike price from each potential outcome in part (a). The option payout will be the greater of this value and zero:

Value of Underlying Asset	*Strike Price*	*Underlying Asset minus Strike Price*	*Greater of Zero and the Difference*
$ 0	$50	−$50	$ 0
$ 10	$50	−$40	$ 0
$ 20	$50	−$30	$ 0
$ 30	$50	−$20	$ 0
$ 40	$50	−$10	$ 0
$ 50	$50	$ 0	$ 0
$ 60	$50	$10	$10
$ 70	$50	$20	$20
$ 80	$50	$30	$30
$ 90	$50	$40	$40
$100	$50	$50	$50

Step 2: The value of the equity of Mom and Pop Grocery Store can be similarly determined by subtracting the face value of the debt from the value of the firm's assets. The value of the equity will be the greater of this value and zero because the lowest value that a corporation's stock can have is zero.

Value of Store's Assets	*Face Value of Debt*	*Asset Value minus $50,000 Debt*	*Greater of Zero and the Difference*
$ 0	$50,000	−$50,000	$ 0
$ 10,000	$50,000	−$40,000	$ 0
$ 20,000	$50,000	−$30,000	$ 0
$ 30,000	$50,000	−$20,000	$ 0
$ 40,000	$50,000	−$10,000	$ 0
$ 50,000	$50,000	$ 0	$ 0
$ 60,000	$50,000	$10,000	$10,000
$ 70,000	$50,000	$20,000	$20,000
$ 80,000	$50,000	$30,000	$30,000
$ 90,000	$50,000	$40,000	$40,000
$100,000	$50,000	$50,000	$50,000

Final Solution: Notice that the payout to a call option holder is extremely similar to the payout to the shareholder of a volatile firm with a great deal of debt. In both cases, the payout is greatest for extremely high outcomes in the value of the underlying assets. In addition, in both cases the losses due to declines in the value of the underlying assets are limited. In the case of a traditional call option, the optionholder simply allows the option to expire worthless. In the case of a shareholder of a firm whose debt greatly exceeds its assets, the shareholder can declare bankruptcy.

Problem 2

A call option is trading that permits the holder to purchase Cantwell Corporation's common stock at $20 per share. The option has 0.5 years to expiration, the risk-free rate is 5%, and the standard deviation of the stock's returns is 0.30. Use the Black-Scholes formula to compute the value of the option if Cantwell Corporation stock is now selling for $25 per share.

Solution to Problem 2

The solution follows the procedure given in the appendix to Chapter 10, which solves the Black-Scholes option pricing model:

$$\text{CALL} = [P \cdot N(d_1)] - [EX \cdot N(d_2) \cdot e^{-rt}]$$

Step 1: Calculate the value of d_1 using the formula for d_1:

$$d_1 = \left[ln\left(P / EX\right) + rt + 0.5\,\sigma^2 t\right] / \sqrt{\sigma^2 t}$$

$$d_1 = \left[ln\left(\$25 / \$20\right) + 0.0475\right] / \sqrt{0.3^2\ 0.5}$$

$$d_1 = \left[.22314 + 0.0475\right] / 0.2121$$

$$d_1 = 1.276$$

Step 2: Calculate d_2 from d_1:

$$d_2 = d_1 - \sqrt{\sigma^2 t}$$

$$d_2 = 1.276 - \sqrt{.3^2 .5}$$
$$d_2 = 1.276 - 0.2121$$
$$d_2 = 1.064$$

Step 3: Use d_1 and d_2 to look up $N(d_1)$ and $N(d_2)$ in Table 10.2:

$$N(d_1) = N(1.276) = 0.899$$
$$N(d_2) = N(1.064) = 0.8563$$

Step 4: Using $r = 5\%$ and $t = 0.5$, compute e^{-rt}:

$$-rt = -0.05 \times 0.5$$
$$-rt = -0.025$$
$$e^{-rt} = e^{-0.025}$$
$$e^{-rt} = 0.9753$$

Step 5: Plug the preceding results into the Black-Scholes equation:

$$\text{CALL} = [P \cdot N(d_1)] - [EX \cdot N(d_2) \cdot e^{-rt}]$$
$$\text{CALL} = [\$25 \cdot .899] - [\$20 \cdot .8563 \cdot .9753]$$
$$\text{CALL} = \$22.475 - \$16.703$$
$$\text{CALL} = \$5.77$$

Final Solution: The value of the call option is approximately \$5.77. Notice that if the option expired today it would be worth \$5 because the underlying asset price exceeds the strike price by \$5. In addition, the option is rather far into the money, meaning that its actual price will sell near its price if it were expiring today. Thus, the value of \$5.77 seems reasonable.

Review Questions

1. What is the difference between a call option and a put option?
2. How are call options related to the equity value of the firm?
3. What does a call option give to the option holder?
4. What is an option seller?
5. List the five variables from the Black-Scholes model that determine option values.

6. Describe the relationship between the value of a call option and the exercise price of the option.
7. Describe the relationship between the value of a call option and the underlying standard deviation of the stock.
8. Describe the relationship between the value of a call option and the option's time to maturity.

Problems

1. The Last Resort Hotel sells, for $25, a coupon that allows the holder to stay for 1 week for $350. The regular price of a 1-week stay is currently $450, but the price varies a great deal due to travel conditions. The coupon is good for 1 year.
   a. What is the call option in the above discussion?
   b. What are the five variables that would determine the value of the above call option?
2. The following option prices were listed for the Jennings Corporation on August 29:

Jennings Corporation—Call Option Prices

NY Close	*Strike Price*	*September*	*October*
$46	$40	7½	7⅞
$46	$45	1½	1⅞
$46	$50	¼	½

   a. From the call options above, identify those that are "in the money" and those that are "out of the money."
   b. Explain why the September option with a strike price of $50 has value.
   c. Explain why the October options have prices or premiums that are higher than those for the September options.
3. A November call option for the Rather Corporation has a price or premium of 1/16. The closing price of Rather's stock is $1.50, and the option's exercise price is $3.00. Is the option "in the money," "out of the money," or "at the money"? Explain.
4. Brokaw, Inc., has a call option that expires in 2 months. Brokaw's stock is currently trading at $53. The exercise price of the call option is $35. Which of the following call option prices are possible: $2, $12, or $20? Explain.
5. Reno Corp. has common stock trading at $50 per share. Suppose you purchase one share of Reno.
   a. Determine the profit or loss on your stock investment in Reno if when you sell the stock the price per share is: $0; $50; $60; or $100.
   b. Make a graph of the profit or loss from your stock investment at each of the prices listed in part (a). Place the four potential stock prices on the horizontal axis, and the profit or loss from each of these four potential stock prices on the vertical axis.
6. Reno Corp. (Problem 5), whose stock is currently trading at $50 per share, also has a call option with a strike price of $50. The call option premium is $10.
   a. Determine the profit or loss on an investment in one Reno call option if at the option's expiration the stock price is: $0, $50, $60, or $100.

b. Make a graph of the profit or loss from investing in the Reno call option. Place the four potential stock prices on the horizontal axis, and the option's profit or loss from each of these four stock prices on the vertical axis.
c. Compare the graph in Problem 6(b) to the graph in Problem 5(b). Relate these graphs to the risk of a call option vis-à-vis the risk of stock investments.

7. Consider Black Jack Harry, an investor who writes (sells) the call option on Reno that you bought in Problem 6.
   a. Determine the profit or loss on Harry's call writing investment if at the option's expiration the stock price is: $0; $50; $60; or $100.
   b. Make a graph of the profit or loss from writing the Reno call option. Place the four potential stock prices on the horizontal axis, and the option writer's profit or loss from these four stock prices on the vertical axis.
   c. Compare the graph in Problem 7(b) to the graph in Problem 6(b). Relate these graphs to the differences between purchasing and writing call options.
8. Assume that there is a call option on IBM Corp. with a strike price of $100 and an expiration date of June 18. What would the call option be worth on June 18 if the stock is worth:
   a. $112
   b. $102
   c. $92
   d. $100
9. Assume that there is a call option on Eastman Kodak Corporation (EK) with a strike price of $50 and an expiration date of July 20. What would the call option be worth on the following dates and at the following stock prices? (Some of your answers should be in the form "greater than $3.")
   a. On July 20 EK is $52
   b. On July 1 EK is $52
   c. On July 20 EK is $50
   d. On June 1 EK is $50
   e. On July 20 EK is $48
   f. On June 15 EK is worth $48
10. Make a graph of the value of a call option on its expiration date. Place the underlying stock price on the vertical axis and the call option price on the horizontal axis. Assume that the strike price is $50.
11. What will happen to the value of a call option on a share of stock if everything else stays constant and:
    a. The underlying stock price rises?
    b. The volatility of the underlying stock rises?
    c. The time to expiration of the option is extended?
    d. The risk-free interest rates rise?
    e. The strike price is increased?
    f. The beta of the underlying stock rises but the total variance remains constant?
12. IBM Corp. is selling at $100 per share, and some strange call options begin trading that have widely varying strike prices and expiration dates.
    a. What is the maximum price for which any of the call options can sell?
    b. What is the minimum price for which any call option can sell?

13. Would the owner of a call option hope that the underlying stock price will rise or fall (select one)? What about a person who has written or sold the call option and does not own the underlying stock?
14. Fill in the blanks from the following list: strike price, stockholders, time to expiration, variance of the firm's underlying asset, call option price, price of underlying assets, debt, debtholders, call option.

    The common stock of a corporation with debt may be viewed as a ________ on the firm's assets. If the ________ wish to exercise their call option, they simply pay off the firm's ________ by paying them the face value of the firm's ________, which represents the exercise or ________ of the option. The time to maturity of the debt may be viewed as the option's ________. The firm's stock price may therefore be computed as a ________, and it will rise whenever there is a rise in the risk-free interest rate, a rise in the firm's ________, or an increase in risk causes the ________ to increase.

15. Using the Black-Scholes option pricing model, compute the values for call options, given the five variables:

	Strike Price	*Underlying Assest*	*Standard Deviation of Underlying Assest*	*Time to Expiration*	*Risk-free Interest Rate*
a.	\$20	\$16	0.40	0.25	0.10
b.	\$20	\$18	0.40	0.25	0.10
c.	\$20	\$20	0.40	0.25	0.10
d.	\$20	\$22	0.40	0.25	0.10
e.	\$20	\$24	0.40	0.25	0.10

16. Using the answers to Problem 15, make a graph with option prices on the vertical axis and the price of the underlying asset on the horizontal axis.
17. Assume that you observed that a call option has a price of \$2.00 when the underlying asset has a price of \$20, the strike price is \$20, the time to expiration is 0.25 years, and the risk-free interest rate is 0.10 (i.e., 10%). Using the Black-Scholes option pricing model and trial and error, estimate what the variance of the underlying asset must be. (*Hint:* Plug in guesses of the variance until the model's answer is near the given option price.)

Discussion Questions

1. Respond to the following statement:

    Call options sound great! Just think, their gains are unlimited but their losses are limited. I just don't understand why option writers would offer such fantastic opportunities.

2. The chapter explains that the firm's equity holders have a call option on the assets of the firm. The text also teaches us that the value of a call option increases with an increase in risk. Putting these two concepts together seems to suggest

that the firm's equity holders are better off when the firm's assets take on additional risk. Why, then, is the risk not bad? Explain.

3. Can a call option have a negative value?
4. Is option trading speculation, and should it be legal?
5. Respond to the following statement:

   It is said that when options reach their expiration date an investor's position is terminated and often the investor can be forced to accept a loss. In contrast, an investor in stocks can always wait until the stock returns to profitability.

6. Dollar price changes in options are almost always less than dollar price changes in the underlying asset, which implies that options are less risky compared with the underlying asset. Percentage price changes in options, however, are almost always greater than percentage price changes in the underlying asset, which implies that options are more risky. Which is correct?

APPENDIX

THE BLACK-SCHOLES OPTION PRICING MODEL

The Black-Scholes option pricing model produces an option price from five variables. The key complexity to the model is the use of the cumulative normal probability function: $N(d)$. The function $N(d)$ is the probability that a standard normally distributed variable will have a value equal to or less than the quantity d. The Black-Scholes formula also shows how d can be calculated.

The value of $N(d)$ is equal to zero when d is equal to negative infinity and is equal to 1 when d is equal to positive infinity. The value of $N(d)$ can be found from a table of cumulative probabilities of the standard normal distribution function or by using a sophisticated calculator or computer. Some financial spreadsheet software packages include functions that compute $N(d)$ from d in a very user friendly manner—making the entire job a snap!

The Black-Scholes option pricing model is:

$$\text{CALL} = [P \cdot N(d_1)] - [EX \cdot N(d_2) \cdot e^{-rt}] \quad \text{(A10.1)}$$

where:

CALL = price of the call option (the premium)

P = price of the underlying asset,

$N(\cdot)$ = cumulative normal probability function,

EX = exercise price of option,

e = the exponential function,

r = risk-free interest rate (continuously compounded)

t = time to expiration,

$$d_1 = [ln(P \div EX) + rt + 0.5\,\sigma^2 t] \div \sqrt{\sigma^2 t}$$

$$d_2 = d_1 - \sqrt{\sigma^2 t}$$

σ^2 = variance of the price changes of the underlying security.

Looking at the model you may now think that the best way to use it is through a computer program; however, it really is not as hard as it looks at first. Follow these steps:

1. Calculate the value of d_1 using its formula and write it down,
2. Use d_1 to calculate the value of d_2 and write it down,
3. Convert d_1 and d_2 to $N(d_1)$ and $N(d_2)$, using Table 10.2, and write them down,
4. Calculate e^{-rt} and write it down.
5. Plug these values into the model.

For example, use the following values:

$$P = \$95.00$$

$$E_x = \$100.000$$

$$t = 0.25$$

$$\sigma = 0.20$$

$$r = 0.10$$

the call option value is determined as follows. First, determine the values for d_1 and d_2:

$$d_1 = \frac{ln(\$95 \div \$100) + (0.10 \cdot 0.25) + (0.5 \cdot 0.04 \cdot 0.25)}{\sqrt{0.04(0.25)}} = \frac{-0.0513 + 0.03}{0.1} = -0.213$$

$$d_2 = -0.213 - \sqrt{0.04(0.25)} = -0.313.$$

Next, determine the values for $N(d_1)$ and $N(d_2)$. Remember that $N(d_1)$ and $N(d_2)$ represent the probability that a standard normally distributed random variable will have a value less than or equal to d_1 or d_2.

$$N(d_1) = N(-0.213) = 0.4157$$

$$N(d_2) = N(-0.313) = 0.3772$$

The value of the call option, therefore, is:

$$\text{CALL} = \$95\ (0.4157) - \$100\ (0.3772)\ e^{-0.1(0.25)}$$

where $e^{-0.1(0.25)} = 0.9753$.

$$\text{CALL} = \$39.49 - \$36.79 = \$2.70$$

TABLE 10.2 Standard Normal Cumulative Probabilities

This table calculates values of $N(d)$ given values for d through a five-step process:

Step 1: If d is negative, remove its negative sign (i.e., use its absolute value).
Step 2: Look at the first column labeled "tenths." Find the row corresponding to the number of tenths in the value d.
Step 3: Find the column with the same number of hundredths at the top.
Step 4: If d was positive, the entry in the appropriate row and column is $N(d)$. If d was negative, subtract the number in the table from 1.
Step 5: For greater accuracy, interpolate using thousandths.

					Hundredths					
Tenths	*0.00*	*0.01*	*0.02*	*0.03*	*0.04*	*0.05*	*0.06*	*0.07*	*0.08*	*0.09*
0.0	.5000	.5040	.5080	.5120	.5160	.5199	.5239	.5279	.5319	.5359
0.1	.5398	.5438	.5478	.5517	.5557	.5596	.5636	.5675	.5714	.5753
0.2	.5793	.5832	.5871	.5910	.5948	.5987	.6026	.6064	.6103	.6141
0.3	.6179	.6217	.6255	.6293	.6331	.6368	.6406	.6443	.6480	.6517
0.4	.6554	.6591	.6628	.6664	.6700	.6736	.6772	.6808	.6844	.6879
0.5	.6915	.6950	.6985	.7019	.7054	.7088	.7123	.7157	.7190	.7224
0.6	.7257	.7291	.7324	.7357	.7389	.7422	.7454	.7486	.7517	.7549
0.7	.7580	.7611	.7642	.7673	.7704	.7734	.7764	.7794	.7823	.7852
0.8	.7881	.7910	.7939	.7967	.7995	.8023	.8051	.8078	.8106	.8133
0.9	.8159	.8186	.8212	.8238	.8264	.8289	.8315	.8340	.8365	.8389
1.0	.8413	.8438	.8461	.8485	.8508	.8531	.8554	.8577	.8599	.8621
1.1	.8643	.8665	.8686	.8708	.8729	.8749	.8770	.8790	.8810	.8830
1.2	.8849	.8869	.8888	.8907	.8925	.8944	.8962	.8980	.8997	.9015
1.3	.9032	.9049	.9066	.9082	.9099	.9115	.9131	.9147	.9162	.9177
1.4	.9192	.9207	.9222	.9236	.9251	.9265	.9279	.9292	.9306	.9319
1.5	.9332	.9345	.9357	.9370	.9382	.9394	.9406	.9418	.9429	.9441
1.6	.9452	.9463	.9474	.9484	.9495	.9505	.9515	.9525	.9535	.9545
1.7	.9554	.9564	.9573	.9582	.9591	.9599	.9608	.9616	.9625	.9633
1.8	.9641	.9649	.9656	.9664	.9671	.9678	.9686	.9693	.9699	.9706
1.9	.9713	.9719	.9726	.9732	.9738	.9744	.9750	.9756	.9761	.9767
2.0	.9772	.9778	.9783	.9788	.9793	.9798	.9803	.9808	.9812	.9817
2.1	.9821	.9826	.9830	.9834	.9838	.9842	.9846	.9850	.9854	.9857
2.2	.9861	.9864	.9868	.9871	.9875	.9878	.9881	.9884	.9887	.9890
2.3	.9893	.9896	.9898	.9901	.9904	.9906	.9909	.9911	.9913	.9916
2.4	.9918	.9920	.9922	.9925	.9927	.9929	.9931	.9932	.9934	.9936
2.5	.9938	.9940	.9941	.9943	.9945	.9946	.9948	.9949	.9951	.9952
2.6	.9953	.9955	.9956	.9957	.9959	.9960	.9961	.9962	.9963	.9964
2.7	.9965	.9966	.9967	.9968	.9969	.9970	.9971	.9972	.9973	.9974
2.8	.9974	.9975	.9976	.9977	.9977	.9978	.9979	.9979	.9980	.9981
2.9	.9981	.9982	.9982	.9983	.9984	.9984	.9985	.9985	.9986	.9986
3.0	.9987	.9987	.9987	.9988	.9988	.9989	.9989	.9989	.9990	.9990

Example: If $d = 0.51$, look in the row with tenths = 0.5 and the column with hundredths = 0.01 to find $N(0.51) = 0.6950$. If $d = -0.89$, locate the value corresponding to 0.89 (0.8133) and subtract it from 1 to determine that $N(-0.89) = 0.1867$.

If the current stock price were \$105 instead of \$95, then the call price would be determined as:

$$d_1 = \frac{ln(\$105 \div \$100) + (0.10 \cdot 0.25) + (0.5 \cdot 0.04 \cdot 0.25)}{\sqrt{0.04(0.25)}} = \frac{0.0448 + 0.03}{0.1} = 0.788$$

$$d_2 = 0.788 - \sqrt{0.04(0.25)} = 0.688.$$

$$N(d_1) = N(0.788) = 0.7846.$$

$$N(d_2) = N(0.688) = 0.7542.$$

The value of the call option, therefore, is:

$$\text{CALL} = \$105\ (0.7846) - \$100\ (0.7542)\ e^{-0.1(0.25)}$$

$$\text{CALL} = \$82.38 - \$73.56 = \$8.82.$$

CHAPTER 11

FINANCIAL LEVERAGE

During the late 1980s there was an explosion in the use of a type of bond known as a *junk bond*, which may be defined as a risky corporate bond. Junk bonds are risky because the corporation has usually issued so much debt that there is a higher than average probability that the corporation will default on some or all of its promised debt payments.

Most junk debt originated from corporate ownership or management battles, especially mergers, in which the corporation's existing assets were purchased from the original owners. Hundreds of billions of dollars changed hands in these mergers and other deals. For example, in one of the largest such corporate ownership changes, the assets of RJR Nabisco, Inc., were purchased with almost $30 billion of new debt such that the assets of the new company were backed by almost 95 percent debt and only 5 percent equity. The investment bankers who acted as intermediaries between the issuing corporation and bond investors earned large and in some cases outrageous transactions fees. A certain percentage of junk bond investors lost money when the issuing corporations experienced financial distress and stopped making promised payments. The media were filled with editorials that decried runaway debt usage by corporations.

The use of junk bonds to finance an acquisition is an example of a corporate financing decision. Other less dramatic examples of corporate financing decisions include the issuing of bonds to finance new projects. Financing has increasingly become a centerpiece of corporate news stories. Modern finance, however, offers some surprising answers to questions concerning the importance of corporate financing decisions.

An Introduction to Corporate Financing

Chapters 1–10 focused almost exclusively on the management of corporate assets. To meet the objective of shareholder wealth maximization, financial managers should invest in projects whose benefits exceed costs, or, in other words, projects with a positive net present value. Net present value was shown to take into account both the time value of money and risk.

This chapter begins a focus on the financing decision. Corporations issue securities to finance their assets. These securities—represented generally by bonds and stocks—come in hundreds of different varieties. Does the choice of a particular set of financing instruments matter? In other words, can firm value be maximized through a particular mix of bonds and stocks? How much time should financial managers spend on the financing decision? How high a dividend should the firm pay to the shareholders? These are all examples of questions that relate to the financing decision.

Here is a preview of the important results that will be developed in the next three chapters:

- Financial leverage is created when the firm borrows money in the form of debt. Financial leverage changes the risk of holding the firm's debt and equity securities, but does not change the risk of the firm as a whole (Chapter 11).
- Using the restrictive assumptions of a perfect market, the decision about how to finance the firm's assets is irrelevant. The implication of this is that corporate managers should spend little time on how to raise money and most of their time on how to invest the money raised (Chapter 11).
- When the restrictive assumptions of a perfect market are relaxed, the preceding conclusion no longer holds. In such a case, the decision of how the firm finances its assets can change the value of the firm and therefore shareholder wealth (Chapter 12).
- The dividend policy of the firm is the decision of which portion of the firm's earnings to pay to shareholders and which portion to retain inside the firm. Under the restrictive assumptions of a perfect market, this decision is irrelevant. When the restrictive assumptions of a perfect market are relaxed, however, the dividend decision can change the value of the firm and shareholder wealth (Chapter 13).

An Overview of Corporate Financing

Chapter 11 follows a balance-sheet view of the firm, emphasizing that a corporation contains assets financed by both debt and equity. As we said early on, the two most important decisions facing financial managers are how to raise the needed money, known as the financing decision, and which assets to acquire with the money raised, known as the investment decision.

The investment decision was touched on in our earlier discussion of capital budgeting. In a nutshell, the firm compares the cost of investment with the benefits of investment. Good projects are those whose present value of benefits exceeds the present value of costs—in other words, those with a positive net present value (NPV).

TABLE 11.1 Long-term Debt of Coca-Cola Inc., 2000

Long-term debt consists of the following (in millions):

		January 2, 2000
10.00%	Medium term notes, fixed rate, due 2000	$ 25,500
8.56%	Medium term notes, fixed rate, due 2002	47,000
6.99%	Line of credit, variable rate, due 2002	46,600
7.14%	Term loan agreement, variable rate, due 2004	85,000
7.14%	Term loan agreement, variable rate, due 2005	85,000
6.85%	Debentures, fixed rate, due 2007	100,000
7.20%	Debentures, fixed rate, due 2009	100,000
6.38%	Debentures, fixed rate, due 2009	250,000
5.75%	Other notes payable, due 2001-2006, fixed rate	13,499
		$ 752,599
	Less Current Portion	28,635
		$ 723,964

Source: Form 10-K for Coca-Cola Inc. filed on December 31, 2000.

financing decision
The decision as to which securities the firm will issue in order to raise money to finance the firm's assets. The financing decision is also known as the capital structure decision or the debt-to-equity decision.

This chapter now shifts to the other major decision—where to obtain the money to invest in positive-*NPV* projects. The decision of where to raise money is called the **financing decision,** the capital structure decision, or the debt to equity decision. These three terms are often used interchangeably.

The Walt Disney Company provides a good example of the types of securities a firm typically uses to raise capital. Disney's capital structure, shown in Chapter 1, includes short term and long term debt and equity securities. Disney is typical of other corporations in the use of many different types of securities in their capital structure. For example, Table 11.1 lists the debt included in the balance sheet category "long-term debt" of The Coca-Cola Company in 2000. These 9 categories do not include short-term debt and other financing commitments of the firm. Window 11.1 provides some detail on common types of securities used in firm financing.

The fact that firms often choose to finance their assets with many different types of securities appears to indicate that how a firm is financed is very important. In other words, observation might suggest that wealth can be created or lost by making good or bad financing decisions; however, these issues need to be examined carefully. By the end of this chapter we hope that you will be convinced that how a firm is financed is not nearly important as how it invests and how it is operated.

To provide an analogy to corporate financing decisions, consider the decision to purchase a car. Most people spend 99 percent of their time deciding

WINDOW 11.1

The Menu of Financing Securities

This window describes financial securities that make up a firm's capital structure. The securities listed here are the more common types and are not meant as an all-inclusive list.

A. Short-Term Securities

1. Accounts Payable: Credit extended by suppliers for the purchase of raw materials and other goods used for the firm's normal operations. The level of accounts payable will fluctuate with the firm's level of purchases. Terms of credit are usually very short term, with 30 days serving as the standard.

2. Notes Payable: Securities usually issued to banks to cover seasonal expenditures related to the firm's working capital.

3. Commercial Paper: Securities issued by financially secure corporations with maturities that range up to 9 months. Commercial paper is usually backed by the value of the firm's assets.

B. Long-Term Securities—Bonds

1. Debentures: Bonds or debt obligations of the firm whose payment is backed only by the earnings of the firm.

2. Secured Bonds: Bonds whose payment is backed by specific assets. A common type of collateral backing a bond is the issuer's property.

3. Callable Bonds: Bonds that can be redeemed by the issuer before maturity. Issuers who exercise their option to call usually pay a special fee or a premium to the holder at the time of the call.

4. Convertible Bonds: Bonds that, at the option of the holder, can be converted into another security, usually shares of common stock.

5. Floating-Rate Bonds: Bonds whose coupon interest rate is tied to an interest rate index and thus can change through time. For example, the bond's coupon payment may be set 2 percent higher than the 90-day Treasury bill rate.

6. Income Bonds: Bonds whose coupon payments are not fixed; rather, they change with the income of the firm. Insufficient income would relieve the firm from making payments to the bondholders, whereas higher-than-expected income would generate higher payments to the bondholders.

7. Zero Coupon Bonds: Bonds that pay no coupon payment. Zero coupon bonds are sold at a price far below their value at maturity. The difference between the bond's selling price and the bond's purchase price represents the return earned on the bond.

WINDOW 11.1 *(continued)*

C. Long-Term Securities—Stocks

1. Common Stock: Securities that represent ownership in a corporation. Holders of common stock are given the right to vote for the firm's board of directors, and they are entitled to share in the residual profits of the firm (after all other claims have been paid), and are thus referred to as residual claimants.

2. Preferred Stock: Stock that pays dividends at some specified rate and whose shares must receive dividends before the holders of common stock.

on which car manufacturer, which car dealership, which car model, and which car options are most desirable, and 1 percent of their time deciding from which bank to borrow the money. The reason that financing is relatively unimportant is that most car loans usually offer similar interest rates. One loan choice is about as good as any other loan choice.

In the case of corporate financing, we will discuss whether a firm's particular choice of instruments is as good as any other choice. One key question is whether or not financing can affect firm value. In other words, does it matter which types of securities and quantities of securities a corporation uses to raise capital. The answer to this question involves a complex set of issues. The approach of modern corporate finance is to build logically from a very simple model to more complex models. The simplest model—one in perfect capital markets—provides such a logical starting point.

Financing in Perfect Markets

perfect markets
Markets that operate under highly restrictive assumptions such as zero tax rates, no transactions costs, and full information of all market participants.

The initial model describes behavior in an environment of **perfect markets.** Perfect markets are synonymous with a set of highly restrictive assumptions regarding how securities are traded, how information is received, and how individuals make decisions.[1] Most notable for this discussion is that no corporate or personal income taxes are paid. Perfect market assumptions, admittedly unrealistic, help to set in place a foundation with which to build more realistic models of capital structure. As part of this foundation, modern finance has proven that, in perfect markets, capital structure does not affect the value of the firm. This is to say that one package of financing securities, such as all equity capital and no debt, is as good as any other package, such as half equity capital and half debt. The form of financing is said to be irrelevant.

[1]Perfect market assumptions can be summarized as follows: First, markets are frictionless in the sense that there are no costs of transacting, no taxes, and no regulations. Second, information regarding securities and markets is free and understood by all participants.

Modern finance has proven that in perfect markets, capital structure does not affect the value of the firm.

An important implication of this is that managers should spend most of their time on the investment decision, such as which assets to acquire, and very little time on the financing decision, such as how those assets should be financed. The rest of this chapter will detail the analysis that leads to this conclusion.

The Traditionalist Versus the Modernist Positions on Capital Structure

The financing decision provides a clear distinction between traditional finance and modern finance. Traditionalists believe that financing decisions are important and that the firm would do well by searching for the package of securities that minimizes the aggregate cost of obtaining capital for the firm. This package of securities is known as the *optimal capital structure*. The traditionalist position focuses on the firm's combined or weighted average cost of capital—the overall cost of financing the firm's assets.

The traditionalists' position is illustrated in Figure 11.1(a), which shows that the firm's cost of capital changes as the use of debt financing inside the firm changes, and in Figure 11.1(b), which shows that that firm value is maximized at some optimal level of debt financing.

FIGURE 11.1 The Traditionalists' View on Financing and Firm Value

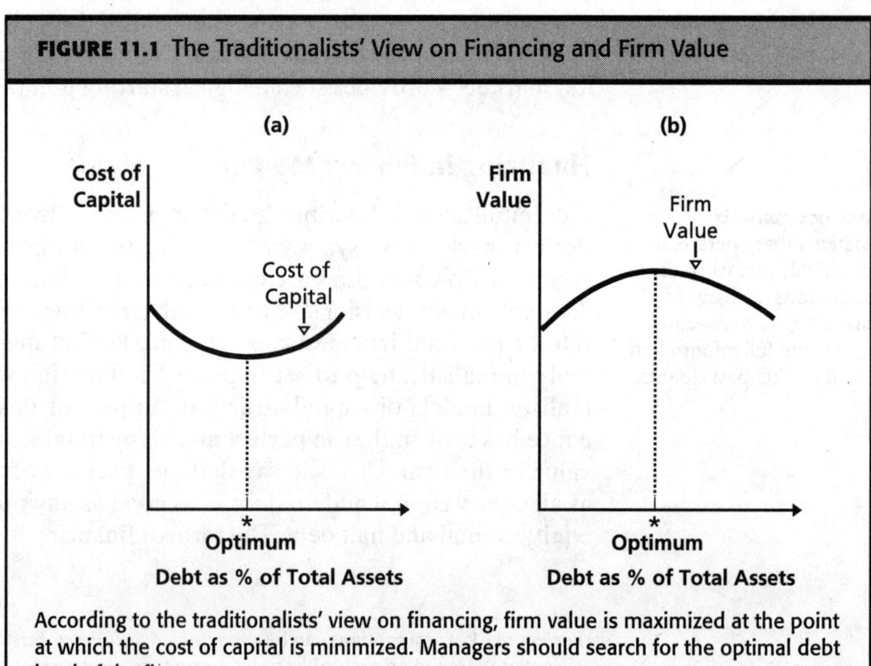

According to the traditionalists' view on financing, firm value is maximized at the point at which the cost of capital is minimized. Managers should search for the optimal debt level of the firm.

Modernists take a much different and, at least initially, a much simpler approach. Modernists claim that the decision is irrelevant—that there is no ideal or optimal capital structure. This is illustrated in Figure 11.2, for both the cost of the firm's capital and the value of the firm.

Modernists believe that, in certain conditions, the firm's cost of capital is the same for any financing mix so that it does not matter what types of securities the firm issues or when it issues them. At a minimum, modernists believe that corporate financial managers can do far more to maximize shareholder wealth by properly managing the firm's real assets than by transacting in financial markets.

The remainder of this chapter will explore the traditionalist and modernist positions in detail. Because both positions are based on financial leverage, or on the use of debt financing, and the effect of financial leverage on the firm, we must first explore the mechanics of financial leverage.

The Mechanics of Financial Leverage

Everyone should be familiar with the concept of physical leverage, which permits heavy objects to be lifted with relative ease (e.g., the use of a car jack to change a tire). The key to leverage is that all of the energy from a large movement, such as the pumping of a jack's handle, is concentrated into a smaller and more powerful movement. The **financial leverage** that results from the use of debt is much like physical leverage.

financial leverage
The use of debt. Financial leverage is created when the firm borrows money in the form of debt.

Financial leverage manipulates risk as physical leverage manipulates energy.

FIGURE 11.2 The Modernists' View on Financing and Firm Value

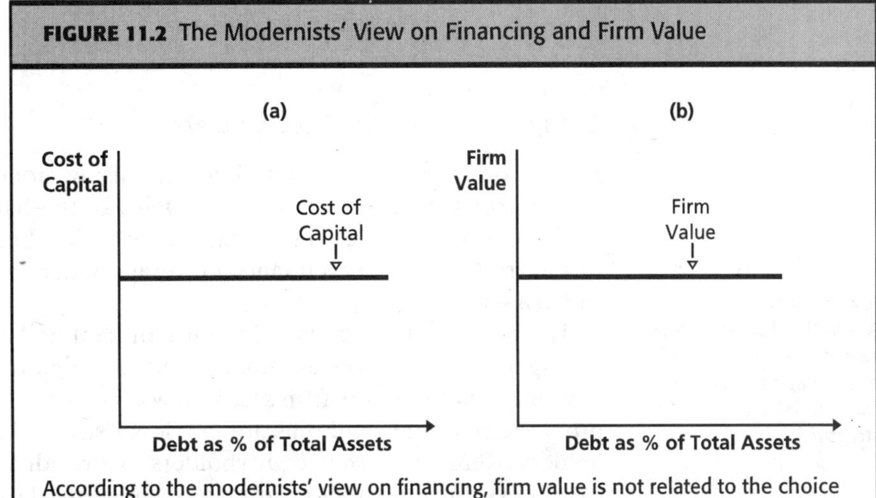

According to the modernists' view on financing, firm value is not related to the choice of financing. One capital structure is as good as any other capital structure.

Being Unlevered: The Case of No Debt

unlevered firm
A firm that finances its assets with equity capital only such that there is no debt in its capital structure.

To understand the concept of financial leverage, let us begin by considering a firm that uses no debt at all. We can call this firm an all-equity firm, or an **unlevered firm.** Because this firm has no debt, its basic balance sheet relationship is simplified:

$$\text{The Unlevered Firm: Assets} = \text{Equity} \tag{11.1}$$

For unlevered firms, owning a portion of the firm's equity is effectively the same as owning a portion of the firm's assets. In other words, because the equityholders own 100 percent of the assets of the firm, the risk and return characteristics of the firm's equity are essentially equal to the characteristics of the assets.

Example 11.1 ________ Consider an individual who sets up a corporation to own and rent out houses. The individual puts up money or equity capital to start the business in the amount of \$100,000 and uses this capital to purchase a \$100,000 house. The risk and return of the individual's \$100,000 in equity capital is identical to the risk and return of the house. If the house, which is the firm's only asset, rises in value by 20 percent to \$120,000, then the individual's equity in the firm also rises by 20 percent to \$120,000. If the rental of the house produces an \$18,000 per year cash flow, then the equityholder will be entitled to the entire \$18,000 cash flow. Because we are in a perfect market, there are no taxes. Ignoring changes in the price of the property, the return on the house, expressed as a percentage, is:

$$\text{Return to Equityholder} = \frac{\$18{,}000}{\$100{,}000} = 0.18\text{, or } 18\%$$

Being Levered: The Case of Debt

Let us now consider that in addition to raising money by issuing equity, the firm borrows money in the form of debt. In the balance-sheet view of the firm, the firm's assets are now financed by both debt and equity. The effect of this borrowing is termed financial leverage, and a firm that borrows is often called a **levered firm.**

levered firm
A firm that finances its assets with both debt and equity capital such that there is debt in its capital structure.

The best way to understand the use of debt and equity is to view debt as having low risk and to view equity as having high risk. Because debtholders have prior claims to the firm's cash flows, they usually expect to receive their promised payments and thus are in a less risky position vis-à-vis the equityholders. Remember that equityholders are residual claimants and receive cash flows only when all prior claims, including those of bondholders, have been satisfied. A corporation that has both debt and equity may be viewed as taking the cash flow stream produced by the firm's assets and dividing or partitioning the cash flow into two streams: (1) a low-risk debt stream and (2) a high-risk equity stream:

$$\text{The Levered Firm:} \qquad (11.2)$$
$$\text{Assets} = \text{(Low-Risk) Debt} + \text{(High-Risk) Equity}$$

Example 11.2 Let us now consider using leverage, or debt, in the previous housing example. Suppose that in addition to equity capital the individual issues a debt security known as a mortgage and uses the proceeds of the debt to purchase assets for the corporation. When money is borrowed, the lender of the money demands a position of priority in receiving the firm's cash flows. The lender, or in this case the mortgage holder or more generally the debtholder, has a fixed claim on the assets of the firm. In contrast, the equityholder has a residual claim.

The equityholder, still with \$100,000 to invest, now considers a new set of assets through the corporation. Rather than buying a single \$100,000 house with the firm's equity, the corporation might combine the \$100,000 in equity with \$100,000 in debt and purchase two \$100,000 houses. Perhaps each house is financed with \$50,000 of debt and \$50,000 of equity. The firm's balance sheet looks like this:

$$\text{Assets} = \text{Debt} + \text{Equity}$$
$$\$200{,}000 = \$100{,}000 + \$100{,}000$$

Because the corporation has two houses, the cash flow stream produced by the assets will be twice the cash flow stream of our previous example, in which the corporation purchased one house and did not use debt. The cash flow stream produced by the firm's assets, however, must now be divided or partitioned into debt and equity streams. If the debt were issued at a cost of 10 percent, then debtholders would be entitled to interest payments of \$10,000 per year (10 percent of \$100,000). Equityholders are entitled to whatever cash flow remains after the debtholders' claims have been satisfied.

The \$10,000 of promised cash flow to the debtholders changes the financial position of the equityholders. We will show specifically that an effect of the financial leverage is to increase the risk of the equityholders' claim.

Let us first examine the good side of financial leverage. If each house produces \$18,000 of cash flow, for a total of \$36,000 for the two houses, then the equityholders will pay \$10,000 to the debtholders and be left with \$26,000. Expressed as a percentage, the return to the equityholders is:

$$\text{Return to Equityholders} = \frac{(\$36{,}000 - \$10{,}000)}{\$100{,}000}$$
$$= 0.26, \text{ or } 26\%$$

Notice that this 26 percent return exceeds the 18 percent return earned in the case of the unlevered firm.

Let us now consider the bad side of financial leverage. Suppose the market for rental properties turns bad, and that the rental receipts for the two houses drop from $36,000 to $15,000. Because the debtholders have prior claims, the equityholders must first satisfy the debtholders' claim through a $10,000 interest payment, leaving a residual cash flow of only $5,000. Expressed as a percentage, the return to the equityholders is:

$$\text{Return to Equityholders} = \frac{(\$15{,}000 - \$10{,}000)}{\$100{,}000}$$

$$= 0.05, \text{ or } 5\%$$

In this case the return of 5 percent falls short of the return that would be earned in the same case for the unlevered firm (7.5%).

Financial Leverage from the Perspective of Debtholders and Equityholders

We will now examine our example of financial leverage from the perspective of both debtholders and equityholders. The debtholders will generally view their claim as virtually assuring a 10 percent return. Their claim is fixed, and although they have no chance of earning a return greater than 10 percent, there is little chance that the real estate market will become so depressed that their promised return is at risk. In fact, the only case in which the debtholders will not receive the 10 percent return is if the corporation defaults on the debt by failing to make the required interest payments. This is a serious consequence and would result in the corporation declaring bankruptcy. Detail on the bankruptcy process is provided in Window 11.2.

In contrast to debtholders, the equityholders view their position as being riskier than just owning a single house because their position contains leverage. The financial risks of two houses are being borne primarily by the equityholders, even though they have only invested an amount of money equal to the value of one house. If things go poorly, then the equityholders still owe the debtholders $10,000 per year and thus will do much worse than if they had not borrowed the money. If things go well, the equityholders can earn much greater cash flows than if they owned a single house.

The association between the concepts of physical leverage and financial leverage should now be clear. A small amount of physical leverage may allow its users to concentrate two times their normal force into their work. In the preceding example, financial leverage is used and twice as much economic risk, such as two houses rather than one, is borne by the equityholders.

The Link Between Financial Leverage and Risk We will now need to get more specific about financial leverage and its effect on risk. Suppose, for instance, that in the previous example each rental house had one unit of risk. Thus, two rental houses have two units of risk, and so forth. Because a corporation is simply a set of contracts, the risk of a firm's assets flows through to

WINDOW 11.2

The Bankruptcy Process

We define *bankruptcy* as a financial situation in which the value of the firm's assets is less than the face value of the firm's debt. To be precise, however, bankruptcy is a complex legal procedure whose details are set forth by the Bankruptcy Act of 1978. In essence, declaring bankruptcy provides temporary protection to the shareholders against legal action taken by the debtholders or creditors.

The bankruptcy process can proceed in one of two ways: liquidation or reorganization. The process of liquidation falls under Chapter 7 of the Federal Bankruptcy Act and is best used when the firm is worth more dead than alive. Under a liquidation, control of the firm's assets is transferred from current management to a court-appointed trustee. The trustee is in charge of selling the assets and distributing its proceeds.

A well-defined pecking order exists to determine the position of the creditors in receiving the proceeds of the liquefied assets of a firm. In general, the claims of the government come first. Next come the claims of secured creditors, such as bonds backed by specific assets of the firm. Next in line are employees' claims on wages, claims on the firm's pension plan, and the claims of unsecured or general creditors. Next to last come the claims of preferred stockholders, and, finally, common stockholders.

In contrast to a liquidation, the firm may instead seek to be reorganized, which is governed by Chapter 11 of the Federal Bankruptcy Act. Reorganizations are usually more complicated than are liquidations, and are usually more in the interest of shareholders and creditors low on the pecking order. A reorganization means that the firm is permitted to continue operations while working on a plan for turning the business around.

During reorganization, the firm is operated either by existing management, a group representing the debtors, or a court-appointed trustee. The plan of reorganization must be accepted by the creditors and the court before it can go into effect. The reorganization plan specifies how the creditors' claims will be satisfied through the reorganized firm. In many cases, the creditors exchange their original claims for a new set of claims. For example, bondholders may exchange their $1,000 face-value bond for an amount of, say, $500, and a new bond that promises to start paying interest some time in the future.

For the sake of keeping the contractual obligations of the firm alive, reorganizations are preferred. Reorganizations make sense if the financial problems of the firm are considered to be temporary—perhaps the result of a local or national economic downturn that is outside the control of the firm's managers. Financial distress that is beyond repair, of course, will most likely lead to the liquidation of the firm's assets.

the suppliers of capital. In the case of no debt, the risk of the assets flows through on a dollar-for-dollar basis to the equityholders:

Unlevered Firm:

Assets	=	*Debt*	+	*Equity*
Risk = 1 unit		Risk = 0 units		Risk = 1 unit
Amount = $100,000		Amount = $0		Amount = $100,000

When the corporation issues debt, however, the risk of the assets becomes partitioned into a high level of risk, represented by equity, and a low level of risk represented by debt. If we assume that the debt was risk-free, such that there is no chance of default, then the risk may be diagrammed as:

Levered Firm with 50% Debt:

Assets	=	*Debt*	+	*Equity*
Risk = 2 units		Risk = 0 units		Risk = 2 units
Amount = $200,000		Amount = $100,000		Amount = $100,000

Notice that the use of debt has the result of partitioning a moderate level of asset risk into securities with lower risk (debt) and higher risk (equity). In this case, the firm used 50 percent debt and we assumed that this doubled the risk of the equity while permitting the debtholders to bear no risk.

Increasing Financial Leverage—The Case of Using More Debt The previous situation can be extended by using more than 50 percent debt. For example, the equityholders may be able to use the corporation to buy four or more houses, utilizing borrowed money to finance the added investment.

The effect of more debt is to produce more leverage, so that a large amount of assets is controlled by a small amount of equity. Let us compare the effects of 50 percent debt with the effects of 75 percent debt and 90 percent debt. As shown in Table 11.2, with 50 percent debt, a 20 percent rise in housing prices will be levered into a 40 percent rise in equity. This is because the risk of $200,000 in houses is being levered into only $100,000 of equity, causing a leverage factor of 2 to 1, or 2.0 for short. We define the **leverage factor** as the ratio between the firm's assets and the firm's equity.

leverage factor
The ratio between the firm's assets and the firm's equity.

Thus, a firm with no debt has a leverage factor of 1.0 rather than 0.0 because the assets in the numerator are equal to the equity in the denominator. A firm with 90 percent debt would have a leverage factor of 10 because the

TABLE 11.2 Financial Leverage and Risks to Equityholders

	0% Debt	*50% Debt*	*75% Debt*	*90% Debt*
Number of homes purchased	1	2	4	10
Total value of homes	$100,000	$200,000	$400,000	$1,000,000
Amount of equity	$100,000	$100,000	$100,000	$ 100,000
Amount of debt	-0-	$100,000	$300,000	$ 900,000
Leverage factor	1.0	2.0	4.0	10.0
Change in equity for:				
20% rise in home values	+20%	+40%	+80%	+200%
20% decline in home values	−20%	−40%	−80%	−100%

assets in the numerator represent 100 percent of firm value and the equity in the denominator represents 10 percent of the firm value. Another way to view the leverage factor is as the inverse of the ratio of equity to assets.

The use of 75 percent debt would create a leverage factor of 4 to 1 because $400,000 in houses is purchased with only $100,000 of equity. In this case a rise of 20 percent in housing prices would be levered into an 80 percent increase in equity value. In terms of the risk diagrams used earlier, the case of 75 percent debt looks like this:

Levered Firm with 75% Debt:

Assets	=	*Debt*	+	*Equity*
Risk = 4 units Amount = $400,000		Risk = 0 units Amount = $300,000		Risk = 4 units Amount = $100,000

Notice that the risk of all four houses is being concentrated or squeezed into the $100,000 of equity held by the owner. We are still assuming that the debt is risk-free.

As we said, the use of 90 percent debt would create a leverage factor of 10 to 1. Note that $1 million in houses is purchased with only $100,000 of equity. In this case, a 20 percent rise in housing prices would be levered into a 200 percent rise in equity value.

Our examples have demonstrated financial leverage and rising housing values. Housing values, however, can move down as well as up. In the case of no debt, a 20 percent decline in housing prices will force a 20 percent decline in equity. When debt is used, the decline in housing values causes equity to decline by more than 20 percent. As shown in Table 11.2, the decline in equity values is 40 percent in the case of 50 percent debt, 80 percent in the case of 75 percent debt, and 100 percent in the case of 90 percent debt.

An interesting result can be obtained by comparing, with 90 percent debt, the change in the value of the equity as housing values move up and down. When housing values increase by 20 percent, equity value increases by 200 percent. When housing values decline by 20 percent, however, equity value decreases by only 100 percent. Why is the change in equity value greater for increases in value than for decreases in value? The reason is that, because of limited liability, the most equity can lose is its full value.

Another result of limited liability is that, with high leverage, some of the risk of the assets is not transferred to the equityholders but instead is transferred to the debtholders. For example, selecting an arbitrary value of 1.25 units of risk to debtholders, our risk diagram looks like this:

Levered Firm with 90% Debt:

Assets	=	*Debt*	+	*Equity*
Risk = 10 units Amount = $1,000,000		Risk = 1.25 units Amount = $900,000		Risk = 8.75 units Amount = $100.000

High Leverage and Debtholder Risk There are several important changes that occurred when we assumed that the added leverage would cause the debtholders to begin to bear risk. First, the math becomes "muddy" because a high leverage factor, say 10 to 1, no longer causes the risk of the equity to increase by the same factor. In this rough example we cannot be sure of an exact value for the relative risks. We illustrated using a factor of 8.75 units of risk in the previous example, but the same point could have been illustrated using a value other than 8.75.

Second, the example brings limited liability into focus. By using the corporate form of business organization, equityholders can transfer risk to debtholders, as is shown in the preceding example. Finally, the example will help us to make clear one of the great puzzles of corporate finance: If the 10-house example had been entirely equity-financed, then the risk diagram would be:

Unlevered Firm with 10 Houses:

Assets	=	*Debt*	+	*Equity*
Risk = 10 units		Risk = 0 units		Risk = 10 units
Amount = $1,000,000		Amount = $0		Amount = $1,000,000

Notice that when we compare buying 10 houses without debt with buying 10 houses with 90 percent debt, the use of leverage causes the risk of each dollar of equity to increase. To be specific, without debt, each $100,000 of equity bears 1 unit of risk. With debt, the $100,000 of equity bears 8.75 units of risk.

We also showed that when a firm takes on large amounts of debt, the riskiness of the debt increases. To be specific, with low leverage, the debt bears no risk, but with 10 to 1 leverage, the debtholder begins to bear risk.

Here is the puzzle: If leverage causes each $1 of debt and each $1 of equity to bear more risk, does it not have to be true that the total amount of risk has increased? The answer is, *no.* Both the debt and equity of a firm can increase in riskiness without total firm risk changing. With 90 percent leverage, both debt and equity become more risky, but the total risk of debt and equity equals that of the risk of assets. Equityholders bear 8.75 units of risk, and debtholders bear 1.25 units of risk. Total units of risk, however, are equal to the total units in the case of no debt. Financial leverage has not caused the risk of the firm to increase; rather, it has only acted to partition total risk between the firm's debtholders and equityholders.

> The risk of the firm is determined by the risk of the firm's assets. The only way to change total risk is to change the assets. Financial leverage will not change total risk—it will only partition it.

Figure 11.3 provides another method of illustrating these relationships for the cases of 0 percent, 50 percent, and 75 percent debt. The slopes of the lines reflect the level of risk because they reflect the effect on the equity value, measured on the vertical axis, caused by a change in asset value, measured on the horizontal axis.

FIGURE 11.3 Financial Leverage and Rates of Return on Equity

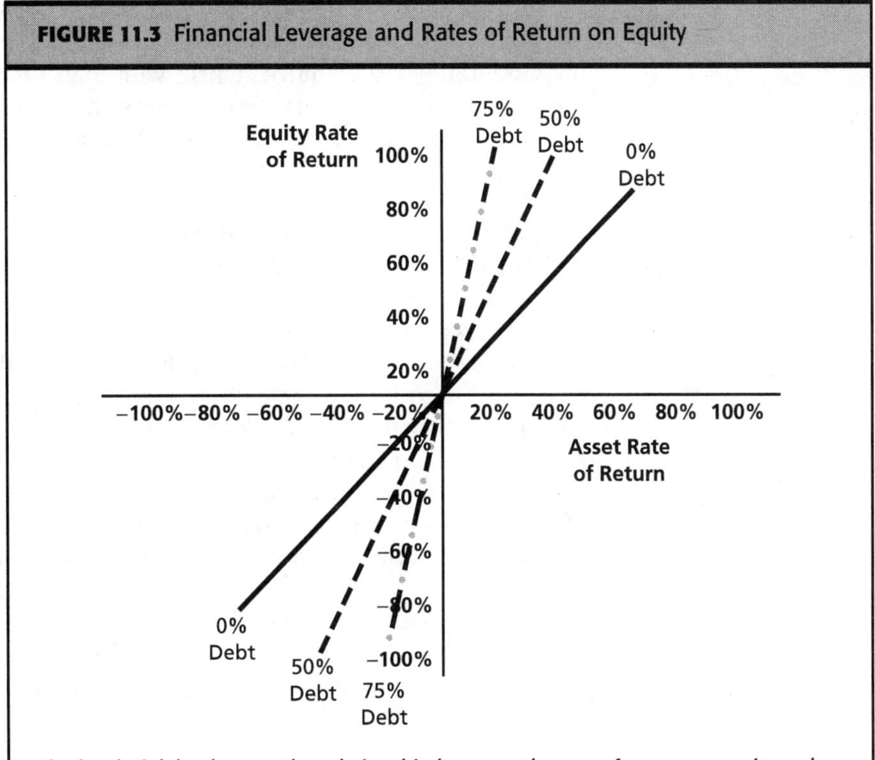

The level of debt changes the relationship between the rate of return on equity and the rate of return on assets. The higher the level of debt, the greater the response of the rate of return on equity to a given change in the rate of return on assets.

In Figure 11.3, the zero percent debt line indicates that a given change in asset value corresponds to an identical change in equity value. For example, a 20 percent increase or decrease in assets corresponds to a 20 percent increase or decrease in equity. Thus, in the absence of debt, the risk of the equity is identical to the risk of the assets. Figure 11.3 also indicates that the use of debt causes asset changes to be magnified or levered into larger equity changes. The steepest line is that of 75 percent debt, illustrating the more dramatic effects of leverage on equity values. For example, a 20 percent increase or decrease in assets corresponds to an 80 percent increase or decrease in equity. For the steep or levered lines, the equity changes are two times greater than the asset changes for the 50 percent line, and four times greater than the asset changes for the 75 percent line.

A Summary of the Mechanics of Leverage

Financial leverage does not change the total amount of risk; rather, it causes the risk of the assets of the firm to be partitioned into risks represented by equity claims and debt claims.

Debt is usually of relatively low risk, whereas equity is of relatively high risk. A firm with low financial leverage usually has very low-risk debt and only moderately risky equity. A firm with high financial leverage can have both riskier debt and equity. Nevertheless, the firm's total risk depends only on the assets, not on the use of financial leverage.

Capital Structure and Firm Value—The Traditionalists' View

In our discussion of the mechanics of financial leverage, we concluded that the use of debt partitions the risk of the assets into the firm's debt securities and equity securities. We can now examine the traditionalists' view of the relationship between the use of debt (the capital structure decision) and the expected return on the firm's securities.

In order to isolate the effect of leverage on return, we assume that the risk of the firm's assets stays constant. In other words, the firm has its investment decisions in place, and is now deciding on the particular way to finance those investments.

Figure 11.4 illustrates the traditionalists' view on the effect of leverage on the expected return of both the debtholder and the equityholder. The line r_D represents the cost of debt, the line r_C is the combined cost of capital, and the line r_E is the cost of equity.

FIGURE 11.4 A Traditionalist's View on Leverage and Expected Return

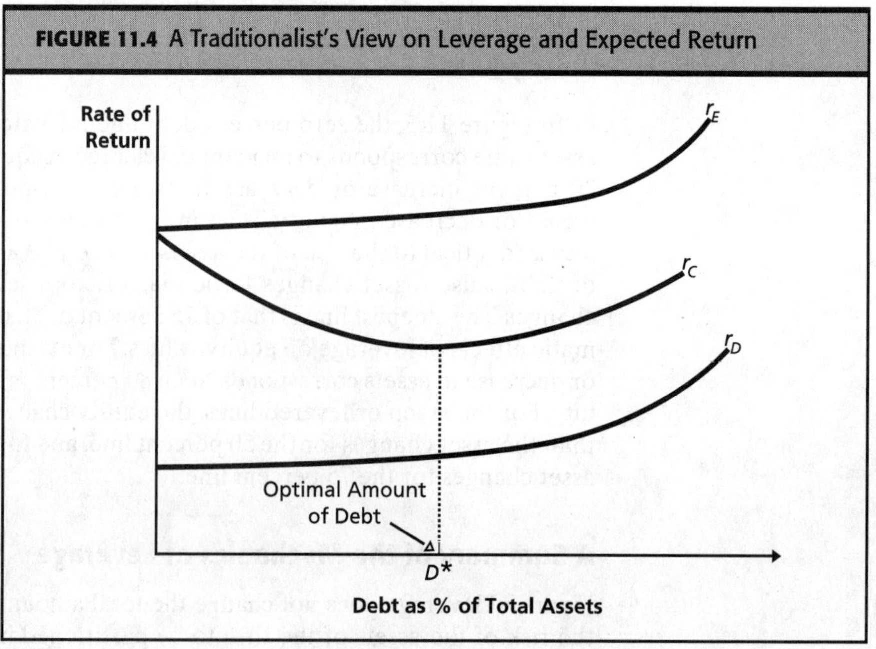

Traditionalists believe that as a firm moves from a position of zero debt to small amounts of debt, leverage increases the equityholders' risk but does not significantly increase the risk borne by debtholders. Because the probability is high that debtholders will receive promised payments, small amounts of debt are considered to be risk-free and debtholders can be persuaded to hold debt at or near the risk-free interest rate (the curve labeled r_D). Traditionalists also believe that the expected return on equity, labeled r_E, will not rise significantly until moderate to large amounts of debt are used.

What about the expected rate of return of the firm as a whole—the curve labeled r_C, which can be viewed as the weighted average of the firm's debt cost, or r_D, and equity cost, or r_E? Traditionalists believe that because debt is cheaper, combining equity with reasonable amounts of debt results in a reduction in the firm's overall cost of capital, or r_C. This would of course be good news because the value of the firm is higher when a lower discount rate is applied to its cash flow stream. Thus, under the traditionalists' argument, the goal of corporate management is to find the level of debt financing that minimizes the firm's cost of capital and maximizes firm value. This amount of debt, sometimes called the firm's **debt capacity,** is given by D^* in Figure 11.4.

debt capacity
The notion that there is some range of debt that maximizes the value of the firm.

Traditionalists believe, however, that too much debt can be a bad thing. Look what happens to the cost of both debt and equity as debt levels go from low to high. First, the cost of debt, which initially did not rise much, now starts to rise substantially as debtholders become highly concerned about the firm's ability to generate enough income to cover promised debt payments. The debtholders' concern is translated into higher required rates of return on debt.

Second, at high debt levels, the cost of equity also rises quickly because equityholders know that high amounts of debt are accompanied by high amounts of fixed interest payments, which increases the chance that they as residual claimants will end up with little or no return on their investment. Thus, following the traditionalists' argument, the overall cost of capital of the firm begins to rise at high levels of debt.

To summarize, traditionalists search for the combination of securities that creates a minimum overall cost of capital. Traditionalists believe that this is accomplished by using an amount of leverage that utilizes the low cost advantage of debt, but which keeps the amount of debt from exceeding the firm's debt capacity and becoming so risky that debt becomes too costly.

Capital Structure and Firm Value— The Modernists' View

The modernists' position on the use of debt and the value of the firm was established by Franco Modigliani and Merton Miller in the late 1950s. Their contributions to finance were so important that their concepts and propositions are known simply by their initials: M&M. Each of them has won a Nobel prize in economics, and the following analyses are highly simplified expositions of the concepts set forth in their work.

In a nutshell, the modernist position states that, under ideal conditions, all capital structures produce the same total cost of capital to the firm and the same total firm value. Said differently, modernists believe that the financing decision is irrelevant.

The modernist position is illustrated in Figure 11.5. In contrast to the traditionalists' position shown in Figure 11.4, there is no precise point at which the cost of equity rapidly rises. The required rate of return on equity rises less quickly when greater debt usage begins to transfer some of the firm's risks to the debtholders.

Notice, in Figure 11.5, that the required return on equity (r_E) begins to flatten out or rise less steeply at higher and higher levels of debt. This reflects the fact that as debtholders begin to bear more and more risk, the increased risk borne by equityholders is reduced.

Within the modernist viewpoint there is no optimum capital structure, and firms do not have a debt capacity. It is not necessary to use debt financing, nor is it unwise to use great amounts of debt financing. The key to this viewpoint is that no matter how a firm partitions the risk of its assets among its securities, the market will still charge the same total amount of money for bearing the same total amount of risk. The logic is that because the risk of the firm's assets is not changing, the overall cost of the firm's capital will also not change.

The modernists' position has been developed using models and deductive reasoning. As the years have progressed, the modernist position has been

FIGURE 11.5 A Modernist's View on Leverage and Expected Return

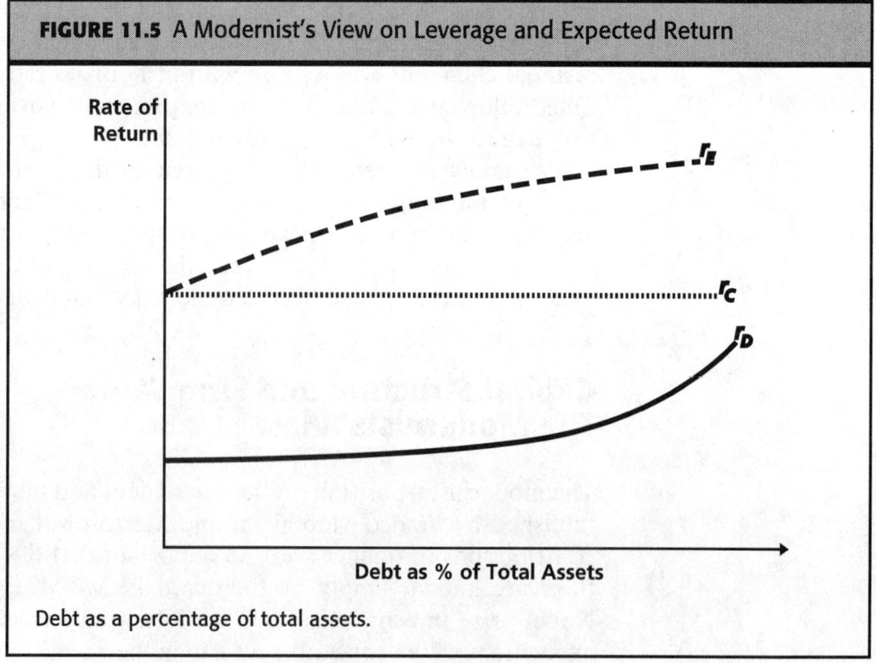

Debt as a percentage of total assets.

demonstrated in different ways and is becoming easier to understand. We will set forth the modernist arguments in three different ways. Each argument, however, leads to the same conclusion: The firm's capital structure decision can neither create or destroy wealth—it is irrelevant.

Capital Structure Irrelevancy Using Market Efficiency and Net Present Value

In an efficient capital market, as introduced in Chapter 2, numerous well-informed investors compete to increase their wealth in a marketplace such that financial securities trade at prices that are neither too low nor too high. If a security is trading at a wrong price, then one side of the trade would be making extra money, known as a positive net present value *(NPV),* and the other side of the trade would be losing extra money, known as a negative *NPV.* This type of mispricing and the transfer of wealth that would result cannot continue in an efficient market.

The implication of market efficiency is that the *NPV* of a security issued in an efficient market is zero. Investors in an efficient market would never purchase a security with a negative *NPV,* and firms would have no reason to sell a security at a price so low as to create a positive *NPV* for the investor. If, by chance, someone did offer to sell a security at too low a price, then buyers would quickly compete to purchase the security, thereby driving the price up until its *NPV* was zero again. The way in which securities are issued is discussed in Window 11.3.

In an efficient market, wealth cannot be increased on a consistent basis by buying and selling mispriced securities. Let us examine market efficiency from the standpoint of the shareholders of a corporation that is issuing securities to investors. Because a corporation is simply a set of contracts through which people transact, when we say that a corporation issues a security, we are really saying that shareholders, acting through a particular set of contracts known as a corporation, are selling securities. Can shareholders hope to sell securities at prices generating positive *NPV*s?

The lesson of market efficiency with respect to this question states that the answer is no. No matter what type of security a corporation issues, or when it is issued, if it is auctioned in a competitive market or if it is issued in such a way as to create an equivalent result, the *NPV* to both the buyer (the investor) and the seller (the shareholders) will be forced to zero. Said differently, shareholders will issue securities to investors at a price equal to the present value of the security's promised cash flows.

The opposing view to that of an efficient market is that shareholders sell securities to investors at a price greater than the present value of the security's promised cash flows. A positive *NPV* to the shareholder, however, must be a negative *NPV* to the investor. The view that shareholders issue securities with positive *NPV*s is tantamount to claiming that investors desire types of securities that have negative *NPV*s. Can these investors really be so misinformed? Clear thinking tells us that the answer is, *no.* Institutions such as

WINDOW 11.3

Issuing Securities—The Investment Banking Process

This window discusses how corporations issue securities. Chapter 1 established that an advantage of the corporate form of business over sole proprietorships and partnerships is its ability to raise additional money for purposes of investment. Sole proprietorships and partnerships, of course, can also raise money through banks and through arrangements with private investors, but on a smaller scale and at higher costs. Corporations often issue new shares of stock or bonds. We will begin by describing how common stock is issued.

For example, consider Arctic Bay Airlines, the only major air carrier servicing the Baffin Bay area in northern Canada. The company's founders recognized the growing interest in vacationing in the Arctic. Indeed, Arctic Bay's business had grown to the point at which it needed money to purchase a second airplane, so the founders decided to raise the money by issuing shares of stock to outside investors. Because Arctic had no shares trading, the issue would be a primary issue. As you will remember, primary issues of stock contrast with secondary issues, or additional shares of stock for companies whose shares are already trading in the market.

The founders of Arctic Bay, even though they are experts in the airline business, know little about issuing securities. The firm, therefore, seeks the advice of experts, known as investment bankers.

Investment bankers serve as a conduit, or intermediary, between the issuer of securities and the investment public. Some well-known investment bankers include Goldman Sachs, Merrill Lynch, and Salomon Brothers. In some cases, the investment banker will purchase the stock from the issuing company at one price and distribute it to the public at a higher price. The difference in price represents the profit to the investment banker. In other cases, the investment banker will enter a best-efforts arrangement, promising to sell as much of the new stock issue as possible without guaranteeing its success. The investment banker's fee is an agreed-upon percentage of the proceeds.

For primary issues of stock, the role of the investment banker begins with preparing the registration statement, the necessary paperwork required by the Securities and Exchange Commission. Next, the investment banker assists the firm in setting the initial price per share for the stock, which is a complex part of primary offerings. Setting the initial offering price too low will underprice the issue, making it easier to sell the stock on the market, but depriving the firm of receiving maximum return from the stock issue. On the other hand, setting the initial offering price too high will overprice the issue and jeopardize the success of the sale of stock to investors.

Issuing costs come in two main types: (1) the compensation earned by investment bankers in the form of the spread between the price paid to the issuer and the offering price to the public, and (2) administrative fees. Studies have found that issuing costs as a percentage of the gross proceeds average 6.2 percent, but are greater for smaller issues. In other words, the fixed costs of issuing securities tend to be high. The total costs for issues of $1 million are more than 15 percent, and the total costs for issues greater than $100 million are 4 percent.

WINDOW 11.3 *(continued)*

Bond issues share many of the characteristics of stock issues. After a registration statement is filed with the Securities and Exchange Commission, the securities are sold to investors. The registration statement must include an indenture—a written agreement between the corporation and the bondholders—that will usually include: (1) the basic terms of the bond, including the maturity date, the face value, the coupon rate, and how it is to be paid, (2) any collateral that the firm uses to protect the bondholder, (3) any restrictions that the debt issue places on the firm, and (4) any call provisions.

pension funds, insurance companies, and mutual funds purchase most of the securities issued by major corporations. These institutions are managed by experienced and highly intelligent professionals who cannot be consistently fooled into purchasing securities with negative *NPV*s.

Thus, modernists believe that major U.S. securities markets are reasonably efficient and that money cannot be made on a consistent basis by attempting to buy or sell securities at market prices. Further, modernists believe that this principle generally holds for the issuance of securities by corporations as well because a corporation is only a set of contracts. Thus, when shareholders use a corporation to issue a security in a perfect market, there is no wealth created, lost, or transferred.

Capital Structure Irrelevancy Using Arbitrage

Another method of defending the irrelevance of capital structure is to consider what would happen if irrelevancy failed to hold. Modernists believe that investors known as arbitragers would enter the market and force irrelevancy in the capital structure. An **arbitrager** is someone who searches for extremely quick and low-risk profits. The modernist belief is that no matter what combination of securities is issued, the combined value of the securities will be equal to the value of the firm's assets.

arbitragers
Investors who search for extremely quick and low-risk profits.

The key to the arbitrage argument is that the person who buys up all of the securities of a corporation, both debt and equity, has, in essence, removed the partitioning of the firm's assets into debt and equity and owns all the firm's securities. Thus, competition will force the total value of the securities to equal the value of the firm's assets. If, instead of purchasing all the firm's securities, investors simply purchase a particular percentage of each security, they are in a position equivalent to having direct ownership of that percentage of the firm's assets.

It should be obvious that if an investor buys up all the securities of the firm, the investor will receive all the cash flows from the firm's assets. Let us now imagine that an investor buys up half of the firm's securities. It is clear that one half of the securities would entitle the investor to exactly half of the cash flows from the firm's assets. In the same manner, an investor who holds any portion of the firm's securities is in a position equivalent to owning directly the same portion of the firm's assets. This is illustrated in Table 11.3.

Table 11.3 demonstrates the partitioning under different economic scenarios such as recession, slow growth, moderate growth, and boom. An investor who owns 10 percent of the firm's equity and 10 percent of the firm's debt would receive exactly 10 percent of the cash flows from the firm's assets, which is equivalent to owning 10 percent of the assets directly.

Example 11.3 Consider Partition, Inc., a fictitious firm with $2 million in assets financed by two different types of securities. Capital structure irrelevance states that the total value of the two types of securities added together must equal $2 million, no matter how they are divided. This can be proven through arbitrage. If Partition's securities were selling for an amount less than the $2 million, then arbitragers would purchase all of the securities, take control of the assets, sell the assets for $2 million, and make a quick profit. The fact that arbitragers have not done this establishes that the securities are not underpriced.

The argument that the securities of Partition, Inc., cannot be overpriced is not as easy to demonstrate, but it can also be shown through arbitrage. In this case, arbitragers can take advantage of overpriced securities either by creating new corporations or by short-selling the securities. For example, the arbitragers could use $2 million of assets to start a new corporation and use the optimal capital structure to issue similar securities that would also sell for more than $2 million, thus earning their profit. On the other hand, there is a process called *short-selling,* detailed in Window 11.4, which would permit the arbitragers to profit. Once again, the absence of such activities in a free and well-functioning market establishes that securities are not significantly overpriced.

One rebuttal to this argument is that the purchase or sale of all of the firm's securities must be difficult for practical and legal reasons. As shown in Table 11.3, however, if an investor purchases, say, 1 percent of each type of security that a firm issues, then the investor has effectively purchased 1 percent of the firm's assets even though the investor will not have legal control of the corporation. It may take longer, and be less dramatic, but the arbitrager could still earn profits if capital structure affected firm value.

TABLE 11.3 Partitioning the Firm's Assets into Debt and Equity Claims: Promised Debt Payment = $50

	Recession	*Slow Growth*	*Moderate Growth*	*Boom*
Value of assets	$40	$100	$120	$140
Payoff of debt	$40	$ 50	$ 50	$ 50
Payoff of equity	$ 0	$ 50	$ 70	$ 90
Payoff of both debt and equity	$40	$100	$120	$140
Value of 10% of assets	$ 4	$ 10	$ 12	$ 14
Payoff of 10% of debt and equity	$ 4	$ 10	$ 12	$ 14

WINDOW 11.4

Short-Selling Securities

An accepted viewpoint in financial markets is that the way to make money is to buy low today and sell high in the future. It is also possible, however, to make money by first selling high and later buying low. In other words, the markets provide opportunities to sell securities first and buy them back at a later date. This is known as short-selling.

Investors will short-sell if they believe that a security's price is overvalued and will soon fall in price. The short-seller sells a security to another investor at the current price with the hope of buying the security back at a later date at a lower price. The difference between the selling price and the buying price represents the gain or loss to the short seller.

One of the most confusing aspects of short-selling is the notion of selling securities that are not owned. Given that the seller does not have physical possession of the security, is selling it not impossible? In short-selling, the answer is, *no.* Owners of stocks or other securities often leave the actual stock certificates with their brokerage firms for safekeeping. The short-seller borrows the securities from the broker and is obligated to return them at a later date. The original owner usually has no knowledge that the securities have been borrowed.

For example, suppose the stock of Neveright is currently selling for $50 per share. Brokerage X has thousands of shares of Neveright in the vault, safekeeping the stock for the investors who expect great things from this company. Suppose that you believe that the share price of Neveright will soon fall to $40 per share and wish to take advantage of this situation. In this case, you borrow 100 shares of Neveright from the broker and sell them in the market for $50. You now have $5,000 from the sale, but also have a liability represented by 100 shares of Neveright that you must return to the vault.

Let us consider the investment aspects of the short-sale. First the good news: If the stock does indeed fall to $40, you go into the market, buy 100 shares of Neveright for $40 a share for a grand total of $4,000, and return the 100 shares to the broker's vault. Compared with the $5,000 you received at the time of the sale, you have just made a $1,000 profit.

Now the bad news. If the stock climbs above its current price of $50, you lose as a short-seller. In fact, you stand to lose $100 for each dollar the stock price rises over its initial value of $50 ($1.00 times 100 shares). If the stock price hits $60, you may decide you've had enough. In this case, you would go into the market, buy 100 shares of Neveright for $60 per share, return the shares to the broker, and suffer a loss of $1,000. Because there is no upper limit to the price of Neveright stock, potential losses to short-selling are unlimited.

The strongest aspect of this argument could be characterized by the question, would it be possible to create a capital structure intentionally such that the combined securities would sell for less than the firm's assets were worth? Suppose that Masochists, Inc., were run by shareholders who desired to create undesirable securities. Each member of the board constructed the security that in their judgment was worst.

For example, one shareholder from Boston might suggest a bond that would pay interest only if his favorite baseball team won the World Series. Another shareholder might suggest preferred stock that would pay double dividends whenever there was a terrible natural disaster and so forth. Of course, there is one security called *common stock* that paid whatever was left over.

Would it be possible that Masochists, Inc., could create such a disgusting capital structure that the total value of its securities would be less than the value of the firm's assets? The answer is, *no!*

Remember that it is possible for any investor to purchase a small percentage of each of the firm's securities. No matter how strange each security was, we know that owning and holding together all of the securities is equivalent to owning the firm's assets. In effect, the investors can strip down or remove any partitioning of the firm's cash flows they do not like. In the case of Masochists, Inc., the arbitrager needs to purchase a percentage of each of the securities in order to remove the effects of the partitioning. Thus, capital structure decisions cannot destroy value even if someone tried to.

Capital structure decisions are simply decisions of how to partition or divide the firm's cash flows. If a partitioning is undesirable, then arbitragers can in effect remove it. If a particular partitioning were viewed as so desirable that it increased wealth, then participants would quickly replicate the idea until the added value was removed. The presence of market participants who would engage in such activities and the rarity with which such activities are performed lend support to the belief that little or no shareholder wealth can be created or destroyed by tinkering with capital structure under ideal conditions.

Capital Structure Irrelevance Using Homemade Leverage

The most compelling argument for capital structure irrelevancy is the homemade leverage argument, which states that any leverage decision made by a firm can be dismantled by or replicated by the investor without the corporation's help. There can therefore be little or no economic advantage to having leverage decisions made at the corporate level in a perfect market.

A dairy analogy is useful in understanding the argument of homemade leverage. Back in the days before homogenization, milk separated naturally into cream and skimmed milk. Consumers were able to either use the products separately or mix them for whole milk, low-fat milk, half and half, and so forth. In effect, consumers could very easily create for themselves the variety of milk products we now buy separately. Today, dairies separate the milk products for the consumer, and if they tried to charge a very high price for this service, competition would encourage a return to the days before homogenization because consumers can do this for themselves.

Just as a dairy now separates milk for us into products with various concentrations of fat, a corporation can partition the cash flows from the firm's assets into securities that contain various concentrations of risk.

The important question is: If a firm chooses not to partition its cash flows into securities represented by debt and equity, then could investors do it themselves? On the other hand, if a firm chooses to partition its cash flows in a manner considered undesirable by some investors, can those investors remove the partitions and reconstruct desirable partitions? The answers are, *yes.*

We have already stated in our arbitrage arguments that the investor can completely strip out partitions by purchasing appropriate proportions of each security to replicate the firm's assets. In this section we shall develop the concept more precisely and with greater flexibility by concentrating on one aspect of capital structure, the debt-versus-equity decision.

Example 11.4

Consider two firms with identical assets. One is an all-equity firm called Boring, Inc. The other firm has significant debt and is called Exciting, Inc. Remember, these firms are considered the same in every way except for the fact that one chooses to include debt in its capital structure and one does not. Is it possible for an investor to use shares of equity in Boring, Inc. to produce the same result as would be obtained by investing directly in Exciting, Inc.? We shall see that the answer is *yes,* due to a process called **homemade leverage.**

homemade leverage
The replication of the corporate leverage decision by the investor at little cost.

Is it also possible that an investor could invest in Exciting, Inc. to produce the same investment results as would be obtained from owning shares in Boring, Inc.? We shall again see that the answer is *yes,* and the process can be called homemade unlevering. Both of these processes demonstrate that because the corporate leverage decision can be replicated or removed by the investor at little cost, there can be no significant advantage for a corporation to levering at the corporate level.

In order to demonstrate these points fully, let us assume that there are three possible states of nature or economic outcomes that investors expect: (1) a recession, (2) normal growth, and (3) an economic boom. Because both firms have identical assets, the values of the assets and the cash flows of each firm will be equal to each other regardless of which state occurs. The specific values are shown in Table 11.4.

Because Boring, Inc. has no debt, the value of its equity and the cash flow it receives flow directly from the assets. Boring, Inc. has outstanding 1,000

TABLE 11.4 The Cash Flows and Values of Boring, Inc. and Exciting, Inc.

State	*Boring, Inc. Future Cash Flow*	*Exciting, Inc. Future Cash Flow*
Recession	$ 500	$ 500
Normal growth	$ 1,000	$ 1,000
Economic boom	$ 1,500	$ 1,500
Current value of debt	$ 0	$ 5,000
Current value of equity	$10,000	$ 5,000
Current total value	$10,000	$10,000

shares of stock such that the equity value per share is equal to the total firm value divided by 1,000.

Exciting, Inc. has $5,000 of debt, which requires an interest payment of $500. Because the debtholders have financed one half of the assets of the firm, Exciting, Inc. has one–half the number of shares of equity outstanding, or 500 shares (assuming the same price per share). The value of the equity per share is equal to the total equity value divided by 500. The cash flows per share of both Boring and Exciting in each of the three states are given in Table 11.5.

Table 11.5 demonstrates that leverage transfers risk to the equityholders. The greater risk to equityholders is demonstrated by the greater variation in the cash flows per share of Exciting, Inc. In a recession, Exciting's cash flow of $500 is equal to the promised payment to the bondholders, leaving the equityholders with nothing. In a boom, the total cash flow to Exciting, Inc. while equal to that of Boring, Inc., is shared with a fewer number of equityholders so that the cash flow per share is greater. This is illustrated in Figure 11.6.

To illustrate homemade leverage and homemade unlevering, consider that it is possible for an investor to buy shares in either firm and then adjust his or her personal debt usage such that the resulting cash flows will be equal to the cash flows that would be received from owning the other firm's equity. An investor who wants to replicate corporate leverage in a homemade fashion borrows; an investor who wants to unlever or strip away the effects of leverage invests relatively less money in stock and puts the remaining money in bonds—in other words, the investor lends.

Suppose an investor has $500 to invest. One alternative is to purchase 10 percent of the equity of Exciting, Inc. for $500 (i.e., to purchase 50 shares for $10 per share). An equivalent alternative, however, is to purchase 10 percent of the equity of Boring, Inc. for $1,000, financing half the purchase by borrowing $500 (i.e., to purchase 100 shares at $10 per share). Panel A of Table 11.6 demonstrates that the cash flows from either alternative are identical regardless of which economic outcome occurs. We are temporarily ignoring the effect of risk on the required rate of return and are assuming that the investor can borrow money at the same interest rate as did Exciting, Inc.

TABLE 11.5 Financial Leverage and Cash Flows

	Boring, Inc. (1,000 shares)			*Exciting, Inc. (500 shares)*		
State	*Total Cash Flow*	*Cash Flow to Debt*	*Cash Flow to Equity per Share*	*Total Cash Flow*	*Cash Flow to Debt*	*Cash Flow to Equity per Share*
Recession	$ 500	$ -0-	$0.50	$ 500	$500	$0.00
Normal growth	$1,000	$ -0-	$1.00	$1,000	$500	$1.00
Economic boom	$1,500	$ -0-	$1.50	$1,500	$500	$2.00

FIGURE 11.6 The Effect of Leverage on Cash Flow to Equity per Share

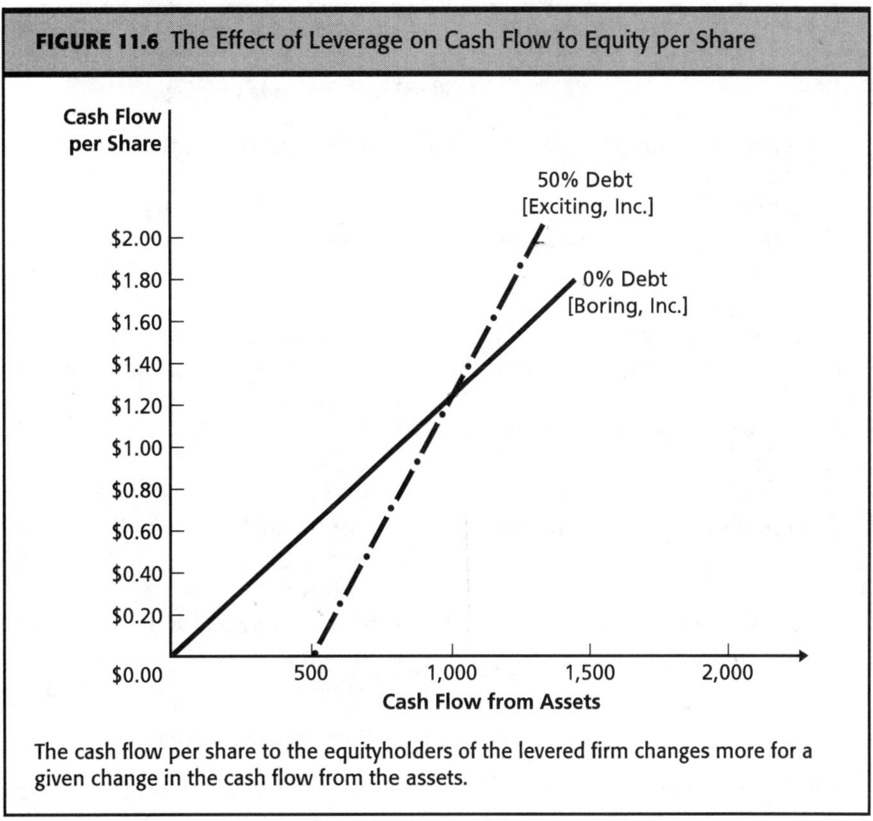

The cash flow per share to the equityholders of the levered firm changes more for a given change in the cash flow from the assets.

In a similar way, Panel B in Table 11.6 illustrates the alternatives available to an investor with $1,000 to invest and who is considering purchasing 10 percent of the equity of Boring, Inc., an unlevered firm. An equivalent alternative, however, is to purchase, for $500, 10 percent of the equity of Exciting, Inc., a firm with debt, and lending $500 by buying bonds—perhaps even bonds of Exciting, Inc. Panel B shows that the cash flows of either alternative are identical regardless of which economic outcome occurs.

The importance of Table 11.6 is that it illustrates that, no matter how a firm partitions the cash flows from its assets into debt and equity streams, the firm is not creating a unique cash flow opportunity. Its securities, therefore, will not be a set of highly valuable instruments that can sell at a premium and thus provide for a lower cost of capital. We know this because Tables 11.5 and 11.6 illustrate that investors can easily partition the cash flow streams from other firms themselves or can remove any undesirable partitions.

Some people argue that it is somehow easier for a corporation to borrow than it is for an individual to borrow money to purchase stock. This is not true. Window 11.5 details the simple way to borrow to buy stocks, known as *using margin*.

TABLE 11.6 Homemade Leverage

Panel A: Homemade Leverage

Alternative 1: Purchase 10% (50 shares) of the equity of Exciting, Inc., a levered firm.

Cash flow—Recession	\$ 0 × 10% = \$ 0 (\$0 per share × 50 shares)
Cash flow—Normal conditions	\$ 500 × 10% = \$ 50 (\$1 per share × 50 shares)
Cash flow—Boom	\$1,000 × 10% = \$100 (\$2 per share × 50 shares)

Alternative 2: Purchase 10% (100 shares) of the equity of Boring, Inc., an unlevered firm. Borrow an amount equal to 10% of the debt of Exciting, Inc., causing \$50 of interest expense.

Cash flow—Recession	Equity:	\$ 500 × 10% =	\$ 50 (\$0.50 × 100 shares)
	Borrowing:		−\$ 50
	Cash flow		\$ 0
Cash flow—Normal conditions	Equity:	\$1,000 × 10% =	\$100 (\$1.00 × 100 shares)
	Borrowing:		−\$ 50
	Cash flow		\$ 50
Cash flow—Boom	Equity:	\$1,500 × 10% =	\$150 (\$1.50 × 100 shares)
	Borrowing:		−\$ 50
	Cash flow		\$100

Panel B: Homemade Unlevering

Alternative 1: Purchase 10% (100 shares) of the equity of Boring, Inc., an unlevered firm.

Cash flow—Recession	\$ 500 × 10% = \$ 50 (\$0.50 × 100 shares)
Cash flow—Normal conditions	\$1,000 × 10% = \$100 (\$1.00 × 100 shares)
Cash flow—Boom	\$1,500 × 10% = \$150 (\$1.50 × 100 shares)

Alternative 2: Purchase 10% (50 shares) of the equity of Exciting, Inc., a levered firm. Lend an amount equal to 10% of the debt of Exciting, Inc., producing \$50 of interest income.

Cash flow—Recession	Equity:	\$ 0 × 10% =	\$ 0 (\$0.00 × 50 shares)
	Lending:		50
			\$ 50
Cash flow—Normal conditions	Equity:	\$ 500 × 10% =	\$ 50 (\$1.00 × 50 shares)
	Lending:		50
			\$100
Cash flow—Boom	Equity:	\$1,000 × 10% =	\$100 (\$2.00 × 50 shares)
	Lending:		50
			\$150

WINDOW 11.5

Buying Stock on Margin

Borrowing money through a brokerage firm to buy stock or other securities is known as *using margin*. Federal regulations (known especially as Regulation T) govern the use of margin.

The key is that the loan is backed by or guaranteed by the securities the investor holds in the brokerage account. The amount of money that can be borrowed is closely governed by the Federal Reserve and individual brokerage firms. Borrowed money can represent up to a particular percentage, say 50 percent, of the total account value.

Regulations also control what securities can be used as collateral. In general, all common stocks of large corporations are acceptable collateral.

The interest rate charged is set by the individual brokerage firm and is often called the "call rate." The rate may change daily and may depend upon the size of the loan—with large loans being charged a lower rate. In general, these interest rates are quite competitive and are only slightly higher than money market interest rates.

More sophisticated analyses have been performed that demonstrate capital structure irrelevancy for risky debt as well as risk-free debt. For example, it is clear that an investor who purchases both the debt (even if it is risky) and equity of a firm in the proper proportions can effectively remove the partition and replicate the cash flow stream of the assets. As we have said, therefore, all of the firm's securities combined must have the same value as the assets, in a perfect market.

In summary, these three cases have shown that, under certain conditions, the firm's capital structure decision is irrelevant. Firm value is not affected by the choice of financing instruments.

Summary

- The study of corporate finance is divided into two primary decisions: the investment decision, or which assets to acquire, and the financing decision, or how those assets are financed. This chapter investigates the effect of the financing decision on the value of the firm.
- The financing decision is sometimes called the capital structure decision. Given the objective of maximizing firm value, the question to be explored is whether or not firm value can be affected by the firm's choice of capital structure.
- Financial leverage is created when the firm borrows money in the form of debt. A corporation that has both debt and equity may be viewed as taking the cash flow stream produced by the firm's assets and partitioning the cash flow into two streams: a low-risk debt stream and a high-risk equity stream.

- Under the restrictive assumptions of perfect markets, both modernists and traditionalists agree that leverage affects the risk of equity. Traditionalists conclude that there is an optimal capital structure. Modernists state that capital structure is irrelevant—there is no best mix of securities that a firm issues to finance assets.

References

Modigliani, F. and M. H. Miller. "Corporate Income Taxes and the Cost of Capital: A Correction." *American Economic Review* 53 (June 1963), 433–443.

———. "The Cost of Capital, Corporation Finance and the Theory of Investment." *American Economic Review* 48 (June 1958), 261–297.

———. "Some Estimates of the Cost of Capital to the Electric Utility Industry, 1954–1957." *American Economic Review* 56 (June 1966), 333–391.

Demonstration Problems

Problem 1

Lindross Salvage Corporation is an all-equity (unlevered) corporation with $10 million in assets and whose performance varies from incurring a loss of $1 million per year to producing a profit of $3 million per year. Please find the range of the rates of return that the shareholders will earn with everything else equal if:

a. Lindross Salvage Corporation remains unlevered, and

b. Lindross Salvage Corporation switches to a capital structure with $3 million of debt and $7 million of equity (assume that the debt has an interest rate of 5%).

Solution to Problem 1

In each case, the problem requires that we determine rates of return for shareholders. We ignore accounting problems and assume that the shareholders' rate of return can be found by dividing the net profit of the firm by the equity of the firm.

Shareholder Rate of Return = Profit or Loss After Interest / Equity

The profit of the firm is found by subtracting the interest cost of the debt, if any. The equity of the firm is given.

Step 1: For the unlevered firm there is no debt and therefore no interest cost or expense. The range in the unlevered shareholders' rate of return is therefore found simply by dividing the possible profit or loss by the quantity of equity:

Lowest Unlevered Rate of Return = −$1,000,000 / $10,000,000

= −10%

Highest Unlevered Rate of Return = $3,000,000 / $10,000,000

= +30%

Step 2: The range of levered rates of return involves the additional step of determining the interest expense and subtracting it from the cash flows produced by the assets.

First, the annual interest expense is found by multiplying the interest rate by the amount of debt:

$$\$3{,}000{,}000 \text{ Debt} \times 5\% \text{ Interest Rate}$$
$$= \$150{,}000 \text{ Annual Interest Expense}$$

Next, the profit or loss net of interest expense is found by subtracting the annual interest expense from the profit or loss that would have occurred had the firm not used debt:

$$\text{Low Outcome: Net Loss} = -\$1{,}000{,}000 - \$150{,}000 = -\$1{,}150{,}000$$
$$\text{High Outcome: Net Profit} = +\$3{,}000{,}000 - \$150{,}000 = +\$2{,}850{,}000$$

Step 3: Finally, the range of rates of return for the levered firm is determined by dividing the net profit or loss by the value of the levered firm's equity. Note that because the firm has $3,000,000 of debt, only $7,000,000 is needed to fund the firm's $10,000,000 of assets.

$$\text{Lowest Levered Rate of Return} = -\$1{,}150{,}000 / \$7{,}000{,}000$$
$$= -16.43\%$$
$$\text{Highest Levered Rate of Return} = \$2{,}850{,}000 / \$7{,}000{,}000$$
$$= +40.71\%$$

Final Solution: The effect of leverage is to widen the range of rates of return from −10 percent and +30 percent to −16.43 percent and +40.71 percent.

Problem 2

Using the results of problem 1, demonstrate homemade leverage and homemade unleverage for an investor with $1,000,000 by finding:

a. how to use the unlevered equity and homemade leverage to produce the same range of returns as is produced by the levered firm.

b. how to use the levered firm and homemade unleverage to produce the same range of returns produced by the unlevered firm.

Solution to Problem 2

In the case of homemade leverage, the investor must find how much money to borrow for additional investment (homemade leverage). In the case of homemade unleverage, the investor does not borrow, rather, the investor lends or buys bonds. The investor must find, specifically, how much money to invest in equity and how much in bonds (lend).

Step 1: In homemade leverage, the investor must borrow enough to offset the fact that the corporation has not borrowed the "desired" amount. In this case, the unlevered firm has no debt and the levered firm has 30% debt.

The key starting point in this problem is to determine the levered corporation's debt usage as a percentage of its equity. In other words, although the corporation has a debt-to-assets ratio of 30 percent, we must find the debt as a percentage of equity (the debt-to-equity ratio):

$$\text{Debt-to-Equity Ratio} = \$3{,}000{,}000 \,/\, \$7{,}000{,}000 = 42.86\%$$

This is the tricky part, because there is a temptation to assume that since the investor has $1,000,000 of his or her own money to invest he or she should simply borrow $300,000, or 30 percent. The borrowed money, however, must be 30 percent of the total amount invested (including the borrowed money itself!). We find the correct amount to borrow by multiplying the investor's funds times the firm's debt-to-equity ratio:

$$\text{Amount Borrowed} = \text{Amount to Invest} \times \text{Debt-to-Equity Ratio}$$

$$\text{Amount Borrowed} = \$1{,}000{,}000 \times 42.86\% = \$428{,}571$$

Thus the total investment by the investor is given as:

$$\text{Original Funds} = \$1{,}000{,}000\ (70\%)$$

$$\text{Borrowed Funds} = \$\ \ 428{,}571\ (30\%)$$

$$\text{Total Invested} = \$1{,}428{,}571\ (100\%)$$

Thus, $428,571 in borrowed money leaves the investor with $1,428,571 of total investment and a percentage debt usage of 30%. If the investor had simply borrowed $300,000, the debt usage would have been only 23% ($300,000/$1,300,000).

Step 2: Now check the preceding result and prove that homemade leverage works, by showing that the $1,428,571 invested in the unlevered firm produces the same result (after interest expense) as $1,000,000 invested in the levered firm.

First, find the profit or loss for $1,000,000 invested in the levered firm. The range is found by multiplying the returns found in the solution to problem 1 by the $1,000,000 invested. Notice that we use the levered returns because homemade leverage seeks to duplicate levered returns.

$$\text{Lowest Return} = \$1{,}000{,}000 \times -16.43\% = -\$164{,}300$$

$$\text{Highest Return} = \$1{,}000{,}000 \times +40.71\% = \$407{,}100$$

We will now check to see if the same results can be found using the performance of the unlevered firm and our homemade leverage. We must find the after-interest expense performance of the borrowed money and investment in the unlevered firm. In order to prove that the results are equal, we must assume that the investor pays the same interest rate as the firm.

	Low Outcome *−10%*	*High Outcome* *+30%*
Total funds in unlevered firm ($1,428,571) times outcome	$−142,857	$ 428,571
Interest expense of borrowed funds ($428,571) at 5%	$− 21,428	$−21,428
Total profit or loss (rounded)	$−164,300	$ 407,100

Ignoring rounding errors, we have demonstrated that homemade leverage using the unlevered firm produces the same net result as investing directly in the levered firm.

Step 3: Next, we prove that investment in a levered firm using homemade unleverage produces the same result as direct investment in an unlevered firm. In homemade unleverage the investor must limit the amount of money placed in the levered firm's equity and must invest the remaining funds in low-risk debt. The key is to determine how much of the total money (in this problem, $1,000,000) should be placed in the levered firm's equity (the remainder will be invested in bonds earning 5%).

Remember, homemade unleverage attempts to replicate an unlevered firm. If the investor placed $1,000,000 in an unlevered firm, it would be tantamount to purchasing $1,000,000 of the firm's assets directly. The levered firm borrows money, however, so a $1,000,000 investment in the equity of the levered firm would involve greater risk. We will now look for the portion of the $1 million that can be invested in the levered firm's equity so as to produce the same risk exposure as having $1 million in the unlevered firm's equity.

The numbers that we are looking for are fortunately related directly to the levered firm's capital structure ratios of 70 percent equity and 30 percent debt. Notice that for every $7 of equity that the levered firm has there is a total of $10 of assets. Thus, in order to perform homemade unleverage, the investor simply invests in equity and debt in the same ratio as is found in the firm.

$$\text{Investment in Equity} = 70\% \times \$1{,}000{,}000 = \$700{,}000$$

$$\text{Investment in Bonds} = 30\% \times \$1{,}000{,}000 = \$300{,}000$$

Thus, the investor can place $700,000 in the levered corporation's stock knowing that the levered firm will use $300,000 of debt to finance a total of $1,000,000 in assets. This will produce the same result as investing the $1,000,000 directly in the unlevered firm's equity. To complete the homemade unleverage, the investor must place the remaining $300,000 in bonds that offer a 5% interest rate.

Step 4: Check to see that the homemade unleverage produces the same results as $1,000,000 invested directly in the unlevered firm. First, compute the profit or loss from investing the full $1,000,000 directly in the unlevered firm:

$$\text{Lowest Return} = \$1{,}000{,}000 \times -10.00\% = -\$100{,}000$$

$$\text{Highest Return} = \$1{,}000{,}000 \times +30.00\% = \$300{,}000$$

We will now check to see if the same results can be found using the performance of the levered firm and our homemade unleverage. We must combine the performance of the equity investment in the levered firm with the $300,000 invested in bonds.

	Low Outcome *−16.43%*	*High Outcome* *+40.71%*
Total funds in levered firm ($700,000) times outcome	$−115,000	$285,000
Interest on $300,000 at 5%	$ 15,000	$ 15,000
Total profit or loss (rounded)	$−100,000	$300,000

Ignoring rounding errors, we have demonstrated that homemade unleverage using the levered firm produces the same net result as investing directly in the unlevered firm.

Final Solution: The homemade leverage solution is to borrow $428,571 in order to invest a total of $1,428,571 in the unlevered firm. This produces the same result as investing $1 million directly in the levered firm. The homemade unleverage solution is to invest $700,000 in the equity of the levered firm and place the remaining $300,000 in bonds (lend). This produces the same result as placing $1 million directly in the unlevered firm.

Review Questions

1. Describe the "capital structure" decision of the firm.
2. How do traditionalists view the firm's capital structure decision?
3. How do modernists view the firm's capital structure decision?
4. What is financial leverage?
5. Why is the equity of the firm also known as residual claims?
6. Why does the presence of debt change the risk of holding equity in a firm?
7. Explain the term *debt capacity* as it relates to the traditionalists' view of capital structure.
8. What is the modernists'—or the M&M—position on the capital structure decision in perfect markets?
9. What is short selling? What direction of prices (up or down) would benefit the short seller?
10. Explain what homemade leverage is, and how modernists use homemade leverage in their arguments.

Problems

1. Donny Donruss has set up a corporation to buy and sell baseball cards. Mr. Donruss, the corporation's only shareholder, puts up $50,000 of his savings to begin the business. Calculate the annual return to Mr. Donruss in each of the following two scenarios:
   a. The market for baseball cards goes on a winning streak, and his business produces a cash flow of $15,000 per year.
   b. The market for baseball cards takes a slide, and his business barely squeaks out a cash flow of $2,500 per year.
2. Chris Russo, the arch-rival of Donny Donruss, sets up a competing corporation to buy and sell baseball cards. Chris has only $25,000 to invest in the business, but wants to open a store that is similar to Donny's. In addition to his $25,000, Chris borrows $25,000 from Topps Bank in the form of debt at a cost of 10 percent. Calculate the annual return to Mr. Russo in each of the following two scenarios:
   a. His business hits a home run and produces a cash flow of $15,000 per year.
   b. His business gets "shut out" and squeaks out a cash flow of $2,500 per year.
3. Let us return again to Mr. Donruss and Mr. Russo. Mr. Donruss operates his $50,000 firm using his own equity. Mr. Russo operates his firm with $25,000 of his own money plus $25,000 of debt at a cost of 10 percent interest.
   a. Calculate Mr. Donruss's and Mr. Russo's rates of return if their respective businesses produce a cash flow of $0, $2,500, $5,000, $7,500, or $10,000 (there is a different rate of return for each cash flow for each business).

b. Plot the relationship between the rate of return on equity (on the *y* or vertical axis) and the four different cash flows in part (a) (on the *x* or horizontal axis) for each business. Give Donruss a solid line, and give Russo a dashed line. What does your graph tell you about the use of debt and the financial risk of a firm?

4. Bobby Binckman owns and operates Soccer Stores of America. He has $150,000 of his own money in the business as equity capital, but because of the use of debt, the total value of his stores is $750,000. Calculate the percentage of debt in the corporation, and the corporation's leverage factor.

5. Buckley Bookstores, Inc., has $50,000 of equity capital, just enough money to open one store. The firm, however, can open more than one store by taking on debt. Assume that Buckley, Inc., can borrow all the money it needs at a cost of 12 percent. Use this information and the following information to complete the following table:

Number of Bookstores Opened	1	2	3	10
Total Value of the Bookstores	$50,000	$100,000	$150,000	$500,000
Amount of Equity	$50,000	$ 50,000	$ 50,000	$ 50,000
Amount of Debt	$ 0	$ 50,000	$100,000	$450,000
Leverage Factor	?	?	?	?
Percentage of Debt	?	?	?	?

6. Felicia Fish is the sole shareholder in Aquarium City. Her equity in the corporation totals $500,000. Given her use of leverage, however, the total value of Aquarium City is $2 million. Calculate the change in the value of Ms. Fish's equity in the firm under the following scenarios:

a. The value of her assets rises by 25 percent.
b. The value of her assets rises by 100 percent.
c. The value of her assets falls by 30 percent.

7. Buchanan, Inc., makes "Republican Brand" footwear. The firm is currently unlevered and is valued at $1 million. The business is doing well and a decision has been made to expand. The two key questions are the size of the expansion and how the expansion is financed.

a. Suppose that the decision is to double the size of the firm, with all expansion funds coming from equity capital. What must the percentage fall in assets be before all of the equity is wiped out?
b. Suppose that the decision is to double the size of the firm, with all of the expansion funds coming from debt. What must the percentage fall in assets be before all the equity is wiped out?
c. Suppose the decision is a tenfold increase in the size of the firm with all of the expansion funds coming from debt. What must the percentage fall in assets be before all the equity is wiped out?

8. We can conceptualize the risk of DataTech by assigning 5 units to the risk of the assets—5 units to equity and 0 units to debt. Suppose that the firm expands, using debt such that the firm is five times its original size, and that after the expansion we find that the firm's debt can now be assigned 0.5 units of risk. Determine from this information the new amount of risk of the firm's assets as well as the new units of risk assigned to the firm's equity.

9. The following table shows how financial leverage acts to partition risk for these four different firms. Complete the table using the information given.

Assets	=	*Debt*	+	*Equity*
Risk = 1 unit Amount = $1,000	=	Risk = ? Amount = $0	+	Risk = ? Amount = $1,000
Risk = 2 units Amount = $2,000	=	Risk = ? Amount = $1,000	+	Risk = 2 Amount = ?
Risk = 5 units Amount = ?	=	Risk = 0.85 Amount = $4,000	+	Risk = ? Amount = $1,000
Risk = 5 units Amount = ?	=	Risk = 0 Amount = $4,000	+	Risk = ? Amount = $1,000

10. The assets of the Kinsley firm have been partitioned into debt claims and equity claims. The payment on the debt will be $25 unless the firm hits bad times, in which case the debt will pay $20. The payoff to equity will be one of three values: $125 under status quo, $175 in good times, and $0 in bad times. Determine your payoff if you purchase 10 percent of Kinsley's equity and debt under the following three cases: status quo, good times, and bad times.

11. As a keen and insightful investor, you decide to short-sell Atlas Corporation because you believe that its shares are about to take a dive. Atlas is currently selling for $50 per share. Determine your profit or loss if you sell 500 shares of Atlas short at $50 per share and the price of Atlas:

a. falls to $40.00.
b. falls to $ 0.25.
c. rises to $1,000.00.

12. Tacos Unlimited currently trades at $100 per share. You think the future direction of the share price is south, and decide to sell its shares short.

a. What is the most you can gain, per share, by selling short?
b. What is the most you can lose, per share, by selling short?

13. The Thomas Corp. has a total value of $5 million, partitioned between debt valued at $2 million and equity valued at $3 million. There are 1.5 million shares outstanding. Total interest on the debt is $400,000. Calculate the cash flow per share to equity if total firm cash flow is $700,000. Repeat the analysis for a total firm cash flow of $405,000.

14. American Graffiti Corporation has 5 million shares outstanding and debt with interest payments of $1.3 million. How much cash flow would the firm need to earn in order to provide a $3.00 cash flow per share to equity?

15. Two firms, With, Inc., and Without, Inc., have assets valued at $20,000 and are similar in every way except that With, Inc., has $5,000 of debt issued at a cost of 10 percent, and Without, Inc., has no debt. With, Inc., has 750 shares outstanding and Without, Inc., has 1,000 shares outstanding. Total cash flow to each firm will either be $0, $2,000, or $4,000. Calculate the cash flow per share to the equity of each firm under each of the three cash flow scenarios.

16. For firms With, Inc., and Without, Inc., in Problem 15 provide a graph of the relationship between cash flow per share to equity (on the *y* or vertical axis) and total cash flow (on the *x* or horizontal axis). Use a solid line for With, Inc., and a dashed line for Without, Inc. What does this graph tell you about leverage and risk to equity holders?

17. Return one last time to firms With, Inc. and Without, Inc. Recall that the firms are identical in every way except that With, Inc., uses debt and Without, Inc., does not. From the information given in Problem 15, calculate the level of total cash flow that will give the same level of cash flow per share to equity for each firm. Verify that your answer is the point where the two lines cross on the graph from problem 16.

18. Giants, Inc., is a successful firm that uses leverage and has assets valued at $1 million. Jets, Inc., is another successful firm similar to Giants except that Jets is unlevered. One evening at a party you overhear a shareholder of Giants telling a shareholder of Jets that his firm is better because it uses debt. Use the concept of homemade leverage to convince this rather obnoxious Giants shareholder that because the assets of the two firms are identical, he would be equally as well off by investing in Jets, Inc. and borrowing.

Set the problem in a way similar to that shown in Table 11.5. That is, assume that Giants, Inc., uses $500,000 of debt at a cost of 10 percent such that interest payments total $50,000. In addition, assume that three cash flow scenarios exist: bad with $50,000, OK with $100,000, and good with $150,000. The first alternative is to purchase 10 percent of the equity in Giants, and the second alternative is to purchase 10 percent of Jets and borrow an amount equal to 10 percent of the debt of Giants.

19. Although Square and Peg appear to be similar corporations, a look at their respective balance sheets will reveal some differences. Square is unlevered with 500 shares outstanding, and Peg has $2,500 of debt at a cost of 10 percent interest and has 250 shares outstanding. You own 5 percent of the equity of Peg.

a. Determine the cash flow from your equity investment in Peg assuming that Peg's total cash flow is $500.

b. Determine the cash flow from equity from the following strategy: Borrow an amount equal to 5 percent of the debt of Peg at 10 percent interest and use the proceeds plus your own money to buy 5 percent of the equity of Square. Assume that Square's total cash flow is $500.

20. Return to the firms Giants, Inc., and Jets, Inc., and that great party you were attending in Problem 18. Now suppose that it is a Jets shareholder who tells a Giants shareholder that his firm is better because it is silly to use debt. Use the concept of homemade unlevering to convince this nice but incorrect Jets shareholder that because the assets of the two firms are identical, he would be equally well off by investing in the equity of Giants and placing the remainder of his or her money in the bank.

Set the problem in a way similar to that shown in Table 11.5. That is, assume that Giants, Inc., uses $500,000 of debt at a cost of 10 percent such that interest payments total $50,000. In addition, assume that three cash flow scenarios exist: bad with $50,000, OK with $100,000, and good with $150,000. The first alternative is to purchase 10 percent of the equity in Jets, and the second alternative is to purchase 10 percent of the equity of Giants and to lend an amount equal to 10 percent of the bonds of Giants.

Discussion Questions

1. Respond to the following statement:

High debt usage by corporations drives up the riskiness of our country's economic base.

2. Respond to the following question:

Highly levered firms outperformed all equity firms in the mid- to late 1980s and underperformed all equity firms in the early 1990s. How can modernists say that debt is irrelevant?

3. Respond to the following question:

   Why are traditionalists incorrect in drawing the required rate of return as bending upward in leverage (a convex shape as shown in Figure 11.4), but modernists are correct in drawing the required rate of return as bending down in leverage (a concave shape as shown in Figure 11.5)?

4. Respond to the following statement:

   There are some financial managers who pay a great deal of attention to the capital structure decision. Capital structure, therefore, is relevant.

5. Respond to the following question:

   Almost all financial analysts view financial leverage as being an extremely important factor when they analyze a firm. How can it be irrelevant?

CHAPTER 12

FINANCING: WHY MIGHT IT MATTER

The firm's top managers are engaged in a power meeting. Everyone has assembled to make a final decision on how the firm will raise the $50,000,000 necessary to finance the acquisition of a small public company.

Three investment banking firms from New York City have submitted proposals. One suggests that the firm issue debt to take advantage of current low interest rates. Another suggests an innovative preferred stock issue because they are in heavy demand by institutions. The final investment banking proposal is for the issuance of common stock because they say this is necessary to prevent the firm's bond rating from deteriorating.

The chief financial officer presents detailed financial analyses to demonstrate the impact of each idea on the firm's earnings per share and financial ratios. Finally, a consensus emerges: The issue needs further study.

This describes a *capital structure decision.* Chapter 11 discussed financial leverage and examined the effect of the firm's capital structure on the value of the firm in perfect markets. It was shown that, in the case of perfect markets, the capital structure decision did not affect firm value and was therefore irrelevant. Any mix of financial securities used to finance the firm's assets is as good as any other mix of securities. Securities simply act to divide or partition the cash flows from the assets.

In this chapter we will examine the firm's capital structure decision in imperfect markets where conditions, most notably taxes, can make capital structure decision a determinant of firm value and therefore shareholder wealth. For example, in some cases, levered capital structures, or capital structures that include debt, act to reduce the firm's total tax payment and are preferred to unlevered capital structures.

The first part of the chapter discusses the potential role of taxes on the choice of capital structure; the second discusses the potential role of other imperfections on the firm's capital structure choice.

The Rationale for Capital Structure Relevance

Chapter 11 detailed the irrelevancy view of capital structure in perfect markets. It was shown that borrowing money was simply selling debt claims on the firm's assets, just as issuing stock is selling equity claims on the firm's assets. Competition would force the sales prices of the debt or equity to be equal to their true values, such that securities would be issued with an *NPV* equal to zero. Because managers cannot increase firm value through issuing securities, the capital structure choice is irrelevant.

The irrelevancy conclusion has important implications. Given that corporate managers are faced with two primary decisions—raising money, or the financing decision, and investing money, or the investment decision—capital structure's irrelevancy suggests that managers should spend most of their time deciding which assets to acquire, and little time deciding how to finance those assets. Further, the concept of capital structure irrelevancy vastly simplifies the theory of how to make optimal investment decisions because capital structure effects can be ignored in the capital budgeting process.

Although the discussion of capital structure in perfect markets was interesting and made things easy, it is now time to bring more real-world situations into our analysis. By "real-world," we mean relaxing some of our previous assumptions by introducing what are known as **market imperfections**. It is important, however, that the effects of these imperfections be developed logically and carefully. This chapter helps the reader deduce the differences between valid reasons and dubious reasons for capital structure relevancy.

market imperfections Conditions related to the operations of markets that violate the assumptions of a perfect market. Examples include the payment of taxes and transactions costs.

The No-Free-Lunch Analogy for Capital Structure Relevance

There is a popular saying in economics—and in everyday life, as well—that there's no such thing as a free lunch. In other words, valuable things always carry a cost; otherwise, they would be free, and people do not regard free things as being valuable, no matter how important they are. This goes for products and services sold in stores, as well as for other kinds of commodities such as air, sunlight, and water.

Let us now apply this economic truth to the debate over capital structure. If someone argues that there is an optimal capital structure—one that maximizes the value of the firm—then the logical question is from where does the value come? In other words, if shareholders receive added wealth in the form of a higher stock price from a particular mix of financial securities, from whence does this value derive? Remember, value must come from somewhere because there are no free lunches.

This chapter will show that because of certain imperfections, there are some logical possibilities as to where wealth could derive, and that a particular financing decision might make shareholders better off. The best example comes from taxes. It is logical to believe that tax laws might exist that would favor one capital structure over another. In this case, a particular tax-saving financial decision might cause wealth to be transferred from the government, or more accurately from taxpayers through the government, to shareholders. In the case of taxes, the cumbersome nature of government, combined with the difficulty of implementing laws that would tax all capital structures equally, makes it plausible that taxes might affect capital structure.

An acceptable theory of why one capital structure is more valuable than another must include both an explanation of where the value comes from as well as why the other participants allow the wealth to be transferred from them.

Example 12.1 ______ The challenge in the argument of capital structure relevancy is to explain where the value comes from as well as why other participants would allow the wealth to be transferred from them. Let us look at this challenge from the standpoint of the three proposals of the investment bankers presented in the opening of the chapter. Do any of these proposals truly provide value to the firm's shareholders?

The first argument was that debt should be used because interest rates are low. This rationale implies that interest rates will soon rise and that the same dollar amount of debt issued later will cost the firm more in interest payments. The logical question, however, is, Why would people willingly purchase the firm's bonds when interest rates are low rather than waiting until interest rates rise? After all, bondholders would surely wish to wait and purchase the bonds after the rates have risen in order to receive the higher interest rate. Would bond investors be so ignorant as to allow the corporation consistently to beat them at an interest rate timing competition? Because we see no logical reason why they would, we dismiss this argument as wishful thinking.

The second argument suggests an innovative preferred stock issue because such stocks are in heavy demand by investors, or, specifically, by certain institutions. The argument implies that the demand is so strong that the preferred stock can be issued to investors at a premium. Why would institutions, however, pay a significant amount of extra money for partitioning the cash flows of the corporation? Could the institutions not find a less expensive way of obtaining the desired characteristics that the preferred stock offers? Would competition from other corporations issuing similar preferred stocks not already have driven down the reward for issuing them? We suspect that you would be very suspicious of such a claim.

Finally, the third proposal is to use a common stock issue to avoid deterioration in the firm's bond rating, which implies that a good bond rating is valuable. At first this sounds believable, but let us take a closer look. What this argument is really saying is that corporations with good credit ratings can borrow money at positive net present values (*NPV*s), whereas corporations with bad credit ratings are confronted with borrowing at negative *NPV*s. If this is true, then it implies that bond investors—those on the other side of the bond issue—consistently accept negative *NPV*s when investing in high-quality bonds and consistently enjoy positive *NPV*s when investing in low-quality bonds. We have never seen evidence that this is how bondholders behave.

None of these proposals by the investment bankers meet our challenge, so we conclude that none of the proposals would increase shareholder wealth. The remainder of the chapter will present the major arguments regarding the relevance of capital structure that have survived logical analysis and scrutiny.

Capital Structure with Corporate Taxes

This section builds a theory of capital structure that includes market imperfections. We begin with taxes. Because the foundation of most of this theory is attributable to the work of Franco Modigliani and Merton Miller (M&M), we will refer to the main analysis of Chapter 11 as M&M without taxes, and will refer to their analysis regarding taxes in this chapter as M&M with taxes.

How Corporate Taxes Are Levied

As discussed in Workshop 2.1, individuals and corporations are taxed on income, and the specific rate of taxation often depends on the income level and residence. The U.S. federal government operates a progressive income tax system, taxing higher income levels at higher marginal tax rates. The levels of progressivity, however, are such that corporations with substantial taxable income are taxed at 34 percent. Because most major corporations have substantial taxable income, most of this chapter we will ignore the lower tax rates and use only 34 percent.

In the discussion in Chapter 2, income refers to taxable income, or revenues less deductible expenses. The firm is permitted to deduct its expenses before it computes its taxes owed, including interest expense, but not including its dividend. It is the ability to deduct interest expense that will drastically alter the results achieved in Chapter 11.

Financial Leverage with Corporate Income Taxes

Let us return to the financial statements of Boring, Inc. and Exciting, Inc. introduced in the previous chapter. Table 12.1 modifies the original analysis to reflect the effect of a 34 percent corporate income tax rate.

The difference between the analysis in Table 12.1 and the corresponding analysis in Chapter 11 is that each corporation must now pay income taxes on profits after interest expense. Because corporations have different amounts of debt, and because interest payments are tax deductible, the otherwise identical corporations pay different amounts of taxes.

Let us now try to replicate the levered firm using homemade leverage as was shown in Chapter 11. Table 12.2 demonstrates the attempt to replicate the equity cash flows from Exciting, Inc. by buying two times the shares of Boring, Inc. using borrowed money. For simplicity we assume that the equity of each firm still sells for $10 per share. Alternative #1 buys the levered stock directly. As before, alternative #2 attempts to replicate the results of alternative #1 using the other corporation's stock.

TABLE 12.1 Leverage and Cash Flow per Share

		Boring, Inc. (1,000 shares)				
State	*Total Cash Flow Before Interest*	*Interest Expense*	*Taxable Income*	*Taxes*	*Net Income*	*After-Tax Equity Cash Flow per Share*
Recession	$ 500	$0	$ 500	$170	$330	$0.33
Normal	$1,000	$0	$1,000	$340	$660	$0.66
Boom	$1,500	$0	$1,500	$510	$990	$0.99

		Exciting, Inc. (500 shares)				
State	*Total Cash Flow Before Interest*	*Interest Expense*	*Taxable Income*	*Taxes*	*Net Income*	*After-Tax Equity Cash Flow per Share*
Recession	$ 500	$500	$ -0-	$ -0-	$ -0-	$ -0-
Normal	$1,000	$500	$ 500	$170	$330	$0.66
Boom	$1,500	$500	$1,000	$340	$660	$1.32

Notice that the final results of the two alternatives in Table 12.2 are not equal, and that homemade leverage no longer works. In a recession, alternative #1 breaks even, while alternative #2 loses $17. Similar results occur in normal conditions and a boom. Each outcome in the homemade leverage alternative, alternative #2, is $17 lower than when the corporation does the borrowing. Borrowing through the corporation is therefore preferred to borrowing through homemade leverage; but where, under homemade leverage, does the $17 go?

The answer is that the $17 went to the government. The decision to use homemade leverage rather than corporate leverage means that the tax savings through the deductibility of interest expense in computing the corporation's taxable income is lost. The $50 interest payment multiplied by the 34 percent tax rate equals the $17 of greater taxes paid using homemade leverage.

Modigliani and Miller demonstrated that, when corporate taxes are introduced, there is a tax advantage to using debt, and the optimal capital structure decision is to use as much debt as possible—even up to 100 percent or all debt!

Example 12.2 Let us imagine a corporation set up by one person who has a great idea about a new way to manufacture a product that cleans props, known as Prop Wash. The paperwork, or articles of incorporation, has been filed, but, as of now, the firm does not have any significant assets, liabilities, or equity.

Suppose that the firm wishes to raise $1 million in order to begin the project of demonstrating the new Prop Wash manufacturing process. Because the project will take advantage of a new and valuable technology, it may be reasonable to assume that the value of the firm's assets with the project will rise to $1.5 million. In other words, the project has an *NPV* of $500,000. The

TABLE 12.2 Homemade Leverage with Corporate Income Taxes

Alternative #1: Corporate Leverage

Buy 10% of Exciting, Inc. Equity for $500 (50 shares).

Cash Flow—Recession	50 shares × $0.00 = $ 0.00
Cash Flow—Normal Conditions	50 shares × $0.66 = $33.00
Cash Flow—Boom	50 shares × $1.32 = $66.00

Alternative #2: Homemade Leverage

Buy 10% of Boring, Inc. Equity Using $500 of Borrowed Money *plus* $500 of Original Money (100 shares).

Cash Flow—Recession	Equity	$33.00	($0.33 × 100 shares)
	Borrowing	−$50.00	
	Net Cash Flow	−$17.00	
Cash Flow—Normal	Equity	$66.00	($0.66 × 100 shares)
	Borrowing	−$50.00	
	Net Cash Flow	$16.00	
Cash Flow—Boom	Equity	$99.00	($0.99 × 100 shares)
	Borrowing	−$50.00	
	Net Cash Flow	$49.00	

$1.5 million represents the present value of the project's total cash flow stream, ignoring taxes, which are projected to be $150,000 per year forever. (We found this using a discount rate of 10 percent and applying the perpetuity formula.) Because the cash flow is earned year after year forever, its present value is determined by dividing the cash flow by the discount rate.

The individual who set up the corporation has the needed $1 million in his personal bank account and is considering whether the money should be moved inside the firm as equity or debt. Remember, no one else is involved. The investor is simply deciding what paperwork is best for tax purposes. The only difference is that if the money were to be called debt, then the firm would be able to pay out cash in the form of interest expense—which for tax purposes would be deductible from income.

Under perfect markets it would make no difference whether the money was contributed as debt or equity; however, with corporate income taxes paid at a rate of 34 percent, the after-tax cash flow stream will depend on whether debt or equity is used. Let us look at the two alternatives: equity and debt.

Calling the Contribution Equity If the $1 million is contributed as equity, then the corporation's annual cash flow of $150,000 would be fully taxable. The corporation's after-tax income would drop to $99,000, as the tax bill on $150,000 of income is $51,000. The value of the equity would be the present value of $99,000 per year forever, which is $990,000. Thus, the present value of the benefits, $990,000, is less than the present value of the costs—$1 million—and the project is unacceptable.

Calling the Contribution Debt If, instead, the $1 million is contributed as debt, and if the cost of debt is 10 percent, then the corporation would incur an interest expense of $100,000 per year. The firm would earn a before-tax profit of $50,000, calculated by taking the $150,000 of cash flow and subtracting $100,000 in interest expense. The after-tax profit, after applying a tax rate of 34 percent, would be $33,000 per year. Applying the perpetuity formula, the value of the equity would be $330,000.

Of course, the investor also owns debt securities. The investor's debt holdings would result in $100,000 per year in interest income, and this perpetuity would be worth $1 million. The value of both the equity and debt securities is $1.33 million. Thus, the present value of the benefits, $1.33 million is greater than the present value of the costs, $1 million, and the project is acceptable.

Summary of Financial Leverage and Corporate Taxation

We return to the question being considered in the Prop Wash example—whether funds should be brought into the corporation as equity or debt. If the $1 million investment is contributed as equity, the value of the equity holdings is $990,000. If the $1 million is contributed as debt, the value of the debt claim plus the value of the equity claim is $1.33 million. The difference of $340,000 results from a $34,000 tax reduction, per year forever, as a result of the use of debt.

Illustrating Financial Leverage and Taxes with an M&M Proposition

In the Prop Wash example, the present value of the tax reduction through the use of debt, or $340,000, is equal to the corporate tax rate of 34 percent multiplied by the value of the debt, or $1 million. This concept is expressed in the following famous proposition introduced by M&M:

$$V_L = V_U + (T_C \times D) \tag{12.1}$$

where:

V_L = the value of a levered firm,

V_U = the value of an unlevered firm,

T_C = the corporate income tax rate, and

D = the value of the permanent debt.

This equation shows that the value of a levered firm is equal to the value of an unlevered firm plus the tax shield from debt.

Let us go through the M&M proposition for the Prop Wash example. If the individual uses equity capital by calling the $1 million contribution stock, then the value of the firm will be $990,000. This is V_U in Formula (12.1) because the firm would be unlevered. The second part of the formula measures the present value of the tax savings that from Formula (12.1) is given by:

$$\text{Tax Shield from Debt} = (34\% \times \$1{,}000{,}000) = \$340{,}000,$$

and the total value of the levered firm is:

$$\$1{,}330{,}000 = \$990{,}000 + \$340{,}000.$$

Thus, the unlevered firm has a value of only $990,000 and would not be worth the $1 million investment required. However, the $34,000 of annual tax savings produces a present value of $340,000 of perpetual tax savings, which gives the levered firm a value of $1.33 million.

Where Does the Extra Value of Leverage Come From? At first, Formula (12.1) gives the impression that debt adds to the value of the firm by providing a tax shield. Whereas this is true in some sense, it seems to imply that the government subsidizes corporate shareholders who use debt. A better way of viewing the tax advantage of leverage could be that the use of debt really only reduces the amount of money the government takes from the equityholders. Remember, without taxes, the project had an *NPV* of $500,000. With taxes, the project had an *NPV* of either -$10,000 or +$330,000, depending upon whether the original $1 million is used as debt or equity. Leverage, therefore, can reduce taxes.

Regardless of how the story is viewed, the moral is clear. There is a tax penalty to using equity in the M&M corporate income tax model, and there is no tax penalty to using debt. The optimal capital structure is to use as much debt as possible so that the government's claim is minimized, thereby transferring the least amount of wealth from the equityholders to the government.

In the M&M income tax model there is a tax advantage to debt, and the optimal capital structure approaches 100 percent debt.

Are Firms Fully Levered? A funny thing happened in the 25 or so years after M&M propositions were developed and refined: There did not seem to be a wild rush by corporations to take on more and more debt in order to take maximum advantage of the tax shield claimed by M&M. Some firms may have fully understood the advantage to debt before the M&M work was published, but, even so, most corporations were far short of 100 percent debt.[1] Thus, it appears that the M&M model with taxes does not explain completely how firms make the capital structure choice.

[1]Of course, a firm that is 100 percent debt financed would be "owned" by the debtholders. In this case, the IRS would likely treat the capital as equity.

The Miller Tax Model

Miller tax model
A theory of capital structure, attributed to Merton Miller, that assumes that the tax advantage to debt at the corporate level is offset by the tax disadvantage to debt at the personal level.

In 1977, Merton Miller proposed an alternative model that included personal taxes in addition to corporate taxes—or income taxes on individuals. This model is known as the **Miller tax model.** Within this model, Miller argued that the tax advantage to debt at the corporate level was actually offset by the tax disadvantage to debt at the personal level. The result in the Miller tax model is that capital structure is once again irrelevant.

> In the Miller tax model, the tax advantages to debt at the corporate tax level are offset by the tax disadvantages to debt at the individual income tax level, such that capital structure is irrelevant to firm value and shareholder wealth.

The crux of Miller's argument rests on the idea that the income tax laws for individuals tend to place a higher tax on interest income received from debt than they do on dividend plus capital gain income received from equity. The reason personal income tax laws provide relief to equityholders is the belief that equityholders are taxed twice—once at the corporate level and once at the individual level. This double taxation of dividends led to tax breaks for equityholders to alleviate the burden. In effect, Miller argued that the tax breaks allowed to lessen the burden of double taxation could be used so vigorously that the personal tax on equity was tremendously reduced. This considerable tax advantage to equity at the personal level fully offsets the government's tax penalty on equity at the corporate level.

Miller developed an equation to describe the value of a levered firm that introduced tax rates on individual income from debt and equity:

$$V_L = V_U + \left[1 - \frac{(1 - T_C)(1 - T_E)}{(1 - T_D)}\right] D \tag{12.2}$$

where:

V_L = the value of a levered firm,

V_U = the value of an unlevered firm,

T_C = the corporate income tax rate,

T_E = the individual tax rate on equity income,

T_D = the individual tax rate on debt income, and

D = the value of the permanent debt.

Formula (12.2) expresses the value of the levered firm as the value of the unlevered firm plus the value of the tax shield.

Notice the difference between the Miller tax model and the M&M with taxes model. By introducing personal taxes, which are given in the model by

T_E and T_D, the increase in firm value related to debt financing is not simply $T_C \times D$. Instead, T_C is replaced by the bracketed expression:

$$\left[1 - \frac{(1 - T_C)(1 - T_E)}{(1 - T_D)}\right]$$

The tax advantage to debt is defined by this bracketed expression multiplied by the amount of debt, or D in Formula (12.2). In Miller's model, the tax advantage to debt is reduced as long as T_E is less than T_D.

There are two extreme cases to Miller's model. First, if individual income tax rates, both T_D and T_E, are set equal to zero or are set equal to each other, then Formula (12.2) simplifies to being identical to Formula (12.1), the M&M model with taxes. (You may prove this to yourself by substituting and simplifying.) In other words, when personal tax rates are such that there is no personal tax disadvantage to debt, then the effect of debt is the same as in the original M&M model.

Second, when the differences in the tax rates are such that:

$$(1 - T_D) = (1 - T_C) \times (1 - T_E)$$

then Formula (12.2) reduces to $V_L = V_U$, which means that capital structure returns to being irrelevant! In other words, this is the Miller tax model discussed earlier, where there is no net tax advantage to debt. You may check this by inserting the right-hand side of the formula above in place of $(1 - T_D)$ in Formula (12.2) and simplifying.

Prop Wash and the Miller Tax Model

We return to our Prop Wash example to illustrate the conditions given by the Miller model. Suppose that the individual who set up the firm was in the 34 percent tax bracket for interest income, such that $T_D = .34$, but was able to shelter equity income such that the equity income was tax free at the individual income tax level in a present value sense. With tax-free equity income, the variable T_E in Formula (12.2) is equal to zero. Because the tax rate on corporate income, given by T_C, is 34 percent, the tax advantage to debt vanishes.

You recall from the Prop Wash example that the issue was whether the person should contribute $1 million in the form of equity or debt. We found that when equity financing was used, the value of the firm was $990,000, but when debt financing was used the value was $1.33 million. Let us now introduce personal taxation. We do this by switching to the Miller tax model. The individual's tax bill now must include the $100,000 of interest on the debt. Given the 34 percent personal tax rate on debt interest, new taxes of $34,000 are collected, and the present value of the $34,000 tax perpetuity is $340,000. When this personal tax liability from debt is subtracted from the $1.33 million firm value, the result is $990,000. This is the same as it was without debt and therefore proves the result of the Miller tax model, which is that debt usage is irrelevant to firm value. The new value of the levered firm can be shown using Miller's equation:

$$\$990{,}000 = \$990{,}000 + \left[1 - \frac{(1 - .34)(1 - .00)}{(1 - .34)}\right] \$1{,}000{,}000,$$

This equation illustrates that the value of the firm under these conditions is the same with or without the use of debt, and that the capital structure choice is irrelevant.

We have analyzed the Miller tax model under two extreme cases—one that produces no tax advantage to debt and another that creates a situation in which the firm should be 100 percent debt financed. Of course, the more likely situation is somewhere between these two extreme cases. When the individual tax rate on debt is greater than the individual tax rate on equity such that T_D is greater than T_E, the gain to the firm from using leverage decreases. Thus, the importance of Miller's model depends on the prevailing corporate and personal tax rates. Window 12.1 details the current corporate and personal tax structure as it relates to Miller's model.

Another illustration of the Miller tax model can be found by inserting personal taxes into the example of homemade leverage using Boring, Inc. and Exciting, Inc. Recall that when corporate tax rates were considered, homemade leverage failed to replicate corporate leverage because the corporate tax advantage to debt was lost. Table 12.3 illustrates the combined effects of corporate and personal taxes on homemade leverage assuming that the personal tax rate on debt income is 34 percent, the personal tax rate on equity income is 0 percent, and the corporate tax rate remains at 34 percent.

Table 12.3 shows that the individual receives the same after-tax net cash flow whether corporate or homemade leverage is used. The shareholder's tax advantage of using debt at the corporate level can now be achieved using personal tax savings. This illustrates the Miller tax model result of capital structure irrelevancy because corporate capital structure decisions are rendered useless by the ability of individuals to repartition the firm.

Which Model Is Better: M&M or Miller?

As we have stated, the M&M with taxes model argues that there is a large tax advantage to using debt. The Miller argument is that this tax advantage at the corporate level is offset by the tax disadvantage to debt at the personal level.

Numerous studies have failed to establish either model as being correct. The view for now could be that the tax advantage to debt at the corporate level is at least partially offset by tax disadvantages to debt at the personal level. Viewed together, perhaps there is a small tax advantage to debt. There are other imperfections, however, that will be discussed throughout the remainder of this chapter. There could be certain other disadvantages to debt that offset any remaining tax advantage.

WINDOW 12.1

Current Income Tax Rates and the Miller Model

The Miller tax model introduces the potential disadvantage to investing in debt when considering personal taxes on debt income. In its purest form, Miller's model shows that the personal tax disadvantage completely offsets the corporate tax advantage of debt such that the capital structure decision is once again irrelevant. This window provides some detail into the U.S. tax code and how it relates to Miller's model.

The Tax Reform Act (TRA) of 1986 had a significant impact on the variables contained in the Miller model, most notably the removal of much of the distinction between the personal tax rate on ordinary income and the personal tax rate on long-term capital gains. The full reintroduction of this tax break is proposed and debated each year and is currently included for federal income tax purposes. Some people argue that the 1986 changes removed much of the punch of the Miller tax model.

There are personal tax advantages to owning stocks rather than bonds, such that personal taxes act to reduce the total tax advantage to debt. One advantage is that because the gains from holding stocks are taxed when the stocks are sold, stock investors can set the time when they want to declare profits. Wise investors can carefully time the sale of their stocks to minimize total taxes. Another is that long term capital gains are taxed at significantly lower rates. Let us take a closer look at how stock investors can minimize or even eliminate personal income taxes on their equity holdings in this way.

Consider an investor who has $100,000 to invest in stocks. Stocks tend to pay a portion of their return in the form of dividends, or distributions of current earnings to shareholders, and perhaps a larger portion in price appreciation as profits are retained and reinvested. Suppose, further, that the investor buys $100,000 worth of stock and borrows money (see the use of margin in Window 11.5) to purchase additional stock. The amount of money borrowed is such that each year the total interest expense on the margin borrowing approximately equals the amount of dividends received on all the stocks.

Each year the investor expects that some stocks will go down and that (ideally) most will go up. Each year the investor sells only those stocks that have gone down—and only enough to be able to declare the maximum allowable $3,000 loss for personal income taxes. If the investor does not need cash, then the money from the proceeds of the sale of stock is used to buy more stock. If the investor needs even more cash, then the stocks that have not gone up or down can be sold without incurring any income tax. Notice that the investor is not really losing on the total portfolio by selling the stocks that fell, but is simply recognizing only the losses for tax reasons. There may be tremendous profits occurring elsewhere in the portfolio.

Finally, many years later, the investor will be left with the winners—the stocks that have gone up a great deal. In order to minimize the income tax on selling these winners, the investor may (1) time the sales for those years in which income or tax rates are low, say in retirement, (2) hold the stocks until death and pass the stocks to beneficiaries such that no taxes are ever paid on the gain, or (3) donate the stocks to a charity in lieu of cash (if the investor were going to donate cash anyway). Thus, whether the investor

WINDOW 12.1 *(continued)*

turns out to be rich, poor, or dies early, even the profitable stocks will not cause a big income tax liability.

Notice that the investor enjoys many early years of being able to benefit tremendously from an annual tax loss of $3,000. The tax on dividend income is eliminated by the deductibility of the margin interest expense. Finally, the investor might realize ultimate profits in a way that causes little or no taxes.

In a present value sense, the investor might even be able to have a negative net tax liability. At a minimum, it should be recognized that common stocks offer personal income tax advantages.

Bankruptcy and Capital Structure

The traditional view of bankruptcy notes that bankruptcy most often occurs when cash flows from the firm's assets are insufficient to cover the cash expenses—including the cash flows owed to the firm's debtholders. Thus, bankruptcy is often viewed as being bad. Because using lots of debt can increase the probability of bankruptcy, it is often surmised that using too much debt is bad.

TABLE 12.3 Homemade Leverage with Corporate and Personal Taxes

Alternative #1: Corporate Leverage

Buy 10 percent of Exciting, Inc. Equity for $500 (50 shares)

	Recession	*Normal*	*Boom*
Pretax cash flow	$0.00	$33.00	$66.00
Personal taxes*	-0-	-0-	-0-
After-tax cash flow	$0.00	$33.00	$66.00

Alternative #2: Homemade Leverage

Buy 10 percent of Boring, Inc. Equity Using $500 of Borrowed Money *plus* $500 of Original Money (100 shares)

	Recession	*Normal*	*Boom*
Pretax cash flow	$33.00	$66.00	$99.00
Interest expense	−$50.00	−$50.00	−$50.00
Tax shield on borrowing†	$17.00	$17.00	$17.00
After-tax cash flow	$0.00	$33.00	$66.00

*The personal tax on equity is assumed to be zero.

†Assumes that the individual can deduct $50 interest expense when filing personal tax returns. Tax rate is 34 percent.

The modernist view recognizes that bankruptcy is a legal event and does not destroy or create value. Ignoring legal costs and in well-functioning markets, proponents of this view therefore, do not perceive increased chances of bankruptcy as a reason to restrain the use of debt.

To provide an analogy, some people hate being in hospitals—perhaps because it brings up memories of their previous pain or that of a loved one. Would it be logical, therefore, for them to move to an extremely remote part of the world where it would be virtually impossible to make use of a hospital? The answer is clearly, *no.* The individuals do not really hate hospitals; they really hate the pain associated with events necessitating hospital visits. Avoiding the hospital will not reduce the amount of pain. The fact is that hospitals actually reduce long-term pain.

Bankruptcy itself is similarly not value-destroying or painful—it is a legal event. The pain associated with bankruptcy is actually a result of the operational losses that are occurring, and bankruptcy does not cause these losses. Equityholders should view bankruptcy as a tool—not as a disaster—and a useful tool at that. In fact, if the shareholders truly believe that the chance of the firm going bankrupt is zero, then they should consider a different organizational form, such as a partnership, as there may be tax benefits to partnerships not enjoyed by corporations.

The idea that bankruptcy is the friend of an equityholder becomes clearer when one realizes that bankruptcy is what a corporation declares in order to protect its shareholders from being liable for the debts of the corporation. Alternatively, bankruptcy is a legal tool that an equityholder can use when confronted with unpaid creditors, expensive union contracts, massive lawsuits, high property taxes, and so forth. The financial news abounds with examples of major corporations that are using bankruptcy as a tool to benefit shareholders. In fact, when a major firm declares bankruptcy, the value of its equity usually rises.

Example 12.3 ________ Consider two firms: TTMAR, Inc. (Take the Money and Run) and NSS (Not So Swift) Partners. Both firms have identical assets of land, equipment, and cash that will permit the development of a gold mine. TTMAR, Inc. is organized as a corporation—giving its owners limited liability. NSS Partners is a partnership in which all partners bear unlimited liability.

TTMAR, Inc. begins the venture in earnest. Money is borrowed, long-term union contracts are signed, and reasonable amounts of insurance are purchased. The owners feel that if they strike gold, there will be plenty of money to pay the interest expense and labor costs; however, they also know their losses are limited. If they fail to strike gold, they simply declare bankruptcy—or perhaps they can threaten to declare bankruptcy, so that creditors will wait and union officials will renegotiate contracts while further exploration of recovery is under way.

NSS Partners is in a different situation. Although all will be well if they strike gold, they fear that they will not strike gold, and that a serious accident, such as a mine collapse, will wipe out the assets of the company and expose every investor to losing all of his or her personal wealth. Imagine losing your house, your pension, and everything else you own simply because a firm that you invested in failed and you did not invest with limited liability.

TTMAR, Inc. and NSS PARTNERS illustrate the value and importance of being able to declare corporate bankruptcy. It should be noted, however, that bankruptcy rules do not provide protection in cases of fraud or for corporate officers or shareholders involved in management.

Bankruptcy and Option Theory

Chapter 10, on option theory, discussed the idea that equity can be viewed as a call option on the firm's assets. Option theory can be an important tool in understanding the effects of corporate bankruptcy. If the assets of a corporation have value greater than the face value of the firm's debt, the equityholders will exercise their option, pay off the debtholders, and claim the residual cash flow. If the assets have insufficient value when a debt payment is due, then the equityholders can simply let their option expire—in other words, declare bankruptcy.

One of the important points of Chapter 10 was that the value of an option increases as the volatility of the underlying asset increases. In terms of the equity of a corporation, this means that the equity of a firm with substantial debt will increase in value if the firm increases the riskiness of its assets. This is an important point embodying the essence of option theory and bankruptcy.

Let us consider the effects on debtholders and shareholders of a levered firm that substantially increases the riskiness of its assets. The debtholders will receive their promised payments only if the assets do not fall too much in value, so if the assets' value substantially decreases, the debtholders stand to lose. Thus, if the riskiness of the firm's assets is increased, the value of the debt must fall. The value of the assets, however, is still the same—only their risk has changed. Thus, the loss in value to the bondholders flows as a gain to the stockholders. The stockholders gain because the greater risk has increased their profit potential, whereas limited liability has protected them from potential losses.

In summary, an increase in the risk of the assets of a firm will cause the value of the equity to rise and the value of the debt to fall. This is a direct wealth transfer from those who do not have the option, the debtholders, to those who own the option, the equityholders. Debtholders are of course smart enough to understand the potential for this wealth loss and will likely take steps to protect themselves.

For example, would a person with assets currently worth \$50,000 take a gamble of flipping a coin to win or lose \$50,000? Most of us would agree that the gamble would be foolish, for reasons fully developed in Chapter 8. Suppose that the person could set up a corporation with \$10,000, however, and take the gamble through the corporation. If the corporation wins the flip, then the investor gains \$50,000 through his or her ownership of the corporation. If the corporation loses the flip, however, then bankruptcy can be declared, and the person will lose only $10,000. Most people would agree that this is an excellent risk because the $50,000 of profit potential remains, but the loss potential has been reduced to $10,000 by the limited liability that corporations have through bankruptcy. It would, of course, be difficult to find somebody foolish enough to offer such a gamble to this corporation.

Risky Projects and the Games Shareholders Can Play

Consider a stockholder of a corporation called Dewey, Cheatum, and Howe, which manufactures fish scalers. The chief economist is predicting that the firm faces extremely volatile times ahead—either sales and profits will skyrocket or they will plummet, based upon a number of economywide and industry factors.

The firm has a substantial amount of debt, a very long-term and expensive union contract, high property taxes, and a potentially huge legal liability revolving around a test case now being tried. At this time there are two proposals the firm is considering: (1) a safe proposal and (2) a risky proposal.

Those advocating the safe proposal argue that, with such difficulties and uncertainties ahead, the firm should prepare itself for potential disaster by issuing lots of stock, using half of the money to pay off all of the debtholders and keeping the other half of the money in low-risk, cash-equivalent securities in order to be protected from future disasters. They note that this strategy will best guarantee the survival of the firm.

Those advocating the risky proposal take the opposite position. They suggest that all available cash be sent immediately to the shareholders as a cash distribution or dividend, arguing that in the next few years it will be revealed whether the firm will enjoy massive profits or losses. If there are profits, then they can be shared among the equityholders. Because there would be fewer equityholders under this proposal, each will receive a huge wealth increase. (Note that debt expenses and labor costs are already locked in.) On the other hand, if the firm begins to experience massive losses, then they can always declare bankruptcy. The huge upside potential profit, therefore, dwarfs the downside potential losses. Further, if times get really tough, then perhaps the firm can bluff bankruptcy and use the lack of cash as a reason to negotiate cost savings with the union, the people suing them, the local tax authorities, and even the creditors.

As a shareholder, which proposal would you support? Option theory teaches us that in cases such as these there is tremendous incentive to use bankruptcy potential to transfer wealth from other people to a firm's shareholders. If bondholders, unions, and legal claimants prefer the safe proposal because they are more likely to benefit, as long as assets remain constant, then stockholders must prefer the risky proposal.

In some cases, however, there may be costs attached to an increased potential for bankruptcy that would affect the decision. Perhaps if Dewey, Cheatum, and Howe accept the high-risk proposal, then the firm would suffer significantly by losing key employees who might seek long-term employment potential with other firms, or would lose large customers who do not want to depend upon a firm that is near bankruptcy. If consumer confidence in a firm's ability to continue its product lines, for example computers or cars, is low, then it may be extremely difficult to attract and retain distributors and customers.

Summary of Bankruptcy and Capital Structure

The point of this section on bankruptcy is that, although debt may increase the probability of bankruptcy, that, by itself, is not necessarily a bad thing from the shareholder's perspective. In fact, bankruptcy laws protect shareholders and should be used wisely. It is possible that some firms will find that they can make their shareholders better off by using debt and by taking advantage of bankruptcy laws. If shareholders are better off, then it must be that some other group is made worse off. What group allows themselves to be taken advantage of by shareholders using bankruptcy laws?

Bondholders are smart people who will likely go to great lengths to protect themselves from being taken advantage of by shareholders. For instance, bondholders place restrictions on the firm when it borrows in the form of provisions written into the bond contract, or by demanding a high interest rate up front to offset such risks. Equityholders attempting to use bankruptcy and capital structure to maximize shareholder wealth will therefore probably not be successful in transferring wealth from new bondholders.

Other groups, however, may not be so well protected. Labor unions, for example, tend to allow themselves to be put into positions in which bankruptcy laws can be used against them to void contracts. Local governments and even the federal government may find themselves subsidizing firms that are so large that their failure is deemed to be contrary to the public good. Legal claimants can clearly be hurt by the use of bankruptcy by corporations.

The total effect on shareholder wealth from high leverage and its resulting bankruptcy potential will depend upon individual circumstances. The bottom line on our bankruptcy discussion is that capital structure may matter in certain extreme cases in which bankruptcy laws can cause wealth transfers to or from shareholders. The key is to look carefully for transfers of wealth that may occur.

Transactions Costs, Agency Costs, and Information Signaling

There are numerous and lengthy issues concerning capital structure that go beyond taxes and bankruptcy costs. We will briefly explore a few of them in this section.

transactions costs
The costs associated with issuing or trading securities such as debt and equity.

Transactions costs, such as the costs of issuing debt and equity or the cost of using homemade leverage, can make capital structure relevant. For small firms, the transactions cost of obtaining capital can be huge. It seems clear, however, that for a major firm with access to the U.S. financial markets there is far more money to be made for shareholders by making wise investment decisions than by attempting to minimize aggregate transactions cost by adjusting the firm's capital structure.

agency costs
The costs involved whenever one person hires another person to perform a task.

Agency costs are involved whenever one person hires another person to perform a task. Individuals obviously attempt to do what they perceive is best for their interests. The person doing the hiring is called the *principal,* and the person hired is called the *agent.* In the case of corporate finance, the principal is usually the shareholder and the agent is the firm's management. Agency costs are involved because the manager's objectives differ from the principal's objectives.

In capital structure analysis, debtholders enter as a third party. The debtholders have still another objective—maximizing the probability that they will be paid. As is obvious from the section on bankruptcy, this objective may run counter to the objectives of the shareholders. Some capital structure arguments are based upon the costs involved in these conflicts. This chapter will not explore these issues, but there will be a rather substantial discussion of agency costs and dividends in Chapter 13.

information signaling
An action taken by the management of a firm that conveys information.

Finally, it is important to realize that the firm's capital structure decisions may involve **information signaling** to the market—causing security prices to change even if the capital structure decision itself does not change true shareholder wealth. For example, if a firm issues debt rather than stock, then its stock price might rise. This is because it might signal that the firm's managers believe that the stock is underpriced and therefore do not wish to issue new stock. It could also signal that the firm is doing very well and needs some tax benefits from debt. The theories and models are numerous and complex.

Some people argue that information signaling is a reason that firms make capital structure decisions. That argument is controversial, but most agree that capital structure decisions do, in fact, signal information whether or not information signaling was the reason for the decisions.

Wrapping Up

We began with the question: Can the financing decision affect the value of the firm? After two chapters of analysis we are still left without a definitive answer to this question.

Let us summarize what we have learned. First, while financial leverage does not change the total amount of risk to the firm, it does cause the risk of the assets to be partitioned into equity risk and debt risk. At low levels of financial leverage, the risk is borne principally by the equityholders. At high levels of financial leverage, the increased risk is shared by both the equityholders and the debtholders. Whereas we cannot determine the point at which the debtholders begin to share "too much" risk, we can point out that debt usage differs significantly across industries. As shown in Table 12.4, financial leverage, measured by the ratio of long-term debt to equity, is as

TABLE 12.4 Debt Usage Across Industry—2000

Industry	*Long-Term Debt To Equity Ratio*
Technology	7%
Major Drugs	21%
Iron and Steel	68%
Aerospace & Defense	71%
Electric Utilities	145%
Airline	155%

Source: Yahoo Finance

low as 7 percent for the technology industry, and as high as 155 percent for the airline industry. This evidence suggests that different industries and different groups of assets can support different amounts of debt.

The system of taxing business income at the federal level provides an incentive for taking on debt. Because the interest payments from debt are tax deductible, firms with debt in their capital structures pay less tax, leaving more after-tax cash flow compared with identical unlevered firms. The system for taxing shareholders and bondholders at the personal level, however, may provide a disincentive for investing in debt. If the personal tax on interest income from debt is high relative to the personal tax on income from stock, then the tax advantage to debt at the corporate level may be completely eliminated by the tax disadvantage to debt at the personal level.

Last, transactions costs, agency costs, and information signaling may provide situations whereby financial leverage will affect firm value.

Whereas finance does not offer an unambiguous answer to the question of capital structure, it does offer useful insights. The well-trained financial manager should understand the logical method of approaching such issues on behalf of the shareholders rather than expecting to apply a simple universal formula to generate an optimal capital structure. Understanding the discussions in this chapter is a starting point for developing the ability to think clearly through these issues.

Summary

- This chapter examines the firm's capital structure decision in imperfect markets. Given certain market imperfections, most notably taxes, it was demonstrated that capital structure can affect firm value and therefore shareholder wealth.
- An acceptable theory of why one capital structure is more valuable than another must include an explanation of both where the value comes from and why the other participants allow the wealth to be transferred from them.
- Modigliani and Miller, in their M&M with taxes model, demonstrated that when corporate taxes are introduced, there is a tax advantage to using debt.

- The Miller tax model adds to corporate taxes the payment of personal taxes, or income taxes on individuals. Within this model, Miller argued that the tax advantage to debt at the corporate level was actually offset by the tax disadvantage to debt at the personal level. The result, in the Miller tax model, is that capital structure returns to being irrelevant.
- Although debt may increase the probability of bankruptcy, that by itself is not necessarily a bad thing from the shareholder's perspective. It is possible that some firms will find that they can make their shareholders better off by using debt and by taking advantage of bankruptcy laws.
- The total effect on shareholder wealth from high leverage and its resulting bankruptcy potential will depend upon individual circumstances. Although bondholders will likely protect themselves from the use of bankruptcy, other groups may not be so well protected. Labor unions, for example, tend to allow themselves to be put into positions in which bankruptcy laws can be used against them to void contracts. Local governments and even the federal government may find themselves subsidizing firms that are so large that their failure is deemed to be contrary to the public good.

Reference

Miller, M. H. "Debt and Taxes," *Journal of Finance* 32(May 1977), 261–276.

Demonstration Problems

Problem 1

Return to Lindross Salvage Corporation introduced in the Chapter 11 Demonstration Problems. Recall that Lindross Salvage Corporation is an all-equity (unlevered) corporation with $10 million in assets and whose performance varies from producing a loss of $1 million per year to producing a profit of $3 million per year.

In Chapter 11, the use of homemade leverage and homemade unleverage was demonstrated in a perfect market. Using a corporate tax rate of 40% and no personal taxes (an M&M tax world), compare the after-tax returns between a $1 million investment in unlevered Lindross Salvage Corporation using homemade leverage and a $1 million direct investment in Lindross Salvage Corporation in which Lindross Salvage Corporation switches to a capital structure with $3 million of debt and $7 million of equity (assume that all debt has an interest rate of 5%).

Solution to Problem 1

The problem suggests that the homemade leverage computations in Chapter 11 be performed in the presence of corporate taxation of 40 percent. We first compute the after-tax performance of a direct investment in a levered firm and then, in Steps 2 and 3, we find the after-tax performance of homemade leverage.

Step 1: First, the after-tax performance of the levered firm is found. The after-tax profit or loss net of interest expense is found by subtracting the corporate taxes from the profit or loss that was shown in Chapter 11 for the case of no taxes.

	Low Outcome	*High Outcome*
Profit before interest and taxes:	$−1,000,000	$+3,000,000
less: Interest	$ 150,000	$ 150,000
Profit before taxes:	$−1,150,000	$+2,850,000
less: Taxes	$ 460,000	$ 1,140,000
Net profit	$ −690,000	$+1,710,000
Return to levered firm shareholders	−9.857%	+24.429%

The third line can be taken directly from the solution in Chapter 11. The fourth line represents taxes at 40%. Federal income tax laws allow certain losses in certain years to offset taxable profits in other years. The final line expresses the profit or loss as a percentage return to the equity investor, assuming that there is $7 million of equity. Notice that income taxes are computed after interest has been deducted.

The percentage returns can be multiplied by $1 million to obtain the range of profits and losses for the investor from directly investing in the levered firm:

	Low Outcome	*High Outcome*
Profit or loss to $1,000,000 investment	$−98,570	$+244,290

Step 2: Compute the after-tax returns to shareholders in the unlevered firm when the firm is taxed at 40%.

	Low Outcome	*High Outcome*
Profit before interest and taxes:	$−1,000,000	$+3,000,000
less: Taxes	$ 400,000	$ 1,200,000
Net profit	$ −600,000	$+1,800,000
Return to levered firm shareholders	−6.000%	+18.000%

Notice that the corporate taxes directly reduce the magnitude of each return by 40% for the unlevered firm.

Step 3: Next, the range of rates of return for homemade leverage is determined. Recall that in the solution to Demonstration Problem 2 in Chapter 11, it was established that homemade leverage would require the investor to borrow money and invest in an unlevered firm. To be specific, we found:

$$\text{Amount Borrowed} = \$1{,}000{,}000 \times 42.86\% = \$428{,}571.$$

Thus, the total investment by the investor is given as:

Original Funds = $1,000,000 (70%)
Borrowed Funds = $ 428,571 (30%)
Total Invested = $1,428,571 (100%)

The returns to the homemade leverage strategy are found by applying the returns in step 2 to the previous investment ($1,428,571) in the unlevered firm and subtracting the interest expense on the borrowed money ($428,571 at 5% per year).

	Low Outcome −6%	*High Outcome* +18%
Total funds in unlevered firm ($1,428,571) times outcome	$ −85,714	$257,143
Interest expense of borrowed funds ($428,571) at 5%	−21,428	−21,428
Total profit or loss	$−107,142	$235,715

Final Solution: Notice that the outcomes from direct investment in a levered firm ($−98,570 and $+244,290) differ from the outcomes using homemade leverage ($−107,142 and $235,715). The difference is that homemade leverage produces approximately $8,572 less cash in each outcome. This is due to the lost tax deduction because the interest payment is deductible for the levered firm but not deductible to the individual using homemade leverage. We can verify the lost tax deduction as the amount of interest expense ($21,428) timcs thc tax rate (40%).

Problem 2

Repeat Problem 1 using a Miller tax world. To be specific, using a corporate tax rate of 40 percent, a personal income tax rate of 0 percent on equity income, and a personal tax rate on interest income of 40 percent, compare the after-tax returns between a $1 million homemade leverage investment in unlevered Lindross Salvage Corporation and a $1 million direct investment in Lindross Salvage Corporation in which Lindross Salvage Corporation switches to a capital structure with $3 million of debt and $7 million of equity (assume that all debt has an interest rate of 5%).

Solution to Problem 2

We repeat the solution performed in Problem 1, except that we incorporate personal income taxes. Any interest paid by the investor can be deducted from his or her personal tax returns; however, equity income to the investor is not taxed. We first compute the after-tax performance of a direct investment in a levered firm and then, in Steps 2 and 3, we find the after-tax performance of homemade leverage.
Step 1: First, we note that the after-tax performance to the investor of a direct investment in the levered firm is exactly the same as was found for an M&M tax world. In other words, a $1 million investment in a levered firm will have no effect on personal income taxes because we have assumed that the tax rate in equity income is zero.

	Low Outcome	*High Outcome*
Profit before interest and taxes:	$−1,000,000	$+3,000,000
less: Interest	$ 150,000	$ 150,000
Profit before taxes:	$−1,150,000	$+2,850,000
less: Taxes	$ 460,000	$ 1,140,000
Net profit	$ −690,000	$+1,710,000
Return to levered firm shareholders	−9.857%	+24.429%
Profit or loss to $1,000,000 investment	$ −98,570	$ +244,290

Step 2: Next, we note that the introduction of personal taxes does not change the before-tax returns from investing in the unlevered firm. For convenience, the results that were determined in the solution to Problem 1 are repeated:

	Low Outcome	*High Outcome*
Profit before interest and taxes:	\$−1,000,000	\$+3,000,000
less: Taxes	\$ 400,000	\$ 1,200,000
Net profit	\$ −600,000	\$+1,800,000
Return to levered firm shareholders	−6.000%	+18.000%

Step 3: Finally, we see the difference when we find the total after-tax returns to the homemade leverage strategy because we must alter the analysis to take into account the effects of personal taxation on the use of debt by the investor. Recall that the total investment by the investor is:

Original Funds = \$1,000,000 (70%)

Borrowed Funds = \$ 428,571 (30%)

Total Invested = \$1,428,571 (100%).

The returns after personal (and corporate) taxes to the homemade leverage strategy are found by applying the returns in Step 2 to the investment (\$1,428,571) in the unlevered firm and subtracting the interest expense on the borrowed money (\$428,571 at 5% per year). We must now take into account, however, that the investor will be able to reduce his or her personal income taxes using the deduction for interest paid.

	Low Outcome −6%	*High Outcome* +18%
Total funds in unlevered firm (\$1,428,571) times outcome	\$−85,714	\$ 257,143
Interest expense of borrowed funds (\$428,571) at 5%	\$−21,428	\$−21,428
Tax deduction for interest expense at 40% tax rate	\$ 8,571	\$ 8,571
Total profit or loss (rounded)	\$−98,571	\$ 244,286

Final Solution: Notice that the outcomes from direct investment in a levered firm (\$−98,570 and \$+244,290) are identical (ignoring rounding errors) to the outcomes from homemade leverage. The reason is that the tax advantage to using debt at the corporate level has been matched by a tax advantage to using debt at the personal level, since both levels have a tax rate of 40 percent.

Review Questions

1. Why do we say that the government is a claimant to the firm's assets?
2. Describe how deductions act to reduce the firm's tax burden.

3. Assume an M&M tax model and explain why the optimal capital structure is one with 100 percent debt.
4. Assume a Miller tax model and explain why the capital structure decision can be irrelevant.
5. Why do the traditionalists argue that too much debt is bad?
6. Why do modernists argue that bankruptcy is a good friend to shareholders?
7. Explain how it is possible that the equity value of a firm can increase at the time the firm announces bankruptcy.
8. Use the call option concept to characterize the equity value of a firm close to bankruptcy.
9. What are agency costs?

Problems

1. Marley, Inc., has total cash flow before tax of $900,000 and no debt. Compute Marley's corporate taxes and cash flow after tax if all corporate income is taxed at 34 percent.
2. Moon Lighting Company is unlevered with 2 million shares outstanding and total cash flow before taxes of $725,000. Compute Moon's taxes owed, net income after tax, and after-tax equity earnings per share if all corporate income is taxed at 34 percent.
3. Suppose that the Moon Lighting Company makes a decision to partition its assets into equity and debt. The firm issues $2 million of debt at a cost of 15 percent. The partitioning does not change the firm's total cash flow before taxes; it remains at $725,000. The number of shares outstanding, however, has been reduced from 2 million to 1 million.
   a. Compute Moon's taxes owed using a tax rate of 34 percent. What accounts for the difference between the taxes owed here and those owed in Problem 2?
   b. Compute Moon's net income after tax and after-tax equity earnings per share.
4. Magnum Headache, Inc., is unlevered, with equity valued at $7 million and with 3.5 million shares outstanding. The firm's cash flow before tax is $1 million. The corporate tax rate is 34 percent. Magnum is considering an exchange of 1 million of its equity for $2 million in debt with an annual interest expense of 10 percent (i.e., an opportunity to become levered). The change, of course, will not affect the firm's cash flow. Calculate the after-tax equity earnings per share for Magnum unlevered and for Magnum levered.
5. Return to Magnum Headache, Inc. It turns out that the firm exchanged equity for debt and became levered, and has decided to make the leverage decision permanent by keeping the debt forever. Using Formula (12.1), calculate the new value of Magnum as a levered firm.
6. Boomer's Boogie Boards is currently unlevered, has equity valued at $5 million, and has total cash flow before tax of $1 million. In order to save on taxes, Boomer's CEO suggests that the firm should issue debt and use the proceeds to retire shares of stock. The capital structure change results in $2 million of new debt with an annual interest expense of 12 percent.
   a. How much in taxes will Boomer save, per year, as a result of the decision to issue debt? Use a corporate tax rate of 34 percent.
   b. Suppose that the debt is permanent, and determine the new value of the firm.

7. Woody's Fish and Tackle is a firm whose equity is valued at $20 million and is levered with $10 million in permanent 10 percent interest debt. How much of Woody's value is derived from the present value of tax savings if the corporate tax rate is 34 percent?

8. Carla's Traveling Circus, Inc., provides entertainment to small cities and towns. The firm, valued at $1.5 million, is levered with $700,000 of debt. Although the corporate tax rate is currently 34 percent, there is speculation that the rate will be raised to 40 percent. Calculate the change in the value of the tax shield if the tax rate increases.

9. Campbell Nuts, Inc., is unlevered with 10,000 shares outstanding. The firm is facing three cash flow scenarios: (1) recession, (2) normal, and (3) boom. Given a corporate tax rate of 34 percent, complete the following table:

State	*Total Cash Flow Before Tax*	*Taxes*	*Net Income*	*After-Tax Equity Ownership per Share*
Recession	$4,000	?	?	?
Normal	?	?	$5,280	?
Boom	?	$4,760	?	?

10. Campbell Nuts, Inc., has added a new look to its balance sheet—debt! The firm now has $25,000 of debt, with an annual interest expense of 12 percent. The number of shares outstanding has been reduced to 7,500. The firm continues to face the three cash flow scenarios given in Problem 9. Given a corporate tax rate of 34 percent, complete the following table:

State	*Total Cash Flow Before Tax*	*Interest Expense*	*Taxable Income*	*Taxes*	*Net Income*	*After-Tax Equity Earnings per Share*
Recession	$4,000	$3,000	?	?	?	?
Normal	?	?	$5,000	?	?	?
Boom	?	?	?	$3,740	?	?

11. A certain group of shareholders of Campbell Nuts, Inc., are not convinced that financial leverage was a good idea. They make the point that, at a certain level of total cash flow before tax, the shareholders are better off without debt. Help this group of shareholders make their point by computing the level of total cash flow before tax that would make shareholders indifferent between being unlevered and levered. (*Hint:* Using the formula for EPS and using given values, set unlevered, after-tax equity earnings per share equal to levered after-tax equity ownership per share, and solve for total cash flow before tax.)

12. Recall the firms Square and Peg from Problem 19 in Chapter 11. These were two firms similar in every way except for their respective capital structures. Square is unlevered with 500 shares outstanding, and Peg has $2,000 of debt with an annual interest expense of 10 percent and has 250 shares outstanding. Suppose that you own 5 percent of the equity of Peg because of its use of leverage. The corporate tax rate is 34 percent.

a. Determine the cash flow from your equity investment in Peg, assuming that Peg's total cash flow is $500.
b. Determine the cash flow from equity from the following strategy: Borrow an amount equal to 5 percent of the debt of Peg at 10 percent annual interest expense and use the proceeds plus your own money to buy 5 percent of the equity of Square. Assume that Square's total cash flow is $500.
c. Compare your answers from (a) and (b). Why is it that homemade leverage no longer works?

13. Recall firms Giants and Jets from Problem 18 in Chapter 11. Giants, Inc., is a successful firm that uses leverage and has assets valued at $1 million. Jets, Inc., is another successful firm similar to Giants except that Jets is unlevered. Show that homemade leverage no longer works if corporate income is taxed at 34 percent. Explain briefly why this is true.

Set the problem in a way similar to that shown in Table 12.2. That is, assume that Giants, Inc., uses $500,000 of debt with an annual interest expense of 10 percent such that interest payments total $50,000. In addition, assume three cash flow scenarios: bad, with cash flows of $50,000; OK, with cash flows of $100,000; and good, with cash flows of $150,000. The first alternative is to purchase 10 percent of the equity in Giants; the second is to purchase 10 percent of Jets and borrow an amount equal to 10 percent of the debt of Giants.

14. Elizabeth Smith has an investment of 1 percent of the bonds of CNS, Inc. CNS has debt totaling $1 million, issued at 9 percent interest. Calculate Elizabeth's tax bill on her interest income, assuming that she is in the 34 percent tax bracket.

15. Emerson Electronics, whose value as an unlevered firm would be $10 million, has $1 million of debt outstanding. Use Formula (12.2) to calculate the levered value of Emerson under the following tax scenarios:

a. The personal tax rate on equity income, T_E, is 34 percent.
The personal tax rate on debt income, T_D, is 34 percent.
The corporate tax rate, T_C, is 34 percent.
b. The personal tax rate on equity income, T_E, is 0 percent.
The personal tax rate on debt income, T_D, is 34 percent.
The corporate tax rate, T_C, is 34 percent.
c. The personal tax rate on equity income, T_E, is 10 percent.
The personal tax rate on debt income, T_D, is 34 percent.
The corporate tax rate, T_C, is 34 percent.

16. In a particular economy, equity income is taxed at 34 percent, debt income is taxed at 34 percent, and corporate taxes are also taxed at 34 percent. How much value per dollar of debt will leverage add to a firm that is currently unlevered? [*Hint*: Use the bracketed expression of Formula (12.2) and substitute $1 for *D*.]

17. In a particular economy, equity income is taxed at 0 percent, debt income is taxed at 34 percent, and corporate taxes are also taxed at 34 percent. How much value per dollar of debt will leverage add to a firm that is currently unlevered? [*Hint*: Use the bracketed expression of Formula (12.2) and substitute $1 for *D*.]

18. In a particular economy, equity income is taxed at 15 percent, debt income is taxed at 34 percent, and corporate taxes are also taxed at 34 percent. How much value per dollar of debt will leverage add to a firm that is currently unlevered? [*Hint*: Use the bracketed expression of Formula (12.2) and substitute $1 for *D*.]

19. Return once more to Giants, Inc., and Jets, Inc., in Problem 13. Redo the homemade leverage analysis incorporating personal taxes. Assume that the personal tax on debt income is 34 percent, and the personal tax on equity income is 0 percent. Set the problem up in a way similar to that shown in Table 12.3.

Discussion Questions

1. A newspaper article quoted a stockholder of a corporation as saying, "The firm is in financial distress—and I view bankruptcy as a friend to the shareholder." It almost sounds as if the stockholder is saying that bankruptcy is a good thing, but we all know that it is not. Why would bankruptcy be referred to as a friend?
2. A politician was heard arguing that a major reason we see firms "levering" is because of the advantage to debt in the corporate tax code. Describe the advantage to which the politician is referring. Do you think the politician has a legitimate point? If he does, then how might the corporate tax code be amended to remove this debt advantage?
3. The chapter argues that when a levered firm increases the riskiness of its assets, the value of the firm's debt decreases such that wealth is transferred from bondholders to stockholders; however, levered firms increase their risk all the time. Think of some ways that bondholders can protect themselves from this potential loss in value.
4. The Almost Gone Corporation produces computers and is near bankruptcy. The shareholders argue that it is in their best interest is to "roll the dice" with whatever capital the firm has left and invest in some extremely risky but negative-*NPV* projects.
   a. Use the feature of limited liability to explain why shareholders, in this case, might have the incentive to invest in certain projects even if *NPV* were negative.
   b. Can you think of a positive-*NPV* project that the shareholders would reject?
   c. From the standpoint of operating the business as a "going concern," discuss some costs to the shareholder's strategy.
5. The board of directors of Lucky, Inc., has just decided to issue additional stock to raise capital for an expansion project. At the same time it is revealed to the board that some land owned by the firm, once considered to be worthless, might contain significant amounts of crude oil worth millions, but that this information must remain confidential for several months. Convince the board that given this new information, they should scrap the plan to issue new stock and issue bonds instead.

CHAPTER 13

THE DIVIDEND DECISION

USF&G is a large insurance corporation headquartered in Baltimore, Maryland. The top management of USF&G was very proud of the company's long history of regularly distributing profits to the shareholders. These cash payments, or dividends, had been sent regularly to shareholders since 1939.

In the late 1980s, things were not going well for insurance companies, and USF&G was no exception. Nevertheless, top management held tenaciously to its large and regular dividends. In fact, by 1990, the stock price had fallen by 67 percent compared with its level in 1989, yet the dividend remained at $3.00 per share per year, the same as in 1989.

Debate raged that the top management of USF&G was destroying the company with its refusal to lower the dividend. Finally, top management was replaced and the dividend was lowered. Huge cost savings programs followed and large layoffs were implemented. Some people even began to question if USF&G would survive.

Chapters 11 and 12 analyzed the firm's capital structure decision—what types and amounts of securities the firm may want to issue to finance its assets. This chapter analyzes the firm's dividend decision—what types and amounts of dividends the firm may want to distribute to its shareholders. The firm's dividend policy, therefore, will refer to decisions regarding the general level and timing of distributing cash to the shareholders.

We will analyze the dividend decision in a manner extremely similar to that of the capital structure decision. You may therefore want to review Chapters 11 and 12 before reading this chapter.

An Overview of the Firm's Dividend Decision

dividend
A distribution from the corporation's assets to the shareholders on a pro rata basis.

cash dividend
A distribution of cash from the corporation's assets to the shareholders.

A **dividend** is a distribution from the corporation's assets to the shareholders on a pro rata basis. Thus, if you owned 1 percent of the firm's stock, you would receive 1 percent of the amount of the distribution. The most common type of dividend is the **cash dividend,** which is a distribution of cash to shareholders. Most of this chapter will be focused on cash dividends, which, stated differently, are transfers from the firm's cash balance into the personal cash balances of its shareholders. The payment of cash dividends is similar to the action of a store owner who may, on occasion, transfer money from the store's cash drawer to his or her wallet.

In addition to cash dividends, corporations issue other types of dividends, such as extra dividends, special dividends, liquidating dividends, and stock dividends, on an annual or irregular basis. Window 13.1 lists and describes the terminology of dividends.

announcement date The date when the firm announces the dividend payment.

The firm's dividend payment procedure is spread out over a number of weeks and follows the upcoming sequence. The board of directors meet and declare a dividend of a certain amount to be paid at a certain date in the future. The date when this decision is made public is known as the **announcement date.** The dividend will be sent to all shareholders who own the stock

WINDOW 13.1

Dividend Terminology

Regular Dividend: Dividends paid on a regular basis, such that shareholders expect the firm to continue such dividend payments in the future.

Extra Dividend: Made in addition to the firm's regular dividend, an extra dividend is paid without an expectation that the firm will continue making the payment in the future.

Special Dividend: Reserved for unique situations, this type of dividend would not be expected to continue in the future.

Liquidating Dividend: A distribution of assets in the form of a dividend, made by companies that expect to terminate operations.

Stock Dividend: A dividend in the form of additional shares of the firm's stock.

Dividend Payout Ratio: The percentage of residual cash flow, or earnings, paid to shareholders in the form of dividends. Companies that choose to reinvest all residual cash flow will have zero payout ratios, but companies that choose to distribute all residual cash flow in the form of dividends will have 100 percent dividend payout ratios. Other companies will have dividend payout ratios between zero and 100 percent.

Dividend Yield: A ratio represented by the firm's annual dividend divided by the firm's stock price.

Dividend Reinvestment Plans ("DRIPS"): The automatic reinvestment of the shareholder's dividends into additional shares of the firm's stock. Dividend reinvestment plans represent an inexpensive way to purchase additional shares of stock, as most companies absorb the brokerage fees or transactions costs involved in the purchase. In addition, some companies offer the stock through these plans at a discount from the current market price.

record date
The date on which shareholders listed on the corporate record will receive the announced dividend.
ex-dividend date
The second business day prior to the date of record. The stock trades without the dividend on the ex-dividend date with the result that new purchasers will not receive legal right to the declared dividend if they purchase the stock on or after this date.
payment date
The date when dividend checks are mailed to all entitled shareholders.

on a particular day—the **record date.** Dividends will be paid to every shareholder listed on the corporate record on the record date.

Because it normally takes a few business days after stock is sold to record the new owner on the corporate record, certain investors who purchase stock near the record date will risk not receiving the dividend. To avoid this potential dividend payment problem, the legal right to dividends remains with the stock until two business days prior to the date of record. The second business day prior to the date of record is known as the **ex-dividend date.** On the ex-dividend date, the stock trades "without" dividend, such that new purchasers—on or after this ex-dividend date—will not receive legal right to the declared dividend.

Because investors purchasing stock on or after the ex-dividend date do not receive the dividend, the stock price falls by the amount of the dividend (approximately) on the ex-dividend date. Thus, there is no immediate monetary advantage to purchasing the stock before the ex-dividend date. Dividend checks are mailed to all shareholders about 2 weeks after the record date. This is known as the **payment date.**

Example 13.1 Suppose that on March 3 the board of directors of the Joepa Corporation announce a quarterly dividend of $0.50 per share ($2.00 annually) to be paid to anyone on the corporate record as of Friday, March 16. Joepa stock trades currently for $25 per share. The announcement date is March 3, and the date of record is March 16.

The ex-dividend date is two business days prior to the record date, or Wednesday, March 14. Investors who purchase Joepa stock on or after this ex-dividend date will not receive the $0.50 per share dividend. To compensate for this, the share price will fall from $25 to $24.50 per share when the stock begins trading on March 14.

Buy and sell orders placed on an exchange will be marked down by the amount of the dividend (unless otherwise requested). Ignoring taxes, you would be indifferent between paying $25 for a share of Joepa and receiving a $0.50 dividend, or paying $24.50 per share and receiving no dividend. Dividend checks are mailed to the shareholders on March 31, the payment date.

Why Are Dividends Special?

How much would you pay for a cow if no one could consume its milk or meat? How much would you pay for a car if no one could drive it? How much, then, would you pay for a share of stock that will never pay a dividend?

Recall from Chapter 4 that the value of a share of stock is equal to the present value of the stock's future cash dividends. Ignoring situations such as liquidations and mergers, cash dividends are the only value that stocks provide directly to investors. Although investors often expect to receive capital gains as part of the return on a common stock investment, the ability of your stock to rise in price and be attractive to other investors is based ultimately upon the expected dividends that the stock will offer to future investors.

Another indication of the importance of dividends is the change in the market price of a stock when a corporation unexpectedly changes its dividend policy. Empirical studies examining changes in stock prices in response to dividend announcements have generally found that stock prices rise when firms announce dividends higher than expected and fall upon announcement of dividends lower than expected. The importance of studying dividends is emphasized by the fact that dividends affect both the firm's capital structure and its assets. Because dividends are distributions of cash, they reduce the firm's assets. The dividend also reduces the retained earnings or equity of a firm, thereby increasing the firm's ratio of debt to equity.

The Dividend Payment Flow

The operating profits from the firm's assets minus the cash flows payable to the firm's debtholders and governments form the total return or net income available to the firm's equityholders. The dividend decision divides this cash flow into that portion sent to the shareholders as a dividend and that portion retained inside the firm and used for other purposes, such as to purchase new assets or to pay off some debt. The amount of the net income that stays within the firm is referred to as *retained earnings.* Figure 13.1 illustrates this concept.

FIGURE 13.1 A Dividend Flow Diagram

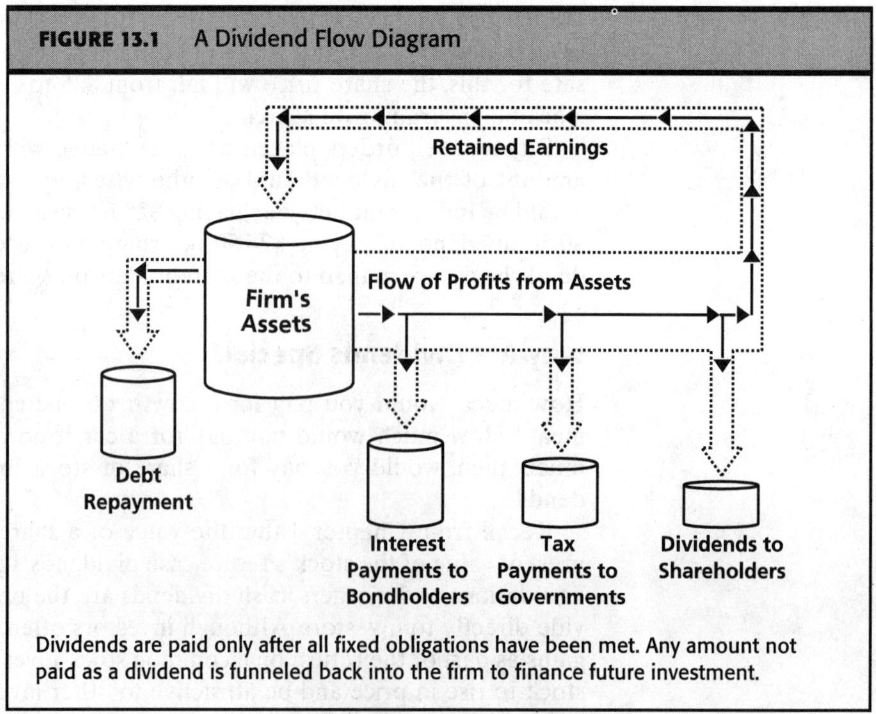

Dividends are paid only after all fixed obligations have been met. Any amount not paid as a dividend is funneled back into the firm to finance future investment.

Thus, the firm's dividend policy is the decision as to which portion, if any, of the firm's earnings should be sent to the shareholders as a dividend and which portion should remain inside the firm as retained earnings. Because the money retained inside the firm generally belongs to the shareholders, and because the decision ultimately rests with the firm's owners, the dividend decision can be viewed as the choice of whether the shareholders would prefer to have their money inside or outside the firm. This is the modernists' view. The money used to pay the dividend always belongs to the shareholder; only its location changes.

In contrast, as we learn in the following section, traditionalists view a dividend as a reward or wage to the firm's owners. Traditionalists believe that dividends are important and that an optimal dividend policy for each firm usually exists. As in the capital structure arguments of Chapters 11 and 12, modernists believe that, in perfect markets, the firm's dividend policy is irrelevant. In a world of market imperfections—especially taxes—modernists carefully construct models that demonstrate either relevance or irrelevance to dividends, depending upon the imperfections assumed.

The Traditionalists' View of Cash Dividends

The most common traditionalist view is that dividends are good for shareholders, and that the goal of an optimal dividend policy is to pay out as much cash in the form of dividends as possible while still maintaining the optimal growth and capital structure of the firm.

bird-in-the-hand theory A theory of dividend payments suggesting that a shareholder would prefer to receive a dollar of dividends today over the hope of more than a dollar of dividends in the future. The argument is that most shareholders prefer a sure amount of cash today to an unsure amount of dividends and capital gains in the future.

The traditionalists' idea that dividends are good for shareholders is often referred to as the **bird-in-the-hand theory,** in reference to the popular saying that a bird in the hand is preferred to two birds in the bush. In terms of finance, this suggests that a shareholder would prefer to receive a dollar of dividends today rather than the hope of more than a dollar of dividends in the future. The argument is that most shareholders prefer a sure amount of cash today to an unsure amount of dividends and capital gains in the future. Following this view, the firm's managers should attempt to pay out as much in dividends as they can in order to reward the shareholders without jeopardizing other objectives.

In the traditionalists' model, the shareholders' desire to be rewarded by dividends also forces management to try hard not to cut the dollar amounts of dividends. Managers reason that no one likes a cut in pay, and shareholders certainly do not want a cut in their reward. Managers are also reluctant to raise dividend payouts in response to a rise in the firm's earnings unless or until they are convinced that the new higher earnings level can be preserved, and, therefore, that a new higher dividend payout is likely to be sustained.

The reluctance to both cut and raise dividends motivates firms to create an optimal dividend policy whereby there is a regular dividend with periodic increases, but with rare (if ever) decreases. The normal percentage of earnings for a large corporation to distribute in the form of dividends is approximately 50 percent. Thus, a stock whose net income divided by the number of shares of common stock is $4.00 might have an annual dividend of $2.00 per share. This dividend would probably be distributed as $0.50 per share every 3 months.

dividend payout ratio The percentage of residual cash flow, or earnings, paid to the shareholders in the form of dividends.

Numerous surveys have been performed to try to establish how firms decide on a dividend policy. One popular view is that the general level of dividends, called the **dividend payout ratio,** and the speed with which dividends adjust to new earnings levels are determined mostly by the types of assets the firm owns and its plans for the future.

Observation does indicate that younger, higher-risk, and research-oriented firms tend to pay less of their earnings as dividends. The stocks in these firms are referred to as *growth stocks* because their low dividends mean that most or all of their return must come from growth in the share price. In contrast, older, more stable, and low-technology firms tend to pay more of their earnings as current dividends. These stocks are referred to as *income stocks* because much of their return comes from immediate dividends or current income.

Other dividend theories that tend to be associated with the views of traditionalists are the **residual dividend theory** and the **target payout ratio theory.** The residual dividend theory states that the amount of dividends paid to shareholders is what's left over from earnings after all positive NPV projects have been financed. Under the residual dividend theory, the firm will pay high dividends in times when earnings are high and/or when the firm has few good projects to invest. They may pay little to no dividends, however, at times when earnings are low and/or the firm has many good projects in which to invest. The target payout ratio theory attempts to smooth out dividend instability that may occur under the residual theory by setting the dividend payout at some fraction of earnings. The precise payout is set so that dividends adjust slowly through time to changes in earnings. In addition, firms with very large short-term increases in earnings might pay out a special dividend that would not be expected to be paid in subsequent years. Both theories are consistent with the view that dividends are special.

The Modernists' Viewpoint— The M&M Model Without Taxes

At about the same time that Franco Modigliani and Merton Miller were developing their famous propositions regarding the irrelevance of capital structure, they also developed similar propositions for dividends and dividend policy. In perfect markets, M&M demonstrated that dividends and dividend policy are irrelevant. As in Chapter 11, we will refer to this view as the M&M without taxes model.

Understanding dividend irrelevance is much simpler than understanding capital structure irrelevance. A dividend is simply a movement of shareholder wealth from inside the firm to outside the firm. Shareholders have always owned the money and are simply taking it home with them.

The simplest proof of dividend irrelevancy is the so-called homemade dividend argument, which we will look at next.

Homemade Dividends in a Perfect Market

homemade dividend An action by the individual investor that replicates or negates a dividend decision by the firm.

The **homemade dividend** argument shows that any dividend action by a firm can be replicated or negated by the individual investor (i.e., that the individual investor can, in effect, produce dividends on his or her own).

Example 13.2 _______

Consider an investor with 500 shares of Skyhook, Inc., a stock that trades for $40 per share. The investor has a total equity value of $20,000. Table 13.1 shows the balance sheet of Skyhook, Inc. in terms of market values. Skyhook has no debt, so in effect the shareholders own all the assets of the firm. Note that the $40 of equity value per share is associated with $4 per share in cash and marketable securities and $36 in other assets.

The purpose of this example is to demonstrate dividend irrelevancy using homemade dividends. We will show that the investor can either negate a dividend that is undesired or can replicate a desired dividend. Thus, if any dividend action of the firm can be easily negated and if investors can create their own dividends, then the specific dividend payment policy of the firm must be irrelevant.

First, let us consider the case of an unwanted cash dividend in a perfect market. Suppose that Skyhook pays a cash dividend of $0.50 per share on January 1. What will happen to the firm's balance sheet and share price? Table 13.2 demonstrates that the value of the firm's assets drops by the amount of the cash dividend, or by $5,000 (10,000 shares × $0.50 per share), and the value of its shares will decline to $39.50.

The investor now owns $19,750 worth of stock (500 shares times $39.50 per share) and a $250 dividend check (500 shares times the $0.50 per share

TABLE 13.1 Balance Sheet of Skyhook, Inc.

Assets	
Cash and marketable securities	$ 40,000
Other assets	$360,000
Total assets	$400,000
Liabilities and Owner's Equity	
Debt	$ 0
Equity (10,000 shares)	$400,000
Total liabilities and owner's equity	$400,000

Value of equity per share = ($400,000/10,000 shares) = $40

TABLE 13.2 Balance Sheet of Skyhook After Dividend

Assets	
Cash and marketable securities	$ 35,000
Other assets	$360,000
Total assets	$395,000
Liabilities and Owner's Equity	
Debt	$ 0
Equity (10,000 shares)	$395,000
Total liabilities and owner's equity	$395,000

Value of equity per share = ($395,000/10,000 shares) = $39.50

dividend) for a total of $20,000. The wealth of every investor in the firm will be unchanged because the new value of the stock ($39.50) plus the cash dividend ($0.50) has the same value as the stock had before the dividend ($40.00).

What if the investor did not want his or her investment in the firm's stock reduced? That investor could negate the dividend by using the dividend check to purchase new shares of stock. For example, the investor could use the $250 check to purchase 6.33 shares of stock (note that in a perfect market there are no brokerage or transaction fees and shares can be divided limitlessly). The investor would now have 506.33 shares of stock worth $39.50 per share for a total of $20,000, and the dividend is negated.[1]

The other type of homemade transaction is the creation of a desired dividend when the firm does not pay a cash dividend. In the previous example, suppose Skyhook decided not to pay a dividend. How could the investor raise the desired $250 in cash? The answer is that the investor could sell 6.25 shares of Skyhook stock and receive a $250 check for the sale. The investor's stock would now be worth $19,750 (493.75 shares times $40.00 per share)—the same amount of cash and stock the investor would have had if Skyhook had paid the $0.50 per share dividend.

It is sometimes argued that a homemade dividend is not the same as a corporate dividend because in the case of a homemade dividend the investor's stock in the company is declining from 500 shares to 493.75 shares, but if the company pays a dividend the investor retains 500 shares of stock. The fallacy

[1]One difference in Skyhook after the dividend payment is that it now has a lower percentage of its assets invested in cash (and therefore has higher risk). It should be noted, however, that Skyhook is expected to produce cash throughout the year from its operations, and its cash balance is expected to return to its level prior to the dividend payment. In other words, the decline in Skyhook's cash account is temporary, and occurs in regular fashion at the time of dividend payments.

in the argument is that, although the number of shares drops in the case of a homemade dividend, the dollar size of the investment is not affected by whether the dividend is homemade or not. It is the dollar size of the investment, not the number of shares, that matters.

It is also argued that such homemade dividends could eventually cause the investor to have to liquidate all of the stock by selling shares a little at a time. Once again, this argument rests on the number of shares held rather than on the dollar size of the investment. A firm reinvesting its residual cash in positive *NPV* projects will find its share price rising. As the price per share rises, the investor will be liquidating fewer and fewer shares each time to create the desired dividend. The number of shares held will not go to zero and the investor's dollar investment will be growing just as if the company paid a dividend and he or she retained 500 shares of the dividend-paying stock.

In summary, modernists believe that, in a perfect market, dividends do not change shareholder wealth, only its location. Because we are not including transactions costs in this argument, the shareholder can easily adjust the location of wealth with or without the company's help; therefore, dividends and dividend policy are irrelevant.

How Can the Firm's Dividend Policy Be Irrelevant?

You may still find it surprising to read that the firm's dividend policy can be irrelevant. Recall that in Chapter 4 it was argued the value of the firm is the discounted value of its future dividend stream. In fact, using the perpetual growth model, the dividend payment played a major role in determining the value of a share of stock:

$$\text{Price per share} = \frac{DIV_1}{r_E - g}$$

where DIV_1 is the next year's dividend, r_E is the expected return on the stock, and g represents the constant growth rate in annual dividends.

In the long run, however, dividend policy really answers the question of when dividends are to be paid. If the current dividend is increased, then there will be less money to reinvest and the growth rate in dividends will fall. In other words, more dividends today means relatively fewer dividends in the future. In terms of the previous model, the rise in dividends will be completely offset by the fall in the growth rate, leaving the share price unchanged. On the other hand, a cut in current dividends will generally lead to a rise in the growth rate of future dividends.

Example 13.3 Suppose that the value of Skyhook could be calculated using the previous perpetual growth model by inserting the $2 annual dividend, a required return on stock of 10 percent, and a growth rate in annual dividends of 5 percent.

$$\$40 = \frac{\$2}{.10 - .05}$$

If Skyhook lowered its dividend to \$1, the growth rate in annual dividends would be expected to rise to 7.5 percent due to the increase in retained earnings. The lower dividend and the higher growth rate in future dividends produces the same share price of \$40.

$$\$40 = \frac{\$1}{.10 - .075}$$

On the other hand, if the dividend were raised to \$4, then we would expect the growth rate in future dividends to fall to zero. A dividend of \$4 and a growth rate of zero percent keeps the stock price at \$40 (with the expected return remaining at 10 percent).

$$\$40 = \frac{\$4}{.10 - .00}$$

For Skyhook, the dividend policy did not change the total present value of the future dividends. Only the timing of these dividends was changed.

What About Superior Investment Opportunities?

Let us take a look at one of the more popular rebuttals to the modernist argument of dividend irrelevancy. It is sometimes argued that one reason dividend policy matters is that high dividends can create a situation in which the firm is unable to invest in all available positive-*NPV* projects. With high dividend payments, too much of the firm's income is being paid to the shareholders rather than retained and reinvested. In a similar way, it is sometimes argued that the payment of low dividends can cause the firm to invest in negative-*NPV* projects because of a lack of good ways to use the firm's cash.

Dividend policy, however, should be viewed as separate from the optimal investment policy. As detailed in Chapter 5, the optimal investment policy is to invest in all positive-*NPV* projects and turn down all negative-*NPV* projects. This can be accomplished regardless of dividend policy in a perfect market.

For example, if the firm pays too large a dividend such that retained earnings cannot finance all its great projects, then the firm can issue new securities to raise the needed funds. In markets with many buyers and sellers, the firm knows that it will raise the funds by issuing securities at a competitive price. The securities of and by themselves will not increase or decrease the value of the firm because the *NPV* of issuing securities in a perfect market is zero. Because the equityholders are the residual claimants of the firm, all wealth created from the positive *NPVs* of the great projects will flow to the equityholders.

On the other hand, if the firm pays too small a dividend such that there are still retained earnings left after the last positive-*NPV* project has been undertaken, the firm can always invest the remaining cash in competitively priced securities whose *NPV* is zero, leaving shareholder wealth unchanged.

Summary of the Modernist Viewpoint on Dividend Policy

As we have seen, the homemade dividend argument demonstrates that, under some restrictive assumptions, a corporation's dividend policy is irrelevant to an investor. We have also shown that a corporation's dividend policy should have no effect on the firm's investment decision. Regardless of the firm's dividend policy, it should invest in all positive-*NPV* projects, reject all negative-*NPV* projects, and use zero-*NPV* projects such as buying, selling, and issuing financial securities to maintain the desired cash.

You should not be surprised to learn that some of the arguments set forth here do not hold when some restrictive assumptions are relaxed. The purpose of the remaining sections of this chapter is to discuss the relaxing of these assumptions in detail. We begin with taxes because they are the most important, and then detail other effects such as bankruptcy costs, agency costs, and other imperfections.

Market Imperfections and Dividend Policy

We will now consider dividend policy in a more realistic world of market imperfections such as taxes. Dividend policy, like capital structure policy, is simply paperwork. By *paperwork* we mean that dividends are not real assets that produce scarce resources. Dividends do not create or destroy wealth—they can, at best, merely transfer wealth because there are "no free lunches." Any argument claiming that shareholder wealth is enhanced, therefore, must also show whose wealth is being lost and why.

The modernists' tax arguments regarding dividends parallel the arguments regarding capital structure very closely. The analysis has the same two models: (1) the M&M with taxes model and (2) the Miller tax model.

The M&M Model with Taxes

We will begin with the M&M with taxes model. As in the case of capital structure discussed in Chapter 12, the M&M with taxes model was set forth in the pioneering work of Modigliani and Miller in the late 1950s and early 1960s.

Unlike the M&M with taxes model for capital structure, there are no direct tax implications to dividend policy related to corporate income tax laws. Corporations must pay income taxes on their entire net income regardless of whether the income is paid out to the shareholders as dividends or reinvested in the firm's assets as retained earnings. Any or all tax implications from the firm's dividend policy, therefore, derive from the payment of personal income taxes.

The dividend policy decision is viewed as the decision as to which proportion of the shareholder's return in the near future will be in the form of dividend income and which proportion will be in the form of retained earnings leading to capital gains. The standard view used in the M&M with taxes model of taxing equity at the individual or personal income tax level is that investors pay a higher tax on dividend income than they do on capital gains. This view was very widely held prior to the income tax revisions of 1986. It is still argued by most as a result of the ability to time capital gains (as detailed in Chapter 12) and as the result of the modest tax break given to capital gains for high income taxpayers. For instance, although personal tax rates on dividends and short term capital gains are currently similar for taxpayers in medium and lower tax brackets, investors can put off realizing a capital gain and therefore delay paying a tax by not selling appreciated stock; however, they cannot usually put off the payment of taxes on dividends received in the current year. Further, long term capital gains are taxed at substantially lower rates. Higher-income taxpayers receive a much lower rate on long term capital gains than on dividends and other ordinary income.

At first glance, the ability to delay and time the realization of capital gains and their lower tax rates may appear to be modest. Wealthy investors in high tax brackets, however, can utilize this feature to create important tax advantages. Thus, the M&M with taxes model for dividends stresses the concept that dividends are taxed at a higher rate in terms of present values than are capital gains and, therefore, investors will prefer to receive no dividends.

In an M&M with taxes model, a zero percent dividend payout policy will maximize shareholder wealth.

Example 13.4 ________ Recall the Skyhook, Inc., example in which the investor was indifferent between a $250 corporate cash dividend and a homemade dividend created by selling off $250 worth of stock. In the M&M with taxes model, the homemade dividend offers a higher after-tax cash flow to the investor, which is illustrated in Table 13.3.

In present value terms, and realizing that taxes on capital gains in the future could be avoided through the techniques of Chapter 12, the tax liability of the investor is minimized by a zero percent dividend payout. This therefore represents the firm's optimal dividend policy.

Thus, our first market imperfection (i.e., personal income taxes that favor capital gains) causes shareholder wealth to be maximized by a dividend policy of zero dividends. Because the individual's tax bill is smallest when the firm pays no dividends, the increased wealth of the shareholders comes from a wealth transfer from the government to the individual.

TABLE 13.3 The Payment of Personal Taxes on Dividends

Situation 1: Investor receives a $250 cash dividend from Skyhook, Inc.
Investor's tax bracket = 30 percent.

Dividend payment	$250.00
Tax on dividend	75.00
After-tax cash flow	$175.00

Situation 2: Investor creates a "Homemade Dividend" of $250 by selling stock.
Stock's original purchase price = $24 per share.
Investor's tax bracket = 30 percent.

Proceeds from the sale of stock	$250.00
Original purchase price of stock	150.00
Capital gain	$100.00
Tax on capital gain (30 percent)	$ 30.00
Proceeds from sale minus tax	$220.00

Result: Homemade dividend pays $45 less in tax and is the preferred choice.

The Miller Tax Model

Despite the widespread teachings of the M&M propositions, firms continue to pay dividends. Part of the explanation is that the United States Internal Revenue Service (IRS) exerts pressure on firms not to avoid dividend payouts for tax-avoidance purposes. It is clear, however, that funds distributed as a result of the tendency of corporations to pay dividends vastly exceed the amounts that would be explained by pressure from the IRS.

When Merton Miller established what is known as the Miller tax model in 1977, he created a model that has important implications for dividends as well. These implications were then fully developed by Miller and Scholes in 1978.

In the Miller tax model, it is argued that the tax advantages of capital gains (e.g., lower rates, the investor's ability to time these gains or to pass the capital gains on through an estate) can be used by investors to create such a powerful tax savings that, for all practical purposes, the personal income tax on capital gains is zero. Miller argues that there are so many tax breaks available to taxpayers that even the tax on dividends can be sheltered easily by the investor. In other words, the taxes on dividends can be avoided using the extraordinary tax breaks from capital gains and other tax-advantaged investments. In this model, the dividend payout decision is irrelevant because investors can avoid any income taxes on their equity returns.

In the Miller tax model, the dividend payout decision is irrelevant since investors can avoid any income taxes on their equity returns.

Example 13.5 ________ Returning to Skyhook and under the Miller tax model, the investor could make portfolio adjustments and ultimately pay no additional income taxes, even if the firm paid a dividend of $250. In Window 12.1 we discussed in detail a portfolio strategy that could accomplish the elimination of taxes on all forms of equity income. Because the investor can avoid any and all taxes on the equity portfolio, it will make no difference to the investor whether or not the firm pays a dividend. Dividend policy is once again irrelevant.

Summary of the Two Tax Models for Dividends

Are the tax advantages to capital gains under current tax laws such that investors would prefer low-dividend-payout stocks? In other words, does the M&M with taxes model hold or, are the tax loopholes so great as to make taxes irrelevant at the personal level? Modernists are not sure of the answers to these questions, but they are sure that these logical arguments are the best way of analyzing the problem.

It is obvious that, under current tax laws, there are not millions of investors in high tax brackets frantically fighting with the managers of corporations to stop paying dividends. We find instead that investors who are in search of tax breaks can find them without having to search out firms with extraordinarily low dividend payout policies. Thus, there does not appear to be a large tax penalty to dividends.

Remember, a firm's dividend policy is paperwork rather than the creation or destruction of real assets. Dividend policy, therefore, can only transfer wealth, not create it. In this section we have discussed whether tax laws allow shareholders to use dividend policy to transfer wealth from the government. Because there is no strong evidence to the contrary, it is safe to conclude that, under current tax laws, whether or not a particular firm pays high or low dividends is not an extremely important issue.

Dividends and Bankruptcy

All of the discussions in this chapter so far have ignored bankruptcy. In other words, the debt of the corporation has been assumed to be risk-free. This section will examine the effects of bankruptcy and financial distress on dividend policy.

Issues of dividends and bankruptcy are virtually identical to the issues regarding debt and bankruptcy. The payment of dividends reduces equity in the firm as well as the cash balance of the firm. Thus, when a firm pays a dividend, it loses cash, one of its safest assets, and increases its financial leverage. Both of these effects would tend to increase the probability of bankruptcy. Because traditionalists view bankruptcy as bad, their position is that a firm should avoid dividend payments that would significantly increase that probability.

Modernists believe that dividends do not create or destroy wealth—they can only transfer it. If some large dividends increase the probability of bankruptcy substantially, it would be worthwhile to examine whether this could benefit shareholders by transferring wealth from other people, such as creditors or unions. Whether a dividend can increase shareholder wealth depends upon the specifics of the situation, as was found in the discussion in Chapter 12 regarding debt.

Bankruptcy and Option Theory

In the absence of other effects, option theory provides a tremendous insight into the dividend controversy. You will recall that one of the major points of Chapter 10 was that a call option fell by more than $0.00 but by less than $1.00 when the underlying asset dropped in value by $1.00. In terms of corporate finance, the firm's equity is the call option and the firm's assets are the underlying asset. This means that the equity of a levered firm, which is a call option on the firm's assets, will drop by less than $1 when the firm's assets are reduced by $1—exactly what a dividend does. Thus, a shareholder of a levered firm can receive a $1 dividend and expect that the market value of the equity will drop by less than $1—making the shareholder wealthier!

From where does the shareholder's wealth increase come? The answer is, it comes from the people who do not hold the option—the debtholders.

The Bankruptcy Option in Practice

Example 13.6 ______ Let us examine in detail how this can happen. Suppose that Skyhook, Inc. has a very similar competitor named Cloudhook, Inc. The only difference between the two firms is that whereas Skyhook has no debt, Cloudhook is loaded with debt, as shown in Table 13.4.

Let us now suppose both firms experience financial distress, causing them to liquidate most of their assets by selling their buildings, land, and so forth, and to move to a rented facility. As part of the liquidation, both firms send $300,000 to their shareholders in the form of a cash dividend. Table 13.5 shows the new balance sheets that would result after the dividend.

The value of the equity of Skyhook dropped by the full $300,000. In other words, the dividend caused no wealth transfer between people—it simply moved the shareholders' money from inside the firm to outside the firm, in the shareholders' personal accounts.

Notice that the equity of Cloudhook, however, dropped by only $99,000 (from $100,000 to $1,000). Cloudhook's shareholders are far better off

TABLE 13.4 Balance Sheets of Skyhook and Cloudhook

Assets	*Skyhook, Inc.*	*Cloudhook, Inc.*
Cash and marketable securities	$40,000	$40,000
Other assets	360,000	360,000
Total assets	$400,000	$400,000
Liabilities and Owners' Equity		
Debt	$-0-	$300,000
Equity	400,000	100,000
Total liabilities and owners' equity	$400,000	$400,000

because they received a $300,000 dividend that was only partially offset by a $99,000 drop in equity. How did the stockholders become better off? As explained earlier, the stockholder's $201,000 wealth increase came from the debtholders, who saw the value of their bonds drop by $201,000.

This example demonstrates that, in theory, stockholders of a levered firm can use dividends to transfer wealth from bondholders to themselves. The driving force is bankruptcy. The removal of so much cash from the firm hurts the value of the bonds tremendously because it is virtually certain that the firm will declare bankruptcy and the bondholders will receive less than they are owed. Note again, however, that wealth has not been destroyed; it was simply transferred—in this case from the bondholders to the stockholders.

In the real world, few such startling opportunities exist because bondholders are careful to protect themselves before they lend money, and governments usually impose laws to protect bondholders from such outrageous cases.

TABLE 13.5 Balance Sheets of Skyhook and Cloudhook

Assets	*Skyhook, Inc.*	*Cloudhook, Inc.*
Total assets	$100,000	$100,000
Liabilities and Owners' Equity		
Debt	$-0-	$99,000
Equity	100,000	1,000
Total liabilities and owners' equity	$100,000	$100,000

Other less obvious cases exist, however, that allow shareholders to benefit from profits by using dividends to distribute them outside the levered firm while keeping the corporation lean on cash. For example, in the case of a potential lawsuit against the firm, legal claimants may settle quickly or not even file a lawsuit if they know that the corporation could not pay a large cash award. In addition, labor unions may negotiate more easily due to the fact that a tough stance could force the firm into bankruptcy. Governments are known for using taxpayers' money to assist a struggling firm. Of course, cases such as these raise ethical issues that shareholders need to explore.

As in the case of the capital structure decision, the ultimate question of whether bankruptcy and dividends can be used to maximize shareholder wealth must be decided on a case-by-case basis. Most creditors are not fools and therefore are not easily separated from their money. The idea of distributing equity, however, by way of dividends outside the firm in the face of huge debt, large lawsuits, unfavorable union contracts, and so forth seems to be plausible.

Dividends and Agency Costs

As discussed in Chapter 12, an agency relationship and agency costs arise when a principal, or shareholder, hires an agent, or manager, to perform a service such as run the firm. Such arrangements may create conflicts in objectives and therefore result in costs. Agency costs are related to both the cost of trying to align objectives and the costs associated with unaligned objectives.

It was stated previously that a dividend represents the decision that the shareholder's wealth is to be held outside rather than inside the firm. In terms of agency theory this decision takes on more importance. The big difference is that, if the earnings are retained inside the firm, an agent has direct and immediate control over these earnings. If the earnings are paid as dividends, then the control of these earnings is in the hands of the principals.

Agency models explain whether agents will correctly invest retained earnings, from a shareholder perspective, by accepting only positive *NPV* projects or will squander some of the money on negative *NPV* projects. Managers might be tempted to squander money on negative *NPV* projects in order to derive personal benefit from them (e.g., lavish executive dining rooms, projects to employ friends and relatives, and pet projects such as wineries, branch offices in Hawaii, and so forth).

Models that attempt to explain the effects of these agency costs differ from finding that retained earnings are squandered to finding that the same amount of money will be squandered whether the firm retains its earnings or has to raise the money by issuing securities. In other words, it is not clear that agency costs can directly explain firm dividend policy. The importance of understanding and effectively setting up agency relationships in modern business, however, is clear. It is possible that agency relationships and the compensation schemes that are set up are the single most important issue in corporate finance.

Dividends and Information Signaling

As we have previously stated, many scholars believe that dividend payments contain a signal about the financial strength of the firm. Information-signaling models and concepts begin with the idea that managers have inside and valuable information regarding the firm that the public does not know. Such information would include unpublished sales and costs figures, knowledge regarding how projects are proceeding, and what types of new projects are being considered.

Managers may be reluctant to announce such news explicitly for fear of disgruntled investors or even lawsuits if things do not turn out well—or, perhaps, they wish to keep the specifics of the information from their competitors. The public's awareness of such information must therefore be achieved by observing the actions of the managers.

It was argued earlier in the chapter that because managers dislike lowering dividends they are very reluctant to raise them until they are rather sure that new dividend and earnings levels can be sustained. Dividends, therefore, are an important signal regarding management's view of the prospects for the firm.

Dividend increases generally signal good news, and dividend cuts or even failure to raise dividends at times may be viewed as bad news. The firm's stock price generally responds by rising on announcements of dividend increases and falling on announcements of dividend cuts. This does not mean that a dividend increase itself creates shareholder wealth, but rather that the dividend signals to the shareholders that the managers believe the firm is worth more than the market perceives.

On the other hand, dividend increases can signal bad news. For instance, a dividend increase could signal that the firm does not have good projects in the works and is therefore paying out cash in the form of a dividend. Dividend cuts can simliarly signal the good news that the firm has great projects and needs cash to finance them. When a signal can be interpreted in more than one way it is called an *ambiguous signal.* Moreover, most signals are ambiguous and need to be examined empirically.

The bottom line on information signaling is that a dividend decision can affect the firm's stock price even though the dividend itself does not create, destroy, or transfer wealth. For example, when a firm announces that it has discovered oil, we would expect its stock price to rise. The announcement itself, however, did not create value—it was always there in the form of undiscovered oil. The announcement simply revealed the information.

Information signaling certainly explains why security prices often move substantially in response to actions that modernists believe are irrelevant. Some even argue that the reason managers make certain dividend decisions is in order to signal certain information to the market. Most people believe, however, that information signaling does not provide a powerful reason to prefer one particular dividend policy over any other.

Stock Dividends and Stock Splits

In a stock dividend—as opposed to a cash dividend—the firm issues additional shares to each shareholder based upon the number of shares currently held. For example, in a 10 percent stock dividend, each investor would receive additional shares to increase share holdings by 10 percent: An investor with 500 shares would receive 50 new shares. Note, however, that no cash has moved outside the firm, and because all shareholders now own 10 percent more total shares, each investor still holds the same percentage of the firm's equity. We would therefore expect the share price to fall in response to the stock dividend—in this case by approximately 10 percent.

Stock dividends do not change anyone's wealth—in the same way that cutting a pie into twice as many pieces does not create more pie. Regardless of how many times the pie is sliced, the total size remains constant. This can also be shown through the balance-sheet relationship:

$$\text{Assets} = \text{Debt} + \text{Equity}$$

Because the stock dividend has no effect on either assets or debt, there can be no effect on equity. In the case of a stock dividend, the value of each share drops, while the number of shares rises, leaving total value unchanged. Thus, stock dividends are clearly irrelevant in a perfect market.

stock split
A large stock dividend. For example, in a two-for-one stock split, the number of each shareholder's shares is doubled, and the price per share falls to half its original level. No money changes hands nor does the percentage ownership of each shareholder change.

A **stock split** is a large stock dividend. For example, in a two-for-one stock split, the number of each shareholder's shares is doubled, and the price per share falls to half its original level. There is also such a thing as a *reverse stock split,* in which the number of each shareholder's shares is reduced, and the price per share rises from its previous level. Once again, no money changes hands nor does the percentage ownership of each shareholder change. Window 13.2 details the mathematics of stock dividends, stock splits, and reverse stock splits. As Window 13.2 emphasizes, the number of shares and share prices do not change by the same percentages.

Traditionalists usually view stock dividends as means by which managers of firms with limited cash reward their shareholders without having to pay large cash dividends. In addition, stock splits and stock dividends may be viewed as an attempt by managers to lower the market price of the stock toward a preferred dollar and cent level—perhaps because it requires lower brokerage fees to trade. Another aspect of stock dividends is that if the cash dividend is kept constant on a per share basis, then a stock dividend is tanta-

WINDOW 13.2

The Mechanics of Stock Dividends and Stock Splits

Stock Dividend: Consider the Malta Corporation, which currently has 1,000 shares of stock outstanding, with each trading at a market price of \$10. To simplify matters, Malta is unlevered, such that the total value of the firm is \$10,000. Malta announces that each shareholder will receive a 10 percent stock dividend. You currently own 10 shares of Malta, and the market value of your holdings is \$100.

Stock Split: Consider the Yalta Corporation, which currently has 1,000 shares of stock outstanding, with each trading at a market price of \$10. To simplify matters, Yalta is unlevered, such that the total value of the firm is \$10,000. Yalta announces a two-for-one stock split, such that for each share originally owned, Yalta will issue one additional share. You currently own 10 shares of Yalta, and the market value of your holdings is \$100.

Reverse Stock Split: Consider the Falta Corporation, which currently has 1,000 shares of stock outstanding, with each trading at a market price of \$10. To simplify matters, Falta is unlevered, such that the total value of the firm is \$10,000. Falta announces a one-for-two reverse stock split, such that for each two shares originally owned, Falta will take one share away. You currently own 10 shares of Falta, and the market value of your holdings is \$100.

The key in each of these situations is that total market value does not change, just the numbers of shares. The stock price after the stock dividend, stock split, and reverse stock split can be found as the product of the old price and the ratio of the number of shares:

$$\text{New Stock Price} = \text{Old Stock Price} \times \frac{\text{Old Number of Shares}}{\text{New Number of Shares}}$$

For Malta (stock dividend), the new stock price is

$$\$10 \times \frac{1}{1.1} = \$9.09,$$

and the total market value of your investment is 11 shares × \$9.09 = \$100, the same as before.

For Yalta (stock split), the new stock price is:

$$\$10 \times \frac{1}{2} = \$5.00$$

and the total market value of your investment is 20 shares × \$5 = \$100, the same as before.

For Falta (reverse stock split), the new stock price is:

$$\$10 \times \frac{2}{1} = \$20.00$$

and the total market value of your investment is 5 shares × \$20 = \$100, the same as before.

mount to a cash dividend increase, because each investor will receive the cash dividend on more shares.

To repeat, stock dividends and stock splits do not significantly create, destroy, or transfer wealth. They are simply types of paperwork that can be used to move prices per share into more desirable levels in order to provide convenience or reduced transactions costs. Important creation of wealth comes from intelligent acquisition and management of real assets.

A Final Wrap-Up

Can the firm's dividend policy affect the value of the firm? The traditional view is, *yes,* that dividends are good for shareholders and that the goal of an optimal dividend policy is to pay out as much cash in the form of dividends as possible, while still maintaining the optimal growth and capital structure of the firm.

The modernist view, however, is that the firm's dividend policy is paperwork, rather than the creation or destruction of real assets. Dividend policy, therefore, cannot create wealth, but questions still remain. Do the tax laws allow shareholders to use dividend policy to transfer wealth from the government? Can dividends be a vehicle through which bankruptcy can be used to maximize shareholder wealth? Can dividends be a vehicle through which agency costs can be minimized, or through which information can be signaled?

As in the case of capital structure in Chapter 12, there are no clear answers to these questions. Rather, this chapter has offered a structured framework within which logical analysis can take place. Equipped with this method of thinking and analyzing, the financial manager will be prepared to make decisions for specific cases.

Summary

- Dividend policy is the decision as to which portion of earnings to pay outside the firm to stockholders and which portion to retain inside the firm. Either way, the shareholder is entitled to the wealth—as a current dividend or as a higher future dividend.
- In the absence of market imperfections, the dividend decision is irrelevant. This is best shown through the argument of homemade dividends. There are, however, several market imperfections, such as taxes, bankruptcy, and agency costs, that seem to play an important role in understanding dividends.
- In the M&M with taxes model, the tax disadvantages of dividends in terms of personal income tax drive the optimal dividend policy to a zero percent payout. In the Miller tax model, the tax advantages of capital gains and other breaks are so powerful that personal-equity income taxes are driven to zero and it becomes irrelevant as to whether or not the firm pays dividends.

- Dividends remove equity and cash from the firm and therefore may increase the probability of bankruptcy. Although this can have both advantages and costs to shareholders, it would generally appear to be beneficial in cases of huge debt burdens, large lawsuits, and impending business collapse.
- Dividends appear to signal information to the market. This is a critical explanation of why security prices tend to change dramatically when a major dividend announcement is made, but does not necessarily say anything about how dividend payments affect firm value.

References

Miller, M. H. "Debt and Taxes." *Journal of Finance* 32 (May 1977), 261–276.

———, and F. Modigliani. "Dividend Policy, Growth, and the Valuation of Shares." *Journal of Business* 34 (October 1961), 1–40.

Miller, M. H., and M. S. Scholes. "Dividends and Taxes." *Journal of Financial Economics* 6 (December 1978), 333–364.

Demonstration Problems

Problem 1
Miles Corporation has the following balance sheet, expressed in market values:

Assets		*Liabilities and Owners' Equity*	
Cash	$ 500,000	Debt	$1,000,000
Fixed assets	$2,500,000	Common stock	$2,000,000
Total assets	$3,000,000	Total debt and stock	$3,000,000

Assuming that there are currently 100,000 shares of common stock, find the current stock price as well as the stock prices that would immediately result from: (a) a $1 cash dividend, (b) a 10 percent stock dividend, (c) a two-for-one stock split, and (d) a one-for-four reverse stock split. (Solve each occurrence separately rather than assuming that all four events happened.)

Solution to Problem 1
Step 1: Find the current stock price. The current common stock price may be found by dividing the total value of the shareholders' equity by the number of shares:

$$\text{Price per Share} = \text{Total Equity Value} / \text{Number of Shares}$$

$$\text{Price per Share} = \$2{,}000{,}000 / 100{,}000$$

$$\text{Price per Share} = \$20.$$

Step 2: Find the stock price after a $1 cash dividend. The price per share of a common stock drops (approximately) by the amount of a cash dividend on the ex-dividend date as discussed in the text.

New Share Price = Old Share Price − Cash Dividend

New Share Price = $20 − $1

New Share Price = $19.

This can be verified by putting together a new balance sheet:

Assets		*Liabilities and Owners' Equity*	
Cash	$ 400,000	Debt	$1,000,000
Fixed assets	$2,500,000	Common stock	$1,900,000
Total assets	$2,900,000	Total debt and stock	$2,900,000

The cash balance has declined by $100,000 to reflect the payment by the corporation of a $1 per share cash dividend on 100,000 shares. The value of the common stock drops by the same amount to keep the balance sheet balanced. The result is that the new total equity value ($1.9 million) divided by the same number of shares (100,000) is $19.

Step 3: The new price of the stock after each of the actions can be found using the procedures and formula shown in Window 13.2:

New Stock Price = Old Stock Price × (Old # of Shares / New # of Shares).

Step 4: For the 10 percent stock dividend, there will now be 110,000 shares because the number of shares has increased by 10 percent. Plugging into the equation:

New Stock Price = $20 × (100,000 / 110,000) = $18.18

Step 5: For the two-for-one stock split, there will now be 200,000 shares because the number of shares has doubled. Plugging into the equation:

New Stock Price = $20 × (100,000 / 200,000) = $10.00

Step 6: For the one-for-four reverse stock split, there will now be 25,000 shares because the number of shares has been quartered. Plugging into the equation:

New Stock Price = $20 × (100,000 / 25,000) = $80.00

Final Solution	
Current Stock Price	$20.00
(a) After cash dividend	$19.00
(b) After stock dividend	$18.18
(c) After stock split	$10.00
(d) After reverse stock split	$80.00

Problem 2

Return to Miles Corporation, which has the following balance sheet expressed in market values:

Assets		*Liabilities and Owners' Equity*	
Cash	$ 500,000	Debt	$1,000,000
Fixed assets	$2,500,000	Common stock	$2,000,000
Total assets	$3,000,000	Total debt and stock	$3,000,000

Continue to assume that there are currently 100,000 shares of common stock. Let us assume, however, that the Miles Corporation has decided not to pay any cash dividends to their shareholders—as a method of demonstrating the firm's financial troubles to their labor union as negotiations draw near. Joan owns 1,000 shares of Miles Corporation stock and counts on the $1 per share dividend to meet ordinary living expenses. Joan paid $20 per share for the stock and is in a 30 percent income tax bracket. Given this information:

a. Demonstrate homemade dividends with no taxes,

b. Compare (1) the after-tax value of Joan's investment using homemade dividends with (2) the after-tax value assuming that a dividend is paid in an M&M tax world (with no taxes on capital gains), and

c. Compare (1) the after-tax value of Joan's investment using homemade dividends with (2) the after-tax value assuming that a dividend is paid in a Miller tax world (with no tax on any equity income).

Solution to Problem 2

Step 1: First, demonstrate homemade dividends with no taxes. Joan now owns 1,000 shares at $20 per share for a total value of $20,000, and she wants a $1 per share dividend so she can have $1,000 cash even though she knows that the share price will drop by the $1 if the firm pays a $1 dividend. Thus, Joan wants to move from the left side to the right side of the following illustration:

Where Joan is:		*Where Joan wants to be:*	
Cash	$ 0	Cash	$ 1,000
Stock	$20,000	Stock	$19,000

Examining the preceding illustration, it is clear that Joan can obtain the $1,000 cash that she desires by selling 50 shares of stock at $20 each:

Proceeds from sale of 50 shares at $20 each	$ 1,000
Remaining value of 950 shares at $20 each	$19,000

This is the same result as would be obtained if the firm has issued a $1 dividend:

Cash from $1 per share dividend on 1,000 shares	$ 1,000
Remaining value of 1,000 shares at $19 each	$19,000

Step 2: Next, we compare the homemade dividend strategy on an after-tax basis with an actual corporate cash dividend. Assuming an M&M tax world, investors are fully taxed on dividend income, but income from capital gains is untaxed.

First, find the after-tax proceeds from selling 50 shares:

Proceeds from sale of 50 shares at $20 each	$ 1,000
Remaining value of 950 shares at $20 each	$19,000
Total after-tax value	$20,000

Now, find the after-tax value of receiving a cash dividend from the corporation:

Cash from $1 per share dividend on 1,000 shares	$ 1,000
Tax liability on $1,000 dividend at 30%	$ −300
Remaining value of 1,000 shares at $19 each	$19,000
Total after-tax value	$19,700

Thus, in an M&M tax world, the investor is better off not receiving a cash dividend so that the $300 tax liability can be avoided.

Step 3: Finally, we compare the homemade dividend strategy on an after-tax basis with an actual corporate cash dividend in a Miller tax world with no tax on equity income. First, find the after-tax proceeds from selling 50 shares:

Proceeds from sale of 50 shares at $20 each	$ 1,000
Remaining value of 950 shares at $20 each	$19,000
Total after-tax value	$20,000

Now, find the after-tax value of receiving a cash dividend from the corporation:

Cash from $1 per share dividend on 1,000 shares	$ 1,000
Tax liability on $1,000 dividend	$ 0
Remaining value of 1,000 shares at $19 each	$19,000
Total after-tax value	$20,000

Thus, in a Miller tax world, the investor is equally well off receiving a cash dividend as liquidating shares because there are no personal taxes on either dividends or capital gains.

Final Solution: Homemade dividends are equally attractive as corporate cash dividends without taxes or in a Miller tax world. Only in an M&M tax world, where it is assumed that capital gains offer a tax advantage and that dividends are taxed, is there a disadvantage to cash dividends and therefore an incentive to use homemade dividends.

Review Questions

1. Describe the dividend decision as a transfer of cash from inside to outside the firm.
2. Contrast the following terms: (a) regular cash dividend, (b) extra dividend, (c) special dividend, (d) stock dividend.
3. What is the ex-dividend date, and what will happen to the market price of the stock on the ex-dividend date? Why?
4. What are retained earnings, and how do they relate to the firm's dividend policy? (*Hint*: Think of shareholders as residual claimants.)
5. Describe how homemade dividends can undo the firm's dividend policy.
6. Why do M&M maintain that, in the presence of taxes, the dividend payout ratio should be zero percent?
7. Why in the Miller model is it stated that, in the presence of taxes, the dividend payout ratio is irrelevant?
8. How are agency costs related to the payment of dividends?

9. Relate signaling theory and manager's information to dividend policy.
10. Do stock dividends or stock splits, in and of themselves, make shareholders better off? Worse off? Explain.

Problems

1. Fill in each blank space with a type of dividend payment. Choose from the following: stock, extra, regular, liquidating, special.

   Dividends that shareholders expect to receive on a periodic basis are called _______ dividends; however, other types of dividends exist. For example _______ dividends are paid in addition to regular dividends, and _______ dividends are reserved for special situations. Further, dividends in the form of shares of stock instead of cash are called _______ dividends. Finally, companies that expect to terminate operations may pay a _______ dividend.

2. Fill in each blank with a dividend related date. Choose from the following: announcement, record, ex-dividend, payment.

   The dividend payment procedure is often spread out over a number of weeks and follows a certain sequence. The date the board of directors meet and make public the firm's intent to pay a dividend is the _______ date. The dividend will be sent to all shareholders who own stock on the _______ date. Because it normally takes three business days after stock is sold to record the name and address of the new owner on the company official list, the two business day prior to the _______ date is known as the _______ date. Dividend payments are mailed to the shareholders about two weeks after the date, known as the _______ date.

3. The dividend payout ratio is the percentage of the firm's residual cash flow paid to the shareholders in the form of a dividend. The annual dividend is usually divided into quarterly chunks. Simon's Suitcases, Inc., has a payout ratio of 60 percent. Calculate Simon's annual and quarterly dividend if its residual cash flow is $4.00 per share.
4. Alfred is a wise investor who picks stocks on the basis of the firm's dividend payout ratio. He invests in a stock only if the dividend payout ratio is at least 40 percent. Help Alfred determine if he should consider the following four stocks for his portfolio:

   1: Quarterly dividend = $0.30 per share, annual residual cash flow = $ 2.00 share.

   2: Quarterly dividend = $2.50 per share, annual residual cash flow = $22.50 share.

   3: Quarterly dividend = $0.75 per share, annual residual cash flow = $ 4.00 share.

   4: Quarterly dividend = $1.25 per share, annual residual cash flow = $12.50 share.

5. Jim Simpson, the founder of Simpson's Saxophones, knows much about saxophones but little about finance. The other day he was alarmed when his company's stock price, which had been $50 per share, fell to $48.50 per share. The reason he was alarmed was because he knew things were going well for the firm, and that no bad news had been released. Explain to Jim how dividends might explain the movement in share price.
6. McMann's Marble Shoppes has stock currently trading at $8.00 per share. The firm has announced a $0.50 quarterly dividend.
   a. What is McMann's expected price per share on the ex-dividend date?
   b. Ruth purchases 500 shares of McMann stock on the day prior to the ex-dividend date. Jerry purchases 500 shares of McMann stock on the ex-dividend date. Given your answer in part (a), show how these investments are equivalent.
7. The following is the abbreviated balance sheet for DiConcini Boats and Yachts.

Cash	$ 500,000	Debt	$ 0
Other Assets	$9,500,000	Equity	$10,000,000
Shares outstanding =	100,000		

DiConcini has just paid a cash dividend of $1.00 per share. Show what will likely happen to the firm's balance sheet and share price after the dividend payment.

Cash	Debt
Other Assets	Equity

8. Recall DiConcini Boats and Yachts. Hatch is an unhappy DiConcini shareholder, as he has no use for the $1 dividend. Hatch owns 1,000 shares. Show how Hatch can (approximately) negate the dividend.
9. Mary-Ellen Kennedy is also a DiConcini shareholder who owns 1,000 shares. Unlike Mr. Hatch, Ms. Kennedy loves dividends. In fact, Mary-Ellen would prefer that the firm double its dividend to $2 per share. Show how she can use homemade dividends to achieve (approximately) her desired dividend.
10. The following is the abbreviated balance sheet for Bryant Mining.

Cash	$ 6,000	Debt	$ 0
Other Assets	$14,000	Equity	$20,000
Shares outstanding =	2,000		

Bryant has just paid a cash dividend of $1.00 per share. Show what will likely happen to the firm's balance sheet and share price after the dividend payment.

Cash	Debt
Other Assets	Equity

11. Refer to Bryant Mining in Problem 10. Becker Shembo owns 100 shares of Bryant, but he decides that he does not want his investment in the firm reduced. Show how Becker Shembo can negate the dividend. Repeat the analysis for a $2 dividend payment.
12. The Duke Football Company has equity valued at $60,000, 10,000 shares outstanding, and a current price per share of $6.00. Duke just paid a $1.00 dividend per share. You own 500 shares of Duke. Show how you can negate the dividend.

13. Sacco Genetech has a policy of retaining after-tax income for future growth opportunities. Sacco has equity valued at $500,000 and has 5,000 shares of stock outstanding. As a shareholder with 100 shares, you desire a dividend to meet cash needs. If your cash needs are $500, show how you can use a homemade dividend to realize the $500.
14. Duffie Dog Collars has 600,000 shares outstanding and a market equity value of $2.4 million. The firm has just paid a dividend of $1.00 per share. As a shareholder with 1,000 shares, however, you desire a $3.00 dividend. Use homemade dividends to create (approximately) the desired dividend.
15. Sandusky Real Estate estimates dividends next year at $1.50. The firm's required rate of return on equity is 12 percent. If the firm's rate of growth in annual dividends is 6 percent, calculate the price per share of Sandusky using the perpetual growth model.
16. The Board of Directors of Sandusky Real Estate (see Problem 15) announces that next year's dividend, expected to be $1.50, will be lowered to $1.00 in order to retain additional funds for investment purposes. Given a required rate of return on equity at 12 percent, calculate the new growth rate in dividends that would produce the share price of $25.
17. J and J Cowboy Paraphernalia, Inc., pays a dividend of $2.00 per share. All of J and J's shareholders are taxed at the rate of 31 percent. Calculate the after-tax proceeds per share of the shareholder's dividend payment.
18. Elvis Humperdinck is a retired tightrope walker. Mr. Humperdinck relies mostly on his dividend check from RRR Corp. to meet living expenses. He owns 10,000 shares of RRR, which pays a dividend of $1 per share, and he is in the 15 percent tax bracket.
    a. Calculate Mr. Humperdinck's after-tax dividend proceeds.
    b. Suppose that the taxing authorities raise Mr. Humperdinck's tax rate to 25 percent. How much higher would the dividend of RRR need to be in order to keep Elvis's after-tax dividend income the same as it was under the old tax rates?
19. Recall Mary-Ellen Kennedy (Problem 9), who owns 1,000 shares of DiConcini, Inc. Ms. Kennedy is in the 31 percent tax bracket.
    a. Compute Ms. Kennedy's after-tax dividend payment per share, assuming that she pays her taxes on time.
    b. Problem 9 illustrated how Ms. Kennedy used homemade dividends to create her desired dividend payment. Show that, considering personal taxes, Ms. Kennedy would be better off creating the homemade dividend than she would be if the firm increased the dividend. Assume her original purchase price for DiConcini was $70.00 per share.
20. Washington Turf is a large corporation with equity valued at $5 million but no debt. Rust Roofing is also a large corporation with $3 million in debt and $2 million in equity. Both companies are close to bankruptcy. Calculate the maximum amount of a liquidating dividend that each firm can make. In which firm would you rather have a $1,000 investment? Explain.
21. Parcells Pools has 5,000 shares of stock outstanding and a current stock price of $5.00 per share. Parcells has no debt. The company is short on cash and announces that, instead of a cash dividend, the firm will pay a stock dividend—one new share of stock for each 10 held.
    a. Calculate the new share price after the stock dividend goes into effect.
    b. L.T., a Parcells shareholder with 100 shares, wonders what the stock dividend means to him. Show L.T. that the stock dividend does not increase his wealth.

22. Madden Airlines is so strapped for cash that it has decided to scrap any plans for a cash dividend and to "reward" its shareholders with a stock dividend. Madden's share price is currently at $10 per share. There are 10,000 shares outstanding and its equity value is $100,000. Madden decides to keep its shareholders happy by providing 10 new shares for each one share held. Patrick Summerhill, a loyal Madden shareholder, has 10 shares before the stock dividend. Explain to Summerhill both the good news and the bad news of the stock dividend.
23. Ryan's Buddy System, a company specializing in social skills training, makes the big announcement: The firm will split its stock two-for-one. Ryan's stock is currently at $150 per share, and there are 1,000 shares outstanding.
    a. What will happen to the price of each share upon the announcement?
    b. Demonstrate that a shareholder with 50 shares does not gain by the split.
24. There are some who believe that firms split their stock in order to bring the per share price down to a trading range affordable to most investors. Darlene's Dance Company is currently trading at $180 per share, but would like to see its shares trade at $45. Design a stock split strategy for Darlene to accomplish its trading range objective.
25. Shula Air Attach, a manufacturer of navigational systems, is near bankruptcy with shares trading at $0.25 each. Shula has 100,000 shares outstanding. The firm's founder, sensing that the end is near, has given up all hope of his goal—to head a firm whose share price is more than $100 per share. Show how the founder can obtain his goal through the reverse stock split.

Discussion Questions

1. Why would the U.S. Internal Revenue Service try to force firms to pay dividends?
2. Which of the following groups of people can be hurt when a firm switches to a high dividend payout strategy in an imperfect market: managers, laborers, creditors, suppliers, pension recipients?
3. How could a stock split signal good news and how could a reverse stock split signal bad news?
4. Stock prices fall by only 20 percent when a firm pays a 25 percent stock dividend. Is this an arbitrage opportunity?
5. Respond to the following:

   Modern corporate finance theory does not apply to firms that currently pay no dividends because the market is obviously pricing their stock based on something other than dividends.

6. Why do the stock prices of large firms that declare bankruptcy usually rise when the announcement is made?
7. Chance and Security are identical twin sisters (with unusual names) who live in the city of Ceteris Paribus, Pennsylvania. It is important, for this problem, to note that it is assumed that these sisters live in a country with well-functioning capital markets. (For the purposes of this problem, assume that they are perfect capital markets.) Further, legal services and other "frictions" involved with bankruptcy do not exist.

   Chance and Security have identical high-level management jobs in identical (but separate) small corporations. Both corporations have a single identical building, identical equipment, identical products, identical financial statements, and so forth.

There is one difference between Chance and Security. The corporation that employs Chance has absolutely no fire insurance. The corporation that employs Security is well insured against losses due to fire. The fire insurance policy for Security's firm states that, in the event of a serious fire, the insurance company will pay Security's firm an amount of money equal to the value of the fire damage to the building.

Chance worries that someday there might be a fire that will destroy the building. In particular, she is rather worried that a large, uninsured loss would drive her firm into bankruptcy, and she worries that she would, therefore, lose her job. Jobs like Chance's and Security's are very difficult and costly to find. On the other hand, Security knows that a serious fire would not drive her firm into bankruptcy because the insurance company can be trusted to provide a prompt and fair settlement.

Chance has sought your advice. Which of the following do you most agree with?

a. Chance should try to talk with other managers of her corporation in order to encourage them to obtain the same type of insurance that Security's firm has.

b. Chance should purchase her own insurance against this loss (assume that this is legal) even though her sister should not purchase such insurance.

c. Chance is in the same position as her sister. She should, therefore, do the same thing that her sister does (which may or may not include the purchase of "private" insurance).

d. Chance should incur the expense of switching jobs before it is too late.

e. Chance should seek advice from someone else.

f. None of the above.

Defend your answer and then attempt to extend the results of this exercise into addressing the following question. In perfect capital markets, who benefits from insurance?

CHAPTER 14

CORPORATE ETHICS AND SHAREHOLDER WEALTH MAXIMIZATION

It seemed like a dream come true. Craig had just graduated from college and was offered a job as a stockbroker at a small but rapidly growing East Coast brokerage firm. He knew it was going to be hard work. The firm offered no guaranteed salary—only commissions on sales. At age 22, Craig had no actual investment experience. He did pass the exam required for a license as a stockbroker, paying $500 for the study materials for the training class that the brokerage firm required. He borrowed the money from his parents, confident that his commissions would enable him to pay it back.

The first few days on the job were far different than Craig had imagined. The brokerage firm specialized in newly issued shares of stock in high-technology ventures. Craig's job consisted of "cold-calling" prospective investors and attempting to get them to invest.

The hours were strange. Work began at 5 P.M. Craig's office was one of about 30 desks in a large room filled with computers and telephones. A computer would dial numbers for Craig until someone answered the phone. Craig would then read word-for-word from a script, as he had been trained:

Hi, Mr. ____________: My name is Craig, with America, Motherhood, and Apple Pie Investment Corporation. How are you today? Fine. Listen, Mr. ____________, the reason I am calling is to let you know about our firm. We specialize in the common stock of small and extremely promising high-technology firms. In the past, our recommendations have produced profits for our clients of up to 200 percent per year. Is 200 percent a return which you would be interested in earning? Great, Mr. ____________, we do not have any such opportunities right now, but when the next great opportunity arises, I'll give you another call.

As the evenings wore on, the computer would dial phone numbers in western time zones so that Craig could continue calling prospective clients until 11 P.M. eastern time.

In the first few weeks, success was rare. While Craig did manage to sell about $2,000 of stock, his sales were to his closest relatives and friends. By watching the techniques of the superstars in the office, however, Craig began to learn the proper technique of cold-calling. Any investor who responded favorably to the first phone call would receive a second phone call urgently pressing the customer to invest quickly in a new venture. The key was to make it seem as if it was now or never, that this opportunity might never be presented again.

Craig found that the rewards for success were phenomenal. In addition to commissions, there were monthly sales contests in which one could win trips to the Bahamas. As commissions came in, Craig was able to pay back the $500 loan to his parents and to enjoy a new type of life-style. He took on a large car payment and larger and larger credit card bills. Craig found that even though he was beginning to make good commissions, his rising debt forced him to push potential clients especially hard.

After several months, some problems began to develop. Many of the stocks he had recommended shot upward in price initially, but collapsed soon afterward and became worthless. He was instructed to push clients who did make money into reinvesting profits in new companies instead of cashing in. He also noticed, however, that the stocks he was recommending to buy were often the same stocks that other brokers in the office were recommending to sell.

A nagging fear in the back of Craig's mind told him that the America, Motherhood, and Apple Pie Corporation was not like the typical brokerage firm and was stretching the rules of investing to the point of being illegal. What could he do? If he quit, he would lose everything he had worked hard for over the last 6 months, and he would never be able to help his friends and relatives earn back the money that they had lost on his first few recommendations. How could he ever expect to get a better job if he blew his first one?

Craig knew better than to discuss his concerns at work, as there seemed to be an unwritten office rule against negative or discouraging comments. Further, the other brokers joked about the ignorance and hard luck of their clients. They seemed to feel that the best way to do business was to worry only about themselves.

Craig's dilemma raises the issue of ethical business behavior. Recall our conclusion in Chapter 1—that the purpose of the corporation is to maximize shareholder wealth. Is wealth maximization still an appropriate objective when ethics are considered? Said differently, was it right for the America, Motherhood, and Apple Pie Investment Corporation to sell stock this way? To help answer this question, this chapter discusses ethics and ethical decision making as it relates to corporate finance and the firm's objective.

Corporate Ethics Introduced

Corporate ethics has been and continues to be a topic of prime importance in business. Business ethics, unfortunately, is traditionally discussed in the context of proper conduct in specific situations, perhaps through case analyses or through surveying business leaders. Although we can draw interesting inferences from cases and surveys, they fail to provide a proper foundation by which to analyze corporate ethics.

In providing such a foundation, we begin by defining *ethics.* According to *Webster's New Collegiate Dictionary,* ethics is "the discipline dealing with what is good and bad and with moral duty and obligation." Thus, discussing ethics is by definition exploring right and wrong. **Corporate** (or business) **ethics** explores establishing right and wrong conduct for situations within a corporate or business environment. Examples of business ethics include (1) with what wages and benefits should firms compensate their employees? (2) to what hiring, promotion, and severance practices should a firm adhere? and (3) what role should a corporation play within its community?

corporate ethics
Ethics is by definition exploring right and wrong behavior. Corporate or business ethics explores establishing right and wrong conduct for situations within a corporate or business environment.

This text does not discuss ethics per se. In other words, we are not trying to teach what is right or wrong. Rather, we are attempting to provide students with a framework with which they can use their understanding of ethics to analyze a situation that occurs in financial management.

For example, Chapter 1 discussed the importance of basing decisions on market prices, and stated that market prices are the product of basic economic principles. Do questions of ethics move us away from using market prices and economic principles? We believe the answer is, *no,* that market values can price ethics just as they can price anything else. Thus, a corporation that maximizes shareholder wealth by maximizing the firm's stock price is making the stock as desirable as possible to investors. We return to this point later in the chapter.

Can Corporations Act Ethically?

We often hear news or commentary that suggests that a certain corporation is practicing unethical behavior. Is this possible? The answer is, *no!* Ethical decisions can be rationally viewed only as being between the people who contract through the corporation, including managers, employees, shareholders, bondholders, customers, and suppliers.

As discussed in Chapter 1, a corporation is a set of contracts linking people together. Corporations, like all forms of business organizations, are legal abstractions that do not have the ability to hurt or to be hurt. Pieces of paper and documents do not have feelings, emotions, or nervous breakdowns—they can only serve as conduits from one person to another. It is not possible for a legal abstraction to do something right or wrong.

Questions of corporate ethical behavior are therefore questions of actions by one person or group of persons within the corporation with respect to their effect on another person or group of persons. For example, we may ask if it is ethical of shareholders (people) to seek wealth maximization. In a similar way, we can ask if bondholders (people) are acting ethically by taking control of the firm when it is in financial trouble. Discussing whether a specific company (e.g., Exxon) is unethical, however, must be viewed as imprecise and requires further specification in order to identify clearly the people involved.

Two Approaches to Corporate Ethics

contractual-rights approach
An approach to the study of ethics in which ethical decisions are applied based upon rights and how those rights should be preserved.

societal-good approach
An approach to the study of ethics whereby ethical decisions are applied based upon whether or not something is viewed as being good for society.

The philosophical underpinnings of ethical thought date back over centuries. This chapter discusses these underpinnings around two general approaches. The first is the **contractual-rights approach,** in which ethical decisions are applied based upon rights and how those rights should be preserved. The second approach is the **societal-good approach,** wherein ethical decisions are applied based upon whether or not something is viewed as being good for society rather than upon rights. A summary of the philosophical roots of ethics and economics is provided in Appendix 14.1.

For example, let us consider the topic of drug testing in the work place, for which the typical question is should employers be allowed to administer drug testing on current or prospective employees? Advocates of the contractual-rights approach would explore this issue by questioning whether employees have a right not to be drug tested and whether employers have a right to hire and retain anyone they want. Advocates of the societal-good approach would explore this issue from the perspective of when and if drug testing leads to a better or worse society.

Other examples of topics involving ethical decisions include universal health care, family leave in the work place, and minimum wage laws, and can be analyzed from the perspective of these two approaches. As authors, we admit that we favor the contractual-rights approach. We will present both approaches, but we must point out that only the contractual-rights approach stands up against the standards of logical analysis discussed in Chapter 1.

The Contractual-Rights Approach to Corporate Ethics

The contractual-rights approach to corporate ethics analyzes behavior on the basis of individual rights, contractually retained. For instance, is it a person's right to drug-test an employee or does it violate the employee's rights? Is health care a right of each employee? Within the contractual-rights approach there is little or no emphasis on whether or not the behavior is good for society.

In discussions of contractual rights, it becomes clear that people differ on what they feel is a true right. For example, from the following two lists ask yourself which group, List 1 or List 2, represents true rights of individuals.

List 1	*List 2*
1. The right to a decent job.	1. The right to unionize.
2. The right to basic health care.	2. The right to own property.
3. The right to quality child care.	3. The right to pay an agreed-upon wage.

Within the contractual-rights view of business ethics, there is general agreement that List 2 represents true rights and List 1 does not. For example, in the United States the discussion of contractual rights is greatly simplified because many of the rights of people are clearly understood. Individual rights in the United States are set forth in the U.S. Constitution and the constitutions of the states. The Constitution declares that people have a right to own, keep, and control the property they have earned in exchange for their labor or which they have been lawfully given by others (e.g., parents).

In contrast, the "rights" in List 1 have not been contracted. Further, List 1 forces people to supply resources against their will to other people. For example, the right to health care or child care is tantamount to forcing other people to provide it or to pay for it. Thus, the rights in List 1 are examples of attempts to violate the rights of other persons. The rights in List 2 are contractual, as they represent the rights of people to control their own bodies and property, when rights are defined in their traditional and constitutional sense.

The Societal-Good Approach to Corporate Ethics

The second approach to corporate ethics is the societal-good approach, in which ethically correct decisions are defined as those that produce the greatest overall benefit to society.

Politicians often use this approach when debating or determining matters of public policy. For example, most people support the idea that corporations should be required to pay at least some minimum wage, based on the idea that it is only fair that a corporation provide this minimum pay to its employees. Notice that this argument focuses on what seems fair rather than on whether society has a right to interfere with the wage rate that the corporation's shareholders pay.

Returning to the drug-testing example, advocates of the societal-good approach would debate whether the responsibilities of certain jobs, such as those of airline pilots or other jobs that put people at risk of injury, are important enough to society that testing should be required. If so, testing would become a requirement for these jobs but not for others.

Debating the Two Approaches to Corporate Ethics

Despite the widespread usage and appeal of the societal-good approach, the debate must be analyzed carefully. Consider the fact that the United States was founded by applying the contractual-rights approach.

The rich and the poor provide a fertile ground for debating the two approaches to business ethics. Compassionate people hate to see groups suffer in poverty while others live in opulence. In fact, it is the desire to force a fairer distribution of wealth that lies at the heart of most societal-good arguments. What many people fail to see, however, is that actions designed to alleviate the economic conditions of the poor can violate individual rights.

WINDOW 14.1

The Corruption of Robin Hood

Most people are familiar with the story of Robin Hood—or so they think. Many people will describe Robin Hood as the legendary Englishman who stole from the rich and gave to the poor, but it may surprise most readers to know that this is not the original story. Some may recall that the story was a little more complicated than simply stealing from the rich and giving to the poor. In fact, most authorities agree that, in the original stories, Robin Hood was taking money from tax collectors and unscrupulous landowners and returning it to the people from whom it had been stolen. Many readers will never have heard of the original version.

There is a very big difference between these versions. In the "stealing from the rich and giving to the poor" version, Robin Hood is admired based upon the idea that poor people are entitled to money held by rich people; therefore, this is not "stealing," but rather is "justice." In the historic version, Robin Hood is admired for risking his life to return stolen money.

What do you believe stealing is? Is it stealing to shoplift from a small store owned by a family, but acceptable to shoplift from big corporations such as Sears? Is it stealing to inflate a claim made to a large insurance company? Would it be stealing if someone stole this book from you right now, sold it, and used the money on the premise that he or she needs the money more than you? As you evaluate these questions, we hope you agree that individual rights belong to everyone according to the U.S. Constitution—even the rich.

Contractual rights belong to everyone—from the poorest to the wealthiest individuals in society. The view that "I" have a right to "my property" but "shareholders" of a corporation do not have the same right to "their property" is implicit in many widely held viewpoints. It is essential as we explore business ethics that we keep reminding ourselves that according to the U.S. Constitution individual rights belong to everyone—even shareholders! To illustrate this important point, we offer the story of Robin Hood in Window 14.1.

Does this mean that in order to adhere to contractual rights a person must stop caring about the poor and doing things for them? The answer is, *no!* The contractual-rights approach does not stand in the way of helping the poor, but rather it says that it is wrong to pass laws that force people to help the poor. Indeed, the United States, under a system of contractual rights, has one of the highest levels of philanthropic giving in the world.

Unrequired Behavior Versus Required Behavior: Oughttas Versus Gottas

Before addressing questions of corporate ethics directly, it is useful to draw a distinction between the concepts *oughttas* and *gottas.* We seek to differentiate ethical conduct we require from other people (the "got to's" or gottas) from the ethical conduct we do not require from others (the "ought to's" or oughttas). Helping an elderly person cross a street is an oughtta. Not running an elderly person over in a crosswalk with your car is a gotta.

Keeping these two concepts separate in our minds helps develop a reasoned approach to corporate ethics. This begins by separating behavior that we pursue ourselves and wish others would pursue from behavior that we require of other people. We can thus categorize a particular ethical dilemma as involving either an oughtta or a gotta. Readers will find that this insight changes their view of ethics.

Oughttas

We start with oughttas, or conduct a person believes is morally correct but which is not legally required. Virtually everyone would agree that, in business, there are many oughttas. For example, people operating within the firm should be courteous to customers and co-workers—saying please and thank you. In addition, people operating within the firm should not knowingly sell a product or service that entails certain dangers without providing an appropriate warning. We could cite many more examples of what most people would agree the corporation ought to do.

Example 14.1 Should Sarah, a trusted employee in a small computer firm, give 2 weeks of notice before leaving the firm for a new job? Sarah's dilemma is a good example of an oughtta. The key to this oughtta is that no matter how much we agree that providing notice to the firm is proper, and no matter how serious the consequences are to other people of not providing notice, forcing an employee to work for 2 weeks after announcing that she is leaving (assuming that the employee did not agree to this condition when accepting the job) would be tantamount to forced work, a clear violation of the Constitution's antislavery amendment. Thus, in the theory of contractual rights, an employee cannot be forced to work against his or her will even if a job is crucial within a small and vital business.

Gottas

Gottas represent required behavior. For example, we require people not to murder or steal. While a discussion of oughttas is fun because no one is being forced to do or not do anything, a discussion of gottas is less fun because it often poses the risk of the denial of one or more persons' rights.

Example 14.2 Can corporations be required to pay income taxes? According to the Sixteenth Amendment to the U.S. Constitution, the answer is, *yes.* The Constitution gives the federal government the right to collect income taxes from people who transact using the corporate form of business organization. Thus, this is a contractual gotta. Of course, people can debate this question in the context of whether or not this gotta is appropriate, but a firm that organizes as a corporation does not have a choice in the matter; it must pay taxes.

This discussion of oughttas and gottas may seem a little unnecessary for understanding business ethics, but it is essential in drawing a clear line between what a person should do and what a person can be forced by society to do. As we will see in the following section, this helps divide the discussion of ethics into two types of decisions: personal ethical decisions and public-policy decisions.

Personal Versus Public-Policy Debates

We now use the ethical approaches of contractual rights and societal good, and the concepts of oughttas and gottas, to clarify the issues of corporate ethics. As Craig from the America, Motherhood, and Apple Pie Investment Corporation found out in the opening to the chapter, ethical dilemmas are faced almost daily by individuals and groups of individuals within the corporation. For instance, shareholders face ethical decisions regarding pollution, the fair treatment of customers, the fair treatment of employees, and so forth.

Personal Ethical Decisions

Like Sarah's decision to give notice, many ethical decisions do not involve illegal behavior; rather, they are personal decisions such as those found in office politics. Most of these issues come down to a conflict between helping yourself and doing what is right for others.[1] How individuals reach a particular decision involves their own ethical belief system (i.e., their own beliefs regarding right or wrong conduct).

Sarah's decision whether or not to provide 2 weeks of notice falls in the category of a personal ethical decision. Because she would not be violating the law or others' rights by leaving the firm without providing 2 weeks of notice, the decision comes down to her own belief system regarding right or wrong conduct.[2]

Public-Policy Ethical Decisions

A different type of ethical decision is a public-policy ethical decision. Public-policy decisions use the government to turn an oughtta into a gotta. As citi-

[1]There is an old joke about someone who is asked to perform unethical behavior for $1 million. After a little thought, the person agreed. The person was then asked to perform the same behavior for $20. The person responded: "No, what type of person do you think I am?" The reply was: "We already know the type of person you are; now we're simply negotiating the price."

[2]Sarah's decision did not involve violating the law. However, sometimes personal ethical decisions, can involve breaking the law, such as the decision to speed to avoid being late for an important appointment.

zens, we participate in making laws subject to the limits placed by the Constitution, and we can even change the Constitution itself by amending it (with the approval of 75 percent of the states).

In terms of public-policy decisions, think of the government as a set of contracts through which people formulate gottas, which require certain types of behavior. Many of the current public-policy debates regarding corporations involve the passage of laws to force some type of behavior. For example, the Family Leave Act (Window 14.2) was passed by the federal government to require that employers grant particular rights and privileges to employees. Other examples of this type include the Americans with Disabilities Act, the Civil Rights Act, and the Clean Air Act. As long as the piece of legislation is constitutional, discussing ethical conduct through these laws is a debate of what is good or bad for society, both within and outside the corporation.

WINDOW 14.2

The Family and Medical Leave Act of 1993

Employee's Provisions

- Allows a worker to take up to 12 weeks of unpaid leave in any 12-month period for the birth of a child or an adoption, to care for a child, spouse, or parent with a serious heath condition or for the workers serious health condition that makes it impossible to perform a job.
- Provides that an employee must be returned to his or her old job or an equivalent position upon returning to work.
- Requires an employer to keep providing health care benefits during the leave, as though the worker were still employed, but does not require the employer to pay the worker on leave.
- Prohibits a worker on leave from collecting unemployment or other Government compensation.
- Covers only a worker who has been employed for at least 1 year and for at least 1,250 hours (25 hours a week).

Employer's Provisions

- Exempts any company with fewer than 50 workers.
- Allows a company to deny leave to a salaried employee within the highest-paid 10 percent of its work force, if letting the worker take the leave would create "substantial and grievous injury" to the business operations.
- Permits an employer to obtain medical opinions and certifications on the need for the leave.
- Allows an employer to ask the employee to repay the health-care premiums paid by the employer during the leave if the employee does not return to work.

We examined a public-policy ethical decision earlier when we asked whether corporations can be required to pay income tax. People, acting through government, have passed laws that force those who contract through the corporation to pay taxes. If society believes that this law is bad, then society can change the law and undo this gotta. A more detailed discussion of personal and public policy ethical decisions is provided in Appendix 14.2.

Corporate Ethics and Shareholder Wealth Maximization

A popular debate in corporate ethics concerns the purpose or goal of a corporation. As detailed in Chapter 1, debating the purpose of the corporation, when this is interpreted literally, does not make a great deal of sense because a corporation is simply a nexus or set of contracts, not a set of people. Although we could detail the goals of all people who contract through corporations, including employees, customers, suppliers, and creditors, we are concerned primarily with discussing the shareholders because they own the corporation. The key question involves the goal of the shareholders with respect to their decision to contract through a particular corporation.

The goal of any person is to make decisions that produce what they perceive to be the most desirable results. Thus, the goal of a corporation is to achieve the most desirable possible results for its shareholders, which may or may not include concern for other people, depending upon the shareholders' ethical beliefs. As is fully developed in Chapter 1, we would generally expect shareholders to desire the greatest possible market value to their stock and therefore their wealth.

Do shareholders have the right to seek maximization of their wealth? The answer based on contractual rights is clearly, *yes!* Shareholders can do whatever they want with their wealth as long as that does not include a violation of society's gottas. The concept of individual private property rights makes the goal of assets or contracts clear: The goal is set by the owner subject to the required behavior or gottas of the society. Shareholders will determine the goal of a corporation because they own the corporation. Of course, we assume that shareholders fulfill their contracts with others (e.g., stakeholders) and that contracts are freely negotiated.

the stakeholder view of the corporation
A view of the corporation originating from the concept that anyone affected by a corporation has a stake in the corporation and should therefore be given the right to influence the corporation.

The societal-good approach to corporate ethics, which is often referred to as **the stakeholder view of the corporation,** attempts to force the shareholders to do the good deeds that other people would like to see done. The word *stakeholder* originates from the concept that anybody affected by a corporation has a stake in the corporation and should therefore be given the right to influence the corporation. As discussed in Chapter 1, we can think of stakeholders as the different groups that contract through the corporation. Thus, while stakeholders have contracts, it is the shareholders that have a residual claim on the firm's cash flows and own the firm. Arguing against shareholder control is implicitly arguing that society itself owns the property and therefore has the right to determine or influence the corporation's goal. This argument can be presented with great intentions, but as the contractual-rights view points out, the stakeholder view violates the rights of the shareholders.

Example 14.3 ________ Given the background of oughttas and gottas, and of personal and public-policy decisions, let us now work through some actual ethical situations facing shareholders within corporations. For example, let us consider the following five corporate ethical questions:

1. Advertising products that some consider to be harmful.
2. Smoking in the work place.
3. Issuing high-risk bonds, sometimes referred to as "junk" bonds.
4. Equal opportunity in hiring practices, especially company policy regarding minority applicants.
5. The disposal of hazardous waste products.

How would these two approaches—societal good and contractual rights—attempt to resolve these ethical issues? The societal-good approach would examine whether laws should be passed to control these behaviors based upon what is best for society. For example, it might be argued that (1) advertising harmful products such as cigarettes and alcoholic beverages might be interpreted as a stamp of approval for their use, (2) second-hand smoke adversely affects the health of all employees, (3) junk bonds have a destabilizing effect on the economy, (4) employment practices need to be fair and equitable, and (5) the local environment must be protected. If widespread agreement exists on these points of view, then people might be tempted to work through government and pass laws that guarantee leaves of absence, that ban all smoking in the work place, that restrict the issuance of certain types of bonds, that require that certain products not be advertised, and that restrict haphazard disposal of waste.

In contrast, the contractual-rights approach first asks whether or not these issues restrict individual rights protected by the Constitution. In other words, does the U.S. Constitution allow governments to interfere with these rights? If the answer is *no,* then from the point of view of contractual rights, people cannot force other people to do these good deeds. If the answer is *yes,* then from the point of view of contractual rights, people can come together to work through government to regulate certain corporate behavior.

In the United States, the Constitution protects the right to ownership of private property. Shareholders are no exception. Thus, corporations cannot be forced to hire or retain people who smoke cigarettes. Further, shareholders have the right to issue debt—including "junk" debt. Because no such contracts exist involving smoking and junk bonds, these situations fall in the category of personal ethical decisions that the corporation's shareholders must make. Shareholders within one corporation could decide to allow cigarette smoking while shareholders within another corporation could decide to restrict such behavior.

In the areas of hiring practices and hazardous waste disposal, however, laws have been passed specifying gottas. Society has acted through government to legislate certain corporate conduct, perhaps because of infringements on the right of people to life and property. These examples illustrate the application of this chapter's principles to contemporary business ethics debates. In the cases of advertising and hazardous waste disposal, the corporation faces penalties if specific guidelines are not followed.

Corporate Ethics and Market Values

We previously discussed whether shareholders have the right to seek maximization of their wealth. We will now discuss whether shareholder wealth maximization is an ethical goal. Some would argue that this goal drives corporations toward highly unethical, and perhaps even illegal, activity.

An essential point, however, is that market values can price ethics just as they can price all other expected cash flows to the firm. Thus, a corporation that maximizes shareholder wealth by maximizing the firm's stock price is making the stock as desirable as possible to investors. If investors care about ethical issues, then they will find the stock of an unethical firm to be less desirable and its stock price will be lower than if it were an ethical firm.

It has become increasingly clear that many investors do care about ethics. With divestiture from certain countries leading the way, ethical concerns have entered corporate boardrooms throughout the world. Window 14.3 discusses socially responsible investing.

Throughout our society we find that ethics are priced. For example, hiring someone to perform an unethical task generally costs more than hiring

WINDOW 14.3

Socially Responsible Investing

The decade of the 1980s witnessed the introduction of investment funds organized around ethical concerns. For example, mutual funds were created to invest only in corporations meeting certain predetermined guidelines such as the corporation's involvement in military weapons systems, in environmental protection, in doing business in certain countries (e.g., South Africa), and in philanthropic activities. These ethical funds were formed under the premise that ethics are valuable, or that all else being equal, the market places a higher value on ethical concerns.

In terms of investment performance, the evidence on ethics funds is far from clear. There is, however, no evidence to support the argument that ethics funds have outperformed the market, where outperforming would be defined as offering a higher return for the same amount of risk. Indeed, if anything, evidence reports that ethics funds have underperformed the market. And although no conclusive evidence exists on the performance of ethics funds, the demand for them is expected to continue for some time.

someone to do honorable work. Are shareholders any different? If not, then the goal of shareholder wealth maximization forces corporate decisions to be made in a way that most satisfies these investors—including their ethical concerns.

In order to maximize shareholder wealth, corporate decisions must be made using the same ethical beliefs that investors have and use in making everyday investment decisions. In other words, market prices are mirrors of or gauges of the values of the free society that produces them. To claim that maximization of shareholder wealth results in unethical behavior is really to claim that the society trading the stock is unethical. In such cases, the real criticism is against the views of society and is unrelated to corporate finance.

Regardless of whether or not shareholders have standards that encourage managers to act ethically, there are other market pressures exerted on a corporation's ethical conduct. For instance, a corporation labeled with "bad" ethical conduct can be hurt by boycotts or other activist activities. There is also some anecdotal evidence that firms can use stated ethical objectives to achieve success in the marketplace. Ben and Jerry's Homemade, the Vermont ice cream producer introduced in Chapter 1, has achieved phenomenal growth due in part to their business philosophy known as caring capitalism. For Ben and Jerry's, however, as well as for any other corporation, this does not mean that the objective of the firm has changed.

Summary

- This chapter discusses corporate ethics and provides a framework for analyzing business decisions involving questions of ethical behavior. Although a discussion of the underpinnings of ethics is beyond the scope of this chapter, the purpose here is to provide a way to think clearly through questions of corporate ethics.
- Two foundations exist from which to study corporate ethics. The contractual-rights approach analyzes behavior on the basis of contracts. In contrast, the societal-good approach analyzes behavior on the basis of its overall benefit to society, and ethical decisions are those viewed as being good for society.
- Under the contractual-rights approach, shareholder wealth maximization remains the appropriate goal of the firm as long as the shareholders, who have the rights of ownership, desire their wealth to be maximized.
- Under the societal-good approach, shareholder wealth maximization may or may not be the appropriate goal, depending on whether the objective most benefits society. This viewpoint often advocates stakeholder objectives.
- Shareholder wealth maximization does not necessarily force unethical behavior but rather mirrors the ethical standards of the society within which the firm operates.

Demonstration Problems

Problem 1

It is often argued that at least some corporations should be required to offer alcohol and drug abuse treatment programs to those employees who voluntarily come forward to request help. Defend this position concisely based upon the societal-good approach.

Solution to Problem 1

The U.S. Constitution establishes the broad mission for people to come together through government to promote the general welfare and to insure domestic tranquillity. When an employee operates a train, or a ship weighing hundreds of tons, or a truck, or an airplane, the general public is placed in extreme danger if that person is impaired by drug abuse. Within these industries, and perhaps in many others, everyone can certainly be made better off by requiring that the employer treat fairly any employees who voluntarily come forward seeking help.

Treatment programs for those persons voluntarily coming forward is the most cost-effective and successful method for alleviating the problem of substance abuse. Even the corporations will be better off, inasmuch as these programs have been proven to be an effective means of reducing the financial consequences of the abuse of drugs and alcohol.

Final Solution: The federal government must set up clear guidelines through which employees in vital industries will be granted access to programs required for their safety as well as for the safety of the general public, which has a stake in the drug-free performance of their duties.

Problem 2

Discuss the same issue as discussed in Question 1, except this time utilize the contractual-rights approach.

Solution to Problem 2

To claim that an employer must provide drug treatment programs to employees is to claim that an employer must spend shareholder money, unwillingly, to provide for services to employees that the employees did not require when agreeing to employment terms.

The U.S. Constitution clearly sets forth that government shall not violate the rights of its citizens, including the right to own private property. The Declaration of Independence holds that the liberties we cherish are self-evident and unalienable.

When a person acting either alone or as a shareholder of a corporation (the employer) hires another person (the employee), this does not abolish the rights of the employer. The employer still has the same rights and protections under the law (ignoring those rights that the employer may have explicitly waived in the employment contract). In other words, just because a person becomes an employer does not mean that the person gives up the right to free speech, a speedy trial, or anything else. An employer has the right to own private property just as an employee does.

How would parents feel if they were suddenly "socked" with a $50,000 drug treatment bill for a babysitter whom they had hired to watch their children? Is child care not a vital job with a direct effect on the health and well-being of our children?

Final Solution: Laws that require an employer to provide services to employees in excess of those agreed upon in the employment contracts violate the rights of the employers. If drug treatment programs are a cost-effective method of alleviating the problems of employees in vital industries, then competition and litigation will "force" employers to provide those programs whose benefits exceed their costs.

Review Questions

1. Can a corporation be ethical or unethical? Explain.
2. Explain the difference between an "oughtta" and a "gotta."
3. Explain briefly the role of the Declaration of Independence and the Constitution as they relate to the contractual-rights approach.
4. Explain the property-rights view of business ethics.
5. Distinguish between personal ethical decisions and public-policy ethical decisions.
6. Can the market price ethics? Explain.
7. If a firm has a goal of shareholder wealth maximization, does this mean that only cash flows should be considered in decision making and that ethical considerations should be ignored?

Problems

1. Based upon your understanding of typical laws, place an "O" in front of those actions better described as "oughttas" (unrequired) and a "G" in front of those actions better described as "gottas" (legal requirements).
   ________ **a.** Making donations to orphans.
   ________ **b.** Paying income taxes.
   ________ **c.** Selling safe and reliable products.
   ________ **d.** Paying employees wages for work performed.
   ________ **e.** Producing products that perform as advertised.
   ________ **f.** Paying wages that permit dignity.
2. Based upon your interpretation of the U.S. Constitution, which of the following are guaranteed rights and which are not rights at all? Use the label *Y* for constitutionally protected rights and *N* for all others.
   ________ **a.** A job.
   ________ **b.** Wasting your food or other assets.
   ________ **c.** Not being fired for voicing one's religious beliefs.
   ________ **d.** Publicly denouncing the actions of a corporation.
   ________ **e.** Adequate health care.
   ________ **f.** Buying, using, and selling property.
   ________ **g.** Firing workers who join a union.
3. For each of the following issues listed indicate whose rights might be violated (e.g., workers, shareholders), and which rights are violated (e.g., property, speech).
   a. Laws that make it illegal for a corporation to pay a worker less than a certain wage (minimum wage legislation).
   b. Laws that limit the ability of shareholders of an existing corporation to sell their firm.
   c. Laws that allow corporations to break their contracts with a labor union when the contract is not in the society's interest.
   d. Laws that prevent discrimination in hiring people.
   e. Laws that prevent employees from being purchased by corporations and forced to work.
   f. Laws that limit corporations from polluting the resources of other people.

g. Laws that require a corporation to negotiate in good faith with a union that has been properly selected by a majority of employees.
h. Laws that force corporations not to pollute or deface their land.
i. Corporate income taxes
j. Individual income taxes
k. Social security taxes.
l. A law that requires only "large" firms to provide reasonable child care and health care to their full-time employees.
m. A law that requires corporations to sell only the safest possible cars and other products regardless of cost.

4. In which of the following situations do you believe that society generally prices ethics (i.e., requires more money to perform unethical tasks). Answer with a *T* for true or *F* for false.

________ **a.** Actors or actresses in sexually explicit shows requiring greater pay than those in documentaries for public TV.

________ **b.** Owners of pawnshops requiring greater returns than owners of soup kitchens.

________ **c.** Slumlords requiring higher returns than luxury apartment owners.

5. Can you think of an ethically wrong thing a corporation (i.e., its shareholders or managers) could do that would lower its stock value even though it caused it to make more money?

6. Make a list of things you do or have done that save money but which put yourself and others in danger. Are you acting ethically?

7. The Keystone Pharmaceutical Company received permission from the FDA to sell Cardizone, a drug that reduces the discomforts of heartache. Research indicates, however, that the drug can cause serious side effects in a small percentage of potential users.

The company's president calls the board together to discuss Cardizone. Three options are proposed:

a. Drop all plans of selling Cardizone. The risk of serious illness or death, although remote, is a risk to which the firm will not be a party.
b. Place a large warning of the potential side effects on the package. It is expected that such a warning will significantly lower usage but will also greatly reduce liability.
c. Put a rather limited warning on the package. Analysis indicates that such a warning would permit higher sales but would provide less protection from lawsuits.

What would you recommend?

APPENDIX 14.1

OVERVIEWING THE HISTORY OF THE PHILOSOPHY OF ETHICS AND ECONOMICS

This appendix overviews the historical contributions to the philosophical underpinnings of ethical issues within economics using the two approaches discussed in the chapter: contractural rights approach and the societal good approach. This distinction, however, can become blurred. For example, some people advocate individual rights based upon the idea that it is good for society. Others detail social contracts through which people will voluntarily subjugate their rights. The key issue is whether rights inalienably belong to the individual or whether they (at least partially) belong to society.

I. The Contractual Rights Approach (deontology) is the nomenclature used to denote economic philosophies based on or driven by private property rights. The most popular advocates of this viewpoint in the last few centuries are summarized shortly. The roots of these philosophical viewpoints go back to Aristotle who viewed the world as rational with rational laws that humans could understand. Aristotle wrote: "How immeasurably greater is the pleasure, when a man feels the thing to be his own; for surely the love of self is a feeling implanted by nature" and that "property should be . . . as a general rule, private."[3]

Thomas Aquinas (1221–1274) proposed three methods by which truth could be ascertained: divine law, natural law, and positive law (observed through human interactions and consequences). Each of these three foundations has been used to build philosophical defenses of economic systems.

John Locke (late 1600s) logically developed rights as being natural (i.e., instinctive). His name is primarily associated with the articulation of particular private property rights (freedom from coercion) and with the defense of these rights as being natural. Locke's concepts, often referred to as "Lock-

[3]See Aristotle, *The Politics*, B. Jowett, trans. (London: Oxford University Press, 1885).

ean," are seen in the U.S. Declaration of Independence and were a background for Kant's (1724–1804) efforts to derive a moral justification of rights based on human reason.

Other defenses of private property rights include efficiency arguments and supernatural ordinance. Adam Smith (c. 1750) is perhaps the premier early advocate of rights based on efficiency arguments—in other words, that rights lead to prosperity and that prosperity helps all. The idea that individual rights should be protected by society for the benefit of the society, however, can also be viewed as a societal good approach in origin.

A final potential defense to private property rights is justice—that such systems produce fair results. Rawls sets forth a view that individuals, pursuing their self-interest, agree to form a social union (a set of social contracts) that includes justice. In other words, people voluntarily enter societies and form governments that subjugate some of their rights to the need for fairness within the society. The reason that people seek justice is not altruism, but rather the self-interest to live in a just society and potentially become a direct beneficiary of the justice.

Other advocates of individual rights include the Austrian School that has been used to denote a viewpoint that emphasizes the individual's behavior (and rights) and the Chicago School that has been used to describe current espousing of a free market, laissez-faire system by Friedman and others.

II. The Societal Good Approach (teleology) is the nomenclature that the authors use to denote economic philosophies driven by opinions with regard to the good of society with limited regard for private property rights. The most popular advocates of this viewpoint in the last few centuries are summarized shortly. The roots of these philosophical viewpoints go back to Plato, who viewed humans as being in a permanent state of illusion and who favored state control. Plato suggested extensive laws to force the public interest and common good and to limit the shortsightedness and other ill effects of selfishness and private advantage.[4]

The philosophical underpinnings of the "societal good" philosophies include the idea that rights are a social concept (i.e., the idea of a right is only relevant when two or more persons are interacting). Because rights (and nontrivial wealth) are a result of social gathering, it is the society's "right" to control economic transactions within that society rather than to subjugate societal goals to absolute private property rights.

The obvious question is on what basis should a society form its decisions regarding economic control. We will discuss three relevant concepts: utilitarianism, justice, and socialism.

In a strict historical sense, utilitarianism can be viewed as the proposition that individuals pursue utility maximization (of outcomes) with regard to

[4]See *Philosophy and Political Economy,* by James Bonar (New Brunswick: Transaction Publishers, 1992).

personal choices. In this sense, utilitarianism is silent with regard to "contractual rights" versus "societal good" and was in fact an outgrowth of the work of Adam Smith. Utilitarianism, however, has been extended to public policy debate by the principle that economic control by society should pursue a goal of maximizing the aggregate utility of society where, for example, the utility of the society might be defined as the sum individual utilities.

Bentham advocated the greatest good for the greatest number of people without clearly describing a philosophical basis. Ricardo (1772–1823), Malthus (1766–1834), and J. S. Mill (1806–1873) were instrumental to the development of utilitarianism and the refinement of an objective. In addition to concerns over an appropriate objective, utilitarians debate whether utility can actually be measured and aggregated. They agree, however, that maximizing happiness of outcomes, not necessarily justice, is the goal. Of course, some people's happiness may depend on the extent that they feel that their economic system is just.

Finally, we relate socialism to the analysis as the attempt to form, control, and evaluate economic systems based on various philosophical understandings of what constitutes an ethically correct system. For example, one idea is that all people are equal in their humanity and, therefore, all people deserve equal resources. In socialism or, more generally, communitarianism, the underlying principle is driven by ethical views of the value of people, society, and community—not by concerns discussed earlier such as the rights of more productive persons to consume more output or the unhappiness that might result. Unlike utilitarians, their objective is not entirely evaluated or measured by outcomes or consequences in terms of happiness, but rather appeals to some other viewpoint of good and justice. The value system used will ultimately be based on some premise of divine law, natural law, or positive law.

APPENDIX 14.2

THE ORIGIN OF INDIVIDUAL RIGHTS

In Chapter 14, we defined a *gotta* as required behavior. Because gottas often result in the denial of certain rights, it is appropriate to ask where required behavior (gottas) originates. History provides a guide in that when people have gathered together to form a society, they have contracted with, or required, other people to behave in certain ways. People agree that a certain type of ethical behavior (an oughtta) is so nice that it should be required of everybody—turning it into a contractual gotta.

People may agree to be subjected to these behavior requirements (gottas) in a voluntary manner, such as when a person immigrates into a country or when shareholders decide to organize as a corporation, or in an involuntary manner, such as when one country conquers and annexes another. An ethical question that merits debate is whether people should ever force others to be subjected to certain required behavior against their will. For example, is taxation without representation moral? Such a debate is unfortunately, beyond the scope of this chapter. We will therefore concentrate on the behavior requirements (gottas) as if they have been voluntarily entered. Thus, a gotta is a rule of a particular society that all of the society's people have (perhaps implicitly) voluntarily agreed to abide by or face the consequences.

In the United States, as well as in other countries, there are agreed-upon limits to the behavior people can require of others (i.e., which oughttas can be turned into gottas). The founders of the United States defined these limits through the Declaration of Independence and through the Constitution. The purpose of these limits is to draw a clear line of distinction between what a person should do and what a person can be forced by society to do.

The United States and some other countries emphasize the role of contractual rights in business ethics; however, not all societies base government on individual rights. When government contracts are formed (e.g., the U.S. Constitution) there are two primary foundations or perspectives that people can use in attempting to turn an oughtta into a gotta. The first is a "contractual-rights" perspective and the second is from a "societal-good" perspective. Free-market economics (and modern finance) is built primarily upon a foundation of individual rights. Socialism, communism, and countries using these systems are built primarily upon a foundation of management for the "good" of the society. In other words, in deciding whether a person should be allowed to do something, a free society asks whether it is the person's right, but a controlled society, in theory, asks whether or not it is in the best interests of the society.

For example, many people might think it is morally wrong for a newspaper to try to increase its circulation and profits by writing numerous extremely negative (but true) articles and opinions about the personal lives of famous people and their families. Most free societies, however, agree that this is a freedom of the press. In a controlled society, the press might be allowed to write only what the ruling class desires.

The alternative viewpoint to the concept of individual rights is often held outside the free world and is enforced by ruling groups in countries known for communism, socialism, fascism, and so forth. Within this alternative, the permitted uses of property and the permitted behavior of people are based upon whether the results of the permission appear to produce a generally improved or worsened society. Thus, a person is allowed to speak, write, pay wages, receive wages, buy goods, sell goods, and so forth only if the action is viewed as benefiting, or at least not hurting, the society's overall good.

Of course, the decision as to whether something is good or bad for society, and therefore whether it is legal or illegal is usually made by the ruling class, and the permitted behavior usually changes as the composition of the ruling class changes.

Now we can link the concepts of oughttas versus gottas with the types of governmental foundations: individual rights versus societal good. In a controlled society the gottas will be whatever oughttas the ruling class desires and can impose on the society. In theory, the government can and will impose on society whatever ethical standards it deems are for the good of the society. In contrast, in an individual-rights or free society, the government is limited to imposing on society only those ethical standards that do not interfere with the guaranteed rights of the individuals.

CHAPTER 15

FINANCIAL ANALYSIS

It has been a busy day at Points of Light, Inc. (POL, Inc.), the nation's only manufacturer of points of light. As part of the firm's ambitious growth program, top management has placed a large order for raw materials, applied for a bank loan, decided to offer an applicant the job of assistant treasurer, and met with a potential new investor. Tomorrow will be a new day during which top management can tackle another set of decisions and responsibilities.

Each of today's actions, however, has set a number of people in motion to perform the challenging task of financial analysis. The firm that received the order for materials, the bank that received POL's loan application, the woman who was offered the job, and the potential new investor all must make important decisions regarding how to contract with POL, Inc.

The consequences of poor financial analysis could be disastrous. To the raw materials supplier it might mean delivery of materials for which the supplier would never receive payment. For the bank it might mean making a loan that would never be repaid. For the prospective assistant treasurer it might mean leaving her current job and moving to a new location for a firm with an uncertain future. Finally, for the prospective investor, it might mean sinking hundreds of thousands of dollars into the equity of a firm that ends up bankrupt.

How do these firms and people make the difficult decision of whether or not to do business with POL, Inc.? In the case of dealing with small firms and in certain other circumstances, the answer is *financial analysis*.

The purpose of this chapter is to provide an overview of financial analysis. Time value of money techniques and capital budgeting serve as prerequisite background material for this chapter. Understanding the firm's financing is also helpful. For those students who have not yet covered Chapters 11–13, and for those students who would like a refresher on this material, Window 15.1, on debt and dividends, provides the necessary background.

WINDOW 15.1

Review of Debt and Dividends

Debt

The two primary securities used by corporations to raise capital are debt securities and equity securities. Debt and equity are financial securities that differ in risk such that the proportions of debt and equity used by the firm determine who bears the firm's risk.

Debt securities are fixed promises of future cash flows and generally carry a lower level of risk. *Equity securities*—more specifically, common stock—are claims to whatever cash flows are left over, if any, after all prior claims have been satisfied. Equity securities, therefore, generally carry a higher level of risk.

A firm with a high proportion of debt is said to have high *financial leverage*. Ignoring the detailed theoretical arguments discussed in Chapters 11 and 12, the use of debt has certain generally accepted results. A firm that uses a high proportion of debt has: (1) a higher probability of going bankrupt because of being unable to meet its obligations, due to the relatively high interest payments it must make to its debtholders; (2) a higher probability of defaulting on (i.e., being unable to pay) its debt payments such that the debt itself becomes more risky; and (3) more volatile residual cash flows such that the equity claims become more risky.

On the other hand, a firm with a low proportion of debt is said to have low financial leverage. Low leverage indicates that the firm, under normal operating conditions, will be able to meet its obligations and thus has a lower probability of bankruptcy. This acts to reduce the relative risk borne by the firm's debt and equity securities.

Analysts therefore view debt usage as an indicator of whether the firm will be able to meet its obligations. This is not to say that debt usage is bad; rather, it can affect who bears the risk. A financial analyst, therefore, needs to take debt usage into account.

Dividends

A *dividend* is a distribution—usually of cash—from the firm to its stockholders. In general, the dividend is viewed as derived from the firm's profits. The amount of dividends that a firm pays out, therefore, determines the percentage of profits that will leave the firm and the percentage that will be retained within the firm. The profits retained within the firm are called *retained earnings*.

With reference to the value of the firm, some argue that cash dividends usually do not matter because the firm's profits belong to the stockholders whether they are paid out as dividends or retained inside the firm. As part of this argument, dividends are simply the transfer of the stockholders' wealth from the firm's cash balances to their private cash balances.

The payment of dividends, however, can affect the ability of the firm to meet its obligations. In simple terms and ignoring the theoretical arguments of Chapter 13, it can be argued that high dividends damage the ability of a firm to meet its obligations. The reason for this is twofold: (1) dividends cause a reduction in the firm's cash balance, which is viewed as the firm's safest asset; and (2) dividends reduce the equity owner's

WINDOW 15.1 *(continued)*

investment in the firm and therefore act to decrease the percentage of equity and increase the percentage of debt in the firm. How much debt to use and the amounts to pay in dividends are the two most important financing issues to be made by financial management. The ultimate effect of debt and dividends on financial analysis is complex.

Two Views of Financial Analysis

financial analysis
The process of extracting decision-making information from existing knowledge such as financial statements.

Financial analysis is the process of extracting decision-making information from existing knowledge such as financial statements. Thus, the purpose of performing financial analysis is to facilitate decision making by transforming raw facts into more useful information. For example, it may be possible to use the raw information in financial statements to predict bankruptcy, or some other potential event.

Who performs financial analysis? First and foremost, firms perform such analysis on themselves in order to better understand their current performance and to plan for the future. Internal analysis would be a way for management to obtain results of operations in its own divisions. Second, financial analysis is performed by external entities dealing with the firm, in such circumstances as deciding whether to extend credit, accept a job offer, or invest in a firm. Finally, firms such as rating agencies and investment houses may perform financial analysis on other firms as a service to their clients. In many cases, it is more cost effective to have a third party perform a single analysis for all of its clients rather than have each client perform the analysis for itself. This is especially true given the fact that many firms lack the expertise to perform such analysis. Window 15.2 details the most popular sources of financial analysis on firms.

Modernists' View of Financial Analysis

In many cases, the essential information being sought in financial analysis by outsiders is the probability that the firm will declare bankruptcy or have other serious problems meeting its obligations. Modern corporate finance theory offers some powerful tools (e.g., option theory) to measure the probability of bankruptcy. (Option theory was introduced in Chapter 10.) Although using option theory to predict bankruptcy is beyond the scope of this text, it is certainly within the scope of most advanced finance courses.

Whatever tools are used in the analysis, modernists believe that it is almost always better for outsiders to perform financial analysis using market

WINDOW 15.2

Sources of Financial Analysis

Credit-Rating Agencies

1. *Standard and Poor's:* A subsidiary of McGraw-Hill, Inc., Standard and Poor's (S&P) provides a range of financial services, most notably ratings on corporate and municipal bonds and common stocks. S&P ratings classify bonds according to risk classes: triple A (AAA), or most financially secure, to single D (D), or in default. In addition, Standard and Poor's uses the modifiers plus (+) and minus (−) to classify debt securities further. Thus, bond ratings signal the probability of default. Ratings on common stocks range from A+ (most financially secure) to D (in reorganization) and signal the potential for future growth and stability of dividend payments. Other financial information provided by S&P includes the compilation of common stock indexes (e.g., the S&P 500), *The Bond Guide, Earnings Forecaster, New Issue Investor, The Stock Guide,* and *Corporation Records.*
2. *Moody's:* A subsidiary of Financial Communication Company, Inc., Moody's provides information similar to that provided by S&P. Moody's is best known for its corporate and municipal bond ratings, which signal the financial strength of the issuer and the probability of default. Moody's also rates common stocks, providing information on each company's background, its current operations, and the outlook for the future.

Information on Commercial Firms

3. *Dun & Bradstreet:* Dun & Bradstreet is a supplier of credit information on commercial firms, including previous credit history and current credit listings. It also provides financial analysis and other financial information, including *Industry Norms and Key Business Ratios,* which provides basic balance sheet and income statement information as well as ratios for industries.
4. *Value Line Investment Survey:* The Value Line Investment Survey is an advisory service best known for its system of ranking thousands of stocks from One (recommend to buy) to Five (recommend to sell). The Value Line ranking system is updated weekly and is based on relative strength in market price movement, earnings momentum, and unexpected changes in earnings. Value Line also provides other types of firm analysis, including history, current developments, and measures of risk such as firm betas. The beta of the firm is a measure of its systematic risk, as detailed in Chapter 9.

Information on Individuals

5. *Experion (formally TRW, Inc.):* Experion is a major corporation providing consumer credit reporting services. Consumer credit reporting provides a credit history for millions of individuals, reporting on amounts of credit outstanding as well as any defaults on past credit.

prices rather than accounting numbers, such as those provided by financial statements.[1] For example, the best way to determine a firm's credit worthiness is to analyze the pricing of its existing debt that trades in the marketplace. Whether a financial analyst prefers to use market prices, assuming that the firm's securities are traded in an active and competitive market, or accounting information found on financial statements is an important consideration.

The argument for using market prices is that self-interest will drive the most talented analysts in the world, equipped with the best information available in the world, to trade any mispriced securities until the mispricing vanishes. Thus, the market prices themselves become conduits of the finest information available.

Some analysts tend to distrust accounting numbers because they can be manipulated by management in an effort to conceal troubles. Instead, these analysts place their greatest trust in market prices, which are determined by people investing real money. For example, if the debt of a firm is regularly being bought and sold at a high price, then a modernist would conclude that the firm must have a small chance of going bankrupt—regardless of other indicators. It is argued that indicators other than market prices, such as talk and accounting numbers, are unreliable.

Traditionalists' View of Financial Analysis

Traditionalists tend to believe that market prices may be either too high or too low, depending upon the errors being made by investors, and that information found on financial statements is not subject to these errors.

The debate over whether market prices provide better answers to the questions asked by outside financial analysts or whether accounting numbers are better has gone on for years and will continue. Nevertheless, even modernists agree that the information found on financial statements must be used when reliable market prices are not available.

Financial Statements

Accountants produce two primary types of financial statements that convey financial information regarding a firm: (1) the balance sheet and (2) the income statement. Both statements are ordinarily reported using accounting

1. It is generally only in cases where the firm's securities are not actively and competitively traded that market prices should not be given primary consideration. Examples of firms that would not have reliable market prices would be very small firms or "privately held" firms whose securities are not traded by numerous investors at publicly known prices.

numbers or book values. These accounting numbers are generally derived from the cost of each item using the complex rules of accounting.

For example, the accounting or book value of land is usually listed as the cost of the land when purchased rather than its value today. In the case of buildings and equipment, the book values are lowered or depreciated each year according to complicated depreciation rules—even if the true values are rising.

The good news about accounting numbers is that to some extent the practices of how to report values are standardized so that different corporations use generally similar methods. The bad news is that the values can bear little resemblance to the true values being measured. This is especially true when the corporation being analyzed has assets that are very difficult to value, such as patents, trademarks, a good reputation, and so forth.

As discussed briefly in Chapter 1, it is also possible to envision financial statements based upon the market values of each item. If correctly implemented, then market-value financial statements would be extremely useful; unfortunately, the enormous difficulty of reporting accurate market prices of untraded items on a consistent basis and the tremendous potential for misuse virtually eliminate their practical usefulness. Thus, for the remainder of this chapter, "values" will refer to accounting or book values rather than market values. Let us now take a closer look at the two primary financial statements.

The Balance Sheet

balance sheet
A listing of all of the assets of a firm and all of the claims to those assets at a particular point in time.

Many people refer to a balance sheet as a snapshot of the firm because it attempts to express all items of value at a particular point in time. The **balance sheet** or balance statement is simply a listing of all of the assets of a firm and all of the claims to those assets at a particular point in time. Assets are anything that can produce future cash inflows to the firm. They are generally listed first, or on the left-hand side of the statement.

The claims to the firm include all fixed debts or liabilities as well as residual ownership, known as preferred and common stocks. These claims are listed last, or on the right-hand side, usually under the title "Liabilities and Owners' Equity." The total value of the assets must equal the total value of the liabilities and owners' equity because all the assets are owned by or claimed by someone. An example of a real-world balance sheet is provided in Chapter 1 for the Walt Disney Company.

Differences in Balance Sheet Detail The distinguishing aspect of balance sheets is their level of detail. Students are sometimes confused by balance sheets because they expect them to look somewhat similar to each other. Balance sheets, however, can differ markedly in appearance depending on whether various categories are lumped together or separated out. For example, in its briefest form, the balance sheet for Points of Light, Inc., after their first year in business would look as follows:

Assets	*Liabilities and Owners' Equity*
Total Assets $1,000,000	Common Stock $1,000,000

On the other hand, this balance sheet could be expanded to cover several pages by listing the different types of assets in extreme detail. Thus, the primary difference between various balance sheet formats is their level of detail.

The primary difference between various balance sheet formats is their level of detail.

Common Balance Sheet Practices A convention of balance sheets is that they list assets and liabilities starting with the shortest maturities and ending with the longest maturities. The reason for this is the importance that financial analysts place on the liquidity of the items.

Another convention is that certain figures are added together or subtracted out to form various subtotals. For example, loosely speaking, assets and liabilities with lifetimes of less than 1 year are often subtotaled under the headings *current assets* and *current liabilities.* Other assets are called *fixed assets,* and other liabilities are entitled *long-term liabilities.*

In addition, assets that have been depreciated or lowered through time are often listed first at their original purchase prices and then lowered to their depreciated or net values. Finally, two or more balance sheets are often overlaid onto a single statement by including a column of figures for each quarter or year. An example of the detail found in a typical balance sheet is provided in Table 15.1. Remember that a balance sheet is simply a listing of the firm's assets, liabilities, and the residual value of the equity. The general concept of a balance sheet is easy to understand even though, as we have said, these statements can differ tremendously because of differences in the level of detail shown.

Complex Aspects of Balance Sheets Detailed balance sheets usually contain a few tricky aspects:

1. Assets that can be liquidated within 1 year and liabilities that may come due within 1 year are often expanded into numerous entries. This is done to provide detail for analysts studying liquidity.
2. Asset categories such as equipment and buildings, which are depreciated through time, are often listed using three lines. The first line lists the sum of the original purchase prices of all of the assets in the category. The second line lists the accumulated depreciation, which represents the sum of all of the years of depreciation on all of the assets in the

TABLE 15.1 A Detailed Balance Sheet for Points of Light, Inc.

Assets	
Cash and marketable securities	$ 852,000
Accounts receivable	2,324,000
Inventory	9,496,000
Total Current Assets	$ 12,672,000
Equipment	$ 42,939,000
Less accumulated depreciation	17,389,000
Net equipment	$ 25,550,000
Buildings	$ 95,921,000
Less accumulated depreciation	65,838,000
Net buildings	$ 30,083,000
Land	$ 73,012,000
Total Fixed Assets	$128,645,000
Total Assets	$141,317,000
Liabilities and Owners' Equity	
Accounts payable	$ 1,465,000
Bank loans	3,960,000
Debt due within one year	2,580,000
Total Current Liabilities	$ 8,005,000
Total Long-Term Debt	$ 27,812,000
Common stock (par value $0.10)	$ 1,000,000
Paid-in-surplus of par	99,000,000
Retained earnings	5,500,000
Total Equity	$105,500,000
Total Liabilities and Owners' Equity	$141,317,000

category. Depreciation is an accounting estimate of the decline in an asset's value due to aging and wear. The third and final line lists the net (or subtracted) value. This last line is the true book value of the assets and is the only value that is summed into the total fixed assets and total assets lines.[2]

2. When a depreciable asset is sold, its cost is removed from the first line and its accumulated depreciation is removed from the second line. Simpler balance sheets in effect report only the third line. Accounts receivable can also be listed in three lines in order to reflect the fact that some of the money might not be collected.

par value
An arbitrary listing of the value of stock per share on the firm's books. Par value has little economic significance.

3. Common stock is often broken into two or three lines based upon a concept known as **par value.** All three lines added together form the book value of the firm's common equity. In general, there are two important reasons to separate common equity into three lines. First, with a line listed as common stock (par value $0.10), the user is able to compute the number of shares of common stock in the corporation. The user simply divides the value for the item by the par value per share. From Table 15.1, there are 10 million shares, found by dividing $1 million by $0.10 par value per share. Second, the user can differentiate between common equity that was contributed to the firm by the sale of shares to investors and common equity that was generated by profits through the years. The sum of the common stock and paid-in-surplus of par is the amount of money raised from selling newly issued shares. The third line is the residual ownership, or retained earnings, generated by the firm's profits and accumulated through the years. It represents the sum of all previous profits less all previous dividends.
4. Balance sheets can be condensed by deducting current liabilities from current assets and reporting only net current assets or net working capital. The net working capital is entered as an asset. Thus, the balance sheet is shorter (current liabilities and current assets do not even appear) and the total figures will not really represent all assets or liabilities.

Summary of Balance Sheets In summary, a balance sheet is a listing of the firm's assets, liabilities, and residual value of the equity; however, tremendous variations in their format as well as such alternatives as those previously listed may tend to be intimidating. With a little practice and by keeping "the big picture" clear in your mind, however, most balance sheets can be understood.

The Income Statement

income statement
A summary of the firm's profit or loss over a certain time period.

An **income statement** is a summary of the transactions that have added accounting value to the firm, known as *profits,* or lost accounting value from the firm, known as *losses.* Whereas a balance sheet tries to express a firm's value at a particular point in time, an income statement attempts to summarize the firm's profit or loss over a certain time period. Thus, an income statement summarizes all of the transactions that affect the accounting value of equity.

Income statements are typically compiled for 1-month, 3-month, 6-month, 9-month, or 1-year intervals. Two or more income statements can be listed together using different columns for the financial figures that correspond to different time intervals. A real-world income statement was provided in Chapter 1 for the Walt Disney Company.

Differences in Income Statement Detail As in the case of balance sheets, income statements differ tremendously in format due primarily to the amount of detail they express, such as whether various categories are lumped together or separated out. For example, in its briefest form, an income statement would look as follows:

Total Revenues	$110,600,000
Total Expenditures	102,788,000
Net Income	$ 7,812,000

Only those types of transactions that earn or lose money are listed. There are many transactions in which a firm may engage that do not make or lose money immediately; therefore, they are not listed on the income statement. Examples include borrowing money, issuing stock, repaying debt, or purchasing assets.

There are two primary types of transactions that can earn or lose money. The first is an ordinary operation, which represents the enterprise of the firm in making and selling its products. The second is an extraordinary event, which represents unusual and major transactions that produce a profit or loss, such as the sale or loss of a major asset. Most income statements differentiate between these two types of transactions.

Ordinary transactions represented by the production and selling of the firm's products are usually provided in somewhat standard fashion across firms. The firm's revenues are often broken into three lines in order to reflect the expectation that some of the money from the sales will never be collected because some customers will never pay. The first line usually lists the total possible revenues from sales, followed by a second line that reflects an allowance for the money that is typically uncollected. The third line is the difference and is entitled the net sales. For condensed income statements, only the third line might be listed.

The firm's ordinary expenses are often detailed in the following way:

Cost of Goods Sold
Selling and General Administrative Expenses
Depreciation

The first category represents the variable costs of production, whereas the second category represents fixed costs of production. Depreciation is often separated out because it is simply an accounting concept, not a cash expense. There is no limit, of course, to the level of detail that could be used to expand this list by breaking out expenses into more specific categories, such as labor versus materials, or into different divisions, product types, and so forth.

Another common practice is to subtotal the revenues and expenses before subtracting interest expense and taxes. The purpose of this is to illustrate how the cash flows being produced from the assets are being divided among the claimants of the firm's cash flows. In this classification, interest goes to bondholders, taxes to the government, and net income to the shareholders.

Earnings Before Interest and Taxes (Operating Income)
−Interest Expense

Profit Before Taxes
−Income Taxes

Net Income

The last figure or line on the income statement is usually viewed as the most important because it is the accounting measure of the change in the value of the shareholder's wealth, hence the expression "the bottom line." Combining the previous characteristics produces the income statement shown in Table 15.2, which illustrates a moderate level of detail.

Complex Aspects of Income Statements As with balance sheets, it is important to remember that most income statements are based upon accounting numbers and accounting rules rather than market values and economic principles. For example, a firm may have a tremendous economic gain because the buildings, land, patents, and trademarks it purchased and developed years ago are now worth a great deal of money. These gains, however, will not be recognized and reported by accountants until the assets have been sold.

Accountants are quicker to report losses even if the assets have not been sold. For example, a bank with huge potential losses on its investments must "write off" or declare the losses even though it might not be allowed to report potential profits on other assets that have risen in value but have not been sold.

Worse yet, some major decisions of when to recognize and report transactions can be left to the discretion of management. In effect, this allows management, in some cases, to exert an enormous amount of control over the

TABLE 15.2 A Moderately Detailed Income Statement

Sales	$110,600,000
Cost of goods sold	45,427,000
Selling and administrative expenses	39,650,000
Depreciation	10,350,000
Earnings before interest and taxes (EBIT)	$ 15,173,000
Interest on debt	3,337,000
Earnings before taxes (EBT)	$ 11,836,000
Taxes	4,024,000
Net income	$ 7,812,000

reporting of the firm's performance. The net result is that in certain circumstances the net income of a firm bears little or no resemblance to its true economic performance for the time period.

Another complexity of the income statement is the distinction between completed transactions, represented by revenues or expenses that have been received or paid, and those that have only been *accrued*, which are represented by revenues earned or expenses incurred that have not been collected or paid in cash as of the date of the income statement. The more serious problem, however, is that many major potential profits and some major potential losses are not reported until and unless a transaction has been agreed to or has occurred.

Finally, income statements often express figures such as net income on a per share basis by dividing the total net income by the number of shares of common stock. The statement may also detail payments to preferred stockholders and the amount of the net income paid to the common stockholders as a dividend rather than retained inside the firm.

Summary of Income Statements

In summary, the formats of income statements vary so tremendously that it is easy to become confused. All income statements, however, are attempts to measure the profit or loss of a firm over a specified time interval. As with any accounting numbers, they are to be viewed realistically and with recognition of their limitations.

Ratio Analysis

A *ratio* is one number divided by another number or, in other words, one number expressed as a proportion of another. For example, throughout life we compute ratios such as miles per gallon and points scored per game. In corporate finance we might divide the total amount of a firm's debt by the amount of its total assets in order to compute the proportion of the firm's total value that is represented by the debt.

Total debt, say an amount of $853,000, may convey very little information regarding the level of a firm's debt usage or health. For example, $853,000 might be a large amount of debt for a small retail firm, but it is a small amount of debt for a large manufacturer. The number must be adjusted or scaled in order to be transformed into a meaningful measure. Ratios provide the solution.

ratio analysis
The use of values taken from financial statements such as the balance sheet and income statements in order to measure certain aspects of a firm's financial condition.

Ratio analysis refers to the use of simple ratios between numbers, such as those in the balance sheets and income statements, in order to measure certain aspects of a firm's financial condition. The four primary aspects that financial analysts study are: (1) the debt usage of the firm, (2) the liquidity of the firm, (3) the profitability of the firm, and (4) the efficiency of the firm.

Standards for Comparison of Financial Ratios

Before detailing each of the four types of ratios, we will first examine the usefulness of the ratio. One of the most troubling aspects of ratio analysis is the difficulty of determining good or bad values. Is there such a thing as a correct value, an optimal value, or even a reasonable range of values?

The answers to these and other related questions depend on how the ratios are used. For instance, after a ratio has been computed for a particular firm, it needs to be compared or judged against some type of target or benchmark ratio, but should these target ratios be taken from theory, from the firm's previous years, or from other firms in the same industry? Do other firms use the same accounting methods? Why should we believe that the other firms in the industry have the correct ratios?

Practices vary and must be tailored to circumstances. In general, however, a firm's financial ratios are analyzed through time in order to ascertain trends, and then compared with industry averages in order to provide indications as to whether the firm is above or below the levels found in the industry. Thus, a performance ratio that is below that of the year before may not be a danger signal if the industry's ratio has fallen by an even larger extent.

Sources for industry ratios include Dun & Bradstreet, Robert Morris Associates, and the U.S. Commerce Department's *Quarterly Financial Report for Manufacturers.* Many of these industry averages are reported for specific industries grouped by four-digit standard industrialized company (SIC) codes. It is important that the industry used as the benchmark match the industry of the firm. In some cases, this is a straightforward comparison inasmuch as the company being analyzed has one major line of business. In other cases, the benchmark is not easily identified because the company being analyzed has a number of business lines. In cases such as these, analysts usually use as an industry benchmark the firm's major line of business.

Ratios will be illustrated by separating the analysis into four major areas: debt usage, liquidity, profitability, and efficiency. Next to each type of ratio will be the corresponding value for the Walt Disney Company and Walt Disney's industry average.

Financial Ratio Example: The Walt Disney Company

Table 15.3 reports financial ratios for the Walt Disney Company in 2000. Industry averages are also reported. Because Disney's main products include theme parks, a television network, full-length films, and consumer products, and no one industry benchmark provides a perfect match, the main line of business is theme parks and the benchmark industry is amusements and recreation for this analysis.

Debt-Usage Ratios As is fully discussed in the chapters on firm financing, and briefly discussed in Window 15.1, it may be important to study the

TABLE 15.3 Common Financial Ratios, The Walt Disney Company, 2000

	Walt Disney	*Industry Average*
Panel A: Debt Ratios (Current Year)		
1. The Debt Ratio $= \frac{\text{Total Debt}}{\text{Total Assets}}$	0.21	Not Available
2. The Debt–to–Equity Ratio $= \frac{\text{Total Debt}}{\text{Total Equity}}$	0.43	0.48
3. Coverage Ratio $= \frac{\text{EBIT}^{\dagger}}{\text{\$ Interest}}$	5.81	9.94
Panel B: Liquidity Ratios (Current Year)		
1. The Cash Ratio $= \frac{\text{Cash}}{\text{Current Liabilities}}$	0.10	Not Available
2. The Quick Ratio $= \frac{\text{Cash + Accounts Receivable}}{\text{Current Liabilities}}$	0.79	0.68
3. The Current Ratio $= \frac{\text{Current Assets}}{\text{Current Liabilities}}$	1.37	1.14
Panel C: Profitability Ratios (5 Year Average)		
1. Net Return on Assets $= \frac{\text{Net Income}}{\text{Average Total Assets}}$	0.040	0.054
2. Net Return on Equity $= \frac{\text{Net Income}}{\text{Average Total Equity}}$	0.086	0.106
Panel D: Efficiency Ratios		
1. Inventory Turnover $= \frac{\text{Sales}}{\text{Average Inventory}}$	33.06	31.15
2. Days Sales Outstanding $= \frac{\text{Average Receivables}}{\text{Annual Sales/360}}$	6.50 days	16.47 days

**Source:* yahoo.marketguide.com
†EBIT = Earnings before interest and taxes.

amount of debt owed by the firm. The most common reason for analyzing debt usage would be to determine the probability that the firm will be able to pay its current and future debts. This information would be useful to current and prospective owners of the firm's debt—including the people who are considering selling their products to the firm on credit.

Two types of ratios measure the amount of debt a firm uses. The most common type of debt ratio expresses some measure of the firm's debt as a proportion of some other value in the firm. These ratios, known as the *debt ratio* and the *debt-to-equity ratio,* are summarized in Panel A of Table 15.3. Analysts concerned about the firm's debt capacity will focus on debt as a percentage of assets. Ratios appropriate for analyzing a particular situation vary and depend upon the purpose of the analysis. For example, the analyst concerned about the ability of the firm to generate cash flow sufficient to make debt payments will focus on ratios that measure interest as a percentage of profitability or cash flow. This is known as a *coverage ratio,* or a ratio measuring the firm's ability to cover fixed interest expense.

Comparisons indicate that Disney has a higher debt usage than the industry average. For example, the coverage of interest expense by earnings is only half as high for Disney compared with the industry. However, the debt to equity ratio tells a slightly different story as Disney's ratio is just below the industry average.

Liquidity Ratios The liquidity of a firm refers to its ability to have sufficient cash to meet current and future needs. Thus, liquidity depends upon the amount of the firm's cash, the amount of other assets that can be quickly converted to cash, whether the firm is making or losing money, the amount of obligations that will require repayment in the near future, and the ability of the firm to raise more cash by issuing securities or borrowing money.

The primary purpose for analyzing the liquidity of a firm is to determine whether it has sufficient liquidity to meet its needs and, therefore, whether it would be a wise decision to extend credit to the firm such as by allowing it to purchase products on credit.

Panel B in Table 15.3 lists the most common measures of liquidity. Notice that the three liquidity ratios differ only by their numerator. Each ratio divides certain liquid assets of the firm by the firm's total current debt. The first ratio includes only the firm's cash, the second ratio adds accounts receivable to cash, and the third ratio includes all of the firm's current assets including inventories. Which ratio or set of ratios a financial analyst will focus on depends upon the purpose of the analysis. The cash ratio might better indicate the firm's ability to meet immediate payments, but the current ratio might be a better indicator of credit worthiness over the next year.

Disney's ratios are somewhat similar to industry averages. The current ratio indicates that Disney's current assets are one-and-a-third that of current liabilities, which is considered to be in the "safe" range of liquidity.

Profitability Ratios The most common profitability ratios are shown in Panel C of Table 15.3, measuring net income as a proportion of (1) average total assets, and (2) average total equity. The first two ratios can provide useful insights into the amount of sales or assets that a particular corporation has used to produce a particular income and perhaps whether these sales and assets are being used efficiently. The third ratio, the return on equity, is perhaps the most common accounting measures of profitability. The return on equity is the accounting measure of the return to the firm's stockholders.

Disney's profitability ratios are below than industry averages. Both ratios—net income to average assets, and return on equity—are about 80 percent of the industry average. These ratios provide signals of weakness.

Efficiency Ratios The ratios in Panel D in Table 15.3 measure the efficiency of the firm. For example, the inventory turnover ratio measures the number of times the average inventory is turned over or sold. A high turnover ratio indicates the advantage of not tying up a lot of its capital in inventory. On the other hand, a low inventory can produce a high turnover ratio, but it may cause problems to the firm such as lost sales and production inefficiencies.

A similar ratio is the receivables turnover, which measures the amount of the firm's revenues tied up in average accounts receivable as well as indicates how many days the firm takes on average to collect its accounts receivable. Disney's low ratio indicates either that the firm's customers are prompt payers, that the firm collects its accounts receivable aggressively, or has less lenient terms of credit.

Disney's inventory turnover is slightly above the industry average. This could indicate that inventory levels are at lower levels, or it could point to a faulty industry comparison due to the uniqueness of Disney's business.

Problems with Ratio Analysis

In addition to problems relating to inaccuracies of accounting numbers, there is a particular problem with ratios that depend on balance sheet values at a single point (stock measures) in time and on income statement items that are measures over time (flow measures). One usually corrects this problem by converting stock measures into flow measures by taking an average of the beginning and ending amounts or more frequent averaging. In addition, some balance sheet values, such as cash, can change substantially through time and can even be manipulated by management to be at certain levels at the end of an accounting period. Thus, a ratio indicating a low level of cash may be the result of a seasonal variation in sales and not a liquidity problem. Of course, breaking down annual ratios into periods within the year, such as computing quarterly or even monthly ratios, can help solve the seasonality problem.

In addition, profitability and efficiency ratios should be used with special caution. It should be remembered that there are no absolute standards for efficiency ratios. For example, a high inventory turnover rate and a low average collection period would appear to indicate efficient management; however, the opposite may be true. What appears as high efficiency may actually be a practice that hurts shareholder wealth. A high inventory turnover rate might indicate that the firm has too little inventory and is experiencing lost sales and production delays when inventories run out. A low average collection period might indicate that a firm has a credit policy that is too restrictive. A restrictive credit policy could cause the firm to lose profitable sales because of its reluctance to extend credit to customers.

Systems of Ratio Analysis

Rather than computing a few ratios and comparing them to some standards, some analysts have developed systems for analyzing ratios in an organized fashion. The objective of these systems is to identify strengths and weaknesses of the firm.

> Systems for analyzing ratios, such as the Du Pont system, attempt to identify the firm's strengths and weaknesses.

For example, the **Du Pont system** was devised by financial managers of the Du Pont Corporation as a tool for systematic ratio analysis. It breaks down the return on equity (ROE) first into three components:

Du Pont system
A system for analyzing ratios in an organized fashion. The objective of the system is to identify strengths and weaknesses of the firm.

$$ROE = \text{Net Income/Equity} = \text{Net Income/Sales} \times \text{Sales/Assets} \times \text{Assets/Equity}$$

This simple mathematical identity is intended to assist the financial analyst in identifying the firm's strengths and weaknesses. The approach begins with ROE, or what many consider the bottom line, and then systematically decomposes this into a measure of profitability, a measure of asset utilization, and a leverage factor. Following the Du Pont system, the analyst compares these broad measures against a peer group and against time, and then searches for additional clues depending on these comparisons. A detailed explanation of the Du Pont system and other systems is beyond the scope of this text; however, students should be aware that such systems exist and may be useful in providing a thorough analysis.

Financial Ratios as a Predictor of Performance

Some analysts use ratios as a method of predicting firm performance. For example, models have been developed using ratios and accounting entries to predict default. These models base their predictions on past history, investigating whether firms that declare bankruptcy share common characteristics. To the extent that these characteristics can be captured in financial ratios, trends in these ratios can be used to predict which firms will or will not default.

Research investigating the ability of financial ratios to predict default has been inconclusive. The best that can be said could be that ratios can provide insights into predicting which firms will run into financial distress.

Statement of Cash Flows

statement of cash flows A financial statement that attempts to organize and convey information regarding all of the changes in the components of the firm's balance sheet.

A lesser-known financial statement known as the **statement of cash flows** is extremely important for financial planning. The statement of cash flows attempts to organize and convey information regarding *all* of the changes in the components of the firm's balance sheet. You may recall that the income statement reflects only those transactions that affect the firm's profit and therefore the value of the firm's equity. The statement of cash flows also includes the transactions that do not immediately affect profits but that can have longer-term implications, such as purchases of assets and raising of capital.

The Statement of Cash Flows as a Summary of Balance Sheet Changes

The statement of cash flows may be viewed as a summary of the changes in the cash and cash equivalent accounts between two balance sheets of a firm at different points in time. For example, Table 15.4 lists the balance sheet of Points of Light, Inc., for 2 years. The final column in Table 15.4 shows the changes in each value. The changes are formed by subtracting the earlier balance sheet values from the later balance sheet values.

The statement of cash flows is an accounting of the cash flows of the firm. It reports the relevant cash flow information in three categories: operating activities, investing activities, and financing activities. It is helpful to think of these categories as roughly relating to the following:

Operating Activities ↔ Income Statements

Investing Activities ↔ Balance Sheet Assets

Financing Activities ↔ Balance Sheet Liabilities and Equity

The statement of cash flows categorizes all of the activities that affect the cash balance and sums their effects. The change in the cash balance indicated in the statement of cash flows should correspond to the change in the cash balance observed between the two balance sheets.

Complex Aspects of the Statement of Cash Flows

There are two rather tough "tricks" in creating a statement of cash flows like the one shown in Table 15.5. First, rather than placing the change in the retained earnings value in the statement, the user includes the firm's net income as an operating activity and its dividends as a financing activity. Note that the change in retained earnings is equal to the net income minus the dividends.

TABLE 15.4 The Balance Sheet for Points of Light over 2 Years (in $000s)

	2002	*2001*	*Change*
Assets			
Cash and securities	$ 852	$ 953	− 101
Accounts receivable	2,324	2,200	+ 124
Inventory	9,496	8,386	+ 1,110
Total Current Assets	$ 12,672	$ 11,539	+ 1,133
Equipment	$ 42,939	$ 31,929	+11,010
Less accumulated depreciation	17,389	15,027	+ 2,362
Net equipment	$ 25,550	$ 16,902	+ 8,648
Buildings	$ 95,921	$ 95,921	0
Less accumulated depreciation	65,838	61,687	+ 4,151
Net buildings	$ 30,083	$ 34,234	− 4,151
Land	$ 73,012	$ 73,012	0
Fixed Assets	$128,645	$124,148	+ 4,497
Total Assets	$141,317	$135,687	+ 5,630
Liabilities and Equity			
Accounts payable	$ 1,465	$ 1,166	+ 299
Bank loans	3,960	4,040	− 80
Debt due within year	2,580	2,580	0
Total Current Liabilities	$ 8,005	$ 7,786	+ 219
Total Long-Term Debt	$ 27,812	$ 25,392	+ 2,420
Common stock	$ 1,000	$ 1,000	0
Paid-in-surplus	99,000	99,000	0
Retained earnings	5,500	2,509	+ 2,991
Total Equity	$105,500	$102,509	+ 2,991
Total Liabilities and Equity	$141,317	$135,687	+ 5,630

TABLE 15.5 A Statement of Cash Flows for Points of Light, Inc. (in $000s)

Operating Activities	
Net Income	5,991
Depreciation	6,513
Investing Activities	
Inventory	(1,110)
Accounts Receivable	(124)
Equipment	(11,010)
Financing Activities	
Dividends	(3,000)
Accounts Payable	299
Long-term Debt	2,240
Bank Loans	(80)
Net Increase (Decrease) in Cash	(101)

Second, depreciable assets complicate the statement of cash flows. You may recall from the discussion of the balance sheet that depreciable assets, such as equipment, are often listed in three lines such as:

Equipment
−Accumulated Depreciation
Net Equipment

Rather than transposing the third line to the statement of cash flows (the net value of the depreciated asset), the statement of cash flows usually contains changes in both of the first two lines. The first line is listed as an investing activity. The change in accumulated depreciation is listed as an operating activity.

Depreciation is one of the most difficult aspects of a statement of cash flows. It is important to recognize depreciation as an unusual item inasmuch as no money leaves the firm in the form of depreciation expense. In the statement of cash flows, depreciation is entered *twice*—with opposite results, which cancel each other out. Depreciation needs to be negated because it is an accounting number rather than an actual cash flow. Depreciation "washes out" of a statement of cash flows because it is subtracted from net income, and then is added back in as an operating activity. In fact, the only importance of depreciation from the perspective of cash flows is that it is tax deductible and therefore reduces the cash spent on income taxes. The concept that the only real consequence of depreciation is its effect on income taxes is an important insight.

The Starting Format for a Statement of Cash Flows

In order to minimize confusion due to the "tricks" discussed earlier, you may find it helpful to begin construction of a statement of cash flows by using the format shown in Table 15.6. This format helps guide you past some of the adjustments necessitated by equity changes and depreciation. You then transpose the changes in the balance sheet items into their appropriate locations. Remember to transpose all values using the correct sign. The numbers should be transposed according to the following location guideline:

Asset Increase ⇒ Enter as a negative investing activity
Asset Decreases ⇒ Enter as a positive investing activity
Liability or Equity Increases ⇒ Enter as a positive financing activity
Liability or Equity Decreases ⇒ Enter as a negative financing activity

The idea is that asset increases involve investment of funds and therefore tend to reduce cash balances. The divestment or reduction in an asset tends to increase cash balances. On the other hand, an increase in a liability tends to raise cash balances, and a decrease in a liability tends to reduce available cash.

Alternative Formats for a Statement of Cash Flows

The statement of cash flows is a relatively new financial statement that replaces the sources and uses of cash statement. Like its predecessor, the statement summarizes the flow of cash in and out of the firm, not just revenues and expenses.

An alternative format to the format for the statement of cash flows is shown in Table 15.7. Table 15.7 highlights the starting cash balance at the top of the statement and ends with the ending cash balance.

Statements of cash flows for large corporations often include extensive detail on noncash revenues and expenses, as well as the effects on accounting income caused by changes in accounting methods or accounting values. Nevertheless, the basic structure and concepts of the statement are similar.

TABLE 15.6 A Format for Starting a Statement of Cash Flows

Operating Activities
Net Income
Depreciation
Investing Activities
Financing Activities
Dividends
Net Increase (Decrease) in Cash

TABLE 15.7 An Alternative Format for a Statement of Cash Flows

Starting Cash Balance

Operating Activities
  Net Income
  Depreciation

Investing Activities

Financing Activities
  Dividends

Ending Cash Balance

Summary of Statement of Cash Flows

As with other financial statements, the variety of formats and detail among firms tends to make the statement appear complex and difficult to understand. Underneath these vastly different appearances, however, each statement of cash flows is essentially the same. Regardless of format, the purpose of a statement of cash flows is clear: It conveys the changes in the balance sheet values in a way that encourages the user to view the firm as having engaged in a variety of activities that affect the cash balance.

In order to understand the purpose of a statement of cash flows, it is better to view it as a link through time between balance sheets:

Current Balance Sheet + Statement of Cash Flows = Forecasted Balance Sheet

The statement of cash flows is an important planning tool. For an existing corporation, the statement of cash flows is the focal point because it forces forecasted balance sheets to be balanced. In the business plan of a new venture, the statement of cash flows is especially useful because it is the tool for estimating future funding needs. Many new business plans incorrectly forecast funding needs as a list of investments and projected initial losses. Without a statement of cash flows, such financial plans are both incorrect and unimpressive to sophisticated venture capitalists considering investing in a new business.

Summary

- Financial analysis is the process of using financial information for decision-making purposes. Most of the information used in financial planning comes from financial statements known as the balance sheet, the income statement, and the statement of cash flows.

- Ratios constructed from financial statements can be used to analyze the debt usage, liquidity, profitability, and efficiency of the firm.
- Financial analysis is sometimes criticized because it relies on accounting numbers that can be manipulated in many different ways. For example, accounting numbers can be used to show that the firm is profitable when it is not. In the absence of reliable market information, however, there may be no other alternative to accounting statements.
- The material in this chapter may at times appear to be reduced to a number of rules that need to be followed. Yet financial analysis is critical to corporate financial management.

Demonstration Problems

Problem 1

As a financial analyst in a small firm, you have been charged with deciding whether credit should be extended to Clayberger Corporation. Clayberger has never before done business with your firm, but recently placed a large order. In fact, your firm's entire history has been as a supplier to one huge, local corporation whose credit is excellent but whose operations are declining. In order for your business to continue to expand, you must reach new customers, such as Clayberger. You have been provided with the following financial statements:

Clayberger Corporation Income Statements (in $000s)

	2003	*2002*	*2001*	*2000*
Revenues	8,614	8,116	7,730	7,436
Expenses	4,307	4,058	3,865	3,718
Depreciation	3,000	2,000	1,000	1,000
EBIT	1,307	2,058	2,865	2,718
Interest	287	248	215	178
Taxes	400	700	1,100	1,050
Net Income	620	1,110	1,550	1,490

Clayberger Corporation Balance Sheets (in $000s)

	2003	*2002*	*2001*	*2000*
Current Assets	3,146	2,746	1,838	1,444
Net Fixed Assets	24,346	18,888	10,486	10,614
Total Assets	27,492	21,634	12,324	12,058
Current Liabilities	1,424	1,858	2,166	2,726
Long-Term Debt	3,987	3,244	2,225	1,178
Equity	22,081	16,532	7,933	8,154
Total Liabilities and Equity	27,492	21,634	12,324	12,058

Your boss is not experienced in financial analysis, but did see that Clayberger's income has been dropping like a rock while its long-term debt has more than tripled. If credit is extended and Clayberger defaults, your boss says ominously that "somebody could lose a job." If your firm does not extend credit to Clayberger, however, your boss worries that Clayberger will turn to your competitor—and if Clayberger turns out to have been a good customer "somebody could lose a job."

Your boss asks for the report to be finished by tomorrow morning. As he picks up his bag and heads to the athletic club with the CEO, you somehow know who will end up losing a job if this decision turns out badly. What steps will you take to analyze the situation?

Solution to Problem 1:

First, following Table 15.3, compute the appropriate debt ratios, liquidity ratios, and profitability ratios as shown in Steps 1–3.

Step 1: Compute the debt ratios from Panel A of Table 15.3 for each year. Note that the total debt includes the current liabilities.

	2003	*2002*	*2001*	*2000*
The Debt Ratio	0.197	0.236	0.356	0.324
Debt-to-Equity	0.245	0.309	0.554	0.479
Equity Multiplier	1.245	1.309	1.554	1.479
Times Interest Earned	4.554	8.298	13.326	15.270

Step 2: For liquidity ratios, compute only the Current Ratio because details of the current assets are not provided.

	2003	*2002*	*2001*	*2000*
Current Ratio	2.21	1.48	0.85	0.53

Step 3: Compute all of the profitability ratios from Panel C of Table 15.3. For simplicity, use only the end-of-year total asset and equity.

	2003	*2002*	*2001*	*2000*
Net Return on Sales	0.072	0.137	0.201	0.200
Net Return on Assets	0.023	0.051	0.126	0.124
Net Return on Equity	0.028	0.067	0.195	0.183

Step 4: Analyze the ratios. First, note that the value of total debt is declining as a percentage even though long-term debt is rising. This is because assets are growing and current liabilities have fallen. The times interest earned ratio is falling, primarily as a result of a drop in income—which is discussed later.

The liquidity ratio is very supportive of Clayberger's creditworthiness because it is rising. A useful step might be to compare the ratio with industry averages.

Finally, efficiency ratios are declining—reflecting the problem of declining net income.

Step 5: Look beyond the ratios to discover why the net income is declining. A closer inspection of the income statement indicates that the cause of the problem is greatly increased depreciation. A close inspection of the notes to the statement might indicate, for example, that the firm is switching from renting equipment to owning equipment. This would explain the higher assets, the higher depreciation, and the lower net income. The cost savings from owning the equipment might be argued to lead to much lower expenses and higher net income, once the one-time expenses of making the transition have been absorbed.
Step 6: Consider becoming a customer of a credit service. These bureaus have both much greater experience at performing financial analysis as well as extensive information on the firm's current and past abilities to pay their bills. In addition, the credit service can provide the information quickly, and the boss wants an answer the next day. A call to the credit agency finds no past histories of delinquency in paying bills.
Step 7: Look to the financial markets—specifically to Clayberger's bond yields and stock price—to see whether trends in these market prices indicate concern with Clayberger's future. Clayberger's stock price is now trading in the middle of its range over the last 52 weeks, and the bonds are trading at yields that are well within the range of the firm's risk class.
Final Solution: Following these seven steps puts you in a position to make the following recommendation: Even though every credit decision comes with some risk, Clayberger is a risk worth taking.

Problem 2

Now return to Clayberger Corporation's financial statements and compute its statement of cash flows for 2003. Because depreciation is included in the net assets figure in this condensed balance sheet, list depreciation as zero for this problem. In addition, assume that the current assets account is comprised of cash only and that the firm paid out all of its income each year in the form of dividends.

Solution to Problem 2:

The solution is to takes figures from the balance sheets and income statement and place them into the format of the Statement of Cash Flows (Table 15.6 or 15.7)
Step 1: Begin by determining the change between year-end 2002 and year-end 2003 in each of the balance sheet accounts; however, do not include changes in entries that are sums of other entries (e.g., total assets):

Clayberger Corporation Balance Sheets (in $000s)

	2003	*2002*	*Change*
Current Assets	3,146	2,746	+400
Net Fixed Assets	24,346	18,888	+5,458
Total Assets	27,492	21,634	
Current Liabilities	1,424	1,858	−434
Long-Term Debt	3,987	3,244	+743
Equity	22,081	16,532	+5,549
Total Liabilities and Equity	27,492	21,634	

Step 2: Select a statement of cash flows format (either Table 15.6 or Table 15.7). For this example, we use Table 15.6:

<u>Operating Activities</u>
Net Income
Depreciation
<u>Investing Activities</u>
<u>Financing Activities</u>
Dividends
Net Increase (or Decrease) in Cash

Step 3: Enter net income figures from the income statement and enter zero, as assumed, for depreciation. As stated earlier, assume that the dividends are equal to the net income. Finally, enter the changes in the net fixed assets as an investing activity (negative because increased assets require cash) and the changes in the two debt categories and equity as a financing activity (increases are listed as positive values because their increases generated cash and vice versa).

<u>Operating Activities</u>	
Net Income	+620
Depreciation	+0
<u>Investing Activities</u>	
Fixed Assets	−5,458
<u>Financing Activities</u>	
Dividends	−620
Current Liabilities	−434
Long-Term Debt	+743
Equity	+5,549

Net Increase (or Decrease) in Cash

Step 4: Sum the column, enter the resulting sum as the change in the cash balance, and then confirm that the result matches the change in cash (current assets) found in the balance sheet.
Net Increase (or Decrease) in Cash +400

Final Solution: The current asset account (cash for this example) gained $400, from $2,746 to $3,146.

Review Questions

1. Provide a one-sentence definition of financial analysis.
2. List the three general aspects of the firm that financial analysts investigate.
3. Why do modernists prefer to use market prices when analyzing the firm?
4. Why do traditionalists prefer to use accounting numbers when analyzing the firm?

5. Describe a situation in which a modernist might advocate using accounting numbers.
6. How do current assets or liabilities differ from fixed assets or liabilities?
7. Explain in one or two sentences what the balance sheet is measuring.
8. Explain in one or two sentences what the income statement is measuring.
9. In its simplest form, what is a financial ratio?
10. Define ratio analysis.
11. List one common ratio in each of the following areas: (1) debt usage, (2) liquidity, (3) profitability, and (4) efficiency. State briefly what each of these ratios is measuring.
12. What type of information is conveyed in the statement of cash flows?

Problems

1. An office party on New Year's Eve overflowed into the accounting department of your corporation, causing ink to be spilled onto a balance sheet. The accountants are furious, especially because they are never invited to the parties. Can you help them by supplying the missing numbers?

The Balance Sheet for Problem #1 (in $000s)

Assets	*Year 2*	*Year 1*	*Change*
Cash and securities	$ 512	$ 453	$ ____
Accounts receivable	$ 1,325	$ ____	$ + 104
Inventory	$ ____	$ 8,386	$ ____
Total Current Assets	$ ____	$ ____	$ + 300
Equipment	$ ____	$ 33,929	$ + 8,010
Less: Accumulated depreciation	$ 12,657	$ ____	$ + 1,362
Net equipment	$ ____	$ ____	$ ____
Buildings	$ 95,129	$ ____	$ 0
Less: Accumulated depreciation	$ ____	$ 51,237	$ + 2,251
Net buildings	$ ____	$ ____	$ ____
Land	$ 73,012	$ ____	$ 0
Fixed Assets	$ ____	$ ____	$ ____
Total Assets	$ ____	$ ____	$ ____
Liabilities and Equity			
Accounts payable	$ ____	$ 1,423	$ + 76
Bank loans	$ 3,664	$ ____	$ − 32
Debt due within year	$ 1,483	$ 1,327	$ ____
Total Current Liabilities	$ ____	$ ____	$ ____
Total Long-Term Debt	$ ____	$ ____	$ ____
Common stock ($.10 par)	$ 1,500	$ 1,500	$ ____
Paid-in-surplus	$ 45,546	$ ____	$ 0
Retained earnings	$ ____	$ ____	$ ____
Total Equity	$ 103,323	$ 102,876	$ ____
Total Liabilities and Equity	$ ____	$ ____	$ ____

2. Net working capital is defined as current assets less current liabilities.
   a. Determine the net working capital for Points of Light Corporation for each year given in Table 15.4.
   b. What would happen to net working capital in the last year if Points of Lights Corporation used $100,000 of cash to pay off $100,000 of bank loans?
   c. What would happen to net working capital in the last year if Points of Light Corporation used $100,000 of cash to buy inventory?
   d. Finally, what would happen to net working capital in the last year if Points of Light Corporation used $100,000 of cash to buy a building?

3. Worn Out Equipment, Inc., has the following year-end balance sheet values for its depreciable assets:

Equipment	$478,213	Buildings	$8,648,382
Less Accumulated Depreciation	265,111	Less Accumulated Depreciation	2,424,171
Net Equipment	$213,102	Net Buildings	$6,224,211

   a. Determine the values for equipment, accumulated depreciation on equipment, and net equipment at the end of the next year if, until that time, the firm does not buy or sell any equipment but expenses another $52,099 of depreciation.
   b. Determine the values for buildings, accumulated depreciation on buildings, and net buildings at the end of the next year if, during the next year, the firm buys a new building for $1.5 million and takes total depreciation (including the new building) of $404,764.

4. The Painted Post Corp. has the following year-end balance sheet values for its buildings and equipment:

Equipment and Buildings	$ 83,324,958
Less Accumulated Depreciation	23,114,145
Net Equipment and Buildings	$ 60,210,813

Determine the values for each account at the end of the next year if, during the next year, the firm buys $12 million of equipment, depreciates all buildings and equipment by $6,545,000, and sells an old building that it had purchased for $10 million, but which had an accumulated depreciation of $6,423,382.

5. Preemptive Rights, Inc., has the following values on its balance sheet:

	Year 2	*Year 1*
Common Stock ($1 Par)	$ 2,564,000	$ 2,400,000
Paid in Surplus of Par	$ 8,439,000	$ 8,000,000
Retained Earnings	$15,435,000	$14,328,000

   a. How many shares of common stock did the firm have in each year?
   b. How many shares of stock did the firm issue during Year 2?
   c. How much money was raised above the $1 par value for these new shares?
   d. What must have been the selling price of each share of the new stock on average?
   e. If the firm paid $500,000 in dividends during Year 2, what was its net income?

6. Thieves have broken into your computer system and have stolen key numbers from your firm's income statement. Can you replace them?

Income Statement for Problem 6

	Year 2	*Year 1*
Sales	$ 2,658,000	$ 2,435,000
Costs of goods sold	$ ______	$ 967,000
Selling and general expenses	$ 867,000	$ 831,000
Earnings before interest and taxes	$ 768,000	$ ______
Interest on debt	$ ______	$ 200,000
Earnings before taxes	$ 558,000	$ ______
Taxes	$ ______	$ 175,000
Net income	$ 335,000	$ ______

7. Referring to Problem 6, during Year 2 the firm paid $100,000 in dividends. The Year 1 year-end retained earnings were $2.5 million. What would be the retained earnings on the firm's balance sheet statements in Year 2?
8. Using the financial statements in Table 15.8 (see page 472), fill in the following debt ratios:

	Year 2	*Year 1*
a. The Debt Ratio	______	______
b. The Debt-to-Equity Ratio	______	______
c. The Equity Multiplier	______	______

9. Using the financial statements in Table 15.8, fill in the following liquidity ratios:

	Year 2	*Year 1*
a. The Cash Ratio	______	______
b. The Quick Ratio	______	______
c. The Current Ratio	______	______

10. Using the financial statements in Table 15.8, fill in the following profitability and efficiency ratios for Year 2:
    a. Net Return on Sales = __________.
    b. Net Return on Assets = __________.
    c. Net Return on Equity = __________.
    d. Inventory Turnover = __________.
    e. Days Sales Outstanding = __________.

11. Use the retained earnings figures and the net income in Table 15.8 to compute the dividends paid in Year 2. What percentage of net income was this dividend?
12. Find the changes between years for each account in the balance sheets in Table 15.8 and use those changes to construct a statement of cash flows.

TABLE 15.8 Balance Sheet for Problems 8–13 (in $000s)

	Year 2	*Year 1*
Assets		
Cash and Securities	$ 512	$ 453
Accounts receivable	1,325	1,215
Inventory	9,001	8,386
Total Current Assets	$ 10,838	$10,054
Fixed Assets	90,001	88,785
Total Assets	$100,839	$98,839
Liabilities and Equity		
Accounts payable	$ 1,301	$ 1,223
Bank loans	3,664	3,550
Debt due within year	1,483	1,327
Total Current Liabilities	$ 6,448	$ 6,100
Total Long-Term Debt	$ 39,100	39,000
Common stock ($.10 Par)	$ 2,000	$ 2,000
Paid-in-surplus	25,500	25,500
Retained earnings	27,791	26,239
Total Liabilitics and Equity	$100,839	$98,839

Income Statement for Problems 8–13 (in 000s)

	Year 2	*Year 1*
Sales	$35,000	$34,000
Cost of goods sold	12,100	11,690
Selling and general expenses	12,450	12,500
Earnings before interest and taxes	$ 10,450	$ 9,810
Interest on debt	5,000	5,490
Earnings before taxes	$ 5,450	$ 4,320
Taxes	2,100	1,700
Net income	$ 3,350	$ 2,620

13. Condense the balance sheets in Table 15.8 by collapsing all current assets and current liabilities into a single figure entitled Net Working Capital. Then, use the condensed balance sheet to construct a statement of cash flows.

Discussion Questions

1. The firm's accountant suggests that by taking less depreciation the firm will be able to increase its net income and therefore have sufficient earnings that the firm will not need to borrow money to fund expansion. You are asked to comment.
2. It is your decision whether to extend a large amount of credit to Comic Adventures in order to fill a large order that they have placed with your firm. Your financial analysis of Comic Adventures, Inc., reveals that the firm's financial ratios have been improving and that they now meet or exceed all industry standards. The market price of both their debt and equity, however, has fallen substantially in recent months. What would you do?
3. Why might an optimal financial ratio for one firm differ from the industry average financial ratio?
4. Why is depreciation listed as a source of cash or funds when it is an expense?
5. Which contains more information about the probability that a firm will be able to pay its debts: the price of one of its bonds or all of its current and past financial statements?

CHAPTER 16

WORKING CAPITAL MANAGEMENT

Jan was in a bind. Tuition was due in 4 days and the penalty for late payment was $100. On top of tuition, the phone bill was due tomorrow or another late payment fee would be assessed. The money to pay the tuition was "locked" into a certificate of deposit (CD), which did not come due for seven more days. If she withdrew the money from the bank, then she would have to pay a substantial interest penalty for early withdrawal.[1]

Despondent, Jan turned to her corporate finance textbook. The pages fell open to the chapter on working capital management. Could the working capital management techniques of a major corporation apply to her personal financial decisions?

Jan suddenly saw hope. She could write the check for the tuition payment, take it to the bursar's office after banking hours, and then transfer the money from the CD to her checking account on the day that the CD matured. The time period or "float" between when the check was written and when the money would be deducted from her checking account might be sufficient to enable the money to be transferred—especially because the time interval included a weekend.

Jan, now excited, continued to flip through the pages in the hope that the telephone bill problem could be solved as well. It was a little tougher, but she found a solution. As a start, Jan figured that she could pressure one of her roommates to pay back the money that she owed her, but that amount of money would not be enough.

Jan was in charge of collecting rent from each of her roommates and turning it over to the landlord. Following the techniques of working capital management, Jan offered one of her roommates (whom everyone not so affectionately called "money bags") a discount if she would pay her share of next month's rent in advance. Jan could pay the telephone bill using the rent money and then pay the rent money when the CD came due. The problem was solved, and she still had time to read a few extra chapters of her corporate finance textbook.

---

[1]Despite the bank's advertisements to the contrary, federal law does not require this penalty.

working capital management
The management of the firm's current assets and current liabilities.

The problems and solutions just described fall under the broad heading of **working capital management**—the topic of this chapter—and the techniques apply to Jan's personal finances as well as to small and large corporations.

An Overview of Working Capital Management

working capital
A firm's investments in current assets.

net working capital
The difference between current assets and current liabilities.

Working capital is defined as a firm's investments in current assets. A related concept is **net working capital,** which is defined as current assets minus current liabilities. Although it is possible to provide very detailed listings, the principal categories of working capital—often referred to as the components of working capital—are shown in Table 16.1. Working capital management refers to the specialized tools and strategies for making decisions with regard to these assets and liabilities.

The Three Tasks of Working Capital Management

The concepts underlying the problems and techniques of working capital management discussed in this chapter are remarkably familiar to most college students. There may be no other place in finance where there is such a similarity between corporate and personal finance. The three tasks or concepts underlying working capital management are:

1. Speeding up receipts of cash
2. Delaying payments of cash
3. Investing excess cash

Implicit in each of these three tasks, however, is the corporate objective to maximize shareholder wealth. Thus, they are to be performed in a manner that takes advantage of the time value of money in an optimal way. In other words, receipts should be speeded up, payments delayed, and cash invested if and only if the advantages outweigh the disadvantages.

The first part of this chapter discusses each of the components or categories of working capital individually in detail. Current assets will be presented first, followed by current liabilities. Chapter 17 will discuss overall working capital forecasting and planning. If things at first appear compli-

TABLE 16.1 Principal Categories of Working Capital

Current Assets	*Current Liabilities*
Cash	Accounts Payable
Marketable Securities	Bank Loans and Notes Payable
Accounts Receivable	Current Debt (due in 1 year)
Inventory	

cated, then remember that the tools in this chapter are familiar to each of us in everyday personal financial management.

Current Asset Management

We will now discuss each type of current asset in detail, beginning with cash, the most liquid category, and ending with inventory, the least liquid category. Liquidity, the speed with which an asset can be converted into cash at a reasonable price, was discussed in Chapter 2.

Cash Management

cash management
The management of the firm's cash position. Cash management recognizes that even though cash is a necessary raw material, too much of it is wasteful.

Cash management plays perhaps the most important role in working capital management. Cash is a necessary asset for running a firm and must be held in sufficient quantity to meet demand. In this sense, cash is held in inventory just as are some other assets, such as the raw materials for production. The concept that drives cash management is that, even though cash is necessary, too much of it is wasteful. In other words, the corporation's capital is a valuable commodity that could be put to work earning better rates of return elsewhere than it earns as cash—little or no interest in a bank's checking account. The goal of cash management is simply to minimize the total cost of providing cash liquidity to the firm.

The EOQ Model for Cash Management All firms need some amount of cash on hand to pay bills, meet their payroll, and to satisfy other needs. Inasmuch as the cash held reduces funds available for investment, the task of the financial manager is to keep enough cash on hand for ordinary current expenses, but to avoid waste due to excessive transactions or large cash balances. There are several techniques available to assist the financial manager in determining the optimal policy. The **economic order quantity (EOQ) model** is one such technique.

economic order quantity (EOQ) model
A technique that determines the optimal amount of cash or any other inventory to order each time the inventory of that item is depleted.

To demonstrate how this model can be used to optimize cash balance, consider a growing firm that spends cash steadily and must replenish its cash balance regularly to maintain its inventories, its payroll, and its advertising. The financial manager of this firm wants to achieve the needed liquidity to meet such expenses, but wants to do so as cost-effectively as possible. This means that cash balances should be as low as possible so that funds can be channeled to profitable investment opportunities.

In analyzing the situation, the financial manager realizes that there are two costs to holding cash: (1) the transactions costs of obtaining cash, and (2) the cost of lost investment earnings incurred by holding cash rather than investing those funds. The transactions costs of obtaining cash are called *order costs* in the EOQ model. The costs of lost earnings are called the *storage costs.* You may be familiar with storage costs under a different name—*opportunity cost*. An economist would say that the opportunity cost of holding cash is the lost earnings, but the terms used here are those that apply in the EOQ model.

To find the firm's optimal level of cash, assume that (1) the firm needs \$10,000 in cash each day to meet expenses, (2) the firm's order costs are \$100 because this is the fee it pays to obtain cash, and (3) the firm's storage costs are \$5 for each \$100 per year that must be kept as cash rather than invested elsewhere. Expressed as a percentage, the cost of lost earnings is 5 percent (\$5/\$100).

With the EOQ model, the financial manager can strike the proper balance between order costs and storage costs such that cash is managed as efficiently as possible. Use $\$X$ to represent the amount of money that the firm needs to replenish its cash balance whenever it runs out of cash. Because the firm uses up \$10,000 of cash per day, it will have to replenish its cash balance every $\$X/\$10{,}000$ days. For example, if $\$X = \$100{,}000$, then the firm must replenish its cash every 10 days. Figure 16.1 shows the change in cash balance $\$X$ through time.

We want to use the EOQ model to find the cash balance $\$X$ that minimizes the sum of the order costs and storage costs. Total costs are given by:

$$\text{Total Cost} = \text{Annual Order Cost} + \text{Annual Storage Cost}$$

Annual order cost is found by taking the firm's annual cash need divided by the order size (the unknown variable $\$X$) multiplied by the cost per order:

$$\text{Annual Order Cost} = \frac{\text{Daily Cash Need} \times 365}{\text{Order Size}} \times \text{Cost of Per Order} \qquad (16.1)$$

FIGURE 16.1 The Flow of Cash in the EOQ Model

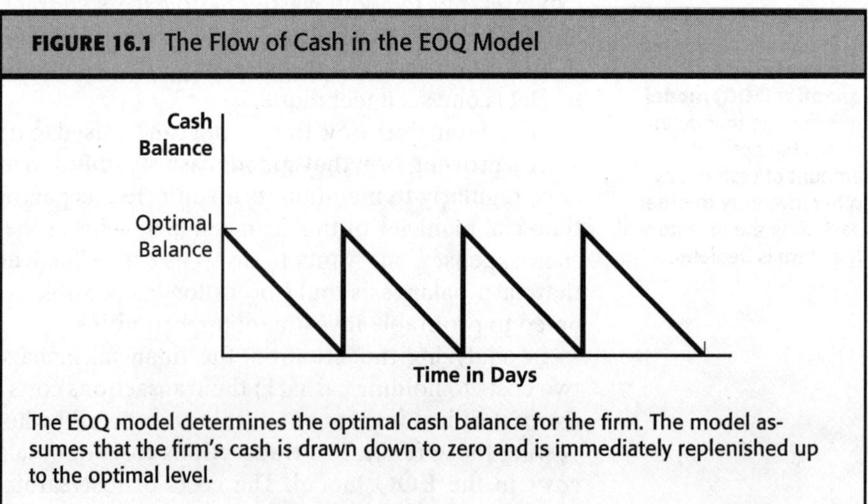

The EOQ model determines the optimal cash balance for the firm. The model assumes that the firm's cash is drawn down to zero and is immediately replenished up to the optimal level.

For the firm in our example, annual order costs are:

$$\text{Annual Order Cost} = \frac{\$10{,}000 \times 365}{X} \times 100$$

Annual storage costs are found by multiplying the average amount of cash held by the cost of holding cash. Because the cash balance starts each "cycle" with $\$X$ and steadily declines to \$0, the average cash balance is the midpoint, or $\$X/2$:

$$\text{Annual Storage Cost} = \frac{X}{2} \times \text{Cost of Lost Earnings} \tag{16.2}$$

For the firm in our example, annual storage costs are:

$$\text{Annual Storage Cost} = \frac{X}{2} \times 5\%$$

Substituting these expressions for annual order costs and annual storage costs into the relationship for total costs we get:

$$\text{Total Cost} = \left[\frac{\$10{,}000 \times 365}{X} \times \$100\right] + \left[\frac{X}{2} \times 5\%\right]$$

The total cost to the firm is a function of, or depends upon, the value $\$X$. A low value of $\$X$ will drive the order costs high. A high value of $\$X$ will create high storage costs. Our objective is to is to find the optimal or least cost value of X.

The optimal solution can be found by using calculus. As with many problems, the idea is to take the derivative of the function and set it equal to zero. Because the derivative measures the rate of change in the function (in our example, the total costs) with respect to a change in a variable (in our case X), finding the value of X where the derivative is zero is finding the value of X at which costs have reached an optimum. Neither increases nor decreases in X will produce lower costs.

We use calculus, therefore, to take the derivative of the previous equation with respect to X, set it equal to zero, and solve for X:

$$\text{EOQ} = \sqrt{\frac{2(\text{Annual Cash Needs})(\text{Cost per Order})}{\text{Interest Rate}}} \tag{16.3}$$

In the example, the optimal order size is:

$$\text{X} = \sqrt{\frac{2(\$10{,}000 \times 365)(\$100)}{.05}} = \$120{,}830$$

Thus, the firm should "order" (or obtain) the amount of $120,830 in cash each time it replenishes its cash. Because the firm uses cash at a rate of $10,000 per day, it will run out of cash approximately every 12 days. The EOQ model assumes that the firm's cash balance is drawn down to approximately zero, and at that time, a new "order" of $120,830 arrives. In practice, few firms allow their cash balance to go to zero, as we did for simplicity in our example. Most keep some minimum amount of cash on hand to meet emergencies. This minimum cash balance is called the *safety stock* in the EOQ model.

In the EOQ model, cash is assumed to flow out at an even rate. There is a cost each time cash is replenished, called the *order cost*, and a cost to maintaining the cash inventory, called the *storage cost*. Storage costs arise because of the low rate of interest the firm earns on its cash balance. The optimal solution minimizes the total sum of these two costs over time.

There is a serious problem, however, with applying the EOQ model to cash management. The EOQ model ignores cash inflows and uncertainty in that all movements of cash are assumed to be outflows and unchanging. Because the EOQ model ignores cash inflows, it is better suited for other types of management problems, such as traditional inventory management. The EOQ model, however, was worth considering as a cash management tool because it lays a foundation upon which to build the model discussed next.

Miller-Orr model
A cash management model that determines an upper and lower limit for the firm's cash balances. In the model, when the upper limit is reached, the cash manager invests the excess cash in a less liquid and more profitable asset. When the lower limit is reached the cash manager needs to replenish the cash balance by liquidating an asset or by borrowing.

The Miller-Orr Model An improved cash management model called the Miller-Orr model addresses some of the problems of EOQ. The **Miller-Orr model** is similar to the EOQ in that it determines when and how much to order and specifies upper and lower limits to the cash balance. The cash balance is allowed to rise or fall randomly as the firm's operations either produce cash inflows or require cash outflows due to random events such as the timing of various transactions and bills. The upper and lower limits for cash balances trigger adjustments in the cash balance. When the model's upper limit is reached, the cash manager invests the excess cash in a less liquid and more profitable asset. When the lower limit is reached, the cash manager replenishes the cash balance by liquidating an asset or by borrowing.

The model determines the optimal cash balance to which the cash level is adjusted when the upper or lower limits are reached. This *target cash balance*, or *return point*, is located one third of the distance from the lower limit toward the upper limit. These concepts are illustrated in Figure 16.2. The lower limit in the Miller-Orr model is set by management and reflects the firm's estimation of the lowest cash balance that should be held. The model generates the target cash balance that minimizes the expected total costs of holding cash.

Formula (16.4) determines the precise specification for the target cash balance according to the Miller-Orr model:

$$\text{Target Cash Balance} = \text{Lower Limit} + \left[\frac{3 \times TCOST \times \sigma^2}{4r}\right]^{1/3} \tag{16.4}$$

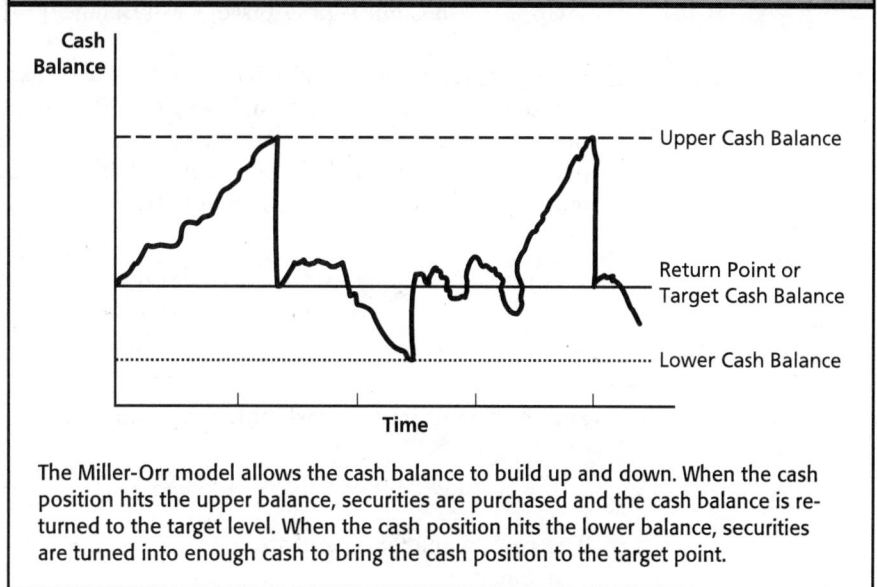

FIGURE 16.2 The Miller-Orr Cash Management Model

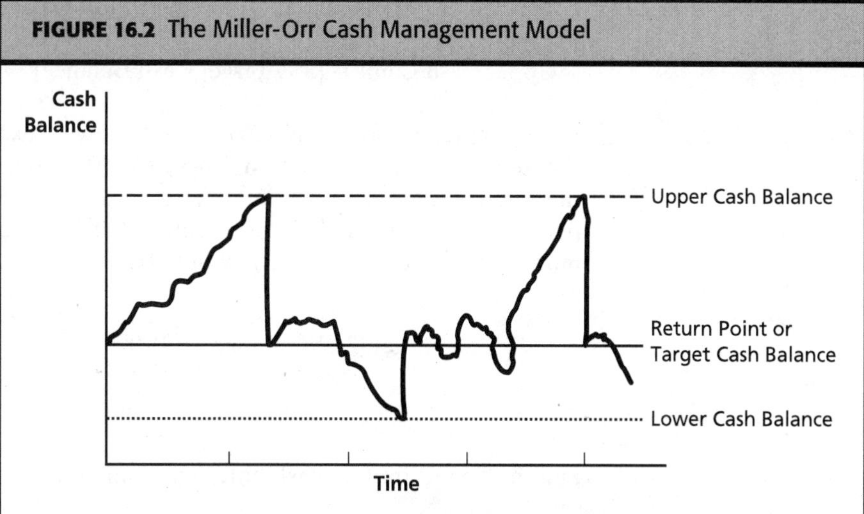

The Miller-Orr model allows the cash balance to build up and down. When the cash position hits the upper balance, securities are purchased and the cash balance is returned to the target level. When the cash position hits the lower balance, securities are turned into enough cash to bring the cash position to the target point.

This target cash balance requires estimation of the volatility of the cash flows given in the formula by the daily variance of cash flows (σ^2), estimation of the daily interest rate (r), and an estimate of the cost of returning the cash balance to its return point ($TCOST$). The variance and interest rate can also be expressed in annual terms.

The Miller-Orr Model generates two important results. First, it suggests that cash balances should be restored to one third the distance from the lower cash balance toward the upper cash balance rather than the midpoint. The reason is the storage cost of cash—the low rate of interest on cash relative to the firm's other assets. By returning the cash balance to a point below the midpoint, the average cash balance is reduced; therefore, the average storage costs are reduced.

The second important result of the Miller-Orr model is to establish the optimal spread between the lower and upper cash balances. A higher upper bound reduces transactions costs as in the EOQ model. A higher upper bound, however, also increases the average cash balance and, therefore, the average storage costs. The Miller-Orr Model solves for the optimal solution when cash balances can rise or fall.

Some calculators are unable to handle numbers as large as those that can result from Formula (16.4). In this case we suggest that Formula (16.4) be broken into the following parts:

$$\text{Target Cash Balance} = \text{Lower Limit} + \left[\frac{(3)^{1/3} \times (TCOST)^{1/3} \times (\sigma^2)^{1/3}}{(4r)^{1/3}}\right]$$

Given the target cash balance, the upper limit of cash is determined as:

$$\text{Upper Cash Limit} = [3 \times \text{Target Cash Balance}] - [2 \times \text{Lower Limit}] \quad (16.5)$$

Example 16.1 For example, suppose that a firm sets the lower cash limit at $1,000, has an estimated daily variance of cash flows of $250, estimates its cost of returning to the target cash balance at $150, and assumes an annual interest rate of 10 percent so that the daily interest rate is 0.0274 percent. Using the Miller-Orr model, the target cash balance would be:

$$\text{Target Cash Balance} = \$1{,}000 + \left[\frac{3 \times 150 \times 250}{4 \times .000274}\right]^{1/3}$$

$$= \$1{,}468.23,$$

and the upper limit on cash holdings would be:

$$\text{Upper Limit} = [3 \times \$1{,}468.23] - [2 \times \$1{,}000] = \$2{,}404.70$$

The cash manager, therefore, knows when and to what level to adjust the cash balance.

Newer models have been developed that attempt to build on the Miller-Orr model by incorporating the predictability of some cash flows. Although Miller-Orr does not address all of the complexities of managing the firm's cash position, it nevertheless provides a good starting point for the study and practice of cash management. All cash management models share the objective of finding the least-cost approach to providing a firm with an adequate cash balance to meet its liquidity needs.

Marketable Securities Management

We previously discussed the corporation's cash balances, such as their funds in checking accounts that earn no interest or a relatively low rate of interest. The second-most liquid category of assets for a corporation is marketable securities.

The marketable securities in which a corporation would typically invest are known as **money market securities.** The money market is not a physical place, such as the New York Stock Exchange; rather, it simply refers to types of securities such as U.S. Treasury bills, repurchase agreements, commercial paper, certificates of deposit, money market mutual funds, and other short-term, relatively low-risk investments. An expanded discussion of marketable securities is included in Window 16.1.

money market securities
Types of securities characterized by short-term maturity of 1 year or less and low risk of default. Examples of money market securities include U.S. Treasury bills, commercial paper, and certificates of deposit.

The advantage of marketable securities over cash is that they generally pay a higher rate of interest. The disadvantage is that they must be liquidated into cash in order to meet an expense, and the process of selling the security and receiving the cash usually takes 1 or 2 days.

WINDOW 16.1

Types of Marketable Securities

This window describes the various types of marketable securities used by firms as part of a cash management strategy. Corporations usually hold marketable securities 'in-waiting' as they search for major investment opportunities and to meet potential cash outflow. Because marketable securities are not viewed as permanent investments they usually have the characteristics of low default risk and short maturity. The choice of which type of marketable security to hold will be determined by the relative risk and tax feature of the security.

1. **Treasury Bills,** as described in Window 4.1, are short-term securities issued and backed by the U.S. Treasury with maturities of 1 year or less issued at a discount from face value. The face value of Treasury bills start at $10,000 and go up from that minimum in increments of $5,000. The income received from Treasury bills, as with all Treasury securities, is exempt from state and local taxes, but not from federal taxes. Because they are issued by the U.S. Treasury, Treasury bills are considered default risk free.
2. **Repurchase agreements (Repos)** are agreements to purchase government securities and then to sell them for an agreed upon price. They are an effective way for corporations with excess cash to invest the cash for very short periods of time, sometimes even for 1 day. Because repos usually represent investments in government securities, the tax status would be the same as for Treasury bills.
3. **Certificates of deposit (CDs)** are securities issued by banks with maturities usually less than 1 year. CDs marketed for larger institutional customers are issued in denominations as low as $100,000, although a $1 million denomination is more common, and are issued by large banks as a financing tool for their business practices. The income received from CDs is generally fully taxable at the state and federal government level. The default risk of CDs depends on the issuer. For example, prime CDs are issued by the most financially secure banks and thus have low default risk, while nonprime CDs are issued by less financially secured banks and have higher relative degrees of default risk. Further, Yankee CDs, CDs issued by a foreign bank with a branch in the United States, may have even higher relative levels of credit risk.
4. **Commercial paper** is a short-term promissory note (maturities ranging from 2 days to 270 days) issued directly by corporations. Like Treasury bills, commercial paper is traded at a discount from its face value. Because these notes are unsecured (there is no physical collateral backing the loan), the commercial paper market is usually confined to large, well-known, financially sound firms. The default risk of commercial paper generally falls on the low end of the risk spectrum. Income from commercial paper is generally fully taxable at the state and federal government area.

The purpose of buying and holding marketable securities may be to provide funds to meet some expenses that are planned at future specific points in time or to meet unexpected expenses. Corporations occasionally hold large amounts of marketable securities "in waiting" as they search for major investment opportunities. When investing cash in marketable securities, it is important for the cash manager or treasurer to determine the probabilities of when the marketable securities might need to be liquidated to meet cash needs.

Example 16.2 Consider Liberal Wines, Inc. (LW), a maker of traditional wines. LW receives somewhat regular cash inflows throughout the year. Many of LW's expenses, unfortunately, are concentrated in the fall, when they pay local farmers for grapes and have enormous labor expenses for beginning production.

We would expect LW's liquidity to follow an annual cycle, with a peak balance of cash and marketable securities in the summer and minimum balances in the fall. We would typically expect LW to invest in marketable securities throughout the year and to liquidate these securities in the fall when the cash is needed.

The Choice of Marketable Securities Once it has been decided how much cash should be invested in marketable securities, the next issue is in which marketable securities should the firm invest. In selecting a marketable security a cash manager typically has three considerations: maturity, credit risk, and income taxes.

Maturity: One of the most difficult decisions the cash manager faces is that involving the maturity of the marketable security. The advantage of investing in longer maturities is that they generally offer higher rates of return. The primary disadvantage of longer-term securities is that they fluctuate more in market price when interest rates change. In other words, longer-term securities have higher interest rate risk. Worse yet, if the security needs to be liquidated before it matures, the corporation might be forced to recognize a very low return or even a loss. These fluctuations in price and therefore in the return on longer-term marketable securities are usually disliked by cash managers and their bosses, such as the CFO and board of directors.

term structure of interest rates
The relationship between yield and time to maturity for similar-risk securities.

The relationship between interest rates and term to maturity is known as the **term structure of interest rates.** History reveals that the average returns of investing in longer-term money market securities are high relative to the small risks they pose. The realities of corporate politics, however, often outweigh this theory of investment such that cash managers are notoriously conservative in bearing this risk of interest rate fluctuation.

Credit Risk: Credit risk is the potential for the issuer of the marketable security to default and be unable to pay back some or all of the investor's principal and interest.

In the United States, securities backed by the U.S. government are considered to be free of credit risk. There are enormous quantities of such securities available, including U.S. Treasury bills and FDIC insured certificates of deposit.

Securities considered to be subject to credit risk include money market obligations of corporations (called *commercial paper*), uninsured certificates of deposit (uninsured because they exceed the $100,000 FDIC insurance limit), obligations of state and municipal governments, and banker's acceptances.

As we would expect, market interest rates adjust such that the securities with higher credit risk offer higher returns. Thus, the cash manager is faced with the dilemma that most higher returns in the money market are only available if credit risk is borne. Despite their conservative nature, cash managers frequently bear minor amounts of credit risk.

Income Taxes: The final major consideration for a cash manager is the effect of income taxes on marketable securities. In general, there are four levels of taxability:

1. Fully taxable—including almost all securities backed by corporations and banks such as commercial paper, CDs, and money market mutual funds that buy them.
2. Free of state income taxes—including direct obligations of the U.S. government.
3. Partially excluded—including dividends from common and preferred stocks, which are substantially tax free and are usually held by cash managers through funds known as dividend capture funds.
4. Tax free—including interest from municipal and state obligations, which are free of federal income tax as well as totally tax free for residents of the municipality or state issuing the securities.

The rates of return offered by securities adjust to offset tax advantages partially. Thus, if everything else is equal, fully taxable securities pay the highest before-tax returns, and tax-free securities pay the lowest returns.

Nevertheless, corporations in high tax brackets are well advised to consider seriously the last two categories. It is important to note, however, that the tax-advantaged securities tend to have higher levels of credit risk. Corporations in low tax brackets (which may be losing money) and nontaxed entities should invest only in the first two categories.

Summary of Marketable Securities Marketable securities provide an excellent opportunity for a cash manager to invest excess cash for the purpose of producing higher returns while maintaining liquidity. There are no easy answers, however, as to how a cash manager should decide among marketable securities, because prices in the money market will adjust such that all securities will be approximately equally desirable. Market conditions and institutional features change. What is unlikely to change is that the decision will continue to involve maturity, credit risk, and taxability.

Accounts Receivable Management

accounts receivable Monies owed to a firm as a result of having sold its products to customers on credit.

Accounts receivable are the monies owed to a firm as a result of having sold its products to customers on credit. For example, consider the sales and collections on sales for a new firm over the first half-year 1996:

Month	*Sales*	*Collections on Sales*
January	$2,000	$0
February	$2,000	$0
March	$2,000	$0
April	$2,000	$2,000 (From January)
May	$2,000	$0
June	$2,000	$2,000 (From February)

Over the first half of the year, sales are $12,000 but collections are only $4,000. Accounts receivable is $8,000.

There are three primary issues in the management of accounts receivable:

1. To whom to extend credit
2. What should be the terms of the credit
3. What procedure should be used to collect the money

We will discuss each of these issues separately.

To Whom to Extend Credit As with any corporate decision, extending credit should be based upon a comparison of costs and benefits. In accounts receivable management, these costs and benefits are a little more complicated than one might initially think. The analysis must build in uncertainty because we are uncertain of future payment, and we will handle this by computing the expected costs and expected benefits through payment probabilities.

The potential cost of extending credit is that the customer will not pay. Although there is a temptation to compute this cost as the full price of the product (the amount owed to the firm), it is almost always more appropriate to use the actual cost of the product, which is illustrated shortly. The potential benefit of extending credit is not just the hope for profit on the one transaction; rather, it is the potential value of the customer for a long-term relationship.

Example 16.3 ______ Assume that Deadbeats, Inc., has just placed an order for 1,200 of your firm's instant post holes. Your firm's selling price of post holes is $10 each, and the total cost is $5 each.

Based upon available information on Deadbeats, Inc. and your financial analysis, it is estimated that there is only a 30 percent chance that Deadbeats will pay. In the event that they are denied credit, you are sure that they will purchase post holes from your competitor. In the event that credit is extended, you would expect them to continue to do business with your firm. In fact, you would expect them to place a similar order each year.

Whether or not Deadbeats pays, the cost to your firm of having extended credit is the manufacturing cost of the product delivered, or $6,000 ($5 times 1,200 post holes), not the $12,000 listed price.

If Deadbeats pays and turns out to be a long-term customer, the benefit to your firm would be a profit of $6,000 per year. Applying the formula for a perpetuity from Chapter 4 and selecting 20 percent as a discount rate, we could roughly estimate the present value of this customer to be $30,000:

$$\text{Present Value of Deadbeat's Business} = \frac{\$6{,}000}{.20} = \$30{,}000.$$

The net present value of the decision to extend credit to Deadbeats, Inc., is found as the expected benefit of the sale minus the expected cost:

$$\begin{aligned} NPV = {} & [\text{Probability of Payment} \times \$30{,}000] \\ & - [(1 - \text{Probability of Payment}) \times \$6{,}000] \end{aligned}$$

Inserting the 30 percent probability of the customer paying produces a net benefit of $4,800:

$$NPV = [0.3 \times \$30{,}000] - [0.7 \times \$6{,}000] = \$4{,}800$$

The analysis indicates that the credit should be extended. In fact, the probability of payment would have to drop to below 16.67 percent before the net present value (*NPV*) of the credit extension decision to Deadbeats is negative.

This example could explain why so many firms are willing to extend credit to consumers. As we have said, the potential loss to the firm is the cost of the product, not its price. Further, the potential benefit may include an ongoing relationship.[2]

We may generalize the formula for the *NPV* of a credit decision as:

$$\begin{aligned} NPV = {} & [\text{Probability of Payment} \times \text{Customer Value}] - \\ & [(1 - \text{Probability of Payment}) \times \text{Cost}] \end{aligned} \qquad (16.6)$$

In the case of a one-time sale where no repeat business is anticipated, the customer value reduces to the profit for the one sale. In practice, however, the credit extension decision can become more complicated and often must

[2]In the case of consumer purchases, the potential interest charges earned on the credit decision would need to be factored into the analysis.

be formalized into a policy that can be implemented consistently. Nevertheless, the decision should be based upon the general principles presented here.

How Much Credit To Extend Similar to the decision of to whom to offer credit is the decision of how much credit to offer. This decision must be made when the customer initially requests credit and when the customer requests additional credit. The fundamental principle that guides financial decisions can be used: marginal benefit versus marginal cost.

Credit should be extended to the point where the marginal cost of the credit equals the marginal benefit. The marginal cost is the additional potential lost costs of the product. Note that the costs of past uncollected sales are sunk costs and should not be included as a marginal costs. The marginal benefits are the potential sales and interest revenues—including the potential to recover past sales that remain uncollected.

Determining the Terms of Credit Once the decision to grant credit has been made, the firm must establish the terms of the credit. These terms are called the *terms of sale* and give the buyer the time period for which, and the price at which, payment is due. While these terms of sale are usually discussed before the transaction is made, they are also listed on the firm's invoice—which is simply the bill for the order.

Example 16.4 Credit terms are often separated into two parts: the credit period and the credit discount. Somewhat complex jargon that looks something like this is used:

2/10; net 30

As shown, the terms of sale are usually presented as a string of numbers or words. In the example, the string needs to be broken up into pairs: The first pair is 2 and 10; the second pair is net and 30. The customer has the option of choosing either of the two payment terms offered.

The first item in each pair denotes the cost. The cost is listed as either a percentage discount or the word net, which means no discount. Thus the "2" in the preceding example indicates that the customer can receive a 2 percent discount, meaning that the seller will accept 98 percent of the billed price as payment in full.

The second number in each pair is the number of days for which the stated discount or net price will be available. In the preceding example, the 2 percent discount will be available only if the discounted price is paid within 10 days.

The second pair in the preceding example, net 30, offers alternate terms in the event that the buyer does not pay within the time period for the first payment option. Net 30 means that the customer must pay the full price within the 20 days following the initial discount period. If not paid by a total of 30 days, this bill will be considered overdue.

There are many terms that can be used to denote the terms of the discount and the terms of the credit sales without the discount. For example:

2/10; net 30; 18% over 30

means that a 2 percent discount applies if the bill is paid within 10 days, that the net amount of credit is due in 30 days, and that annual interest of 18 percent will apply to any credit balance beyond 30 days. In addition:

5/10 − EOM; net 45

means that a 5 percent discount applies if paid within 10 days of the end of the month (EOM), but that the net amount of credit is due within 45 days.

As the examples show, most terms of sale offer the buyer an incentive to pay early. The advantage of including this incentive is that it increases the speed with which payments will be made and also may decrease the probability that collection efforts will be required or that payment will never be made.

As with all other financial decisions, a correct decision is made when all costs and benefits are included, using market prices and adjusted for time and risk. The issues involved with selecting a credit policy are too numerous to detail, but they are all based upon a common-sense application of the principles detailed throughout this text.

One key issue is the interest rate implied by the discount. For example, offering a 2 percent discount to accelerate payment by 20 days amounts to an annual time value of money of well more than 36 percent. How this interest rate is computed is discussed in detail later in the section on accounts payable.

factoring of accounts receivables
The selling of all or part of the firm's accounts receivables to another firm at an agreed-upon price. The buying firm is the factor and has developed an expertise in collection.

lock boxes
Collection locations spread geographically so as to reduce the amount of time required for checks mailed to the firm to be deposited and cleared. Lock boxes are typically post office box addresses from which deposits go directly to a bank on the day of receipt.

Collection Efforts Virtually anyone who has ever loaned money has learned the difficulty of collecting it. Collection of accounts receivable is an important process for a corporation and requires a well-designed and well-implemented policy.

One technique is the **factoring of accounts receivables.** In a typical factoring arrangement, one firm will sell their accounts receivable(s) outright to another firm for an agreed-upon price. There is usually no recourse in such transactions, such that the buyer (also known as the factor) takes the loss if the purchaser of the goods does not ultimately pay for them. The buyer of accounts receivables obviously has developed an expertise in collections.

Another technique to expedite the receipt of accounts receivable is to utilize **lock boxes.** Lock boxes are payment collection locations spread geographically so as to reduce the amount of time required for checks mailed to the firm to be deposited and cleared. The lock boxes are typically post office box addresses from which deposits go directly to a bank on the day of receipt. The reduction of mailing time and check clearing time for the banks can produce significant savings when large sums of money are involved. A challenging working capital management problem is obviously the decision of how many lock boxes should be used and where they should be located.

Payments of accounts receivable should be closely monitored to detect potential problems such as would be indicated by slow payments.

Following up on slow-paying customers is an important function of the credit department. Procedures should be carefully developed and consistently implemented. These procedures can include control of credit limits, dunning letters, telephone calls, and held shipments.

Summary of Accounts Receivable Accounts receivable are the monies owed to a firm as a result of having sold its products to customers on credit. The three primary issues in accounts receivable management are to whom to extend credit, the terms of the credit, and the procedure that should be used to collect the money. In most cases, these issues can be placed in the context of *NPV,* or the comparison of the present value of the benefits with the present value of the costs.

Inventory Management

The three primary types of inventory are raw materials, work in process, and finished goods, which are represented by the cumulated costs of items before, during, and after production, respectively.

The benefit of an inventory is to assure that goods will be available as required. The primary costs of an inventory are the opportunity cost of the capital used to finance the inventory, ordering costs, and storage costs. Inventory management seeks to maximize the net benefit—the benefits minus costs—of the inventory. All benefits and costs should be measured using market prices adjusted for time and risk.

The EOQ model reviewed earlier in this chapter represents the foundation model for conventional inventory management. In recent years, the concept of meeting demand on a continuous basis rather than having stockpiles of inventory has frequently been advocated. These inventory techniques, such as **just-in-time** inventory management, seek to maximize the net benefit through superior management.

just-in-time
A technique that seeks to maximize the net benefit of inventory through superior management, such as reducing inventory to near-zero levels.

Inventory management is an extremely important function within most businesses. The discipline is usually taught in business courses and labeled inventory control and management, production management, operations research, management science, or quantitative business.

Current Liability Management

We will now detail the management of each of the current liabilities. In general, the categories will be discussed from most liquid to least liquid, as they are usually listed on a balance sheet.

Accounts Payable Management

accounts payables
Short-term liabilities that the firm has incurred as a result of buying products on credit from other corporations.

Accounts payables are short-term liabilities that the firm has incurred as a result of buying products on credit from other corporations. This is the other side of the transactions previously detailed under accounts receivable. The accounts payable decision is rather straightforward. If a firm is offered several payment alternatives, then the goal of accounts payable management is to select the payment alternative that maximizes shareholder wealth.

Using credit usually involves a cost that can be expressed as an interest rate. In theory, there is a benchmark interest rate, which, if paid by a firm, would generate a zero net present value. The goal of accounts payable management is to accept an extension of credit whenever the interest rate implied by the credit is less than the benchmark rate, and to reject other extensions of credit.

Determining the Implied Interest Rate of an Account Payable As detailed in the subsection on accounts receivable, firms extend credit using a potentially complex jargon. Using a time line and a financial calculator, however, greatly simplifies the process.

Most extensions of credit can be reduced to the idea that there are one or more deadlines by which a particular amount of money must be paid or else the amount due will increase. Extensions of credit may be illustrated on a time line as follows. Each payment amount is listed above the last date that it will be accepted as payment in full. For example, if on March 1 a firm purchases $100,000 of products on the credit terms 2/10; net 30, the firm can pay $98,000 on March 11 or $100,000 on March 31:

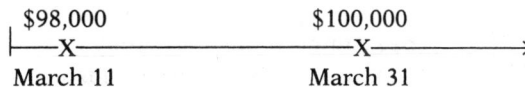

```
 $98,000                 $100,000
|---X---------------------X-------->
 March 11                March 31
```

The decision to pay on the second date may now be viewed as the ability of the firm to borrow $98,000 and to repay the money in the form of $100,000 in 20 days. Note that 20 days can be turned into years by dividing by 365. The number of years is (approximately) 0.0548.

The interest rate may be determined using a financial calculator by entering $98,000 as *PV,* $100,000 as *FV,* and 0.0548 as the number of years and computing the interest rate. The answer is approximately 44.58 percent. Our analysis reveals that if the firm pays $100,000 on March 31, then it has effectively borrowed money at an interest rate of 44.58 percent. This would certainly be larger than any benchmark and would therefore hurt shareholder wealth. The firm should not accept the extension of credit, and the account payable should be paid on March 11.

To summarize, the decision to accept credit is no different from other types of investment decisions; however, two mistakes are common in accounts payable analysis and must be avoided. First, the time period used to compute the interest rate should be the number of days between the two decision points, or 20 days in the above example. This is the true number of days for which the second payment option delays payment. Second, the base of the loan should not be the net amount of the loan ($100,000 in the preceding example), instead it should be the discounted amount of the loan ($98,000 in the example). Students should use a time line until these points are clear.

With only two potential payment dates, the problem is whether or not to defer the payment from the first date to the second date. A potential complexity is that there can be more than two potential payment dates such that there are several payment-deferral intervals, and because only one alternative can be accepted, they must be ranked. As discussed in Chapter 5, the net present value technique is often necessary to make ranking decisions.

Determining the benchmark interest rate is conceptually straightforward. The firm should use the interest rate that would be demanded in a competitive market in order to receive credit under similar conditions. For example, the interest rate on commercial paper of the firm or of similar firms would provide an approximate benchmark.

There are other issues involved in accounts payable management such as coordinating the timing of payments with other cash flows to assist the treasurer in maintaining the target level of liquidity for the firm. The biggest decision, however, is selecting optimal payment options.

Bank Loan and Notes Payable Management

Firms often borrow money on a short-term basis to meet seasonal or other temporary cash needs. Financial management of these accounts involves attaining arrangements that permit overall firm liquidity at a minimum cost.

compensating balances
A requirement of banks that a percentage of the loan be kept in a non-interest-bearing account as long as the loan is outstanding.

Years ago, this subject was made complex by arrangements known as **compensating balances,** whereby banks required that a percentage of the loan be kept in a non-interest-bearing account over the life of the loan. Compensating balances increased the cost of the loan; however, this practice has become rare. Today, management of bank loans and other short-term credit involves choosing a lending institution with competitive loan rates, competitive fees, and the services most desired by the firm.

Current Debt Management

Portions of long-term debt issues that become due within 1 year are listed as a current liability under a heading such as current payments on long-term debt. The payments may be required because the debt is maturing or because of regular debt repayment requirements, known as *sinking fund provisions,* under the terms of the debt contract. Working capital management involves planning how these obligations will be met.

Summary

- Net working capital is defined as current assets minus current liabilities. The three primary forces that emerge from working capital management are the desire to maximize shareholder wealth by accelerating cash inflows, delaying cash outflows, and maintaining an optimal level of liquidity.

- A liquid firm is one with sufficient cash to pay its bills; however, too much liquidity has certain costs, known as opportunity costs. In the case of working capital management, it may be optimal to maintain a low level of liquidity, which causes occasional problems but which minimizes opportunity costs. Models to help determine the optimal amount of liquidity to hold include the EOQ Model and the Miller-Orr model.
- Examples of liquidity management include maintaining optimal levels of cash and optimal levels of inventory.
- Optimal management of working capital requires the decision maker to incorporate all advantages and disadvantages adjusted for time and risk.

Demonstration Problems

Problem 1

Kramer Industries experiences regular cash outflows of $50,000 per day as it expands its chain of Cosmo Coffee Shops across the country. To obtain cash the firm must sell marketable securities and incur a transactions cost of $100. Further, the firm earns no interest on its cash balance while it earns 6% on its marketable securities. Using the EOQ model, find the optimal order amount.

Solution to Problem 1:

The optimal order amount, or EOQ, is found by inserting the known values into Equation (16.3).

Step 1: The annual cash need is 365 days times $50,000 per day, or $18.25 million.

Step 2: Multiply together two times the annual cash need and the cost per order ($100) and divide the resulting product by the annual interest rate (0.06) to produce 60,833,333,333.

Step 3: Take the square root of the answer to Step 2: $246,644.

Final Solution: The firm should replenish its cash balance approximately every 5 days with $246,644 of cash.

Problem 2

Abbey Corporation has set a minimum cash balance of $1,000. The daily variance of cash flows is $1 million, the transaction cost of adjusting the cash balance is $1,000, and the interest rate is 15 percent. Use the Miller-Orr model to find the target cash balance and upper cash balance.

Solution to Problem 2

The target cash balance is found by inserting the given figures into Formula (16.4). The upper cash balance is then found by inserting into Formula (16.5).

Step 1: The primary problem with applying Formula (16.4) can be that some calculators will not handle such large numbers. We use the next formula in the text in order to avoid this problem:

$$\text{Target Cash Balance} = \text{Lower Limit} + [3^{1/3} \times TCOST^{1/3} \times (\sigma^2)^{1/3} / (4r)^{1/3}]$$

Substituting $1,000 for the lower limit, $1,000 for *TCOST,* $1 million for σ^2, and 15 percent for r gives:

$$\text{Target Cash Balance} = \$1{,}000 + [1.442 \times 10 \times 100 / 0.8434]$$

Each of the figures can be raised to the 1/3 power by using the y^x key and setting x = .33333. Solving the preceding produces:

$$\text{Target Cash Balance} = \$2{,}709.94$$

Step 2: This is the target cash balance that the firm should adjust to each time it reaches the upper or lower limit. The upper cash balance limit is found as follows using Formula (16.5):

$$\text{Upper Limit} = [3 \times \text{Target Cash Balance}] - [2 \times \text{Lower Limit}]$$

$$\text{Upper Limit} = \$6{,}129.81$$

Final Solution: The firm should replenish its cash balance to $2,710 whenever the balance falls below $1,000 and should invest the excess cash above $2,710 whenever the cash balance exceeds $6,129.81.

Review Questions

1. Provide a one-sentence definition of net working capital.
2. What are the three tasks or concepts that underlie working capital management?
3. Rank a typical firm's current assets from the most to the least liquid.
4. Describe, in a few sentences, the goal of cash management.
5. What is the objective of the cash management model known as the EOQ model?
6. In nonstatistical nontechnical terms, explain how the Miller-Orr model differs from the EOQ model.
7. What is the money market? List at least two securities that trade in the money market.
8. In selecting the appropriate marketable security, which three qualities should the cash manager consider?
9. Define the "term structure of interest rates."
10. What is credit risk? Do U.S. Treasury bills contain credit risk? Do certificates of deposits or commercial paper contain credit risk? Explain.
11. What are the costs and benefits of extending credit in the form of an accounts receivable?
12. In accounts receivable management, explain the term "3/15; net 45."
13. What are lock boxes and how can they be used in managing accounts receivable?
14. What is accounts payable, and what is the goal of accounts payable management?

Problems

1. Abnormal Growths, Inc., is consuming cash at the rate of $10,000 per day. Each time the firm sells securities to obtain the cash, it costs them $250. The interest rate is 10 percent. Answer the following using the EOQ model.
   a. How much cash should the firm obtain each time it sells securities?

b. How many orders will be placed each year?
c. What would be the total annual order costs?
d. What would be the average cash balance size?
e. What would be the annual storage cost or lost opportunity cost on the cash balance?
f. How much money would the firm lose each year if it replenished its cash balance daily with $10,000?
g. How would your answer to (a) change if the interest rate fell to 5 percent?

2. Caton Corporation's management has decided that the firm's minimum cash balance should be $50,000. A financial analyst has applied the Miller-Orr model and has determined that the firm's target cash balance should be $75,000.
   a. What would the firm's upper limit cash balance be?
   b. If the cash balance began to exceed the upper limit, what would the firm do and what would be the new cash balance?
   c. If the cash balance began to fall below the lower limit, what would the firm do and what would be the new cash balance?
3. Carder Corporation's management has determined that their minimum cash balance should be $10,000. The daily variance of the cash flows is $50,000, the daily interest rate is 0.0003, and the transaction cost of returning to the target cash balance is $500. Using the Miller-Orr model, determine:
   a. The target cash balance
   b. The upper limit
4. Return to Carder Corporation from Problem 3. Interest rates have risen to a daily rate of 0.0004. Find the new target cash balance and upper limit for the firm, assuming that all other variables remain the same.
5. Like many other models in finance, the Miller-Orr model produces an answer and requires the inputting of several other variables. Fill in the missing value, treating each line as a separate problem.

	Lower Limit	*Transaction Cost*	*Daily Variance*	*Daily Interest Rate*	*Target Cash Balance*
a.	$50,000	$100	$100,000	0.0003	_______
b.	$75,000	$100	$100,000	0.0003	_______
c.	$50,000	$800	$200,000	0.0004	_______
d.	$50,000	$600	$400,000	0.0005	_______

6. Suppose that 1-year CDs (certificates of deposit) now offer 8 percent interest and 2-year CDs now offer 9 percent interest (both compounded annually or expressed as effective annual interest rates).
   a. How much would $10,000 grow in two years if invested in the 2-year CD?
   b. How much would $10,000 grow to in one year if invested in the 1-year CD?
   c. Suppose that a cash manager invested $10,000 in a 1-year CD and then took the proceeds at the end of that year [the answer to 5(b)] and reinvested the money in another 1-year CD for a total of a 2-year investment. What interest rate would the new 1-year CD have to offer after the end of the first year such that the cash manager would end up with the same amount of money at the end of the second year as compared with the answer in 5(a)?
7. Unlucky Louie is a cash manager who invests in relatively long-term bonds in an effort to earn extra interest on his firm's working capital. Using the tools of Chapter 4, find the present value (i.e., market price) of a $10,000 zero coupon bond under the following circumstances.

a. The bond's cash flow is due in 1 year, and annually compounded interest rates are 8 percent.
b. The bond's cash flow is due in 2 years, and annually compounded interest rates are 8 percent.
c. The bond's cash flow is due in 1 year, and annually compounded interest rates are 9 percent.
d. The bond's cash flow is due in 2 years, and annually compounded interest rates are 9 percent.

8. Returning to Unlucky Louie in Problem 7, suppose that he buys the 1-year bond when interest rates are 8 percent and that interest rates immediately rise by 1 percent. In percentage terms, how much did his investment decline in value?

9. Returning again to Unlucky Louie in Problems 7 and 8, suppose that he bought the 2-year bond when interest rates were 8% and that interest rates immediately rose by 1 percent. In percentage terms, how much did this 2-year investment decline in value?

10. Returning once again to Unlucky Louie in Problems 7–9, there is a general rule in finance that when interest rates climb by 1 percent the price of zero coupon bonds falls by a percentage slightly smaller than their maturity. Verify that this is true by computing how much Unlucky would have lost as a percentage of the original purchase prices if he had bought one-half-year, 3-year, and 5-year zero coupon bonds just before the interest rates rose from 8 percent to 9 percent.

11. Unlucky Louie has decided to try his cash management skills in other areas of investments. Louie notices that 1-year U.S. Treasury bills offer an annualized yield of 8 percent at the same time that an alternative 1-year investment offers a return of 10 percent (assume annual compounding).
a. By how much would $100,000 grow in 1 year if invested in the U.S. Treasury bill?
b. By how much would $100,000 grow in 1 year if invested in the alternative that offers a 10 percent return?
c. Assume that the U.S. Treasury bill cannot default but that the alternative investment has a 97 percent chance of paying fully and a 3 percent chance of paying nothing. What is the expected cash flow from investing $100,000 in the alternative investment?
d. What would be the expected cash flow from a third 1-year investment of $100,000 that offers a 90 percent chance of a 15 percent return, a 5 percent chance of paying back only 50 cents on each dollar invested, and a 5 percent chance of returning nothing?

12. Elkland Corporation is in a 34 percent federal income tax bracket and is comparing the after-tax yields between a municipal money market mutual fund offering 6 percent and a U.S. government money market mutual fund offering 3 percent more before tax. The municipal fund's 6 percent return is both a before-tax return and an after-tax return because the returns from this fund are free of both federal and state income taxes. The U.S. government fund, however, is taxable for federal income tax purposes (but not for state tax purposes).
a. Compute the after-tax returns for the U.S government bond fund if its pretax return is 9 percent. Ignoring all other consideration such as risk, which investment offers the higher after-tax return?
b. Assume that interest rates rise such that the municipal fund offers 12 percent while the U.S. government fund offers 15 percent. Which fund would you now prefer on the basis of after-tax returns alone?

13. Hornby Corporation is in a 34 percent federal income tax bracket and a 6 percent state income tax bracket. Ignoring interactions such as the ability to deduct some taxes in computing other taxes, compute the after-tax returns for each of the following alternatives.
    a. A totally tax-free municipal fund that offers 7 percent.
    b. A U.S. government fund that is federally taxable but tax-free at the state level and which offers 10 percent before taxes.
    c. A corporate fund that is fully taxable at both levels and offers 11 percent before taxes.
14. As a financial analyst at Presho, Inc., you are asked to determine whether credit should be extended to Fly By Nights, Inc. They have ordered $50,000 of products, which have a cost to your firm of $30,000. Based upon your analysis of Fly By Nights, Inc., credit history, you estimate that the probability of being paid is 50 percent. You do not expect them ever to order products from your firm again because you have been told that they have a one-time need for your products. Based upon expected cash flows, what is your decision?
15. Returning to Fly By Nights, Inc., a further analysis reveals that if Fly By Nights can remain in business for the next year, they will surely order and surely pay for $500,000 of similar products with similar costs in 1 year if and only if you will help them through this year. Based upon expected cash flows only, what is your decision?
16. Compute the annual interest rate implied by the following credit terms:
    a. 2/15; net 30.
    b. 2/30; net 60.
    c. 2/10—EOM; net 90 (purchased on the 10th of the month).
    d. 2/10—EOM; net 90 (purchased on the 31st of the month).

Discussion Questions

1. What are the costs and benefits of having liquidity, and why is there a theoretical optimal level of liquidity?
2. What are the reasons that a firm's cash flow would be cyclical?
3. Why would a firm buy very short-term securities in its cash management department while buying very long-term securities in its pension management?
4. Is a corporation shirking its responsibilities to pay taxes when it buys municipal securities that are free of income taxes?
5. If a firm extends small amounts of credit to all prospective customers in order to build relationships and learn about credit worthiness, what types of customers will it attract?
6. Optimal inventory management means never having to say that you are sorry that you are out of something." Please comment.
7. Referring to the Miller-Orr model: Would a target cash balance halfway between the lower and upper limits minimize the number of times the firm would incur the expense of adjusting its cash balance? Why is the midway point not used in the Miller-Orr model?

Discussion Questions

CHAPTER 17

CORPORATE FINANCIAL PLANNING

Like many hard workers, Dave Hershel had always dreamed of starting his own business. During his long and successful career as an engineer in several high-tech firms, Dave had demonstrated an ability to develop valuable product lines. His most recent idea was related to his favorite hobby: skiing. The product was a combination of "space-age" material and electronics that would adjust the clothing's insulation automatically to provide the consumer with ideal protection from winter weather conditions.

Soon after his children finished college Dave sought and received a patent for the product. He then took most of his savings and invested them in manufacturing operations to bring the product to market. Combining his wife's keen marketing skills with his production skills and with patent protection, it was unimaginable that the product could fail—even though he had heard that the vast majority of new businesses fail in their first few years.

At first, the Hershels thrived through a very successful mail order campaign using advertisements in skiing magazines and through targeted mailing lists. One difficulty over the first few years was the seasonal nature of the business. Checks poured in during the fall and winter months when most of the products were shipped; however, few checks came in during the spring and summer months, during which fixed expenses such as rent and salaries continued, and inventories grew requiring more cash. The Hershels eventually learned how to plan for seasonal cash flows.

The "big break" came after 6 years: The Hershels landed a massive contract with one of the nation's largest retailers that called for the Hershels to provide ever-increasing quantities of their product. Dave projected that this contract would produce earnings starting at $500,000 in the first year and rising to more than $1 million by the third year. The Hershels' dream of financial independence seemed at hand.

The Hershels unfortunately never realized their dream. They had failed to make a financial plan and had not realized the need for working capital. The mail-order business did not require much working capital because checks came in before products were produced and shipped. The retailer, however, would pay for the products several months after they were shipped. The

Hershels simply did not have enough money to produce the large quantities of skiwear requested. After a few frustrating years, the retailer switched to obtaining similar products from a large firm that had developed a still-newer technology.

Despite all that Dave Hershel had going for him, his hopes and years of hard work were scuttled by a lack of financial planning. In this chapter we'll look at the process of corporate **financial planning,** which consists of short-term planning and long-range planning. Short-term financial planning emphasizes the cash budget and projections of cash balances. As Dave Hershel's story demonstrates, cash planning is essential to the sustained liquidity of the business. Long-range financial planning focuses on the entire balance sheet and is essential to the judicious procurement and deployment of resources. We begin with short-term financial planning.

financial planning
The process of planning the major financial aspects of a corporation over long periods of time, such as 3–5 years.

Short-Term Financial Planning and the Cash Budget

Cash and near-cash assets, such as marketable securities, are critical to the maintenance of a firm's liquidity. As discussed in Chapter 16, liquidity is essential for the optimal management of the firm's resources. Too much liquidity, however, tends to be a waste of the firm's resources relative to its ability to produce returns elsewhere within the firm. Too little liquidity can cause a firm to miss minor opportunities such as the ability to receive discounts for paying bills early and/or can have major consequences such as the inability to make scheduled payments on the firm's debt.

The answer, then, is to budget the firm's cash in order to plan for needed levels of liquidity. The **cash budget** is nothing more than a schedule of anticipated cash inflows and outflows over a short future period, such as several months or quarters. Table 17.1 illustrates a simplified format for a cash budget, from the beginning cash balance to the ending cash balance. Because the cash flows from operations change from quarter to quarter, the firm's cash balance will also change.

cash budget
A schedule of anticipated cash inflows and outflows over a short period of time into the future, such as several months or quarters.

TABLE 17.1 Simplified Cash Budget, Showing Operational Cash Flows (numbers in 000s)

	2003				*2004*
	Q1	*Q2*	*Q3*	*Q4*	*Q1*
Beginning Cash Balance	____	____	____	____	____
Cash inflows from operations	$740	$600	$250	$600	$760
Cash outflows from operations	($600)	($610)	($650)	($310)	($610)
Net cash flow from operations	$140	($ 10)	($400)	$290	$150
Ending Cash Balance	____	____	____	____	____

The key issue in cash budgeting is developing the best plan that will keep the cash balance within the range of allowable cash balances throughout the year. As detailed in Chapter 16's discussion of cash management, most firms set an allowable range for their cash balance that provides a trade-off between cash becoming too low and too high.

The purpose of the cash budgeting process is to forecast and plan for transactions that are needed to maintain the firm's target cash balance in an optimal manner. The firm establishes a hierarchy of priorities that will be done if the cash balance begins to go outside its range. A simplified example would be:

Locations for Excess Cash	*Source for Needed Cash*
Invest first \$100,000 in money market mutual funds (MMMF) selected internally	First \$150,000 of borrowing through line of bank credit
Additional cash placed in marketable securities with outside money manager	Next \$100,000 using unsecured bank loan
	Additional funds using notes.

When the firm's cash balance falls to the lower limit, the firm meets cash needs by first transferring funds from the money market mutual fund and then meets additional needs by liquidating some or all of its marketable securities. After marketable securities have been liquidated, the firm begins to borrow using the sources in the sequence listed earlier. In the opposite case, in which the cash balance reaches the upper limit, the firm would first pay off borrowed funds (starting with the last funds borrowed, which would be the most expensive) before it switched to purchasing marketable securities.

Although the process may appear complex at times, the cash budgeting process is conceptually quite simple. Many of the concepts of short-term financial planning mirror the concepts of personal finance. In essence, the manager attempts to keep the firm's liquidity within the range that maximizes shareholder wealth. The process both keeps the cash balance within its target range and directs the firm to invest the excess cash in vehicles that either enhance return or minimize risk-adjusted cost.

Example 17.1 ______ A useful first step in setting up the cash budget is to work through the cash balances, using the projections of net cash flows from operations that would occur if no other working capital decisions were made. This is shown in Table 17.2. The firm's initial cash balance is provided as a given. The firm's cash flows are typically provided as inputs to the cash budget (in other words, they are *exogenous* to the process). Notice that the initial cash balance of \$50 in the first quarter of 2003 begins the process that ends in the first quarter of 2004 with a cash balance of \$220.

In the example, the firm is planning for a seasonal cash flow pattern in which the firm's ending cash balance would start at \$190, would fall to a low

TABLE 17.2 A First Pass at a Cash Balance (no borrowing or lending) (numbers in 000s)

	2003 Q1	2003 Q2	2003 Q3	2003 Q4	2004 Q1
Beginning Cash Balance	$ 50[a]	$190	$180	($220)	$ 70
Cash inflows from operations	$740	$600	$250	$600	$760
Cash outflows from operations	($600)	($610)	($650)	($310)	($610)
Net cash flow from operations	$140	($ 10)	($400)	$290	$150
Ending Cash Balance	$190	$180	($220)	$ 70	$220

[a]The amount $50 was not part of the model but was supplied outside of the model.

of −$220 in the third quarter, and would rise to a high of $220 in the first quarter of 2004. The seasonal pattern of cash flows that produces this variation is illustrated in Figure 17.1.

The seasonality is clearly causing an unacceptable range of cash balances. Remember, the key to managing the cash budget is to adhere to a target range for the cash balance per quarter. For example, suppose the firm sets a range of $0 to $100 for its cash balance. Table 17.3 indicates that the firm must borrow cash during part of the year, and invest excess cash during other parts of the year to keep the cash balance within its target range. Table 17.3 illustrates the borrowing and investing that the cash budget indicates would be needed during the year to stay within the target. Notice that money was borrowed and invested according to the priority previously listed.

FIGURE 17.1 A Seasonal Pattern of Ending Cash Balances

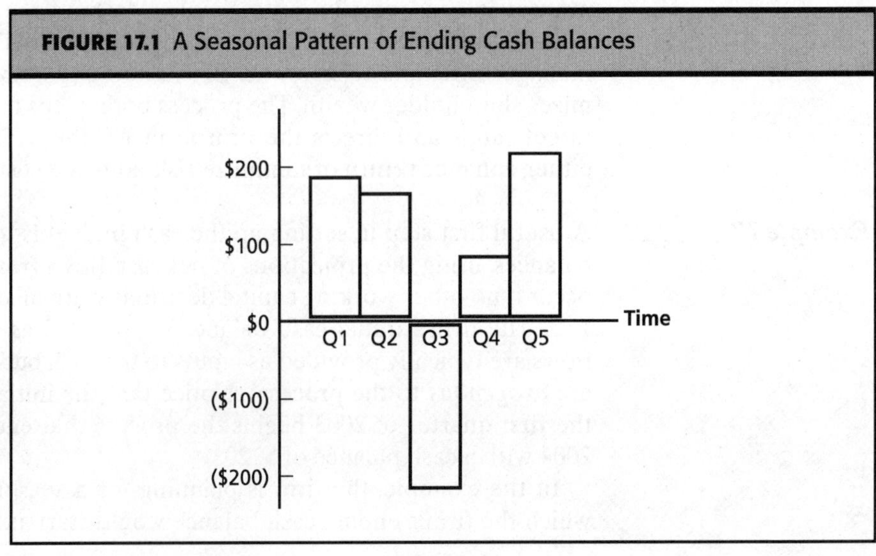

TABLE 17.3 The Completed Cash Budget (numbers in 000s)

	2003				2004
	Q1	*Q2*	*Q3*	*Q4*	*Q1*
Beginning Cash	$ 50	$100	$ 90	$ 0	$ 70
Cash inflows from operations	$740	$600	$250	$600	$760
Cash outflows from operations	($600)	($610)	($650)	($310)	($610)
Net cash flow from operations	$140	($ 10)	($400)	$290	$150
Cash Buildup	$190	$ 90	($310)	$290	$220
To MMMF	$ 90	$ 0	($ 90)[a]	$ 0	$100
To securities	$ 0	$ 0	$ 0	$ 0	$ 20
From bank line	$ 0	$ 0	$150	($150)[b]	$ 0
From unsecured loan	$ 0	$ 0	$ 70	($ 70)[c]	$ 0
Ending Cash Balance	$100	$ 90	$ 0	$ 70	$100

[a]Negative $ 90 refers to selling off $90 of MMMFs to meet liquidity needs.
[b]Negative $150 refers to the payment of the bank line from the cash buildup.
[c]Negative $ 70 refers to the payment of the loan from the cash buildup.

For example, in the first quarter of 2003, the cash buildup of $190 allows for $100 to stay in the cash balance as well as for the excess of $90 to be placed in the money market mutual fund (MMMF). The third quarter of 2003, however, indicates that cash has fallen below zero to ($310), a full $310 below the lower target range of $0. In order to adhere to the cash target, the firm needs to (1) liquidate the $90 placed in the MMMF, (2) borrow $150 from its bank line, and (3) borrow $70 in the form of an unsecured bank loan. In the fourth quarter of 2003, the cash buildup of $290 is used to pay off both the bank line of credit and the unsecured bank loan. Finally, in the first quarter of 2004, the cash buildup of $220 allows $100 to be placed again into the MMMF and $20 to be placed into securities, leaving an ending cash balance at the upper end of the target, or at $100.

In actual practice, borrowing to maintain a minimum cash balance and investing of excess cash affects the cash flows in the same period as well as in subsequent periods. This is because the interest income and interest expense are based upon the balances. A simple model includes interest revenue and interest expense based upon balances from the previous period. A sophisticated cash budgeting model will include these cash flows based upon the balance in the same (concurrent) period.

The goal of the cash budgeting process is to develop a forecast and plan for borrowing and investing cash. In particular, the cash budget can signal to the manager when the firm needs to seek long-term financing to meet working capital needs, which enables the manager to make necessary arrangements and to monitor the firm's liquidity condition relative to a plan. Thus,

TABLE 17.4 Sales Forecasts (numbers in 000s)

	Jan 03	*Feb 03*	*Mar 03*	*Apr 03*	*May 03*	*Jun 03*
Sales Forecast	$50	$60	$70	$90	$80	$60

the firm has a meaningful measure of its current liquidity by comparing actual liquidity with that of the plan. Finally, the cash budgeting process can provide insights into the length of time that excess cash can be invested and thereby provide guidance as to the appropriate length of maturity and other aspects of the investment securities that will be used.

Cash Forecasting

A cash budget will only be as good as the cash flow forecasts used to create it. The most critical input could be the forecast of cash revenues from sales. Growing firms and those with highly variable cash revenues struggle with the lag between payment of the costs of production and the receipt of revenues from sales.

A classic cash forecasting task is to convert a forecast of monthly sales into a forecast of monthly cash inflows, using the firm's collection experience. For example, a firm that extends credit terms such as 2/10, net 30 may find that 30 percent of its sales are collected in the first month, 50 percent in the second month, and 15 percent in the third month, and that 5 percent are never collected. To illustrate, consider the sales forecasts in Table 17.4. The cash inflows can be forecasted by applying the percentages of its collections (stated earlier), as shown in Table 17.5.

TABLE 17.5 Cash Forecasts from Sales (numbers in 000s)

	Jan 03	*Feb 03*	*Mar 03*	*Apr 03*	*May 03*	*Jun 03*
Sales Forecast	$50	$60	$70	$90	$80	$60
Collections from Cash Sales (30%)	$15	$18	$21	$27	$24	$18
Collections from Last Month (50%)	$60[a]	$25	$30	$35	$45	$40
Collections from Two Months Ago (15%)	$21[b]	$18[a]	$ 7.5	$ 9	$10.5	$13.5
Total Collections	$96	$61	$58.5	$71	$79.5	$71.5

[a]Sales in December 2002 were $120.
[b]Sales in November 2002 were $140.

The bottom line, "Total Collections," is then used as input into the cash budget. Similar cash schedules can be produced for other cash flows, such as the costs of manufacturing, by incorporating the delay between when a firm arranges for its materials and when it must pay for them. All such cash schedules become inputs into the cash budget.

Long-Range Financial Planning

Long-range financial planning encompasses the planning of all major financial aspects of a firm over long periods of time, typically 3–5 years. The concept of long-range financial planning is really quite simple. Most large corporations use an iterative technique in which projections are tested and adjusted in search of the best plan. In overview, the process works like this: First, the user inputs a number of assumptions or parameters into a particular model about how various items such as revenues, expenses, and investments will change through time. Second, these assumptions are used to forecast future balance sheets. Third, a financial analysis technique such as ratio analysis is applied to determine the desirability of the results of the forecast.

The process is then repeated by modifying the assumptions and repeating the forecast and analysis stages until the users are confident that they have found the best available plan. This whole process is computerized so that numerous new forecasts can be generated with just a few changes to the parameters of a computer program.

The computer model used specifies certain relationships between variables and how the variables change through time. For example, one model might assume that revenues will grow at a constant percentage growth rate through time, whereas a more complex model will allow the user to input two or more stages of growth with different growth rates in each stage.

The Accounting Mechanics of a Financial Planning Model

It is possible to use corporate financial planning models with little or no knowledge of their underlying mechanics, just as it is possible to drive a car without knowing how the engine works. The best financial managers, however, like the best race car drivers, understand both how their tools work as well as how to operate them.

Table 17.6 illustrates highly condensed versions of a firm's current balance sheet as well as the forecasts of the next period's income statement and statement of cash flows, which were produced by a computer model. Notice that the working capital and fixed assets are assumed to increase by 10 percent. In most models, the user would simply input these growth rates and the computer would convert them to dollar values. The user can then alter the figures by inputting alternative growth rates.

The essential element to long-range financial planning is the statement of cash flows, discussed in Chapter 15. The statement of cash flows keeps the

TABLE 17.6 Current and Forecasted Financial Statements, Simplified Tools, Inc. (in $000s)

Panel A: Condensed Balance Sheet—12/31/02	
Net working capital	$ 80
Fixed assets	830
Total Assets	$910
Long-term debt	$400
Equity	510
Total Debt and Equity	$910
Panel B: 2003 Forecasted Income Statement	
Revenues	$187
Expenses	132
Net income	$ 55
Panel C: 2003 Forecasted Statement of Cash Flow	
Starting Net Working Capital	$ 80
Operating Activity	
Net Income	$ 55
Depreciation	$ 20
Investing Activity	
Fixed assets	−$ 83
Financing Activity	
Dividends	−$ 4
Debt	$ 20
Ending Net Working Capital	$ 88

balance sheet balanced as they are forecasted through time. The statement of cash flows is discussed in this chapter under the assumption that the accounting statements are prepared using a cash method rather than an accrual method. The cash method of accounting recognizes cash transactions only while the accrual method of accounting recognizes accrual transactions, some of which may not have yet been consummated with cash. In the more typical case of accrual-based accounting that statement of cash flows would have an extra section that summarizes these effects.

Condensing the Balance Sheet

In long-range financial planning it is essential to focus on the major financial issues. In order to simplify the models, corporations commonly condense their balance sheets for financial planning purposes. To be specific, corporations often collapse all of their current assets and current liabilities into a single figure: *net working capital.* Net working capital would typically be positive and entered as a current asset. Notice in Table 17.6 that the balance sheet is condensed by using net working capital and the statement of cash flows also incorporates this measure.

The idea behind this condensation of the balance sheet is that the components of net working capital can vary significantly over short periods of time. For example, a firm might use a lot of cash to pay down its accounts payable and short-term bank loan. Notice that although these types of actions change the firm's current assets and current liabilities, net working capital remains unchanged. In a long-range financial planning sense, it is important to the firm that its net working capital is appropriate. The components of that net working capital can be managed when the time arrives. One consequence of using a highly condensed balance sheet is that it dramatically simplifies the statement of cash flows. In fact, because the analysis is focusing on net working capital rather than cash, the statement could be called, more appropriately, a statement of funds.

Most computerized corporate financial planning models may be viewed as following this process:

1. The inputted forecasts of revenue and expense growth rates (along with tax rates, depreciation, and so forth) are used to forecast the "next" income statement.
2. The income statement is combined with other growth-rate forecasts of assets and liabilities to generate a balanced statement of cash flows.
3. The statement of cash flows is "overlaid" onto the previous balance sheet in order to produce the next balance sheet. This new forecasted balance sheet then becomes the basis upon which to forecast another time period into the future.
4. The computer then returns to Step #1 and repeats the process by forecasting another time period into the future until the financial statements have been forecasted for the desired number of periods.

In order to simplify the concepts, we've implied that the financial planning process produces a single forecast. In actual usage, most financial plans would produce a spectrum of forecasts based upon various scenarios, such as high, moderate, and low-growth. The spectrum of scenarios is usually input by the user as a range of values for certain parameters, such as growth rates.

An Example of Compiling a Forecast

Let's look at a highly simplified financial planning model that produces the forecast for only one scenario at a time. The income statement and statement of cash flows from Table 17.6 are produced by the model using the inputted parameters and can be used to construct the next balance sheet, as illustrated in Table 17.7. The computer model would then use the inputted growth rates

TABLE 17.7 Forecasting the Balance Sheet, Simplified Tools, Inc. (in $000s)

Net working capital	$ 88
Fixed assets	893
Total Assets	$981
Long-term debt	$420
Equity	561
Total Debt and Equity	$981

to forecast the next income statement and the statement of cash flows, and the process would repeat itself.

The key financial statement for financial planning is the statement of cash flows. The model requires that the flows be balanced so that forecasted balance sheets are balanced. We will next show that all of the items in the statement of cash flows except one are explicitly forecasted by the model. The remaining variable is known as the "slack" variable, and it takes on whatever value is necessary to balance the statement.

The Slack Variable

All but one of the values in the forecasted balance sheet were explicitly forced into their values by assumptions in the model. It was noted earlier that the working capital and fixed assets grew at the user-supplied growth rate of 10 percent. It is a little more difficult to realize that the change in the value of the equity was also forced because it was assumed to be equal to the net income of the firm minus its dividend. (This is the definition of retained earnings and we are assuming that the firm does not wish to issue new stock.)

Thus, all of the items in the statement of cash flows were automatically and directly determined by the parameters inputted by the user, except the change in the debt. In the preceding model, debt is the **slack variable,** because its value is implicitly determined by the requirement that the statement of cash flows be balanced. In other words, debt took the value necessary to keep the statements balanced. The slack variable is usually the focus of the financial planning process.

slack variable
A variable whose value is implicitly determined by the requirement that the statement of cash flows be balanced.

Different models have different slack variables, but the most common are the amount of debt, the amount of dividends, and the amount of equity. The choice of which to use as the slack variable has varying effects:

- When *debt* serves as the slack variable, the model will show the user the amount of debt that will accumulate throughout the years, given all of the other decisions such as growth rates, dividend policy, and so forth. The user will obviously then analyze the debt usage to determine whether the debt usage would be reasonable.

- When the *dividend* amount serves as the slack variable, the model will show the user how much the firm can pay out in dividends, given all of the other decisions regarding growth rates, debt usage, and so forth.
- Finally, when the *equity* amount serves as the slack variable, the model will show the user how much equity the firm will have to issue throughout the years or can repurchase, given the other decisions.

Using a Financial Planning Model

Although most financial planning models may be viewed as having a key slack variable whose future values are determined based upon all of the other inputs, the real process of meeting future financial needs of a firm is not as simple as allowing the slack variable to be whatever it needs to be. In the real world, corporations are usually interested in planning *all* of the variables, including the slack variable, whether it is debt usage, dividend payout, or equity usage.

This is where the iterative process becomes so important. After the computer model has generated a financial plan or a range of financial plans, the user then performs a financial analysis to determine if the plan offers an optimal level of profitability and the desired capital structure (debt versus equity financing). If a variable other than the slack variable appears to be unreasonable, then the user can alter this variable by changing the parameters that determine it or its components. Of course, when one variable is changed other variables will be affected, especially the slack variable. Or, if the forecasted values of the slack variable appear unreasonable, the user can modify the parameters that explicitly determine other variables, which will cause the slack variable to change. For example, if debt usage is the slack variable and the forecasts indicate debt usage that is "too high," then the user may alter other parameters, such as lowering the dividend payout rate, lowering the firm's growth rate, and so forth.

This iterative process allows the user to experiment. The goal is to produce a financial plan that is viable for a range of scenarios—which reflects the potential outcomes of variables that are outside the control of the financial manager such as interest rates, general economic performance, and the like.

The Planning Process of a New Business

As the chapter's lead story indicated, financial planning is an essential element of starting a new business. A good business plan usually addresses, in writing, a variety of concerns, such as marketing and business organization, as well as financial issues. Entrepreneurs typically use the formal business plan in an attempt to obtain financial backing from external sources such as venture capital firms. Venture capitalists and other potential providers of external capital are usually well trained in finance and will study the financial plan of the new business both to ascertain the stated plans for the firm and to judge the financial sophistication and competence of the people proposing the business. Thus, the financial plan can be an important signal of the quality of the people and the budget.

A financial plan is more than a schedule of the cash that the firm will need to fund initial asset acquisitions and to meet the first few periods of operating losses. It is a forecast of cash needs generated from forecasted financial statements in general and the statement of cash flows in particular. The financial planning process outlined in this chapter is the basis of a competent financial plan and can be an essential ingredient to the success of funding and operating a new venture.

Summary of the Financial Planning Process

Long-range planning is a necessary component of corporate strategy, and the planning horizon is dictated by the needs of the business. For example, for some firms, such as electric utilities, a plan of 3–5 years or longer is considered to be a long-range plan. For other firms, such as start ups, a planning horizon of 1–2 years may be adequate. For most corporations, however, it is very difficult to develop realistic projections into the future.

Financial plans differ tremendously with regard to the level of detail, the parameters assumed to affect the firm, and the relationship between the parameters and the firm's performance. Nevertheless, the general concepts remain unchanged. Corporate financial planning is designed to bring together and modify the investment, financing, and operational plans of the firm and to ensure that, under reasonable scenarios, plans can operate together in a sensible fashion.

Summary

- Cash budgeting requires the scheduling of anticipated cash inflows and outflows over a short time into the future, such as several months or quarters. Cash budgeting is complicated by the fact that sales and cash collection of sales often do not occur in the same time period.
- Long-range financial planning guides the overall balance sheet of the firm. Long-range financial planning examines the major acquisitions of assets, procurement of funding, and the dividend policy of the firm. Planning is an iterative process that uses inputs that project the future financial statements of the firm. Next, the projections are analyzed in order to evaluate the desirability of the results. Inputs can then be experimented with in order to find the best plan.

Demonstration Problems

Problem 1

Woodelves Corporation invests excess cash—which it defines as cash in excess of \$500,000—in Treasury bills. Woodelves also keeps its cash balance at or above

$100,000 by borrowing money through a bank loan. Woodelves does not use the Miller-Orr model, but simply keeps its cash balance within these boundaries. Of course, before Woodelves Corporation uses a bank loan it makes sure that it has liquidated its Treasury bills. In addition, before Woodelves Corporation buys Treasury bills it makes sure that its bank loan is paid off. Woodelves Corporation now (December 31) has a cash balance of $250,000. Woodelves Corporation is experiencing dramatic growth. This unfortunately creates immediate expenses, but revenues will not be received for several months. During the next 6 months, Woodelves expects the following net cash flows:

Jan	*Feb*	*Mar*	*Apr*	*May*	*Jun*
−$75,000	−$125,000	−$150,000	−$200,000	+$300,000	+$700,000

Woodelves now owns $200,000 of Treasury bills and has completely paid off its bank loan. Construct a cash budget in order to help the treasurer of Woodelves make plans for managing the firm's cash.

Solution to Problem 1

Notice that if our cash balance were allowed to "wander" in response to the cash flows without limits, the hypothetical balances would be:

Hypothetical End-of-Month Cash Balances

Dec	*Jan*	*Feb*	*Mar*	*Apr*	*May*	*Jun*
$250,000	+$175,000	+$50,000	−$100,000	−$300,000	+$0	+$700,000

These figures were found by starting with the given end-of-December cash balance of $250,000 and then adding in cash inflows (positive numbers) and subtracting out cash outflows (negative numbers).

The problem with the previous "solution" is that the firm does not want the cash balance to drop below $100,000 or to rise above $500,000. The cash budget determines the combinations of bank loans and Treasury bills that will be used to keep the cash balance within its bounds.

Step 1: Design a cash budget using a format such as Table 17.3 and the specific features for the firm:

Cash Budget for Woodelves Corporation

Month	*Jan*	*Feb*	*Mar*	*Apr*	*May*	*Jun*
Starting cash	+$250,000					
Net cash flow	−$ 75,000	−$125,000	−$150,000	−$200,000	+$300,000	+$700,000
Cash buildup						
To T-bills						
To bank loan						
From T-bills						
From bank loan						
Ending cash balance						

This allows excess cash to be used to repay the bank loan or to buy Treasury bills. Cash deficiencies can be met by liquidating Treasury bills or by borrowing money.
Step 2: We now work through each month using the figures and procedures given in the problem. For example, January's $75,000 cash need can be met without lowering the firm's cash balance below the $100,000 lower limit. The cash balance falls by $75,000, from $250,000 to $175,000, in order to meet the $75,000 cash outflow. In February, however, the firm expects an outflow of $125,000 that would lower the cash balance below its target. The cash balance can be restored to its minimum value of $100,000 by liquidating $50,000 of the $200,000 of Treasury bills that are owned. Thus, the cash budget should now look like this:

Cash Budget for Woodelves Corporation

Month	*Jan*	*Feb*	*Mar*	*Apr*	*May*	*Jun*
Starting cash	+$250,000	$175,000				
Net cash flow	−$ 75,000	−$125,000	−$150,000	$−200,000	+$300,000	+$700,000
Cash buildup	+$175,000	$ 50,000				
To T-bills	$0	$0				
To bank loan	$0	$0				
From T-bills	$0	$ 50,000				
From bank loan	$0	$0				
Ending cash balance	$175,000	$100,000				

Step 3: As the expected cash outflows continue, the Treasury bills are completely liquidated and the firm begins to borrow cash through its bank loan. Completed though the end of April, the cash budget should look like this:

Cash Budget for Woodelves Corporation

Month	*Jan*	*Feb*	*Mar*	*Apr*	*May*	*Jun*
Starting cash	+$250,000	$175,000	$100,000	$100,000		
Net cash flow	−$ 75,000	−$125,000	−$150,000	−$200,000	+$300,000	+$700,000
Cash buildup	+$175,000	$ 50,000	−$ 50,000	−$100,000		
To T-billls	$0	$0	$0	$0		
To bank loan	$0	$0	$0	$0		
From T-bills	$0	$ 50,000	$150,000	$0		
From bank loan	$0	$0	$0	$200,000		
Ending cash balance	$175,000	$100,000	$100,000	$100,000		

The Treasury bills were completely sold off in March, and in April the firm needed to borrow $200,000 to meet its minimum cash balance. These calculations come from the same sense of logic and priorities that guide our daily cash decisions in our personal-finance lives.
Step 4: Finally, in the last 2 months the firm's operations are bringing in more cash than is being spent. The result is that the firm first replenishes its cash balance to its maximum ($500,000), then repays the bank loan and begins buying Treasury bills as shown in our final budget:

Cash Budget for Woodelves Corporation

Month	*Jan*	*Feb*	*Mar*	*Apr*	*May*	*Jun*
Starting cash	$250,000	$175,000	$100,000	$100,000	$100,000	$400,000
Net cash flow	−$ 75,000	−$125,000	−$150,000	−$200,000	+$300,000	+$ 700,000
Cash buildup	+$175,000	+$ 50,000	−$ 50,000	−$100,000	+$400,000	+$1,100,000
To T-billls	$0	$0	$0	$0	$0	$400,000
To bank loan	$0	$0	$0	$0	$0	$200,000
From T-bills	$0	$ 50,000	$150,000	$0	$0	$0
From bank loan	$0	$0	$0	$200,000	$0	$0
Ending cash balance	$175,000	$100,000	$100,000	$100,000	$400,000	$500,000

Final Solution: The firm meets cash drains by liquidating its Treasury bills and then borrowing money. When money starts coming in, the firm pays off the bank loan and begins buying Treasury bills again. At all times the actual cash budget is kept within the desired range.

Problem 2

Harlow Corporation has an especially simple balance sheet because it has no debt:

Harlow Corporation 12/31/02

Net Working Capital	$ 100,000	Debt	$ 0
Fixed Assets	1,000,000	Equity	1,100,000
Total Assets	$1,100,000	Total Debt and Equity	$1,100,000

Harlow Corporation has developed the following projections of net income for the next 3 years:

2003	*2004*	*2005*
$75,000	$100,000	$125,000

Finally, Harlow Corporation projects that in order to meet future demands it will need to expand its fixed assets by $50,000 per year. Its net working capital can stay constant.

Use this information to compute a statement of cash flows and balance sheets for next year. Assume that Harlow Corporation wishes to avoid debt. Management hopes that its plans for expansion can be met by retaining earnings and then paying out any further income in the form of dividends. For simplicity, ignore taxes and depreciation.

Solution to Problem 1

This is a classic and extremely simplified financial projection. The key to completing the exercise is to begin by forming the statement of cash flows and recognizing that dividends are the "slack" variable in this problem. In other words, we use the statement of cash flows for the purpose of computing the dividend that can be paid. This comprises Steps 1 and 2. Then, in Step 3, we use the statement of cash flows to forecast the next future balance sheet.

Step 1: The statement of cash flows is best begun using a format such as:

Harlow Corporation 2002 Statement of Cash Flows

Operating Activity
Net income
Investing Activity
Financing Activity
Dividends
Change in Net Working Capital

Step 2: Fill in the information that is known from the problem:

Operating Activity	
Net income	$75,000
Investing Activity	
Fixed assets	−$50,000
Financing Activities	
Dividends	?
Change in Net Working Capital	$0

Notice that net income, depreciation, and changes in assets are already given. In this simplified example, it is relatively easy to see that we need to find the level of dividend payment that will make the column sum to the bottom line (the change in net working capital). A dividend payment of $25,000 keeps the statement balanced:

Harlow Corporation 2002 Statement of Cash Flows

Operating Activity	
Net income	$75,000
Investing Activity	
Fixed assets	−$50,000
Financing Activities	
Dividends	$25,000
Change in Net Working Capital	$0

Step 3: Next we use the 2002 statement of cash flows to form the year-end balance sheet. We recognize that assets rose by $50,000 and that equity (retained earnings) rose by the quantity: net income less dividends.

Harlow Corporation 12/31/03

Net working capital	$ 100,000	Debt	$ 0
Fixed assets	1,050,000	Equity	1,150,000
Total Assets	$1,150,000	Total Debt and Equity	$1,150,000

Final Solution: We find that, given an income of $75,000, Harlow can meet its cash needs for expansion ($50,000) and still have money available for a $25,000 dividend.

Review Questions

1. What is a cash budget, and what is the purpose of such a budget?
2. Provide a one-sentence definition of corporate financial planning.
3. What is the "slack" variable, and how is it used in the financial planning process?

Problems

1. Winterfest Ski Corporation has seasonal net cash flows from operations that are projected as follows:

	2005	*2006*	*2007*
First quarter	+150,000	+160,000	+170,000
Second quarter	−120,000	−190,000	−100,000
Third quarter	− 10,000	− 15,000	− 20,000
Fourth quarter	+ 10,000	+110,000	+120,000

The cash management policy at Winterfest Ski Corporation is as follows:

a. A minimum cash balance of $50,000 should be kept and money should be borrowed using a line of credit at the bank if needed to maintain this balance.

b. Cash in excess of $100,000 should be invested in marketable securities.

c. No more than $100,000 should be invested in marketable securities. When this limit has been reached, the excess cash should be sent to the shareholders as a dividend.

The firm's cash balance is currently $100,000, and there is no investment in marketable securities and no loan outstanding to the bank. Use the following format to project the firm's cash balances, loan balances, marketable securities balances, and dividends. We have finished the first quarter and begun the second quarter for you. You may ignore interest paid on the loan or received on the investments.

Year and Quarter

	2005–1	*2005–2*
Beginning Cash	$100,000 (1)	$100,000
+ Operating cash inflow	150,000 (1)	0
+ New bank loan	0 (2)	
+ Market securities sold	0 (2)	
Available Cash	250,000 (3)	
− Operating cash outflow	0 (1)	120,000
− Loan repayment	0 (1)	0
− Market securities bought	100,000 (3)	0
− Dividends	50,000 (3)	
Cash Uses	150,000 (3)	
Ending Cash	100,000 (2)	

Notes:

1. These figures were directly or indirectly given.
2. These figures became clear when it was realized that there would be excess cash.
3. These figures were deduced through the need to balance the statement and the priorities set forth in the firm's policy.

2. Return to Winterfest Ski Corporation in Problem 1, repeat the exercise under the assumption that the firm will receive 2 percent interest each quarter on the funds kept in marketable securities and will pay 3 percent interest each quarter on the bank line of credit. These interest payments and receipts, however, will not occur until the quarter that follows and will be based upon the balance at the end of the previous quarter. Use the following format, which we have partially completed.

Year and Quarter

	2005–1	*2005–2*	*2005–3 through 2007–4*
Beginning Cash	$100,000 (1)	$100,000	
+ Operating cash inflow	150,000 (1)	0	
+ New bank loan	0 (2)		
+ Market securities sold	0 (2)		
+ Interest on previous securities	0 (1)	2,000	
Available Cash	250,000 (3)		
– Operating cash outflow	0 (1)	120,000	
– Loan repayment	0 (1)	0	
– Market securities bought	100,000 (3)	0	
– Interest on previous loan	0 (1)	0	
– Dividends	50,000 (3)		
Cash Uses	150,000 (3)		
Ending Cash	100,000 (2)		

Notes:
1. These figures were directly or indirectly given.
2. These figures became clear when it was realized that there would be excess cash.
3. These figures were deduced through the need to balance the statement and the priorities set forth in the firm's policy.

3. What problems would be introduced if, for Winterfest Ski Corporation, we assumed that the interest receipts and payments would occur in the quarter in which the funds were invested and borrowed?
4. Lagged Loot, Inc., collects 35 percent of all sales in the month of the sale, 45 percent in the second month, and 15% in the third month; 5 percent is never collected. Lagged Loot had sales of $154,000 in both October and November and $186,000 in December. It is now December 31, and the following sales projections have been given to you:

Jan	*Feb*	*Mar*	*Apr*	*May*	*Jun*
$200,000	$180,000	$170,000	$200,000	$200,000	$200,000

Compute the expected cash flows from sales for each of the first 6 months of the year.

5. Manweg's Grocery Store collects 100 percent of all sales in the month of the sale. Most of the expenses it incurs, however, are paid for on a delayed basis. Manweg's pays 50 percent of its bills in the month in which they are received, 45 percent in the second month, and 5 percent in the third month, and its expenses are 95 percent of sales. Manweg's is projecting cash flow for the first 6 months of the year. It is now December 31 and the following past sales and sales projections have been given to you:

Nov	*Dec*	*Jan*	*Feb*
$550,000	$650,000	$400,000	$400,000

Ma	*Apr*	*May*	*Jun*
$400,000	$400,000	$575,000	$600,000

Compute the expected cash flows from both sales and expense and net them for each of the first 6 months of the year.

6. Returning to Manweg's Grocery Store, the firm had a cash balance of $50,000 on December 31. Manweg's hopes to be able to buy $100,000 of equipment on April 30 using cash but does not want its cash balance to fall below $25,000.
   a. Will the firm be able to buy the equipment?
   b. How would your answer change if the firm received 1 percent interest on its cash balance each month (added to the cash balance on the first of each month based upon the ending balance of the previous month) and received a delay in the payment on the equipment purchase until June 1?

7. Chugging Along, Inc., is attempting to forecast its financial future and develop a financial plan. The firm's most recent income statement and balance sheet have been constructed. Highly condensed versions are shown in the Tables. For simplicity, we are ignoring depreciation.

Chugging Along, Inc.
2005 Condensed Income Statement

	(in $000s)
Revenues	$ 100
Expenses	80
Net income	$ 20

Chugging Along, Inc.
12/31/05 Condensed Balance Sheet

	(in $000s)
Net working capital	$ 50
Fixed assets	150
Total Assets	$200
Long-term debt	$ 0
Equity	200
Total Debt and Equity	$200

The president of Chugging Along, Inc., is rather confident that revenues will grow by $10,000 per year. Expenses tend to run about 80 percent of revenues. It is, therefore, rather straightforward to construct a forecast of next year's income statement:

Chugging Along, Inc.
2006 Forecasted Income Statement

	(in $000s)
Revenues	$ 110
Expenses	88
Net income	$ 22

You have been asked to compile a forecast of the balance sheet for the end of the next year. You are told that net working capital will need to expand by $5,000, but that fixed assets will not need to expand because there is already excess capacity. You are also told that the firm desires to grow without taking on new debt and that any profits not needed to fund growth should be sent to the shareholders as a dividend. Begin by computing the statement of cash flows for 2006 using the given format. (*Hint*: All variables are determined except the dividend amount, which must be set equal to the number that will sum to the change in net working capital.)

Chugging Along, Inc.
2006 Forecasted Statement of Cash Flows

Operating Activities	
Net income	$______
Depreciation	$ 0
Investing Activity	
Fixed assets	$______
Financing Activities	
Dividends	$______
Debt	$______
Change in Net Working Capital	$______

8. Returning to Chugging Along, Inc. in Problem 7, now use the forecasted statement of cash flows for 2006 to construct the firm's condensed balance sheet for the end of 2006. Use the same format as was used in the 2005 balance sheet.

9. Returning one last time to Chugging Along, Inc., the president asks you to forecast all three financial statements for 2007 using the same formats and forecasts as were used for 2006. In other words, revenues are expected to grow by another $10,000, net working capital is expected to grow by another $5,000, and so forth.

10. Johnny Checkpay has had his last bad day at work. Starting tomorrow, Johnny is putting his life savings into starting up his own company. The first thing he is going to do is put together a financial plan as part of the business plan he will take to the bank in an effort to obtain the financing that he needs. Johnny already knows the type of balance sheet he will need to get started:

Checkpay, Inc.
Starting Condensed Balance Sheet

	(in $000s)
Net working capital	$ 100
Fixed assets	100
Total Assets	$ 200
Bank loan	$ 100
Equity	100
Total Debt and Equity	$ 200

Thus, Johnny knows that in order to obtain the net working capital and fixed assets he needs he will require a $100,000 bank loan in addition to his life savings of $100,000. Johnny has also forecasted the income statements he expects for the first 4 years (we ignore depreciation and taxes):

Checkpay, Inc.
Forecasted Condensed Income Statements

(in $000s)

	Year 1	*Year 2*	*Year 3*	*Year 4*
Revenues	$ 100	$ 200	$300	$450
Expenses	170	230	300	360
Net income	$−70	$−30	$ 0	$ 90

Johnny plans to go to the bank with a request for a $200,000 loan. He arrived at the amount by adding together the $100,000 immediate need for money to purchase assets as well as an additional $100,000 to cover the losses he expects to suffer in the first 2 years as the company gets going. Other than needing money to cover unexpected losses, can you think of anything that Johnny is forgetting?

11. Returning to Checkpay, Inc. in Problem 10, Johnny returns from the bank very disappointed. It seems that the bank's analyst has questioned his financial plan. Upon questioning, Johnny had admitted that his plans for growth would require additional net working capital even though he proved that no additional fixed assets would be needed. Johnny forecasts that he will need to expand his net working capital by $20,000 per year to meet growth.

Construct a forecast of the first 4 years of statements of cash flow and the first 4 years of balance sheets. Use these statements to show Johnny how much of a bank loan he will ultimately need because it is new bank loans that must be used to meet capital needs. (The bank loan is the slack variable that will allow these financial statements to balance.) Ignore additional interest expense.

12. Returning to Checkpay, Inc., Johnny has discovered that his original projections of expenses were based upon only the first $100,000 of loans. Assuming that the interest rate is 10 percent and that Johnny is allowed to borrow more money as it is needed, how much will he have needed to borrow by the end of the third year to meet his growth goals and to pay the interest? You may assume that the interest on the bank loan is paid in the year following the loan and is based upon the previous year's ending balance of the loan. [*Hint*: This requires that each year's income statement be revised to add an interest expense (equal to 10 percent of the previous year's ending bank loan amount more than $100,000) to the original expense projections. This will cause the equity account to become negative.] We have done the first statements to help get you started. (The bank loan amount was entered last so as to cause the column to sum to the last line.)

Checkpay, Inc.
Statement of Cash Flows Projection for Year 1

Operating Activities	
Net income	−$70
Investing Activity	
None	
Financing Activities	
Bank loan	$90
Change in Net Working Capital	$20

Checkpay, Inc.
Forecasted Condensed Balance Sheet, End of Year 1

Net working capital	$120
Fixed assets	100
Total Assets	$220
Bank loan	$190
Equity	30
Total Debt and Equity	$220

Checkpay, Inc.
Forecasted Income Statement, Year 2

Revenues	$ 200
Original expenses	230
Additional interest expense	9
Net income or loss	$−39

13. Perform a rough financial analysis of the debt usage, liquidity, and profitability of Checkpay, Inc. How would you suggest that Johnny revise his plans in order to provide for a more reasonable financial future?

Discussion Questions

1. It is often said that cash budgets should be projected only weeks or months into the future. Please comment.
2. Would it not be a lot simpler to maintain a large balance of marketable securities earning competitive rates of interest to ensure adequate liquidity and to avoid the whole budgeting process altogether?
3. Why can a firm's need for capital exceed the total of its projected losses and initial assets?
4. Can long-range financial planning be adequately accurate to justify the time spent on the process?

CHAPTER 18

INTERNATIONAL FINANCE

Willy World Amusement Parks, Inc. had earned a reputation for providing high-quality amusement entertainment in the United States through the operation of five parks in highly competitive markets near major cities. Even though competing theme parks have moved into choice European and Asian locations, Willy World has been slow to react. The management at Willy World was at one time studying the possibility of opening a major park somewhere outside the United States. Possible locations that were considered included South America and Eastern Europe.

The dollar amount of investment required to open a first-class operation was a staggering $1 billion. This amount of money, however, was not far from the cost of a new theme park in the United States. Willy World's management was not primarily concerned with the amount of investment; rather, they looked at the international aspects of the venture. How could they plan for construction costs in a country that had a different currency? What types of risks would Willy World face due to fluctuations in currency values once the park began operating? What if the government of the country collapsed or decided to nationalize foreign assets? What types of regulations and liability exposures would they face outside the United States?

These questions had no easy answers, and operating within the borders of the United States had allowed the firm to avoid issues of international operations. Management was concerned, however, whether Willy World could continue to be a world-class competitor without foreign expansion.

After months of careful study, management decided to take the safe course, abandon plans for an international park, and focus on an entirely domestic operation. This decision proved costly because it soon became clear that the firm lost market share in the amusement park industry. Willy World's stock price fell to a new low at a time when their competitors were doing well. Finally, the decision to go international was imposed on Willy World when a multinational firm bought them out. Willy World's top management team was replaced by a new set of managers who announced a goal of expanding Willy World's operations throughout the world.

Multinational operations are quite common in corporations today. For example, in 1995, 40 percent of Coca-Cola's sales came from its domestic operations, but 60 percent of sales were earned in its international divisions. This chapter examines corporate financial decisions in a multinational context.

An Overview of International Finance

How does international finance differ from domestic finance? The answer is, not very much. In fact, most of the principles of modern corporate finance remain unchanged whether they are being applied to decision making inside the United States, outside the United States, or between the United States and another nation. The decision to operate outside the domestic market, however, does introduce some new and unique issues, such as handling different currencies. As we shall see, the fact that nations have different currencies is the primary issue in international corporate financial management.

We begin our development of international corporate finance by studying foreign currency exchange for immediate transactions, which are simpler in that there is no passage of time and little risk. The passage of time and risk will then be introduced to foreign currency exchange. The final sections of the chapter discuss political risk and practical considerations.

The Economics of Multiple Currencies

Corporate decision making through net present value (*NPV*) requires the discounting of all relevant costs and benefits using market values. In domestic situations, total revenues are determined by multiplying the number of units sold by the market price, which is measured in the decision maker's own currency. For example, a U.S. farmer harvesting 25,000 bushels of grain will compute total grain revenues by multiplying the amount of grain by its dollar price per bushel:

$$\begin{array}{ccccc} \text{Value of Grain} & = & \text{Bushels of Grain} & \times & \text{Price per Bushel} \\ \$100{,}000 & = & 25{,}000 & \times & \$4 \end{array}$$

We will examine next how the value of goods and services in one currency can be converted into another currency.

foreign exchange market
A market where currencies of one country are exchanged for currencies of another. The foreign exchange market is a network of dealers linked by telephones and computers.

The Foreign Exchange Market

Currencies of one country are exchanged into currencies of another in the **foreign exchange market,** which is not a centralized location, but is instead a network of dealers linked by telephones and computers. Major holders and traders of currency include large money-center banks who exchange directly through the foreign exchange markets. Smaller users of currency, such as small businesses and tourists, exchange indirectly through smaller financial intermediaries such as community banks and local exchange offices.

The price at which currencies are traded is usually determined by the forces of supply and demand. A decreasing number of countries attempt to control their economies by making it illegal to trade their currency at any exchange rate other than the official exchange rate set by the government. These governments usually set exchange rates that reflect a much higher value to their currency than would occur in a free market. In cases such as these, it is common for **black markets** to arise that trade the currency at exchange rates driven by supply and demand. The price of the currency on these markets is often much lower. For example, black market currency values might be 20 percent of the values set by the official exchange rate.

black market
A market consisting of the illicit buying and selling of goods and services in violation of legal controls.

Exchange Rates

When a firm's product or service is located in a foreign country, the computation of the market value of the resource must be determined in two steps. First, the product or service must be valued in foreign currency using the price of the resource in the local currencies.

$$\text{Foreign Currency Value} = \text{Number of Units} \times \text{Foreign Price per Unit} \quad (18.1)$$

Next, the foreign currency value must be translated into the equivalent domestic currency value—the currency of the decision maker. This is accomplished by multiplying the foreign currency value by the exchange rate between the foreign and domestic currencies:

$$\text{Domestic Currency Value} = \text{Foreign Currency Value} \times \text{Exchange Rate}$$

Example 18.1 ______

Consider a U.S. truck manufacturer with international operations in Great Britain. If the division in Great Britain produces 1,000 small trucks at a cost of £5,100 (5,100 pounds), the foreign currency cost would be:

$$\text{Cost of Trucks in Foreign Currency} = 1{,}000 \times £5{,}100 = £5{,}100{,}000$$

where £ is the symbol for British pounds. The cost in dollars would be determined by exchanging the foreign currency into the domestic currency. In this case, the transaction requires turning British pounds into U.S. dollars. If the exchange rate between British pounds and U.S. dollars is 1 pound = \$1.5205, then the total cost in dollars of producing trucks in Great Britain would be:

$$\begin{aligned}\text{Cost of Trucks in Domestic Currency} &= £5{,}100{,}000 \times \$1.5205\\ &= \$7{,}754{,}550\end{aligned}$$

Thus, a cost of £5.1 million is equivalent to a cost of approximately \$7.7 million.

foreign exchange rate
The rate at which one currency can be traded for another.

Most nations have their own currency, and most currencies can be traded in the foreign exchange market.[1] The rate at which one currency can be traded for another is called the **foreign exchange rate.** An exchange rate is the price of one currency in terms of another, and exchange rates can be expressed in terms of either currency. Figure 18.1 illustrates foreign exchange rates as listed in the *Wall Street Journal* as of Friday, May 11, 2001, and Thursday, May 10, 2001, the previous trading day.

In the preceding example, on Friday, May 11, 2001, $1.4207 in U.S. dollars could be exchanged into one British pound. As Figure 18.1 illustrates, however, we could also express the relationship between pounds and dollars by saying that $1 U.S. was worth approximately 0.7039 British pounds. This is found by taking the inverse of 1.4207. Similar calculations can be made from the other 50 or so currencies listed in Figure 18.1. For instance, on May 11, 2001, $0.008161 in U.S. dollars could be exchanged into 1 Japanese yen, and $1 U.S. was worth approximately 122.53 yen.

As shown in Figure 18.1, exchange rates can change through time. On Thursday, May 10, 2001, it would have taken $1.4225 to purchase one British pound, $0.0018 more than the next day. Because less dollars are required to purchase pounds on Friday than on Thursday, we say that the dollar strengthened against the pound. The opposite was true for the Japanese yen. On Thursday, May 10, 2001, $0.008151 would have purchased one Japanese yen, a change of – $0.00001 from the subsequent trading day. Because more dollars are required to purchase yen on Friday than on Thursday, we say that the dollar weakened against the yen.

To summarize, transacting in a foreign currency is as simple as shopping for groceries. Just like apples, foreign currencies have prices that allow traders to express their value and transact in the currency of their choice. Foreign exchange rates allow one currency to be turned into another. Note that foreign exchange rates allow the value of goods in one country to be easily compared with the value of goods in another country. The comparison of goods between countries using exchange rates is discussed next in detail.

The Spot Market for Foreign Exchange

spot market
A market in which exchange takes place immediately.

In the previous discussion, the currency in one country was exchanged immediately into the currency of another country. The foreign exchange was therefore obtained through the spot market. A **spot market** is nothing more than a market where exchange takes place immediately.[2]

Most students are familiar with trading in spot markets. A large majority of transactions in which we engage result in a nearly immediate exchange. For example, a consumer goes to the store and exchanges money for gro-

[1]The formal introduction of Europe's single currency was motivated, in part, by the complexities and costs of different currencies.

[2]In the case of the spot market for foreign exchange, the process actually takes about 2 days.

FIGURE 18.1 Foreign Exchange Rates

CURRENCY TRADING

Friday, May 11, 2001

EXCHANGE RATES

The New York foreign exchange mid-range rates below apply to trading among banks in amounts of $1 million and more, as quoted at 4 p.m. Eastern time by Reuters and other sources. Retail transactions provide fewer units of foreign currency per dollar. Rates for the 12 Euro currency countries are derived from the latest dollar-euro rate using the exchange ratios set 1/1/99.

	U.S. $ EQUIV.		CURRENCY PER U.S. $	
Country	**Fri**	**Thu**	**Fri**	**Thu**
Argentina (Peso)	1.0009	1.0003	.9991	.9997
Australia (Dollar)	.5219	.5239	1.9159	1.9086
Austria (Schilling)	.06369	.06406	15.702	15.609
Bahrain (Dinar)	2.6525	2.6525	.3770	.3770
Belgium (Franc)	.0217	.0219	46.0317	45.7602
Brazil (Real)	.4374	.4432	2.2860	2.2565
Britain (Pound)	1.4207	1.4225	.7039	.7030
1-month forward	1.4199	1.4212	.7043	.7036
3-months forward	1.4170	1.4186	.7057	.7049
6-months forward	1.4139	1.4152	.7073	.7066
Canada (Dollar)	.6457	.6480	1.5487	1.5432
1-month forward	.6455	.6478	1.5493	1.5438
3-months forward	.6451	.6475	1.5501	1.5445
6-months forward	.6447	.6472	1.5511	1.5452
Chile (Peso)	.001655	.001659	604.20	602.65
China (Renminbi)	.1208	.1208	8.2771	8.2771
Colombia (Peso)	.0004223	.0004227	2368.00	2365.50
Czech. Rep. (Koruna)				
Commercial rate	.02549	.02563	39.237	39.017
Denmark (Krone)	.1174	.1181	8.5165	8.4655
Ecuador (US Dollar)-e	1.0000	1.0000	1.0000	1.0000
Finland (Markka)	.1474	.1483	6.7847	6.7446
France (Franc)	.1336	.1344	7.4851	7.4410
1-month forward	.1335	.1343	7.4880	7.4440
3-months forward	.1334	.1342	7.4939	7.4498
6-months forward	.1334	.1341	7.4988	7.4565
Germany (Mark)	.4481	.4507	2.2318	2.2186
1-month forward	.4479	.4506	2.2327	2.2195
3-months forward	.4475	.4502	2.2344	2.2213
6-months forward	.4472	.4498	2.2359	2.2232
Greece (Drachma)	.002572	.002587	388.76	386.54
Hong Kong (Dollar)	.1282	.1282	7.7996	7.7997
Hungary (Forint)	.003407	.003415	293.55	292.83
India (Rupee)	.02134	.02136	46.860	46.825
Indonesia (Rupiah)	.0000887	.0000896	11278	11165
Ireland (Punt)	1.1127	1.1193	.8987	.8934
Israel (Shekel)	.2411	.2412	4.1470	4.1460
Italy (Lira)	.0004526	.0004553	2209.47	2196.44

	U.S. $ EQUIV.		CURRENCY PER U.S. $	
Country	**Fri**	**Thu**	**Fri**	**Thu**
Japan (Yen)	.008161	.008151	122.53	122.69
1-month forward	.008190	.008179	122.10	122.26
3-months forward	.008246	.008233	121.27	121.46
6-months forward	.008331	.008316	120.04	120.25
Jordan (Dinar)	1.4069	1.4069	.7108	.7108
Kuwait (Dinar)	3.2520	3.2541	.3075	.3073
Lebanon (Pound)	.0006604	.0006604	1514.25	1514.25
Malaysia (Ringgit)-b	.2632	.2632	3.8000	3.8000
Malta (Lira)	2.1964	2.2036	.4553	.4538
Mexico (Peso)				
Floating rate	.1086	.1087	9.2110	9.1960
Netherlands (Guilder)	.3977	.4000	2.5146	2.4998
New Zealand (Dollar)	.4230	.4263	2.3641	2.3458
Norway (Krone)	.1092	.1095	9.1611	9.1351
Pakistan (Rupee)	.01630	.01630	61.350	61.350
Peru (new Sol)	.2781	.2772	3.5955	3.6070
Philippines (Peso)	.01990	.01978	50.250	50.550
Poland (Zloty)-d	.2498	.2522	4.0035	3.9650
Portugal (Escudo)	.004371	.004397	228.77	227.42
Russia (Ruble)-a	.03451	.03450	28.980	28.983
Saudi Arabia (Riyal)	.2666	.2666	3.7505	3.7506
Singapore (Dollar)	.5516	.5505	1.8130	1.8165
Slovak Rep. (Koruna)	.02026	.02038	49.361	49.078
South Africa (Rand)	.1254	.1258	7.9750	7.9475
South Korea (Won)	.0007710	.0007657	1297.00	1306.00
Spain (Peseta)	.005267	.005298	189.86	188.74
Sweden (Krona)	.0976	.0976	10.2497	10.2490
Switzerland (Franc)	.5713	.5739	1.7503	1.7425
1-month forward	.5718	.5743	1.7489	1.7411
3-months forward	.5727	.5753	1.7461	1.7383
6-months forward	.5743	.5768	1.7411	1.7337
Taiwan (Dollar)	.03042	.03042	32.870	32.870
Thailand (Baht)	.02199	.02198	45.485	45.500
Turkey (Lira)-f	.00000087	.00000087	1152000	1145000
United Arab (Dirham)	.2723	.2723	3.6730	3.6730
Uruguay (New Peso)				
Financial	.07663	.07663	13.050	13.050
Venezuela (Bolivar)	.001400	.001402	714.31	713.36
SDR	1.2614	1.2666	.7928	.7895
Euro	.8764	.8816	1.1410	1.1343

Special Drawing Rights (SDR) are based on exchange rates for the U.S., German, British, French , and Japanese currencies. Source: International Monetary Fund.

a-Russian Central Bank rate. b-Government rate. d-Floating rate; trading band suspended on 4/11/00. e-Adopted U.S. dollar as of 9/11/00. f-Floating rate, eff. Feb. 22.

(Source: From *The Wall Street Journal*, Friday, May 11, 2001. Reprinted by permission of *The Wall Street Journal*,

ceries. The store receives the money immediately and the consumer receives the groceries immediately—making this a spot transaction in a spot market.

On the other hand, someone may sign an agreement in which the exchange will not take place until some point in the future (e.g., a contract for lawn care service that will be performed and paid for at points in the future). Later in the chapter we will discuss other markets in which transactions agreed to today do not take place until weeks, months, or even years into the future.

Perfect Markets and the Law of One Price

The foreign exchange market allows participants to convert a given currency, such as U.S. currency, into the currency of virtually all other major countries and vice versa. Foreign exchange markets therefore allow people to purchase goods from throughout the world by starting with a single currency, such as U.S. dollars. This subsection will discuss the impact we would expect currency transactions to have on relative values throughout the world.

Chapter 1 introduced the economic principle called the *law of one price,* which states that, in a perfect market, competition will drive the price of two identical assets to be equal. Because there are no trading costs in perfect markets, anything other than equal prices would quickly vanish through the actions of people buying the underpriced asset and selling the overpriced asset.

For example, let us consider gold. Assume that the price at which U.S. dollars can be exchanged for an ounce of gold is approximately \$400. How much, therefore, would we expect gold to be priced in other currencies? Given perfect markets (i.e., markets with no trading costs), the value of gold would be equal regardless of the currency in which its value is expressed.

Example 18.2 ______ In U.S. markets suppose that gold trades at \$400 per ounce and French francs trade at \$0.20. By taking the inverse of the exchange rate, we can calculate that five French francs are worth \$1 U.S. According to the law of one price, we can determine the price of gold in Paris in terms of French francs. Given that an ounce of gold in U.S. dollars costs \$400, we can apply the law of one price by multiplying the price of gold in U.S. dollars by the price of U.S. dollars in terms of francs:

$$\begin{array}{cccc} \text{French Franc} & \text{Price of Gold} & & \text{Price of Dollars} \\ \text{Price of Gold} = & \text{in U.S. Dollars} & \times & \text{in French Francs} \\ 2{,}000 \quad = & \$400 & \times & (5 \text{ Francs per Dollar}). \end{array}$$

Thus, the law of one price permits us to specify the Paris price of gold at 2,000 francs. On the other hand, if we observed first that the price of gold in Paris was 2,000 francs and that the price of a franc in terms of U.S. dollars was \$0.20, then we could apply the law of one price to find the price of gold in terms of U.S. dollars:

$$\text{U.S. Dollar Cost of Gold} = \text{Price of Gold in French Francs} \times \text{Price of Francs in U.S. Dollars}$$

$$\$400 = 2{,}000 \times \$0.20$$

The Law of One Price and Arbitrage Opportunities

arbitrage
An opportunity to make profits with very little risk.

In the preceding example the price of gold was exactly the same whether the buyer used U.S. dollars or French francs. Why would we expect the prices to be equal? The answer is that if they were substantially different there would be an **arbitrage** opportunity—an opportunity to make profits with very little risk.

What would happen if the law of one price failed to hold? For example, suppose that the price of gold in U.S. dollars is $400, that the exchange rate between dollars and francs is $0.20 = 1 franc, and that an ounce of gold could be purchased in France for 1950 francs. In this case, the dollar price of gold in Paris is $390:

$$\$390 = 1{,}950 \text{ Francs} \times \$0.20.$$

Given perfect markets, how could an individual take advantage of such a situation? The individual could earn an arbitrage profit by engaging in these three transactions: (1) trading $390 dollars for 1950 francs on the foreign exchange markets, (2) buying an ounce of gold in Paris for the 1950 francs, and (3) selling the gold in the United States for $400 per ounce, leaving a riskless profit of $10 per ounce.

In a similar fashion, an arbitrage profit can be made if the price of gold in U.S. dollars is $400, the exchange rate between dollars and francs is $0.20 = 1 franc, and an ounce of gold in France costs 2,050 francs. In this case, the dollar price of gold in Paris is $410:

$$\$410 = 2{,}050 \text{ Francs} \times \$0.20.$$

Given perfect markets, the individual could earn an arbitrage profit by engaging in these three transactions: (1) buying an ounce of gold in the United States for $400, (2) selling the gold in Paris for 2,050 francs, and (3) exchanging the 2,050 francs for $410, leaving a riskless profit of $10 per ounce.

Such easy profits, unfortunately, do not exist in the real world. In the first arbitrage situation, the holder of the gold would not be willing to sell the gold for 1,950 francs if more money could be made by selling gold elsewhere and converting one currency into the currency of choice using the foreign exchange market. In addition, the buyer of the gold would not pay $400 if it could be purchased elsewhere for a cost in terms of U.S. dollars of $390. The tiny differences in prices that do exist in the real world are only big enough to pay for the time and expenses of being an arbitrageur—unless you are one of the best in the world. In perfect markets the law of one price will hold even with multiple currencies.

In perfect markets the law of one price will hold even if multiple currencies are involved.

In other words, for those assets traded in perfect or near-perfect markets, the prices of identical assets being traded in different currencies will be equal to each other if they are converted into a common currency using foreign market exchange rates.

Imperfect Markets and the Law of One Price

Would we expect the prices of all goods in different countries selling for different currencies to reflect the law of one price, using market exchange rates? The answer is, *no*! Most goods do not sell in perfect or near-perfect markets. How closely prices behave to the law of one price depends upon the type of good and the trading costs—in other words, the lack of perfection in the markets.

For widely traded, highly similar assets, such as precious metals and oil, we would expect prices to obey (approximately) the law of one price. This is because well-developed markets exist for the trading of such assets such that they can be transported around the world easily at relatively low costs.

For less often traded goods, dissimilar goods, or goods that are not easily transportable, however, we could expect price differences such that the law of one price fails to hold. For example, we would expect tropical fruit, a rare product in some northern countries, to sell for a higher price in Canada than in Brazil, when converted to a common currency. In other words, the U.S. dollar cost of tropical fruit in Canada is likely to be greater than the U.S. dollar cost of tropical fruit in Brazil. Even more so, we would expect the price of services such as manual labor, haircuts, and medical care to differ between countries because they are even less able to be transported.

In theory, perfect markets would be expected to produce identical prices. For assets that trade in near-perfect markets, the law of one price will approximately hold. For assets that do not trade in perfect markets, such as perishable foods and services, prices can differ when converted into a common currency.

Purchasing Power Parity

We have learned that virtually any currency can be used to buy any good. This is accomplished by simply exchanging currencies in the foreign exchange market. We next ask whether overall prices in one country must equal overall prices in another country. To put this another way, do different currencies have equal purchasing power?

purchasing power of a currency
The value of a currency in purchasing goods directly, without first being exchanged into another currency.

For the purposes of this discussion, the **purchasing power of a currency** refers to the value of the currency in purchasing goods directly—without first being exchanged into another currency. Thus, purchasing power refers to the overall cost level of those goods that are offered for direct sale in the given currency. For example, the purchasing power of the French franc would refer to the amount of goods that could be used to purchase goods directly (mostly in France) without having to convert the francs into another currency.

High purchasing power obviously allows the holder to purchase more goods than does low purchasing power. The degree of purchasing power can be assessed through the following question: If $1,000 is converted into French francs and is used to buy goods in Paris, then how many goods could be purchased relative to what the U.S. dollars would have purchased in New York City?

One answer to this question is that to the extent that the markets are well functioning, spending the $1,000 in the United States would be roughly equivalent to converting the $1,000 into francs and spending the money in Paris. Although France may have some goods that are relatively inexpensive, such as fine wine, and some that are relatively expensive, such as land, supply and demand pressures would force France to have the same overall purchasing power as the United States for a given level of wealth.

According to this argument, a U.S. dollar will have the same overall purchasing power in the United States as it does when converted to the local currency and spent in Paris, Japan, or Mexico. The argument that all currencies must have the same overall purchasing power is known as the **purchasing power parity** theorem. Proponents of this theorem argue that if one currency had a higher overall purchasing power, then competition would force its exchange rates up until it had the same purchasing power as all other currencies.

purchasing power parity
A theory stating that the purchasing power of a currency in one country will have the same power when converted to another currency and spent in another country.

Clear thinking reveals that the notion of purchasing power parity can never hold exactly in imperfect markets. As we have said, some goods are not easily transportable and thus cannot have equal purchasing power around the globe (e.g., tropical fruit). Even more important, there is no such thing as an overall cost level that can be compared between countries. Can every country offer the same beauty, climate, medical care, safety, or culture? We are sure that you will agree that the answer is no.

We do know that goods in near-perfect markets will sell at near-equal prices throughout the world, and that goods in imperfect markets can vary in price depending upon imperfections in the markets in which they trade.

Multiple Currencies and the Passage of Time

The previous section focused on the economics of multiple currencies in the absence of both time and risk. The purpose of this section is to introduce to the discussion the passage of time. Although we will occasionally mention risk in this section, a more detailed analysis of risk will occur later.

Example 18.3 ________ Consider Melissa's Fashions, Inc. which is a firm specializing in the importing and exporting of clothes. Melissa's Fashions is headquartered in the United States and has recently arranged to import a line of clothing from France to be sold domestically. The firm has agreed to purchase the clothing for 5 million French francs, and to sell it to a U.S. retailer for $1 million.

At the time the arrangement is made, the exchange rate between dollars and francs is \$0.18 = 1 franc. Given this exchange rate, Melissa's Fashions will make a profit on the transaction of \$100,000:

$$\text{Profit} = \$1{,}000{,}000 - (5{,}000{,}000 \text{ Francs} \times \$0.18)$$
$$= \$100{,}000$$

Even though this appears to be a good arrangement for the firm, one potential problem is that all payments will occur in 60 days—and the exchange rate between dollars and francs might change. If the exchange rate should rise to \$0.21 = 1 franc, Melissa's Fashions would have a loss of \$50,000:

$$\text{Loss} = \$1{,}000{,}000 - (5{,}000{,}000 \text{ Francs} \times \$0.21)$$
$$= \$50{,}000$$

What would happen if the exchange rate fell to \$0.16 = 1 franc? The answer is that there would be a profit of \$200,000:

$$\text{Profit} = \$1{,}000{,}000 - (5{,}000{,}000 \text{ Francs} \times \$0.16)$$
$$= \$200{,}000$$

Thus, when a transaction with multiple currencies occurs at a distant point in the future, it can be viewed as exposing the firm to foreign exchange risk, which is the fluctuations in profit and loss caused by fluctuations in the foreign exchange rate.

Forward Contracts

There is an interesting security known as a forward contract that solves the potential problem of foreign exchange risk quickly and easily, and greatly simplifies the discussion of multiple currencies through time. To put it simply, a **forward contract** allows someone to exchange future units of one currency for future units of another currency at a price agreed upon today. In other words, where spot market foreign exchange rates allow people to trade currencies today, forward foreign exchange markets allow people to agree today to trade currencies at some point in the future.

forward contract
A contract that allows the exchange of future units of one currency for future units of another currency at an agreed-upon price today.

For example, Melissa's Fashions could enter a forward contract that would lock in the French franc exchange rate to be used in 60 days. The firm could use the forward market to buy 5 million francs in 60 days for \$0.18 each such that the dollar price of the franc exchange is \$900,000. Because the firm will receive \$1 million in 60 days, the clothing transaction will net the firm a sure \$100,000 profit. Because all of Melissa's Fashions revenues and expenses would now be locked in relative to U.S. dollars, the firm would be protected from fluctuations in the foreign exchange rates. These transactions are summarized in Table 18.1.

Thus, in situations where future revenues and/or expenses are known and are expressed in foreign currencies, a firm can usually eliminate foreign exchange risk by locking in exchange rates using forward contracts.

Futures Contracts

futures contract
A contract similar to a forward contract that allows participants to make agreements today to exchange currencies (or other commodities) in the future.

There is another type of contract, called a **futures contract,** which is very closely related to a forward contract. In fact, futures contracts and forward contracts are so similar that many people view them as the same concept. Both contracts allow the participants to make agreements today to exchange currencies (or other commodities) in the future. Window 18.1 discusses both of these contracts and their differences in detail.

Forward and futures contracts provide a simple and clear solution to the problem of major multiple currencies when there is a significant passage of time between the date of the agreement and the date of payment. The decision maker can use forward or future exchange rate contracts to convert the future prices into a common currency.

For example, let us return to Melissa's Fashions and consider a typical futures contract arrangement. Suppose the firm had agreed to import and sell clothing over the course of 1 year in four shipments corresponding to the four seasons. The firm agrees to accept four quarterly shipments of clothes from France at a cost of 5 million francs and will deliver these shipments to retailers in the United States for $1 million each. The first exchange of funds will take place in 2 months, the next in 5 months, the third in 8 months, and the final in 11 months. How would Melissa's Fashions be able to accept such

TABLE 18.1 Using Forward Contracts to Eliminate Foreign Exchange Risk

Today

Agree to buy clothing for 5,000,000 francs payable in 60 days.	Agree to sell clothing for $1,000,000 to be received in 60 days.

Spot Exchange Rate: $0.18 = 1 Franc
Profit If Transacted Today: $1,000,000 − (5,000,000 × $0.18) = $100,000

Problem: All payments to occur in 60 days. Spot exchange rate in 60 days is uncertain.

Solution: Enter the forward foreign exchange market. Agree to buy francs in 60 days for $900,000 in the forward markets. Forward transaction locks in a profit of $100,000.

WINDOW 18.1

Forward Contracts and Futures Contracts

The basic features of the forward and futures contracts are the same—both allow for prices in the future to be locked in today. There are, however, important differences between these contracts. This window presents a brief discussion of these differences.

1. **Forward contracts** are agreements between two parties; therefore, the terms of the contracts can be tailored to suit the needs of the participants. Futures contracts trade on organized exchanges (backed by clearinghouses) and the exchanges set the specific terms, such as the size of each contract and the time of expiration.

For example, suppose that Melissa's Fashions, Inc. trades with a Mexican clothing manufacturer and takes on Mexican peso foreign currency risk that spans 3.5 months. A forward market arrangement would allow the firm to lock in a rate of Mexican peso exchange in exactly 3.5 months. In contrast, the choices available in the organized futures markets might not include a 3.5 month contract for Mexican pesos. In this case, if Melissa's Fashions were to use futures contracts, the firm would need to find the contract that comes closest to the foreign currency risk it is trying to remove.

2. In **futures contracts,** the organized exchange guarantees the agreements of both parties, while no such guarantees exist in forward contracts. If Melissa's Fashions enters a forward contract to eliminate foreign exchange risk, the firm has accepted the risk that the other party will fail to convert the currency as promised. Even though forward contracts can be tailor-made to eliminate foreign currency risk through time, these contracts introduce another type of risk known as default risk. Because the clearinghouse guarantees that all futures participants will honor their agreements, virtually no such default risk is introduced with futures contracts.

3. Futures contracts require a daily "settling-up" process, whereas forward contracts settle up only at maturity. The daily settling-up process works as follows: At the end of each day's trading, the clearinghouse calculates the profit or loss of each position as if these positions were to end. Settling-up provides a financial safeguard to ensure that futures traders will live up to their promises. With forward contracts there is no settling-up process.

a business arrangement given the uncertainty regarding future exchange rates between francs and dollars?

The answer is found by using futures prices to "lock in" a foreign exchange rate for turning francs into dollars. For example, Table 18.2 provides a set of futures prices for French franc foreign exchange in 2 months, 5 months, 8 months, and 11 months. These prices show a stable dollar relative to French francs. According to this set of futures prices, Melissa's Fashions can use the futures market to lock in an exchange rate at each of the four trading dates, guaranteeing a profit of $100,000 in each transaction.

TABLE 18.2 Melissa's Fashions, Inc.: Using Futures to Remove Foreign Exchange Risk

Maturity	*Futures Exchange Rate*
2 months	0.18
5 months	0.18
8 months	0.18
11 months	0.18

The Clothing Transaction

1. Firm agrees to pay 5,000,000 francs for clothing.
2. Firm has an agreement to sell the clothing for $1,000,000.
3. Firm locks in the rate of foreign exchange today for future transactions.

Profit in 2 months: $1,000,000 – (5,000,000 × 0.18) = $100,000
Profit in 5 months: $1,000,000 – (5,000,000 × 0.18) = $100,000
Profit in 8 months: $1,000,000 – (5,000,000 × 0.18) = $100,000
Profit in 11 months: $1,000,000 – (5,000,000 × 0.18) = $100,000

Of course, the futures price of French franc foreign exchange need not be constant through time. For instance, Table 18.3 shows a set of futures prices whereby the dollar strengthens against the franc (it takes fewer and fewer dollars to purchase francs). Using these futures prices to remove foreign exchange risk, Melissa's Fashions locks in a different profit in each of the four transactions. Because the price of French francs in dollars declines through time, futures market transactions will guarantee a profit of $100,000 in 2 months, $150,000 in 5 months, $200,000 in 8 months, and $250,000 in 11 months.

Finally, Table 18.4 shows another possible set of futures prices whereby the dollar weakens against the franc through time (it takes more and more dollars to purchase francs). Because the price of French francs in dollars rises through time, futures market transactions will guarantee a profit of $100,000 in 2 months, $50,000 in 5 months, and $0 in 8 months, and a loss of $50,000 in 11 months.

Tables 18.2–18.4 demonstrate that foreign exchange risk related to timing can be removed by using futures contracts to convert the currencies into fixed dollar costs. If future exchange rates reflect a stable dollar relative to francs, then profits will remain constant. If future exchange rates reflect a strengthening dollar relative to francs, then profits will increase through time in our example. If future exchange rates reflect a weakening dollar relative to francs, then profits will decrease through time. Melissa's Fashions can use the prices in the futures markets to determine whether or not to arrange for the clothing shipment.

TABLE 18.3 Melissa's Fashions, Inc.: Using Futures to Remove Foreign Exchange Risk

Maturity	*Futures Exchange Rate*
2 months	0.18
5 months	0.17
8 months	0.16
11 months	0.15

The Clothing Transaction

1. Firm agrees to pay 5,000,000 francs for clothing.
2. Firm has an agreement to sell the clothing for $1,000,000.
3. Firm locks in the rate of foreign exchange today for future transactions.

Profit in 2 months: $1,000,000 − (5,000,000 × 0.18) = $100,000
Profit in 5 months: $1,000,000 − (5,000,000 × 0.17) = $150,000
Profit in 8 months: $1,000,000 − (5,000,000 × 0.16) = $200,000
Profit in 11 months: $1,000,000 − (5,000,000 × 0.15) = $250,000

TABLE 18.4 Melissa's Fashions, Inc.: Using Futures to Remove Foreign Exchange Risk

Maturity	*Futures Exchange Rate*
2 months	0.18
5 months	0.19
8 months	0.20
11 months	0.21

The Clothing Transaction

1. Firm agrees to pay 5,000,000 francs for clothing.
2. Firm has an agreement to sell the clothing for $1,000,000.
3. Firm locks in the rate of foreign exchange today for future transactions.

Profit in 2 months: $1,000,000 − (5,000,000 × 0.18) = $100,000
Profit in 5 months: $1,000,000 − (5,000,000 × 0.19) = $ 50,000
Profit in 8 months: $1,000,000 − (5,000,000 × 0.20) = $ 0
Profit in 11 months: $1,000,000 − (5,000,000 × 0.21) = −$ 50,000

Forward and Futures Contracts as a Double-Edged Sword

As demonstrated earlier, different foreign currencies do not present major difficulties in the absence of risk because forward and futures markets allow firms to lock in today the rate of foreign exchange in the future. In practice, however, there may be two problems with using forwards and futures.

The first problem is *commitment*. Forward and futures contracts commit their participants to an exchange even if the need to exchange currency vanishes. For example, suppose that after Melissa's Fashions enters into futures contracts, the French clothing manufacturer or the American retailer goes out of business. Because the clothes will not be delivered, there is no longer a need for foreign exchange. Melissa's Fashions, however, is committed to buy 5 million francs each quarter for a year as a result of the futures contracts.

The second problem is *regret*. Look at Table 18.2, where Melissa's Fashions uses futures contracts to lock in foreign exchange at a price of $0.18. How would top management and the shareholders react if during the next year the dollar strengthens against the franc such that the spot exchange rate of French francs for dollars drops to $0.15? The answer is, not very well, as the firm would have had higher profits ($250,000 to be exact) if the futures contracts were not used. This is demonstrated in Table 18.5.

TABLE 18.5 The Potential for Regret When Using Forward or Futures Contracts

Problem—Foreign Exchange Risk: Firm will receive clothes and will pay 5,000,000 francs in 60 days.

Firm will sell clothes for $1,000,000 in 60 days.

Solution: Use the futures market to lock in a profit. Enter a 2-month futures contract to "buy" 5,000,000 francs for $0.18 each. Use the 5,000,000 francs to pay for the clothes at a cost of $900,000.

Result of Using the Futures Transaction: Receive clothes for $1,000,000 at a guaranteed cost of $900,000. Profit is locked in at $100,000.

Potential Regret: Suppose the dollar price for francs in 60 days falls such that francs can be purchased for $0.15 each. In the absence of a futures agreement, the cost in dollars of receiving the clothes is:

$$5{,}000{,}000 \times 0.15 = \$750{,}000,$$

such that profit would have been:

$$\$1{,}000{,}000 - \$750{,}000 = \$250{,}000$$

The futures agreement results in profits $150,000 below what they would have been in the absence of holding futures contracts.

Table 18.5 illustrates that the futures contract is a commitment to pay \$0.18 per franc even though the spot market price is \$0.15. Remember, the purpose of the futures contract was to eliminate or hedge away the risk of currency fluctuations.[3] Of course, had the dollar strengthened against the franc such that the spot market price of a franc were \$0.20, the profit on the clothing transaction in the absence of the futures contract would have been completely wiped out.

To the Rescue: Options on Foreign Currency Risk

Foreign exchange options allow users to avoid or lessen the problems just discussed. A foreign exchange option allows its holder the option to exchange a given amount of one currency for another without the obligation to do so. These options follow most of the same concepts and principles detailed in Chapter 10 on options.

Example 18.4 _______ Melissa's Fashions, Inc. could use options on French francs in order to protect itself from foreign exchange risk. The option would allow Melissa's Fashions to exchange U.S. dollars for 5 million French francs at or near each of the four quarterly transaction dates. Each option would specify the amount of currency to be exchanged, the rate of exchange, and the time period. If the clothing deal fell through or if the dollar price per franc fell in value, Melissa's Fashions could walk away from its option to exchange francs for dollars by letting the option expire. On the other hand, if the dollar price per franc went up in value, Melissa's Fashions would be protected because they had locked in a purchase price for the francs required to purchase the clothing.

Of course, there are no free lunches in the real world. As shown in Chapter 10, the buyer of an option must pay a price, called a *premium,* for the privilege of owning the option. The person who sells or writes the option will demand this premium as a compensation for offering the option.

In the highly efficient markets of foreign exchange it cannot be said that options, futures, or forwards will allow anyone to earn abnormal profits consistently. These markets simply allow their users to eliminate or hedge away the risks inherent in contracting while using multiple currencies.

Interest Rates and the Law of One Price

In the near-perfect markets of foreign exchange and government bonds, the law of one price forces a relationship between international interest rates and exchange rates known as interest rate parity. The concept of interest rate

---

[3]Even worse, these contracts will sometimes produce separate accounting "losses," which will cause some uninformed people to think that the manager is speculating in the futures markets.

interest rate parity
A theory stating that risk-free bonds of various currencies must offer the same return when "translated" into a common currency using forward contracts.

parity is similar to purchasing power parity. **Interest rate parity** states that risk-free bonds of various currencies must offer the same return when "translated" into a common currency using forward contracts.

For example, consider two government-guaranteed zero coupon bonds with identical maturities of 1 year, but issued by different countries. To simplify the analysis, assume that each bond is risk-free. Government bonds of the United States and England might provide somewhat realistic examples. We know that an American investor can earn a risk-free return in U.S. dollars by simply purchasing a U.S. government bond. The investor pays U.S. dollars today for the bond and receives U.S. dollars in the future. If the interest rate on this U.S. government bond is 10 percent, then the investor can invest $100 and receive a guaranteed payment of $110 in 1 year.

Is it possible for the American investor to use the British bond and foreign exchange markets to create an equivalent risk-free investment with a guaranteed return of U.S. dollars? The answer is, *yes,* by following three steps: (1) convert dollars to pounds using the spot foreign exchange market, (2) buy the British bond using the pounds, and (3) enter into a forward foreign exchange contract, which allows the conversion of pounds received from the British bond into dollars in 1 year when the bond matures. The forward contract must be established at the same time that the bond is purchased so that the investor's future exchange rate can be locked in. These two equivalent alternatives are pictured on a time line in Figure 18.2.

There are an infinite number of combinations of exchange rates and interest rates that would permit the British bond to pay the same return in U.S. dollars as the U.S. bond. For example, if the current spot exchange rate allows 0.8 British pounds to be exchanged for each U.S. dollar, if the forward exchange rate will allow 0.816 British pounds to be exchanged for each dollar in 1 year, and if the British bond pays 12.2 percent interest, then the payoff of a $100 investment in the British bond is equivalent to the payoff of a $100

FIGURE 18.2 Creating an Equivalent Risk-Free Investment

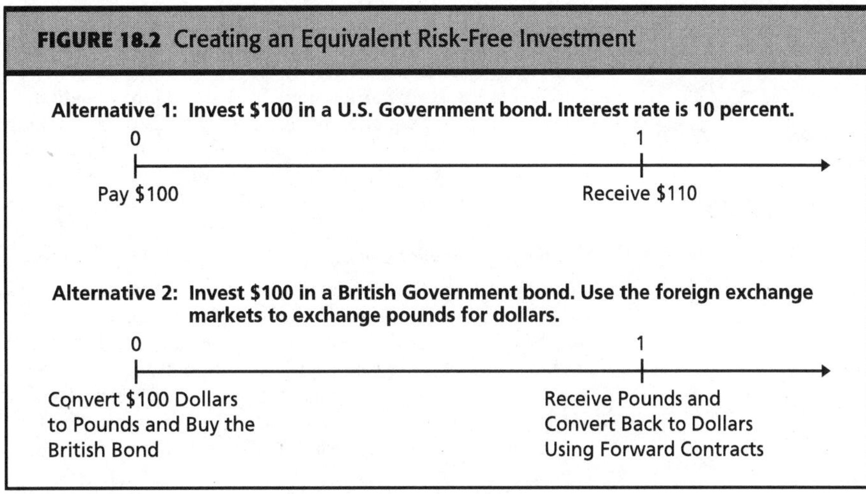
Alternative 1: Invest $100 in a U.S. Government bond. Interest rate is 10 percent.
0
1
Pay $100
Receive $110
Alternative 2: Invest $100 in a British Government bond. Use the foreign exchange markets to exchange pounds for dollars.
0
1
Convert $100 Dollars to Pounds and Buy the British Bond
Receive Pounds and Convert Back to Dollars Using Forward Contracts

investment in the U.S. government bond. This payoff is shown in the following transactions:

1. Convert \$100 using 0.8 exchange rate into 80 pounds
2. Invest 80 pounds at 12.2 percent bond return
3. Receive 89.76 pounds at British bond maturity
4. Convert 89.76 pounds, using a forward exchange rate, of 0.816 into \$110

Notice that the British bond investment returns the same dollar amount as the U.S. bond investment. Even though the British bond earns a higher interest rate (12.2 percent vs. 10 percent), the higher return is offset when converting pounds back into dollars.

The Interest Rate Parity Theorem

The relationship between interest rates and exchange rates described earlier can be generalized into the interest rate parity theorem:

$$\text{The Ratio Between Interest Rates} = \text{The Ratio Between Forward and Spot Foreign Exchange Rates}$$

$$\frac{(1+\text{Domestic Yield})}{(1+\text{Foreign Yield})} = \frac{\text{Spot Exchange Rate}}{\text{Forward Exchange Rate}} \quad (18.2)$$

The interest rate parity theorem[4] states that international interest rate differences will be equal to differences between current and forward exchange rates.[5] Thus, futures and forward exchange rates reflect interest rate differentials between the two countries. In the previous example of British bonds and U.S. bonds, the interest rate parity theorem is:

$$\frac{(1.100)}{(1.122)} = \frac{0.800}{0.816}$$

[4]Three details regarding Equation (18.2) are: (1) the equation is shown for a 1-year horizon—in order to adjust the equation for multiple periods or fractional periods, both the expressions in parenthesis would be raised to a power equal to the number of periods, (2) the exchange rates are expresses in the equation in terms of foreign currencies per one unit of domestic currency—if the exchange rates are expressed as domestic currency per foreign unit, then the interest rate ratio must be inverted, and (3) the equation is often factored differently. Thus, although the equation can appear quite differently, it is still economically equivalent.

[5]Some people think of the forward exchange rates as "guesses" of subsequent spot rates. In other words, they think that, because the forward exchange rate in the previous example was 0.816, it must be true that market participants are estimating that the spot exchange rate is expected to rise to 0.816 during the next year. The viewpoint that forward prices are forecasts of subsequent spot prices has become so popular that it has even received a name: *the expectations theory of forward rates.* This "theory," however, ignores risk and is therefore fundamentally flawed. It is, at best, a crude approximation when dealing with forward contracts that contain systematic risk.

Summary of the Forward, Futures, and Options Markets

The problem of future cash inflows or outflows denominated in a major foreign currency[6] is easily solved. The firm can either sell in advance an undesired currency in the forward market or it can prepare in advance for an outflow by contracting to purchase the currency in the forward market. The prices of forward foreign exchange contracts are determined by relative interest rates between the currencies.

Some corporations may wish to handle foreign exchange problems by purchasing options that allow the holder to exchange between currencies if exchange rates move against them but which allow the option holder to transact in the spot market if exchange rates move in a favorable direction.

Multiple Currencies with Time and Risk

Given our focus on corporate finance, and given that corporations are owned by shareholders, the most important question is how shareholders perceive the risk of transacting in foreign markets with different currencies. For instance, how does a shareholder of a major computer firm view the risks of commitments to sell major equipment at prices fixed in a foreign currency? In this section we will formally discuss foreign exchange risks.

A Review of the Theory of Risk

Chapters 8 and 9 discussed the theory of risk in detail. To review, the most important lesson of these chapters is that there are two types of risk—systematic risk and diversifiable risk. *Systematic risk* is that variation in an asset's return that is correlated with the performance of the overall economy. *Diversifiable risk* is all other variation.

The ability to eliminate diversifiable risk through diversification leads to the conclusion that little or no added return should be demanded for bearing diversifiable risk. Systematic risk, however, is what ultimately flows through to shareholders and exposes them to the concern that they will have too little wealth if there is a general economic downturn. Only systematic risk requires a reward.

Another term for systematic risk is *market risk* because it is the variation in return that is correlated with the entire economy or stock market. Market risk is measured by beta, and beta is used in an equation known as the capital asset pricing model in order to estimate a required rate of return.

---

[6]Currencies of some smaller countries are not widely traded and can introduce a significant problem. The size of these transactions, fortunately, is relatively small, and often the corporations in these countries are accustomed to contracting using major currencies.

The International Capital Asset Pricing Model

In Chapters 8 and 9 the overall performance of the economy was viewed as the performance of the stock market as captured by the S&P 500 stock portfolio or perhaps the overall U.S. economy. In theory, however, the market should comprise all assets, including stocks, bonds, real estate, automobiles, and clothing. Further, the market should include all of the wealth of the world—the international market portfolio—not just the wealth in the United States.

For the purposes of this chapter, market risk will be defined relative to the entire world economy. Thus, an asset will have systematic risk only to the extent that the performance of the asset is correlated with the overall world economy. All other risk will be considered as diversifiable risk. The required return on such an asset can be determined through **the international capital asset pricing model.**

the international capital asset pricing model
An asset valuation model built on the theory that an asset will have systematic risk only to the extent that the performance of the asset is correlated with the overall world economy. All other risk will be considered as diversifiable risk.

The notion that we should view the capital asset pricing model (CAPM) in an international context, with the market defined as the global portfolio, should be evident. The model itself would predict that investors would seek diversification and would therefore invest internationally. In fact, the more unrealistic view of the capital asset pricing model is to apply the model only to the economy of a single country such as the United States.

Systematic Risk and Multiple Currencies

The key question in a formal analysis of international systematic risk is whether or not systematic risk increases when contracting with or operating in foreign countries, as compared with otherwise similar domestic situations. For example, if a U.S. firm contracts to buy products from or sell products to a foreign firm, does it affect the systematic risk of the firm whether the transaction is fixed in terms of dollars or in a foreign currency?

The traditional view of international transactions is that they expose a firm to the fluctuations or risk inherent in foreign currencies. Thus, the decision of a firm to trade or operate internationally is often focused on the resulting exposure of the firm to foreign exchange risk. In other words, risk is viewed solely in terms of values measured in the decision-maker's domestic currency.

Remember, however, that any contract using a foreign currency can be transformed into a fixed dollar arrangement by buying and selling through the forward market. This is illustrated as:

$$\begin{array}{c}\text{Contract Fixed in}\\\text{Foreign Currency}\end{array} + \begin{array}{c}\text{Forward}\\\text{Contracts}\end{array} = \begin{array}{c}\text{Contract Fixed in}\\\text{Domestic Currency}\end{array}$$

Thus, the decision of a firm to enter into international transactions in foreign currencies can be viewed as being economically similar to the decision to buy and sell forward contracts on foreign exchange rates.

Do contracts fixed in U.S. dollars have different levels of systematic risk relative to the world economy than do contracts fixed in yen, francs, pounds, lira, and so forth? Do forward contracts between two currencies have a positive beta? The evidence from international markets tends to indicate that transactions expressed in foreign currencies do not increase the systematic risk of a corporation. Firms considering projects with international aspects, therefore, should not necessarily require a higher rate of return when discounting cash flows for decision-making purposes. In fact, international operations and trade tend to decrease the total risk to a firm by diversifying away some of the risk of the firm's domestic economy. Thus, a multinational corporation tends to be more diversified than an entirely domestic corporation because the multinational firm is less sensitive to the economic performance of a single country.

It is clear that a portfolio of international securities offers an investor enhanced diversification. Moreover, using a myriad of available mutual funds, shareholders of corporations are easily able to diversify across investments in various countries into a global portfolio. Because investors can accomplish this at little or no cost for themselves, it is not the job of domestic corporations to diversify into international transactions on behalf of their shareholders simply for the sake of diversification.

Political Risk

We have just discussed the systematic risk and diversification of international transactions, focusing on the extent to which the returns of assets from various countries differed in terms of systematic risk and the amount of diversification that they offered.

This section will discuss a very different analysis of risk: political risk. **Political risk** is the risk that actions by a foreign government will have a negative impact on a firm's wealth. An example of political risk is the danger that an operation in a foreign country will be nationalized or seized by the existing government or by a new government through a coup d'état.

political risk
The risk that actions by a foreign government will have a negative impact on a firm's wealth.

Overview of Political Risk

Financial analysis in major developed nations takes for granted individuals' right to private property and their general protection from seizure by the government. Nationalization is the process whereby certain private property is seized by a government for the "good of the people," with little or no compensation to the original owner. To the citizens and governments of poor nations, the concept has a certain appeal, especially where a high percentage of the wealth in the nation is owned by an especially small percentage of the people or by the shareholders of foreign corporations.

Nationalization, however, is not the only form of political risk. Increased taxes or regulations can also harm shareholder wealth. In fact, nationalization can be viewed as a more complete form of taxation revision in which the tax rate is raised to 100 percent!

It is important to distinguish between high tax rates and uncertain tax rates. There is no problem in making a decision regarding investment in an environment of high tax rates, as long as the rates are stable. The investor simply takes taxes into account when estimating future cash flows. Political risk, however, is the risk that the tax rates will rise dramatically or that nationalization will occur after the investment is made. From the perspective of the country that hosts foreign assets, there is an obvious temptation to want to confiscate foreign wealth. Countries with political stability and a clearly defined process for legislating taxes therefore have less political risk regardless of the level of their taxes.

Political Risk and Investment Decisions

As with all other potential expenses, the expected consequences of political risk must be incorporated into the estimation of a project's cash flows whenever the risk is viewed as being nontrivial. The higher the political risk and therefore the higher the probability of an adverse change in taxation, the lower should be the estimated cash inflows. The greater the political risk, the less desirable the investment.

The degree of political risk depends in part upon the type of asset located in the host country. Assets that are of little value to the host country run a lower risk of being seized. A foreign operation that depends upon the parent company would therefore have less political risk than a relatively autonomous operation. An example of a foreign asset carrying little political risk would be a foreign marketing office that depends on the sales office of the parent company. An example of a foreign asset carrying high political risk would be a low-technology manufacturing operation that can operate independently from the parent.

Innovative Financial Arrangements

Most political risk occurs from the incentives of governments to seize assets, and innovative financing arrangements can reduce political risk by reducing this incentive. The key is to ensure, directly or indirectly, that as large as possible a percentage of any losses due to seizure will be borne by the host country itself.

For example, political risk is reduced if the host country provides a portion of the project's financing. If such financing is provided, then it may be useful to have a clause stating that, in the event of nationalization, any debts to the citizens of the host country would be forgiven. This clause is especially helpful when the parties providing the financing have some influence on the government.

Practical Considerations of International Financial Management

As we have said, engaging in international trade is not as simple as engaging in domestic trade. We will briefly review two issues that are directly or indirectly related to international finance. (There are a host of other issues such as shipping, marketing, and management that are important, but they outside the scope of this text.)

Payment for Goods

The decision to extend credit to a foreign customer is more risky than the decision to extend credit to a domestic customer, due to difficulty in obtaining information regarding the customer and difficulty in collection.

banker's acceptances and irrevocable letters of credit
Financial instruments often used to facilitate international trade. The banker's acceptance and letter of credit represents a third-party guarantee of payment by the importer to the exporter.

Banker's acceptances and **irrevocable letters of credit** are often used for international trade. In both situations, payment of the bill is guaranteed by a bank. It is the responsibility of the buyer to arrange for one of these forms of guarantee.

Receipt of Goods

The decision to purchase goods from a foreign operation is the opposite side of the previous transaction. If the foreign seller does not extend credit, the domestic buyer can arrange for either a banker's acceptance or an irrevocable letter of credit. It is then important to ensure that payment will not be made until satisfactory receipt of the goods has occurred.

Summary

- The primary financial problem that occurs in international finance is multiple currencies. In international transactions, the costs and benefits of a decision can be expressed in more than one currency or in a currency other than the currency of the shareholders. Proper decision making can be accomplished by converting all the costs and benefits into a common currency, adjusted for time and risk.
- Foreign exchange markets provide the opportunity to trade between currencies. In order to convert a current cost or current benefit into a desired currency, the decision maker multiplies the foreign currency by the spot rate of exchange between the currencies.
- The prices in various currencies of any good traded in a well-functioning market should be approximately equal when converted into a common currency using market exchange rates. This is an extension of the law of one price, which is a natural result of competition. Goods that are dissimilar, expensive to transport, and otherwise trade in highly imperfect markets, however, can have substantially different prices in different places.
- Purchasing power parity states that all currencies have approximately equal overall purchasing power when converted using market exchange rates. Overall

purchasing power refers to the ability to purchase a common spectrum of goods for an ordinary lifestyle. Thus, the theory of purchasing power parity states that the law of one price will hold for overall purchasing. Because so many goods are traded in highly imperfect markets, however, there is no reason to believe that purchasing power parity will hold.

- Financial managers can convert future costs and benefits into a desired currency using the forward or futures markets for foreign exchange. Forward and futures contracts allow the corporation to agree today and negotiate a price today for a transaction that will not be completed until some predetermined point in the future, such as a certain number of months hence.
- The law of one price can be applied to government bonds in various currencies because the bonds trade in rather well-functioning markets. This is also expressed as the interest rate parity theorem, which states that the ratios between interest rates across currencies will be determined simultaneously with the ratios between spot and forward exchange rates.
- When future benefits and costs are uncertain, currency differentials become more difficult to resolve. Foreign exchange options give the holder of the option the opportunity to exchange at predetermined prices, but not the obligation. Thus, the risk of currency differentials can be controlled at a cost.
- The international capital asset pricing model views the systematic risk of an asset as being determined by the correlation of the asset's return with the world economy. Within this model, currency differentials do not introduce substantial systematic risk; therefore corporations do not need to be overly concerned about currency differentials. The model predicts that shareholders do not need to be protected against the risks of fluctuations in the value of various currencies because this risk is largely diversifiable and can be completely resolved by the shareholder without the help of the corporation.
- Political risk is the danger that the host country will seize, nationalize, confiscate, or heavily tax the benefits of a firm's foreign operation. This risk can be reduced through innovative financing arrangements that reduce the host country's benefit in such actions. An example would include the financing of foreign operations using money from the host country.
- International business involves a myriad of practical financial issues, of which the major ones are arranging receipt of payment for goods delivered to a foreign customer and arranging payment for goods received from a foreign supplier.

Demonstration Problems

Problem 1

Overland Corporation anticipates receiving 10 million British pounds in exactly 3 months. The current value of a British pound in American dollars is \$1.80. The corporation is considering the following alternatives:

a. Lock in an exchange rate for the pounds using a forward contract or a futures contract with an exchange rate of \$1.80

b. Lock in a potential exchange rate for the pounds using a foreign exchange option that would allow the 10 million pounds to be converted into American dollars at an exchange rate of \$1.80

c. Do nothing and accept the foreign exchange risk

Compute the ultimate American dollar value of the 10 million British pounds to Overland Corporation using each of the 3 strategies. Examine three scenarios in which the value of the pound drops to $1.50, rises to $2.10, and stays at $1.80 at the end of the 3 months. Ignore the costs of purchasing the foreign exchange option.

Solution to Problem 1

Step 1: The first strategy locks in a guaranteed value for British pounds to Overland Corporation of $1.80. Thus, whether the British pounds rise in value, fall in value, or stay at the same value, Overland will convert the pounds to American dollars at the locked-in exchange rate of $1.80. Thus, in 3 months the firm would receive $18 million.

Step 2: The second strategy has Overland purchase a foreign exchange option that will be used by the firm only in the event that the British pounds fall in value:

Scenario 1: Pound drops to $1.50
Result: Firm uses option to convert pounds to dollars at $1.80 and therefore receives $18 million.

Scenario 2: Pound stays at $1.80
Result: It makes no difference whether or not the firm uses the option because either way Overland can convert pounds to dollars at $1.80 and therefore receive $18 million.

Scenario 3: Pound rises to $2.10
Result: Firm does not use option; rather, it converts pounds to dollars at $2.10 and therefore receives $21 million.

Step 3: The third strategy has Overland do nothing to protect itself. The firm will therefore receive value based in American dollars, which depends upon whatever the market exchange rate is in 3 months.

Scenario 1: Pound drops to $1.50
Result: Firm converts pounds to dollars at $1.50 and therefore receives $15 million.

Scenario 2: Pound stays at $1.80.
Result: Firm converts pounds to dollars at $1.80 and therefore receives $18 million.

Scenario 3: Pound rises to $2.10
Result: Firm converts pounds to dollars at $2.10 and therefore receives $21 million.

Final Solution: The final position viewed in American dollars is:

		Outcome	
	Scenario 1 (1.50)	*Scenario 2 ($1.80)*	*Scenario 3 ($2.10)*
Strategy (a): Futures	$18,000,000	$18,000,000	$18,000,000
Strategy (b): Option	$18,000,000	$18,000,000	$21,000,000
Strategy (c): Nothing	$15,000,000	$18,000,000	$21,000,000

Notice that futures (or forwards) contracts eliminate the risk if the foreign currency is received. Remember, however, that if the deal falls through, they the firm may end up with an unhedged futures contract loss. Under the option, the firm would not lose money if the deal fell through and it has the chance of benefiting from favorable movements. Options, however, can be expensive. Finally, doing "nothing" exposes the firm (or perhaps its shareholders) to the risk of fluctuations in the value of British pounds.

Problem 2

The 1-year risk-free interest rate in the United States is 3 percent on a particular day. The German 1 year risk-free interest rate in Euros is 9 percent. The current spot foreign exchange rate is that each Euro is worth $0.65 and therefore that each dollar is worth 1.53846 Euros. Find the forward exchange rate for 1 year from today using interest rate parity theory.

Solution to Problem 2

The solution can be found by inserting the three known values into the interest rate parity equation, Formula (18.2), and solving for the unknown fourth variable. The primary complexity is figuring out whether to use the foreign exchange rate expressed in the domestic currency or the foreign currency. In our form of the formula it is necessary to express both the spot exchange rate and the forward exchange rate in the foreign currency (i.e., in our example use 1.53846 Euros per American dollar).
Step 1: Write down Formula (18.2):

$$\frac{(1 + \text{Domestic Yield})}{(1 + \text{Foreign Yield})} = \frac{\text{Spot Exchange Rate}}{\text{Forward Exchange Rate}}$$

Step 2: Enter 3 percent as the domestic yield, 9 percent as the foreign yield, and 1.53846 as the spot foreign exchange rate:

$$1.03 / 1.09 = \$1.53846 / (\text{Forward Exchange Rate})$$

Step 3: Arrange the equation to place the unknown variable on the left side:

$$\text{Forward Exchange Rate} = 1.53846 \times (1.09/103)$$

Step 4: Solve for the forward rate:

$$\text{Forward Exchange Rate} = 1.628$$

Step 5: Convert the exchange rate to American dollars, if desired, by taking its inverse: $0.6142.
Final Solution: The forward foreign exchange rate is $0.6142, expressed as American dollars per Euro, or 1.628, expressed as Euros per American dollar. Thus, the higher foreign interest rate is fully offset by a decline in the Euros in the futures market relative to the spot market.

Review Questions

1. What is traded in the foreign exchange market?
2. Describe a "black market," and explain how it comes about.

3. Explain how an exchange rate can be used to transform one currency into another currency.
4. Explain the relevance of the law of one price in foreign exchange transactions.
5. Would we generally expect the prices of all world goods to obey the law of one price? Why or why not?
6. What is purchasing power parity, and what are its implications?
7. Explain how forward or futures contracts can eliminate foreign exchange risk through time.
8. List and explain briefly two potential problems associated with using forward or futures contracts to remove foreign exchange risk.
9. Explain how options on foreign exchange can be used to avoid the two problems with forward or futures contracts in Review Question 8. Why would a firm ever use forward or futures contracts if options exist?
10. What is interest rate parity and what are its implications?
11. Discuss systematic risk in the context of an international market portfolio.
12. Provide an example of political risk.
13. What is "nationalization" and how does it relate to political risk?
14. Describe how innovative financing can reduce political risk.
15. How do letters of credit facilitate international trade?

Problems

1. P & T Corporation is a specialty firm with a worldwide reputation for providing protection to egos. They are considering the import of equipment that costs 120,000 German marks and performs the same as a domestic model that costs $80,000.
   a. Which alternative has lower cost if the exchange rate is such that each German mark is worth $0.60?
   b. Which would be cheaper if the exchange rate were $0.70 per German mark?
   c. What would the exchange rate have to be expressed as a dollar cost per German mark in order to make the alternatives have equal cost?
   d. What would be the equivalent exchange rate from Part (c) that would express U.S. dollars in terms of German marks?
2. Use the exchange rates given in Figure 18.1 to convert the following values into U.S. dollars using the Friday columns.
   a. 140,000 Canadian dollars into U.S. dollars
   b. 340,000 Euros into U.S. dollars
   c. 804,000 Japanese yen into U.S. dollars
   d. 145,000 Swiss francs into U.S. dollars
3. Use the exchange rates given in Figure 18.1 to convert the following values from U.S. dollars into the listed currency, using the Friday columns.
   a. $123,000 into Canadian dollars
   b. $150,000 into Euros
   c. $8,000 into Japanese yen
   d. $456,000 into Swiss francs
4. If the price of an ounce of gold were $1,000, use the exchange rates listed for Friday in Figure 18.1 to find the price of gold in the following currencies. Assume perfect markets.
   a. Australian dollars
   b. British pounds

c. Euros
d. Mexican pesos
e. South African rands

5. Suppose that the price of gold in U.S. dollars is $1,000, that the exchange rate between Australian dollars and U.S. dollars is $0.75 = 1 Australian dollar, and that an ounce of gold can be purchased in Australia for 1,300 Australian dollars. Show how an investor can earn an arbitrage profit in this situation.

6. Matthew's Sports Importing Emporium Incorporated (Mat's) is considering signing contracts that will obligate the firm to purchase 100,000 Euros' worth of electronic time-keeping equipment at the end of each calendar quarter for the next 2 years. Mat's is also signing a contract with a major university system that will purchase this equipment from Mat's at a price of $75,000 (U.S.) per quarter.

a. What would Mat's profit or loss be each quarter if the exchange rate is $0.60 per Euro throughout the life of the contract?

b. What would Mat's profit or loss be if the value of the Euro rose by $0.05 per quarter starting at $0.65 in the first quarter and ending at $1.00 in the eighth quarter?

7. Returning to Mat's in Problem 6, suppose that futures markets offer the following prices for Euros at the following times to delivery:

Quarters in Future	*Futures Price of Euro*
1,2,3	$0.65
4,5,6	$0.75
7,8	$0.80

a. Compute and aggregate the profit or loss for each quarter if Mat's buys the necessary Euros through the futures market.

b. Would your answer change if the price of each futures contract fell by $0.05 before Mat's entered any contracts? Please detail.

8. Returning to Problems 6 and 7, suppose that Mat's entered the futures contracts given in the table in problem 7 and that the price of Euros immediately fell to $0.60 for all contracts and stayed there for the next 2 years.

a. What aggregate profit or loss would Mat's have for the eight quarters if Mat's entered the contracts using the prices from the table in Problem 7?

b. What aggregate profit or loss would Mat's have for the eight quarters if Mat's did not use futures contracts but instead used the actual spot rates that occurred ($0.60)?

c. Viewed at the end of the eight quarters, if Mat's entered into the futures contracts as discussed earlier, what aggregate profit or loss was caused by this effort to protect itself from currency fluctuations?

9. Drunken Sailor Oil Corporation is negotiating the purchase of 1 million barrels of oil to be delivered and paid for in exactly 1 year. Drunken Sailor Oil Corporation is willing to pay $25 per barrel because they can sell the oil in advance to oil refineries. For political reasons, the oil exporter wants the contract expressed in French francs.

a. What price per barrel of oil expressed in French francs is equivalent to $25 if the French franc exchange rate is $0.25?

b. If the contract is signed at a price of 110 French francs per barrel and the oil corporation does not use futures contracts, in terms of U.S. dollars how much will it pay for the 1 million barrels of oil if the exchange rate per French franc rises to $0.30?

c. If the oil corporation buys the French francs in the futures markets for $0.26, how much will the oil cost in U.S. dollars (if the price of the oil was 110 francs)?

10. Returning to Drunken Sailor Oil Corporation in Problem 9:

a. If the oil corporation locks in an exchange rate of $0.26 per French franc but the exchange rate falls to $0.20 at the end of the year, how much money will the firm have lost due to its decision to use futures contracts?

b. If the oil corporation locks in an exchange rate of $0.16 per French franc and the exchange rate rises to $0.25 at the end of the year, how much money will the firm have gained due to its decision to use futures contracts?

11. Returning to Problems 6–8, how could Mat's have used options contracts to hedge against adverse currency fluctuations? Please give specific times and amounts.

12. Returning to Drunken Sailor Oil Corporation in Problems 9 and 10, the firm's treasury department has suggested the purchase of an option that would enable the firm to exchange $24.75 million U.S. dollars into 110 million French francs at the end of the year. The option would cost the firm $2 million.

a. What is the exercise or striking price (exchange rate) for this option expressed as U.S. dollars per French franc?

b. Including the cost of the option, what would be the total cost of the oil in U.S. dollars if, at the end of the year, the exchange rate were $0.16 per French franc?

c. Including the cost of the option, what would be the total cost of the oil in U.S. dollars if, at the end of the year, the exchange rate were $0.23 per French franc?

d. Including the cost of the option, what would be the total cost of the oil in U.S. dollars if, at the end of the year, the exchange rate were $0.26 per French franc?

e. Including the cost of the option, how much money would the option have saved the firm if, at the end of the year, the exchange rate were $0.27 per French franc?

13. Gret Wayneski can earn 6 percent interest in Canada or 8 percent interest at a U.S. bank. Both rates are risk-free. The current values of a Canadian dollar and U.S. dollar are equal. What would the 1-year forward price of a Canadian dollar be in terms of U.S. dollars if markets were perfect?

14. Returning to Gret Wayneski in Problem 13, what would the 1-year forward price of a Canadian dollar be in terms of U.S. dollars if markets were perfect and if the interest rates were reversed (i.e., the Canadian interest rate were 8 percent and the U.S. interest rate were 6 percent)?

15. Using the interest rate parity theorem, fill in the missing values.

	Domestic Yield	*Foreign Yield*	*Spot Exchange Rate*	*Forward Exchange Rate*
a.	10%	15%	$0.50	_____
b.	18%	12%	_____	$0.25
c.	15%	_____	$0.20	$0.21
d.	_____	10%	$0.44	$0.40

16. The U.S. risk-free interest rate is 8 percent, and a portfolio that reflects the world economy has an expected return in U.S. dollars of 18 percent. The U.S. stock market has an expected return of 24 percent.

- **a.** Using the international capital asset pricing model, should a U.S. firm's beta be computed against the world economy portfolio or the U.S. economy portfolio?
- **b.** If Project Trunk, located in the United States has an "international" beta of 0.5, what required rate of return should be used (expressed as a percentage rate of U.S. dollars)?
- **c.** Assume that Project Trunk has a beta with the domestic economy of 0.8 and find the required rate of return according to the domestic CAPM (expressed as a percentage rate of U.S. dollars).

17. The British risk-free interest rate is 0 percent and a portfolio that reflects the world economy has an expected return in British pounds of 10 percent. The British stock market has an expected return of 7 percent.

- **a.** According to the international capital asset pricing model, should a British firm's beta be computed against the world economy portfolio or the British economy portfolio?
- **b.** If a British project (named Project Boot) has an "international" beta of 0.5, what required rate of return should be used (expressed as a percentage rate of British pounds)?
- **c.** Assume that Project Boot has a "domestic" beta of 1.5 and find the required rate of return according to the domestic CAPM (expressed as a percentage rate of British pounds).

18. Referring to Problems 16 and 17, for simplicity assume that the British pound and U.S. dollar now trade on a par basis (i.e., the exchange rate is 1.0).

- **a.** What would be the 1-year forward exchange rate using the risk-free interest rates in Problems 16 and 17 and the interest rate parity theorem? Express the exchange rate as the number of U.S. dollars required to purchase 1 British pound.
- **b.** Express your answer to (a) as a percentage change relative to the starting exchange rate ($1.00).

19. Use the forward exchange rate found in Problem 18(a) and the percentage change in 18(b) in answering the following questions:

- **a.** Use the change in the forward exchange rate to convert the required rate of return in U.S. dollars from Problem 16(b) into a required rate of return in British pounds by subtracting 18(b) from the answer to 16(b).
- **b.** Compare your answer in 19(a) with your answer in 17(b) and discuss.
- **c.** Use the forward exchange rate to convert the required rate of return in U.S. dollars from Problem 16(c) into a required rate of return in British pounds by subtracting 18(b) from the answer in 16(c).
- **d.** Compare your answer in 19(c) with your answer in 17(c) and discuss.

20. Based upon your answers to Problems 16–19, compare the international capital asset pricing model with domestic capital asset pricing models. It may help your analysis to assume that Projects Trunk and Boot are identical except that Project Trunk is located in the United States and Project Boot is located in England. Which model appears to be correct? What is the source of the difference?

Discussion Questions

1. Do the issues presented in this chapter on international finance change the underlying principles and concepts of modern corporate finance?
2. Some Americans receiving pensions move to less-developed countries in search of a higher standard of living. Does this refute the purchasing power parity theorem?
3. Firm Hops and Firm Barley both trade extensively with foreign countries. Firm Hops has a policy of using the futures market to lock in profits in U.S. dollars; Firm Barley has a policy not to use futures markets and to accept the risk of foreign exchange. As a shareholder, how would you evaluate the decision to invest in Firm Hops as compared with Firm Barley?
4. Return to Firm Hops and Firm Barley in Question 3. Recall that firm Hops uses the futures market to eliminate foreign exchange risk, but firm Barley does not. As a manager, how would you analyze the decision to accept a job with Firm Hops as compared with Firm Barley?
5. Scoundrel Savings and Loan invested in assets that paid out cash in foreign currencies and borrowed money using certificates of deposits that promised U.S. dollars. Scoundrel's manager, I. M. Leavin, claims to have hedged this foreign currency risk by exchanging the foreign currencies for U.S. dollars in the futures markets. In the first year, however, the futures contract lost tens of millions of dollars, and the firm's other operations only made a few million dollars of profit, according to the financial statements. Is there any explanation other than that I. M. Leavin mismanaged the firm?
6. Plastico, Inc., produces plastic exchanges used in common assembly processes. The market for these exchanges in the United States has dried up. The firm, however, has an opportunity to produce and sell their product in a foreign country that recently moved from a "planned" economy to a "market" economy. What types of added risk would the firm face if they begin operations in the foreign country? What can they do to lessen such risks?
7. The European Community (EC) combined many different currencies into a single currency. What are the advantages and disadvantages of such a move?

Discussion Questions

CHAPTER 19

MERGERS AND OTHER REORGANIZATIONS

Merger activity in the United States reached a heightened pace in the second half of the decade of the 1980s. During those years, countless financial headlines cited stories of mergers that were changing the face of American business. Of the more than 4,000 acquisitions that took place in 1988, however, none captured more attention than the takeover of RJR Nabisco, Inc., the food and tobacco conglomerate, by Kohlberg, Kravis, and Roberts (KKR). This takeover was unique because RJR Nabisco was one of the largest Fortune 500 industrial companies, with annual sales of more than $10 billion. The takeover of a company as large as RJR Nabisco, inconceivable at one time, was now a reality.

The story of RJR's takeover was fascinating: RJR's chief executive officer (CEO), F. Ross Johnson, had a key role in the ultimate sale of the company. RJR was doing well under Mr. Johnson's direction, and his success as a CEO allowed him to build a close relationship with the board of directors. In fact, this close relationship with the board led Johnson to make a critical mistake. Johnson announced a plan to lead a group of investors to take over the company. The specifics of the plan—known as a leveraged buyout (LBO)—would raise the vast sums of money needed to accomplish the buyout by issuing debt.

There were two major problems with Johnson's LBO plan. First, it was disclosed that the LBO would have made Mr. Johnson and other top managers at RJR Nabisco exorbitantly wealthy. Second, and more important, it became known that the LBO would require RJR Nabisco to scale down by selling off a major part of its existing business.

The Johnson-led LBO plan attracted other groups of investors to consider the takeover of RJR Nabisco. In cases such as these, the board of directors has the responsibility to consider all reasonable bids, and to select the bid that is in the best interest of the shareholders. The bidding process for RJR resembled that of an auction, with one group, say KKR, announcing a bid, and another group outbidding them. Of course, the higher the bid, the better off were RJR Nabisco's shareholders, as they would receive a higher price for their shares. The rounds of bids for the takeover of RJR Nabisco are summarized in the following table:

Price per Share Bid to Take Over RJR Nabisco, Inc.
(Pre-Bidding Price per Share = $56)

Group	*Round 1*	*Round 2*	*Round 3*	*Round 4*	*Round 5*
F. Ross Johnson	$ 75	$100	$101	$108	$112
KKR	$ 90	$ 94	$106	$108	$109
First Boston	****	$105	DROPPED OUT		

First Boston, which entered the bidding process in Round 2, was the first to drop out. The board of directors at RJR Nabisco concluded, at the end of Round 2, that the two remaining bids were substantially equivalent, and that other factors would be used to determine which bid to accept.

Here, KKR held the advantage. KKR announced that, as winners, they would keep the main part of the company together, would allow current shareholders the opportunity to retain partial ownership of the firm, and would agree to provide protection for the firm's employees. F. Ross Johnson's group was asked to do the same but refused. In the end, KKR was declared the winner and took control by paying to the shareholders $109 per share for stock that weeks earlier traded for $56 per share. F. Ross Johnson, the man who had landed the top spot at RJR only the year before, was replaced as CEO.[1]

This chapter will examine mergers and other forms of corporate reorganizations. The traditional view of mergers is contrasted with the modernist view. Where traditionalists tend to focus on the effect of mergers on competition and on society, modernists focus on mergers as vehicles to change the control of the firm's assets. Other types of reorganizations, such as divestitures and liquidations, will also be discussed.

The Market for Corporate Control

market for corporate control
The study of corporate reorganizations, defined as a change in the control of one or more of the firm's major assets.

Corporate reorganizations is a general term that includes mergers, divestitures, and liquidations. The study of corporate reorganizations is also known as the study of the **market for corporate control,** defined for the purposes of this chapter as a change in the control of one or more of the firm's major assets. The most common type of corporate control change could be the

1. A complete account of KKR's leveraged buyout of RJR Nabisco can be found in the book *Barbarians At The Gate: The Fall of RJR Nabisco*, by Burrough and Helyar, Harper and Row, New York, 1990.

merger
The combination of two firms into a single firm.

divestiture
The removal of part of the firm's current operations. The removal can be accomplished by the sale of assets to another firm, the setting up of a separate corporation to control the sold assets, or the liquidation of the assets.

merger, or the combination of two firms into a single firm. Corporate mergers seem to occur in waves or in periods of high activity. The mid 1990's has seen a resurgence of merger activity.

Table 19.1 reports merger and divestiture activity annually from 1993 to 1999. A **divestiture** is the removal of part of the firm's current operations. The removal can be accomplished by the sale of assets to another firm, the setting up of a separate corporation to control the sold assets, or the liquidation of the assets. Divestitures will be discussed in detail later in the chapter. Leveraged buyouts, also discussed later, are the buyout of a target firm financed through the issuance of large amounts of debt.

From just over $400 billion in 1993, merger activity experienced an eightfold increase to over $3.4 trillion in 1998. The value of merger transactions in the 1990s totaled over $10.5 trillion. Divestiture activity experienced a 320% increase between 1993 and 1999, growing from slightly over $200 billion to just under $700 billion. Leveraged buyouts grew somewhat to $58 billion in 1999. With the recent volume of reorganization experience as background, we next discuss mergers in the context of corporate finance.

Mergers and Corporate Finance

In many ways, the decision to reorganize a corporation is no different from other investment and financing decisions. In a nutshell, corporate reorganizations should be evaluated by comparing the present value of benefits with the present value of costs.

Why, then, do we discuss mergers in a separate chapter? For one, mergers generate a great deal of media coverage and public-policy debate. Govern-

TABLE 19.1 Corporate Reorganization Activity (Values in $billions)

Year	*Merger Activity Value in Billions*	*Divestiture Activity Value in Billions*	*Leveraged Buyouts Value in Billions*
1993	420	213	2
1994	525	237	11
1995	896	365	24
1996	1,059	319	17
1997	1,610	616	24
1998	2,480	555	27
1999	3,401	678	58

Source: Statistical Abstract of the United States, Table N. 882. U.S. Department of Commerce, Accounting and Statistics Administration.

mental leaders, members of the media, and business leaders appear to be captivated by mergers and other corporate reorganizations. Further, many people view corporate reorganizations as events that can have major impacts on individual firms and on the economy in general. For instance, mergers can result in the closing of a plant or in the general reduction in a firm's workforce. People perhaps believe that they should try to understand these events in order to try to influence them. In addition, finance scholars are especially interested in corporate reorganizations because they offer the equivalent of a laboratory in which to test our understanding of finance.

Whatever the reason, students of finance need to be introduced to the issues surrounding corporate reorganizations and to the special vocabulary that serves these issues.

Friendly Versus Hostile Mergers

Mergers can be friendly agreements between the board of directors representing the acquiring company and the board of directors representing the target company. In contrast to friendly agreements, boards may not agree to be combined and a hostile fight for control may ensue. In such a case, the acquiring company attempts to gain control of the target firm without the approval of the target's board of directors.

Friendly Mergers In a friendly merger, the management of the two firms agree in principle to be combined into one firm. Friendly mergers usually result from a consensus that the two firms are worth more together than the sum of the two firms held separately. This is called **synergy.** By merging, the combined firm benefits from the synergy of the merger.

synergy
The notion that two firms are worth more together than the sum of the two firms held separately.

In the case of a friendly merger, the two boards will issue a statement outlining the terms of the agreement and ask for stockholder approval. If the stockholders of the target firm agree to be acquired, then they will sign over the ownership rights of those shares to the acquiring firm. In return for their shares, the shareholders of the target firm will usually either receive cash or the common stock of the acquiring firm.

Unfriendly or Hostile Mergers In an unfriendly or hostile takeover, the acquiring firm makes an offer to buy stock directly from the shareholders of the target firm. These offers sometimes occur after friendly overtures have been rebuffed.

tender offer
An offer to buy stock directly from the shareholders of the target firm in order to gain control of the target firm.

In the context of a hostile merger, the offer to buy stock is called a **tender offer.** The objective of the tender offer is to persuade the shareholders of the target company to "tender" enough shares to the acquiring firm to enable it to take control of the company. Chances for success are greatly improved when the acquiring firm sets the price of the tender offer well above the current market price of the target firm's shares. The control of the firm is transferred when the acquiring firm accumulates enough stock to vote in a new board of directors and set a new direction for the target firm.

The management of the firm to be acquired, or target firm management, may resist a hostile takeover, due at least partly to the fact that the change in control will likely result in a replacement of current management with a new management team. The resistance to takeovers can come in many forms, ranging from a recommendation to the shareholders not to tender their shares, to antitakeover measures. **Antitakeover measures** are enacted in order to make it more difficult for a firm to be merged with another firm. Window 19.1 lists and discusses the most common antitakeover measures.

antitakeover measures Measures enacted in order to make it more difficult for a firm to be merged with another firm.

The next section will review the more traditional approach to mergers, to be followed by some modernist perspectives.

WINDOW 19.1

Common Antitakeover Measures

1. Poison Pills: Acts of target management whose purpose is to make the target firm less appealing to the acquiring firm. An example of a poison pill is the right given to the target's shareholders to buy more stock in the target firm at a bargain price. The right to buy these shares is usually contingent on the target firm losing control.

2. Golden Parachutes: Compensation to the top management of the target firm in the event that the target firm loses control. This compensation package can be of large magnitude, and is usually viewed as an attempt to make the target firm less susceptible to being taken over.

3. Scorched Earth Strategy: The sale of a profitable division or other prized assets in the target firm in order to make it less appealing to the acquiring firm.

4. Targeted Repurchases: The purchase of the shares of the target firm from the acquiring firm at a premium price. A condition of the purchase is that the potential acquirer leave the target firm intact. Targeted repurchases are also known as *greenmail.*

5. Changes in the Corporate Charter: The corporate charter contains the laws that govern the firm, and includes provisions that govern the transfer of control. The corporate charter can be changed so that a large majority, say 80 percent, of the shareholders must approve the merger. This type of change is known as a *super majority provision.* Because it is difficult for any group to acquire such a large percentage of approval, takeovers become less likely to occur.

6. Staggered Board: The classification of the board of directors into groups such that only one group is reelected each year. The acquiring firm can therefore not quickly control the board of the target even after obtaining a majority of the shares.

The Traditional View of Corporate Reorganizations

Most early analysis of mergers focused on the potential impact of merger activity in reducing competition and therefore harming the public good. Merger analysis traditionally attempted to explain why firms were being combined, and what impact the merger would have on the competitive forces of the industry.

Types of Mergers

vertical mergers
Mergers between firms in related industries but at different points in the production and distribution process.

horizontal mergers
Mergers between two firms in the same industry.

conglomerate mergers
Mergers between firms in unrelated industries.

One way to study the impact of mergers is to categorize the relationship between the two firms being merged. **Vertical mergers** are mergers between firms in related industries but at different points in the production and distribution process. For example, if a paper manufacturer merges with a publisher, the combined firm would span a larger portion of the entire process of producing printed material. These mergers were popular in the early part of this century.

In contrast, **horizontal mergers** are mergers between two firms in the same industry. The merger of two automobile manufacturers would be an example of a horizontal merger. Finally, **conglomerate mergers** are mergers between firms in unrelated industries that result in larger and more diversified firms. Conglomerate mergers were especially popular in the 1960s.

Classifying mergers in this way focuses on the tendency of horizontal and vertical mergers to reduce competition and therefore to harm the public good. For example, if a firm becomes the only firm within an industry, then it is said to be a monopoly and may be able to raise prices and profits at the expense of consumers. An industry comprised of a small number of firms is said to be an oligopoly. Oligopolies can also lessen competition and may harm consumers.

Merger Law

Given that mergers have the potential to reduce competition and harm the public good, people have acted through government in an attempt to discourage such activity. Under the goal of promoting the public good, laws have been enacted to curtail mergers that would significantly and adversely affect competition. For example, a merger that would combine the top producers in an industry such that the combined firm would control more than 50 percent of the market would not be allowed under such law. Window 19.2 details the legislation in the United States directed at merger activity that has the potential to reduce competition.

Government's role in regulating merger activity changes as administrations (i.e., as presidents) change. For example, some argue that the Reagan Administration (1981–1989) began a view that antitrust laws are a drain on the economy, and allowed most mergers to take place without government

WINDOW 19.2

Mergers and Antitrust Laws

A series of laws have been enacted in the United States to ensure that mergers do not act to "restrain trade" or monopolize activity in the market. Such laws are known as *antitrust laws.* The first antitrust law dates back to the Sherman Act of 1890, and others include the Federal Trade Commission Act of 1914 and the Clayton Act of 1914. The Clayton Act forbids the acquisition of assets that could potentially result in a significant decrease in competition, such as in creating a monopoly. Because the Clayton Act focuses on the potential for competition to be lessened, it has become the act that is most cited regarding questions of competition as a result of a merger. Under the Clayton Act, enforcement officials must show only that the probable effect of the merger will be to reduce competition.

Antitrust laws are enforced by the Justice Department's Antitrust Division. A civil suit brought by the Justice Department against an anticompetitive merger, if successful, will result in divestment. A criminal suit will result in more severe punishment. In most cases, the Justice Department will meet with firms considering a merger and will provide an opinion regarding whether legal action is likely to ensue.

A second antitrust enforcement body is the Federal Trade Commission (FTC). As a regulatory agency, its decisions are binding but can be appealed through the courts. The FTC will usually conduct investigations concerning potential mergers, and, like the Justice Department, will issue its opinion indicating the likely response to a proposed merger.

Finally, Securities and Exchange Commission (SEC) regulations attempt to promote competition through disclosure to the public of all information pertaining to the likelihood of a merger. For example, the SEC requires any investor accumulating five or more percent of another firm's common stock to disclose such information by filing a form. Other filing rules of the SEC provide additional information regarding the potential for a merger.

interference. This could partially explain why mergers move in waves, as experienced in the mid 1990's.

The Medium of Exchange in a Merger

There are numerous ways to finance a merger. The acquiring firm may purchase the shares of the acquired firm using cash. The cash may be raised from a new issue of securities by the acquiring firm or, in the case of small acquisitions, may be raised from working capital.

The acquisition is often accomplished by offering securities in the merged firm in exchange for the shares of the acquired firm. The most simple exchange of securities occurs when the shareholders of the acquired firm simply exchange their shares for new shares of common stock in the acquiring firm. A ratio of exchange is set such that shareholders of the acquired firm will receive a stated number of shares in the merged firm.

The shares of the acquired firm may sometimes be financed through a blend of cash and securities.[2] The package of securities often includes bonds or preferred stocks in addition to cash or common stock.

Motivations for Mergers—The Traditionalists' View

According to traditionalists, mergers can be motivated by factors related to anticompetition, synergy, and tax shields. After discussing these factors, we offer two irrational motivations for mergers.

Anticompetitive Reasons One reason to merge is to reduce competition and therefore reap the financial benefits of being in a less competitive industry. The typical example of this type of merger is the acquisition by one of the leading firms in an industry of one of its largest competitors. Examples include the automotive industry and the airline industry.

As discussed in Window 19.2, antitrust laws in the United States and other nations are designed to control horizontal mergers that reduce the competitive forces in the industry. It is usually argued that firms of significant size can control the market such that prices are higher and service levels are lower than would be expected in competitive markets. Enforcement of these laws, however, is less than 100 percent effective, and reduced competition is a potential motivation for mergers that cannot be dismissed entirely.

Synergistic Motivations An important economic justification for a merger clearly is synergy, which refers to the potential for the combination of two objects to be worth more than the sum of the parts. The synergy is usually expected to result from economies of scale, whereby average costs are lower in large firms than in smaller firms. Economies of scale can result from the use of more advanced or specialized equipment, from the fact that a large plant can purchase raw materials in larger quantities with larger discounts, or from the ability to operate a large plant more efficiently.

For example, a retail store or manufacturer may find that certain expenses rise more slowly at higher and higher levels of sales. Thus, it can be argued that a merger allows the combined firms to reach a higher level of production, become more cost efficient, and therefore be more valuable to the shareholders. In terms of finance, synergy therefore refers to the potential for the value of two merged firms to be greater than the sum of their values as individual firms.

It is also argued that synergy makes the firms' combined operations more efficient by eliminating certain expenses that are shared by the combined

2. For example, the takeover of RJR Nabisco by KKR for $109 per share was financed through the following package: $81 per share in cash, convertible bonds valued at $10 per share, and preferred shares valued at $18 per share.

firms. For example, if two firms being merged both have a sales force, numerous regional sales offices, and several manufacturing facilities, then it might be possible to consolidate certain overlapping facilities.

Unused Tax Shields Unused tax shields provide still another motivation for mergers. Federal income tax laws limit the ability of a firm to take advantage of losses for tax purposes unless the firm has offsetting profits elsewhere. A merger can provide a method of allowing one firm to use its losses to offset the profits and potential tax liabilities of another. Thus, again, the value of the combination of the firms would be greater than the combination of their individual values. This special type of synergy would in fact be due to a transfer of wealth from the government through reduced aggregate taxes.

Irrational Motivations The three motivating forces we just discussed are rational in that they provide a valid explanation of the sources of the gains from the merger. For example, it is rational to believe that tax laws are constructed in a manner in which some corporate actions can be more advantageous than others. Mergers, however, are sometimes attributed to factors that must be considered irrational because they cannot provide a convincing explanation of the derivation of gains. Two examples of irrational reasons for mergers are (1) diversification and (2) earnings-per-share bootstrapping.

When Sears launched a corporate strategy in the early 1980s to acquire financial service firms, it was argued that the principal motivation behind such moves was in diversifying the firm's operations. The argument was that insurance, real estate, and brokerage services would diversify the firm's earnings away from its retail operation. It was further argued that diversification would increase the value of the firm. Why, then, is diversification an irrational motivation for a merger?

The problem with diversification is that it is far more cost effective for shareholders to diversify their own portfolios by owning shares in several firms. For example, if Sears' shareholders desired to diversify into real estate, then they could have purchased shares in a real estate firm directly without the expenses of acquiring Coldwell Banker. In other words, the shareholders could have easily accomplished the benefits of diversification on their own.

Another irrational motivation for a merger is an attempt to use the merger to boost a firm's accounting earnings. For example, a firm with stagnant profits might attempt to acquire another with high earnings in the hope that the combined firm will have a higher earnings per share and therefore a higher market value to the stock.

This explanation implies that financial analysts are concerned with accounting numbers in such a simplistic fashion that they would place a higher value on the combined firms than they did in pricing the firms separately. The earnings-per-share explanation implies that shareholders will benefit, but there is no solid explanation concerning the source of their added value.

In summary, diversification and accounting games are highly questionable motivations for merger. True economic gains from mergers are more likely to result from cost reductions and other operational synergies.

Legal and Tax Aspects of Mergers

The antitrust legislation discussed in Window 19.2 is designed to discourage or prevent certain mergers from occurring, and it can become a tricky part of the mechanics of mergers.

For example, in the case of hostile takeovers, the management of a target firm may attempt to block the merger. Public announcements by target firm management often indicate that the desire to avoid a merger is attributable to potential effect of the merger on the employees, the community, or even the long-run health of the corporation itself. A more realistic explanation of managerial resistance could be concern for their own careers.

Management can use antitrust legislation as a shield against hostile mergers by engaging in a business that is closely regulated. For example, a large manufacturing concern, such as a major producer of copying machines, may acquire a closely regulated firm, such as an insurance business, so that government approval will be required for the combined firm to be acquired. The management can then enlist the aid of politicians who serve the corporation's community to prevent a hostile takeover.

Shifting to taxes, there are two levels of tax concerns in relation to mergers: corporate income taxes and personal income taxes. As we have discussed, corporate income tax laws serve as a potential motivation for mergers because losses of one firm can be used to offset taxable profits of another firm when they merge.

On the other hand, highly progressive income tax structures can discourage mergers, since larger firms tend to have higher profits, which are taxed at higher rates in a progressive tax system. The U.S. corporate tax rates, however, are reached at such a low level of income that most U.S. corporations pay tax at virtually the same rate.

There are also personal income tax implications to mergers. When a firm is acquired, it is possible that the acquired (target) firm's shareholders will have to pay personal income taxes on the proceeds from selling their shares. Structuring the deal such that the merger does not cause a taxable exchange is a frequent solution to this potential tax liability.

The Modernists' View of Mergers

Modernists do not view mergers as attempts to gain efficiency, but as battles for the control of the corporation's assets. Whereas efficiency gains fall in the category of rational motivations, the same efficiencies can be gained without the expenses associated with mergers. For instance, economies of scale can be achieved through the formation of joint ventures.

joint ventures
The combination of resources through a partnership arrangement rather than through a legal combination of the acquiring and target firm.

Joint ventures are similar to mergers in that resources are combined, but they differ in that they achieve this combination through a partnership arrangement rather than through a legal combination of the acquiring and target firm. Further, joint ventures do not result in complete changes in managerial control.

Examples of joint ventures include the partnership between Toyota and General Motors, in which an idle GM plant in California was set up to produce Toyota cars, and the agreement between IBM, Motorola, and Apple to produce RISC chips. Firms can also cooperate through licensing arrangements, as did IBM and Apple Computer, who found that both sides benefit by allowing their computers to use similar software.

Because most of the advantages of merger activity could be accomplished with joint ventures, which would avoid the cost of mergers, modernists look to reasons beyond efficiency to explain mergers. Modernists believe that mergers can be explained by (1) managers attempting to advance their careers, and (2) shareholders attempting to gain from replacement of an inefficient management team.

Mergers Motivated by Managers

In a perfect world, it might be expected that managers would perform their jobs exactly as directed by shareholders. In other words, managers would maximize shareholder wealth and in so doing would benefit by being regarded as excellent performers. In the real world, however, it is difficult for shareholders of a widely held public corporation to understand fully the performance of their managers, to reward their managers in proportion to their performance, or to select new managers based upon their past performance.

As a practical matter, therefore, corporate managers of widely held corporations have an incentive—and are often permitted—to seek objectives significantly different from shareholder wealth maximization. This subject is studied in conjunction with agency theory and has been discussed at various points in the earlier chapters of the book. It is important to remember, for this discussion, that managers of a widely held corporation may be viewed as having been entrusted with the assets of a major firm, which they will often operate in order to benefit themselves even at the cost of harming the shareholders they serve.

There is an obvious motivation for managers to want "their" firm to acquire other firms. Because the management team of the acquiring firm usually manages the target firm, the merger serves as a type of promotion as job responsibilities are enlarged. Managers of merged firms often enjoy higher compensation, greater prestige, greater power, and the satisfaction of moving up the corporate ladder.

On the other side of the merger transaction, the management teams of target firms usually lose prestige and power in the battle for control. If the merger was hostile, the acquired managers can at best usually hope for a golden parachute that will provide financial benefits but will not provide traditional career advancement. If the merger was friendly, there is a greater chance that target firm managers will remain in their jobs or be offered an especially good compensation package or golden parachute.

In the battle for corporate control, managers of widely held firms battle to be the acquirer and to avoid being the acquired firm. A management team often recognizes that a company's acquisition is inevitable and begins looking for the best deal. The mergers that result are often friendly takeovers in which the management teams divide up the spoils of the merger. In other words, the economic benefits are often shared by the acquiring and acquired management teams, and not necessarily by the shareholders of the respective firms.

Mergers Motivated by Owners

Some mergers are motivated by an attempt by the shareholders of a closely held firm to acquire the assets of a widely held firm. The motivation for the merger is to gain control of the inefficiently operated firm (the target firm) from its shareholders so that the inefficient management team can be replaced. The acquiring firm hopes to buy the firm at a price that has become depressed, to replace the inefficient management team, and make other changes such that the benefits of the merger will exceed the cost.

The Leveraged Buyout by Outsiders In the opening of this chapter we discussed a situation in which a small group of investors, represented by the firm Kohlberg, Kravis, and Roberts, sought and eventually won control of RJR Nabisco, one of the largest Fortune 500 firms. How were they able to accomplish such a task? The answer is that they raised a large amount of money by issuing new debt, and used the proceeds from the debt issue to buy RJR Nabisco's common stock. The stock was then retired, making RJR Nabisco a privately held corporation rather than one publicly held. Because "going private" is accomplished through the use of debt, such a transaction has become known as a **leveraged buyout** (an LBO).

leveraged buyout
The buyout of a target firm financed with money raised through the issuance of large amounts of debt; sometimes referred to as a levered buyout. The proceeds from the debt issue are used to purchase the target firm's common stock, whereby the target firm is no longer a publicly held corporation, but rather becomes a privately held firm.

Financial leverage was discussed in Chapter 11 as a way to manipulate risk through the use of debt. In a sense, LBOs are extremely risky transactions because the new private firm must generate enough cash flow to pay significant amounts of debt interest payments. Of course, if the private firm is managed efficiently and effectively, the leverage works to the advantage of the new shareholders, inasmuch as the residual cash flow that remains gets shared by a small group.

The LBO will also create additional tax shields that originate from the interest paid on the new debt. As shown by Modigliani and Miller and discussed in Chapter 12, tax shields have the potential of increasing firm value. Recall, however, that the tax benefits enjoyed by debt at the corporate level can potentially be offset or even eliminated at the personal tax level.

Whether or not tax shields provide an incentive for LBO transactions therefore depends, at least partly, on this unresolved debate regarding tax shields and their effect on firm value.

Finally, many people question whether LBOs have been a success, which is a difficult question to answer for at least two reasons. First, part of the success of the LBO depends on factors outside of management's control. LBOs tend to be successful in a growing economy, but they tend not to be successful in recessionary economies. Second, it is difficult to assess the health of the private firm, given that its stock price can no longer be observed.

The Leveraged Buyout by Insiders Management teams that are operating inefficiently sometimes recognize that, with the proper incentives, they could manage the firm in a manner that would significantly increase its value. The managers are willing to make these extremely difficult changes only if they can be the primary beneficiaries of the enhanced value. In an effort to exploit these opportunities, the managers can attempt to perform an LBO on their own firm.

The basic characteristics of the insider-initiated LBO are the same as those initiated by outsiders. The management-led team raises large amounts of money through new debt, and uses the proceeds from the debt to purchase the firm's publicly traded shares. The success of the insider-led LBO depends on the ability of the management team to use the incentives of the LBO to increase firm value.

Mergers and Changes in Shareholder Wealth

Numerous empirical studies have been performed that attempt to determine how shareholders have been affected by mergers. These studies shed light on the modernists' view of mergers motivated by owners. This subsection summarizes some of the empirical evidence.

Target-Firm Shareholders Most studies that examine the merger's effect on shareholders agree that target-firm shareholders gain when the merger is announced. The gain is largest when the merger involves an unfriendly attempt by the acquirer to gain control, but is also large for friendly mergers. These results are summarized in Table 19.2.

The percentages listed in Table 19.2 represent "abnormal" returns earned by the shareholders. Abnormal returns are measured as the actual return minus the expected return. In other words, abnormal returns are those returns earned above and beyond what was reasonable to expect given the risk of the firm. The extremely large abnormal returns in Table 19.2 make it quite clear that the shareholders of the target firm benefit upon the announcement of the merger.

Do the abnormal returns shown in Table 19.2 prove that mergers are motivated by attempts to remove managers of poorly run firms? Maybe. This conclusion, however, assumes that these abnormal returns derive from the

TABLE 19.2 The Effect of Merger Announcements on Target Firm Shareholders

	Abnormal Stock Price Returns Around Merger Announcements (target shareholders)
Tender Offer (unfriendly)	39%
Merger (friendly)	27%

Source: "The Market For Corporate Control: A Review of the Evidence," in Peter Dodd, *The Revolution in Corporate Finance,* ed. Joel Stern and Donald Chew (1992: New York: Basil Blackwell). Reprinted by permission of Blackwell Publishers.

expectation that the acquiring group will improve upon the operation of the target firm.

Another explanation of the results in Table 19.2 is that the abnormal returns are wealth transfers from another group. For instance, the gain to the shareholders of the target firm might not come from improved performance expected after the merger; rather, it could come from the pockets of the shareholders of the acquiring firm. This could occur if the acquiring firm pays too much for the right to control the assets of the target firm, which we will examine next.

Acquiring-Firm Shareholders Most merger studies show that gains to shareholders of acquiring firms are not nearly as large as gains to target shareholders. In fact, many studies show that acquiring-firm shareholders do not gain at all at the time of the merger announcement. These results are shown in Table 19.3. They indicate that the shareholders of the acquiring firms receive small negative abnormal returns at the time of the merger announcement. The abnormal returns, however, are so small that they can be considered to be zero in a statistical sense.

Looking at the results of both Table 19.2 and 19.3, mergers appear on net to be value enhancing. On average, mergers increase the value to the shareholders of target firms while not significantly reducing the value to the shareholders of acquiring firms. This supports the modernist view that mergers are a technique to remove inefficient managers from control.

Do the Tables Tell the Entire Story?

Although the combined results in Tables 19.2 and 19.3 suggest that mergers are value enhancing, it is possible that the gain in value comes from other groups; not from the removal of target firm managers. For instance, it is possible that the gains to target shareholders come from the bondholders of the target firm, or from the federal government in the form of tax shields. Finally, the gains could also be transfers from other groups, such as employee

TABLE 19.3 The Effect of Merger Announcements on Acquiring Firm Shareholders

	Abnormal Stock Price Returns Around Merger Announcements (acquiring shareholders)
Tender Offer (unfriendly)	−1%
Merger (friendly)	−1%

Source: "The Market For Corporate Control: A Review of the Evidence," in Peter Dodd, *The Revolution in Corporate Finance,* ed. Joel Stern and Donald Chew (1992: New York: Basil Blackwell). Reprinted by permission of Blackwell Publishers.

unions—if the merger will break a lucrative union contract—from pension holders, or even from plaintiffs in a pending lawsuit.

Some empirical studies have examined these issues and have been unable to develop support for a specific source of the value transfer. Thus, although the issue has not been completely resolved, the modernist viewpoint has survived a great deal of empirical scrutiny.

The Ethics of Corporate Takeovers

Modernists view corporate reorganizations in general and merger activity in particular as inevitable activities within a free market. These battles occur so that assets can be put to their best use. Winning corporate control is one method by which shareholders replace inefficient management and take advantage of synergistic opportunities.

There are, however, several groups that attempt to enter the battle and disrupt this process. These other groups, known as stakeholders, argue that they are affected by, and therefore have a stake in, the outcome of the battle for control. Because the shareholders have direct legal ownership of the corporations, these stakeholders attempt to use government to interfere with the rights of shareholders to control their own company.

Management, labor unions, local citizens, and local politicians attempt to use government control to block corporate reorganizations that they perceive have undesirable consequences. A good example of this is the antitakeover law passed in 1990 in the state of Pennsylvania, which created penalties on firms that attempted to take over a Pennsylvania-based company. Research estimates that Pennsylvania Senate Bill 1310 caused a large loss to shareholders of Pennsylvania firms. The long-term consequences of government control have been shown time and time again to be detrimental to society.

Entrenched and inefficient management, as well as the board of directors, will often utilize the resources of the firm in an attempt to prevent these reorganizations under the rallying cry that the reorganization is bad for the firm's long-term future. Managers and directors, however, have fiduciary responsibilities requiring them to make decisions that benefit the people who have hired them—the shareholders. Corporate reorganization battles, therefore, are increasingly being fought in courtrooms and through government legislation.

The modernist view is that government interference in the battle for corporate control weakens the economy and reduces the competitiveness of the country in the global marketplace.

A Modernists' Fairy Tale

Once upon a time, there was a highly regarded manufacturer of food products nestled in Pennsylvania. The company had been run for years by the family that had established the firm in 1914 as Stoltzfus's Foods and had worked hard to maintain the quality and efficiency that were the hallmark of its reputation.

In the early 1960s, the firm went public and changed its name to Good Old Boys, Inc. (GOB, Inc.). In other words, the family sold the vast majority of its ownership through a public offering of common stock. GOB, Inc. became a widely held public corporation with thousands of shareholders. The family stepped down from managing the firm and was replaced by a new management team of highly educated professionals.

In 1964, GOB, Inc. was rich with cash from the continued success of its food products, which enjoyed a tremendous reputation and an extremely loyal following during its 50-year history. Starting in 1964, and continuing though the late 1960s and 1970s, the firm gobbled up other firms in a frenzy of highly priced acquisitions under the guidance of its new management team.

The market price of the common stock of GOB, Inc. unfortunately, performed rather dismally during and after its enormous merger activity. Financial analysts complained that the company was poorly managed; however, management generally did not feel it needed to respond to financial analysts or even shareholders, for that matter. Management cited costly and cumbersome union contracts and dynamic global factors as reasons for past problems, but it offered optimistic assessments of the long-term effects of its latest strategic changes.

Some shareholders noticed that, each year, certain unprofitable divisions were sold to enable the purchase or development of new and more promising divisions. It appeared, however, that each new division ended up as one of the unprofitable divisions that later needed to be sold.

Shareholders of GOB, Inc. expressed displeasure with the stock's performance at the annual shareholder's meetings, but they were unable to effect changes. Shareholders who attempted to pass resolutions in opposition to the managers' decisions were strongly rebuffed by management, which utilized its ability to make virtually unlimited mailings of its viewpoint to its shareholders.

GOB's management defended its enormous salaries, citing the size of the firm and the salaries of managers of other similarly sized firms. Management complained that financial markets, driven by financial institutions, were attempting to pressure the firm into shortsighted decisions that would destroy the firm's long-run health.

Finally, in 1992, a small consulting firm, backed with millions of dollars of capital obtained from high-risk debt issues, launched a bid to acquire the firm. Management fought diligently to save the firm and enlisted the help of state and federal politicians to block the right of GOB's shareholders to sell it. In fact, Pennsylvania had even passed a law restricting the rights of shareholders to sell their firms.

In the end, top managers were promised spectacular financial packages if they would stop fighting the merger—and they finally approved, stating publicly that it was inevitable and that the agreement would minimize the negative impact of the merger on the communities involved. The politicians even seemed to approve of the final merger agreement—especially those raising campaign funds.

In retrospect, the change in corporate control saved the firm. The successful product lines were retained, and those product lines that had no competitive advantage were spun off or sold outright. Although the firm that survived was much smaller and operated with a far smaller labor force, it seemed obvious that the alternative to the smaller, better managed firm was no firm at all. With the new owner/managers in charge, it seemed as though everyone would live happily ever after.

Divestitures and Liquidations

Although we emphasize mergers in this chapter, other forms of corporate reorganizations include divestitures and liquidations. A *divestiture* is defined as the sale of assets from a firm, and thus can be considered the antithesis of a merger. A firm may divest itself of an asset by selling it directly or by spinning the asset off as a separate corporation. For example, a bank, utility, or other highly regulated corporation may find it advantageous to remove the nonregulated portion of the business from the highly regulated parent corporation. The shares in the newly formed corporation can be sold by the parent firm or sent directly to its shareholders in the form of a dividend.

Divestitures can also result from the perception that a certain segment of a corporation's business no longer fits. This is especially true for firms that have gone through a conglomerate merger strategy and found, in hindsight, that certain divisions have not been adding to the value of the firm, but have been instead detracting from firm value. This type of divestiture may also lead to a management buyout, whereby the managers of the sold division purchase the division themselves, and reorganize the division as its own firm.

liquidation
The selling of some or all of the assets.

A liquidation will occur if the assets that the firm chooses to divest are worth more dead than alive. In a **liquidation**, the firm sells some or all of its assets and distributes the cash to the firm's claimants. In a *voluntary* liquidation, the cash usually goes to the shareholders. If the firm liquidates assets as part of bankruptcy proceedings, the cash usually goes to the bondholders and other creditors. In the latter case, the rules concerning how the assets are to be liquidated come under the general heading of bankruptcy, and were discussed in Window 11.2.

Summary

- Mergers are one type of corporate reorganization. Other types of corporate reorganization include divestitures, liquidations, and bankruptcy.
- Throughout modern economic history, mergers have tended to occur in waves and have been the subject of public policy debate and legislation. Merger waves have tended to be differentiated by types of mergers such as vertical, horizontal, and conglomerate.
- Mergers also differ by whether the acquired management approves of the merger (a friendly merger) or fights the merger (a hostile takeover). The financing of the mergers also differs.
- In the mid-to-late 1980s there was a wave of merger activity financed by the use of large amounts of debt. These mergers included leveraged buyouts, in which the money used to buy the shares of the publicly traded corporation comes from newly issued debt.
- There are several important motivations for mergers, including the replacement of inefficient management and the synergies of combining assets and operations. There are also several motivations offered for mergers that fail to survive deductive scrutiny. Among these questionable motivations for mergers are diversification and manipulation of accounting data.
- The clearest understanding of mergers could result from the application of agency theory. Within this modernist view, mergers are viewed as battles for corporate control: Managers are assumed to have interests that differ from the shareholders. Many mergers can be viewed as the acquisition of an inefficiently operated firm, with entrenched management and widely dispersed shareholders, by a more closely held corporation. The evidence on mergers and the effects on shareholder wealth supports this view. Other mergers can be viewed as the acquisition of one widely held firm by another widely held firm, without regard to the effect on shareholder wealth.

Demonstration Problems

Problem 1

A foreign airline has offered to acquire a major U.S. airline at a huge premium relative to the price at which the airline's stock is currently trading. Discuss this potential merger from the traditionalist viewpoint.

Solution to Problem 1

There might be several factors that would motivate such a merger, but first we must consider the potential impact on the air traveler in particular and the nation's economy in general.

If the U.S. airline and the foreign airline now serve similar markets, then this merger might reduce competition and cause higher air fares. Even if the airlines have complementary markets, however, the United States could suffer from having more and more of its airline industry owned and controlled by foreign corporations. Thus, the merger plans need to be modified or scrapped entirely if the interests of consumers or the nation as a whole could be seriously and adversely affected.

Next, let us examine the merger from an investor's perspective. We need to examine why the merger has been proposed and what the potential benefits and costs are to the firms involved. For example, the merger might be very healthy for each of the companies if it would permit easier connecting schedules, shared ticketing and maintenance facilities, and so forth. These "synergies" are operational because they improve the performance ability of the firm's operations and offer cost savings.

From a financial perspective, the merger might provide the U.S. airline with better access to financing from European sources (or vice versa) and might bolster the airline's dismal income statement and balance sheet. The merger would also make sense if it allowed the U.S. corporation to take advantage of the tax losses that are now going unused. Finally, it might make sense from a diversification perspective because the merged firms would be less vulnerable to huge losses from regional problems, such as reduced air travel or increased competition.

In summary, there can be real advantages to allowing firms to merge when the obvious benefits of such mergers can be passed on to society in general or at least will not harm society. When mergers create monopolistic power groups (or oligopolies), however, it is necessary for government to intervene and ensure through legislation that competition will continue.

Problem 2

Now discuss this potential merger from a modernist perspective.

Solution to Problem 2

It is not necessary to worry about the long-run impact of this merger on the air traveler or the overall United States. As long as governments stay out of it, competition will eventually provide air travelers with the services they desire at a price consistent with providing the services. Time and time again, it is shown that government control and interference hurts the economy in the long run rather than helping it. We should allow free competition and trade regardless because it is the shareholders' firm and it is up to them if they want to sell it.

What is interesting about this merger is the motives of the people. Why is the management of the foreign airline anxious to buy that particular domestic carrier? What are the motivations of the managers and shareholders of the U.S. airline facing acquisition?

The idea of cost-saving operational synergies or better financial capabilities is just a "smoke screen." The firms can form joint ventures without the merger in order to exploit operational synergies—many firms have already formed such "partnerships." In terms of financial statements, Wall Street investors are not easily fooled by simply combining them. Whatever the airlines can accomplish as merged firms can be accomplished as independent firms.

Why have the managers of the foreign airline sought control of another firm? If their shareholders desired ownership of the U.S. airline, they were free to purchase shares in the airline by themselves, and they could have done so at a price much lower than the merger costs. The managers could be building their egos (and their salaries) by trying to create an "empire," or the managers of the foreign airline could realize how incompetent these American managers are, and they know that by purchasing the airline they can dramatically improve its performance.

It is clear that the shareholders of the U.S. airline can simply "vote" with their shares. The shareholders are probably anxious to sell their shares to the foreign airline and reap the tremendous gain.

Perhaps the most telling indication is the response of the management of the U.S. airline to the proposal. If these managers fight the merger, then regardless of what they say it seems clear that they are the incompetent managers who are worried more about their careers than the shareholders that hired them. If the American managers support the merger (at the best possible price), then it seems clear that it is the foreign firm whose managers have motives that are suspect.

Review Questions

1. What is the difference between a merger and a divestiture?
2. A firm that makes computers merges with a firm that designs computer software. Is this a vertical, horizontal, or conglomerate merger?
3. What is the purpose of antitrust legislation?
4. Are all mergers friendly agreements? Explain.
5. What is synergy, and how does synergy relate to mergers?
6. What is a tender offer, and how is it used as a merger strategy?
7. List and describe at least three antitakeover measures.
8. Explain how unused tax shields can provide a motivation for mergers.
9. Why is diversification considered an irrational motivation for mergers?
10. How does a joint venture differ from a merger?
11. Use agency costs to explain the modernist view of mergers as motivated by managers.
12. What is a levered buyout (an LBO)?
13. Do shareholders of target firms gain at the time of the merger announcement? How about shareholders of acquiring firms? Why?

Discussion Questions

1. Chapter 1 introduced the law of conservation of value, which states that the market value of a combination of assets must be equal to the sum of the market values of all the assets held in isolation. Given this law, how can we explain merger activities?
2. Antitrust legislation is designed to promote market competitiveness. Assume that you work for the Justice Department and are given the responsibility of

deciding whether or not a particular merger should take place. What criteria would you use to determine the effect of the merger on competition?

3. Synergy was discussed as a rational or valid reason to merge. Make a list of industries that you believe would be prime candidates for "synergy-related" mergers. Now make a list of industries that you believe would not be good candidates for "synergy-related" mergers. Explain.
4. A manager was quoted as saying, "Our company's recent LBO has really changed things around here. We seem to be 'watching our pennies' like never before." Why would an LBO result in a firm's having to "watch its pennies"? Is this good or bad? Explain.
5. The chairman of the Federal Reserve went before a congressional committee to argue that allowing banks to diversify out of their traditional lines of business by merging with other types of financial service firms (insurance, real estate, investment banking) would result in a less risky banking industry. Would this be a valid reason for bank mergers? Why or why not?
6. In 1990, the state of Pennsylvania passed an act that essentially insulated corporations headquartered in Pennsylvania from being taken over. Who is the winner as a result of such legislation? Who is the loser?

CHAPTER 20

FINANCIAL ENGINEERING

Try-N-Save Food Stores, a supermarket chain, announced a new corporate strategy of competing with some of its largest competitors. The strategy called for construction of bigger facilities and thus required large amounts of new debt capital. Given the relationship between the balance sheet and the income statement, the firm's capital costs under the new strategy will be dominated by interest expense on existing and new debt.

Try-N-Save's financing strategy was to use primarily long-term debt. The firm's management was adamant about locking in fixed interest expense over long periods of time, in order to stabilize profits. Short-term debt usually offered a lower interest rate and the firm's ability to obtain short-term financing was excellent. Management, however, was willing to pay higher long-term rates to remove the risk of rising interest expense if short-term interest rates went higher.

Most members of the board of directors were surprised when the firm's bright young CFO spoke of an idea that could provide both the benefits of locking in long-term rates and short-term prices. Major banks from New York City were offering what were known as "swap" agreements. These vehicles allowed a firm like Try-N-Save to switch a variable (or short-term) rate expense for a fixed (or long-term) rate expense. Thus, the firm could obtain short-term financing and then "swap" the variable cost of the debt for a fixed-debt cost.

Over the years, Try-N-Save's CFO began to understand more and more about swaps and other products, generally called *derivatives*. As interest rates rose and fell, the CFO seemed to be developing a knack for timing the swap and derivative contracts. In fact, as the years went by, the CFO began to take larger and larger derivative positions and was able to make more and more money. The derivative positions increasingly had nothing to do with managing the interest rate expense of the firm—they were undertaken to speculate on future movements in interest rates.

All was going well when a large and sudden interest rate change occurred. The results were disastrous for Try-N-Save's derivative positions. The new interest rates caused tens of millions of dollars of losses—more than wiping out all of the profits on previous derivatives trades and jeopardizing the liquidity and viability of the firm's core supermarket business. At first the CFO tried to cover up the losses—taking even larger positions in the hope that the interest rates would reverse and the losses be recouped. The losses only increased, however, until all derivative positions had to be liquidated at a huge loss.

It took years to complete all of the investigations and litigation surrounding the derivatives trading. The CFO was replaced, several board members resigned, and employees throughout the organization suffered. Despite their many potential benefits, derivatives were never used again at Try-N-Save.

The derivatives used by Try-N-Save's CFO obviously provided opportunities for spectacular gains—as well as for spectacular losses. The term *financial engineering* refers to vehicles (such as those derivatives) and to the theory underlying their use, which have arisen in finance in the attempt to find ever-more-sophisticated solutions to managing risk. To some, the very words *financial engineering* may seem confusing. They may ask, what is there in finance that can be engineered? The answer, as you'll see in this chapter, is quite a lot.

An Overview of Financial Engineering

As we learned in Chapter 1, finance can be defined as *applied economics*—a field of knowledge where real-world decisions that include the passage of time and risk are addressed. The term *engineering* originated from the application of the science of physics to real-world or useful purposes, such as building a bridge. People extend the term *engineering* to describe any process in which knowledge is used to solve practical problems. Thus, the term *financial engineering* is somewhat redundant and could be used to describe any application within finance. Nevertheless, in the field of finance, financial engineering has come to be known as a specific approach to identifying and controlling risk. **Financial engineering** focuses on the development and control of risk exposures using graphs or profiles. Options and other derivatives play a central role in financial engineering.

financial engineering
Financial activity that focuses on the control of environmental risk exposures using options and other derivatives.

Environmental Risk and Core Business Risk

Financial engineers often divide corporate business risk into two categories: environmental risk and core business risk. **Environmental risk** refers to the risk that results from events outside the control of the firm and its management. An example of environmental risk would be the change in the market price of a firm's major raw material. In contrast, **core business risk** is risk caused by events over which the firm has some level of control. Examples of core business risk include cost overruns and marketing failures. The distinction between core business risk and environmental risk is more than just managerial control. A core business risk tends to be unique to the firm or at least unrelated to a market price. An environmental risk tends to be related to a specific market price that extends beyond the firm, and would affect many firms in the same industry. Let us look at a concrete example:

environmental risk
The risk that results from events outside the control of the firm and its management, such as a change in the market price of a firm's major raw material.

core business risk
The risk, caused by events over which the firm has some level of control, that tends to be unique to the firm or unrelated to a market price.

Example 20.1 HiHo Silver Corporation supplies silver-plated electronic components to the automotive industry. It has developed long-term relationships with several parts manufacturers. The firm's primary source of sales is contracts negotiated annually. For example, their largest current contract calls for the delivery of 1.2 million silver-plated engine knockers per month, at a price guaranteed for a full year by a contract that is negotiated each June.

The current direct cost of producing each engine knocker is about \$3 and consists of about \$1 of labor, \$0.50 in silver, and \$1.50 in other materials. Because the firm sells the engine knockers for about \$5 each, the firm has \$2 per engine knocker to cover the other expenses of the firm (utilities, taxes, administration, etc.) and to contribute to the costs of the firm's capital (bond interest and shareholder profits).

Even though the labor charges and the costs for other materials have been stable and seem likely to remain stable, the price of silver has not. In fact, over the last 25 years, the firm has seen market prices of silver range between \$50 and \$3 per ounce. Because each engine knocker uses 0.1 ounces of silver and because the price of silver when the current contract was signed was around \$5 per ounce, the cost of silver for each unit was estimated at \$0.50; however, if the firm is forced to pay, say, \$20 per ounce for silver, all profits would be wiped out because its contracts require the firm to deliver massive quantities of the engine knockers at only \$5 per unit.

Besides changes in the price of silver, the firm faces risks such as labor strikes, failure to win new contracts, inefficient production due to poor management, and so forth. These risks should be within the control or influence of the management and so are usually considered core business risks. Because HiHo exerts no power over the market price of silver, however, it would be an example of environmental risk. Financial engineering focuses on the types of risks that can be linked to fluctuations in specific market prices (i.e., in environmental risks).

In summary, financial engineers focus on the environmental risks that a firm faces. They seek to understand and control the impact of fluctuations in key market prices on the shareholders of the firm's wealth (i.e., on the market value of the firm's equity).

Risk Exposure Profiles

risk exposure profiles Graphical or tabular expressions of the relationship between the financial health of a firm and a key market price or rate; the main tool used in financial engineering. This is sometimes called *risk profiles* or *exposure files.*

Risk exposure profiles are the financial engineer's main tool in understanding environmental risks and in engineering solutions to those risks. Sometimes called *risk profiles* or *exposure files*, **risk exposure profiles** express the relationship between the financial health of a firm and a key market price or rate. They often are presented as graphs, with changes in the market value of the firm on the vertical axis and changes in a key market price or rate on the horizontal axis. Figure 20.1 is a risk exposure profile showing the relationship of the firm's equity value (i.e., its stock price) to a key market price of a major raw material. In the figure, note that when the price of the raw material

FIGURE 20.1 Risk Exposure Profile Example

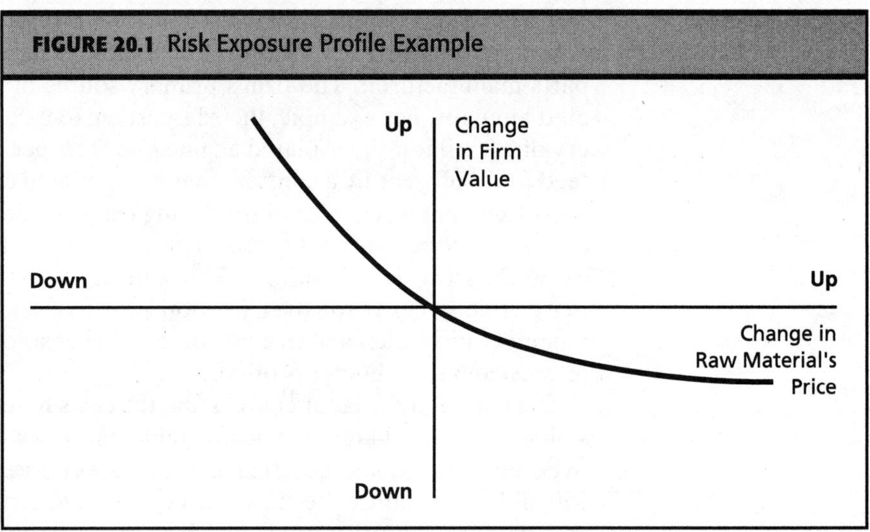

reaches a particular level the firm's equity stops being sensitive to additional price increases. Why? Because at a high enough price, the firm could switch to an alternative raw material (whose price we assume as fixed). Let us apply this idea to our example of HiHo Silver Corporation and the risk of changes in the price of silver.

Example 20.2 HiHo Corporation's CFO has constructed a list of the firm's contracts. This list indicates that the firm has committed to selling a total of 40 million units of silver-plated electronic components over the next 12 months. Because the price of silver has been stable at $5 per ounce, the impact of a sudden, long-term change in the price of silver will have a dramatic effect on the value of existing contracts. This risk exposure profile is shown in Table 20.1. The data

TABLE 20.1 Risk Exposure Profile for HiHo Silver Corporation

Change in Silver Price	*Impact on Firm Value*
−$ 3	+$12,000,000
−$ 2	+$ 8,000,000
−$ 1	+$ 4,000,000
$ 0	$ 0
+$ 1	−$ 4,000,000
+$ 2	−$ 8,000,000
+$ 3	−$12,000,000
+$ 4	−$16,000,000
+$ 5	−$20,000,000
+$10	−$40,000,000

FIGURE 20.2 Risk Exposure Profile—HiHo Silver Corp

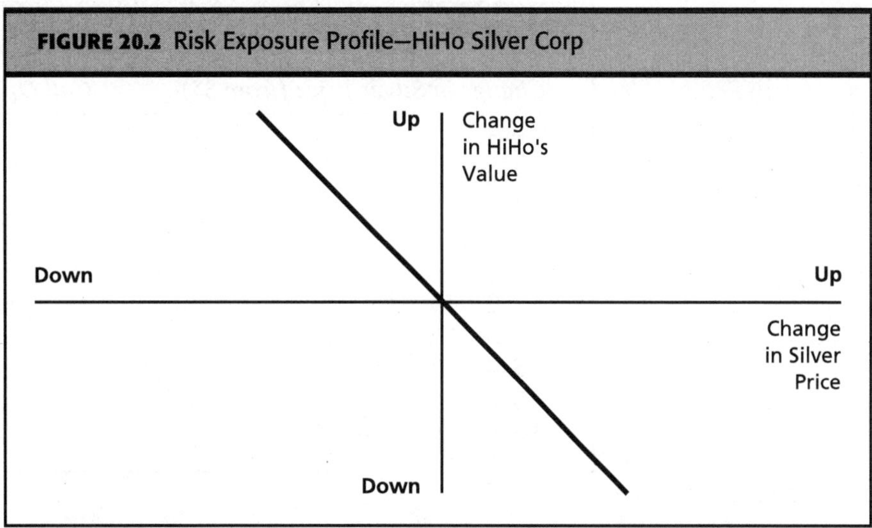

in the table are found by multiplying the changes in the silver price times the number of ounces (0.1) per unit times the number of units and subtracting the product from $0.

The risk exposure profile can be graphed as illustrated in Figure 20.2. This risk exposure profile captures in a single picture the risk that the firm faces from changes in the price of silver.

Combining Risk Exposure Profiles: An Introduction

derivatives
Financial securities whose values derive from the value of an underlying asset; used in financial engineering to hedge environmental risk exposures.

Understanding the risk faced by a firm and expressing that risk in a risk exposure profile are steps that help the financial engineer define the problem. The goal, then, is to find a way to control the risk. The solution can often be found with **derivatives,** securities whose values derive from the value of an underlying asset. The financial engineer identifies a group of derivative securities whose price is also related to the key market price. From these derivatives the financial engineer selects one or more derivatives that, when combined with the firm's current risk exposure profile, will produce a superior risk exposure profile. In this section, we will present a general introduction to this process. We will explain it in greater detail later in the chapter.

Example 20.3 ________ Management of HiHo Silver Corporation has studied the risk exposure profiles in Table 20.1 and Figure 20.2 and is convinced that the risk from rising silver prices is greater than they want to bear. The firm has therefore asked a member of the finance staff who understands financial engineering to design a plan to reduce the firm's exposure.

Numerous alternatives are studied, and the firm decides to use a *call option* to reduce the risk of a rise in the price of silver. Call options, which were discussed in Chapter 10, are financial contracts that allow the holder to purchase a

TABLE 20.2 HiHo's Profit and Losses from Purchasing Call Options on Silver

Change in Silver Price (from $5)	*Call Option Profit and Loss*
−$ 3	−$ 1,000,000
−$ 2	−$ 1,000,000
−$ 1	−$ 1,000,000
$ 0	−$ 1,000,000
+$ 1	−$ 1,000,000
+$ 2	+$ 3,000,000
+$ 3	+$ 7,000,000
+$ 4	+$11,000,000
+$ 5	+$15,000,000
+$10	+$35,000,000

given item at a specified price on or before its expiration date. In this example, HiHo Silver Corporation could purchase a call option on 4 million ounces of silver at $6 per ounce. The cost of the option is $1 million. Possible profits and losses from the call option relative to the price of silver are shown in Table 20.2.

Losses on the call option position can go no higher than the option's $1 million purchase price. This loss would be incurred if the price of silver remains at or below $6 per ounce. In that case, the option expires worthless. Profits on the call option would occur if the price of silver rises above $6 per ounce. To be specific, the profit on the call option will be equal to 4 million ounces times $1 per ounce by which the price of silver rises above the $6 strike price minus the $1 million purchase price. Figure 20.3 expresses the profit or loss relationship for this call option in graphical form.

FIGURE 20.3 Risk Exposure Profile for Silver Call Option

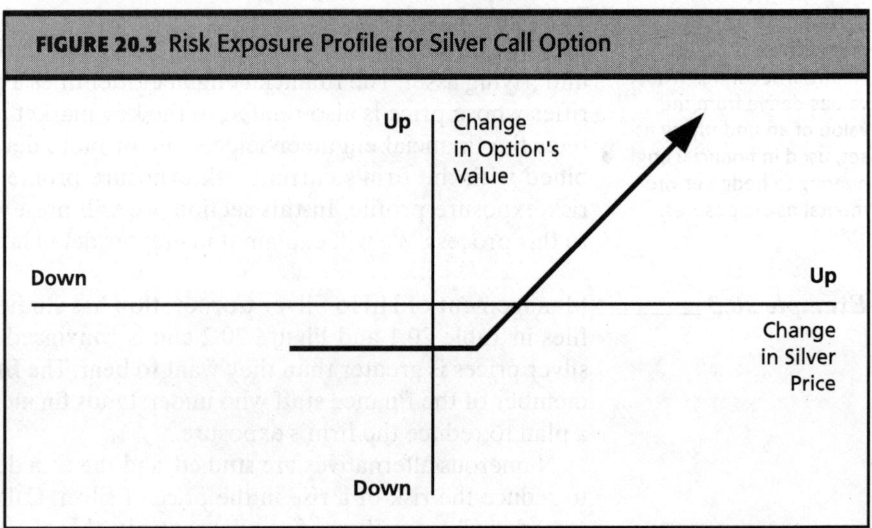

FIGURE 20.4 Combined Risk Exposure Profile—HiHo Silver Corp. with Call Option for Silver

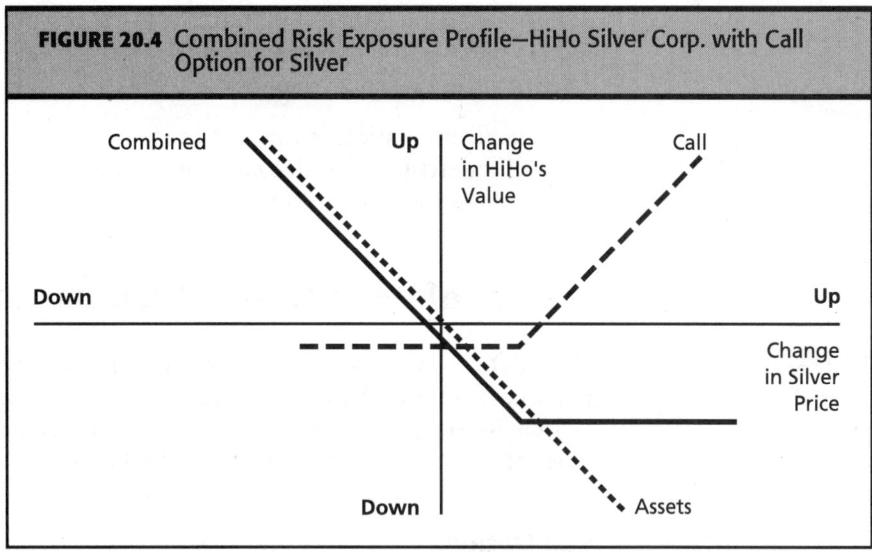

Finally, we reach the key step in financial engineering: We combine the risk exposure profile of the firm (Fig. 20.2) with the profit or loss diagram of the call option (Fig. 20.3). The result is the *combined* risk exposure profile of the firm if it adopts the financial engineered solution, shown in Figure 20.4.

The exact way to combine these diagrams is an important skill in learning financial engineering that will be detailed later in the chapter. For now, note that values used to form Figure 20.3 can be found by combining the profit or loss from changes in the price of silver with the profit or loss of the call option. This combination is shown in Table 20.3. Notice that the firm has reduced to $5 million its exposure to losses from silver price increases. The cost

TABLE 20.3 HiHo's Combined Risk Exposure Profile with the Call Option Position

Change in Silver Price	*Impact on Firm Value*	*Profit/Loss of Call Option*	*Combined Impact*
−$ 3	+$12,000,000	−$ 1,000,000	+$11,000,000
−$ 2	+$ 8,000,000	−$ 1,000,000	+$ 7,000,000
−$ 1	+$ 4,000,000	−$ 1,000,000	+$ 3,000,000
$ 0	$ 0	−$ 1,000,000	−$ 1,000,000
+$ 1	−$ 4,000,000	−$ 1,000,000	−$ 5,000,000
+$ 2	−$ 8,000,000	+$ 3,000,000	−$ 5,000,000
+$ 3	−$12,000,000	+$ 7,000,000	−$ 5,000,000
+$ 4	−$16,000,000	+$11,000,000	−$ 5,000,000
+$ 5	−$20,000,000	+$15,000,000	−$ 5,000,000
+$10	−$40,000,000	+$35,000,000	−$ 5,000,000

of this protection is the $1 million cost of the call option. The impact of the $1 million purchase on the firm's performance is best seen in the case where the price of silver does not change.

Thus, the combination of the risk exposure profile of the firm with that of a particular derivative (in this case, the call option on silver) produces an improved risk exposure profile.

The Use of Derivatives in Financial Engineering

The HiHo Silver example illustrated a highly simplified situation and one potential solution of many. The remainder of this chapter investigates financial engineering more deeply. We will begin by discussing all of the basic types of derivatives, with call options first in the lineup.

Call Options

Chapter 10 provided a detailed discussion of call options. Recall that a *call option* is the right to purchase an underlying asset. The purchaser will lose the entire purchase price or premium of the call option if the option expires with the price of the underlying asset equal to or lesser than the option's strike price. If the underlying asset's price at the option's expiration exceeds the strike price, then the profit or loss is the underlying asset's price, minus the sum of the strike price and the price for which the options were purchased.

For the purpose of understanding financial engineering, we cover two additional aspects of call options in this chapter: profit and loss diagrams and writing a call.

Option Profit and Loss Diagrams Profit and loss diagrams are an important tool for understanding options. A *profit and loss diagram for a call option* has the option's profit or loss on the vertical axis and the price of the option's underlying asset (at the option's expiration) on the horizontal axis. This is depicted in Figure 20.5. Option diagrams such as that in Figure 20.5 are found by plotting the profits and losses that an option holder would receive by establishing the position at a particular price and holding the option to expiration. Another way of constructing the diagram is to begin with the terminal value of an option relative to the price of the underlying asset (see Fig. 10.3) and shift the diagram downward by subtracting out the purchase price (i.e., premium) of the option.

Let us compare the call option profit and loss diagram in Figure 20.5 with the risk exposure profile depicted in Figure 20.1. First, note that the option's profit and loss diagram has the vertical axis on the left side, but the risk exposure profile has the vertical axis in the center. Second, note that the option's profit and loss diagram focuses on the option's strike price, but the risk expo-

FIGURE 20.5 Profit/Loss Diagram for Owning a Call Option

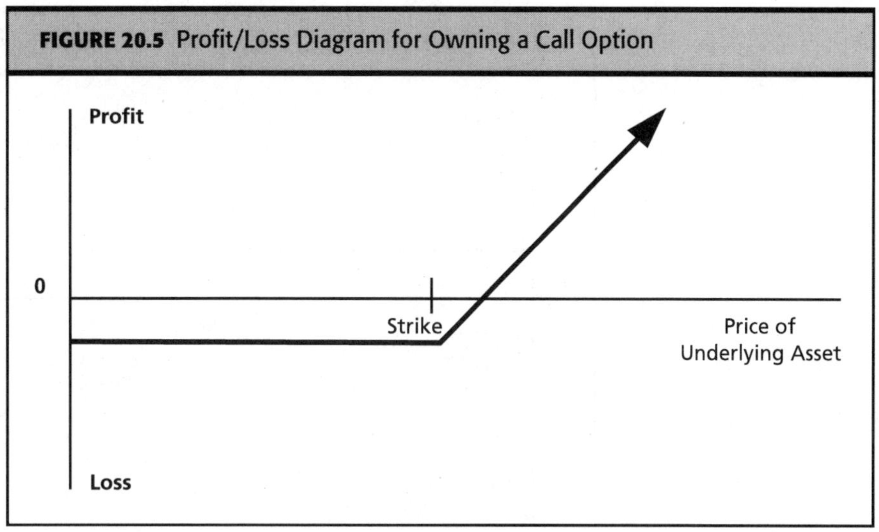

sure profile focuses on the current price of the relevant market price (the "no change" price).

The shape of the profit and loss diagram of the call option embodies its essence. Because potential profits are unlimited, the diagram rises toward infinity to the right as the price of the underlying asset heads toward infinity. To the left, however, the diagram levels out to the maximum loss that an option buyer can suffer: the cost of the option. The relationship has a "kink" directly below the strike price where the option begins to pay off. Note that the kink is the place where the flat line begins its ascent.

Throughout this chapter, options are analyzed by first developing a profit and loss diagram analogous to Figure 20.5. Then, when attempting to financially engineer the risk of a firm, we overlay the option diagrams onto the risk exposure profiles of the firm.

Short Call Options Every call option has both a buyer and a seller. The person who establishes and sells a call option is known as the *call writer.* The call writer receives a selling price, or *premium*, for the call when it is sold. If the option position remains open until expiration, the call writer will then be responsible for the amount, if any, by which the price of the underlying asset exceeds the strike price of the option.

The profit and loss diagram for writing (i.e., selling) a call option uses the same axes as any other option diagram. Figure 20.6 illustrates the diagram for a call writer. Notice that as the underlying asset's price rises to the right toward infinity, the potential loss to the call option writer moves toward infinity. This demonstrates the huge potential losses of writing options. If the underlying asset stays at or below the strike price, however, then the option writer receives a profit equal to the premium received for writing the call.

FIGURE 20.6 Profit/Loss Diagram for Writing a Call Option

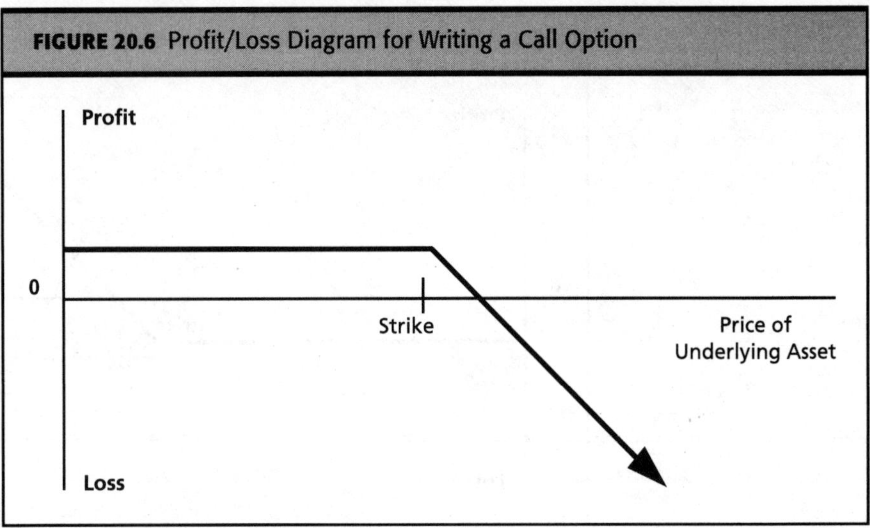

Finally, note that Figure 20.6 is a mirror image of Figure 20.5. Because a normal option is a contract between two parties, it is a "zero-sum game": Any profit that one of the parties receives must be exactly offset by a loss to the other party. Of course, this ignores transaction costs, taxes, and other market imperfections. Each derivative security discussed in this chapter (options and futures and forward contracts) can be purchased ("held long") or written ("held short"). The diagram for the long side (owning the security) is a mirror image of the diagram for the short side (owing the security).

Put Options

Whereas a call option is the right to purchase an underlying asset, a *put option* is the right to sell an underlying asset. A call option benefits from rises in the price of the underlying asset, whereas a put option benefits from *declines* in the price of the underlying asset.

For example, a put option on IBM stock with a strike price of $100 would allow the holder of the put option to sell IBM at $100 to the person who wrote the put option. If the price of IBM falls to $90 as the option expires, then the put option can be used to give its holder a $10 better sales price; hence, it is worth $10. If the price of IBM's stock is at or above the put's strike price of $100 as the put expires, however, then the put is worthless because the stock can be sold for at least as much money in the market without the option.

The profit and loss diagram for buying a put option uses the same axes as any other option diagram. Figure 20.7 illustrates the diagram for a long position in a put. Notice that as the underlying asset's price falls to the left, the potential profit to the put buyer rises. This indicates the large potential prof-

FIGURE 20.7 Profit Loss Diagram for Owning a Put Option

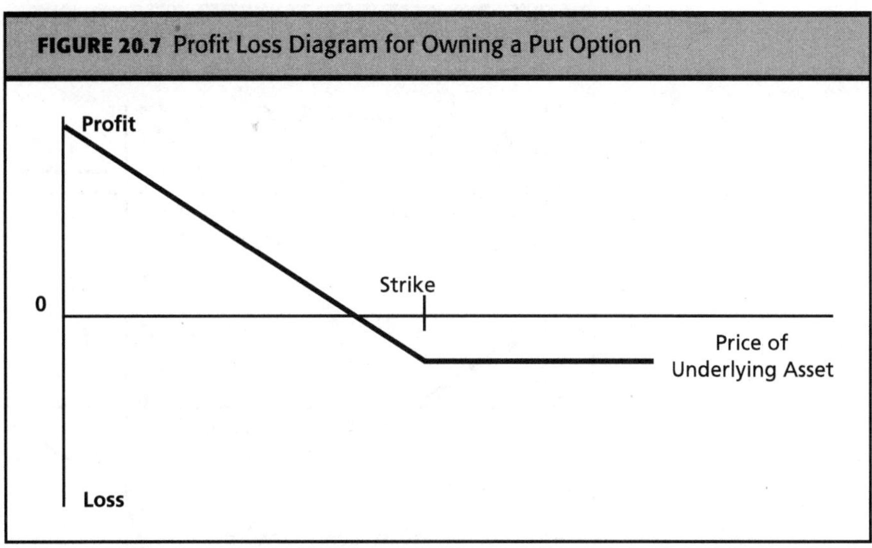

its of buying puts. If the underlying asset stays at or above the strike price, however, then the put holder suffers a loss equal to the premium paid for buying the put.

The writer or seller of the put option receives a premium and then is liable to have to purchase the underlying asset if the put purchaser decides to exercise the put. Thus, like a call writer, a put writer has a small profit potential and a large (but less likely) loss potential. The difference is that the price of a call option tends to move *with* the underlying asset, whereas the price of a put option tends to move *against* the price of the underlying asset.

Figure 20.8 illustrates six different derivative profit and loss diagrams—diagrams of all the derivatives discussed in this chapter. The diagram for writing a put option is in panel D of the figure. Note the large loss potential to the left, as the underlying asset falls, and the small profit potential to the right, as the underlying asset rises and the put option expires worthless. Panels A and B review the diagrams for being long (+) and short (−), respectively, a call option. Panels C and D illustrate being long (+) and short (−), a put option. Panels E and F will be discussed in the next section.

Forward Contracts and Futures Contracts

Call options and put options are two major types of derivatives. In this section we will complete our overview of derivative securities with the third major type, known as either a forward contract or a futures contract. We looked at these derivatives briefly in Chapter 18 and discussed the minor differences between them (see Window 18.1). Readers who have not already done so should study those subsections as a preparation for this subsection. We will review some of the concepts here, briefly.

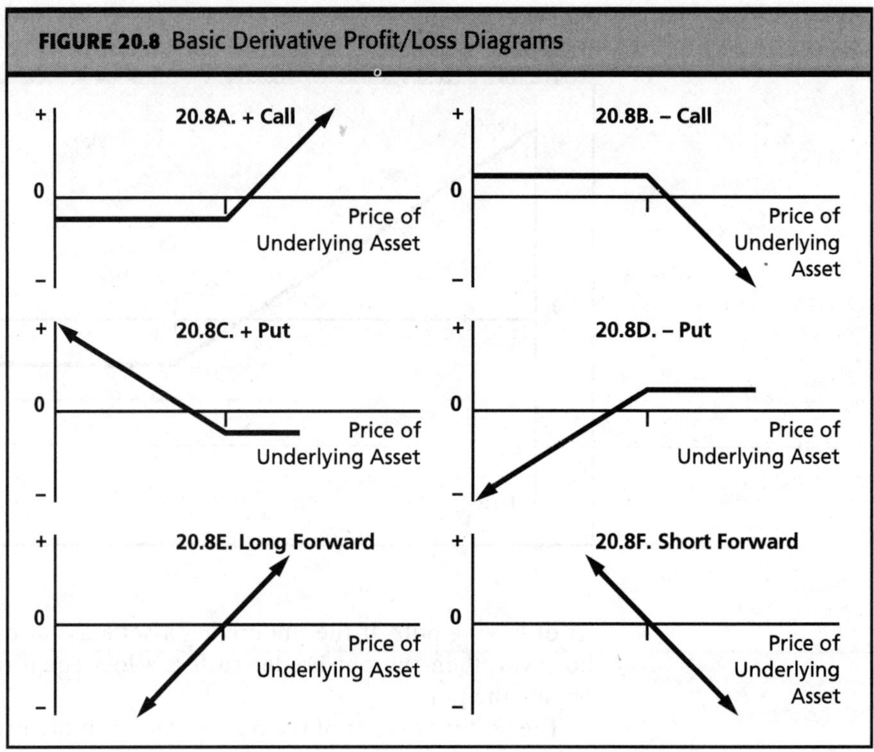

A *forward contract* is an obligation to buy or sell a security at a prespecified price (the forward price) on a particular date (the delivery date). For example, the long side of an agricultural forward contract may be a cereal manufacturer who agrees to buy a certain amount of corn for $5 per bushel on a particular date. The short side of the forward contract might be a farmer who promises to deliver and sell the corn for $5 per bushel.

A *futures contract* has the same design as the forward contract, but they are standardized such that they appeal to a wide range of market participants. Futures contracts trade for more commonly used commodities and on organized exchanges with specific trading rules. In contrast, forward contracts trade for almost any commodities and are usually arranged by the participants themselves, not organized exchanges.

Unlike an option, a forward or futures contract is *not* an *opportunity* to buy or sell; rather, it is a total *obligation* to buy or sell. The long position in a forward is an obligation to buy, and the short side is an obligation to sell. The long position is *required* to buy the underlying asset whether the market price rises or falls, and the short side is *required* to deliver the asset. In general, a person holding a long position in a forward contract faces the same price risks as a person who actually buys and holds the underlying asset.

Example 20.4 _______ Let us return to HiHo Silver Corporation. You may recall the dilemma that HiHo Silver Corporation faced by having contracts that required the delivery of 40 million silver-plated engine knockers over the next year. The problem was that if the price of silver rose significantly, then the corporation could be destroyed by having to purchase the 4 million ounces of silver at high prices while the sales prices of the units were locked in at $5 per unit.

One solution that you may have thought of earlier was for HiHo Silver Corporation to purchase the 4 million ounces of silver as the contracts were being signed, using the market price for silver available at that time ($5 per ounce), and store the silver until it is needed. When a security or commodity is purchased with immediate delivery and payment, it is said to be a *cash* or *spot transaction* in the *cash* or *spot market*. The purchase of 4 million ounces of silver at $5 per ounce would be such a transaction.

There are two problems, however, with purchasing and stockpiling the silver. First, HiHo would incur the costs of a safe storage facility. Second, HiHo would use a large amount of cash, on which no interest would be earned. Buying the silver when it is needed would enable the firm to hold the cash for other uses in the meantime.

As you suspected, forward contracts come to the rescue. Because a forward contract is an agreement for the short side to deliver a specified product to the long side at a prespecified price and date, HiHo Silver Corporation can purchase (i.e., "take long positions in") a variety of forward silver contracts for the amount of silver that is needed at various dates in the future. The forward contract locks in the purchase price for the long side and locks in the sales price for the short side.

Thus, a forward contract is a convenient deal by which delivery of the product and payment for the product occur at some future point in time rather than at the time that the deal is struck. Because most common stocks are purchased with a 3-day settlement period (i.e., the customer pays in three business days and the stock is transferred into the account in 3 days), a stock purchase is a trivial example of a forward contract. The reason that it is trivial is that three days would ordinarily be a virtually inconsequential amount of time.

Most forward contracts are for months or even years. What happens to the market price after the contract is entered determines whether or not the forward contract turns out to have been a benefit or a burden. For example, the farmer who has agreed to sell corn at $5 a bushel likely will be distressed to see the price of corn rise to $7 per bushel; he would have been much better off without the forward contract. This type of risk is known as *regret*.

As the delivery date arrives, one side of the forward contract will see that the forward contract has become a benefit and the other side will see that the forward contract is a burden. For example, if the price of corn rises to $8 per bushel, the farmer with a short position in a forward contract at $5 per bushel will experience a loss of $3 per bushel in the forward contract by being forced to sell at $5 per bushel rather than the subsequent market price of $8. On the other hand, the cereal manufacturer will experience a $3 gain because it will be able to buy the corn at $5 rather than $8.

The profit and loss of the long side of a forward contract can be diagrammed against the price of the underlying asset, as illustrated in Panel E of Figure 20.8. Note that a long position in a forward contract produces virtually unlimited gains as the underlying asset's price rises and substantial losses as the underlying price falls. Note, too, that this is the same price risk faced by somebody who simply owns the underlying asset. On the other hand, the short side of a forward contract experiences the mirror image, as illustrated in Panel F of Figure 20.8. The short side gains from declines in the market price of the underlying asset and suffers from price rises in the underlying asset.

Combining Derivative Positions

Figure 20.8 summarized the six diagrams that represent the long and short sides of the three major types of derivatives that are the "building blocks" for financial engineers: call options, put options, and forward contracts. In this section we will discuss and diagram *combinations* of positions. As a simple example, when a person writes a call option one day and almost immediately buys an identical call option, the two positions completely offset each other. Throughout this chapter we refer to a position in more than one security as a *combination.* A position in two of the same derivatives (such as two call options), however, technically would typically be called a *spread*. The term *combination* typically refers to a position involving two or more *types* of derivatives (such as a call and a put).

Even though virtually any combination of derivatives can be combined and diagrammed, several common combinations are useful to study. For example, if a person purchases a call for $1 and a put for $2 on the same asset with the same strike price ($100) and expiration date, the resulting combination is known as a **straddle**. One way of diagramming a combination is to form a chart of values relative to the price of the underlying asset. In the preceding straddle, we could use option theory to determine the profits and losses of the options at the expiration date at various prices for the underlying asset. The profits and losses for our sample straddle are shown in Table 20.4. A diagram of the straddle can then be formed by plotting the profits and losses, as shown in Figure 20.9.

straddle
The combination of a call option and a put option on the same underlying asset with the same exercise price and expiration date.

A quicker method, but one that requires some practice, involves plotting the combination *directly* on the axes rather than forming a table as earlier. The diagram of a combination can be formed by overlaying the component positions onto a diagram and then forming the combination by netting out the profits and losses of the components. A straddle could be diagrammed as follows: (1) diagram a call, (2) diagram a put, and (3) add to-

TABLE 20.4 A Derivative Combination Known as a Straddle

Price of the Underlying Asset	*Call Option Profit/Loss*	*Put Option Profit/Loss*	*Straddle Profit/Loss*
$ 90	−$1	+$8	+$7
$ 95	−$1	+$3	+$2
$ 98	−$1	$0	−$1
$ 99	−$1	−$1	−$2
$100	−$1	−$2	−$3
$101	$0	−$2	−$2
$102	+$1	−$2	−$1
$105	+$4	−$2	+$2
$110	+$9	−$2	+$7

gether the profits and losses (the losses would be negative numbers) to form the straddle.

Figure 20.9 illustrates the process. There are two key elements: First, make sure that all of the components match up correctly to the axes. In other words, make sure the diagrams of any options kink above their strike prices and that the option premiums correspond to the scale of the vertical axis. Second, combine the profits and losses of each of the components at various points along the horizontal axis and then connect the points. At several values of the underlying asset (points along the horizontal axis) it is especially

FIGURE 20.9 Profit/Loss Diagram for Owning a Straddle

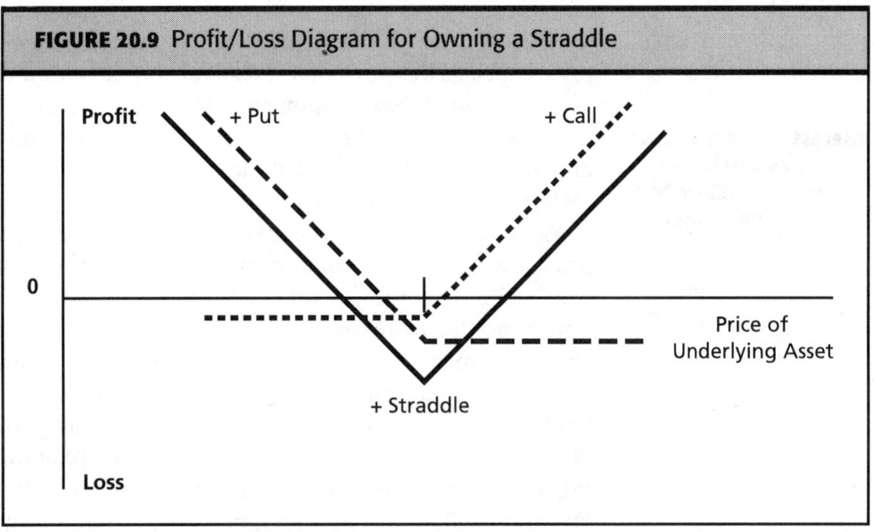

FIGURE 20.10 Various Combination Profit/Loss Diagrams

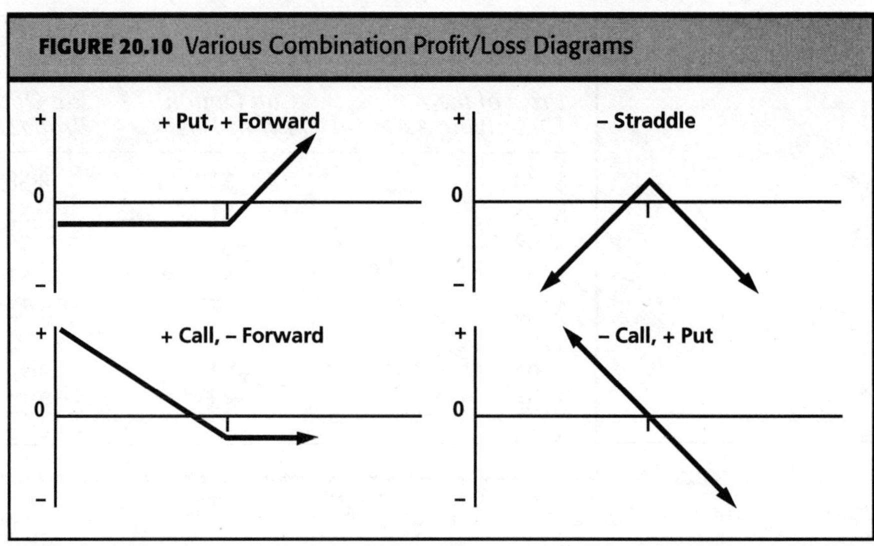

easy to combine profits and losses: prices at which the option diagrams kink (strike prices), prices at which the options break even, and the leftmost and/or rightmost side. In the previous example, values of the underlying asset at $98, $100, and $101 are easiest.

Figure 20.10 illustrates several common combinations of call options, put options, and/or forward contracts.

Interest Rate Derivatives

Our discussion of derivatives to this point has focused on derivatives based on prices, such as the price of a stock. Substantial amounts of derivatives, however, are increasingly based upon *rates* such as interest rates and foreign exchange rates. **Interest rate derivatives** have their own terminology. Because financial engineers commonly deal with interest rate risk and foreign exchange risk, this section provides a brief overview of interest rate derivatives.

interest rate derivatives Derivatives based upon interest rates (rather than prices of commodities).

A call option on a price gives the holder the opportunity to pay the strike price and receive the underlying asset. A call option holder on a rate, however, such as an interest rate, cannot exactly take ownership of a rate. The call option holder instead receives the amount by which the actual market rate exceeds a specified rate, times some amount of money.

For example, consider an interest rate called LIBOR—the London Interbank Offered Rate—which is a particular average of interbank interest rates on U.S. dollars measured in London. There are actually six rates corresponding to maturities from 1 to 6 months. These interest rates have become an international standard by which market participants measure the time value of money and form contracts. We can, roughly speaking, view these rates as being highly similar to more common short-term interest rates in the United States such as Treasury bill rates, CD rates and the prime rate.

A LIBOR call option must specify two things: (1) a rate, say 8 percent, above which the holder receives money, and (2) the amount of money (called the *notional principal*) upon which the percentage payout is be based, for example, $1 million. The holder of the call receives 1 percent of the $1 million for each percent by which the LIBOR rate exceeds the rate specified in the call, multiplied by the length of time in years. Thus in our example, if the 6-month (half year) LIBOR ended up at 10.5 percent, then the call holder would receive (10.5% −8%) ×$1,000,000 ×(0.5 years), or $12,500.

Likewise, a LIBOR put option holder receives payouts if and when the rate falls below the strike rate. A forward or futures contract on an interest rate requires payments from the long position holder to the short position when rates fall and vice versa.

swap
A type of forward contract in which one party is required to pay the other based upon increase or decrease in some variable rate, such as LIBOR, against another (usually fixed) rate.

A **swap** is a type of forward contract in which one side of the contract is required to pay based upon the amount by which some variable rate, such as LIBOR, *exceeds* another (usually fixed) rate, and conversely, the other side of the swap is required to pay when the variable rate is *under* the other rate. Thus, as in the case of a regular forward contract, each side of a swap is obligated to pay when the rate (or a spread between rates) moves in a particular direction. The profit and loss diagram of a swap would show virtually unlimited profits and losses as the rate is varied.

cap
A maximum rate established to limit payments in a swap or other agreement.

floor
A minimum rate established to limit payments in a swap or other agreement.

collar
The combination of a cap and a floor, to keep payout rates bounded on both sides.

Caps and floors are often used to establish limits to the payments in a swap or other agreement. A **cap** establishes a maximum rate, and a **floor** establishes a minimum rate for the purposes of determining a payout. Both a cap and a floor can be used as a **collar** to keep rates bounded on both sides.

As you have seen, there are a tremendous number of terms and complexities involved. This section on the use of derivatives in financial engineering is not intended to provide a comprehensive understanding of the topic (which could take one or more books!), but rather to provide an introduction and overview. In addition to being able to recognize some of the key terms and concepts, the key point to remember is this: A huge variety of derivative contracts has emerged to provide the financial engineer with great flexibility in managing risk. In fact, if a derivative does not already exist that meets the needs of a financial engineer, it is likely that one of the major investment banks will gladly construct one. The only problem might be the price for such custom engineering.

Delta Hedging

Throughout this chapter the ability of derivatives to control or hedge risk is analyzed using the payoffs of the derivatives when they expire or settle. Another common risk control or hedging technique is to focus on the relationship between the current market prices of the derivative and the underlying asset. Window 20.1 expands on this frequently used concept.

WINDOW 20.1

Hedging With Option Deltas

A very common aspect of option analysis involves a risk measure called *delta.* Delta measures the relationship between the current price of an option and the current price of the underlying asset. For example, a particular call option on IBM stock might rise $0.25, everything else equal, if the price of IBM's stock rises $1.00. This would indicate a delta on this call option of 0.25.

The importance of delta is that it can be used to develop a hedge ratio between a stock and an option such that the combined prices of the stock and options will be unaffected by changes in the price of the stock.

For example, because the preceding call option has a delta of 0.25, it would be necessary to write (i.e., establish a short position in) four call options to hedge each share of stock:

$$\text{Hedged Position} = + \text{One Share Stock} - 4 \text{ Call Options}$$

Note that if the price of the stock rose by $1 the price of each call would rise by $0.25, and because four calls are held short, the net gain or loss would be zero:

$$\text{Total Price Change} = + \$1 - (4 \times \$0.25) = \$0$$

On the other hand, if the price of the stock fell by $1 the price of each call would fall by $0.25, and because four calls are held short, the net gain or loss would again be zero:

$$\text{Total Price Change} = -\$1 + (4 \times \$0.25) = \$0$$

In the parlance of calculus, delta is the derivative of an option price with respect to the price of the underlying asset. In the case of the Black-Scholes call option pricing model, detailed in the appendix to Chapter 10, the delta is simply equal to $N(d_1)$. You may recall that $N(d_1)$ is the second term found in the Black-Scholes model (Eq. A10.1).

Chapter 10 discussed the tendency of a call option to rise or fall by more than 0 cents and less than $1.00 for each $1 rise or fall in the price of the underlying asset. Delta quantifies that concept by denoting the exact change. Thus, in the case of ordinary call options, delta is always between 0.00 and 1.00.

The hedge ratio that can be used to establish a risk-free portfolio with stocks and options is found as −1 times the inverse of delta:

$$\text{Hedge Ratio} = -1 / \text{Delta}$$

Thus, in the previous example of a call option with a delta of 0.25, the risk-free hedge required four short call options for each share of stock held long. In the case of an in-the-money call option with a delta closer to 1 (e.g., 0.80) the hedge ratio would be −1.25, which indicates that only 1.25 call options need to be shorted to hedge a share in

WINDOW 20.1 *(continued)*

the underlying asset. For an out-of-the money call option with a delta of only 0.10, the hedge ratio of −10.0 indicates that 10 call options must be written to hedge each share.

The deltas of puts are negative, which indicates that the prices of puts move inversely with the price of the underlying asset. Sophisticated option hedging typically uses more than one risk measure or derivative in hedging and controlling risk. Because these risk measures or derivatives are denoted with letters of the Greek alphabet, like delta, gamma, theta, and vega, they are often referred to as "the Greeks."

Financial Engineering and Financial Theory

What does financial theory have to say about financial engineering? To answer that question, now that we have overviewed derivatives and risk exposure profiles, let us return to the HiHo Silver Corporation. Throughout the chapter we discussed several possible solutions, including buying call options, purchasing the silver in advance, and going long with forward contracts.

Another alternative for managing HiHo Silver's risk of a change in the price of silver could include changing the corporation's policy. Thus, new contracts with customers could specify that the price of the product be allowed to fluctuate based upon the price of silver. For example, the price of each unit might be set at $4.50 plus 0.1 times the prevailing price of an ounce of silver. The problem with this idea is that it passes the risk of silver price changes on to the customer—in this case, the automotive parts manufacturers. Those manufacturers would have to bear the risk or pass it along to the automotive companies when they enter contracts for their parts that also depended upon the price of silver.

The question may ultimately be viewed as who can best bear the risk. In other words, who will bear the risk while demanding the least added return? Derivative markets provide an ideal vehicle for the transfer of risk from people who do not wish to bear the risk to the people who will bear the risk for the least added return. There is reason, therefore, to believe that financial engineering using derivatives makes sense.

A final alternative worth discussing, however, is that perhaps the risk should be allowed to flow through to the shareholders of HiHo Silver Corporation by not hedging the risk at all. In other words, allow the profits and losses of the firm to fluctuate based upon the price of silver. This alternative is based on the assumption that the firm's shareholders own diversified portfolios and therefore the risk will be diversified away within their portfolios. One of the conclusions of Chapters 8 and 9 was that shareholders should hold highly diversified portfolios of stocks and are in a good position to do so (e.g., by using mutual funds). In a perfectly diversified portfolio, the unsystematic or unique risk of one stock would be completely diversified away, so that the shareholder would be unharmed by that firm's risk. By allowing unique risks to flow through to shareholders, corporations are avoiding the time, effort, and transactions costs of managing the risk inside the corporation. Thus, from the perspective of shareholder wealth maximization, financial theory would question financial engineering itself as a legitimate function for the firm to undertake.

Several motivations for financial engineering remain, however, even if we assume that shareholders own highly diversified portfolios. First, it can be argued that some risks are so large that they put the financial health of the firm in jeopardy. This argument requires that the financial distress of a firm or even bankruptcy be damaging to a firm's shareholders. In our discussion of financial distress and bankruptcy (Chapters 10, 12, and 13), we concluded that whether or not it was in the best interest of the shareholders to take chances at going bankrupt was best analyzed on a case by case basis. In some situations involving large amounts of debt, potential legal claimants, or long-term union contracts, it can actually be in the shareholders' best interests to take advantage of the option-like characteristics of common stock by taking risks. In other cases, perhaps risks should be engineered.

Another defense of financial engineering follows from the preceding discussion, but focuses on the firm's management: Putting the financial health of the firm in jeopardy generally has a negative effect on managers who would generally perceive the firm's bankruptcy as having a negative impact on their careers. This is an agency issue. Recall that shareholders contract (as principals) with the managers (as agents) in order to align their financial interests. The goal is to motivate managers to make decisions that maximize shareholder wealth. Shareholders, of course, want managers to feel financial pressure from the consequences of events over which the managers have some level of control (core business risks). By definition, however, environmental risks are somewhat beyond the control of the managers. By subjecting the managers to the financial consequences of *all* of the firm's risk, the shareholders incur potentially negative consequences:

1. *The managers will demand higher compensation.* The higher compensation required by managers (as well as the loss of some managers and the failure to attract others) may exceed the transactions costs and other costs of engineering the environmental risks inside the corporation (i.e., the costs of the financial engineering process). Shareholders may therefore, find financial engineering to be cost effective.
2. *The managers will make decisions that do not maximize shareholder wealth.* Particularly troublesome is the potential for managers to make decisions (reject projects, overprice proposals, etc.) that avoid environmental risks at the expense of shareholder wealth. Financial engineering gives managers a cost-effective way to control risks that, although harmless to diversified shareholders, could be devastating to the manager's compensation plan and prospective career.

For these reasons, and perhaps simply from the realistic perspective that managers have a high degree of effective control of the decision to financially engineer the firm's risks, financial engineering appears to be a topic that will be an important part of corporate finance. In fact, as global competition heats up and as profit margins thin out due to greater efficiency and improved technologies, financial engineering may become an even more important function.

Summary

- Financial engineering is the application of risk management tools, especially the use of derivative securities, to manage the risks of a corporation.
- Risk exposure profiles are used to illustrate the effect of particular market prices on the value of the firm. Derivative securities, such as calls, puts, and forward contracts, can then be used to engineer the risk exposure profile of the firm towards a more desirable relationship. Understanding each type of derivative security and how to combine the derivatives with each other and with the firm's environmental risk exposure profile is therefore essential.
- Theory calls into question the entire motivation for controlling risk at the corporate level rather than simply passing the risk through to the firm's diversified shareholders. Agency theory and the costs of financial distress, however, offer explanations for the popularity of financial engineering.
- Financial engineering appears to be a topic of increasing future interest.

Demonstration Problems

Problem 1

Aldershof Smelting & Minting refines gold and produces gold coins. Aldershof sells these gold coins throughout the United States at prices that vary with the price of gold. Having developed numerous regular customers throughout the years, Aldershof's revenue in terms of units sold is remarkably stable.

Aldershof's CFO, however, is concerned with the lag between when the unrefined gold is purchased and when the gold coins are sold. Changes in the price of gold during this lag expose the firm to risk; unrefined gold purchased when gold prices are high is sometimes sold as coins when gold prices have fallen.

Aldershof's CFO signs a contract each year that locks in the necessary raw materials based upon the price of gold at that date. During the year the firm sells the gold products at prevailing prices. Aldershof reports that the firm has purchased and will process the equivalent of 20,000 ounces of gold during the contract year. The current market price of gold is $400, and that price was used to sign the annual contract for the raw materials and plan production. The CFO is concerned that by the time the gold is processed and sold as coins, the price will have changed. Specifically, falling gold prices will cause losses to the firm and rising gold prices will cause extra profits.

Assume that all of the gold sold throughout the next year will be sold at one price—a price that may be higher or lower than $400 per ounce. Compile a risk exposure profile for Aldershof S & M.

Solution to Problem 1

Step 1: Identify the market price that best measures the environmental risk that the firm faces. In this case, the market price of gold is in U.S. dollars.

Step 2: Compute the changes in the firm's value from changes in the market price. This is accomplished by multiplying the change in the price of gold per ounce times the number of ounces used (20,000) as indicated in the following table:

Change in Gold Price	*Impact on Firm Value*
−$200	−$ 4,000,000
−$100	−$ 2,000,000
$000	$ 0
+$100	+$ 2,000,000
+$200	+$ 4,000,000
+$300	+$ 6,000,000
+$400	+$ 8,000,000
+$500	+$10,000,000

Step 3: Place the change in the firm value on the vertical axis and the change in the price of gold on the horizontal axis, and plot the values. The result is shown in Figure 20.11.

Problem 2

Continuing with Aldershof S & M (from the preceding Demonstration Problem), Aldershof's CFO has learned about two possible ways to hedge the firm's risk of gold price changes: It can buy a put option on gold, or it can write a call option on gold. Both option positions have a market value of $1 million and a strike price of $400, the current market price. Using risk exposure profiles, determine which strategy is better.

FIGURE 20.11 Original Risk Exposure Profile—Aldershof S & M

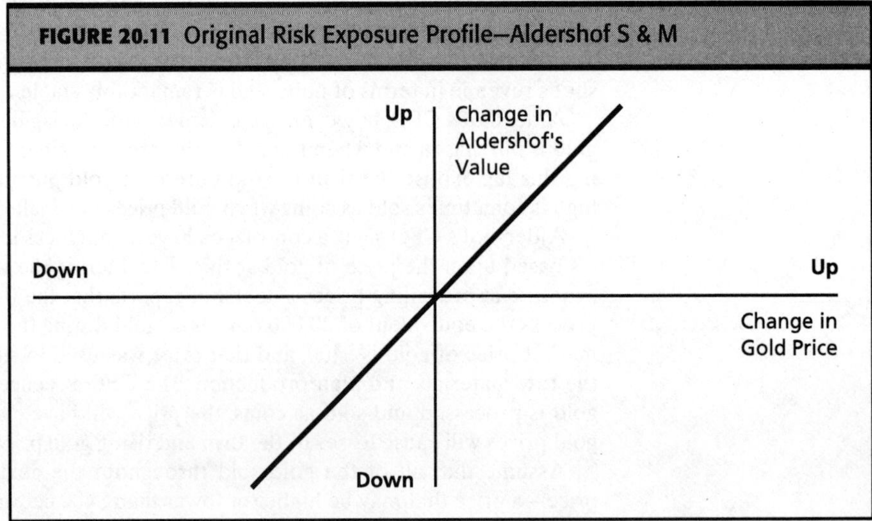

Solution to Problem 2

The slow but sure way is to form a table with four columns: the change in the price of gold, the change in the firm's value, the change in the option position's value, and finally, the combination of the firm value column and the option value column.

The quicker way is to graph the risk exposure profile for the firm and the option profit/loss diagram and then combine them into a third relationship. We will demonstrate the latter method.

Step 1: Considering the purchase of a put option first, use the profit and loss diagram from Panel C of Figure 20.8 and overlay the relationship onto the risk exposure profile from Figure 20.11. Be sure to place the put diagram on the risk exposure profile with the "kink" in the relationship at the vertical axis because the strike price of the option is equal to the current price of gold (the "no change" value).

Step 2: At various locations along the horizontal axis, sum the profits and/or losses from the two known relationships and plot the result. Then connect the points using straight line segments, paying attention to the slopes of the two relationships and the kink point in the option.

For example, at the vertical axis, the combination of zero profit for the firm's assets and a loss in the put would net to a loss equal to the purchase price of the put. That point can be marked as a starting point.

Moving from the vertical axis to the right, notice that the loss on the put stays constant while the firm's original risk exposure profile indicates gains at a 45-degree angle. Thus, the combination of the two profiles will also gain at a 45-degree angle toward the right. Of particular convenience is the point to the right of the vertical axis where the loss on the put equals the profit from the firm's assets. That should be the point where the combination diagram crosses the horizontal axis.

Moving left from the vertical axis, examine the point where the put diagram crosses the horizontal axis. At that point the put has no profit or loss, so the loss of the combination will equal the loss from the firm's original risk exposure profile.

Moving to the left of the vertical axis, note that the option and the firm's original risk exposure profile move in opposite directions at 45-degree angles—canceling each other out and resulting in a level line for the combination.

Step 3: Finally, connect the known points with straight line segments, paying attention to the slopes of the two known relationships. The result is shown in Figure 20.12.

Step 4: Next, consider the writing of a call option. Start, again, by using the profit and loss diagram from Panel B of Figure 20.8 and overlaying the relationship onto the risk exposure profile from Figure 20.11. Again, be sure to place the option diagram on the risk exposure profile with the "kink" in the relationship at the vertical axis because the strike price of the option is equal to the current price of gold (the "no change" value).

Step 5: At various locations along the horizontal axis, sum the profits and or losses from the two known relationships and plot the result. Then connect the points using straight line segments, paying attention to the slopes of the two relationships and the kink point in the option.

For example, at the vertical axis, the combination of zero profit for the firm's assets and a profit in the call would net to a profit equal to the proceeds from writing the call. That point can be marked as a starting point.

Moving from the vertical axis to the left, notice that the profit on the call stays constant, but the firm's original risk exposure profile indicates losses at a 45-degree angle. Thus, the combination of the two profiles will also lose at a 45-degree angle toward the left. Of particular convenience is the point to the left of the vertical axis

FIGURE 20.12 Combined Risk Exposure Profile–Aldershof S & M with a Long Position in a Put

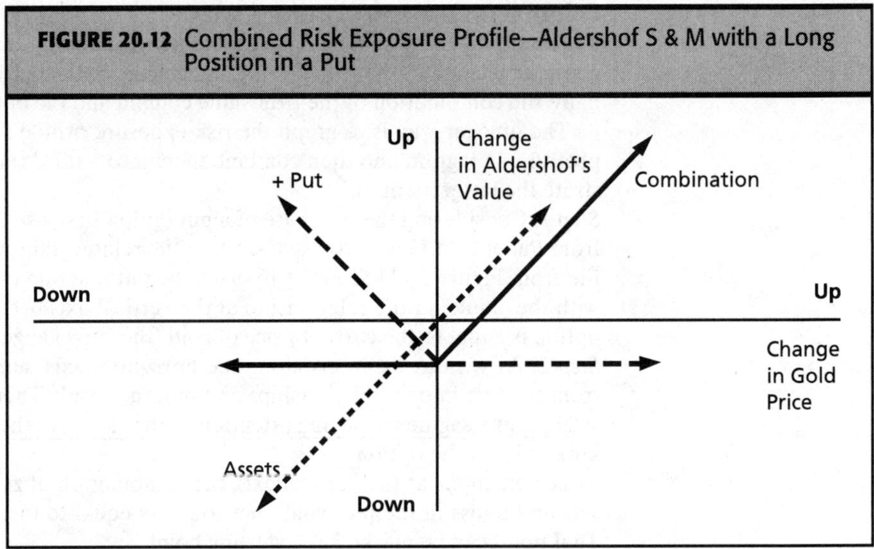

where the profit on the call equals the loss from the firm's assets. That should be the point where the combination diagram crosses the horizontal axis.

Moving right from the vertical axis, examine the point where the call diagram crosses the horizontal axis. At that point the call has no profit or loss, so the profit of the combination will equal the profit from the firm's original risk exposure profile.

Moving to the right of the vertical axis, note that the option and the firm's original risk exposure profile move in opposite directions at 45-degree angles—canceling out each other and resulting in a level line for the combination.

Step 6: Finally, connect the known points with straight line segments, paying attention to the slopes of the two known relationships. The result is shown in Figure 20.13.

FIGURE 20.13 Combined Risk Exposure Profile–Aldershof S & M with a Short Position in a Call

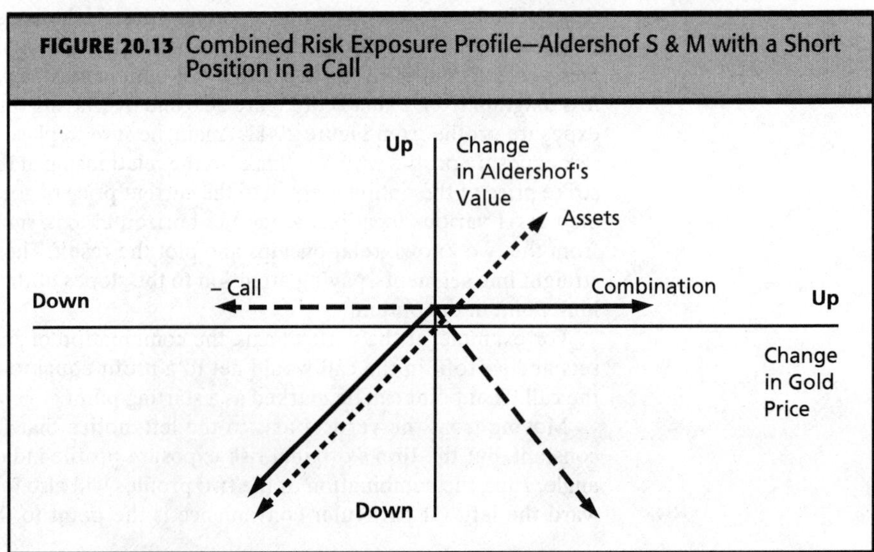

Final Solution: Note, in Figure 20.12, that the purchase of a put results in a limited loss exposure while retaining much of the large profit potential—much like owning a call option. The writing of a call (in Fig. 20.13), however, limits the profit exposure while retaining much of the downside risk—much like writing a naked put. Both options positions reduce the risk, but the purchase of a put (Fig. 20.12) probably offers a final risk exposure profile that would be preferred by Aldershof S & M.

Review Question

1. What is financial engineering, and what is it used for?
2. What is a core business risk? What is an environmental risk?
3. What is a risk exposure profile, and what is its purpose?
4. How is a call option's profit and loss diagrammed?
5. What is a put option?
6. How are long positions in calls, puts, and forward contracts diagrammed?
7. How are short positions in calls, puts, and forward contracts diagrammed?
8. How are positions combined into a single diagram?
9. According to financial theory, why might shareholders desire that their firm perform financial engineering?
10. True or False: "Firm Q losses money for each dollar the price of its chief raw material rises over its current price. Firm Q should limit this risk by writing a call option." Explain your answer.

Problems

1. Charge-O-Rama Corporation's value is linked to interest rates as follows:

Change in Interest Rate	*Change in Firm Value*
−5%	−$ 9,200,000
−4%	−$ 9,000,000
−3%	−$ 8,000,000
−2%	−$ 6,000,000
−1%	−$ 3,000,000
0%	$ 0
+1%	+$ 3,000,000
+2%	+$ 6,000,000
+3%	+$ 9,000,000
+4%	+$12,000,000
+5%	+$15,000,000

   a. Construct a risk exposure profile for Charge-O-Rama Corporation.
   b. What derivatives might you suggest to the CFO of the firm?

2. If the strike price of an option is $50 and the premium or market price of the same option is $*X*, what value would the underlying asset have to be worth when the option expires in order to cause the option to break even (in other words, for the final option price to equal the original option price of $*X*) for:

a. Owning a call option?
b. Owning a put option?
c. Writing a call?
d. Writing a put?

3. Use the information from Problem 2 to find the following:
   a. At what price(s) of the underlying asset, if any, can the four option positions earn a profit of $X? (Solve each position separately.)
   b. At what price(s) of the underlying asset, if any, can the four option positions earn a profit of $2X? (Solve each position separately.)
4. Form profit and loss diagrams of the following positions:
   a. Short a call option.
   b. Long a share of stock.
   c. Both long a share of stock and short a call option. (This position is called a *covered call.*)
5. Form profit and loss diagrams of the following option positions. Assume that all the positions have the same underlying asset and the same expiration date.
   a. Long a call with a strike price of $50 and long a put with a strike price of $50.
   b. Long a call with a strike price of $50 and long a put with a strike price of $40.
   c. What would the diagrams of each of the preceding positions be if the long positions were changed to short positions?
6. Form profit and loss diagrams of the following option positions. Assume that all the positions have the same underlying asset and the same expiration date.
   a. Long a call with a strike price of $50 and short a put with a strike price of $50.
   b. Short a call with a strike price of $50 and long a put with a strike price of $50.
7. Form profit and loss diagrams of the following option positions. Assume that all the positions have the same underlying asset and the same expiration date.
   a. Long a call with a strike price of $50 and short a call with a strike price of $55.
   b. Short a put with a strike price of $50 and long a put with a strike price of $55.
   c. What would the diagrams of each of the preceding positions be if the long positions were changed to short positions and the short positions were changed to long positions?
8. Form profit and loss diagrams of the following option positions. Assume that all the positions have the same underlying asset and the same expiration date.
   a. Long two calls with a strike price of $50, short one call with a strike price of $45, and short one call with a strike price of $55.
   b. Long one call with a strike price of $50, long one call with a strike price of $55, short one call with a strike price of $45, and short one call with a strike price of $60.
   c. What would the diagrams of each of the preceding positions be if the call positions were changed to put positions?
9. Condor International, an American firm, has recognized the firm's tremendous exposure to the risk of fluctuations in the value of the French franc because a substantial portion of the firm's assets are managed in France. Although the assets have stable values in terms of the French franc, when these asset values are converted into U.S. dollars, the exchange rate between the two currencies causes enormous fluctuations in the U.S. dollar value of the assets. The firm wants a strategy to eliminate this risk. The value of the assets is 3.5 billion francs. The current exchange rate is 1 franc to $0.20 U.S. dollars.
   a. Construct a risk exposure profile with the exchange rate as the environmental risk.
   b. What derivative strategy would you suggest?

10. Suppose that Condor International from Problem 9 uses derivatives offered by a large bank (the Bank of Butztown) to completely hedge the risk caused by fluctuations in the exchange rate between U.S. dollars and French francs. What effect, if any, would that hedging activity have on:
    a. A shareholder with all of her money in the stock of Condor International?
    b. A shareholder with all of his money in the stock of the Bank of Butztown?
    c. A shareholder with some money in the stock of Condor International and some money in the stock of the Bank of Butztown?
11. Form a profit and loss diagram of the following position (assume that all of the derivatives have the same underlying asset, the same expiration date, and the same strike price): long a call, short a put, and short a forward contract.

Discussion Questions

1. Why is financial engineering used primarily for environmental risks?
2. Has increased volatility in market prices been a major impetus for the increased attention on financial engineering?
3. Why can an option position show a loss when the underlying asset's price has not changed?
4. Why would anyone ever enter into a straddle?
5. Could a person "beat the market" by waiting to buy straddles until markets are volatile and selling straddles while markets are stable?
6. If financial engineering is primarily a risk management tool and if shareholders own diversified portfolios, why would a corporation attempting to maximize shareholder wealth be concerned with risk management?

INDEX